Second Edition

Applied Sport Psychology

Personal Growth to Peak Performance

Jean M. Williams, editor
University of Arizona

Mayfield Publishing Company

Mountain View, California
London • Toronto

Library of Congress Cataloging-in-Publication data:

Applied sport psychology: personal growth to peak performance / Jean
    M. Williams, editor. — 2nd ed.
    p.   cm.
    Includes bibliographical references and index.
    ISBN 1-55934-132-7
    1. Sports—Psychological aspects. 2. Coaching (Athletics)
    I. Williams, Jean M. (Jean Marie)
    GV706.4.A66   1992   92-35585
    796'.01—dc20

Manufactured in the United States of America
10   9   8   7   6   5   4

Mayfield Publishing Company
1240 Villa Street
Mountain View, California 94041

Sponsoring editor, Erin Mulligan; production service, The Book Company; manuscript editor, Ellen Silge; text designer, Wendy Calmenson;
cover photographer, Tim Davis; cover designer, Jeanne M. Schreiber. The
text was set in Stone Serif by Harrison Typesetting and printed on
50# Finch Opaque by Banta Company.

Contents

PART THREE—PSYCHOLOGICAL CONSIDERATIONS: REFERRAL, DRUG ABUSE, BURNOUT, INJURY, AND TERMINATION FROM ATHLETICS

21 When to Refer Athletes for Counseling or Psychotherapy 299

Steven R. Heyman

22 Drug Abuse in Sport: Causes and Cures 310

Mark H. Anshel

23 Athletic Staleness and Burnout: Diagnosis, Prevention, and Treatment 328

Keith P. Henschen

24 Stress, Injury, and the Psychological Rehabilitation of Athletes 338

Robert J. Rotella, Steven R. Heyman

25 Career Termination in Sports: When the Dream Dies 356

Bruce Ogilivie, Jim Taylor

Author Index 367

Subject Index 375

Preface

An increasing number of coaches and athletes are turning to applied sport psychology to gain a competitive edge—to learn, among other things, ways to manage competitive stress, control concentration, improve confidence, increase communication skills, and promote team harmony. Not until the 1980s had the level of scientific and experiential knowledge about psychological interventions for enhancing performance become sufficient to warrant books that attempt to translate this knowledge into practical suggestions and exercises.

The first edition of *Applied Sport Psychology: Personal Growth to Peak Performance* was one of the first books written specifically to introduce coaches and sport psychologists to psychological theories and techniques that could be used to enhance the performance and personal growth of athletes from youth sport to elite levels. The book focused primarily on three dimensions: (1) techniques for developing and refining psychological skills to enhance performance and personal growth, (2) suggestions for establishing a learning and social environment that would enhance the effectiveness of coaches and maximize the skill and personal growth of athletes, and (3) special issues such as staleness and burnout, psychology of injury and injury rehabilitation, and retirement from athletics. The second edition continues to have the same focus, but has been expanded to cover more topics. For example, new chapters have been added on training youth sport coaches, improving communication, referring athletes for professional counseling, and drug abuse in sport.

Applied Sport Psychology is particularly well-suited as a text for classes in applied sport psychology and psychology of coaching. The book will also be a valuable reference for practicing coaches and sport psychologists who did not have the opportunity for such training in their own formal education. Here are some of the reasons that we think this second edition continues to be exceptionally well-suited for these classes.

Written Specifically for Sport Psychologists and Coaches

The growing body of knowledge and interest in applied sport psychology is perhaps best indicated by the fifty plus books published in the last decade on mental skills for peak performance. Most of these books continue to be written primarily for the athlete. Their coverage is thus not comprehensive enough for the sport psychologist or coach who must apply psychological constructs across a wide variety of situations and deal with many different athletes. Books previously written for sport psychologists and coaches are typically general textbooks that attempt to cover the entire field of sport psychology. Thus their coverage of applied issues—and particularly psychological interventions for enhancing performance and personal growth—is superficial compared to the in-depth coverage provided in this text.

Based on the Latest Research and Practice

This new edition reflects the latest research and practice in applied sport psychology. In fact, the knowledge and experiential base in applied sport psychology has expanded so greatly since the first edition of the book that most of the revisions of the original chapters resulted in extensive changes. Each chapter has been written or updated as of January 1992.

Although the primary focus is on application, theoretical and research foundations have been provided in each chapter, whenever appropriate. When using the book as a textbook for a graduate course, the instructor may want to supplement the book with readings from the research studies cited by the contributors.

Comprehensive Coverage of Topics

No other text in applied sport psychology encompasses the comprehensive approach taken here. The first chapter discusses the past, present, and future of sport psychology. The remainder of the book is divided into three parts.

Part One covers learning, feedback, motivation, desirable leadership behaviors, group dynamics, and effective communication. For clarity and simplicity, some of these chapters have been written in the vernacular of the coach. The reader is cautioned, however, not to conclude that these chapters are only useful for coaches. Sport psychologists frequently find it necessary to work with coaches in areas such as improving communication skills, building team rapport, and fostering more effective leadership behaviors. Also, the same principles of learning, motivation, and social interaction that help to increase a coach's effectiveness apply to the sport psychologist teaching mental skills and interacting with athletes. Thus the knowledge and insight gained from reading the chapters in Part One are equally as appropriate for current and prospective sport psychologists. In those instances where we have addressed only the coach, it should be assumed that we are also addressing the sport psychologist.

Part Two of the book addresses mental training for enhancing performance. This section begins with a chapter on the psychological characteristics of peak performance; other chapters discuss identifying ideal performance states, setting and achieving goals, managing stress and energy levels, training in imagery, identifying optimal attentional styles, controlling concentration, and building confidence. The section concludes with a chapter on the integration and implementation of a psychological skills training program.

Part Three addresses the referral of athletes for professional counseling, drug abuse in sport, athletic staleness and burnout, psychological considerations in injury and rehabilitation, and termination from athletics. This section is unique because coaches and sport psychologists have only recently begun to address and explore these facets of the athlete's career. No sport psychology book has dealt with all of these issues, even though they are crucial to athletes' performance and personal development.

The appropriateness of these chapters for certain courses will depend on the students' backgrounds and interests. The book was planned to provide a complete coverage of psychological theories, techniques, and issues relevant to the enhancement of athletes' performance and personal growth. We intend for the reader, or course instructor, to select those chapters that are appropriate for their course. For example, Chapters 2 and 3 concern motor skills learning and principles of reinforcement and feedback; this material might be redundant if the reader already has a thorough background in motor learning. Chapter 5 on coach–parent relationships may interest only those individuals who are working, or plan to work, in a setting where athletes are still living with their parents; whereas Chapter 25 on termination from athletics may interest only individuals who work with athletes who are nearing retirement or dropping out of athletics.

Written by Leading Experts in Sport Psychology

The contributors to this volume are leading scholars and practitioners in sport psychology. They work with athletes from youth sport to Olympic and professional levels, and most have illustrious backgrounds as elite athletes and/or coaches.

Integrated Organization and Writing Style

The book has the major advantage of drawing upon the diverse expertise and perspectives of 31 sport psychologists and two motor learning experts, but it avoids the common disadvantage of disparate coverage and diverse writing styles frequently found in edited textbooks. The content and sequencing of chapters has been carefully coordinated to assure comprehensive coverage and progressive development of concepts, yet eliminating undesirable overlap and inconsistency in terminology. Writing focus, styles, and organization have been standardized as much as possible. Each chapter cites appropriate research and theory, makes application to the world of sport, and provides examples and training exercises whenever appropriate. Each chapter also begins with an introduction that highlights the content of the chapter and ends with a conclusion or summary of the major psychological constructs and skills and study questions for students.

Application Examples

The numerous examples given throughout the book greatly facilitate the translation of psychological theory and constructs into everyday practice. Many of these examples involve well-known professional and amateur sportspeople. The examples cut across more than 40 sports and provide important anecdotal evidence that can be used to motivate athletes to develop psychological skills for their sport. These real-life examples are frequently supplemented with hypothetical examples created by the authors to clarify appropriate applications.

Applied Sport Psychology Provides Many Benefits

The rewards are many for those who choose to dedicate themselves to the pursuit of athletic excellence through use of the theories and techniques of applied sport psychology. Coaches and athletes acknowledge the importance of mental factors in athletic development and performance, yet the time athletes actually spend practicing mental skills belies this view. In publishing this book, we have made a serious effort to help abolish that inconsistency by supplying the knowledge necessary for providing a salutory and beneficial psychological climate. The benefits that can be derived from this text will arise not just in athletic performance, but in overall performance outside of athletics and, perhaps most importantly, in general personal growth and increased sense of self-worth.

Acknowledgments

I wish to thank all the contributors who participated in this project and thus shared their vast expertise with the readers. Whatever contribution this book continues to make to applied sport psychology and to the field of athletics will be in large measure a consequence of their efforts.

I am also indebted to the fine editorial staff at Mayfield Publishing Company, most particularly Erin Mulligan and Thomas Broadbent, for their support and skill.

Finally, my thanks to the following colleagues for their insightful reviews of the manuscript: Gerald D. Guthrie, Portland State University; Bruce D. Hale, Pennsylvania State University; Ralph A. Vernacchia, Western Washington University; and M. Jane Miner, University of Utah.

Jean M. Williams

Contributors

Jean M. Williams is a professor in the Department of Exercise and Sport Sciences at the University of Arizona. She teaches courses in sport psychology, stress management, and psychological training for peak performance. Dr. Williams has been a consultant for numerous intercollegiate athletes and teams. She has over 10 years of collegiate coaching experience in men's and women's fencing, including the coaching of nationally ranked teams. Dr. Williams has edited two books in sport psychology and published numerous research and professional articles. She is past chair of the AAHPERD Sport Psychology Academy and secretary-treasurer of the AAASP.

Mark H. Anshel is a senior lecturer of sport psychology in the Department of Human Movement Science at the University of Wollongong, New South Wales, Australia. He received his Ph.D. at Florida State University and immigrated to Australia from the United States in 1988. His primary research interests include examining the causes of drug use in sport and coping with acute stress in sport and exercise settings. In addition to his published research articles and book chapters, he has written the textbook *Sport Psychology: From Theory to Practice* and is editor of the *Dictionary of the Exercise and Sport Sciences*. He has consulted with several university sports teams and individual athletes over the years in the United States, Australia, and Singapore and is a full member of the Australian Psychological Society, NASPSPA, and AAASP.

Stephen H. Boutcher is a senior lecturer in the Department of Human Movement at the University of Wollongong in Wollongong, Australia. Dr. Boutcher's research interests include attentional mechanisms underlying performance, the effect of exercise on emotion, and the influence of exercise on chronic disease. His applied interests include the use of aerobic exercise to alter sedentary lifestyle and the development of performance routines in closed-skill sports.

Linda K. Bunker is a professor of physical education and Associate Dean for Academic and Student Affairs at the University of Virginia. She is a certified sport psychology consultant (AAASP) and has worked extensively with professional golfers and tennis players. Dr. Bunker is a well-known scholar in the areas of applied motor learning and sport psychology. She has written over 100 articles and has authored 10 books, including *Advanced Golf: Steps to Success*, *Coaching Golf Effectively*, *Mind Mastery for Winning Golf*, *Motivating Kids Through Play*, and *Parenting Your Superstar*. Her involvement in sport is active as well as scholastic. She is on the advisory board of the Women's Sports Foundation and the Melpomene Institute. Formerly a nationally ranked tennis player and three-sport athlete at the University of Illinois, Dr. Bunker remains an avid tennis player when she is not on the links.

Albert V. Carron is a professor of physical education at the University of Western Ontario, where he teaches sport psychology at the undergraduate and graduate level. Dr. Carron's main area of research interest is group dynamics. His specific focus is on group cohesion, leadership, and coach–athlete compatibility. In addition to 74 research articles Dr. Carron has authored 5 books. Among them are *Motivation: Implications for Coaching and Teaching* and *Group Dynamics*. Dr. Carron has been active in the sport sciences in Canada and the United States. For example, he has been a president of the Canadian Association of Sport Sciences, a member of the Sports Medicine Council of Canada, on the executive board of the AAASP, on the editorial board of the *Journal of Sport and Exercise Psychology*, and a section editor for the *Canadian Journal of Sport Sciences*. He was recently named a Fellow in the Canadian Society for Psychomotor Learning and Sport Psychology and the American Academy of Physical Education.

P. (Chella) Chelladurai is a professor of sport management in the School of Health, Physical Education, and Recreation at Ohio State University. He conducts research in the areas of organization theory and organizational behavior, including leadership in sports. Dr. Chelladurai is the author of *Sport Management: Macro Perspectives* and is currently the editor of the *Journal of Sport Management*. He is a Corresponding Fellow of the American Academy of Physical Education. As a youth in India, he was a national basketball player, coach, and referee.

Mark. G. Fischman is an associate professor in the Department of Health and Human Performance at Auburn University. He received his doctorate in motor learning from Pennsylvania State University. Dr. Fischman is associated with the Motor Behavior Center at Auburn, where he conducts research on theories of response programming and the visual and proprioceptive control of one-hand catching. Dr. Fischman is a former collegiate swimmer and has coached collegiate and age-group swimming.

Daniel Gould is a professor in the Department of Exercise and Sport Science at the University of North Carolina at Greensboro. A specialist in applied sport psychology, he focuses his research on competitive stress and anxiety, athlete motivation, and the effectiveness of psychological skills training interventions for coaches and athletes. He is also heavily involved in coaching education and children's sports. Dr. Gould has been consultant to elite international athletes in a wide variety of sports ranging from figure skating and dressage to

wrestling and baseball. Formerly a wrestler and football and baseball player, he remains an avid fitness enthusiast. Dr. Gould was the founding co-editor of *The Sport Psychologist*. He served as president of the AAASP, chaired the USA Wrestling Science and Medicine Committee, and presently serves on the U.S. Olympic Coaching Development Committee.

Dorothy V. Harris, now deceased, was a professor and coordinator of the graduate program in sport psychology at Pennsylvania State University. She was a world-renowned educational sport psychologist, past president of NASPSPA, a member of the Managing Council of the International Society of Sport Psychology, ISSP treasurer, and editor of the ISSP Newsletter. Dr. Harris was a prolific author who wrote two books, edited five, and contributed to numerous others. She was also an accomplished speaker. She spent a sabbatical at the Olympic Training Center in 1980 and continued to work with numerous Olympic and national teams and athletes.

Keith P. Henschen is a professor in the Department of Exercise and Sport Science at the University of Utah and director of the sport psychology graduate program. He has published numerous research articles and has spoken extensively on the practical applications of sport psychology. His research interests include intervention strategies, athlete performance assessment, and performance psychology for the handicapped. Dr. Henschen is a consultant for numerous college and professional sport teams. He is currently the co-chairman of the Sport Psychology Committee for The Athletic Congress (TAC).

Steven R. Heyman is a licensed clinical psychologist and a professor in the doctoral program in clinical psychology at the University of Wyoming. He was the director of clinical training at Wyoming from 1984 to 1988. Dr. Heyman's interests in sport psychology developed from his personal involvements with high-risk sports, including scuba diving, hang gliding, and sky diving. His research interests within sport psychology include personality and performance, high-risk sports, and hypnosis. He has worked primarily with individual athletes, including swimmers, boxers, football players, and power lifters.

Thelma Sternberg Horn received her doctorate in sport psychology from Michigan State University and is currently an associate professor with the Department of Physical Education, Health, and Sport Studies at Miami University in Ohio. Her research interests center around children's perceptions of their physical competence and the influence of teacher, coach, and parent behavior on children's psychosocial growth. She is also working on an interdisciplinary project designed to examine the relationship between exercise and stress reactivity in adolescent subjects. Dr. Horn is an associate editor for the *Journal of Sport and Exercise Psychology* and has also recently edited the book *Advances in Sport Psychology*. Prior to her graduate work in sport psychology, Dr. Horn taught physical education and English at the high school level in Michigan and Colorado. She has had extensive coaching experience at both interscholastic and intercollegiate levels and continues to work as a consultant and clinician with coaches and teachers in youth sport programs.

Vikki Krane is an assistant professor of health, physical education, recreation, and dance at Bowling Green State University. She completed her doctorate in exercise science at the University of North Carolina at Greensboro. Her main research interests concern the relationship between anxiety and athletic performance, as well as coping and psychological skills utilized by athletes. Dr. Krane has consulted with athletes in a variety of collegiate team sports and with golfers, track and field athletes, and adolescent figure skaters. She has also conducted seminars for high school and youth sport coaches. A former collegiate soccer player, Dr. Krane has coached high school and collegiate soccer.

Daniel M. Landers is a Regents' Professor of exercise science and physical education and is director of the interdisciplinary doctoral program in exercise science at Arizona State University. He was the founding editor of the *Journal of Sport and Exercise Psychology*. Dr. Landers served on a National Academy of Science committee and is a member of the Sport Psychology Committee of the U.S. Olympic Committee. His research has focused on the arousal–performance relationship, including attention/concentration and stress-reducing coping strategies. He has served as a sport psychologist

for collegiate teams, professional teams, and national Olympic teams in the United States, Canada, and Korea.

Curt L. Lox received his M.S. degree from Miami University in Ohio and is currently working toward a doctorate degree in kinesiology at the University of Illinois, Urbana-Champaign. His research interests center around the psychological aspects of exercise and sport behavior including self-efficacy, attributions, and emotion. Mr. Lox has coached at the youth and high school levels, has served as a consultant with coaches and players at the high school and college levels, and has experience as a counselor in the clinical setting.

Betty Mann received her doctorate from Springfield College, where she is an associate professor. She is the associate director of graduate programs and serves as the coordinator for graduate studies in physical education. Her areas of expertise are sport psychology, sport law, and administration. Dr. Mann has made numerous presentations on leadership and has written articles about that topic. She has coached women's basketball at the college and high school levels and taught middle school physical education.

Mimi Murray is currently Buxton Professor at Springfield College. Dr. Murray has been a very successful gymnastics coach: Her teams at Springfield College won three Division I National Championships; she was selected to coach the U.S. team for the World University Games and was named "Coach of the Year." She authored *Gymnastics for Women: The Spectator, Gymnast, Coach and Teacher*. She has been a television sports commentator. As a sport psychology consultant, Dr. Murray has published many articles and lectured throughout the world and has worked with Olympic and professional athletes including the U.S. Equestrian Team. She is listed on the U.S. Olympic Committee's Sport Psychology Registry and she is currently the president of the AAHPERD.

Robert M. Nideffer has been a professor on the faculties of the University of Rochester, the California School of Professional Psychology, and California State University at San Diego. He has been involved in sport psychology since 1969 and is currently self-employed as the president of Enhanced Performance Systems. Dr. Nideffer has published extensively in the sport psychology and stress management areas, with 10 books and over 100 articles to his credit. He has worked with Olympic-level and professional athletes in a wide variety of sports and has been a member of policy-setting committees in the United States, Canada, and Australia.

Bruce C. Ogilvie is professor emeritus in the Department of Psychology at California State University at San Jose. Dr. Ogilvie is a world-renowned pioneer in applied sport psychology; he has researched, consulted, and published in the area of performance and the high-performance person since 1955. He has contributed over 150 publications on issues including children in sport, identification of psychological factors that contribute to performance success, and the development of performance-enhancing strategies. Dr. Ogilvie has served as team psychological consultant for numerous U.S. Olympic teams as well as professional football, basketball, baseball, hockey, and soccer teams. He has also been a private-practice consultant for elite athletes from various sports.

Joseph B. Oxendine has been the chancellor of Pembroke State University since 1989. After competing in three sports at the college level, he played professional baseball for three years in the Pittsburgh Pirate minor league system. Dr. Oxendine served for 30 years at Temple University as professor, department chairman, and founding dean of the College of Health, Physical Education, Recreation and Dance. He has conducted research on practice conditions, information feedback, and the role of arousal on motor performance. He has written three books, including *Psychology of Motor Learning* and *American Indian Sports Heritage*.

Erik Peper is the associate director of the Institute for Holistic Healing Studies at California State University at San Francisco and is the director of the Biofeedback and Family Therapy Institute. His research focuses on biofeedback and applied psychophysiology to enhance optimal performance, and he has published numerous books and articles, including *Mind/Body Integration, From the Inside Out: A Self-Teaching and Laboratory Manual for Biofeedback*, and *Creating Wholeness: A Self-Healing Workbook Using Dynamic Relaxation, Images and Thoughts*. Dr. Peper is a consultant to musicians, artists, and athletes. He was a consultant to the U.S. Rhythmic Gymnastics Team. He is past president of the Biofeedback Society of America.

Kenneth Ravizza is a professor in the Department of Health, Physical Education, and Recreation at California State University at Fullerton. His research examines the nature of peak performance in human movement activities. Dr. Ravizza has been a sport psychology consultant with the Fullerton gymnastics, softball, and baseball teams for over a decade. He worked with the 1984 and 1988 Olympic Women's Field Hockey Teams, the 1988 Olympic Equestrian Team, and two figure skaters for the 1992 Olympics. He has worked with the California Angels for the past seven years. He has also developed and presented stress management programs for health care and school staffs, cancer patients, battered women, private business groups, and prison inmates.

Robert J. Rotella is the director of the sport psychology program at the University of Virginia. Dr. Rotella was named twice to "Outstanding College Athletes of America" and was awarded All-American honors in lacrosse. He has also coached high school basketball and college lacrosse teams. His research interests have focused on stress, anxiety, and self-confidence and sport performance. Dr. Rotella has written numerous books and articles on applied sport psychology; his books include *Mind Mastery for Winning Golf* and *Scientific Foundations of Coaching*. He has also served as consultant for the University of Virginia athletic teams, the University of Notre Dame, and professional athletes from football, basketball, baseball, and golf.

Andrea Schmid is professor of physical education at California State University at San Francisco. A two-time Olympian, she received gold, silver, and bronze medals in gymnastics. She coached the 1975 U.S. world championship team and judged 10 world championships and 2 Olympic Games in rhythmic gymnastics. She has published books and articles and given lectures on sport psychology at national and international conferences. Her research focuses on optimal performance. She is a member of the Federation of International Gymnastics and is the international consultant to the U.S. Gymnastics Federation. Dr. Schmid has served as sport psychology consultant to several college athletes and the U.S. Olympic rhythmic gymnasts and synchronized swimmers.

Ronald E. Smith is professor of psychology at the University of Washington, where he has served as the director of Clinical Psychology Training and is currently head of the Social Psychology and Personality area. He received his bachelor's degree from Marquette University and his Ph.D. in personality and clinical psychology from Southern Illinois University. He completed his advanced clinical training at the UCLA Neuropsychiatric Institute. Dr. Smith's major research interests are in personality, stress and coping, performance enhancement, and sport psychology research and intervention. He has written more than 100 scientific articles and book chapters and has authored or co-authored 10 books. Since 1986, Dr. Smith has directed a psychological skills training program within the Houston Astros Player Development Program and currently works as a roving minor league instructor for the Astros. He is the team counselor for the Seattle Mariners. In a recent poll of sport psychologists, Dr. Smith was named one of the top 10 sport psychologists in North America. Dr. Smith is a Fellow of the American Psychological Association, the American Psychological Society, and the AAASP, of which he is past president. He is also the recipient of a Distinguished Alumnus Award from the UCLA Neuropsychiatric Institute for his contributions to the field of psychology.

Frank L. Smoll is a professor in the Psychology Department at the University of Washington. His research has focused on developing and testing intervention programs designed to improve the quality of youth sports. While attending Ripon College, he played on championship basketball and baseball teams. In the area of applied sport psychology, Dr. Smoll has extensive experience in conducting psychologically oriented coaching clinics (Coach Effectiveness Training) and workshops for parents of young athletes. He is actively involved as a consultant to numerous youth sport organizations.

William F. Straub is president of Sport Science International. He is actively involved in helping athletes improve their individual and team performances. A former professor of biomechanics and sport psychology, Dr. Straub spent 14 years teaching physical education and coaching interscholastic teams. He played professional baseball in the St. Louis Cardinal farm system and was a three-sport athlete in college. Straub has published extensively in scholarly journals and has edited two books. He chaired AAHPERD's Sport Psychology Academy and is a Fellow of the American College of Sports Medicine, the AAASP, and the American Psychological Society. As a consultant, Dr. Straub has worked for Cornell University, SUNY-Cortland, the Washington Redskins, Adirondack Red Wings, and the Phildelphia Eagles.

Jim Taylor earned his doctorate in psychology from the University of Colorado, Boulder. He is currently an associate professor and sport psychologist in the School of Psychology at Nova University in Ft. Lauderdale, Florida. Dr. Taylor's research interests include the use of hypnosis and mental imagery in enhancing performance, career termination, coaching stress, and slumps and momentum. He has published over 80 articles in popular and professional publications and has given more than 70 workshops and presentations throughout the United States and in Europe. A former alpine ski racer who competed internationally, he is also a second-degree black belt in karate. He has worked with many junior-elite, collegiate, professional, world-class, and recreational athletes in tennis, skiing, baseball, swimming, golf, water skiing, and other sports. Dr. Taylor has been a consultant for several national governing bodies, including the U.S. Ski Team and the U.S. Tennis Association.

Robin S. Vealey is an associate professor in the Department of Physical Education, Health, and Sport Studies at Miami University in Ohio. Dr. Vealey's research interests include personality influences on achievement behavior in sport, particularly self-confidence, achievement goals, and competitive anxiety. She has also published in the areas of coaching behavior and the effectiveness of psychological training with athletes and coaches. Dr. Vealey has worked as a sport psychology consultant for the U.S. Nordic Ski Team, conducted clinics for U.S. Field Hockey, and is involved in psychological skills training with athletes and teams at Miami University. She is editor of *The Sport Psy-*

chologist and is a national instructor for the American Coaching Effectiveness Program. Prior to beginning a career in sport psychology, Dr. Vealey achieved national recognition as a collegiate basketball player and coach.

Susan M. Walter is a graduate student in sport psychology in the Department of Physical Education, Health, and Sport Studies at Miami University. After working at the Harvard University Business School as an exercise specialist, Ms. Walter focused her studies in the areas of sport psychology and motor learning. Her research interests include self-confidence, motivation, and imagery. She completed a B.A. at Hope College in Michigan, where she played field hockey and received all-league and regional honors.

Robert Weinberg is a professor and chair of the Department of Physical Education, Health, and Sport Studies at Miami University in Ohio. He has published over 80 journal articles as well as 5 books and 8 book chapters. He serves on the editorial boards of several sport psychology journals, including the *Journal of Applied Sport Psychology, The Sport Psychologist*, and the *Journal of Sport and Exercise Psychology*. He has served as president of the AAASP and chair of the AAHPERD Sport Psychology Academy. He is a Certified Consultant, AAASP and a member of the U.S. Olympic Committee's Sport Psychology Registry. He has worked extensively with young athletes developing psychological skills in a variety of individual and team sports. He has been a varsity athlete in tennis, football, and basketball and has coached these three sports.

David P. Yukelson is an applied sport psychology practitioner with the Academic Support Center for Student-Athletes at Pennsylvania State University, where he provides counseling and support to coaches and athletes in the areas of mental skills training, motivation and self-confidence, stress management, and responsible decision making. A Fellow and Certified Consultant in the AAASP and past president of NASPE's Sport Psychology Academy (AAHPERD), Dr. Yukelson also serves as a consultant for the U.S. Men's and Women's National and Junior Elite Racewalking Teams (TAC) and is a national faculty member with the American Coaching Effectiveness Program. His research interests include mental skills training, individual and group motivation in sport, life skill development and the student-athlete, and psychological considerations and the injured athlete.

Nathaniel Zinsser is presently the psychologist for the Performance Enhancement Center at the U.S. Military Academy in West Point. He is a graduate of the doctoral program in applied sport psychology at the University of Virginia and has served on the physical education faculties of East Stroudsburg University in Pennsylvania, the University of Virginia Division of Continuing Education, and William Patterson College in New Jersey. Dr. Zinsser contributes an advice column to the magazine *Sports Illustrated for Kids*; advises collegiate and nationally ranked athletes on the topics of confidence, concentration, and mental preparation; and has written the first sport psychology handbook for young athletes, *Dear Dr. Psych*. His research deals with the evolution of self-confidence in athletes and with the maintenance of commitment to training regimens and behavior change programs.

Sport Psychology: Past, Present, Future

Jean M. Williams, *University of Arizona*
William F. Straub, *Sport Science International*

Within the past 25 years, a new field of sport science has been recognized. It is called **sport psychology**, and it is concerned with both the psychological factors that influence participation and performance in sport and exercise and the psychological effects derived from them. Sport psychologists study motivation, personality, aggression and violence, leadership, group dynamics, exercise and psychological well-being, thoughts and feelings of athletes, and many other dimensions of participation in sport and physical activity. Among other functions, modern-day sport psychologists teach sport psychology classes, conduct research, and work with athletes, coaches, and exercise participants to help improve performance and enhance the quality of the sport and exercise experience.

Coaches were interested in the psychological aspects of athletic competition even before there was a science called sport psychology. For example, in the 1920s Knute Rockne, the football coach of the fighting Irish of Notre Dame, popularized the pep talk by making it an important part of his coaching. We should note, however, that Rockne did not attempt to psych up his team for every contest. He only used the pep talk for special occasions. Coaching interest in contemporary sport psychology also involves more than a mere concern for psyching up athletes for competition.

Applied sport psychology focuses on only one facet of sport psychology, that of identifying and understanding psychological theories and techniques that can be applied to sport and exercise to enhance the performance and personal growth of athletes and physical activity participants. Applied sport psychologists are part of a complex interrelationship between psychological theory, application, historical context, social influence, and the individual behavior of the applier and the recipient (Goldstein & Krasner, 1987).

The area of applied sport psychology has grown tremendously in recent years, as evidenced by the numbers of coaches and athletes now looking to sport psychology for a competitive edge. These individuals are turning to various psychological training programs to learn, among other things, ways to manage competitive stress, control concentration, improve confidence, and increase communication skills and team harmony. The goal of psychological training is to learn to consistently create the ideal mental climate that unleashes those physcial skills that allow athletes to perform at their best. The authors of subsequent chapters will discuss the factors introduced here and also present other psychological principles and techniques that can be used to enhance performance and personal growth. But, first, in this chapter we will provide a brief overview of the past, present, and future of sport psychology. Primary emphasis will be given to sport psychology practices in North America and the countries of Eastern Europe. The coverage is not all-inclusive but selective to the focus of the book.

History of Sport Psychology in North America

According to Mahoney (1989), sport psychology's conceptual roots lie in antiquity. For example, in early Greek and Asian cultures the interdependence of mind and body was not only acknowledged but emphasized as central to both performance and personal development. However, the scientific foundation of sport psychology emerged primarily during the last 25 years. Although modern sport psychology's roots and development lie largely within the domains of physical education and exercise science, psychologists conducted many of the earliest and most influential sport psychology investigations.

Coleman Griffith, a psychologist who is considered by many to be the grandfather of sport psychology in North America, was the first person to research sport psychology over an extended period of time. Griffith was hired by the University of Illinois in 1925 to help coaches improve the performance of their players. He wrote two books, *Psychology of Coaching* (1926) and *Psychology of Athletics* (1928), that are considered to be classics. He also established the first sport psychology laboratory in North America and taught the first course in sport psychology. By modern definition, Griffith was as much interested in motor learning as he was in sport psychology. Besides studying reaction time and flexibility, Griffith corresponded with Notre Dame coach Rockne about psychological and motivational aspects of coaching and athletics. Later Griffith served as a team psychologist and researcher for the Chicago Cubs baseball team. His personality study of the Cubs is of particular interest and importance since it was the forerunner of one of the first research emphases in sport psychology.

Following Griffith's work and up until the 1960s very little writing occurred in sport psychology, except for occasional research studies on personality and stress and a book, *Psychology of Coaching*, published in 1951 by John Lawther, a psychologist who also headed the Pennsylvania State University basketball team. Coaches were particularly interested in Lawther's treatment of such topics as motivation, team cohesion, personality, feelings and emotions, and the handling of athletes.

The 1960s: Birth of Applied Sport Psychology and Supporting Organizations

During the 1960s, two San Jose State University psychologists, Bruce Ogilvie and Tom Tutko (1966), created considerable interest in sport psychology with their research and their book *Problem Athletes and How to Handle Them*. According to Ogilvie, this book "moved the coaching world off dead center." After extensively researching the personality of athletes, Ogilvie and Tutko developed the controversial Athletic Motivation Inventory, a paper-and-pencil test that purported to measure the motives of athletes. Despite some criticism of their work, Ogilvie and Tutko were the leading applied sport psychologists of the 1960s. They did considerable consulting with college and professional teams and did much to foster public interest in sport psychology. Because of Ogilvie's many contributions, he has been called the father of applied sport psychology in North America.

The 1960s also witnessed the first attempts to bring together groups of individuals interested in sport psychology. In the early part of the decade, sport psychology began to organize on an international level with the formation of the International Society of Sport Psychology (ISSP) in Rome. Dr. Ferruccio Antonelli, an Italian psychiatrist, was elected the first president and provided leadership during the early years. The ISSP publishes the *International Journal of Sport Psychology* and hosts worldwide meetings. These gatherings provide a forum for sharing research and fostering the exchange of ideas by sport psychologists from different countries.

The second meeting of the ISSP was hosted in 1968 at Washington, D.C. by the newly formed North American Society for the Psychology of

Sport and Physical Activity (NASPSPA). The first annual meeting of NASPSPA was held in 1967 prior to the American Alliance for Health, Physical Education, Recreation and Dance (AAHPERD) conference in Las Vegas, Nevada. Dr. Arthur Slatter-Hammel of Indiana University was the first president. NASPSPA's annual meetings are well attended by scholars in motor learning and control, motor development, and sport psychology.

The late 1960s also saw the formation of the Canadian Society for Psychomotor Learning and Sport Psychology (CSPLSP). Founded by Robert Wilberg at the University of Alberta in 1969, CSPLSP was initially under the auspices of the Canadian Association for Health, Physical Education and Recreation, but it became independent in 1977. The members and leaders of NASPSPA and CSPLSP were extremely influential in building the research base in sport psychology and gaining acceptance of the field. The 1970s saw sport psychology being added to the conference programs of the American College of Sports Medicine (ACSM) and AAHPERD. The Sport Psychology Academy (SPA) within AAHPERD was the first group for which a major goal was to bridge the gap between the researcher and practitioner by providing an opportunity for sport psychologists to share their research and expertise with coaches and physical education teachers.

The 1970s: Flourishing Field Moves Toward Interactionism and Cognitive Focus

The decade of the 1970s was the period in which sport psychology in North America began to flourish and be recognized more widely as a separate discipline within the sport sciences. Systematic research by ever-increasing numbers of sport psychologists played a major role in this coming of age. In fact, the primary goal of sport psychologists in the 1970s was advancing sport psychology's knowledge base through experimental research. We should note, however, that there was no clear focus or agreement as to what the knowledge base should be. Consequently, research topics were very diverse and were directed toward many target populations. Topics typically came from mainstream psychology.

The earlier interest in personality research declined in the 1970s because of heated debates about the validity of personality traits and the paper-and-pencil tests used to assess the personality traits of athletes. Many sport psychologists continued to believe that internal mechanisms (i.e., traits) govern behavior, but these psychologists also became aware of the effect of environmental variables. The **interactionism paradigm**, which considers person and environmental variables and their potential interaction surfaced and began to gain credibility. Today interactionism is the most viable approach to the understanding of athlete behavior.

In the late 1970s and early 1980s sport psychology began to reflect a more cognitive focus by devoting increasing attention to athletes' thoughts and images. How athletes think influences how they perform. Negative thinking, the "I can't" attitude, seems to be associated with performance failure. The 1983 New York City Marathon provides an excellent example of how inner dialogue can influence the performance of runners. Geoff Smith, an Englishman, led for most of the race. Within approximately 300 meters of the finish line, Rod Dixon, a New Zealander, passed Smith and won the race. The difference between first and second place was 9 seconds, or about 50 yards. William P. Morgan (1984), a well-known sport psychology authority, indicated that Dixon's success may have been aided by his cognitive strategy. According to newspaper reports, Dixon stated, "With a mile to go I was thinking, 'A miler's kick does the trick,' and 'I've got to go, I've got to go.'" By contrast, with 600 yards to go, Smith is reported to have said, "My legs have gone." Later Smith noted, "I was just running from memory. I thought I was going to stumble and collapse." In fact, Smith did collapse at the finish line. Today many sport psychologists who work in the area of applied sport psychology have developed techniques to train athletes to think positively by focusing on what they want to happen as opposed to what they do *not* want to happen. Perhaps the results of the 1983 New York Marathon would have been different if Smith had employed these techniques.

The growth of cognitive sport psychology has also led to renewed interest in visualization. Athletes who naturally visualize themselves performing well or who are trained to image successful performances appear to both learn and perform better. Consequently, imagery and cognitive interventions have become an integral part of most mental training programs. See Chapters 16 and 17 for a detailed description of how these procedures work and how they can be trained.

The interest in cognitive sport psychology paralleled an increase in field research in sport psychology, which advanced knowledge in the area. Research has been conducted on topics such as identifying coaching behaviors most effective in promoting learning and personal growth, discovering ways to enhance team harmony and coach—athlete communications, learning how to set and use goals, determining psychological characteristics of successful performers, and developing psychological training techniques for enhancing performance and personal growth.

The 1980s: Growth in Field Reflected in Increased Research and Acceptance

An important development of the 1980s was better documentation of the effectiveness of psychological interventions at enhancing performance (see the chapters that follow and a meta-analysis by Greenspan and Feltz, 1989, for examples of this documentation). In addition to this performance enhancement research, the 1980s saw increased attention given to exercise and health psychology issues such as the psychological effects of exercise and overtraining, factors influencing participation in and adherence to exercise programs, exercise addiction, psychology of injury and injury rehabilitation, and the relationship of exercise to stress reactivity. Although much still needs to be learned and tested in regard to these topics in applied sport psychology, important advances have been made. The advances that are integral to enhancing athletic performance and personal growth will be discussed specifically in the following chapters.

Journals and books. The preceding description of research topics in sport psychology is one indication of the growth in the field of sport psychology, but perhaps the best reflection of the quality and volume of work in any academic area is the number of research journals devoted strictly to the discipline and the number of books published in the area. In 1979 the *Journal of Sport Psychology* was established as the second journal in sport psychology; its name was changed in 1988 to *Journal of Sport and Exercise Psychology* to reflect an expanding research base dealing with exercise and health psychology issues. The tremendous growth in applied sport psychology is exemplified by the establishment of *The Sport Psychologist* in 1987 and the *Journal of Applied Sport Psychology* in 1989. Both of these journals are devoted exclusively to applied sport psychology. *The Sport Psychologist* publishes research and articles that deal primarily with performance enhancement questions, and the *Journal of Applied Sport Psychology* encompasses the areas of social, health, and performance enhancement. The number of books dealing with applied sport psychology also has grown tremendously. For example, in a 1991 critique of only psychological skills training books in applied sport psychology, Sachs identified 48 books.

USOC recognition. Considerable growth and recognition of applied sport psychology also occurred because of publicity stemming from sport psychologists working with athletes, particularly Olympic athletes. In 1978 the United States Olympic Committee (USOC) recruited expert advisers in four branches of sport science: biomechanics, exercise physiology, nutrition, and sport psychology. This development was the first indication of the USOC's interest in using sport psychologists to help elite athletes enhance their performance. Later, in 1983, the USOC established an official Sport Psychology Committee and a registry of qualified sport psychologists. Following intensive review of an individual's credentials and experiences, he/she could be recognized as either a research, educational, or clinical sport psychologist. As a result of the USOC's development of its sport psychology program, sport psychologists played an increasingly prominent and visible role in the 1984 and 1988 Olympics (see Suinn, 1985, and issue #4, 1989, *The Sport Psychologist*). Television and written coverage of various sport psychology topics and interventions with Olympic athletes also created considerable interest among professionals and laypersons. Involvement by sport psychologists in the Olympic movement and on the professional level (see issue #4, 1990, *The Sport Psychologist*) and intercollegiate level continues to grow.

Formation of AAASP. The interest and knowledge base in sport psychology also is reflected by the number and quality of its national and international organizations. In addition to the ISSP, NASPSPA, CSPLSP, SPA, and ACSM, the Association for the Advancement of Applied Sport Psychology (AAASP) was formed in 1985. John Silva, a University of North Carolina sport psychologist, played the primary role in forming AAASP and served as its first president. The purpose of AAASP is to provide a forum to address applied aspects of sport psychology such as the promotion of applied research in the areas of social, health, and performance enhancement psychology; the promotion of the appropriate application of these research findings; and the examination of professional issues such as ethical standards, qualifications for becoming a sport psychologist, and certification of sport psychologists. Another objective is to promote the field of sport psychology within general psychology and to encourage membership from interested individuals trained in general psychology and other relevant disciplines as well as sport psychologists trained through physical education and exercise and sport science departments. AAASP appears to have met the latter objective, as 40% of its 650+ membership comes from individuals with degrees in psychology or equivalent departments.

Additional support for the growing recognition of sport psychology within mainstream psychology comes from the American Psychological Association (APA). In 1987 the APA officially recognized a sport psychology division, Division 47. Division 47 provides APA members with an opportunity to share research and discuss relevant sport psychology issues.

The 1990s: Continued Growth Spawns Certification Criteria

The 1990s have thus far been characterized by continued growth in sport psychology research and application of sport psychology knowledge. The implementation in 1991 by AAASP of guidelines for certified consultants should prove to be a milestone of the 1990s for sport psychology. The certification criteria provide minimum professional training and experience standards for individuals who wish to be certified by AAASP to provide services such as performance enhancement interventions for athletes. The criteria include a doctoral degree from an accredited institution of higher education and knowledge of the (1) scientific and professional ethics and standards; (2) sport psychology subdisciplines of intervention/performance enhancement, health/exercise psychology,

and social psychology; (3) biomechanical and/or physiological bases of sport; (4) historical, philosophical, social, or motor behavior bases of sport; (5) psychopathology and its assessment; (6) basic skills in counseling; (7) skills and techniques within sport or exercise; (8) skills in research design, statistics, and psychological assessment; (9) biological bases of behavior; (10) cognitive-affective bases of behavior; (11) social bases of behavior; and (12) individual behavior. Also required is a supervised experience with a qualified person (i.e., one who has an appropriate background in applied sport psychology), during which the individual receives training in the use of sport psychology principles and techniques.

Necessary levels of preparation in the preceding content areas generally require successful completion of at least three graduate semester hours or their equivalent. However, up to four upper-level undergraduate courses may be substituted for this requirement, except for the internship, sport psychology, and research design experiences. The sport psychology knowledge requirement must be evidenced by three courses or two courses and one independent study of which two of the courses must be taken at the graduate level. Also, entire courses may not be required for the ethics and sport skills knowledge areas. Whether or not the AAASP's certifying criteria and procedures will be widely accepted remains to be seen. The challenge of the 1990s will be to derive some consensus regarding the training of sport psychologists and the services they are qualified to provide.

History of Sport Psychology in Eastern Europe

Sport psychology in the former iron curtain countries of Eastern Europe is of particular importance to people interested in peak performance. These nations have a long history of giving a great deal of attention to the applied aspects of sport psychology—more specifically, the enhancing of elite athletes' performance through applied research and direct intervention. As a consequence of this emphasis, sport psychologists in Eastern Europe play an active role at all levels in the selection, training, and competitive preparation of athletes.

Sport psychology in Eastern Europe is a highly esteemed field of academic and professional concern as evidenced by state support and the acceptance of sport psychologists in national psychological associations. In some nations, sport psychologists have even been awarded the title of academician, a title that elevates the recipient to the level of a national hero. All of this was because in these countries sport excellence was considered to be an important propaganda tool in advancing the Communist political system, and sport psychologists were viewed as central figures in facilitating the athlete's quest for excellence.

Vanek and Cratty (1970) reported that the first interest in sport psychology in Eastern Europe can be traced to a physician, Dr. P. F. Lesgaft, who described in 1901 the possible psychological benefits of physical activity. The first research articles were published by Puni and Rudik in the early 1920s. The Institutes for Physical Culture in Moscow and Leningrad were also established in the early 1920s, and the beginning of sport psychology can be traced to them.

Garfield (Garfield & Bennett, 1984), who visited with a group of Soviet sport psychologists and physiologists while lecturing in Milan in 1979, reported that "the extensive investment in athletic research in the communist countries began early in the 1950s as part of the Soviet space program" (p. 13). Russian scientists successfully explored the possibility of using ancient yogic techniques to teach cosmonauts to control psychophysiological processes while in space. These techniques were called **self-regulation training** or **psychic self-regulation** and were used to voluntarily control such bodily functions as heart rate, temperature, and muscle tension, as well as emotional reactions to stressful situations such as zero gravity. Nearly 20 years passed before these methods were systematically applied to the Soviet and East German sport programs. According to Kurt Tittel, director of the Leipzig Institute of Sports (a 14-acre sport laboratory employing 900 people, over half of whom are scientists), new training methods similar to psychic self-regulation were responsible for the impressive victories by East German and Soviet athletes during the 1976 Olympics (Garfield & Bennett, 1984).

Salmela (1984) reported that sport psychology research in Eastern European countries has been more limited in scope than in North America because of greater governmental control. Rather narrowly focused five-year research plans were deter-

mined by the state with the advice of its sport psychologists. All sport psychology researchers within the country were required to coordinate and streamline their research efforts to accomplish the stated research objective. Salmela (1981) also indicated that this research focus tended to be of a field variety and applied primarily toward top-level achievement in sport. This is not surprising considering each state's heavy emphasis on sport excellence and the easy access by sport psychologists to elite athletes. Most of the Eastern European sport institutes where athletes are trained have teams of sport psychologists. Salmela (1984), on a visit to a major sport institute in Bucharest, Romania, reported meeting with a team of eight sport psychologists. A sport psychology faculty of that size is considered normal for that type of sport institute. In contrast, in North America it is uncommon for an institution to have more than one or two people specifically trained in sport psychology.

Although most North American sport psychologists would find government-dictated research endeavors abhorrent, a large-scale, unified approach to a particular research topic does have advantages. Salmela (1984) cited one positive example that was a consequence of knowledge gained from a constrained focus of attention. All Eastern European countries successfully inaugurated as many as 30 hours of theory and practice of training in self-control for all elite athletes. Equivalent types of programs have been implemented on only a limited basis in North America.

The exact training techniques employed by Eastern European sport psychologists are not known; however, a recent book by a Russian sport psychologist indicates that autogenic training, visualization, and autoconditioning (self-hypnosis) are key components (Raiport, 1988). Because of government-funded research and widespread integration of sophisticated mental training programs with rigorous physical training, many authorities believed Eastern Europe was ahead of North America and the rest of the world in the development and application of applied sport psychology. Whatever gap initially existed has been rapidly closing as North Americans complement their growing research base with experience in implementing performance-enhancement interventions with athletes. With the 1990s bringing the termination of communist control in Eastern Europe and the break-up of the Soviet Union, the future status of sport and sport psychology in what previously were called the iron curtain countries is impossible to predict accurately. Considering the extensiveness of state support prior to the 1990s and the underlying political motivation in promoting excellence in sport, the future of sport psychology in Eastern Europe may not be as bright as its past.

Future Directions in North American Sport Psychology

What will be the future of sport psychology in North America? Will sport psychologists take a more active role in educating coaches and athletes regarding psychological training techniques for enhancing performance and personal growth? What should be the future directions in sport psychology research? Will the effectiveness of performance-enhancement techniques be rigorously tested? Will we continue to bridge the gap between research and practice? What will be the impact on graduate curriculums of AAASP's recently implemented certification standards? Will the training of future sport psychologists more rigorously merge the disciplines of psychology and sport science? Will extensive coursework in sport psychology and supervised internships be required? Who will house graduate programs in sport psychology? Will future sport psychology practitioners be certified? Will the acceptance of sport psychology by mainstream psychology continue to grow? Will the demand for sport psychologists increase? For example, will college and professional teams hire more sport psychologists and will businesses start hiring sport psychologists? If so, what kinds of services will future sport psychologists be qualified to provide? How can the various organizations in sport psychology complement each other? These and other questions abound as we consider the future of sport psychology.

As these questions indicate, the field of sport psychology is undergoing considerable change. Its future nature and scope hinge upon answers to the preceding questions. Although at this time it is impossible to provide definitive answers, a study by Straub and Hinman (in press) that queried ten of North America's leading sport psychologists (Gould, Landers, Martens, Nideffer, Ogilvie, Orlick, Scanlan, Singer, Smith, and Weinberg) provides important information regarding these questions

as well as other concerns. All respondents believe that the next 10 years are absolutely critical to the growth of sport psychology. Scanlan emphasizes that "effort will require the contribution, indeed coordinated actions, of all members of the field."

Some of the sport psychologists hold strong opinions about future research directions. Nideffer, for example, postulates an interface between biomechanics, exercise physiology, and psychology. He believes that "studies will be designed to examine the effects cognitive processes have on physiological and biomechanical processes in complex environments." The focus, according to Weinberg, should be on bridging the gap between research and practice. Gould and Martens support the use of qualitative and tacit knowledge. Singer, in agreement with Gould, Weinberg, and Martens, speculates that there will be more research in "real" settings and sport-simulating laboratory situations. Exercise or health psychology, Landers and Gould suggest, will be a highly viable subarea due to widespread grant support. Landers and Smith indicate that sport psychology will become a truly interdisciplinary field positioned between exercise science and psychology. Smith expects to see a continued acceptance of sport psychology within mainstream psychology, resulting in more fruitful, and very welcome, interactions between psychology and sport sciences.

Orlick states that sport psychology is headed toward more and more applications and integration of mental skill training into daily physical and technical practice settings. According to him, the mental links to excellence in sport will be adopted by many other domains. Orlick also indicates that the opportunity to develop relevant mental skills approaches for young children will begin to gain much attention, once people recognize its potential value.

The education of sport psychologists continues to be a major concern. Singer indicates that the main challenge facing sport psychologists is to establish a bona fide curriculum that is reasonably standardized. This curriculum, Singer suggests, is needed to produce the scholarly base, competencies, and practitioner skills for the would-be sport psychologist. Sport psychology, Singer continues, needs acceptance for its legitimacy. Weinberg also believes that the development of professional standards/certification is needed. (Note: The survey of these sport psychologists was completed before the implementation of AAASP's certification procedures.)

Nideffer and Landers believe that, in the future, students will receive their terminal degrees in APA-approved programs in counseling or clinical psychology. Landers also sees students receiving a second degree in exercise science. Nideffer contends that a turf battle is taking place between psychology and physical education. This friction, he believes, is causing students to earn two Ph.D.'s, one in the sport sciences and the other in psychology. The recommended courses, according to Nideffer, are excessive. Instead of licensing and/or certifying the general title "sport psychologist," Nideffer suggests that individuals should be certified on the basis of specific functions that their education and experience would qualify them to perform. Some persons, for example, would be certified to make use of psychological tests in sport settings. Others, Nideffer indicates, would be certified to practice relaxation strategies with athletes. This approach would limit training and experience and would not require everyone to have a Ph.D. in sport psychology and in sport science. Ogilvie says that we must demand that every person who professes to be a sport psychologist serve an internship under supervision before being permitted to practice. Course content at the graduate level, according to Singer, will be designed cooperatively by psychology and sport science departments.

Most of these leading sport psychologists are concerned about the job market. Nideffer and Weinberg predict that sport psychologists will be hired by businesses to teach stress management, team building, and decision making under pressure. Weinberg indicates that there will be an expanding job market in academic counseling and working with Olympic athletes. Ogilvie believes the future looks bright for those trained to treat problems of obesity, stress, and physical rehabilitation within a thriving sports medicine clinic staff. Gould, however, states that people who gravitate toward the field often have unrealistic expectations, for example, working with professional teams to make large sums of money. Singer, on the other hand, believes there will be more active involvement with high school, college, professional, and international teams.

In contrast to the above opinions, Ogilvie, Smith, and Martens worry about the viability of the future job market in academia. Ogilvie states that the Ph.D. opens the door to an academic appointment, but with the financial state of higher education even these positions are limited. However, according to Ogilvie, the tremendous interest in the psychology of wellness has the potential for opening opportunities for applied sport psychologists. Smith indicates that there is still no appreciable demand for sport psychologists within psychology departments. The situation will only change, Smith contends, if sport psychology research finds its way into mainstream psychology journals.

Scanlon summarizes well when she says, "What I hope to see in the next decade is an enthusiastic, vital group of 'pioneers' making significant strides in developing, articulating, and disseminating a scientifically sound knowledge base that is truly unique to sport psychology." The generation of new theory, research, and applications that are sport psychology specific is perhaps the field's greatest challenge. All ten sport psychologists agree that this unique body of knowledge is essential to academic, professional, and public credibility and impact.

There are divergent views among the sport psychologists about the effectiveness and future directions of professional organizations. Nideffer, for example, states that he believes there will be a merging of organizations in the future, with sport psychology probably controlled by the APA. Criteria for membership, licensure, certification, and the like will be controlled by Division 47.

Weinberg, Singer, and Smith, on the other hand, indicate that the different sport psychology organizations (e.g., NASPSPA, AAASP, ISSP) serve different functions and therefore should maintain their own identities. They suggest that there is a need for cooperation and integration. Singer does not see the need for unification but indicates that it would be ideal if the leaders of the professional societies would meet periodically.

Scanlon states that the formation of new organizations reflects the growth of the field. She indicates that organizations such as NASPSPA, SPA, AAASP, and Division 47 provide diversity of interest and opportunities. However, Scanlon continues, sport psychology is too small to "cut the pie into too many pieces." Martens states that the splintering of organizations has seriously impaired the field. As a result of splintering, Landers says, sport psychology is not influential enough to affect social policy or policy within sporting agencies such as the USOC. Despite the varied opinions, the respondents all agree with Scanlon's suggestion that we need to be communicating, accepting and assimilating diversity, and growing together.

Gould desires to spend less time focusing on political issues (e.g., turf battles) and to direct attention to basic values and questions underlying work in the field. We should study, Gould suggests, how to provide better and more effective services to coaches, athletes, and exercisers. In addition, Gould desires more meaningful research. Considering the many challenges facing sport psychology, the next decade should be very exciting for sport psychologists and the individuals who benefit from their services.

Summary

Sports psychology, the youngest of the sport sciences, is concerned with the psychological factors that influence participation in sport and exercise and with the psychological effects derived from participation. Today many athletes and coaches look to sport psychology for a competitive edge by seeking psychological training programs in order to learn, among other things, ways to manage competitive stress, control concentration, improve confidence, and increase communication skills and team harmony.

The roots of sport psychology in North America go back to Coleman Griffith, a psychologist who was hired in 1925 by the University of Illinois to help improve the performance of its athletes. Griffith taught the first course in sport psychology, established the first sport psychology laboratory in North America, and wrote the first psychology of coaching book. Following Griffith's contributions in the 1920s and 1930s, very little happened in sport psychology until the 1960s. The 1960s witnessed the first attempts to bring together groups of individuals interested in sport psychology, which resulted in the formation of several sport psychology associations. During the 1970s, sport psychology in North America began to flourish. Systematic research by increasing numbers of sport psychologists played a major role in this coming of age. Research topics were very diverse and were channeled toward many populations.

During the 1980s a shift occurred from primarily laboratory to field research. It became very popular to apply psychological theories and techniques to sport to enhance the performance and personal growth of athletes. Increased attention also was given to exercise and health psychology issues.

The growth in applied sport psychology resulted in the formation of an additional sport psychology organization (AAASP) and two new journals. An additional consequence was greater concern regarding professional issues such as trying to identify minimal standards for training and certifying sport psychologists. During this same time, sport psychology became more acceptable to mainstream psychology and an increasing number of psychologists became active in sport psychology.

In contrast, sport psychology in the countries of Eastern Europe has a long history of devoting a great deal of attention to enhancing the performance of elite athletes through applied research and direct intervention. Sport psychologists in these countries are viewed as central figures in facilitating an athlete's quest for excellence. Thus, they are held in great esteem because sport excellence was considered an important propaganda tool in advancing the Communist political system of Eastern Europe. With the break-up of communist party control in Eastern Europe, it is not possible to predict if future government support of sport psychology researchers and practitioners will be as extensive as what occurred previously.

Based on Straub and Hinman's (1991) investigation of ten of North America's leading sport psychologists, future directions in sport psychology were presented. Although these sport psychologists are optimistic about the future of the field, there are a number of concerns that need to be addressed if sport psychology is to continue to grow and prosper. The education of sport psychologists, certification requirements, job market, continued development of a unique scientifically sound knowledge base, and other concerns were mentioned.

Study Questions

1. Define what is meant by applied sport psychology.

2. What is the goal of psychological training?

3. List at least four organizations and four research journals in sport psychology.

4. Briefly describe the development of sport psychology in North America.

5. Contrast the development of sport psychology in Eastern Europe to that in North America.

6. Discuss at least five concerns regarding the future of sport psychology.

References

Garfield, C. A., & Bennett, H. Z. (1984). *Peak performance*. Los Angeles: Tarcher.

Goldstein, A. P., & Krasner, L. (1987). *Modern applied psychology*. Elmsford, N.Y.: Pergamon.

Greenspan, M. J., & Feltz, D. L. (1989). Psychological interventions with athletes in competitive situations: A review. *The Sport Psychologist, 3,* 219–236.

Griffith, C. R. (1926). *Psychology of coaching.* New York: Scribner.

Griffith, C R. (1928). *Psychology of athletics.* New York: Scribner.

Kroll, W., & Lewis, G. (1970). America's first sport psychologists. *Quest, 13,* 1–4.

Lawther, J. D. (1951). *Psychology of coaching.* Englewood Cliffs, N.J.: Prentice-Hall.

Mahoney, M. J. (1989). Sport psychology. In I. Cohen (Ed.), *The G. Stanley Hall lecture series* (vol. 9) (pp. 97–134). Washington, D.C.: American Psychological Association.

Morgan, W. P. (1984). Mind over matter. In W. F. Straub & J. M. Williams (Eds.), *Cognitive sport psychology* (pp. 311–316). Lansing, N.Y.: Sport Science International.

Ogilvie, B., & Tutko, T. (1966). *Problem athletes and how to handle them.* London: Pelham.

Raiport, G. (1988). *Red gold: Peak performance techniques of the Russian and East German Olympic victors.* New York: Tarcher.

Sachs, M. L. (1991). Reading list in applied sport psychology: Psychological skills training. *The Sport Psychologist, 5,* 88–91.

Salmela, J. H. (1981). *The world sport psychology sourcebook.* Ithaca, N.Y.: Mouvement Publications.

Salmela, J. H. (1984). Comparative sport psychology. In J. M. Silva III & R. A. Weinberg (Eds.), *Psychological foundations of sport* (pp. 23–24). Champaign, Ill.: Human Kinetics.

Straub, W. F., & Hinman, D. A. (1992). Profiles and professional perspectives of ten leading sport psychologists, *The Sport Psychologist, 6,* 297–312.

Suinn, R. M. (1985). The 1984 Olympics and sport psychology. *Journal of Sport Psychology, 7,* 321–329.

U.S. Olympic Committee (1983). U.S. Olympic Committee establishes guidelines for sport psychology services. *Journal of Sport Psychology, 5,* 4–7.

Vanek, M., & Cratty, B. J. (1970). *Psychology and the superior athlete.* New York: Macmillan.

Motor Skill Learning for Effective Coaching and Performance

Mark G. Fischman, *Auburn University*
Joseph B. Oxendine, *Pembroke State University*

E ffective coaching depends on many factors. Coaches must have excellent knowledge of their sport and be innovative strategists, skilled motivators, and effective personal counselors. However, at the core of successful coaching is an understanding of the motor learning process. First and foremost, effective coaches must be good teachers. Most sports comprise a diverse array of complex motor skills. Athletes enter the sporting arena with different abilities and prior experiences. The coach must understand both how the novice performer acquires brand new skills and how the experienced athlete maintains peak performance on well-learned skills. This understanding will enable the coach to structure effective practices and to provide clear, effective feedback to the athlete about performance errors. The understanding also will enable the sport psychologist to help coaches critique whether or not their behaviors and learning and practice environment maximize the potential growth of their athletes.

This chapter's goal is to present coaches and sport psychologists with information concerning the essentials of motor skill learning. We begin by describing a three-phase model of the learning process and then proceed to the two topics that are the most critical determinants of skill learning and

performance: practice considerations and feedback. Clearly, there are a wealth of other topics that are also important for motor skill learning. However, the topics chosen were selected because of their immediate relevance to the practical world of coaching. The principles and recommendations presented in this chapter are based on knowledge derived from motor learning research, but with the understanding that in some areas the current state of research may be less than adequate for making generalizations to applied sport settings.

Phases of Motor Skill Learning

Motor skill learning should be understood as a set of internal processes, associated with practice or experience, leading to relatively permanent changes in skilled movement behavior. Because motor learning is internal, taking place within the athlete's central nervous system, we cannot observe learning directly. We can, however, monitor an athlete's *performance*, which is observable behavior, and draw an inference about learning. For example, a beginning swimmer's first attempts at the butterfly stroke will likely proceed in an awkward, step-by-step manner. As the swimmer practices, form, timing, and coordination improve. By monitoring these changes in performance we infer that the swimmer is learning. It is also important that the changes in performance be relatively permanent; that is, the athlete should be able to demonstrate the skill repeatedly, even after a period of no practice.

As athletes progress from the novice stage to an advanced level, they go through different phases or steps. The clearest model of this process was developed by Fitts and Posner (1967; Fitts, 1964), who described three phases in motor skill learning: the cognitive, the associative, and the autonomous phases. However, it would be misleading to think of these phases as distinct because, as learning progresses, one phase blends gradually into another, so that no clear transitions between them are evident (Christina & Corcos, 1988; Fitts & Posner, 1967). Thus, the phases of learning should be thought of as a continuum, with some overlap occurring between the cognitive and associative phases and between the associative and autonomous phases. It is doubtful that there would be any overlap between the cognitive and autonomous phases within a particular skill.

The Cognitive Phase

In the cognitive, or beginning, phase of skill learning, learners focus on gaining an understanding of how the skill is to be performed. The coach or teacher explains or describes the skill. In addition, he/she will typically provide demonstrations, films, charts, or other visual cues to help the learners "picture" the new skill. During this period the learners use cognition, or mental processes, to gain an understanding of how the task is to be performed. The cognitive phase is characterized by much verbal activity by the learners; they "talk" themselves through the movements. In fact, Adams (1971) used the term **verbal-motor** to describe this phase of learning.

When athletes listen to an explanation of a skill new to them and then observe a demonstration of the skill, they begin to develop a **motor program** for that skill. A motor program is an abstract representation of the skill, similar to a computer program, and contains a set of instructions to guide movement. These instructions are written in the language of the athletes' nervous system and muscular system and allow the athletes to begin

practicing the skill. At first the motor program may be very crude, containing just enough details to allow the athletes to make a "ballpark" response. There are also likely to be errors in the program, just as there would be in the initial attempts to write a complex computer program. However, with practice and feedback, both from the athletes' sensory systems and supplemented by information feedback from the coach, the motor program is revised so that it gradually becomes more effective at controlling performance.

This process is characterized by much conscious attention to the details of movement. The learners are not free to devote their attention to other aspects of the environment, such as positions of teammates or movements of defensive players. The dominant sensory system in the cognitive phase of learning is *vision*; we visually monitor our limbs when first practicing a new skill. For example, observe a young child learning to dribble a basketball: The child intently watches both the hand and the ball, knowing that without such visual guidance, the dribble will be lost. Vision of the limbs is also important in the beginning phase of learning skills that do not involve manipulating another object, such as learning a new gymnastics routine.

One of the critical aspects during the cognitive phase of learning is the demonstration of the new skill for the learners. There is much truth in the saying "a picture is worth a thousand words," and a demonstration will help learners create a reference image of the skill so that practice can begin. A good demonstration can be an effective tool in helping learners gain a basic understanding of the skill. However, a correctly performed demonstration does not necessarily ensure that the athletes' attention was focused on the most important part of the demonstration. The coach must tell the athletes *specifically* what to look for, whether it be the pattern of racket movement in a looped tennis backswing, the position of the recovery elbow in the crawl stroke, or the entire pattern of coordination in a baseball swing. A favorite example of how a demonstration, although executed correctly, can ultimately backfire comes from a series of cartoon drawings of a dog being trained in proper bathroom protocol (see Singer, 1982). The first picture shows the dog, lifting its leg, having an "accident" on a living room chair. In the second picture the dog and his owner are outside by a tree in the yard.

The third illustration shows the man demonstrating the proper technique—use the tree. In this picture the dog is paying careful attention to the demonstration, or so it seems. The final picture shows the dog, back in the house, again using the chair. But this time the dog is up on its hind legs! Something went wrong. The demonstration was correct, but what the "coach" thought he was demonstrating was not what the "athlete" was seeing. The athletes' attention must be drawn to the most critical aspect of the demonstration.

The cognitive phase of learning is a relatively short period in the overall learning process. It may last only a few minutes, as in teaching a simple skill to older athletes, or it may involve a longer period if the skill is complex and the athletes are very young. The cognitive phase is complete when the athletes can reasonably execute the skill the way it was demonstrated and can now begin practicing (Christina & Corcos, 1988).

The Associative Phase

The associative, or intermediate, phase of skill learning is a much longer period than the cognitive phase, ranging from perhaps a few hours to learn simple skills to several years for mastering complex ones. During this phase the learner practices the skill to the point that it is performed both accurately and consistently. Instruction during this phase mainly involves planning and implementing effective practice conditions. With the proper practice and feedback, you can expect each athlete's motor program for the skill to become better developed than it was in the cognitive phase of learning.

As learners progress through the associative phase, they will have to attend less and less to the physical execution of the skill. As the movements become more automated, some attention can be devoted to other aspects of the environment, such as planning strategy. Visual control of movement, which was dominant during the cognitive phase of learning, is gradually replaced by **proprioceptive control**, or "feel." Returning to the example of learning to dribble a basketball, the child can now effectively dribble the ball without looking at the ball or his/her hand and could probably dribble it with the eyes closed. Were proprioceptive cues not available during the early phase of learning? They were available, but the athletes were simply not yet sensitive to them. It takes many practice trials before athletes come to associate the feel of their movements with the outcomes that these movements produce. Schmidt (1975) referred to the generation of "expected sensory consequences," meaning that we expect our movements to feel a certain way, and we can use such sensory feedback to evaluate the correctness of our movements.

During the associative phase of learning, athletes gradually eliminate extraneous movements and errors. They improve their speed, accuracy, coordination, and consistency. Closed skills, which are those performed in a relatively stable, predictable environment such as bowling, target archery, free throw shooting, and tennis serving, become more consistent, while open skills, in which the environment is changing and unpredictable, become more diversified. Examples of open skills include returning a punt in football, executing a breakaway in field hockey or soccer, and driving through heavy rush-hour traffic. In general, athletes improve their performance during this phase to the point of mastery.

The Autonomous Phase

The autonomous, or advanced, phase of learning emerges when the learner can perform the skill with perfection (or at a maximal level of proficiency). As the term implies, performance is quite automatic; the learner seems to require very little conscious thought or attention to the details of movement. In fact, asking highly skilled performers to consciously focus on their movements will seriously disrupt performance, especially in high-speed activities such as performing a routine on the uneven bars in gymnastics or executing a dodge and kick for goal in soccer.

In the autonomous phase the learners' understanding of the skill is excellent. Their motor program for generating the correct movements is highly developed and well established in memory. Free from having to concentrate on executing the skill, they can concentrate on other things besides technique. For example, the NBA's Michael Jordan can dribble the basketball downcourt at full speed on a fast break and change course by dribbling behind his back. He does this without looking at the ball and while planning the best strategy for getting the ball to the basket. During such a play he considers the position and movements of his opponents as well as his teammates. He considers delivering a bounce pass to the right or to the left or perhaps faking in one direction and, if the defensive player takes the fake, driving for the basket himself, or pulling up short and shooting a 15-foot jump shot. He also has the option of slowing down and taking the ball outside to set up a new play. Jordan does all this while dribbling the ball at full speed, *giving no thought to the mechanics of dribbling*, and there is rarely an error in the dribble itself. He is "programmed" to perform the fundamental skills of basketball, which include dribbling. A similar analysis would apply to Diego Miradona bringing a soccer ball down the field or to Katarina Witt, the figure skater, performing a complex routine. They perform their skills while devoting little thought to the actual movements involved.

Each of these tasks—basketball dribbling, soccer, and figure skating—is a complex motor skill that requires some native ability as well as a great deal of practice before one reaches the autonomous phase. Yet each of these experts began as a novice, comparable to a child beginning to walk, or an American adult in a Chinese restaurant attempting to use chopsticks for the first time. Progressing from the cognitive through the associative and arriving at the autonomous phase of learning requires an amount of practice and a period of time that depend on the abilities of the individual, the complexity of the task itself, the learner's prior movement experiences, and the efficiency of the learning environment. Certainly high-speed dribbling, complex figure skating maneuvers, and a two and a half gainer dive require more time and practice to master than does a vertical jump or a simple swan dive. In the next section of this chapter we consider some of the aspects of this most important variable, practice, in the skill-learning process. For now, suffice it to say that some speculate that it requires from 8 to 15 years and over a million repetitions to produce high-level performance in major sports such as football, basketball, baseball, and gymnastics (Kottke et al., 1978).

Instruction during the autonomous phase of learning basically serves two purposes: first, to help the athletes maintain their level of skill, and, second, to motivate the athletes to continue to want to improve. Once a consistently high level of skill is achieved, it must be maintained not only during a single season but also from season to season. Recall that our definition of motor learning referred

to changes in skilled behavior that are relatively permanent. Also, it would be a mistake to assume that learning has ended in the autonomous phase and that performance cannot be improved. While the level of competence an athlete may achieve in a skill has certain limits, and performance may be approaching some arbitrary standard of perfection, the progression to this point usually occurs so gradually that it is rarely possible to claim that athletes have reached their highest level of achievement (Christina & Corcos, 1988). However, because of the difficulty in improving performance as one approaches the highest levels of skill, even though practice continues, athletes may lose motivation to strive for improvement. Thus, the role of the coach as a motivator becomes very important during this phase of learning.

An understanding of the motor learning process and the phases of skill learning is important for teaching new skills to novice athletes. However, an understanding of the phases of learning is also important when a coach desires to *change* a highly skilled athlete's well-learned technique. Making a minor change in technique, such as widening a baseball player's batting stance, is simple and can usually be accomplished easily. Having a tennis player change from an Eastern forehand grip to the continental grip should also be accomplished with little difficulty. This is because changes such as these require very little relearning. However, when you ask athletes to make a major change in technique, such as going from a two-hand backhand in tennis to a one-hand backhand, you are essentially asking them to return to the cognitive phase of learning and progress through the associative and autonomous phases again. When you consider that it may have taken years of practice to perfect the motor program for the original technique, you realize that learning the new technique will require a great deal of time. Major changes in technique should probably be undertaken during the off season.

When athletes are in the process of relearning a skill, performance will initially suffer. This can be very discouraging and the athletes may hold the coach responsible. The coach should be prepared to accept this responsibility and take some of the pressure off the athletes by providing much encouragement. Ultimately, when relearning is accomplished, the athletes' performance should be better than it was with the old technique.

Practice Considerations

Most writers agree that the single most important factor in the control of learning is **practice**, the repeated performance of a skill so as to become proficient. In general, the greater the number of practice trials, the better the learning. However, practice by itself is not enough to enable athletes to learn a skill correctly. For practice to be effective, the athletes must be motivated to learn. The old adage that "practice makes perfect" is not necessarily true; athletes must practice with the *intent* to improve. This means that skill learning involves more than simply going through the motions physically. A good example of this principle can be seen in a motor skill that most adults perform daily throughout their lives—handwriting. The handwriting of one of the authors (Fischman) is no better now than it was when he was in the sixth grade, over 30 years ago, although he has performed it thousands of times since. In fact, many colleagues suggest that it may even be worse. Without the intent to improve, practice can lead to a mediocre level of proficiency or, worse, a deterioration of skill (Christina & Corcos, 1988).

Given athletes who are motivated to learn, the coach is faced with the task of organizing and scheduling practice so that maximal learning occurs. The next sections of this chapter present several topics important in organizing effective practice sessions. One topic that we will not cover here is mental practice, the cognitive rehearsal of a skill without overt movement. This important topic is covered later in this book (see Chapter 16).

Teaching Several Skills: Blocked Versus Random Practice

In most sports, athletes are challenged to learn a variety of different skills. Swimmers, for example, must learn four strokes, along with starts and turns. Gymnasts must learn many routines on several pieces of equipment. Tennis players must learn forehand and backhand groundstrokes, several different serves, net play, and appropriate strategies. Golfers are charged with learning to hit many different clubs over a variety of distances and often through various obstacles. Novice athletes have to learn the many skills of their sport before the first competition. Experienced athletes have to practice these many skills in order to maintain peak performance.

Considering the large number of skills that are comprised in most sports and the often restricted practice time available, coaches are forced to teach more than a single skill in a week; often, several skills must be taught in a single practice session. How can a coach sequence the practice of several tasks during the practice period to maximize learning?

Suppose that an age-group swim team practices four times a week for an hour per session. The coach would like to devote two weeks to teaching the four competitive strokes: butterfly, backstroke, breaststroke, and freestyle. A commonsense approach to scheduling would be to practice the butterfly for two sessions, then the backstroke for two sessions, and so on until all four strokes are completed. This schedule of practice is called **blocked practice**, where all the trials of a given task are completed before moving on to the next task. Actually, the order in which the strokes are practiced could be arbitrary, as long as practice on one stroke is completed before beginning practice on the next stroke. Intuitively, blocked practice seems to make sense because it allows the swimmers to concentrate on one stroke at a time without worrying about interference from the other strokes.

An alternative approach to scheduling would be to practice all four strokes within each practice period, but to do so in a random order so that the swimmers never practice the same stroke on two consecutive trials. This is called a **random practice** schedule. It is important to note that at the end of our two-week period, both practice schedules would have provided the same amount of practice on each of the four strokes. Random practice would appear to present a more difficult environment for the learner because of the constant switching between tasks.

Which of these practice schedules might produce more efficient learning in our swimmers? At first glance, the obvious answer would be blocked practice, and, if we plotted the swimmers' performance of the four strokes over the two-week learning period, we would probably find better performance under blocked practice. However, a sizable body of research seems to contradict this intuitive view about practice. The results of many laboratory-based experiments indicate that blocked practice produces better acquisition performance than random practice, but poorer long-term learning, as measured by delayed retention and **transfer**, the application of the practiced skill in a new situation (Lee & Magill, 1983; Shea & Morgan, 1979; Shea & Zimny, 1983). This phenomenon is known as the **contextual interference** effect, based on the early work of Battig (1966). For a comprehensive review of contextual interference see Magill and Hall (1990).

Essentially, contextual interference proposes that making the practice environment more difficult for the learner, as with random practice, leads to better learning, even though performance during acquisition is depressed. This is certainly a counterintuitive idea, and we are challenged to understand how a practice structure that degrades acquisition performance can produce more learning.

Recent attempts to explain why random practice is more effective than blocked practice for learning suggest two possible mechanisms. First, when several tasks are present in the learners' working memory at the same time, the learners have to use more elaborate processing strategies to keep the tasks distinct. This more effortful processing produces better memory representations of the tasks (Shea & Zimny, 1983). Second, when learners practice a task on trial 1 but do not repeat that task until several trials later, there may be some forgetting of the "solution" to the task. The learners are forced to go through more solution generations with random practice, which ultimately leads to better retrieval (Lee & Magill, 1983).

While most of the research support for contextual interference comes from laboratory-type tasks, there are several recent attempts to apply the laboratory findings to more real-world sport skills, such as learning different badminton serves (Goode & Magill, 1986; Wrisberg & Liu, 1991), and learning to toss beanbags to a target (Pigott & Shapiro, 1984). Results from these studies are, in general, supportive of the laboratory-based findings in that random practice produced better retention and transfer than blocked practice. We certainly need more field-based research in a variety of sports before we can be truly confident about the learning benefits of random practice. Nevertheless, the available research should encourage coaches to at least think about some of their deeply rooted traditional practice methods. Sometimes we can be led astray by following the intuitively obvious.

Teaching Several Variations of a Skill: Variable Practice

In the preceding discussion the coach's goal was to teach several *different* tasks. There are also times, however, where only a single task is to be learned during a practice session, such as shooting a jump shot, kicking a field goal, or fielding a ground ball. How should the coach structure practice for these situations to maximize learning?

Consider the task of developing one of the skills needed by a shortstop in softball, specifically, fielding a ground ball and throwing to first base. This task essentially involves perceiving a stimulus (the ground ball), moving the body in front of the ball, getting down to field it, and making an accurate throw. Coach A believes that the best way to learn this task would be to practice under **constant** conditions. She will give her shortstop 100 ground balls to field, but each one will be thrown by a pitching machine, have a constant velocity, come to the same spot on the field, and have exactly the same bounce and roll characteristics. Coach A feels that this type of practice will allow her shortstop to master the fundamentals of fielding and to "groove" her response.

Coach B adopts a **variable** practice approach. She will also give her shortstop 100 balls to field, but each one will be hit by a batter, come to different spots on the field so that the player has to move both left and right, and possess different bounce and roll characteristics. Coach B reasons that in the real game, no two ground balls are exactly alike, so variability of practice would be more likely to produce the specific skills needed by a shortstop. This type of drill more realistically simulates actual game conditions. It is also possible that in an actual game a shortstop will have to field a ball that is slightly different from any of the 100 variations experienced during practice. Coach B's shortstop would be more likely to experience success at this "novel" task than coach A's shortstop because of all the practice received at similar versions of the task.

What is actually being learned through variable practice is more than simply the specific actions practiced. The shortstop develops a general capability to produce "fielding" responses, a capability that enhances generalizability, allowing athletes to transfer their learning to actions not specifically experienced in practice. According to schema theory (Schmidt, 1975, 1988, 1991), variable practice allows the learner to discover relationships among environmental conditions (my location on the field, speed and bounce characteristics of the ball, distance from first base), what she "told" her muscles to produce (how fast to move, where to put my glove, how hard to throw), and the outcomes that these movements produced (missed/caught the ball, threw too far or too short). Through variable practice the athlete's understanding of these relationships becomes stronger and she develops a set of "schemas," or rules, that relate the initial environmental conditions, such as distance of the throw, to the force and trajectory requirements that must be selected to produce a correct throw. When the shortstop is called on to execute a "new" fielding response, one that she has never experienced before, her variable practice experiences allow her to better estimate the response specifications needed by her motor program to produce the new response. The athlete who has experienced only one version of the task, through constant practice, may be able to execute that version very well but will be limited in developing a repertoire of responses that may be needed in the criterion activity.

Before we leave the topic of variable practice, a word of caution may be in order. When learners have no prior experience in an activity, such as may be common with very young children or even adult novices, then it may be advantageous to begin with constant practice at one version of the task—shooting a jump shot from one spot on the court, for example, before introducing variable practice. Initial constant practice will allow the pure beginner to master the "basics" of the skill and pass through the cognitive phase of learning. Once this is accomplished, however, variable practice should be introduced to develop the schemas needed in the actual sport.

Whole Versus Part Practice

Many of the sport skills an athlete must learn are quite complex, such as a floor exercise routine in gymnastics, a reverse lay-up in basketball, or a forward double somersault with two twists in diving. Even a relatively simple skill, such as a two-foot putt in golf, may seem very complex to the beginner. One of the most important decisions for a coach is whether to present all aspects of such skills to the athlete at once for practice or to divide the skill into smaller, meaningful units that can be practiced separately and then combined into the whole skill.

Whole and part methods of practice should be thought of as the extreme ends of a continuum. The **whole** method requires that the athletes practice the activity or skill in its entirety, as a single unit. At the other end of the continuum, the **part** method requires that the athletes practice each component of the activity or skill separately and then combine the parts into the whole skill. Between these two extremes we have a variation known as the **progressive-part** method, in which the first two parts of a skill are practiced separately and then combined and practiced as a unit. The third part is practiced next and then combined with the first two, and so on until the skill is complete.

There are distinct advantages to both the whole and part methods of practice, and there are circumstances under which one or the other is preferable. The essential advantage of the whole method is that ultimately the separate parts of the skill, once learned, are more likely to be performed in a smooth, continuous fashion. Undue adherence to the part method is likely to develop a series of well-learned components that are disconnected and are performed in a disjointed and segmented fashion when combined into a whole. Learning a skill requires both learning the individual parts and *connecting* them into a cohesive unit.

The part method of practice is of greatest value when a skill is very complex or involves separate, independently performed parts. For example, a gymnastics floor exercise routine is suited to the part method of practice because each individual trick can be practiced independently. Also, the gymnast can devote more practice time to particularly difficult tricks in the routine without practicing the easier ones, thus making practice more efficient. However, as Gestalt psychologists emphasized years ago, "the whole is greater than the sum of its parts." The successful gymnastics or figure skating routine is more than a series of well-executed individual movements. The transitions between individual elements must be executed smoothly so that the entire performance "flows" as a coherent unit. Most serial activities of reasonably long duration are characterized by an inherent timing or rhythmic structure among certain components. The coach must be careful to identify the components within the routine that "go together" and have the athletes practice them as a unit so as not to disrupt this essential timing. Before breaking a skill down for part practice, it is important to demonstrate the whole skill so the athletes see how the parts fit into the whole.

While the whole may be greater than the sum of its parts, it may also be different than its parts. For example, teaching the swimming strokes would seem to be suited to the part method of practice because the arm and leg actions can be practiced independently. However, in the front and back crawl strokes, the kick, when practiced in drills with a kickboard, is performed in a vertical plane. In the whole stroke, though, the kick occurs in a diagonal plane because of the body roll (Counsilman, 1968). Therefore, how much transfer of learning can we expect between the kick performed in isolation and the kick as performed in the whole stroke?

The transfer of learning principle underlies the use of part methods of practice. In some cases the part of a task practiced in isolation is nearly identical to that part in the whole task; thus, transfer from the part to the whole should be almost perfect. In other situations the isolated part may be quite different from the whole task, leading to very little transfer. The amount of transfer from parts of a skill to the whole skill, and thus the effectiveness of part practice, depends on the nature of the skill.

One advantage of teaching complex activities by the part method is that it usually provides the learners with a sense of having accomplished something. The more success athletes experience, the more motivated and confident they are likely to become. Building confidence is a critical factor in successful athletic performance.

The decision to practice a motor skill as a whole or by parts should be based on the nature of the skill *and* the nature of the learner. Christina and Corcos (1988) provide several excellent suggestions for how to do this. In general, the whole method is favored (a) if the skill is not too complicated and can be understood in a meaningful way; (b) if the skill is not too dangerous and can be practiced with a reasonable degree of success (many gymnastics and diving routines, certain wrestling maneuvers, and pole vaulting, for example, because of the potential for injury, lend themselves to part practice); (c) if you are working with capable athletes, highly motivated, who have an ex-

tensive background in various sports; and (d) if the athletes' attention span is long enough to deal with the whole.

There are clearly times when parts of an activity should be practiced separately. For example, when one particular skill or phase of the overall activity is causing difficulty, concentration and practice on this particular component are appropriate for a time. This allows additional practice where it is most needed. However, too much part practice on an isolated component can cause it to become disconnected from the surrounding components. The coach should seek to integrate the troublesome part back into the whole skill as quickly as possible.

Feedback: Its Functions and Use in Skill Learning and Performance

If practice is number one in importance for successful motor skill learning, then running a close second is **feedback**, the information athletes receive about their performance. Without feedback, learning is practically nonexistent. After all, if people do not know how they are doing, there is no reason for them to change their behavior. Furthermore, if they arbitrarily make a change, there is no assurance that it will be in the right direction. Since the time of Thorndike's (1931) experiment with line drawing, other researchers (Bennett, Vincent, & Johnson, 1979; Salmoni, 1980; Trowbridge & Cason, 1932) have repeatedly shown the essential nature of information feedback. Thorough reviews of the published research on feedback and motor learning can be found in Oxendine (1984); Salmoni, Schmidt, and Walter (1984); and Newell and McGinnis (1985).

Kinds of Feedback

Information available to athletes about their movements can be of two types: intrinsic feedback and extrinsic feedback. **Intrinsic feedback** is information athletes receive as a natural consequence of moving; it is provided by the athletes' own sensory systems. For example, when basketball players shoot the ball, they can *feel* the proprioceptive sensations coming from their muscles, joints, and tendons. They can *hear* the sound of the ball hitting the rim, or perhaps swishing through the net. Finally, they can *see* whether the ball went into the basket or not. All these sensations provide the athletes with information about the outcome of their shot in terms of achieving the environmental goal. In many sports, information about the success in achieving some goal is readily apparent to performers intrinsically. For example, it is easy to see where the arrow lands in the archery target, whether one clears the bar in the high jump, how many pins are knocked down in bowling, or whether the tennis ball lands in the service area. In such activities it is not necessary for anyone to provide information as to the results of the performances. Such information is clearly evident to the athlete.

Extrinsic feedback is information athletes receive that is not a natural consequence of executing a response. It must be provided by some external source such as a coach, teammate, stopwatch, judge's score, videotape replay, and so on. Extrinsic feedback is supplied beyond intrinsic feedback and supplements the information naturally available. It can provide information about the outcome of the performance or about the movement pattern that the athletes have just made.

In many sports the performers have no clear idea of how well they are doing. In track, the runner does not know his/her time in a 400-meter trial run until informed by another person or a clock. Neither does the long jumper know the distance of the jump until a measure is taken and reported by an official. Gymnasts, divers, and figure skaters have minimal information about the quality of their performance until they receive the judges' scores or are informed by the coach or other observers.

The extrinsic feedback a coach gives athletes should not be redundant with the intrinsic feedback the athletes have already obtained. It is absurd for a football coach to tell a receiver, "You dropped the ball." The athlete knows this. Feedback should provide specific information directed at correcting errors or reinforcing correct performance. For example, a bowler sees that the ball is repeatedly veering off into the left gutter but has no idea of what is causing it. A coach may be able to point out that during the follow-through the arm is pulling across the left shoulder, therefore pulling the ball off to the left. Consequently, focusing attention on a follow-through that is straight past the visual line may correct the problem.

Functions of Feedback

Feedback serves at least three important functions in skill learning and performance: (a) motivation, (b) reinforcement or punishment, and (c) error correction information.

Feedback as motivation. How hard would you try or how long would you persist at learning a task in which you had no idea how well you were performing? Feedback can play a powerful role in energizing and directing athletes' behavior in a particular task. A casual comment from a coach, such as "You're doing great, Jason—only two more repeats to go!" can help Jason get through a gruelling practice and perhaps put out even a little more effort. Notice that this comment is of a general nature in that it did not convey specific information about Jason's performance. Nevertheless, the extra effort such feedback can cause athletes to bring to the task can only benefit them in terms of increased performance.

Feedback can also influence motivation in terms of goal setting and goal evaluation. Most athletes, with the help of their coaches, set performance goals for themselves, both immediate and long-range. Feedback (intrinsic or extrinsic) informs the athletes about their progress toward those goals. If the feedback indicates that the athletes are improving, then this kind of information can be very satisfying to them, causing them to try to improve present performance until the goal is achieved. If the feedback indicates very little or no improvement is occurring, then this can either lower the athletes' incentive to keep trying to learn the skill or it may reveal that the original goals were unrealistic and need to be adjusted. More about motivation and goal setting will be covered in later chapters of this book.

Feedback as reinforcement or punishment. **Reinforcement** is any event that *increases* the likelihood that a specific action will occur again under similar circumstances. **Punishment** is just the opposite: It is any event that *decreases* the likelihood that a specific action will occur again. The reinforcing and punishing properties of feedback operate according to Thorndike's (1927) empirical **law of effect**, which essentially says that actions followed by rewarding consequences tend to be repeated, while actions followed by unpleasant, or punishing, consequences tend *not* to be repeated.

An example of intrinsic feedback that may serve as reinforcement is the satisfaction of seeing your tennis serve go untouched for an "ace" because you served it exactly where you wanted to and sensing (via proprioception) that your body moved just as you intended it to move when executing the serve. To experience these rewarding sensations again you will try to perform the serve in the same way in the future under similar conditions.

Examples of extrinsic feedback that may serve as reinforcement are compliments or praise from the coach, like "Good job," "Nice shot," "Your form was excellent that time," and "Way to hustle!" and nonverbal types of communication, such as a thumbs up, a smile, or a high five. Athletes receiving these kinds of rewarding extrinsic feedback right after performing a skill will try to perform the skill in the same way in the future under similar circumstances.

Based on the preceding discussion, it should be easy to see how intrinsic and extrinsic feedback can also operate as punishment. When Hilary lands on her back following a dive, her pain receptors provide powerful feedback that an error occurred. She may or may not know precisely what was wrong, but she knows she must change something on her next attempt to avoid this unpleasant experience. Intrinsic feedback does not necessarily have to be associated with physical pain in order to be offensive. When Mike attempts a field goal, seeing the ball veer off wide to the left and feeling the sensations associated with that kick should also be unpleasant and cause Mike to modify his next attempt. Essentially, athletes will try to avoid punishing feedback by learning not to perform the response being punished.

In the preceding examples extrinsic feedback from coaches, such as verbally expressing disapproval of the incorrect performance or nonverbally expressing disapproval (shake of the head, scowl) could also serve as punishment to stop Hilary and Mike from repeating their errors. The important point about using extrinsic feedback as punishment is that the coach should punish the undesirable behavior—the performance error—and not the athlete. The coach should praise sincere effort and any part of the skill that was performed correctly, thereby reinforcing these desirable aspects of the performance.

Feedback as error correction information. There is little doubt that the most important component of feedback for motor skill learning is the information it provides about patterns of movement, specifically, errors in the movement pattern. This feedback about errors, prescribing ways for modifying performance, is the reason why the coach's role as a teacher is so important for skill learning. Only a skilled teacher can know the correct technique—the proper movement pattern—to provide information feedback.

In some sports, because of the nature of the scoring system, the criterion for successful performance *is* the movement pattern itself. Examples include diving, figure skating, gymnastics, and synchronized swimming. Because it is impossible to receive a high score in these sports without producing technically correct patterns of movement, the coach's extrinsic feedback must be directed at helping the athletes achieve the correct mechanics. In other sports, however, successful performance outcomes are possible even in the absence of textbook-perfect movement patterns. For example, it does not matter how a basketball player shoots the free throw as long as the ball goes into the basket, how a runner swings her arms as long as she crosses the finish line first, or how a golfer grips the club as long as a 250-yard drive straight down the fairway results. Nevertheless, the probability of producing successful performance outcomes is greater when athletes use proper mechanics than when they use improper mechanics. Therefore, coaches should teach and reinforce the use of correct fundamental movement patterns in *all* sports.

How does information feedback operate in skill learning? What does information about errors cause the learner to do? First and foremost, giving information helps to guide the learners toward the movement goal (Salmoni, Schmidt, & Walter, 1984; Schmidt, 1991). This is very important during the early stages of learning, when performance errors are quite large and tend to occur often. Continued use of extrinsic feedback from the coach helps keep errors to a minimum and allows them to be corrected quickly, thus bringing performance close to the goal and helping to maintain it there. While this would seem to be good for learning, recent studies have shown that the guidance properties of feedback may cause learners to become too dependent on the feedback, using it as a "crutch," so that performance can only be maintained when the feedback is present (Lee, White, & Carnahan, 1990; Salmoni, Schmidt, & Walter, 1984; Schmidt et al., 1989). When the feedback is withdrawn, as it must be during actual competition, the athletes may have trouble performing. The constant provision of extrinsic feedback may also distract athletes from processing their own sensory feedback. If the athletes know that the coach will give feedback on every practice attempt, they simply have to wait for it, without attending to the rich sources of intrinsic feedback that can be so important for learning.

The practical implications here seem clear. A high frequency of extrinsic feedback is important during the early stage of learning to bring performance close to the goal. As proficiency increases, extrinsic feedback should gradually become less and less frequent so that the athlete learns to become less dependent on it for successful performance (Winstein & Schmidt, 1990). When a high degree of proficiency is attained, the athletes need only an occasional dose of information feedback to be certain that performance is correct.

Some Techniques for Giving Information Feedback

Providing timely and effective feedback to learners is not a simple matter. Even when the movement faults are obvious to the coach and the appropriate corrective responses are clear, transmitting this information to learners so that they can comprehend and use it is not always easy. Frequently learners are unable to translate the verbiage into meaningful movement behavior. At other times learners simply may not believe what they are being told. Consequently, the ability to effectively communicate feedback to learners is often as troublesome as actually detecting the movement errors. The ability to analyze what learners are doing wrong and how to correct it and to communicate this information (i.e., giving feedback) to those learners are two of the coach's most important teaching responsibilities.

Before giving athletes extrinsic feedback designed to correct errors in performance, the coach should first do a careful, thorough analysis of the athletes' technique. Christina and Corcos (1988)

advocate a three-step process for analyzing skill technique. The first step is to compare the athletes' technique with correct technique. The key here is to focus on the *basic movement pattern*, rather than small idiosyncrasies in individual style. The coach asks, "Is the athletes' technique fundamentally sound?" It may take several observations of the skill to evaluate the seriousness of observed errors, but the coach should avoid the mistake of offering feedback too quickly. Errors in technique should be corrected if they will substantially improve performance or increase safety.

The second step in analyzing technique is to select one error to correct at a time. With beginners especially there are probably several performance errors occurring simultaneously. If one tried to give feedback about every error on a trial, one would probably overload the learners with too much information, resulting in very little correction on the next trial. Given multiple errors, where does one begin? The coach should try to identify the error that is most fundamental or critical and give feedback only about it. Very often, one error is the cause of other errors, and if this critical error can be corrected, the others may be eliminated. When the fundamental aspect is mastered, then attention can be devoted to the next most important error.

When multiple errors seem unrelated, a good strategy is to select the one that is easiest to learn and leads to the greatest improvement. The benefits here may be twofold. First, the athletes' respect for the coach's knowledge may be enhanced, and, second, improved performance will contribute to the athletes' motivation to continue learning the skill.

Another strategy, one that works for skills that last several seconds, is to identify the critical error that occurs earliest in the sequence. For example, in diving, if the approach on the board is incorrect, the takeoff, the dive itself, and the entry are likely to be incorrect. The approach should be corrected first.

The final step in analyzing technique is to determine the cause of the error and what the athletes must do to correct it. Causes of errors can range from the relatively simple, such as forgetting to concentrate on some aspect of the skill, to the very difficult, such as a subtle change in mechanics. If the coach determines that forgetting is the cause of an error, then the correction is a simple reminder to the athletes. "Square up your racket to the net" may be all a young tennis player needs to correct a short volley. Determining the cause of a nonpropulsive breaststroke kick, on the other hand, may be more difficult because the problem may lie in poor body position, incorrect timing, positioning of the ankles, and so on. Further analysis, perhaps through filming, may be called for.

If the coach cannot isolate the cause of an error or is uncertain about how to correct it, he/she should not experiment with random suggestions. If the hasty suggestions do not lead to improved performance, the athletes may come to doubt their coach's ability, as well as experience a great deal of frustration. Coaches should think through the situation carefully and watch the performance many times before saying anything.

Giving Feedback Effectively to Correct Errors

The three-step process described above should be completed before saying anything to the athletes. After the coach has done this, it is time to give feedback. We favor a "sandwich" approach to giving feedback to athletes. The sandwich begins with a compliment about effort and any parts of the technique that were correct. Although the coach is about to give information to correct an error, he/she also wants to reinforce correct performance.

Next, the coach gives simple, precise, error correction information. We advocate the "KISS" principle—"Keep It Short and Simple." Feedback must provide sufficient information to benefit the athletes, but it must not provide too much or it may become confusing. Also, the coach should be sure to verify the athletes' understanding of the

feedback by asking them to repeat it and explain how they will make the correction.

Finally, the sandwich finishes with some encouragement. The coach should motivate athletes to learn the recommended correction because this will lead to improved performance. Notice that our feedback sandwich simply takes advantage of the three functions of feedback, with error correction information being sandwiched between reinforcement and motivation.

A teacher or coach who can provide accurate and understandable feedback is important to performers at all levels of the performance scale, from novice to elite. Clearly, the beginner in any sport needs early and consistent instruction as well as regular feedback. What is not as often understood is that performers at average and even advanced levels also need feedback. Major league pitchers at the peak of their careers sometimes run into slumps that are not attributable to any physical or emotional problem they can detect. At this point the pitching coach must set aside a period to work with such pitchers and attempt to determine what they are doing differently and how the problem can be corrected. At this high level of performance, problems are usually very subtle; errors in technique are so slight that only a highly skilled coach can detect them.

The baseball coach who trots out to the mound to confer with a pitcher who has started throwing wildly may have noticed that the pitcher is overstriding, or that the pitcher is leaning too far backward to get more speed on the ball, or that he is releasing too early. Only a very knowledgeable coach, and one who is thoroughly familiar with the particular player, is able to provide this type of helpful information.

Summary

This chapter has focused on one of the most important roles of a coach, that of a teacher of motor skills. The motor learning process is incredibly complex, and we have attempted to provide a basic understanding of that process. We began by describing a three-phase model of motor skill learning, consisting of the cognitive (beginning), asso-

ciative (intermediate), and autonomous (advanced) phases. Understanding the phases of learning is important both for teaching novice athletes a brand-new skill and for changing well-learned techniques of highly skilled athletes.

Practice and feedback are two of the most important determinants of motor learning and performance, and we have provided some guidelines for structuring effective practice sessions and for providing effective feedback to learners. In some instances, current research findings run counter to some of our long-held beliefs about practice and feedback.

Study Questions

1. Briefly describe Fitts and Posner's three phases of motor skill learning.
2. Give an example of how vision is used during the cognitive phase of learning.
3. What are the important points to remember when demonstrating a new skill for learners?
4. How is proprioception, or "feel," important in motor performance?
5. What are the effects of asking highly skilled performers to consciously attend to their movements?
6. Explain why the coach's role as motivator is so important during the autonomous phase of learning.
7. Describe how a coach should proceed to change a highly skilled athlete's well-learned technique.
8. How could one use blocked practice to teach several skills? Random practice? Which would be more effective and why?
9. Give an example of how a coach could use variable practice to teach several variations of a skill.
10. What are schemas, and how does variable practice contribute to their development?
11. What general guidelines should a coach consider in deciding to use the whole method versus the part method of practice?
12. What are the two major types of feedback? Give three examples of each type.
13. How can feedback be used as motivation in skill learning?
14. How can feedback be used as reinforcement or punishment in skill learning?
15. How can feedback be used to correct errors in performance?
16. Briefly describe Christina and Corcos's three-step process for analyzing skill technique.
17. Briefly describe the "sandwich" approach to giving feedback to athletes.

References

Adams, J. A. (1971). A closed-loop theory of motor learning. *Journal of Motor Behavior, 3,* 111–149.

Battig, W. F. (1966). Facilitation and interference. In E. A. Bilodeau (Ed.), *Acquisition of skill* (pp. 215–244). New York: Academic Press.

Bennett, I. C., Vincent, W. J., & Johnson, C. J. (1979). Effects of precision of grading systems on learning a fine motor skill. *Research Quarterly, 50,* 715–722.

Christina, R. W., & Corcos, D. M. (1988). *Coaches guide to teaching sport skills.* Champaign, Ill: Human Kinetics.

Counsilman, J. E. (1968). *The science of swimming.* Englewood Cliffs, N.J.: Prentice-Hall.

Fitts, P. M. (1964). Perceptual-motor skill learning. In A. W. Melton (Ed.), *Categories of human learning* (pp. 243–285). New York: Academic Press.

Fitts, P. M., & Posner, M. I. (1967). *Human performance.* Belmont, Calif.: Brooks/Cole.

Goode, S., & Magill, R. A. (1986). Contextual interference effects in learning three badminton serves. *Research Quarterly for Exercise and Sport, 57,* 308–314.

Kottke, F. J., Halpern, D., Easton, J. K. M., Ozel, A. T., & Burrill, C. A. (1978). The training of coordination. *Archives of Physical Medicine and Rehabilitation, 59,* 567–572.

Lee, T. D., & Magill, R. A. (1983). The locus of contextual interference in motor-skill acquisition. *Journal of Experimental Psychology: Learning, Memory, and Cognition, 9,* 730–746.

Lee, T. D., White, M. A., & Carnahan, H. (1990). On the role of knowledge of results in motor learning: Exploring the guidance hypothesis. *Journal of Motor Behavior, 22,* 191–208.

Magill, R. A., & Hall, K. G. (1990). A review of the contextual interference effect in motor skill acquisition. *Human Movement Science, 9,* 241–289.

Newell, K. M., & McGinnis, P. M. (1985). Kinematic information feedback for skilled performance. *Human Learning, 4,* 39–56.

Oxendine, J. B. (1984). Psychology of motor learning (2nd ed.). Englewood Cliffs, N.J.: Prentice-Hall.

Pigott, R. E., & Shapiro, D. C. (1984). Motor schema: The structure of the variability session. *Research Quarterly for Exercise and Sport, 55,* 41–45.

Salmoni, A. W. (1980). The effect of precision of knowledge of results on the performance of a simple line drawing task for children and adults. *Research Quarterly for Exercise and Sport, 51,* 572–575.

Salmoni, A. W., Schmidt, R. A., & Walter, C. B. (1984). Knowledge of results and motor learning: A review and critical reappraisal. *Psychological Bulletin, 95,* 355–386.

Schmidt, R. A. (1975). A schema theory of discrete motor skill learning. *Psychological Review, 82,* 225–260.

Schmidt, R. A. (1988). *Motor control and learning: A behavioral emphasis* (2nd ed.). Champaign, Ill: Human Kinetics.

Schmidt, R. A. (1991). *Motor learning and performance: From principles to practice.* Champaign, IL: Human Kinetics.

Schmidt, R. A., Young, D. E., Swinnen, S., & Shapiro, D. C. (1989). Summary knowledge of results for skill acquisition: Support for the guidance hypothesis. *Journal of Experimental Psychology: Learning, Memory, and Cognition, 15,* 352–359.

Shea, J. B., & Morgan, R. L. (1979). Contextual interference effects on the acquisition, retention, and transfer of a motor skill. *Journal of Experimental Psychology: Human Learning and Memory, 5,* 179–187.

Shea, J. B., & Zimny, S. T. (1983). Context effects in memory and learning movement information. In R. A. Magill (Ed.), *Memory and control of action* (pp. 345–366). Amsterdam: North-Holland.

Singer, R. N. (1982). *The learning of motor skills.* New York: Macmillan.

Thorndike, E. L. (1927). The law of effect. *American Journal of Psychology, 39,* 212–222.

Thorndike, E. L. (1931). *Human learning.* New York: Appleton-Century-Crofts.

Trowbridge, M. H., & Cason, H. (1932). An experimental study of Thorndike's theory of learning. *Journal of General Psychology, 7,* 245–260.

Winstein, C. J., & Schmidt, R. A. (1990). Reduced frequency of knowledge of results enhances motor skill learning. *Journal of Experimental Psychology: Learning, Memory, and Cognition, 16,* 677–691.

Wrisberg, C. A., & Liu, Z. (1991). The effect of contextual variety on the practice, retention, and transfer of an applied motor skill. *Research Quarterly for Exercise and Sport, 62,* 406–412.

A Positive Approach to Enhancing Sport Performance: Principles of Positive Reinforcement and Performance Feedback

Ronald E. Smith, *University of Washington*

*M*uch of human interaction consists of attempts to influence the behavior of other people. Influence attempts occur constantly in virtually every life setting. Sometimes the attempts are directed at influencing attitudes, motives, values, or emotions. At other times, social interactions or task performance are the targets of influence attempts.

Sport is a setting where all these targets of influence—cognitions, emotions, motivational factors, and behaviors—are relevant. Influence attempts occur constantly as athletes interact with teammates, coaches, and their opponents. In the discussion to follow, I will focus on influence attempts directed by coaches to their athletes. I will attempt to provide a conceptual framework to which other topics in this book, such as goal setting (Chapter 13) and intervention programs directed toward coaches and parents (Chapters 4 and 5) may be related. My focus will be primarily on enhancing sport performance, although, as we will see, this goal is intimately related to the social-psychological climate created by interactions among coaches and athletes.

Coaches try to influence their players in many important ways. One of their most important goals is to create a good learning situation where athletes can acquire the technical skills needed to succeed as individuals and as a team. Another priority for most coaches is to create a social environment where the participants can experience positive interactions with one another. This is certainly a key factor in building team cohesion; in making athletes more receptive to technical instruction; and in fostering a supportive environment where athletes can develop teamwork, dedication, "mental toughness," and other valued traits. Indeed, virtually everything coaches do can be viewed as attempts to increase certain desired behaviors and to decrease undesirable behaviors.

The "psychology of coaching" can essentially be regarded as a set of strategies designed to increase a coach's ability to influence the behavior of others more effectively. It is often said that, stripped of its jargon and complexities, psychology is basically the application of common sense. I believe that the principles to be discussed in this chapter—positive (as opposed to aversive) control, reinforcement, and performance feedback—make good sense. But, more importantly, they have been shown in many scientific studies to be among the most effective ways to increase motivation, morale, enjoyment of the athletic situation, and performance.

Positive and Aversive Approaches to Influencing Behavior

There are two basic approaches to influencing the behavior of others. Psychologists refer to these as **positive control** and **aversive control** (Bandura, 1986; Smith, 1993). Both forms of control are based on the fact that behavior is strongly influenced by the consequences it produces. Responses that lead to positive or desired consequences (from the perspective of the responder) are strengthened and their likelihood of occurring in the future is increased. In more technical terms, **positive reinforcers** are consequences that increase the future probability of behaviors that produce them. Conversely, behaviors that result in undesirable or unpleasant consequences (as perceived by the responder) are less likely to recur. **Punishment** is thus defined as a consequence that weakens or suppresses a behavior that produces it. Positive reinforcement and punishment are the respective cornerstones of positive and aversive control of behavior. Positive and aversive control, in turn, underlie what we have termed the positive approach and the negative approach to coaching (see Chapters 4 and 5 of this book and Smoll & Smith, 1987).

The positive approach is designed to strengthen desired behaviors by motivating players to perform them and by reinforcing the behaviors when they occur. The second approach, the negative approach, involves attempts to eliminate unwanted behaviors through punishment and criticism. The motivating factor in this approach is fear. Observational studies of coaches indicate that most coaches use a combination of positive and aversive control (Smith et al., 1983).

In our society, aversive control through punishment is perhaps the most widespread means of controlling behavior. Our entire system of laws is backed up by threats of punishment. Similarly, fear of failure is one means of promoting school achievement, social development, and other desired behaviors. The reason that punishment is the glue that holds so much of our society's fabric together is that, for the most part, it seems to work. It is the fastest way to bring behavior under control. In sport it finds one mode of expression in the negative approach to coaching.

So frequently in sport we hear the statement, "The team that makes the fewest mistakes will win." And, indeed, this is usually the case. Many coaches therefore develop coaching tactics that are oriented toward eliminating mistakes. The most natural approach is to use aversive control. To get rid of mistakes, we simply punish athletes who make them. The assumption is that if we make players fearful enough of making mistakes, they are more likely to perform well. We do not have to look far to find examples of highly successful coaches who are "screamers" and whose teams seem to perform like well-oiled machines. Other less experienced coaches may therefore conclude that this is the most effective way to train athletes. They too adopt this aspect of the successful coaches' behavior, perhaps to the exclusion of other teaching techniques that probably are the true keys to the success of the screamers.

Negative Side Effects of Punishment

There is clear evidence that punishment and criticism can decrease unwanted behaviors. Unfortunately, the evidence is equally compelling that punishment has certain undesirable side effects that can actually interfere with what a coach is trying to accomplish.

Most important is the fact that punishment works by arousing fear. If used excessively, punishment promotes the development of fear of failure, and this is undoubtedly the least desirable form of athletic motivation. If fear of failure becomes the predominant motive for athletic performance, it not only decreases enjoyment of the activity but also increases the likelihood of failure. The athlete with a high fear of failure is motivated not by a positive desire to achieve and enjoy "the thrill of victory" but by a dread of "the agony of defeat." Athletic competition is transformed from a challenge into a threat. Because high anxiety disrupts motor performance and interferes with thinking, this athlete is prone to "choke" under pressure because he/she is concentrating more on the feared consequences of mistakes or failure than on what needs to be done in a positive sense. Research has shown that athletes having high fear of failure not only perform more poorly in competition but also are at greater risk for injury, enjoy the sport experience less, and are more likely to drop out (Orlick & Botterill, 1975; Smith & Smoll, 1990). The research literature also shows that the quickest and most effective way to develop fear of failure is by punishing people when they fail (McClelland, 1985). Thus, coaches who create fear of failure through the use of punishment may, ironically, increase the likelihood that their athletes may indeed make the very mistakes they are trying to prevent. Moreover, high levels of fear may have a generally depressing effect on behavior and make athletes afraid to take risks of any kind.

Punishment has other potential side effects that most coaches wish to avoid. A predominance of aversive control makes for an unpleasant teaching situation. It arouses resentment and hostility, which may be masked by the power differential that exists between coach and athlete. It may produce a kind of cohesion among players based on their mutual hatred for the coach, but most coaches would prefer other bases for team cohesion. It is even possible that players may consciously or subconsciously act in ways that sabotage what the coach is trying to accomplish. Moreover, coaches occupy a role that is admired by athletes, and they should not overlook their importance as models for young people who are developing socially. The abusive screamer is certainly not exhibiting the kinds of behaviors that will contribute to the personal growth of athletes who emulate the coach.

Does this mean that coaches should avoid all criticism and punishment of their athletes? Not at all. Sometimes these behaviors are necessary for instructional or disciplinary purposes. But they should be used sparingly and with a full appreciation for the potential negative side effects that we have discussed. I believe the negative approach should never be the primary approach to athletes. This is particularly the case where child athletes are concerned, but it also applies at higher competitive levels, including professional sports (Smith & Johnson, 1990).

My observation has been that while abusive coaches may enjoy success and may even be admired by some of their players, they run the risk of losing other players who could contribute to the team's success and who could profit personally from an athletic experience. Those who succeed through the use of aversive control usually do so because (a) they are also able to communicate caring for their players as people, so that the abuse is not "taken personally"; (b) they have very talented athletes; and/or (c) they are such skilled teachers and strategists that these abilities overshadow their

negative approach. In other words, such coaches win in spite of, not because of, the negative approach they espouse.

The Positive Alternative

Fortunately, there is an alternative to the negative approach. As a means of influencing behavior, it can accomplish everything that aversive control does, and much more, without the harmful side effects. The **positive approach** is aimed at strengthening desired behaviors through the use of encouragement, positive reinforcement, and sound technical instruction carried out within a supportive atmosphere. From this point of view the best way to eliminate mistakes is not to try to stamp them out with punishment, but, rather, to strengthen the correct or desired behaviors. The motivational force at work here is a positive desire to achieve, rather than a negative fear of failure. Mistakes are seen not as totally negative occurrences but as, in the words of John Wooden, "stepping stones to achievement" that provide the information needed to improve performance. The positive approach, through its emphasis on improving rather than on "not screwing up," fosters a more positive learning environment and tends to promote more positive relationships among coaches and athletes. Research has clearly shown that athletes like positive coaches better, enjoy their athletic experience more and report higher team cohesion when playing for them, and perform at a higher level when positive control techniques are used (Martin & Hyrcaiko, 1983; Smith & Smoll, 1990).

The cornerstone of the positive approach is the skillful use of positive reinforcement to increase motivation and to strengthen desired behaviors. Another highly effective technique is the use of performance feedback.

Positive Reinforcement: Getting Good Things to Happen

As noted earlier, positive reinforcement is any consequence that increases the likelihood of a behavior that it follows. For our present purposes, positive reinforcement can be viewed as related to the more familiar concept of "reward," as long as we keep in mind that a consequence that may be rewarding from the perspective of one person may not function as a reinforcer for another person who is not motivated to receive that consequence. Thus, a compliment from a coach who is despised by her players may have no positive impact on their behavior. (Likewise, rat food is a highly effective reinforcer for the white rat but notoriously ineffective for children.) Reinforcement can take many possible forms: verbal compliments, smiles, or other nonverbal behaviors that convey approval, increased privileges, awards, and so on.

The effective use of reinforcement to strengthen behavior requires that a coach (a) find a reinforcer that works for a particular athlete and (b) make the occurrence of reinforcement dependent upon performance of the desired behavior. The relations between behaviors and their consequences are termed **reinforcement contingencies**.

Choosing Effective Reinforcers

Choosing a reinforcer is not usually difficult, but in some instances the coach's ingenuity and sensitivity to the needs of individual players might be tested. Potential reinforcers include social behaviors such as verbal praise, smiles, nonverbal signs such as applause, or physical contact such as a pat on the back. They also include the opportunity to engage in certain activities (such as extra batting practice) or to use a particular piece of equipment.

Social reinforcers are most frequently employed in athletics, but even here the coach must decide what is most likely to be effective with each player. One player might find praise given in the presence of others highly reinforcing, whereas another might find it embarassing. The best way for a coach to find an effective reinforcer is to get to know each player's likes and dislikes. In some instances a coach may elect to praise an entire unit or group of players; at other times, reinforcement may be directed at one player. If at all possible, it is a good idea to use a variety of reinforcers and vary what one says and does so that the coach does not begin to sound like a broken record. In the final analysis, the acid test of one's choice of reinforcer is whether it affects behavior in the desired manner.

The effectiveness of verbal reinforcement can be increased by combining it with a specific description of the desirable behavior that the athlete just performed. For example, a coach might say, "Way to go, Bob. Your head stayed right down on the ball on that swing." In this way the power of the reinforcement is combined with an instructional reminder of what the player should do. This also cues the athlete to what the coach wants him/her to concentrate on.

Selecting and Reinforcing Target Behaviors

Systematic use of reinforcement forces coaches to be specific in their own minds about exactly which behaviors they want to reinforce in a given athlete at a particular time. Obviously, they will not want to reinforce everything an athlete does correctly, lest the power of the reinforcer be diluted. The most effective use of "reward power" is to strengthen skills that an athlete is just beginning to master. In many instances complex skills can be broken down into their component subskills, and coaches can concentrate on one of these subskills at a time until each is mastered. For example, a football coach might choose to concentrate entirely on the pattern run by a pass receiver, with no concern about whether or not the pass is completed. This is where a coach's knowledge of the sport and of the mastery levels of individual athletes is crucial. Athletes can enjoy lots of support and reinforcement long before they have completely mastered the entire skill if coaches are attentive to their instructional needs and progress. Such reinforcement will help to keep motivation and interest at their maximum.

Shaping

We have all marveled at the complex behaviors performed by animals in circuses, at amusement parks, and in the movies. These behavioral feats are brought about by the use of a positive reinforcement procedure known as **shaping**, or the **method of successive approximations**. At the beginning of training the animal was incapable of anything even approximating the desired behavior. The trainer began with some behavior the animal was already performing and began reinforcing that behavior. Then, over time, the requirements for reinforcement were gradually altered so that the animal had to perform acts that more and more closely resembled the final desired behavior, until that behavior had been "shaped" by the systematic application of reinforcement. Consider, for example, this description by a trainer of how killer whales are taught to jump through a hoop situated high above the surface of the water.

> The animals you're seeing are not geniuses, although they may look like it at times. Actually, what you're seeing is the end product of very systematic training. We use a method known as *shaping* to gradually build the complex behaviors you see. This means that we reinforce, with a juicy fish, behaviors that get closer and closer to the desired trick. For example, no dolphin or killer whale, regardless of how brilliant, is going to jump spontaneously through a hoop ten feet above the water. We have to gradually shape her, first by immediately and consistently rewarding her when she swims into the area near the hoop, then when she breaks water, and so on. In other words, she has to come closer and closer to what we want her to eventually do in order to get her fish. This is basically how all animal acts are developed, whether here at Sea Life Park or in a circus. We can eventually put together long **behavior chains** in which a number of responses are run off in sequence, with reinforcement at the end of the chain (Smith, 1993, p. 324).

The products of shaping go far beyond rats pressing bars and pigeons pecking discs in Skinner boxes, and even beyond the feats performed by trained animals. Humans also learn many complex behaviors through shaping. Shaping is involved in learning a language and in developing educational skills. If we want to train children to be mathematicians, we do not expect them to solve complex calculus problems spontaneously. We start by teaching them basic arithmetic operations, and we successively build on what they have already learned. On a broader level, our acquisition of the behaviors, values, and attitudes of our society involves a great deal of shaping on the part of parents, teachers, and peers.

Shaping can also be used to shape athletic skills. The procedure is to start with what the athlete is currently capable of doing and then gradually require a more skillful level of performance before reinforcement is given. It is important that the shift in demands be realistic and that the steps be small enough so that the athlete can master them and be reinforced. For example, a youth baseball coach may at first praise novice infielders whenever they stop a ball. As proficiency increases, however, she may require that the players field the ball in the correct position, and later that they field the ball cleanly in the correct position and make an accurate throw. Used correctly, shaping is one of the most powerful of all the positive control techniques.

An Example of a Successful Positive Reinforcement Program

The systematic use of positive reinforcement to improve the performance of a youth football team's offensive backfield was described by Komaki and Barnett (1977). Three different plays run out of the wishbone offense were selected by the coach. Each of the plays was broken down into five stages judged to be crucial to the execution of the play and was presented to the players accordingly. For example, one of the plays included the following stages: (1) quarterback–center exchange, (2) quarterback spin and pitch, (3) right halfback and fullback lead blocking, (4) left halfback route, and (5) quarterback block. Breaking down the plays in this manner allowed the coach to respond to the elements that were run correctly and to give specific feedback to the players about their execution of each of the five stages.

During the first phase of the experiment, data were carefully collected on how often the stages of each play were executed correctly. Then the coach began to systematically apply reinforcement procedures to Play A. Each time the play was run in practice, the coach checked off which of the elements had been successfully executed and praised the players for the stages that were run successfully. Reinforcement was not applied when Plays B and C were run. After a period of time the reinforcement procedure was shifted to Play B only, and later to Play C only. Applying the technique to only one play at a time permitted a determination of the specific effects of reinforcement on the performance of each of them.

A comparison of the percentage of stages executed correctly before and after introduction of the reinforcement procedure indicated that performance increased for all three plays, but only after reinforcement was introduced. The level of performance for Play A improved from 61.7% to 81.5% when reinforcement was applied, but execution of B and C did not improve until reinforcement was also applied to them. When this occurred, execution of play B improved from 54.4% to 82.0%, and execution of Play C improved from 65.5% to 79.8%. Clearly, the systematic use of reinforcement led to a substantial improvement in performance. Other studies have shown similar performance improvement in gymnastics, swimming, baseball, golf, and tennis (see Martin & Hyrcaiko, 1983).

Schedules and Timing of Reinforcement

One of the most frequently asked questions is how often and how consistently reinforcement should be given. Fortunately, a great deal of research has been done concerning the effects of so-called **schedules of reinforcement** on behavior change. Reinforcement schedules refer to the pattern and frequency with which reinforcement is administered. Although there are many different kinds of schedules, the most important distinction is between continuous and partial schedules. On a **continuous schedule**, *every* correct response is reinforced. On **partial schedules**, some correct responses are reinforced and some are not.

A coach has two related challenges. First, athletes must be instructed in specific skills until they master them. Then, the coach must figure out ways to maintain the skills so that athletes will continue to perform them at a high level of proficiency. A knowledge of the effects of reinforcement schedules can assist in meeting both challenges.

During the initial stages of training, reinforcement is best given on a continuous schedule. The frequent reinforcement not only strengthens the desired response but also provides the athlete with frequent feedback about how he/she is doing. Once the behavior is learned, however, reinforcement should be shifted to a partial schedule. Research has shown that behaviors reinforced on partial schedules persist much longer in the absence of reinforcement than do those that have been reinforced only on a continuous schedule (Skinner, 1969). For example, people will put a great many coins into slot machines, which operate on partial schedules. In contrast, they are unlikely to persist in putting coins into soft drink machines that do not deliver, for these machines normally operate on a continuous schedule. Thus, the key principle

in using schedules is to start with continuous reinforcement until the behavior is mastered, then to shift gradually to partial reinforcement to maintain a high level of motivation and performance (Martin & Pear, 1992).

The timing of reinforcement is another important consideration. Other things being equal, the sooner after a response that reinforcement occurs, the stronger are its effects on behavior. Thus, whenever possible, a coach should try to reinforce a desired behavior as soon as it occurs. If this is not possible, however, he/she should try to find an opportunity to praise the athlete later on.

Reinforcing Effort and Other Desirable Behaviors

The preceding discussion has emphasized the use of reinforcement to strengthen skills. It is important to realize, however, that reinforcement can be used to strengthen other desirable behaviors. For example, the positive approach can be used to reduce the likelihood of disciplinary problems by reinforcing compliance with team rules. There is no reason why a coach should not recognize and reinforce exemplary conduct on the part of particular athletes or the team as a whole. One of the most effective ways of avoiding disciplinary problems is by strengthening the opposite (desired) behaviors through reinforcement (Smoll & Smith, 1987).

Similarly, instances of teamwork and of players' support and encouragement of one another should be acknowledged and reinforced from time to time. Doing so not only strengthens these desirable behaviors but also creates an atmosphere in which the coach is actually serving as a positive model by supporting them. Research has shown that the best predictor of liking for the coach and desire to play for him/her in the future is not the won-lost record of the team but how consistently the coach applies the positive approach and avoids the use of punishment (Smith & Smoll, 1991).

I have saved one of the most important points of all until last. *What* coaches choose to reinforce is of critical importance. It's easy to praise an athlete who has just made a great play. It is less natural to reinforce one who tried but failed. A good principle is to reinforce effort as much as results. After all, the only thing athletes have complete control over is the amount of effort they put forth; they have only limited control over the outcome of their efforts. Coaches have a right to demand total effort, and this is perhaps the most important behavior of all for them to reinforce. If athletes have had good technical instruction, are free from self-defeating fear of failure, and are giving maximum effort (all of which should be promoted by the use of the positive approach), then performance and winning will take care of themselves within the limits of the athletes' ability. John Wooden, the legendary "Wizard of Westwood," placed great emphasis on this concept:

> You cannot find a player who ever played for me at UCLA that can tell you he ever heard me mention "winning" a basketball game. He might say I inferred a little here and there, but I never mentioned winning. Yet the last thing that I told my players, just prior to tipoff, before we would go on the floor was, "When the game is over, I want your head up — and I know of only one way for your head to be up —and that's for you to know that you did your best.... This means to do the best YOU can do. That's the best; no one can do more.... You made that effort.

Reinforcement and Intrinsic Motivation

An important distinction is often made between **intrinsic motivation** and **extrinsic motivation**. When people are motivated to perform an activity for its own sake, they are said to be intrinsically motivated. When they perform the activity only to obtain some external reward, they are extrinsically motivated.

Concerns are often raised about the potential negative impact of positive reinforcement on intrinsic motivation. If external rewards are suddenly introduced for performance of a behavior that is intrinsically rewarding, a person may come to attribute his/her performance to the extrinsic reward and cease performing the behavior if the external reward is withdrawn. Thus, in one study, children who loved drawing with pens were offered external reinforcement (a "good player" award for drawing with the pens). Later, when the good player award was withdrawn, the children showed a sharp decrease in their tendency to draw with the pens (Lepper & Greene, 1978).

Most of us would like athletes to be intrinsically motivated to participate in athletics. Is it pos-

sible that the positive approach, with its emphasis on reinforcement from the coach, could undermine their "love of the game" for its own sake?

It now appears that if extrinsic reinforcement is given to acknowledge a specific level of performance, it is unlikely to undermine intrinsic motivation. Rather, it provides important information to an athlete he/she has met a standard of excellence and thereby provides a basis for positive self-reinforcement by the athlete. Positive internal self-evaluations can strengthen behavior and also maintain and even increase intrinsic motivation (Cervone, 1992). Thus, it is a good idea for coaches to instill self-pride in their athletes with statements like "Great job! You ought to feel proud of yourself for that effort." There is considerable evidence that standards for self-reinforcement are often adopted from other people, and a coach can be an influential source of standards of excellence that can be internalized by the athletes, particularly if he/she has developed a strong positive relationship with them.

Performance Feedback

As we have seen, positive reinforcement serves not only as a reward for desirable behavior but also as a form of performance feedback. In other words, by providing "knowledge of results," it communicates the message that performance has met or exceeded the coach's standards. When it is possible to measure desired and undesired behaviors objectively, the coach can utilize the highly effective tool of performance feedback to increase motivation and performance.

In recent years there has been a surge of interest in objective feedback as a technology for improving job performance in business and industry. The evidence indicates that performance feedback is a highly effective tool. A review of 18 scientific studies carried out in a variety of job settings found increases in objective performance indicators averaging 53% after systematic performance feedback procedures were instituted (Kopelman, 1982–83). Specific work behaviors improved an average of 78%, and overall productivity an average of 16%. These increases were recorded over intervals ranging from eight weeks to four years.

Performance feedback is a prominent feature of what many successful coaches do. For example, psychologists Roland Tharpe and Ronald Gallimore (1976) charted all of John Wooden's behaviors during 15 practice sessions. They found that 75% of Wooden's comments to his players contained instructional feedback. Most of his comments were specific statements of what to do and how the players were or were not doing it. Indeed, Wooden was five times more likely to inform than to merely praise or reprimand.

How Feedback Motivates

There are a variety of reasons why objective feedback is consistently effective in motivating increased performance. For one thing, feedback can correct misconceptions. Athletes, like other people, often have distorted perceptions of their own behavior. Objective evidence in the form of statistics or numbers can help correct such misconceptions and may motivate corrective action. For example, it can be a sobering experience for a basketball player who fancies himself a great ball handler to learn that he has more turnovers than assists.

Feedback also creates internal consequences by stimulating athletes to experience positive (or negative) feelings about themselves, depending on how well they performed in relation to their standards of performance. Athletes who are dissatisfied with their level of performance may not only be motivated to improve but will experience feelings of self-satisfaction that function as positive reinforcement when subsequent feedback indicates improvement. Such self-administered reinforcement can be even more important than external reinforcement from the coach in bringing about improved performance (Cervone, 1992). Promoting self-motivation in athletes also reduces the need for coaches to reinforce or punish. When feedback is public, as in the posting of statistics, the actual or anticipated reactions of others to one's performance level can serve as an additional motivator of increased effort and performance. Improvement is also likely to result in reinforcement from teammates.

A final motivational function of objective feedback is in relation to formal goal-setting programs. Because goal-setting is discussed in detail elsewhere (Chapter 13) in this volume, I will simply point out that successful goal setting programs almost always involve clear feedback that informs

workers as to their performance in relation to the goal (Locke & Latham, 1990). Without such feedback, goal setting does not improve performance, and without clear and specific goals that are either assigned by others or set internally, performance feedback has little effect on performance. For example, in a study by Bandura and Cervone (1983), subjects engaged in a strenuous aerobic task on an arm-powered exercise bicycle. Four experimental conditions were created by the presence/absence of challenging assigned goals and the presence/absence of performance feedback. Over the three performance periods the subjects with both assigned goals and feedback improved their level of performance 59%. The performance improvements in the other three experimental conditions ranged from 20–25%. It thus appears that the presence of both challenging goals and performance feedback provides a powerful motivational boost to task performance. Such motivation is maximized if people also have a high level of self-efficacy (the belief that they can succeed) and if the goal is highly prized (Cervone, 1992). In the study just described, the largest performance increases on the aerobic task occurred for subjects who (a) had both goals and feedback, (b) were performing below the goal, (c) were dissatisfied with this state of affairs and, (d) had high self-efficacy for improvement.

Instructional Benefits of Feedback

Feedback has not only motivational but also instructional effects. It helps direct behavior. Objective performance feedback provides information about (a) the specific behaviors that should be performed, (b) the levels of proficiency that should be achieved in each of the skills, and (c) the athlete's current level of proficiency in these activities. This instructional function of feedback can be especially valuable when execution of a given skill is broken down into its stages or components, as was done in the football study described earlier. When the skill is a highly complex one, such as hitting a baseball, objective feedback on how frequently a hitter executes each of the essentials (e.g., keeping the bat in the correct position, shifting one's weight correctly, striding with the hips closed, keeping one's head down during the swing) can be very valuable in pinpointing areas of strength and weakness so that attention can be directed toward correcting mistakes. The information provided by subsequent objective feedback allows both coach and athlete to monitor progress in a more useful fashion than by depending on a more global measure of proficiency, such as batting average.

Implementing a Performance Measurement and Feedback System

As in the application of positive reinforcement programs, a successful feedback program requires that coaches identify specific and measurable behaviors or consequences. What they give feedback on must be something that can be counted. The performance measures can be fairly global (e.g., number of rebounds per minute) or more specific and dealing with subskills (e.g., percentage of rebound plays in which the opponent is boxed out). Because successful execution does not always result in a successful outcome, it is sometimes preferable to use a measure of successful execution. For example, some baseball coaches keep statistics on the percentage of times the batter hits either a line drive or a hard ground ball in preference to emphasizing batting average. In other words, the coach selects the specific behaviors he/she wants to track and then develops a system for measuring them. At this stage it is important to communicate with players so that they are in agreement with the coach that the behaviors are important ones. A coach should try to elicit suggestions from the athletes so that they feel a sense of involvement in the program.

In many instances, coaches can choose between measuring either a desired behavior or its undesirable counterpart. In line with the positive approach to coaching, I strongly recommend choosing the correct behavior for feedback rather than the mistake (or, at the very least, presenting both). This puts a coach in the position of reinforcing improvement rather than punishing or criticizing mistakes. It also focuses players' attention on what they should do rather than on what they should *not* do.

The measurement and feedback systems coaches choose are limited only by their own ingenuity and awareness of the specific behaviors that they want to promote. Some coaches have developed "total performance indexes" that include a variety of behaviors. For example, basketball coach Lute Olson has devised an index in which negative behaviors such as turnovers, missed free throws, and defensive mistakes are subtracted from positive behaviors such as points scored, rebounds, and assists. Coach Don James has a highly detailed performance feedback system that involves the percentage of plays during games and scrimmages in which each of his football players successfully carried out his specific assignment. The measures are derived from game films and posted after every game and scrimmage. They also provide an objective basis for selecting starters and allocating playing time.

Finally, it is important to note that performance feedback measures can be derived not only for individual players but also for subgroups or even for the team as a whole. Such measures can help to promote team cohesion by emphasizing the importance of teamwork and by providing a specific measure of group performance. As we saw in the Bandura and Cervone (1983) study, a negative discrepancy between the goal and the subjects' performance stimulated the greatest amount of performance improvement. In another study, subjects received information on how both they and their group were doing in relation to specific individual and group goals. Performance improvement was stimulated by negative performance–goal discrepancies on the part of either the individual or the group. When the group was lagging behind, subjects tried harder to do their part to improve group performance. When individuals were not achieving their individual goals, they felt compelled to work harder, to "pull their share of the load" (Matsui, Kayuyama, & Onglatco, 1987). This suggests the effectiveness of establishing both individual and group performance goals.

There are many ways in which positive reinforcement and performance feedback techniques can be applied to sports. Given the success they have enjoyed in a wide variety of performance settings, these strategies have the potential to increase coaching effectiveness at all competitive levels, from children's programs to the demanding and exacting realm of elite and professional sports.

Summary

In this chapter we have focused on some of the advantages of a positive approach to coaching, which involves the use of reinforcement to (a) strengthen desired behaviors and (b) promote the development of a positive motivation for success rather than fear of failure. We have also seen that objective performance feedback on specific aspects of performance is a highly successful motivational and instructional technique. Both systematic reinforcement and objective feedback require that the coach identify specific behaviors that are important to individual and team success. This is in itself a highly desirable practice, for it focuses both the coach's and the athletes' attention on exactly what needs to be mastered and executed. It also promotes goal setting based on specific behaviors rather than on more general goals that are difficult to measure. Systematic use of positive reinforcement and objective feedback has yielded impressive results in many performance settings, including sports, and their utilization is appropriate at all competitive levels of athletics.

Study Questions

1. In what ways can coaching be reduced to attempts to influence behavior?

2. Define positive reinforcement and contrast it with punishment in terms of its effects on behavior and the motivational factors that underlie its effectiveness.

3. What are the direct effects and undesirable side effects of punishment?

4. What are reinforcement contingencies, and how are they applied in shaping?

5. Summarize the schedules of reinforcement described in the text, as well as their effects on performance.

6. What is the importance of reinforcing effort rather than focusing entirely on outcome?

7. How can the positive approach be used to reduce disciplinary problems?

8. Differentiate between intrinsic and extrinsic motivation. Under what conditions can intrinsic motivation be undermined by positive reinforcement, and what can be done to reduce this danger?

9. What are the effects of performance feedback on task performance, and what are the mechanisms whereby feedback is assumed to motivate behavior? What is the instructional value of feedback?

10. What are some of the key principles in implementing a performance feedback program? How are these related to the positive approach to coaching?

References

Bandura, A. (1986). *Social foundations of thought and action: A social cognitive theory.* Englewood Cliffs, N.J.: Prentice-Hall.

Bandura, A., & Cervone, D. (1983). Self-evaluative and self-efficacy mechanisms governing the motivational effects of goal systems. *Journal of Personality and Social Psychology, 45,* 1017–1028.

Cervone, D. (1992). The role of self-referent cognitions in goal setting, motivation, and performance. In M. Rabinowitz (Ed.), *Applied cognition.* New York: Ablex.

Komaki, J., & Barnett, F. T. (1977). A behavioral approach to coaching football: Improving the play execution of an offensive backfield on a youth football team. *Journal of Applied Behavior Analysis, 10,* 657–664.

Kopelman, R. E. (1982–83). Improving productivity through objective feedback: A review of the evidence. *National Productivity Review, 24,* 43–55.

Lepper, M. R., & Greene, D. (1978). *The hidden costs of reward: New perspectives on the psychology of motivation.* Hillsdale, N.J.: Erlbaum.

Locke, E. A., & Latham, G. P. (1990). *A theory of goal setting and task performance.* Englewood Cliffs, N.J.: Prentice-Hall.

Martin, G. L., & Hyrcaiko, D. (1983). *Behavior modification and coaching: Principles, procedures, and research.* Springfield, Ill.: Thomas.

Martin, G., & Pear, J. (1992). *Behavior modification: What it is and how to do it.* Englewood Cliffs, N.J.: Prentice-Hall.

Matsui, T., Kakuyama, T., & Onglatco, M. L. U. (1987). Effects of goals and feedback on performance in groups. *Journal of Applied Psychology, 72,* 407–415.

McClelland, D. C. (1985). *Human motivation.* Glenview, Ill.: Scott Foresman.

Orlick, T., & Botterill, C. (1975). *Every kid can win.* Chicago: Nelson-Hall.

Skinner, B. F. (1969). *Contingencies of reinforcement: A theoretical analysis*. New York: Appleton-Century-Crofts.

Smith, R. E. (1993). *Psychology*. St. Paul, Minn.: West.

Smith, R. E., & Johnson, J. (1990). An organizational empowerment approach to consultation in professional baseball. *The Sport Psychologist, 4*, 347–357.

Smith, R. E., & Smoll, F. L. (1990). Athletic performance anxiety. In H. Leitenberg (Ed.), *Handbook of Social and Evaluation Anxiety* (pp. 417–454). New York: Plenum.

Smith, R. E., & Smoll, F. L. (1991). Behavioral research and intervention in youth sports. *Behavior Therapy, 22*, 329–344.

Smith, R. E., Zane, N. S., Smoll, F. L., & Coppel, D. B. (1983). Behavioral assessment in youth sports: Coaching behaviors and children's attitudes. *Medicine and Science in Sports and Exercise, 15*, 208–214.

Smoll, F. L., & Smith, R. E. (1987). *Sport psychology for youth coaches: Personal growth to athletic excellence*. Washington, D.C.: National Federation of Catholic Youth Ministries.

Tharpe, R. G., & Gallimore, R. (1976). What a coach can teach a teacher. *Psychology Today, 9*, 74–78.

Educating Youth Sport Coaches: An Applied Sport Psychology Perspective

Frank L. Smoll, *University of Washington*

Ronald E. Smith, *University of Washington*

D uring the past several decades, youth sport programs have grown tremendously. More than 20 million U.S. boys and girls between the ages of 6 and 18 participate in nonschool sports (Martens, 1986), and there is no reason to believe that participation has reached a peak or that a decline is likely to occur. The rising participation by youngsters has been accompanied by a greater degree of adult involvement. Consequently, these programs have become an extremely complex social system that has attracted the attention of researchers interested in studying the impact of sport competition on psychosocial development (see Fine, 1987; Gould & Weiss, 1987; Smoll, Magill, & Ash, 1988; Smoll & Smith, 1978; Weiss & Gould, 1986).

Much of the controversy that surrounds youth sports concerns the roles that adults play in the process. There is, however, general agreement that an important determinant of the effects of participation is the relationship between coach and athlete (Martens, 1987; Seefeldt & Gould, 1980; Smoll & Smith, 1989). The way coaches structure the athletic situation, the goal priorities they establish, the attitudes and values they transmit, and the behaviors they engage in can markedly influence the effects of sport participation on children. Coaches not only occupy a position of centrality in the athletic setting, but their influence can extend into other areas of the child's life as well. For example, because of the number of single-parent families, coaches frequently occupy the role of a substitute parent.

Most athletes have their first sport experiences in programs staffed by volunteer coaches. While many of these coaches are fairly well versed in the technical aspects of the sport, they rarely have had any formal training in creating a healthy psychological environment for youngsters. Moreover, through the mass media, these coaches are frequently exposed to college or professional coaches who model aggressive behaviors and a "winning is everything" philosophy that are highly inappropriate in a recreational and skill development context. Because the vast majority of youth coaches have desirable motives for coaching (Martens & Gould, 1979; Smith, Smoll, & Curtis, 1978), one can assume that their limitations result primarily from a lack of information on how to create a supportive interpersonal climate. It is here that sport psychologists are capable of making significant contributions, by developing and conducting coach training programs that positively affect coaching practices and thereby increase the likelihood that youngsters will have positive sport experiences.

This chapter begins with an overview of the development and assessment of a cognitive-behavioral intervention designed to assist youth sport coaches in relating more effectively to young athletes. Next, consideration is given to principles and techniques for implementing psychologically oriented coach training programs. The chapter concludes with a brief discussion of procedures for evaluating coach training programs and mechanisms for maximizing attendance. Although the focus throughout is on youth sports, the various methods and approaches are applicable to sport psychology workshops for coaches at virtually all levels of competition, including the professional ranks (Smith & Johnson, 1990).

Developing and Testing a Coach Training Program

A crucial first step in developing a training program is to determine what is to be presented. In this regard, a fundamental assumption that guided our work is the belief that a training program should be based on scientific evidence rather than intuition and/or what we "know" on the basis of informal observation. An empirical foundation for coaching guidelines not only enhances the validity and potential value of the program, but it also increases its credibility in the eyes of consumers. For purposes of illustrating practical issues in program development and evaluation, we will describe our approach to generating an empirical data base and employing cognitive-behavioral techniques to present the program and assess its effects.

Theoretical Model and Research Paradigm

In the early 1970s, recognition of the potential impact of youth coaches on athletes' psychological welfare prompted several scientific questions that we felt were worth pursuing. For example, what do coaches do, and how frequently do they engage in such behaviors as encouragement, punishment, instruction, and organization? What are the psychological dimensions that underlie such behaviors? And, finally, how are observable coaching behaviors related to children's reactions to their organized athletic experiences? Answers to such questions are not only a first step in describing the

behavioral ecology of one aspect of the youth sport setting, but they also provide an empirical basis for the development of psychologically oriented intervention programs.

To begin to answer such questions, we carried out a systematic program of research over a period of several years. The project was guided by a mediational model of coach–athlete interactions, the basic elements of which are represented as follows:

Coach Behaviors → Athlete Perception
and Recall → Athletes' Evaluative Reactions

This model stipulates that the ultimate effects of coaching behaviors are mediated by the meaning that athletes attribute to them. In other words, what athletes remember about their coach's behaviors and how they interpret these actions affects the way that athletes evaluate their sport experiences. Furthermore, a complex of cognitive and affective processes is involved at this mediational level. The athletes' perceptions and reactions are likely to be affected not only by the coach's behaviors, but also by other factors, such as the athlete's age, what he/she expects of coaches (normative beliefs and expectations), and certain personality variables, such as self-esteem and anxiety. In recognition of this, the basic three-element model has been expanded to reflect these factors (Smoll & Smith, 1989). The expanded model, which is presented in Figure 4-1, specifies a number of situational factors as well as coach and athlete characteristics that could influence coach behaviors and the perceptions and reactions of athletes to them. Using this model as a starting point, we have sought to determine how observed coaching behaviors, athletes' perception and recall of the coach's behaviors, and athlete attitudes are related to one another. We have also explored how athlete and coach characteristics might affect these relations.

Measurement of Coaching Behaviors

Several research groups have used behavioral assessment techniques to observe the actual behaviors of youth coaches and their effects on young athletes (e.g., Allison & Ayllon, 1980; Buzas & Ayllon, 1981; Komaki & Barnett, 1977; Koop & Martin, 1983; Rushall & Smith, 1979; Shapiro & Shapiro, 1985). In order to measure leadership behaviors, we developed the Coaching Behavior Assessment System (CBAS) to permit the direct observation and coding of coaches' actions during

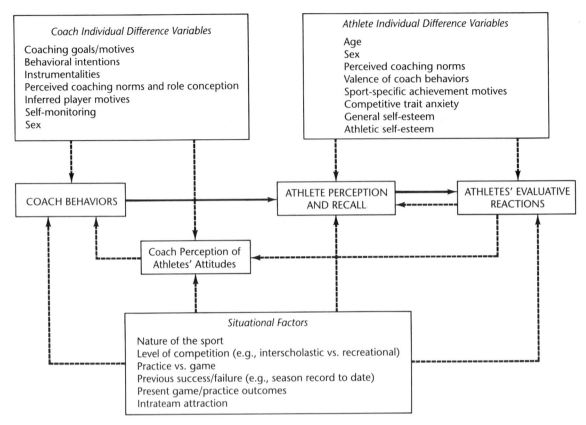

Figure 4-1 **A model of coaching behaviors, their antecedents, and their effects, with hypothesized relations among situational, cognitive, behavioral, and individual difference variables** *Source: Smoll & Smith, 1989.*

practices and games (Smith, Smoll, & Hunt, 1977). The behavioral categories were derived from content analyses of numerous audiotaped "play-by-play" reports of coaches' actions during practices and games. Both the measurement approach and some of the categories derive from a social-behavioral orientation, and the categories incorporate behaviors that have been shown to affect both children and adults in a variety of nonathletic settings (Bales & Slater, 1955; Komaki, 1986; White, 1975).

The CBAS contains 12 categories divided into two major classes of behaviors. **Reactive** (elicited) behaviors are responses to immediately preceding athlete or team behaviors, while **spontaneous** (emitted) behaviors are initiated by the coach and are not a response to a discernible preceding event. Reactive behaviors are responses to either

desirable performance or effort (reinforcement, nonreinforcement), mistakes and errors (mistake-contingent encouragement, mistake-contingent technical instruction, punishment, punitive technical instruction, ignoring mistakes), or misbehaviors on the part of athletes (keeping control). The spontaneous class includes general technical instruction, general encouragement, organization, and general communication. The system thus involves basic interactions between the situation and the coach's behavior. Use of the CBAS in observing and coding coaching behaviors in a variety of sports indicates that the scoring system is sufficiently comprehensive to incorporate the vast majority of overt leader behaviors, that high interrater reliability can be obtained, and that individual differences in behavioral patterns can be discerned (Chaumeton & Duda, 1988; Cruz et al., 1987;

Horn, 1984, 1985; Rejeski, Darracott, & Hutslar, 1979; Smith et al., 1983; Wandzilak, Ansorge, & Potter, 1988).

Basic Research: Coaching Behaviors and Children's Evaluative Reactions

Following development of the CBAS, a field study was conducted to establish relations between coaching behaviors and several athlete variables specified in the conceptual model (Smith, Smoll, & Curtis, 1978). Fifty-one male Little League Baseball coaches were observed by trained coders during 202 complete games. A total of 57,213 individual coaching behaviors were coded into the 12 categories, and a behavioral profile based on an average of 1,122 behaviors was computed for each coach.

Several self-report measures were developed to assess coaches' beliefs, attitudes, and perceptions. These were combined into a questionnaire that the coaches completed at the end of the season. Coaches' self-perception of their behaviors was of primary importance. This was assessed by describing and giving examples of the 12 CBAS behaviors and asking coaches to indicate on a 7-point scale how often they engaged in the behaviors in the situations described.

Data from 542 players were collected after the season during individual interviews and questionnaire administrations carried out in the children's homes. Included were measures of their recall and perception of the coach's behaviors (on the same scales as the coaches had rated their own behavior), their liking for the coach and their teammates, the degree of enjoyment they experienced during the season, and their general self-esteem.

At the level of overt behavior, three independent behavioral dimensions were identified through factor analysis—supportiveness (made up of reinforcement and mistake-contingent encouragement), instructiveness (general technical instruction and mistake-contingent technical instruction *versus* general communication and general encouragement), and punitiveness (punishment and punitive technical instruction *versus* organizational behaviors). The first two dimensions correspond closely to the classic leadership styles of relationship orientation and task orientation emphasized in leadership theories such as Fiedler's (1967) contingency model, situational leadership (Hersey & Blanchard, 1977), and the

vertical dyad linkage model of Graen and Schiemann (1978) and identified in other research on leadership behavior (e.g., Stogdill, 1959).

Relations between coaches' scores on these behavioral dimensions and player measures indicated that players responded most favorably to coaches who engaged in higher percentages of supportive and instructional behaviors. Players on teams whose coaches created a supportive environment also liked their teammates more. A somewhat surprising finding was that the team's won-lost record was essentially unrelated to how well the players liked the coach and how much they wanted to play for the coach in the future. On the other hand, players on winning teams felt that their parents liked the coach more and that the coach liked them more than did players on losing teams. Apparently, winning made little difference to the children, but they knew that it was important to the adults. It is worth noting, however, that winning assumed greater importance beyond age 12, although it continued to be a less important attitudinal determinant than coach behaviors.

Another important issue concerns the degree of accuracy with which coaches perceive their own behaviors. Correlations between CBAS observed behaviors and coaches' ratings of how frequently they performed the behaviors were generally low and nonsignificant. The only significant correlation occurred for punishment. Children's ratings on the same perceived behavior scales correlated much more highly with CBAS measures than did the coaches'! It thus appears that coaches have limited awareness of how frequently they engage in particular forms of behavior, and that athletes are more accurate perceivers of actual coach behaviors.

Finally, analysis of the children's attraction responses toward the coaches revealed a significant interaction between coach supportiveness (the tendency to reinforce desirable performance and effort and to respond to mistakes with encouragement) and athletes' level of self-esteem (Smith & Smoll, 1990). Specifically, the low self-esteem children were especially responsive to variations in supportiveness in a manner consistent with a self-enhancement model of self-esteem (Shrauger, 1975; Swann, 1990; Tesser, 1988). This finding is consistent with the results of other studies that, collectively, suggest that self-enhancement motivation causes people who are low in self-esteem to be especially responsive to variations in supportiveness because of their greater need for positive feedback from others (Dittes, 1959; Brown, Collins, & Schmidt, 1988; Tesser & Campbell, 1983).

Applied Research: Testing a Coach Training Program

Sweeping conclusions are often drawn about the efficacy of intervention programs, in the absence of anything approximating acceptable scientific evidence. We therefore felt it was important not only to develop an empirical foundation for a coach training program but also to measure its effects on coaches and the youngsters who play for them.

In the second phase of our research the results from the observational study formed the basis for a cognitive-behavioral intervention designed to train coaches to provide a more positive and socially supportive athletic environment for their young athletes (Smith, Smoll, & Curtis, 1979). Thirty-one Little League Baseball coaches were randomly assigned to an experimental (training) or to a no-treatment control group. During the preseason intervention program, which is known as Coach Effectiveness Training (CET), behavioral guidelines derived from the initial research were presented and modeled by the trainers. In addition to the information-modeling portion of the program, behavioral feedback and self-monitoring procedures were employed in an attempt to increase the coaches' self-awareness of their behaviors and to encourage them to comply with the coaching guidelines. To assess the effects of the experimental program, CBAS data were collected throughout the season and behavioral profiles were generated for each coach. Postseason outcome measures were obtained from 325 children in individual data collection sessions in their homes.

On both observed behavior and player perception measures, the trained coaches differed from the controls in a manner consistent with the coaching guidelines. The trained coaches gave more reinforcement in response to good performance and effort, and they responded to mistakes with more encouragement and technical instruction and with fewer punitive responses. These behavioral differences were, in turn, reflected in their players' attitudes. The average won-lost percentages of the two groups of coaches did not differ, since success at this level is largely determined by the "luck of the player draft." Nevertheless, the trained coaches were better liked and were rated as

better teachers. Additionally, players on their teams liked one another more and enjoyed their sport experience more. These results seemingly reflect the more socially supportive environment created by the trained coaches. Perhaps most encouraging was the fact that children who played for the trained coaches exhibited a significant increase on a measure of general self-esteem as compared with scores obtained a year earlier, while those who played for the untrained coaches showed no significant change.

A replication of our research on the efficacy of CET has recently been conducted (Smoll et al., in press). The subjects were 18 coaches and 152 children who participated in three Little League Baseball programs. One league (8 teams) was designated the experimental group. The no-treatment control group included 10 teams from two other leagues. Prior to the season, the experimental group coaches participated in CET. To assess the effects of CET, preseason and postseason data were collected for 62 and 90 children in the experimental and control groups, respectively.

The study yielded four major results. First, we found player-perceived behavioral differences between trained and untrained coaches that were in accordance with the behavioral guidelines. Thus, as in previous research (Smith, Smoll, & Curtis, 1979), the experimental manipulation was successful in promoting a more desirable pattern of coaching behaviors. Second, the behavioral differences resulting from the CET program were accompanied by player evaluative responses that favored the trained coaches. They were better liked and were rated as better teachers by their players, their players reported that they had more fun playing baseball, and a higher level of attraction among teammates was found despite the fact that their teams did not differ from controls in won-lost records. Third, consistent with a self-esteem enhancement model, low self-esteem children who played for the trained coaches exhibited a significant increase in general self-esteem over the course of the season; low-esteem youngsters in the control group did not change. Fourth, the children who played for the CET coaches reported lower levels of competitive anxiety than did the control children (Smoll, Smith, & Barnett, 1991).

An extension of the above study was completed one year following the CET intervention (Barnett, Smoll, & Smith, 1992). At the beginning of the next baseball season, dropout rates were assessed for youngsters who had played for the two groups of coaches. If a child was not playing baseball, a brief home interview was scheduled. During this session the children completed a questionnaire designed to assess their reasons for discontinuing participation. The results revealed a 26% dropout rate among the control group children, a figure that is comparable to those obtained in previous youth sport attrition studies (Gould, 1987). In contrast, an attrition rate of only 5% was found for the children who had played for the CET coaches. There was no difference in won-lost percentages between dropouts and returning players; thus the attrition was not a consequence of a lack of team success. Moreover, evidence suggested that the withdrawal was a function of the players' sport experience rather than something that occurred during the nine-month interim. Finally, the questionnaire responses revealed that dropouts in the control group more often reported reasons for withdrawing that were associated with having a negative reaction to their sport experience the previous year.

In summary, the research discussed above, guided by a heuristic leadership model, has demonstrated significant and replicable relations between adult leadership behaviors and children's evaluative reactions to their athletic experiences. Furthermore, the results obtained from the experimental field studies indicate that cognitive-behavioral methods can be employed to train coaches to relate more effectively to young athletes and that psychological intervention can have a positive impact on a social system that is an important part of the lives of many children.

Implementing Sport Psychology Workshops for Youth Coaches

Creating a Receptive Attitude and a Cooperative Atmosphere

The most basic objectives of CET, and of other psychologically oriented coach training programs, are (a) to communicate coaching principles and problem-solving skills in a way that is easily comprehended and (b) to maximize the likelihood that coaches will adopt the information. Thus, the importance of creating a positive learning environment cannot be overemphasized. Even the very

best program is of little value if presented in a way that creates antagonism and defensiveness on the part of coaches.

There are several considerations in setting the stage for a successful session. The primary key is to convey respect for the participating coaches. They really deserve it! We point out to them that even though they may not be explicitly told so, people are aware of the valuable contributions they are making, and that their efforts are appreciated. Indeed, without their unselfish involvement, there could be no organized youth sports.

Next, at the very outset of a training session, it should be emphasized that the coaches themselves have a great deal to offer as a result of their own experiences and associated practical knowledge. We attempt to take advantage of their expertise by encouraging them to share it with the group. In conducting a CET workshop as a two-way sharing of information, coaches are treated as an integral part of the session rather than a mere audience. The open atmosphere for exchange promotes active versus passive learning, and the dialogue serves to enhance the participants' interest and involvement in the learning process.

A final key to successful program implementation is to put a considerable amount of sincere enthusiasm into leading the session. When a trainer truly enjoys his/her pedagogical role, the pleasurable feeling ultimately carries over to the coaches. In such an atmosphere, attention and audience involvement are likely to be enhanced, increasing the enjoyment of coaches and trainer alike.

In contrast to the above, there are three strategies that are virtually guaranteed to create hostility and resistance from coaches. One is to approach them in a condescending manner. In other words, the thing not to do is communicate how much you think you know and how little they know. An associated implication concerns the way a trainer is introduced at the beginning of a session. We recommend against presenting an extensive listing of credentials and professional accomplishments, which tends to convey an air of elitism. Another contraindicated approach is to intimate that your training program is designed to protect athletes from coaches. As noted earlier, most volunteer coaches have commendable motives for coaching, and they generally make positive contributions to children's well-being. A final mistake is to convey the impression that what the coaches have been doing is incorrect. Rather, we emphasize that many options are available for dealing with particular coaching situations, and although all of these tactics may work in *some* cases, certain procedures have a greater likelihood than others of being successful. By counteracting the notion of "right versus wrong," we stress the importance of flexibility and thus attempt to make coaches receptive to alternative ways of responding to specific circumstances.

Orientation to the Psychology of Coaching

In introducing the psychology of coaching, workshop participants should understand the importance of their role as coaches. Some coaches tend to underestimate their influence, and they must be reminded of the many ways in which they can affect young athletes. Information and increased awareness of what they are doing can help them to optimize the desirable effects they can have on children.

Because the term *psychology* means different things to different people, we attempt to remove some of the misunderstanding associated with sport psychology. In so doing, the "psychology of coaching" is described as a form of human interaction; that is, coaches attempt to influence athletes in ways that optimize the physical and psychosocial outcomes of sport participation. Sport psychologists are then portrayed as behavioral scientists who, among other things, seek to understand coach–athlete relationships for the purpose of deriving guidelines designed to improve the quality of that interaction. The task for the trainer and the participating coaches is to explore viable approaches for influencing athletes in the most desirable fashion.

An orientation to the psychology of coaching includes consideration of the topic of winning. The conventional notion of success in sports involves achieving a victorious outcome. But when winning games becomes the sole or primary goal in youth sports, children can be deprived of important opportunities to develop their skills, enjoy participation, and to grow as people. Because of the educational potential of sport, children can learn from both winning and losing. But for this to occur, winning must be placed in a *healthy* perspective. We have therefore developed a four-part philosophy of winning that is taught in CET (Smoll & Smith, 1981):

1. *Winning isn't everything, nor is it the only thing.* Young athletes cannot get the most out of sports if they think that the only objective is to beat their opponents. Although winning is an important goal, it is *not* the most important objective.

2. *Failure is not the same thing as losing.* It is important that athletes do not view losing as a sign of failure or as a threat to their personal value.

3. *Success is not synonymous with winning.* Neither success nor failure need depend on the outcome of a contest or on a won-lost record. Winning and losing pertain to the outcome of a contest, whereas success and failure do not.

4. *Children should be taught that success is found in striving for victory (i.e., success is related to effort).* Youngsters should be taught that they are never losers if they give maximum effort.

This philosophy is designed to maximize young athletes' enjoyment of sport and their chances of deriving the benefits of participation, partly as a result of combating competitive anxiety (Smoll & Smith, 1988). Although seeking victory is encouraged, the ultimate importance of winning is reduced relative to other participation motives. In recognition of the inverse relation between enjoyment and postcompetition stress, *fun* is highlighted as the paramount objective. The philosophy also promotes separation of the athlete's feelings of self-worth from the game outcome, which serves to help overcome fear of failure.

Because they tend to project adult values onto children, many coaches seem to believe that how their athletes feel about them hinges on how successfully the team performs. Yet, as noted earlier, our own research has shown that coaches for whom players enjoyed playing most, and who were most successful in enhancing youngsters' self-esteem, actually had won-lost records that were about the same as coaches who were less liked and less effective in promoting feelings of self-worth (Smith, Smoll, & Curtis, 1978). Differences in coaching behaviors consistently accounted for significantly more variance in player attitudes toward the coach than did won-lost records. Stressing this finding to coaches tends to make them more receptive to the philosophy of winning that we espouse.

Presenting a Conceptual and Empirical Basis for the Program

We not only believe in the importance of establishing an empirical foundation for training guidelines, but we also feel that the ability to present supportive data increases the credibility of the guidelines for the coaches. In describing the development and testing of CET to coaches, we place the empirical findings within the conceptual framework that has guided our work. As previously noted, this model emphasizes functional relations between coaching behaviors, athletes' perceptions of those behaviors, and athletes' reactions to their sport experiences. As a prelude to presenting behavioral guidelines, we customarily familiarize coaches with the core components of the mediational model and describe the Coaching Behavior Assessment System. This provides coaches with a set of perceptual categories for organizing their own experiences and self-perceptions. After establishing a familiarity with potential behaviors, coaches can be informed of how the various behaviors affect young athletes, and this, in turn, sets the stage for the presentation of coaching guidelines.

A number of considerations underlie our commitment to presenting empirical results. First, expertise and trustworthiness are two critically important variables in communicating credibility (Hovland, Janis, & Kelley, 1953). Both are enhanced when data are presented rather than intuitive beliefs. Coaches acquire greater confidence in a training program when they know the content does not merely comprise "armchair" psychology and/or athletic folklore. Second, the presence of empirical data arouses the curiosity and involvement of the participants. Coaches show a great deal of interest in the research, which stimulates their active involvement in the workshop. Also, presentation of unexpected results prevents either the trainer or the coaches from believing that they already know "all of the answers." Third, the research findings form a useful frame of reference for the behavioral guidelines. Better understanding as well as increased credibility of the guidelines seems to result when coaches know how they were derived. Fourth, the ability to demonstrate empirically that certain behaviors have positive effects on children arouses the expectation that the coaches can produce similar effects if they themselves apply the behavioral guidelines. This may

increase their motivation to learn and apply the information.

There are some practical points to be aware of in presenting a conceptual model and empirical results. Obviously, a trainer should use lay terms and avoid scientific jargon. It is best to present data as simply as possible and to avoid technical details. In addition, appropriate use of audio-visual aids enhances any presentation. Diagrams and cartoons illustrating certain concepts and tables summarizing important principles serve to facilitate comprehension and retention.

Behavioral Guidelines and Their Presentation

CET was conceptualized and designed within a cognitive-behavioral framework (Bandura, 1986). The core of the program consists of a series of empirically derived behavioral guidelines (i.e., coaching dos and don'ts). The coaching guidelines are based primarily on social influence techniques that involve principles of positive control rather than aversive control and the conception of success or "winning" as consisting of giving maximum effort (Smoll & Smith, 1987). The behavioral guidelines, which are summarized in Appendix 4-A, emphasize the desirability of *increasing* four specific target behaviors: reinforcement (for effort as well as for good performance), mistake-contingent encouragement, corrective instruction (given in an encouraging and supportive way), and technical instruction (spontaneous instruction in the techniques and strategies of the sport). Coaches are also urged to *decrease* nonreinforcement, punishment, and punitive instruction, as well as to avoid having to use regimenting behaviors (keeping control), by establishing team rules early and reinforcing compliance with them. The guidelines are placed in a goal context of increasing positive coach–athlete and athlete–athlete interactions, developing team cohesion, and developing in athletes a positive desire to achieve rather than a fear of failure.

Didactic instruction. In a CET workshop, which lasts approximately 2½ hours, behavioral guidelines are presented both verbally and in written materials (printed outline and 12-page pamphlet) given to the coaches. The pamphlet supplements the guidelines with concrete suggestions for communicating effectively with young athletes, gaining their respect, and relating effectively to their parents. The importance of sensitivity and being responsive to individual differences among athletes is also stressed. The written materials serve to (a) help keep the workshop organized, (b) facilitate coaches' understanding of the information, (c) eliminate the need for coaches to take notes, and (d) give coaches a tangible resource to refer to in the future. Also, audio-visual aids, such as content slides and cartoons illustrating important points, clarify and emphasize key ideas and add to the organizational quality of the session.

In introducing coaching guidelines we emphasize that they should not be viewed as a "magic formula," nor that mere knowledge of the principles is sufficient. We stress that the challenge is not so much in learning the principles; they are relatively simple. Rather, the challenge is for the coach to integrate the guidelines into his/her own coaching style. When coaches believe that adoption of the guidelines is a result of their own dedication and effort, they are more likely to attribute behavioral changes to themselves rather than to the trainer. This approach is supported by evidence that self-attributed behavioral changes are more enduring than those attributed to some outside causal agent (Deci & Ryan, 1987).

As noted earlier, CET workshops are conducted with an interactive format. Efforts are specifically made to draw coaches into a discussion of the guidelines as opposed to using a lecture-type approach. This is accomplished by directing questions to the coaches and then relating their responses to the written materials. To use this instructional style a trainer must be well versed in the practical ramifications of the guidelines, their applicability to various kinds of coaching situations, and the kinds of questions they are likely to elicit from coaches.

A practical problem occurs when coaches ask questions that are basically unrelated to the topic being covered. For example, during a discussion of principles of reinforcement, a coach might inquire about formulating team rules. Our experience indicates that answering such questions disrupts the sequencing and continuity of concepts, which causes confusion for some coaches. A tactful procedure is to politely ask that the coach write down the question and to indicate on the program outline where he/she should repeat the query.

Credibility and persuasiveness. A primary goal of our instructional approach is to change coaches' attitudes about some of their roles and responsibilities and about their use of certain coaching behaviors. Several aspects of the persuasion process are thus utilized that have proven to be effective in a variety of intervention contexts (see Worchel, Cooper, & Goethals, 1988). In terms of personal characteristics, a highly *credible* communicator is more effective in changing attitudes than one with low credibility. Individuals who are best qualified to conduct psychologically oriented coach training programs are sport psychologists/consultants who have been certified by a professional organization (e.g., Association for the Advancement of Applied Sport Psychology). In addition, competent trainers often have a formal affiliation with an academic institution. Such qualifications and the associated prestige provide some degree of credibility. It is not surprising then that coaches seem to be more receptive and responsive to recommendations presented by a sport psychologist as opposed to a recreation director or a youth league administrator.

Credibility is a multifaceted concept that seems to be a function of at least *expertise* and *trustworthiness*. We endeavor to establish expertise in CET by substantiating the content with empirical evidence from our own work and from the research of other sport psychologists as well. With respect to trusting a communicator's intentions, credibility increases when the communicator does not appear to be purposefully trying to persuade the target. We therefore present information and coaching guidelines objectively, and, as noted earlier, we specifically avoid a "right versus wrong" orientation. In addition, because unexpected stands are generally seen as more trustworthy, we inform coaches that although we have been studying coach–athlete interactions for more than 15 years, we simply do not have all the answers, and in some cases one must admit that "I don't know." The honesty of such disclosures likely contributes to credibility.

The *similarity* between a communicator and the target of the message, along with the communicator's *likability*, are two other factors that affect the power of persuasion. To increase the degree of similarity with coaches, we customarily dress fairly casually. More importantly, while leading discussions we share examples from our own experiences as athletes and coaches, and we often phrase comments with a "we," not a "you," perspective. In regard to likability for a communicator, this particular attribute does lead to greater persuasion. Because liking works by identification, we try to create a warm, friendly rapport with the coaches, and we use humorous anecdotes whenever possible—not primarily for entertainment, but as an educational tool to illustrate certain points.

In addition to characteristics of the communicator, several facets of the message affect its persuasiveness. Coaches are generally not opposed to the points of view advocated in CET, so we usually present *one-sided* communications. In some instances, however, a *two-sided* message is conveyed. This involves more than just acknowledging that another side exists. Rather, opposite approaches are analyzed in order to point out their deficiencies as well as their strengths. Using *rhetorical questions* is another way of influencing attitudes. We ask coaches rhetorical questions (questions to which no answer is expected) to stimulate their thinking and to make them pay closer attention to a communication. For example, "What is the best way to maintain order and teach self-discipline?" Finally, *novelty* of information affects the message's impact. Some coaches may have had previous exposure to some of CET's behavioral guidelines. We attempt to make the principles seem unique by using diagrams, charts, and cartoons for their presentation.

Modeling. The didactic instruction described above contains many *verbal* modeling cues that essentially tell coaches what to do. To supplement the didactic verbal and written materials, behavioral information is transmitted via *behavioral* modeling cues (i.e., actual demonstrations showing coaches how to behave in desirable ways). Such cues may be presented by either a live model or a symbolic model (e.g., films, videotapes, cartoons), as many forms of modeling have been shown to be highly effective in changing behavior (Bandura, 1986; Perry & Furukawa, 1986).

Role playing. In CET, modeling is frequently used in conjunction with later role playing of positive behaviors (e.g., Edelstein & Eisler, 1976; Nay, 1975). Coaches are kept actively involved in the training process by presenting critical situations and asking them to role play appropriate ways of responding. This form of behavioral rehearsal has great promise in facilitating acquisition of desired behaviors, in providing the opportunity to practice the behaviors, and in establishing an increased level of participant involvement during the workshops.

Group problem solving. Another potentially useful procedure is group problem solving. Critical incidents in written form may be provided by the trainer or solicited from the coaches. The coaches are then divided into small groups that are asked to discuss various ways of dealing with the critical incidents. Done in a supportive and reinforcing atmosphere, this can be an extremely useful method for increasing the behavioral repertoire of coaches and their ability to deal with common critical situations. In the group problem-solving process, it is important to discuss the rationales for various behavioral options that are available. In this way, coaches can learn not only how to deal with problematic situations but the rational bases for potential solutions.

Increasing Self-Awareness and Compliance with Coaching Guidelines

One of the striking findings from our initial research was that coaches had very limited awareness of how often they behaved in various ways (Smith, Smoll, & Curtis, 1978). Indeed, ratings made by players correlated more highly with observed behaviors than did coaches' self-ratings of their behaviors. Thus, an important component of a training program should be an attempt to increase coaches' awareness of what they are doing as well as their motivation to comply with behavioral guidelines. In CET, coaches are taught the use of two proven behavioral change techniques, namely, behavioral feedback (Edelstein & Eisler, 1976; McFall & Twentyman, 1973) and self-monitoring (Kanfer & Gaelick-Buys, 1991; Kazdin, 1974; McFall, 1977).

Behavioral feedback. In our preliminary study of the efficacy of CET, behavioral feedback procedures were incorporated (Smith, Smoll, & Curtis, 1979). Observers trained in the use of the CBAS developed behavioral profiles for each of the experimental group coaches, and these were made available to the coaches so that they were able to see the distribution of their own behaviors. Unfortunately, this kind of detailed and objective feedback is usually not available in nonresearch settings. However, it is possible to inform coaches about how to obtain feedback from various sources. For example, coaches can be encouraged to work with their assistants as a team and share descriptions of each others' behaviors. They can discuss alternate ways of dealing with difficult situations and athletes and prepare themselves for dealing with similar situations in the future. Other potential feedback procedures include soliciting input from athletes and provision of feedback by a league committee.

Self-monitoring. **Self-monitoring** (observing and recording one's own behavior) has the potential for increasing coaches' awareness of their own behavioral patterns and repeatedly focusing their attention on specific guidelines. Also, it may be an effective behavior change procedure in itself (Kanfer & Gaelick-Buys, 1991; Kazdin, 1974; Thoresen & Mahoney, 1974). Because of this, self-monitoring procedures were included in our experimental field studies (Smith, Smoll, & Curtis, 1979; Smoll et al., in press). As a part of CET workshops, coaches are given brief self-monitoring forms that they are encouraged to complete immediately after practices and games (see Appendix 4-B). Self-monitoring is restricted to desired behaviors in light of evidence that tracking of undesired behaviors can be detrimental to effective self-regulation (Cavior & Maribotto, 1976; Gottman & McFall, 1972; Kirschenbaum & Karoly, 1977). Coaches are encouraged to engage in self-monitoring on a regular basis in order to achieve optimal results.

Additional procedures. In addition to feedback and self-monitoring, some other procedures might be valuable for increasing awareness and compliance with guidelines. For example, intermittent follow-up meetings might be held with coaches during which they discuss their experiences in utilizing the guidelines and the effects the behaviors seem to be having on their athletes. Follow-up may also occur through telephone contacts with individual coaches by the trainer. Finally, brief questionnaires may be designed and sent to coaches. Such questionnaires can be used not only to elicit information from the coaches but also may contain "refresher" points designed to maintain or increase compliance with coaching guidelines.

Workshop Evaluation

Systematic evaluation of a coaching workshop not only provides a basis for substantiating the efficacy of a training intervention, but it also provides a mechanism for program modification and improvement. It is ironic, however, that consumers of the programs often believe in their value so strongly that they view formal evaluation as unnecessary. Consequently, a commitment to participate in assessment procedures should be an explicit part of the training agreement.

Although a comprehensive description of program evaluation methods is beyond the scope of this chapter, a number of procedures are highly applicable. The simplest and most direct approach is to collect coaches' ratings of the value of the program and its individual components. A checklist used for evaluating CET is included in Appendix 4-C. Of considerably greater utility are measures of knowledge gained from the program. Knowledge tests, including the ability to apply the principles in relevant situations, can be administered prior to training and at succeeding intervals following the training.

Beyond the question of comprehension is the more salient issue of the extent to which the program results in actual behavior change. Our dual approach has been to use the CBAS to collect naturalistic behavioral data and to obtain athletes' perceptions of coaching behaviors. Further, athlete individual difference variables (e.g., self-esteem, trait anxiety) may be employed both as dependent variable measures and as moderator variables to help answer the important question of how different kinds of children are affected by trained coaches.

Maximizing Workshop Attendance

Our experience in offering CET has shown that youth coaches are committed to providing a positive experience for youngsters. It is also reassuring to note that coaches are willing to spend time to acquire additional information and do take advantage of the availability of workshops. An advantage of the CET approach is that it is a brief program that focuses on a relatively small number of critical principles and guidelines that clearly make a difference.

One issue encountered in implementing a workshop is to decide when it should be scheduled. This question was addressed in a study of 1,227 coaches (Universities Study Committee, 1978). Ninety percent of the respondents felt that training sessions should be offered before the season began rather than during the season. Fifty-one percent of the respondents felt that the best time of the week to schedule programs was on week nights, while 28% preferred Saturday mornings.

Some youth sport organizations have adopted policies that require coaches to attend training programs. In lieu of mandatory certification, administrators have employed simple yet effective tactics to boost attendance. For example, charging coaches a modest fee is always advisable. Interestingly, some individuals do not believe that a workshop is worth attending if it is offered for free. A preregistration system, with a reduced admission fee as an inducement, also seems to evoke commitment on the part of coaches. Another administrative ploy is to distribute organizational materials (e.g., team rosters and game schedules) at a training session. Finally, relative to CET, the core content focuses on a series of behavioral guidelines that can be applied in a wide variety of leadership situations, including child rearing. Because parents can also derive benefits from the intervention, they are encouraged to attend workshops along with their child's coach.

A Final Word

Given the ever-expanding nature of organized youth sports, the need for effective coach training programs is obvious. Likewise, the large coach turnover from year to year ensures a continuing demand for intervention. In concluding this chapter, it is appropriate to restate our firm belief that extended efforts to improve the quality and value of coach training programs are best achieved via well-conceived and properly conducted evaluation research. Future collaboration between sport psychologists and youth sport organizations will not only serve to advance understanding of the effects of competition but will also provide for enriched opportunities for children in sport.

Study Questions

1. Describe the core components (three basic elements) of the mediational model of coach–athlete interactions that served to guide the coaching behaviors research.

2. What are the two major classes of behaviors included in the CBAS, and what is the difference between them?

3. Following development of the CBAS, a field study was conducted to establish relations between coaching behaviors and childrens' evaluative reactions. Describe the basic research procedures, and discuss the major findings with respect to (a) the structure of overt coaching behaviors, (b) relations between coaching behaviors and players' attitudinal responses, (c) the role of winning relative to players' attitudes, (d) the degree of accuracy with which coaches perceived their own behaviors, and (e) the role of self-esteem as a mediator variable in coaching-behavior–player-attitude relations.

4. Describe the research design and methodology incorporated in the studies that tested the efficacy of CET. What were the results with respect to (a) behavioral differences between trained and untrained coaches, (b) won-lost records, (c) players' evaluative reactions to trained and untrained coaches, (d) self-esteem effects, (e) competitive anxiety differences between youngsters who played for trained and untrained coaches, and (f) attrition (dropout) rates?

5. In implementing sport psychology workshops for youth coaches, the trainer should create a positive learning environment. What are some ways to foster a receptive and cooperative attitude on the part of coaches? What approaches should be avoided?

6. Describe the components of Smoll and Smith's (1981) healthy philosophy of winning, and in-

dicate how this orientation is designed to combat competitive anxiety.

7. In conducting a CET workshop, what is the rationale/justification for presenting empirical results to coaches?

8. Briefly describe the major behavioral guidelines (i.e., coaching dos and don'ts) that form the core of CET.

9. What are the advantages of conducting coach training programs with an interactive format, and how might this be accomplished?

10. With respect to changing coaches' attitudes during a training program, explain how the following aspects of the persuasion process might be taken into account: (a) credibility (expertise and trustworthiness) of the trainer, (b) similarity between the trainer and the coaches, (c) likability of the trainer, (d) one-sided versus two-sided communications, (e) use of rhetorical questions, and (f) novelty of information.

11. Describe the procedures that can be utilized to increase coaches' self-awareness and their compliance with coaching guidelines.

12. Why is it important to evaluate coaching workshops, and what procedures can be used?

References

Allison, M. G., & Ayllon, T. (1980). Behavioral coaching in the development of skills in football, gymnastics, and tennis. *Journal of Applied Behavior Analysis, 13*, 297–314.

Bales, R. F., & Slater, P. (1955). Role differentiation in small decision-making groups. In P. Parson & R. F. Bales (Eds.), *Family, socialization, and interaction process* (pp. 259–306). Glencoe, Ill.: Free Press.

Bandura, A. (1986). *Social foundations of thought and action: A social cognitive theory*. Englewood Cliffs, N.J.: Prentice-Hall.

Barnett, N. P., Smoll, F. L., & Smith, R. E. (1992). Effects of enhancing coach–athlete relationships on youth sport attrition. *The Sport Psychologist, 6*, 111–127.

Brown, J. D., Collins, R. L., & Schmidt, G. W. (1988). Self-esteem and direct versus indirect forms of self-enhancement. *Journal of Personality and Social Psychology, 55*, 445–453.

Buzas, H. P., & Ayllon, T. (1981). Differential reinforcement in coaching tennis skills. *Behavior Modification, 5*, 372–385.

Cavior, N., & Marabotto, C. M. (1976). Monitoring verbal behaviors in a dyadic interaction. *Journal of Consulting and Clinical Psychology, 44*, 68–76.

Chaumeton, N. R., & Duda, J. L. (1988). Is it how you play the game or whether you win or lose?: The effect of competitive level and situation on coaching behaviors. *Journal of Sport Behavior, 11*, 157–173.

Cruz, J., Bou, A., Fernandez, J. M., Martin, M., Monras, J., Monfort, N., & Ruiz, A. (l987). Avaluacio conductual de les interaccions entre entrenadors i jugadors de basquet escolar. *Apunts Medicina de L'esport, 24*, 89–98.

Deci, E. L., & Ryan, R. M. (1987). The support of autonomy and the control of behavior. *Journal of Personality and Social Psychology, 53*, 1024–1037.

Dittes, J. (1959). Attractiveness of a group as a function of self-esteem and acceptance by group. *Journal of Abnormal and Social Psychology, 59*, 77–82.

Edelstein, B. A., & Eisler, R. M. (1976). Effects of modeling and modeling with instructions and feedback on the behavioral components of social skills. *Behavior Therapy, 7*, 382–389.

Fiedler, F. E. (1967). *A theory of leadership effectiveness*. New York: McGraw-Hill.

Fine, G. A. (1987). *With the boys: Little League Baseball and preadolescent culture*. Chicago: University of Chicago Press.

Gottman, J. M., & McFall, R. M. (1972). Self-monitoring effects in a program for potential high school dropouts: A time series analysis. *Journal of Consulting and Clinical Psychology, 39*, 273–281.

Gould, D. (1987). Understanding attrition in children's sport. In D. Gould & M. R. Weiss (Eds.), *Advances in pediatric sport sciences* (pp. 61–85). Champaign, Ill.: Human Kinetics.

Gould, D., & Weiss, M. R. (Eds.). (1987). *Advances in pediatric sport sciences: Vol. 2. Behavioral issues*. Champaign, Ill.: Human Kinetics.

Graen, G., & Schiemann, W. (1978). Leader member agreement: A vertical dyad linkage approach. *Journal of Applied Psychology, 63*, 206–212.

Hersey, P., & Blanchard, K. H. (1977). *Management of organizational behavior* (3rd ed.). Englewood Cliffs, N.J.: Prentice-Hall.

Horn, T. S. (1984). Expectancy effects in the interscholastic athletic setting: Methodological considerations. *Journal of Sport Psychology, 6*, 60–76.

Horn, T. S. (1985). Coaches' feedback and changes in children's perceptions of their physical competence. *Journal of Educational Psychology, 77*, 174–186.

Hovland, C. I., Janis, I. L., & Kelley, H. H. (1953). *Communication and persuasion*. New Haven, Conn.: Yale University Press.

Kanfer, F. H., & Gaelick-Buys, L. (1991). Self-management methods. In F. H. Kanfer & A. P. Goldstein (Eds.),

Helping people change: A textbook of methods (4th ed.) (pp. 305–360). New York: Pergamon.

Kazdin, A. E. (1974). Self-monitoring and behavior change. In M. J. Mahoney & C. E. Thoresen (Eds.), *Self-control: Power to the person* (pp. 218–246). Monterey, Calif.: Brooks/Cole.

Kirschenbaum, D. S., & Karoly, P. (1977). When self-regulation fails: Tests of some preliminary hypotheses. *Journal of Consulting and Clinical Psychology, 45,* 1116–1125.

Komaki, J. L. (1986). Toward effective supervision: An operant analysis and comparison of managers at work. *Journal of Applied Psychology, 71,* 270–279.

Komaki, J., & Barnett, F. T. (1977). A behavioral approach to coaching football: Improving the play execution of the offensive backfield on a youth football team. *Journal of Applied Behavior Analysis, 10,* 657–664.

Koop, S., & Martin, G. (1983). Evaluation of a coaching strategy to reduce swimming stroke errors with beginning age-group swimmers. *Journal of Applied Behavioral Analysis, 16,* 447–465.

Martens, R. (1986). Youth sport in the USA. In M. R. Weiss & D. Gould (Eds.), *Sport for children and youths* (pp. 27–33). Champaign, Ill.: Human Kinetics.

Martens, R. (1987). *Coaches guide to sport psychology.* Champaign, Ill.: Human Kinetics.

Martens, R., & Gould, D. (1979). Why do adults volunteer to coach children's sports? In G. C. Roberts & K. M. Newell (Eds.), *Psychology of motor behavior and sport—1978* (pp. 79–89). Champaign, Ill.: Human Kinetics.

McFall, R. M. (1977). Parameters of self-monitoring. In R. B. Stuart (Ed.), *Behavioral self-management: Strategies, techniques and outcomes* (pp. 196–214). New York: Brunner/Mazel.

McFall, R. M., & Twentyman, C. T. (1973). Four experiments on the relative contributions of rehearsal, modeling, and coaching to assertion training. *Journal of Abnormal Psychology, 81,* 199–218.

Nay, W. R. (1975). A systematic comparison of instructional techniques for parents. *Behavior Therapy, 6,* 14–21.

Perry, M. A., & Furukawa, M. J. (1986). Modeling methods. In F. H. Kanfer & A. P. Goldstein (Eds.), *Helping people change: A textbook of methods* (3rd ed.) (pp. 66–110). New York: Pergamon.

Rejeski, W., Darracott, C., & Hutslar, S. (1979). Pygmalion in youth sport: A field study. *Journal of Sport Psychology, 1,* 311–319.

Rushall, B. S., & Smith, K. C. (1979). The modification of the quality and quantity of behavior categories in a swimming coach. *Journal of Sport Psychology, 1,* 138–150.

Seefeldt, V., & Gould, D. (1980). *Physical and psychological effects of athletic competition on children and youth.* Washington, D.C.: ERIC Clearinghouse on Teacher Education.

Shapiro, E., & Shapiro, S. (1985). Behavioral coaching in the development of skills in track. *Behavior Modification, 5,* 211–224.

Shrauger, J. S. (1975). Responses to evaluation as a function of initial self-perceptions. *Psychological Bulletin, 82,* 581–596.

Smith, R. E., & Johnson, J. (1990). An organizational empowerment approach to consultation in professional baseball. *The Sport Psychologist, 4,* 347–357.

Smith, R. E., & Smoll, F. L. (1990). Self-esteem and children's reactions to youth sport coaching behaviors: A field study of self-enhancement processes. *Developmental Psychology, 26,* 987–993.

Smith, R. E., Smoll, F. L., & Curtis, B. (1978). Coaching behaviors in Little League Baseball. In F. L. Smoll & R. E. Smith (Eds.), *Psychological perspectives in youth sports* (pp. 173–201). Washington, D.C.: Hemisphere.

Smith, R. E., Smoll, F. L., & Curtis, B. (1979). Coach effectiveness training: A cognitive-behavioral approach to enhancing relationship skills in youth sport coaches. *Journal of Sport Psychology, 1,* 59–75.

Smith, R. E., Smoll, F. L., & Hunt, E. B. (1977). A system for the behavioral assessment of athletic coaches. *Research Quarterly, 48,* 401–407.

Smith, R. E., Zane, N. W. S., Smoll, F. L., & Coppel, D. B. (1983). Behavioral assessment in youth sports: Coaching behaviors and children's attitudes. *Medicine and Science in Sports and Exercise, 15,* 208–214.

Smoll, F. L., Magill, R. A., & Ash, M. J. (Eds.). (1988). *Children in sport* (3rd ed.). Champaign, Ill.: Human Kinetics.

Smoll, F. L., & Smith, R. E. (Eds.). (1978). *Psychological perspectives in youth sports.* Washington, D.C.: Hemisphere.

Smoll, F. L., & Smith, R. E. (1981). Developing a healthy philosophy of winning in youth sports. In V. Seefeldt, F. L. Smoll, R. E. Smith, & D. Gould (Eds.), *A winning philosophy for youth sport programs* (pp. 17–24). East Lansing, Mich.: Michigan Institute for the Study of Youth Sports.

Smoll, F. L., & Smith, R. E. (1987). *Sport psychology for youth coaches.* Washington, D.C.: National Federation for Catholic Youth Ministry.

Smoll, F. L., & Smith, R. E. (1988). Reducing stress in youth sport: Theory and application. In F. L. Smoll, R. A. Magill, & M. J. Ash (Eds.), *Children in sport* (3rd ed.) (pp. 229–249). Champaign, Ill.: Human Kinetics.

Smoll, F. L., & Smith, R. E. (1989). Leadership behaviors in sport: A theoretical model and research paradigm. *Journal of Applied Social Psychology, 19,* 1522–1551.

Smoll, F. L., Smith, R. E., & Barnett, N. P. (1991, October). *A new empirical evaluation of coach effectiveness training.* Paper presented at the meeting of the Association for the Advancement of Applied Sport Psychology, Savannah, Ga..

Smoll, F. L., Smith, R. E., Barnett, N. P., & Everett, J. J. (in press). Enhancement of children's self-esteem through social support training for youth sport coaches. *Journal of Applied Psychology.*

Stogdill, R. M. (1959). *Individual behavior and group achievement.* New York: Oxford University Press.

Swann, W. B., Jr. (1990). To be known or to be adored? The interplay of self-enhancement and self-verification. In R. M. Sorrentino & E. T. Higgins (Eds.), *Handbook of motivation and cognition: Foundations of social behavior* (vol. 2) (pp. 408–488). New York: Guilford.

Tesser, A. (1988). Toward a self-evaluative maintenance model of social behavior. In L. Berkowitz (Ed.), *Advances in experimental social psychology* (vol. 21) (pp. 69–92). Orlando, Fla.: Academic Press.

Tesser, A., & Campbell, J. (1983). Self-definition and self-evaluation maintenance. In J. Suls & A. G. Greenwald (Eds.), *Psychological perspectives on the self* (vol. 2) (pp. 1–32). Hillsdale, N.J.: Erlbaum.

Thoresen, C. E., & Mahoney, M. J. (1974). *Behavioral self-control.* New York: Holt, Rinehart, & Winston.

Universities Study Committee. (1978). *Joint legislative study on youth sports programs: Phase III. Agency sponsored sports.* East Lansing, Mich.: Michigan Institute for the Study of Youth Sports.

Wandzilak, T., Ansorge, C. J., & Potter, G. (1988). Comparison between selected practice and game behaviors of youth soccer coaches. *Journal of Sport Behavior, 11,* 78–88.

Weiss, M. R., & Gould, D. (Eds.). (1986). *Sport for children and youths.* Champaign, Ill.: Human Kinetics.

White, M. A. (1975). Natural rates of teacher approval and disapproval in the classroom. *Journal of Applied Behavior Analysis, 8,* 367–372.

Worchel, S., Cooper, J., & Goethals, G. R. (1988). *Understanding social psychology* (4th ed.). Chicago: Dorsey.

Summary of Coaching Guidelines

I. **Reactive Coaching Behaviors: Responding to Athlete Behaviors and Game Situations**

A. Good plays

Do: Provide *reinforcement*!! Do so immediately. Let the athletes know that you appreciate and value their efforts. Reinforce effort as much as you do results. Look for positive things, reinforce them, and you will see them increase. Remember, whether children show it or not, the positive things you say and do remain with them.

Don't: Take their efforts for granted.

B. Mistakes, screw-ups, boneheaded plays, and all the things the pros seldom do

Do: Give *encouragement* immediately after mistakes. That's when the youngster needs your support the most. If you are sure the athlete knows how to correct the mistake, then encouragement alone is sufficient. When appropriate, give *corrective instruction*, but always do so in an encouraging manner. Do this by emphasizing not the bad things that just happened, but the good things that will happen if the player follows your instruction (the "why" of it). This will make the athlete positively self-motivated to correct the mistakes rather than negatively motivated to avoid failure and your disapproval.

Don't: *Punish* when things are going wrong!! Punishment isn't just yelling. It can be any indication of disapproval, tone of voice, or action. Athletes respond much better to a positive approach. Fear of failure is reduced if you work to reduce fear of punishment.

Don't: Give corrective instruction in a hostile or harsh manner. That is, avoid *punitive instruction*. This is more likely to increase frustration and create resentment than to improve performance. Don't let your good intentions in giving instruction be self-defeating.

C. Misbehaviors, lack of attention

Do: Maintain order by establishing clear expectations. Emphasize that during a contest all members of the team are part of the activity, even those on the bench. Use reinforcement to strengthen team participation. In other words, try to prevent misbehaviors by using the positive approach to strengthen their opposites.

Don't: Get into the position of having to constantly nag or threaten athletes in order to prevent chaos. Don't be a drill sergeant. If an athlete refuses to cooperate, deprive him or her of something valued. Don't use physical measures, such as running laps. The idea here is that if you establish clear behavioral guidelines early and work to build team spirit in achieving them, you can avoid having to repeatedly *keep control*. Youngsters want clear guidelines and expectations, but they don't want to be regimented. Try to achieve a healthy balance.

II. **Spontaneous Coaching Behaviors: Getting Positive Things to Happen and Creating a Good Learning Atmosphere**

Do: Give *technical instruction*. Establish your role as a caring and competent teacher.

Try to structure participation as a learning experience in which you are going to help the athletes develop their abilities. Always give instruction in a positive fashion. Satisfy your athletes' desire to become the best they can be. Give instruction in a clear, concise manner and, if possible, demonstrate how to do it.

Do: Concentrate on the activity. Be "in the game" with the athletes. Set a good example for team unity.

Don't: Give either instruction or encouragement in a sarcastic or degrading manner. Make a point, then leave it. Don't let "encouragement" become irritating to the athletes.

Note. These guidelines were excerpted from the printed materials that are given to CET workshop participants. They are discussed in greater detail elsewhere (see Smoll & Smith, 1987, pp. 23–39).

Coach Self-Report Form

Complete this form as soon as possible after a practice or game.

For items 1, 2, and 3 not only think about what you did, but also consider the kinds of situations in which the actions occurred and the kinds of athletes who were involved.

1. Approximately what percentage of the times they occurred did you respond to good plays with REINFORCEMENT? _____

2. Approximately what percentage of the times they occurred did you respond to mistakes/errors with each of the following communications?

   A. ENCOURAGEMENT only _____

   B. CORRECTIVE INSTRUCTION given in an encouraging manner _____
      (Sum of A plus B should not exceed 100%)

3. About how many times did you reinforce athletes for effort, complying with team rules, encouraging teammates, showing "team spirit," etc.? _____

4. How well did your team play tonight? (Check one)

_____	_____	_____	_____	_____
Very poorly	*Not very well*	*Average*	*Quite well*	*Very well*

5. How positive an experience *for the kids* was this practice/game?

_____	_____	_____	_____	_____
Very negative	*Somewhat negative*	*Neutral*	*Somewhat positive*	*Very positive*

6. How positive an experience *for you* was this practice/game?

_____	_____	_____	_____	_____
Very negative	*Somewhat negative*	*Neutral*	*Somewhat positive*	*Very positive*

7. Is there anything you might do differently if you had a chance to coach this practice/game again? (If so, briefly explain.)

_____

_____

_____

_____

_____

_____

Coach Effectiveness Training: Workshop Evaluation

Background Information

1. Sport _____

2. Years of experience coaching the sport _____

3. Age _____

4. Sex _____

IMPORTANT: *In rating this workshop, please respond to each item carefully and thoughtfully. Keep the purpose of each section in mind as you rate the workshop.*

For each item, circle one response: E   = Excellent
                                   VG = Very Good
                                   G   = Good
                                   F   = Fair
                                   P   = Poor
                                   VP = Very Poor

Section 1: To Provide a General Evaluation

1. The workshop as a whole was:	1.	E	VG	G	F	P	VP
2. Clarity of workshop objective was:	2.	E	VG	G	F	P	VP
3. Amount you learned in the workshop was:	3.	E	VG	G	F	P	VP
4. Relevance and usefulness of workshop content was:	4.	E	VG	G	F	P	VP
5. Interest level in the workshop was:	5.	E	VG	G	F	P	VP
6. Conduciveness of workshop atmosphere to learning was:	6.	E	VG	G	F	P	VP
7. Value for coaches who will attend future workshops:	7.	E	VG	G	F	P	VP

Section 2: To Provide Diagnostic Feedback to the Workshop Leader

8. Workshop organization was:	8.	E	VG	G	F	P	VP
9. Explanations by leader were:	9.	E	VG	G	F	P	VP
10. Leader's use of examples and illustrations:	10.	E	VG	G	F	P	VP
11. Quality of questions or problems raised:	11.	E	VG	G	F	P	VP
12. Coach confidence in leader's knowledge was:	12.	E	VG	G	F	P	VP
13. Leader's enthusiasm was:	13.	E	VG	G	F	P	VP
14. Answers to coaches' questions were:	14.	E	VG	G	F	P	VP
15. Leader's enhancement of coach interest in the material was:	15.	E	VG	G	F	P	VP
16. Leader's preparation for the workshop was:	16.	E	VG	G	F	P	VP
17. Encouragement given coaches to express themselves was:	17.	E	VG	G	F	P	VP

Section 3: To Provide an Estimate of the Impact of the Workshop

18. Your degree of motivation to apply what you learned in the workshop:	18.	E	VG	G	F	P	VP
19. Expected value of the workshop for improving your coaching:	19.	E	VG	G	F	P	VP
20. Anticipated effect that the positive approach will have on your athletes:	20.	E	VG	G	F	P	VP

Section 4: To Provide a Specific Evaluation, Rate the Value of each Workshop Component

21. Objectives of youth sports:	21.	E	VG	G	F	P	VP
22. The importance of a coach:	22.	E	VG	G	F	P	VP
23. Orientation to the psychology of coaching:	23.	E	VG	G	F	P	VP
24. Developing and testing CET:	24.	E	VG	G	F	P	VP
25. A healthy philosophy of winning:	25.	E	VG	G	F	P	VP
26. Expectations and imitation:	26.	E	VG	G	F	P	VP
27. Behavioral guidelines for coaches:	27.	E	VG	G	F	P	VP
28. Increasing self-awareness:	28.	E	VG	G	F	P	VP

Comments:

_____

_____

_____

_____

_____

_____

Enhancing Coach–Parent Relationships in Youth Sports

Frank L. Smoll, *University of Washington*

A	thletic competition for children is a firmly established part of our society. Organized youth sports in the United States actually go back to the early 1900s. The first programs were instituted in public schools when it was recognized that physical activity was an important part of education. Gradually, sponsorship and control of many sports shifted to a host of local and national youth agencies (Berryman, 1975). In moving from the sandlot to the more formalized programs that now exist, the youth sport explosion has touched the lives of millions of children and adults alike (Martens, 1986).

Although coaches have the most direct contact with children within the sport environment, parents are instrumental in determining children's sport involvement (Lewko & Greendorfer, 1988; McPherson & Brown, 1988). The "athletic triangle," consisting of coach, athlete, and parent, is thus a natural aspect of youth sports, and a coach's role in relating to parents is very important to the success of a program. Through their cooperative efforts, many parents productively contribute. Unfortunately, however, the negative impact that some parents have is all too obvious. Some parents, out of ignorance, can undermine the basic goals of youth sport programs and rob youngsters of benefits they could derive from participation. Coaches

are in a position to channel parents' genuine concerns and good intentions in a way that heightens the value of athletes' sport experience.

This chapter provides information to assist coaches in working effectively with parents, thereby increasing the chances of a desirable sport outcome for all concerned. After completing this chapter, one should have a better understanding of (a) the difference between youth and professional models of sport, (b) the objectives of youth sports, including a healthy philosophy of winning, (c) parent roles and responsibilities, (d) how to achieve effective two-way communication with parents, and (e) how to organize and conduct sport meetings with parents.

Developmental Versus Professional Models of Sport

A fundamental issue requiring clarification is the distinction between youth and professional models of sport. Youth sports are believed to provide an educational medium for the development of desirable physical and psychosocial characteristics. These programs are viewed as microcosms of society in which children can learn to cope with realities they will face in later life. Thus, athletics provide a setting within which an *educational process* can occur.

On the other hand, professional sports are a huge commercial enterprise. The goals of professional sports, simply stated, are to entertain and, ultimately, to make money. Financial success is of primary importance and depends heavily on a product orientation, namely, winning. Is this wrong? Certainly not! The professional sports world is a part of the entertainment industry, and as such it is valued in our society.

What, then, is the problem? Most of the negative consequences of youth sports occur when adults erroneously impose a professional model on what should be a recreational and educational experience for children. When excessive emphasis is placed on winning, it is easy to lose sight of the needs and interests of the young athlete.

Objectives of Youth Sports

Participation in youth sports yields many benefits. Some of them are physical, such as attaining sport skills and increasing health and fitness. Others are psychological, such as developing leadership skills, self-discipline, respect for authority, competitiveness, cooperativeness, sportsmanship, and self-confidence. These are many of the positive attributes that fall under the heading of "character." Many people agree with former Dallas Cowboy coach Tom Landry that "the greatest contribution that sports can make to young athletes is to build character. The greatest teacher of character is on the athletic field." Youth sports are also an important social activity in which children can make new friends and acquaintances and become part of an ever-expanding social network. Furthermore, the involvement of parents in the athletic enterprise can bring families closer together and strengthen family unity. Finally, of course, youth sports are (or should be) just plain *fun!*

The basic right of the child athlete to have fun in participating should not be neglected. One of the quickest ways to reduce fun is for adults to begin treating children as if they were varsity or professional athletes. Coaches and parents alike need to keep in mind that young athletes are not miniature adults. They are children, and they have the right to play as children. Youth sports are first

and foremost a play activity, and children deserve to enjoy sports in their own way. In essence, it is important that programs remain child-centered and do not become adult-dominated.

What about *winning*? The common notion in sports equates success with victory. However, with a "winning is everything" philosophy, young athletes may lose opportunities to develop their skills, to enjoy participation, and to grow socially and emotionally. As emphasized in Chapter 4, well-informed coaches realize that success is not equivalent to winning games, and failure is not the same as losing. Rather, the most important kind of success comes from striving to win and giving maximum *effort*. The only thing athletes can control is the amount of effort they give. They have incomplete control over the outcome that is achieved. Athletes should be taught that they are never "losers" if they give maximum effort in striving for excellence. This philosophy of success is relevant to parents as well as coaches. In fact, it may be more important for parents to understand its meaning. They can apply it to many areas of their child's life in addition to athletics.

What are some criteria for determining when winning is out of perspective? Martens (1978) addressed this question in his book *Joy and Sadness in Children's Sports*. He indicated that winning is out of perspective (a) when a display of comradeship with an opponent is considered a sign of weakness, or when laughter is judged to be a lack of competitiveness; (b) when a coach instructs athletes in strategies designed to take unfair advantage of an opponent; (c) when youngsters are given drugs, coaxed to cheat, and intimidated to excel; and (d) when winning the game becomes more important than winning friends, respect, self-confidence, skill, health, and self-worth. When winning is kept in perspective, the child comes first and winning is second (Martens & Seefeldt, 1979). In this case, rather than focusing on a won-lost record, the most important sport product is the quality of the experience provided for young athletes.

What about the objectives that young athletes seek to achieve? A survey of more than 100,000 youth sport participants in the state of Michigan indicated that young athletes most often participated in organized sports for the following reasons: (a) to have fun, (b) to improve their skills and learn new skills, (c) to be with their friends or make new friends, and (d) to succeed or win (Universities Study Committee, 1978). Coaches may wish to give these consideration when establishing goals for the season. Furthermore, coaches should be aware that none of these outcomes is achieved automatically through participation in sports. Coaches, parents, and sport officials should be part of a team trying to accomplish common goals. When everyone works together to reduce chances of misunderstanding and problems, the objectives can be attained. In this regard, parents should be encouraged to view their involvement in youth sports as an integral part of their child-rearing responsibilities.

Parents' Roles and Responsibilities

When a child enters a sport program, the mother and/or father automatically takes on some obligations. Some parents do not realize this at first and are surprised to find out what is expected of them. Others never realize their responsibilities and miss opportunities to help their children grow through sports, or they may actually do things that interfere with their children's development.

To begin, parents must realize that children have a right to participate in sports. This includes the right to choose *not* to participate (Martens & Seefeldt, 1979). Although parents might choose to encourage participation, children should not be pressured, intimidated, or bribed into playing. In fulfilling their responsibility, parents should counsel their children, giving consideration to the sport selected and the level of competition at which the children want to play. And, of course, parents should respect their children's decisions.

Parents can enjoy their children's participation more if they acquire an understanding and appreciation of the sport. This includes knowledge of basic rules, skills, and strategies. Coaches can serve as valuable resources by answering parents' questions and by referring parents to a community/school library or a bookstore for educational materials. In addition, coaches should devote part of an early season practice to a lecture/demonstration of the fundamentals of the sport, and parents having little background in the sport should be encouraged to attend this session.

Parents often assume an extremely active role in youth sports, and in some instances their influence becomes an important source of children's stress (Passer, 1984; Scanlan, 1986; Smith, 1984). What might constitute the underlying basis of parent-induced stress? All parents identify with their children to some extent and thus want them to do well. Unfortunately, in some cases the degree of identification becomes excessive. The child becomes an extension of the parents. When this happens, parents begin to define their own self-worth in terms of how successful their son/daughter is. The father who is a "frustrated jock" may seek to experience through his child the success he never knew as an athlete. Or the parent who was a star may be resentful and rejecting if the child does not attain similar achievements. Some parents thus become "winners" or "losers" through their children, and the pressure placed on the children to excel can be extreme. A child *must* succeed or the parent's self-image is threatened. Much more is at stake than a mere game, and the child of such a parent carries a heavy burden. When parental love and approval are dependent on adequacy of performance, sports are bound to be stressful (see Smith, Smoll, & Smith, 1989; Smoll & Smith, 1990).

Coaches may be able to counteract this tendency by explaining the identification process to parents. Tell them that if they place excessive pressure on children, they can decrease the potential that sports can have for enjoyment and personal growth. A key to reducing parent-produced stress is to impress on parents that youth sport programs are for young athletes and that children and youth are not adults. Parents must acknowledge the right of each child to develop athletic potential in an atmosphere that emphasizes participation, personal growth, and fun.

To contribute to the success of a sport program, parents must be willing and able to commit themselves in many different ways. Al Rosen (1967), a former Major League Baseball player, developed some questions that can serve as thought-provoking reminders of the scope of parent responsibilities:

1. *Can the parents give up their child?* This requires putting the child in the coach's charge and trusting him/her to guide the child's sport expe-

rience. It involves accepting the coach's authority and the fact that the coach may gain some of the child's admiration and affection that the child once directed solely at the parent. This responsibility does not mean that parents cannot have input, but the coach is the boss! If parents are going to undermine the coach's leadership, it is best for all concerned not to have their child join the program.

2. *Can the parents admit their shortcomings?* Parents must be convinced that the proper response to a mistake or not knowing something is an honest disclosure. For example, if their child asks a question about sports and they do not know the answer, they should not be afraid to admit it. An honest response is better than a wrong answer. Coaches and parents alike should show children that they realistically accept whatever limitations they have. Surely nobody is perfect, but sometimes children do not learn this because adults fail to teach them.

3. *Can the parents accept their child's triumphs?* Every child athlete experiences "the thrill of victory and the agony of defeat" as part of the competition process. Accepting a child's triumphs sounds easy, but it is not always so. Some parents do not realize it, but fathers in particular may be competitive with their sons. For example, if a boy does well in a contest, his father may point out minor mistakes, describe how others did even better, or bring up something more impressive from memories of his own sport achievements.

4. *Can the parents accept their child's disappointments?* In addition to accepting athletic accomplishments, parents are called upon to support their children when they are disappointed and hurt. This may mean watching them lose a contest while others triumph, or not being embarrassed, ashamed, or angry when their 10-year-old cries after losing. When an apparent disappointment occurs, parents should be able to help their children see the positive side of the situation.

5. *Can the parents give their child some time?* Some parents are very busy, which becomes a problem because they are interested and want to encourage their children. To avoid disappointment and potential conflicts, the best advice

coaches can give them is to deal honestly with the time-commitment issue and not promise more time than they can actually deliver. Coaches should recommend that parents ask their children about their sport experiences and make every effort to watch some of their contests.

6. *Can the parents let their child make his/her own decisions?* This is an essential part of growing up and a real challenge for parents. Coaches should encourage parents to offer suggestions and guidance about sports, but ultimately within reasonable limits, they should let the child go his/her own way. All parents have ambitions for their child, but they must accept the fact that they cannot dominate the child's life. Sports can offer an introduction to the major process of letting go.

7. *Can the parents show their child self-control?* Parents should be reminded that they are important role models for their children's behavior. It is not surprising that parents who lose control of themselves often have children who are prone to emotional outbursts and poor self-discipline. Coaches can hardly be expected to teach sportsmanship and self-control to youngsters whose parents obviously lack these qualities.

The most noticeable parent problem is misbehavior at contests. As part of their responsibilities, parents should watch their children compete in sports. But their behavior must meet acceptable standards. In this regard, Martens and Seefeldt (1979) recommend the following rules:

1. Parents should remain seated in the spectator area during the contest.

2. Parents should not yell instructions or criticisms to the children.

3. Parents should make no derogatory comments to players, parents of the opposing team, officials, or league administrators.

4. Parents should not interfere with their children's coach. They must be willing to relinquish the responsibility for their child to the coach for the duration of the contest.

Good sportsmanship among spectators is a goal worth working for. Parents have the obligation not only to control their own behavior but also to remind others, if necessary. When parents misbehave, it is the duty of other parents and league administrators to step in and correct the situation. The rule of thumb for all spectators is that nothing in their actions should interfere with any child's enjoyment of the sport.

Two-Way Communication

Parents have both the right and the responsibility to inquire about *all* activities that their children are involved in, including sports. For this reason, coaches should be willing to answer questions and remain open to parent input. *Communication is a two-way street.* If coaches keep the lines of communication open, they will be more likely to have constructive relations with parents.

Fostering two-way communication does not mean that parents are free to be disrespectful toward coaches in word or action. Rather, it is an open invitation for parents to express their genuine concerns with the assurance that they will be heard by the coach. There is, however, a proper time and place for parent–coach interaction. That time is not during practice or a contest, and it is never in the presence of the youngsters. Coaches should tell parents what times and places are best suited for discussions.

The most common cause of coach–parent conflicts is the difference in a coach's and parent's opinion about the young athlete's abilities. In this regard, the use of a performance measurement system (described in Chapter 3) not only provides valuable feedback to athletes but can be an objective source of performance evaluation for parents. Nevertheless, sometimes parents will disagree with what coaches are doing. The main thing is for coaches not to get defensive. They should listen to what the parents have to say. They might find some of their suggestions helpful. However, even if they do not agree, coaches can at least *listen*. They should realize that they have the final say and that no coach can please everyone. No one can ask any more than what coaches ask of their athletes—doing the very best job they can and always looking for ways to improve.

In establishing good relations with parents, coaches should be aware that most parents are really enthusiastic and have a true concern for their children. Sometimes, however, parents sim-

ply do not realize the trouble they are causing. Instead of being angry with them, good coaches recognize that such parents have a problem—one that the coaches can help solve. The task is to point out to these people, tactfully and diplomatically, the negative influences of their actions and get them to become more constructive and helpful. Some common types of problem parents are identified below, along with recommendations for dealing with them.

Disinterested Parents

Distinguishing characteristics.   The most noticeable characteristic of disinterested parents is their absence from team activities to a degree that is upsetting to their child.

What coaches should do.   Coaches should find out why the parents do not participate and contribute. They should avoid the mistake of misjudging parents who are actually interested but have good reasons (work, sickness, etc.) for missing activities. Explaining the value of sports and how they can draw children and parents closer together may provide parents with a new interest in the activities of their children. In this situation the athletes need help, too. Coaches should encourage them and show that they are really interested in them as people.

Overcritical Parents

Distinguishing characteristics.   Overcritical parents often scold and berate their child. Such parents are never quite satisfied with their child's performance. They give the impression that it is more "their" game than it is the athlete's.

What coaches should do.   As discussed earlier, some parents unconsciously relate the success or failure of their child with their own success or failure. As a result, they are often hard on their children. Coaches should attempt to make overcritical parents aware of this problem as tactfully as possible. They can explain how constant criticism can cause stress and emotional turmoil for the youngster, turmoil that actually hinders performance. They can tell the parents why they prefer to use praise and encouragement to motivate and instruct young people, and how parents can do the same.

What coaches can say. "Mr. Jones, I know you're only trying to help Billy, but when you criticize him, he gets so nervous that he plays worse, and that certainly takes any fun out of it for him." *Or,* "Mr. Jones, if you were to encourage your son instead of criticizing him so much, sports would be a lot more enjoyable for both of you. After all, it's the kids' game. They play for fun, and too much criticism spoils it for them."

Parents Who Scream from Behind the Bench

Distinguishing characteristics. Some parents seem to have leather lungs and large vocal chords. They often sit directly behind the bench, which makes them a distinct danger to the well-being of coaches' eardrums. They frequently rant and rave and virtually drown out everyone else speaking in the area, including the coach. Everyone is the target for their verbal abuse—team members, opponents, coaches, officials.

What coaches should do. Coaches must not get into an argument with a screaming parent. It will not do any good and will probably make things worse. During a break in the contest (half time, between periods), coaches can calmly, tactfully, and privately point out to the screamer that such yelling is a poor example for the young athletes. Coaches can ask other people to help out by working with this person during games. Also, coaches can give the disruptive parent a job that will help the team (scouting opponents, keeping stats, looking after equipment, etc.). This may provide a greater sense of responsibility and help the screamer to keep quiet. If the screaming persists, coaches should seek assistance from league administrators.

What coaches can say. "I know it's easy to get excited, but these kids are out here to have a good time. Try not to take the game so seriously, OK?" *Or,* "Listen, why don't we get together after the game and you can give me some of your ideas on coaching. I'd rather have them afterward because during the game they're very confusing."

Sideline Coaches

Distinguishing characteristics. Parents who assume the role of sideline coaches are often found leaning over the bench making suggestions to athletes. They may contradict your instructions and disrupt the team.

What coaches should do. Again, coaches should not confront such a parent right away. Coaches should advise their athletes that during practices and games they are the coach and they want their athletes' full attention. Listening to instructions from others may become confusing. Coaches should tell the parent privately how confusing it is for the athletes when two or more people are telling them what to do. Coaches might ask the parent to be either a full-time assistant coach or a full-time spectator.

What coaches can say. "Ms. Jones, I appreciate your concern and enthusiasm for the team. But when you are coaching Kay from the sidelines, it becomes confusing and distracting to her. I know you've got some good ideas, and I want to hear them. But please, after the game."

Overprotective Parents

Distinguishing characteristics. Most often, overprotective parents are the mothers of the athletes. Such parents are characterized by their worried looks and comments whenever their son/daughter is playing. Overprotective parents frequently threaten to remove their child because of the dangers involved in the sport.

What coaches should do. Coaches must try to eliminate the fear of injury by reassuring the parent that the game is fairly safe. They can explain the rules and equipment that protect the athlete and point out how good coaching, program administration, and officiating add to the safety of the sport.

What coaches can say. "Ms. Jones, we try to make the game as safe as possible for the athletes. You've got to remember that I wouldn't be coaching kids if I didn't care about them or if I thought the sport was dangerous for them." *Or,* "Ms. Jones,

I care about each one of these kids, and I would never let any of them do anything that I thought would endanger them."

The Coach–Parent Meeting

Coaches unselfishly devote a tremendous amount of time and effort to providing a worthwhile life experience for youngsters. All too often, they are asked to do "just one more thing." However, successful coaches are aware of the importance of securing the aid and support of well-informed parents. Rather than facing the task of dealing with problem parents, a preseason meeting is the *key* to reducing the chance of unpleasant experiences. In other words, having a coach–parent meeting is well worth the additional time and effort!

This section is a *guide* for planning and conducting effective coach–parent meetings. Because each coach is unique, we urge coaches to evaluate the information and suggestions and make modifications to suit their personal situation.

Purpose of the Meeting

The overall objective of a coach–parent meeting is to improve parents' understanding of youth sports and what the coach is trying to accomplish. Their input can then increase the value of sport participation for their children's physical, psychological, and social development.

Planning and Preparation

One reason for being hesitant about conducting a coach–parent meeting is that a coach might feel insecure about leading a group of adults. This is not unusual. People are often unwilling to do things for which they have had little training or previous experience. Coaches who have held meetings with parents indicate that it is not an overtaxing experience, and the benefits make the meeting a good investment.

It will take approximately 1¼ hours to cover the necessary topics. The meeting does not have to be elaborate to be successful. However, the importance of being well prepared and organized cannot be overemphasized. To improve organizational quality, the coach should develop and follow a written program outline.

The coach should schedule the meeting as early in the season as possible, and be sure that the facility selected is easily accessible and has a meeting room of adequate size, with appropriate features (seating, lighting, etc.). Should athletes attend the meeting? Some coaches have no objections and believe it helps improve communication among all those involved. Other coaches find it more productive to conduct the meeting without the athletes present. The coach's personal preference will determine the policy adopted. However, if the athletes are excluded, the coach should make special arrangements for parents who might not be able to attend without their children. For example, an additional room might be sought in which the children could be shown an educational sport film under the supervision of an assistant coach.

Parents should be sent a personal letter of invitation, including brief statements about the objective of the meeting, its importance, and information about the date, time, location, directions, and attendance by youngsters. A team roster, with addresses and telephone numbers should accompany the letter. Follow-up telephone calls are recommended to remind parents about the meeting. This could be accomplished by enlisting the aid of parents to set up a chain calling system.

Content and Conduct of the Meeting

As stated earlier, effective communication is based on two-way sharing. Therefore, in conducting the meeting, the coach should draw parents into discussion instead of lecturing to them. The coach can do this by (a) encouraging parents to ask questions and (b) directing questions to them from time to time. Also, in creating an open atmosphere for exchange, it is very important to show respect for the parents. They should feel that they are a contributing part of the meeting rather than a mere audience.

Opening (5 minutes). The coach begins the meeting by introducing himself/herself and the assistant coach(es). In welcoming the parents, it is important to let them know that their interest and concern are appreciated. In praising their attendance, the coach can point out that they are taking an important step toward ensuring a quality sport experience for their children. Next, the coach establishes credibility by giving pertinent background information. The coach tells them about his/her experience in the sport, experience as a coach, and special training that he/she has had (e.g., workshops, clinics). Finally, the coach points out the purpose of the meeting, and tells them how he/she will provide information about fundamentals of the sport (invite them to attend a practice session).

A note of caution is in order. If a coach is conducting a coach–parent meeting for the first time, or might have little experience in leading adults, he/she should not begin the meeting by announcing this as a personal shortcoming or by asking for the parents' tolerance. Such statements may reduce their trust and support in him/her as their child's coach. Self-degrading remarks may also cause parents to question the coach's ability to conduct the meeting. To gain respect, the coach must show confidence in leading the session.

Objectives of youth sports (10 minutes).   After the opening remarks, there should be a discussion of the objectives of children's athletics, including a healthy philosophy of winning. The coach should focus on those goals and values that are a major part of his/her coaching. Also, the coach should find out which objectives the parents would like to have emphasized. As pointed out earlier, if coaches and parents work together to reduce misunderstandings, the objectives can be achieved.

Details of the sport program (10 minutes).   The coach presents details about the operation of the sport program. In addition to other items that he/she might think of, consideration should be given to the following: (a) equipment needed and where it can be purchased, (b) sites and schedules for practices and contests, (c) length of practices and contests, (d) team travel plans, (e) major team rules and guidelines, (f) special rule modifications to be used at this level of competition, (g) medical examinations, (h) insurance, (i) fund-raising projects, (j) communication system for cancellations, etc., and (k) midseason and postseason events.

The coach should also provide information about what is expected of the athletes and parents relative to the program details. Some coaches find it useful to organize a parent committee, giving this committee the task of coordinating parent involvement in many activities of the season.

Coaching roles and relationships (10 minutes). Parents will benefit from knowing about the coach's style. In addition to describing the *positive approach* that he/she will be using (see Chapter 4), the coach should encourage parents to reinforce this approach in interactions with their children.

Parents' roles and responsibilities (20 minutes). Informing parents about their roles in youth sports and the responsibilities the coach expects them to fulfill is the most important part of the meeting. The coach should discuss the following topics, which were covered earlier in this chapter:

1.   Counseling children about sports selection and the level of competition at which they want to play—conferring with and *listening* to them.

2.   Dangers of overidentification by parents with their children—the negative impact of this process.

3.   Parent commitments—the seven important questions (see pages 60–61) to which parents must be able to honestly answer "yes."

4.   Rules for parent behavior at contests—the coach is responsible for the team, and the parents are responsible for their own behavior.

Coach-parent relations (5 minutes).   The coach should tell parents of his/her willingness to discuss any problems that might arise—that all-important two-way communication! He/she should let them know what times and places are best suited for discussions.

Closing (20–30 minutes).   The coach–parent meeting should be concluded with a question–answer session. There is an effective technique for starting a question–answer period. The coach can take the lead in raising questions. He/she can stimulate parent involvement by asking the first few questions and then guiding the discussion. If the coach does not know the answer to a question, he/she should not be ashamed to admit it. The parents will appreciate the honesty. Rather than giving a weak or incorrect response, he/she can indicate that it is a question to which the coach and parent can both seek an answer. Perhaps someone in the audience will be able to provide the answer. The coach should not give the impression that he/she must address and answer every question. Finally, at the end of the meeting, the coach remembers to thank the parents again for attending.

The coach–parent meeting is a vitally important tool for developing parent involvement and support. A successful meeting will help solidify the athletic triangle (the coach-athlete-parent triad) and lead to a positive youth sport experience.

Follow-up Meetings

If possible, it is highly desirable to schedule a mid-season meeting with parents. This will provide an opportunity to present refresher points, discuss the athletes' progress, and cooperatively seek solutions to existing problems.

A postseason celebration is an excellent way to end the season. This could take the form of a family dinner planned by the parents. In addition to having good fellowship and fun, the coach could take some time to obtain parents' evaluations of the program and his/her coaching. In the conversations, the coach asks parents to point out things that went well and gets their suggestions for making improvements.

Summary

This chapter has dealt with a frequently neglected aspect of youth sports, namely, interactions between coaches and parents. Consideration was given to promoting effective coach–parent relationships in order to improve the quality of athletes' sport experiences. In so doing, the following major points were emphasized:

1. Coaches and parents play important roles in young athletes' sport experiences.

2. In a developmental model, sports provide an arena for learning, where success is measured in terms of personal growth and development.

3. Participation in youth sports can improve physical skills and fitness, build "character," promote social competence, bring families closer together, and provide enjoyable recreational experiences for young people.

4. Fun is the essence of play, and it constitutes the core of successful youth sport experiences.

5. Young athletes should be taught that they are never "losers" if they give maximum effort in striving for excellence.

6. Most youth participate in sports to have fun, to learn new skills, and to make new friends. The goal of winning is relatively unimportant to them as compared with these other objectives.

7. Parents should not pressure, intimidate, or bribe their children into playing a sport.

8. Parents should learn basic sport rules, skills, and strategies.

9. Coaches should serve as valuable resources and answer parents' questions as well as possible.

10. A key to reducing parent-produced stress is to impress on them that youth sports are for the young athletes.

11. Parents must be able to endorse their child's participation in youth sports and support the coach's program.

12. Parents must conform to acceptable standards of behavior at contests.

13. In working with parents, it is essential to develop and maintain open, healthy communication with them.

14. Effective communication is a two-way street requiring both speaking and listening skills.

15. Holding a preseason coach–parent meeting is the key to avoiding unpleasant experiences.

16. The main objective of a coach–parent meeting is to improve parents' understanding of youth sports.

Study Questions

1. What are the components of the "athletic triangle," and what impact does this triad have on youth sports?

2. Describe the major differences between developmental and professional models of sport. Why is it important that coaches and parents understand these distinctions?

3. What responsibilities do parents have with respect to counseling their children about sports selection and guiding their entry into specific programs?

4. Explain the overidentification process that might underlie parent-induced stress in youth sports.

5. Discuss the implications of the following sport-related responsibilities of parents: (a) giving up their child, (b) admitting shortcomings, (c) accepting their child's triumphs, (d) accepting their child's disappointments, (e) giving their child some time, (f) allowing their child to make decisions, and (g) demonstrating self-control.

6. What are the four rules that define acceptable standards of parent behavior at youth sport contests?

7. What are some keys to establishing and maintaining open channels of communication with parents of young athletes?

8. Describe the distinguishing characteristics of the following types of problem parents and indicate how they might be dealt with: (a) disinterested parents, (b) overcritical parents, (c) parents who scream from behind the bench, (d) sideline coaches, and (e) overprotective parents.

9. What is the main purpose of a preseason coach–parent meeting?

10. What are the most important considerations in planning a coach–parent meeting?

11. Briefly describe the content of each of the following components of a coach–parent meeting: (a) opening, (b) objectives of youth sports, (c) details of the sport program, (d) coaching roles and relationships, (e) parent roles and responsibilities, (f) coach–parent relations, and (g) closing.

12. What kinds of follow-up meetings can be held with parents, and of what value are they?

References

Berryman, J. W. (1975). From the cradle to the playing field: America's emphasis on highly organized competitive sports for preadolescent boys. *Journal of Sport History, 2,* 112–131.

Lewko, J. H., & Greendorfer, S. L. (1988). Family influences in sport socialization of children and adolescents. In F. L. Smoll, R. A. Magill, & M. J. Ash (Eds.), *Children in sport* (3rd ed.) (pp. 287–300). Champaign, Ill.: Human Kinetics.

Martens, R. (1978). *Joy and sadness in children's sports.* Champaign, Ill.: Human Kinetics.

Martens, R. (1986). Youth sport in the USA. In M. R. Weiss & D. Gould (Eds.), *Sport for children and youths* (pp. 27–33). Champaign, Ill.: Human Kinetics.

Martens, R., & Seefeldt, V. (1979). *Guidelines for children's sports.* Washington, D.C.: American Alliance for Health, Physical Education, Recreation and Dance.

McPherson, B. D., & Brown, B. A. (1988). The structure, processes, and consequences of sport for children. In F. L. Smoll, R. A. Magill, & M. J. Ash (Eds.), *Children in sport* (3rd ed.) (pp. 265–286). Champaign, Ill.: Human Kinetics.

Passer, M. W. (1984). Competitive trait anxiety in children and adolescents: Mediating cognitions, developmental antecedents and consequences. In J. M. Silva & R. S. Weinberg (Eds.), *Psychological foundations of sport and exercise* (pp. 130–144). Champaign, Ill.: Human Kinetics.

Rosen, A. (1967). *Baseball and your boy.* New York: Funk & Wagnalls.

Scanlan, T. K. (1986). Competitive stress in children. In M. R. Weiss & D. Gould (Eds.), *Sport for children and youths* (pp. 113–118). Champaign, Ill.: Human Kinetics.

Smith, R. E. (1984). Theoretical and treatment approaches to anxiety reduction. In J. M. Silva & R. S. Weinberg (Eds.), *Psychological foundations of sport and exercise* (pp. 157–170). Champaign, Ill.: Human Kinetics.

Smith, R. E., Smoll, F. L., & Smith, N. J. (1989). *Parents' complete guide to youth sports.* Reston, Vir.: American Alliance for Health, Physical Education, Recreation and Dance.

Smoll, F. L., & Smith, R. E. (1990). Psychology of the young athlete: Stress-related maladies and remedial approaches. *Pediatric Clinics of North America, 37,* 1021–1046.

Universities Study Committee. (1978). *Joint legislative study on youth sports programs: Phase II. Agency sponsored sports.* East Lansing, Mich.: Michigan Institute for the Study of Youth Sports.

The Self-Fulfilling Prophecy Theory: When Coaches' Expectations Become Reality

Thelma Sternberg Horn, *Miami University*
Curt Lox, *University of Illinois*

*I*n 1968 Rosenthal and Jacobson published the results of an experiment they had conducted with teachers and students in 18 elementary school classrooms. This research study, which was appropriately titled "Pygmalion in the Classroom," had been designed to determine whether the academic progress of students could actually be affected by their teachers' expectations or beliefs concerning their intellectual abilities. To investigate this issue, Rosenthal and Jacobson informed the sample of teachers that certain children in each of their classes had been identified, via scores on a standardized test of academic ability, as latent achievers or "late bloomers" who could be expected to show big gains in academic achievement over the coming school year. In actuality, the identified children had been selected at random from the total group, and there was no reason to expect that they would show any greater academic progress than their classmates. At the end of the school year, however, many of the targeted children, especially those in the lower elementary grades, had made greater gains intellectually than had children who were not so identified. Rosenthal and Jacobson concluded that the false information given to the teachers had led them to hold higher expectations for the targeted children and then to act in ways that would stimulate better performance from those students. Thus, the authors were suggesting that the teachers' expectations served as self-fulfilling prophecies by initiating a series of events that ultimately caused the expectations to be fulfilled.

The publication of this study elicited considerable interest among other researchers, some of whom responded with criticism of the Pygmalion study for a variety of methodological and statistical flaws (Elashoff & Snow, 1971; Thorndike, 1968). The ensuing controversy concerning the legitimacy of the self-fulfilling prophecy phenomenon stimulated an impressive amount of research during the next two decades. Although most of these investigations were oriented toward the study of expectancy effects in the academic classroom, some of them were conducted in physical education classrooms or in competitive sport contexts (Cousineau & Luke, 1990; Horn, 1984; Markland & Martinek, 1988; Martinek, 1988; Martinek & Johnson, 1979; Martinek & Karper, 1984, 1986; Rejeski, Darracott, & Hutslar, 1979). Within the last decade, several excellent reviews of this literature have been compiled (Brophy, 1983; Cooper & Tom, 1984; Harris & Rosenthal, 1985; Martinek, 1981, 1989; Weinstein, 1989). Based on a thorough examination of the expectancy research, the authors of these reviews have generally concluded that teachers' expectations certainly do have the potential to affect the academic progress of individual students. However, the reviewers are also careful to point out that the self-fulfilling prophecy phenomenon does not occur in all instructional situations. Many teachers and coaches are not "Pygmalion-prone" and thus do not allow their expectations to affect the performance or the achievement of their students and athletes.

Such variation among teachers and coaches implies that those who are aware of and understand the self-fulfilling prophecy phenomenon can avoid becoming Pygmalion-type coaches or teachers. Therefore, it is the purpose of this chapter to present coaches with information concerning the expectation–performance process. In the following pages, we will examine how coaches' expectations or judgments of their athletes can influence the athletes' performance and behavior. Specifically, we will identify (a) the processes by which coaches form expectations concerning individual athletes, (b) the ways in which such expectations influence the coaches' behavior, (c) the processes by which expectancy-biased coaches' behavior can affect the athletes' performance and psychological growth, (d) how the athletes' performance and behavior can ultimately conform to the coaches' original expectations, and, finally, (e) how expectancy effects can be particularly negative for selected athletes. The chapter will conclude with a discussion of the ways in which coaches can individualize their interactions with athletes so as to avoid behaving in expectancy-biased ways and thus to facilitate the performance of all athletes.

The Expectation–Performance Process

According to the self-fulfilling prophecy theory, the expectations that coaches form about the ability of individual athletes can serve as prophecies that dictate or determine the level of achievement each athlete will ultimately reach. Several researchers who have studied the self-fulfilling prophecy phenomenon in educational contexts (Brophy, 1983; Cooper & Tom, 1984; Harris & Rosenthal, 1985) have proposed a sequence of steps to explain how the expectation–performance connection is accomplished. These models or sequences of events can be adapted to describe how the self-fulfilling prophecy phenomenon can also occur in sport settings.

Step 1. The coach develops an expectation for each athlete that predicts the level of performance and type of behavior that athlete will exhibit over the course of the year.

Step 2. The coach's expectations influence his/her treatment of individual athletes. That is, the coach's behavior toward each athlete differs according to the coach's belief concerning the athlete's competence.

Step 3. The way in which the coach treats each athlete affects the athlete's performance and rate of learning. In addition, differential communication tells each athlete how competent the coach thinks he/she is. This information affects the athlete's self-concept, achievement motivation, and level of aspiration.

Step 4. The athlete's behavior and performance conform to the coach's expectations. This behavioral conformity reinforces the coach's original expectation, and the process continues.

We will now examine each of these steps in detail.

Step 1: Coaches Form Expectations

At the beginning of an athletic season most coaches form expectations for each athlete on their teams. These expectations are really initial judgments or assessments regarding the physical competence or sport potential of each athlete and are based on certain pieces of information that are available to the coach. In particular, the research indicates that teachers, and by implication coaches, most often use two types or categories of information.

The first category contains what we can label as **person cues** and includes such informational items as the individual's socioeconomic status, racial or ethnic group, family background, sex, physical attractiveness, body size, and style of dress. The exclusive use of any or all of these person cues to form judgments about an athlete's physical competence would certainly lead to inaccurate and very stereotypic expectations (see last section of this chapter). Fortunately, according to the research on expectancy effects, it is likely that most coaches do not form their expectations solely on demographic or physical appearance cues but also use behaviorally based information. Thus, most coaches additionally use **performance information** such as the athlete's scores on certain physical skills tests, the athlete's past performance achievements (e.g., previous season statistics or related sport accomplishments), as well as other teachers' or coaches' comments concerning the athlete's performance and behavior. Coaches also base initial impressions of athletes on observation of their behavior in practice or tryout situations (e.g., observation of the player's motivation, enthusiasm, pleasantness, response to criticism, interaction with teammates).

Although the initial expectations formed by most coaches are based on information from a variety of sources, individual coaches probably differ in regard to the weight they assign to each source. That is, some coaches may particularly value the comments of other coaches in evaluating an athlete during recruitment or at the beginning of the season, whereas other coaches may place greater emphasis on the player's physical attributes (e.g., speed, size, strength, body build). Therefore, two coaches could form very different sets of expectations for the same athlete on the basis of what sources of information each valued most.

It obviously follows, then, that a coach's initial judgment of an athlete may be either accurate or inaccurate depending on the source(s) of information used. Accurate assessments of a player's competence generally pose no problem as they usually do not adversely affect the player's subsequent performance. However, inaccurate expectations (i.e., expectations that are either too high or too low) that are *also* inflexible can be very disruptive for the athlete and can interfere with his/her optimal athletic progress. Consider, for example, the coach who misjudges a particular athlete at the beginning of the season and falsely believes that individual to be less competent than he/she really is. If the coach's expectation or judgment is flexible (i.e., changes when the athlete demonstrates better performance than expected), then the initial false

Example 1

The new coach of a junior high basketball team is informed by the principal that the team has two point guards returning from last year. The first player, Greg, is described as a talented athlete, while the other player, Robert, is portrayed as having been a member of last year's squad "only because he was the coach's son." At practice the first day, Robert dribbles fast up the court but then loses control of the ball. The coach, who has developed the expectation that Robert is not a talented athlete, sees this error as proof of Robert's lack of innate basketball ability. Thus, the coach responds by telling Robert to slow down. Moments later, Greg also mishandles the ball during the same dribbling drill. The coach, who believes Greg to be an excellent dribbler, assumes that the error occurred because the basketball is either worn and slippery or overinflated (and thus difficult to dribble). Based on this perception, the coach orders that the ball not be used again and that Greg should get another ball and try again.

expectation does not cause a problem. In contrast, a coach who is very inflexible and resistant to modifying her/his initial beliefs may well "see" only what she/he expects to see from that player. That is, all evidence of skill errors by the athlete will reinforce the coach's belief that the athlete is incompetent, and all skill success will either be ignored or simply considered by the coach to be "lucky" events and not indicative of the athlete's sport skill. This type of situation is illustrated in Example 1. In this example the coach's initial expectations or judgments concerning the relative basketball ability of both Greg and Robert are formed on the basis of information provided by a colleague. These initial expectations, which may *not* be accurate, cause the coach to *perceive* the two players' performance differently. Such differential perceptions, in turn, affect the way in which the coach reacts or responds to that player. This type of situation leads to the second step in the sequence of events comprising the self-fulfilling prophecy phenomenon.

Step 2: Coaches' Expectations Affect Their Behavior

The expectations that coaches typically form for each athlete at the beginning of an athletic season do not necessarily or automatically act as self-fulfilling prophecies. Expectations do, however, have the potential for doing so if they affect the coaches' treatment of their athletes.

Much of the research on the self-fulfilling prophecy phenomenon has focused on this issue by asking the crucial question "Do teachers and coaches treat students or athletes they believe have high ability (i.e., high-expectancy individuals) differently from students or athletes they believe have low ability (i.e., low-expectancy individuals)?" Generally this question has been studied by observing and recording the type, frequency, and quality of instructional behavior that teachers and coaches exhibit toward individual students and athletes. Again, the overall conclusion from this research (see reviews by Brophy, 1983; Cooper & Tom, 1984; Harris & Rosenthal, 1985; Martinek, 1981, 1989) indicates that *some* teachers and coaches do indeed show differential instructional behaviors to these two groups of students and athletes. Applying the results of this research to the athletic setting, we could expect the Pygmalion-type coach to show differential behavior to high- and low-expectancy athletes in regard to (a) the frequency and quality of interactions the coach has with the individual athletes, (b) the quantity and quality of instruction given to each athlete, and (c) the frequency and type of performance feedback given to each athlete.

In the first behavioral category, **frequency and quality of coach–athlete interactions**, a Pygmalion-prone coach typically shows less tendency to initiate interpersonal contact (either of a social or a skill-related nature) with athletes he/she believes to be less skilled. As a result, the coach spends significantly more time with athletes who are highly skilled (see Example 2 of expectancy-based communication). In addition, the quality of coach–athlete interactions may also differ, with high-expectancy players being shown more warmth and positive affect (e.g., smiling, head nodding, and personal contact) than their low-expectancy teammates.

Perhaps of greater consequence is the differential treatment that high- and low-expectancy players may receive in regard to the **quantity and quality of instruction**. If a coach firmly believes that certain players on her/his team do not have the requisite athletic competencies to be successful (i.e., the low-expectancy players), that coach may,

---

Example 2

Kim and Sue, who are teammates on their school's varsity basketball team, stay after practice to play a game of one-on-one. Their coach comes over to watch. When Kim (a high-expectancy athlete) executes a successful fake and drive, the coach responds with approval but also stops the game to provide Kim with further instruction (i.e., what she should do in a similar situation if the weak side defender had moved across the key). Later when Sue (a low-expectancy player) executes the same successful fake and drive, the coach responds with approval only ("Good move, Sue") but then goes on to show Kim *how she should have prevented or defended against such an offensive move.*

---

first of all, reduce the amount of material and/or skills those players are expected to learn, thus establishing a lower standard of performance for them. Second, the coach may allow the low-expectancy players less time in practice drills. As a result, these athletes may spend relatively more practice time in nonskill-related activities such as shagging balls, waiting in line, and keeping score. Finally, the coach may be less persistent in helping low-expectancy athletes learn a difficult skill. The Pygmalion-prone coach tends to give up on a low-expectancy player who fails after two or three attempts to learn a new skill but will persist in working with a high-expectancy player who is having the same difficulty (see Example 3).

In addition to differences in the quality of instruction, researchers have also found differences in the **type and frequency of feedback** that coaches give to high- and low-expectancy players.

Example 3

During a practice scrimmage, Kim (the high-expectancy player in Example 2) is having problems running a particularly difficult offensive pattern. The coach stops the team drill and spends three or four minutes helping Kim learn the pattern. When Sue (the low-expectancy athlete) later evidences the same difficulty, the coach removes her from the scrimmage team by saying to another player, "Sally, come here and take Sue's place. Let's see if you *can run this play."*

One of the primary ways in which coaches respond differently to individual athletes is in their use of praise and criticism. Some researchers investigating expectancy issues in the classroom or in the motor skill instructional setting (Brophy & Good, 1970; Cooper & Baron, 1977; Martinek & Johnson, 1979; Martinek & Karper, 1982; Rejeski, Darracott, & Hutslar, 1979) have found that teachers and coaches give high-expectancy students and athletes more reinforcement and praise after a successful performance than they do low-expectancy individuals. In contrast, other researchers have found that low-expectancy students and athletes are the ones who receive proportionately more reinforcement (Horn, 1984; Kleinfeld, 1975; Martinek, 1988; Weinstein, 1976). However, some of these latter researchers have additionally noted that the higher frequency of reinforcement or praise given by coaches and teachers to these low-expectancy individuals may actually be qualitatively suspect because the reinforcement is often given inappropriately (i.e., given for a mediocre performance or for success at a very easy task) (see Example 4). Therefore, it appears that Pygmalion-prone coaches may (a) provide low-expectancy athletes with less frequent reinforcement and/or (b) give them less appropriate and less beneficial feedback after successful performances.

Observation of teachers' and coaches' feedback has also revealed differences in the amount of corrective or technical instruction given. In the sport setting such differential treatment may be especially evident in the feedback coaches provide

---

Example 4

During the course of a varsity volleyball match, a hitter approaches the net for a spike. Seeing her opponents put up a single block, she reaches out to "tip" the ball around the block. No point is scored, but the ball is kept in play. The athlete, who is a high-expectancy player, is told by her coach, "O.K., Keisha, at least you kept the ball in play. But next time you go up against a single block, hit the ball. Your spike is good enough to get it through that block." If, however, a low-expectancy player executes the same play, the Pygmalion-type coach might respond with approval only: "Great work, Jackie, you kept the ball away from the block. That was smart."

Example 5

Dan and Pete have both joined an age-group swimming team. Although both swimmers begin the season at the same level of performance, their coach has very high expectations for Dan's improvement and ultimate success because of his "natural" physical attributes. The coach does not have the same high expectations for Pete. At the first meet of the season, both swimmers take fifth place in their respective events. The coach responds to Dan's performance by telling him that he can considerably reduce his time if he improves his technique on the turns. The coach concludes with the comment, "We'll work on those turns all next week so you'll be ready for the next meet." In contrast, the coach responds to Pete's fifth place performance by saying, "Good job, Pete. Hang in there."

---

their athletes following a performance. As illustrated in Example 5, high-expectancy performers receive informational and corrective feedback that tells them how to improve their performance. In contrast, low-expectancy performers receive a positive communication from the coach but no accompanying technical information to tell them what they can do to improve their performance. These differences in feedback responses may well be due to the different expectations the coach holds for the various athletes. For example, because the coach fully expects Dan's performance to improve, he is more apt to provide Dan with technical information to help him achieve skill success. However, the low expectations the coach holds for Pete lead the coach to believe that corrective instruction may be fruitless and certainly not useful for Pete.

Finally, coaches may also differ in the type of attribution they use to explain the cause of the high- and low-expectancy athletes' successful or unsuccessful performances. Although this aspect of performance feedback has received very little research attention, we certainly might speculate that a coach's beliefs concerning the competence or incompetence of selected players on his or her team would induce that coach to verbalize different attributions for the athletes' performance outcome. For instance, the coach in Example 6 holds different perceptions or expectations concerning the physical competence of Scott (a high-expectancy

Example 6

During a baseball game, Steve (a low-expectancy athlete) hits a pitched ball sharply toward the left side of the infield. The shortstop makes a nice backhanded move for the ball and fields it. Although he then slightly mishandles it, he does throw it hard to first for a close play, with the runner (Steve) being called safe. The coach comments, "What a break, Steve! We were lucky he [the shortstop] bobbled it, or you would have been out." However, in a similar situation with Scott (a high-expectancy player) as the batter/runner, the coach responds to the same performance by exclaiming, "Way to hit the hole, Scott, and great speed! You beat the throw again!"

player) and Steve (a low-expectancy player). These expectations lead the coach to attribute these players' performance to different causes. When Steve reaches first base safely, the coach immediately, and in this case verbally, attributes that success to the opposing team's error (i.e., a lucky break for Steve). In comparison, the coach verbally attributes the same performance by Scott to Scott's ability (i.e., his batting prowess and speed). Similarly, the coach's response to these athletes' performance errors may also be affected by the coach's judgment of each player's ability. In Example 7 the coach attributes Scott's lack of success in stealing a base to poor positioning and thus suggests that the performance can be corrected. The coach attributes similar failure by Steve to Steve's lack of ability (i.e., his lack of speed).

Example 7

Later in the game described in Example 6, Scott (the high-expectancy player) attempts to steal second without the coach's giving a steal sign. Scott is easily thrown out. As he reaches the dugout, the coach tells him, "Good try, Scott. That would have been a good pitch to steal on, but you didn't have a big enough lead to go. Next time, you should. . . ." When Steve (the low-expectancy player) attempts the same performance, the coach angrily responds, "What are you doing out there? I didn't tell you to go. . . you're too slow to steal second, especially on that catcher."

These examples illustrate how the expectations that coaches form for individual athletes on their teams can affect coaches' perceptions of actual events. Such different perceptions, in turn, can lead to differences in coaches' responses to athletes' performances.

Although the research clearly suggests that some teachers and coaches treat high- and low-expectancy athletes and students differently, we need to exercise caution in regard to those findings. Specifically, we must not jump to the conclusion that it is essential for coaches to treat all athletes on their teams in exactly the same way. Because athletes differ in their skills as well as in their personalities, coaches are well advised to individualize their instructional behavior to accommodate the uniquenesses of each athlete. Therefore, it is important at this point to emphasize that observable differences in a coach's behavior toward individual athletes on his/her team do not automatically imply that the coach is acting in a biased manner and that the progress of her/his athletes will be impeded. If the differences in the coach's behavior are designed to and actually do facilitate the performance and achievement of *each* athlete, then such differential coaching behavior is appropriate. However, if the differential treatment an athlete or a group of athletes *consistently* receives from their coach in practices and game limits the athletes' ability or opportunity to learn, then such differential coaching behavior is dysfunctional, and the coach's expectations may be serving as self-fulfilling prophecies.

Step 3: Coaches' Behavior Affects Athletes' Performance and Behavior

The third step in the sequence of events in the self-fulfilling prophecy phenomenon occurs when a coach's expectancy-biased treatment of an individual athlete affects that athlete's performance and psychological growth. It is easy to understand how the biased behavior described in the preceding section is likely to maximize the athletic progress of high-expectancy athletes while limiting the achievements of their low-expectancy teammates. Players who are *consistently* given less effective and less intensive instruction or who are allowed less active time in practice drills will not show the same degree of skill improvement as their teammates who are given optimal learning opportunities. In

Examples 2 and 3, Kim and Sue are obviously not being given the same quality of instruction. If this instructional behavior is typical of the treatment that these athletes receive from their coach over the season, we might well anticipate that after a certain period of time, Kim's basketball skills will be considerably better than Sue's. Their coach will attribute these skill differences to what she believes to be the innate differences in Kim and Sue's basic athletic talent. Given the observed variation in the coach's instructional behavior toward these two athletes, it is equally likely that the coach's original expectation or judgment concerning each athlete's sport potential actually *determined*, rather than just *predicted*, the level of achievement that Kim and Sue reached. The coach's expectations, then, served as self-fulfilling prophecies by setting in motion a series of events (i.e., consistent differences in the quality of instruction) that ultimately caused the original expectations to be fulfilled.

In addition to the negative effects that a coach's biased instructional behavior has on an athlete's rate of learning and level of achievement, such behavior can also affect the athlete's psychological growth. Recent research in sport psychology has demonstrated that the type of instructional behaviors a coach exhibits in games and in practices is associated with changes in athletes' self-concept and perceived competence over the course of a season (Horn, 1985, 1987; Smith, Smoll, & Curtis, 1979). This association between coaches' behavior and athletes' self-perceptions is quite consistent with several developmental and/or social psychological theories (Eccles, Jacobs, & Harold, 1990; Harter, 1981; Schunk, 1984) which suggest that the evaluation or feedback that adults provide is an important source of information that children and adolescents use to determine how competent or incompetent they are.

In the athletic setting, then, the type of feedback that coaches give to individual athletes may affect the athletes' self-perceptions (e.g., their self-confidence, self-efficacy, and anxiety) by communicating to the athletes how competent or skilled the coach thinks they are. Occasionally, of course, the coach communicates this evaluative information directly to the athletes. More commonly, however, coaches communicate their judgments or beliefs concerning the athletes' abilities in more subtle or indirect ways. Specifically, the coach's reinforcement patterns (i.e., the level of performance

or type of behavior the coach rewards) provide athletes with information that tells them how skilled the coach thinks they are. In Example 4, Keisha and Jackie have demonstrated the same level of performance, but each receives a different response from the coach. This differential feedback may be communicating to these athletes what standard of performance each is expected to achieve. Jackie, who is clearly reinforced for that level of performance, may be receiving information telling her that she is at the maximum level she is capable of achieving. However, Keisha is led to believe that her performance, while acceptable, can and should be improved because she has the requisite skills to perform at a higher level.

Similarly, the amount and frequency of corrective instruction a coach provides after a skill error may also tell each athlete how competent or skillful the coach thinks he/she is. In Example 5, for instance, the coach responds to Dan's fifth-place performance with corrective feedback, thus overtly telling him that his performance can be improved with effort and covertly supplying him with the perception that he is capable of a higher level of skill. In contrast, although the coach gives Pete a positive and encouraging response for a similar level of performance, the coach does not provide Pete with the additional information to tell him that he can improve his performance and that he is capable of achieving at a higher level. Thus, the coach has indirectly communicated his expectations or judgments concerning each athlete's level of ability.

In a study investigating coaches' feedback in the interscholastic athletic context (Horn, 1984), it was found that junior high softball coaches gave their low-expectancy female athletes proportionately more reinforcement or praise in response to skill successes during games than they gave their high-expectancy athletes. In response to skill errors, however, these coaches provided their high-expectancy athletes with more criticism and corrective instruction but tended more frequently to ignore (give no response to) the mistakes of their low-expectancy athletes.

These findings are consistent with research reported in the educational psychology literature (Meyer, 1982) that has demonstrated that differential feedback responses do indeed provide performers with information concerning their abilities. Individuals who received more reinforcement than other performers for the same level of performance were perceived by themselves and others to have lower ability. In situations where performers exhibited the same performance errors, the individuals who received criticism were perceived by themselves and others to be more competent than those who received a neutral response following failure. It appears, then, that the evaluative feedback given by coaches to individual athletes is indeed providing the athletes with information concerning their competence. Certainly the differential feedback that low- and high-expectancy athletes receive from Pygmalion-prone coaches may affect the athletes' perceptions or beliefs concerning their own skill competence.

Finally, as noted in the previous section, coaches may also communicate their beliefs concerning athletes' skill ability by the attributions they make for their athletes' performance. Such attributions provide each athlete with information concerning his/her competence. When a coach attributes an athlete's successful performance to the athlete's innate ability (e.g., Example 6) the athlete develops a high expectancy for future success and a positive attitude toward the sport activity. In contrast, when a coach attributes successful performance to luck, the attribution does not encourage an athlete to believe that he/she can attain the same performance in the future and provides the athlete with no information concerning personal competence. Similarly, a coach who attributes an athlete's skill error to lack of effort, lack of practice, or some other athlete-controlled factor will do more to facilitate future motivation, decrease feelings of helplessness, and encourage a positive attitude than attributing the athlete's failure to lack of ability. In Example 7, Scott's performance failure is attributed by his coach to incorrect skill execution (a controllable and correctable error), whereas Steve's failure is attributed to his lack of speed (a less controllable and less correctable cause). The differential messages carried via these coaching communications may affect each athlete's future performance and motivation.

Step 4: The Athlete's Performance Conforms to the Coach's Expectations

The final step in the chain of events in the self-fulfilling prophecy phenomenon occurs when the athlete's performance and behavior conform to the coach's original expectation. This behavioral conformity is, in itself, a very important component in the chain of events because it reinforces for the coach that his/her initial judgment of the athlete was accurate. This confirms for the Pygmalion-prone coach that he/she is a very astute judge of sport potential and can recognize true athletic talent at the beginning of the season. Unfortunately, such "success" may reinforce or intensify the coach's Pygmalion tendencies.

As a final point in regard to the self-fulfilling prophecy process, it is important to recognize that all athletes do *not* allow their coach's behavior or expectations to affect their performance or psychological responses. Just as all coaches are not Pygmalion-prone, so, too, all athletes are not susceptible to the self-fulfilling prophecy. Earlier research in the coaching effectiveness area (as summarized in Smoll & Smith, 1989) has suggested that the self-perceptions of some athletes are more easily affected by their coach's evaluative feedback than are the self-perceptions of their teammates. It is likely that individuals who tend to be very dependent on their coach's feedback to provide them with information concerning their competence would be most easily "molded" by their coach's expectations. In contrast, those athletes who are resistant to the Pygmalion process may not use the coach's feedback as a sole source of information to tell them how competent they are. If these "resistant" athletes do receive biased feedback from a coach, they may respond by discounting that information and using other informational sources (e.g., feedback from peers, parents, or other adults) to form their perceptions of how competent or skilled they are. Thus, even if a coach shows biased treatment of an individual athlete, the self-fulfilling prophecy process will short-circuit if the athlete is resistant to the coach's bias. It is important to note, then, that all four steps in the sequence are essential if the self-fulfilling prophecy phenomenon is to occur in the athletic setting.

Sport Applications

The research and theory detailed in the previous pages describe the processes by which coaches' expectations and behavior can affect the performance and psychological growth of individual athletes on their team. Much of this information is based on research work that has been conducted in the academic classroom and which is then applied to the sport domain. Although there are certainly many similarities between these two instructional contexts, there are also some factors that make each domain unique. In this section of the chapter, three expectancy-related issues that are particularly relevant to the sport context are discussed. These issues are especially important because they describe how selected groups of athletes may be at an especially high risk for negative expectancy effects.

Expectancy Effects in Youth Sport Programs

Although Pygmalion-prone coaches can almost certainly be found at any level within the sport system (e.g., from youth sports through the professional level), the negative effects of a coach's expectancy-biased behavior may be particularly devastating at the younger age levels. There are three reasons why this may be the case. First, because children's initial experience with any particular sport is typically through a youth sport program, their interest in and enjoyment of that particular activity is being formed. Ineffective or expectancy-biased feedback from the coach during these early years may cause a child to develop extremely negative feelings about that activity and subsequently to discontinue participation before he/she has had an ample opportunity to learn the skills.

Second, a series of research studies recently conducted with children ranging in age from 8 to 18 years (Horn, 1991; Horn & Hasbrook, 1986; Horn & Weiss, 1991) shows that the self-perceptions of younger children (i.e., those under the age of 10) are based, to a large extent, on the feedback of significant adults. That is, these children are very much apt to evaluate how "good" or "bad" they are at a sport or physical activity based on what their parents, coaches, or teachers say to them. For example, a child in this age range is apt to say "I know that I am a good runner because my mom says I am" or "I don't think that I'm a very good soccer player because my coach is always yelling at me." Thus, for children under 10, the feedback of a coach can have quite significant effects on the child's self-esteem and self-confidence in that sport.

Third, based on research information obtained from the motor development literature (e.g., Ulrich, 1987), children in the early and mid-childhood years (i.e., 4 to 10 years) should be acquiring a variety of fundamental motor and sport-specific skills. Specifically, children should be learning to throw, catch, kick, jump, and run using mature and efficient movement patterns. In addition, this is a good time for children to learn some fundamental sport-specific skills (e.g., dribbling, passing, trapping). If children do not acquire these fundamental motor and sport skills during the formative years, it will be difficult for them to participate with any degree of skill in the more competitive sport programs such as those offered to children after the age of 10 years. Because Pygmalion-prone coaches tend to act in ways that impede the skill progress of their low-expectancy players, these children will be prevented from learning the necessary fundamental motor and sport skills. This, in turn, serves as a limiting factor in regard to their subsequent participation in the more advanced sport programs. Thus, again, the negative effects of a coach's expectancy-biased behavior may be particularly devastating in the early and mid-childhood years.

Maturational Rates and the Sport Expectancy Process

A second expectancy issue, which is certainly related to the first, is that children vary considerably in the rate at which they grow and mature. Those children who are "early" maturers will reach full physical maturation two to three years earlier than children who mature at a more "average" rate. Furthermore, children who are "late" maturers will not reach full physical maturation until two or three years later than their average maturing peers and four to five years later than the early maturing child. Obviously, then, within any given chronological age group there will likely be considerable variation in children's physical status. On a seventh-grade basketball team, for example, all children may be between 12 and 13 years old chronologically, but they certainly may differ in terms of their biological and physical status. The early maturing 12-year-old may be at a stage of physical development comparable to that of the average 14- or 15-year-old child. In contrast, a late maturing 12-year-old may be at a stage of development comparable to that of a 9- or 10-year-old child. Given such obvious differences in rate of maturation, the early maturer is likely to be motorically more proficient than the late maturer. It is important to know, however, that the late maturing child is at a temporary disadvantage only. That is, she/he will eventually catch up to and may even surpass her/his early maturing peers in physical size and athletic performance. Unfortunately, however, because the late maturing child in many youth sport programs is falsely diagnosed by unknowledgeable coaches to be a low-expectancy athlete (i.e., a child who is not now and never will be physically competent), that child may not receive optimal instruction, adequate playing time, or effective performance feedback and may even, in fact, be "cut" from the program. Thus, even though the late maturing child could develop into a very proficient athlete, she/he may be inhibited from doing so because of expectancy-biased coaching behaviors. Therefore, we should consider late maturing children to be at an especially high risk for negative expectancy effects.

Sport Stereotypes and the Expectancy Process

A third expectancy issue concerns selected stereotypes that are related to the performance and behavior of individuals in sport situations. The two most pervasive stereotypes in the sport setting are those concerning race and gender. In regard to race, it is commonly believed that African-American individuals are "naturally" gifted in the sport and physical activity area. Although this may initially appear to be a positive stereotype, there are certain negative ramifications for those African-American children who are not "as good as they are supposed to be." An African-American child who, for example, does not score *higher* than his Euro-American (white) peers on a series of sport skills tests may be perceived by his/her coach to be either lazy or "untalented." That is, even though he may have performed as well as his Euro-American peers, he is perceived by the Pygmalion-prone coach to be less than adequate. Such perceptions may be reflected in the fact that African-American athletes in some programs must either make the starting line-up or they will be cut from the team (i.e., they will not make the team

unless they are significantly more talented than the other athletes). Thus, African-American children may be held to a higher standard of performance in the sport and physical activity arena because of the stereotypes concerning their physical prowess.

Another aspect of racially biased stereotypes is that involving perceptions concerning athletes' mental capabilities. Specifically, although African-American athletes are perceived to be very competent in regard to physical capabilities (e.g., speed, reaction time, strength), it is the Euro-American athletes who are perceived to be better in regard to mental capabilities (i.e., they are believed to be better decision makers and leaders). Pygmalion-prone coaches who subscribe to such racial stereotypes will act in ways that reflect these biased beliefs. Thus, African-American athletes may not be considered for sport leadership or decision-making positions (e.g., football quarterback, basketball point guard, volleyball setter, baseball catcher). Even if they are given the opportunity to practice or play at such positions, their "mistakes" will be perceived as evidence of their innate inability to perform well in these roles rather than as an indicator that they may need more instruction or practice to acquire the necessary skills.

The situations described in the above paragraphs only illustrate some of the race-related stereotypes that abound in the sport context. These examples were provided to show that expectations based on race are not accurate and certainly can inhibit the progress of individual athletes or groups of athletes.

In regard to gender stereotypes, it is commonly believed that females are less physically capable than males. Although these beliefs are based to some extent on research showing that postpubertal males and females do differ on selected physical characteristics (e.g., height, body composition, limb length) (Malina, 1984), they are also based on inaccurate stereotypes concerning the performance and behavior of females. In particular, the available research indicates that there are very few physiological or biological differences between boys and girls prior to puberty (particularly before 10 years of age) (Malina, 1984). Despite these research findings, many teachers, coaches, and parents continue to believe that girls from early childhood on are not "naturally talented" in the physical activity area. Due to such stereotyped beliefs, girls in coeducational youth sport programs may be more apt to be treated as low-expectancy athletes. That is, they may be given less instruction by their coaches in practice and less playing time in games. When they do play in games, they may be relegated to positions where they are inactive for large amounts of time. Even on single-sex (all-girl) teams, a coach's stereotyped belief that girls are not and cannot be physically competent may cause her/him to establish lower standards of performance for them and to give greater amounts of inappropriate praise (i.e., to accept and praise mediocre performance accomplishments). Again, such expectancy-biased behavior is particularly negative during the childhood years because girls may then be less apt to develop the necessary fundamental motor and sport skills. As was indicated earlier in this section, failure to acquire these skills during the childhood years serves as an inhibitor of sport performance in the postpubertal years. Thus, as several researchers and writers have recently suggested, the rather large differences in the physical performance capabilities of postpubertal males and females may be due as much to inadequate instruction, participation, and training during the childhood years as to actual physiological and/or biological differences between males and females (Smoll & Schutz, 1990; Thomas & French, 1985). Furthermore, although there certainly are postpubertal sex differences in strength, speed, power, and endurance, this does not necessarily mean that all girls are less strong and/or less fast than all boys. Thus, coaches who develop expectations concerning the physical competencies of children and adolescents based solely or primarily on gender ignore the reality that there is as much (or more) variation within each sex as there is between sexes. Thus, coaches' expectations should be based to a greater extent on characteristics specific to each individual child rather than on the race or sex to which that child belongs.

The information provided in this section clearly indicates that selected children may be more apt to be perceived as low-expectancy athletes by their coaches than are other children. The specific concern here is that because such expectancies are either based on inaccurate stereotypes (e.g., race and gender) or on coaches' lack of knowledge concerning the physical growth and maturation process, these expectancies do have

the potential to seriously inhibit children's sport development. Thus, we need to consider such children as at greater risk for negative expectancy effects than their peers.

Behavioral Recommendations for Coaches

The information on how coaches' expectations and behavior can affect the performance and psychological growth of individual athletes on their team can and should be used to promote positive coach–athlete interactions. Therefore, the following recommendations are offered to coaches and prospective coaches for their use in evaluating and perhaps modifying their own behavior in the athletic setting.

1.   *Coaches should determine what sources of information they use to form preseason or early season expectations for each athlete.* Performance-based information sources are generally more reliable and accurate predictors or indicators of an individual's physical competence than are such person cues as the athlete's sex, racial or ethnic heritage, socioeconomic status, or physical appearance.

2.   *Coaches should realize that their initial assessments of an athlete's competence may be inaccurate and thus need to be revised continually as the season progresses.* As the research literature in the motor learning area suggests, individuals do not always learn or progress at the same rate. Some individuals may show rapid progress early in the season but then slow down or even plateau towards the middle and end of the season. Other athletes may start slowly but then evidence a rapid increase in performance during the latter part of the season. Given such interindividual variation in learning and performance rates, it is obvious that expectations based on initial assessments of an athlete's capabilities may soon become inaccurate. Thus, coaches at all levels of play should maintain a certain degree of flexibility in regard to their expectations or judgments concerning individual athletes' abilities.

3.   During practices, *coaches need to keep a running count of the amount of time each athlete spends in non-skill-related activities* (i.e., shagging balls, waiting in

line, sitting out of a scrimmage or drill, etc.). Certainly it is advisable for coaches to ask a friend or another coach to observe their practices and record the amount of time a starter (usually a high-expectancy athlete) and a nonstarter (usually a low-expectancy athlete) spend in practice drills.

4. *Coaches should design instructional activities or drills that provide all athletes with an opportunity to improve their skills.* In planning practice activities, the Pygmalion-type coach typically uses skill drills that are most appropriate for the highly skilled players. When the less skilled athletes cannot keep up, the coach then gives up on these athletes because he/she believes that their failure is inevitable because of low skill abilities. The more effective coach, upon finding that his/her less skilled players cannot master the skill, will implement instructional activities designed to help them ultimately achieve success (e.g., break the skill down into component parts, employ performance aids, and/or ask the athlete to stay a few minutes extra after practice for more intensive work).

5. As a general rule, *coaches should respond to skill errors with corrective instruction* that tells each athlete what she/he can do to improve the skill performance. Also, praise and criticism should be given contingent to or consistent with the level of performance that was exhibited.

6. *Coaches should emphasize skill improvement as a means of evaluating and reinforcing individual athletes* rather than using absolute performance scores or levels of skill achievement. To the degree that a coach conveys the attitude that *all* athletes can *improve* their skill performance, no matter what their present level, then positive expectations can be communicated to each athlete.

Summary

Coaches' preseason judgments of individual athletes can serve as self-fulfilling prophecies by initiating a series of events that cause the coaches' initial expectations to become reality. This self-fulfilling prophecy phenomenon can be most detrimental when a coach forms an initial expectation that is inaccurate and underestimates an athlete's true ability. The coach's biased judgment of the athlete's sport potential, in turn, causes the coach to provide that player with less frequent and less effective instruction. Not only does such biased coaching behavior ultimately interfere with the athlete's opportunity to learn, but it also has a negative effect on his/her motivation and self-confidence. When the athlete subsequently exhibits an inability to perform well and a lack of motivation in practice situations, the coach's original but false judgment of incompetence is fulfilled.

Fortunately, the research that has been conducted in academic classrooms as well as in physical activity settings shows that all coaches are not Pygmalion-prone. That is, some coaches do not allow their preseason judgments of individual athletes to affect the quality of their interaction with those players. It seems likely that coaches who are made aware of the effects that their expectations may have on athletes and who are trained to monitor their own instructional behavior may become more effective in working with individual athletes. The results of this research demonstrate that it is important that researchers and coaches more closely examine coaching behavior as one of the major factors that affect the performance and psychological growth of young athletes.

Study Questions

1. Identify and briefly describe the four steps in the expectation–performance process.

2. What sources of information might a coach use to form initial expectations for individual athletes on her/his team?

3. If a coach's initial expectations for an individual athlete can vary along two dimensions (accuracy and flexibility), briefly describe the consequences of the four possible combinations.

4. Should coaches form expectations at the beginning of the season for individual athletes? Why or why not?

5. What are the three primary ways in which coaches' expectations influence their behavior to individual athletes?

6. Do all coaches show expectancy-biased behavior? Explain what is meant by the term "Pygmalion-prone" coach.

7. Why might the negative effects of a coach's expectancy-biased behavior be particularly devastating for children in youth sport programs?

8. Explain what the term "late-maturing" child means and then explain why she/he is at an especially high risk for negative expectancy effects.

9. Describe the stereotypes in the sport setting that are associated with race. Explain how such stereotypes may affect selected groups of athletes.

10. Provide some examples showing how girls may be given less effective instruction, practice, and feedback by "Pygmalion-prone" coaches.

11. What actions might a coach take to avoid or eliminate Pygmalion-prone behaviors?

References

Brophy, J. (1983). Research on the self-fulfilling prophecy and teacher expectations. *Journal of Educational Psychology, 75,* 631–661.

Brophy, J., & Good, T. (1970). Teachers' communication of differential expectations for children's classroom performance: Some behavioral data. *Journal of Educational Psychology, 61,* 365–374.

Cooper, H., & Baron, R. (1977). Academic expectations and attributed responsibility as predictors of professional teachers' reinforcement behavior. *Journal of Educational Psychology, 69,* 409–418.

Cooper, H. M., & Tom, D. Y. H. (1984). Teacher expectation research: A review with implications for classroom instruction. *The Elementary School Journal, 85,* 77–89.

Cousineau, W. J., & Luke, M. D. (1990). Relationships between teacher expectations and academic learning time in sixth grade physical education basketball classes. *Journal of Teaching in Physical Education, 9,* 262–271.

Eccles, J. S., Jacobs, J., & Harold, R. D. (1990). Gender-role stereotypes, expectancy effects, and parents' role in the socialization of gender differences in self-perceptions and skill acquisition. *Journal of Social Issues, 46,* 183–201.

Elashoff, J., & Snow, R. (1971). *Pygmalion reconsidered.* Worthington, Ohio: Jones.

Harris, M., & Rosenthal, R. (1985). Mediation of interpersonal expectancy effects: 31 meta-analyses. *Psychological Bulletin, 97,* 363–386.

Harter, S. (1981). The development of competence motivation in the master of cognitive and physical skills: Is there still a place for joy? In G. C. Roberts & D. M. Landers (Eds.), *Psychology of motor behavior and sport—1980* (pp. 3–29). Champaign, Ill.: Human Kinetics.

Horn, T. S. (1984). Expectancy effects in the interscholastic athletic setting: Methodological considerations. *Journal of Sport Psychology, 6,* 60–76.

Horn, T. S. (1985). Coaches' feedback and changes in children's perceptions of their physical competence. *Journal of Educational Psychology, 77,* 174–186.

Horn, T. S. (1987). The influence of teacher-coach behavior on the psychological development of children. In D. Gould & M. Weiss (Eds.), *Advances in pediatric sport sciences* (vol. 2) (pp. 121–142). Champaign, Ill.: Human Kinetics.

Horn, T. S. (1991, October). *Sources of information underlying personal competence judgments in high school athletes.* Paper presented at the annual meeting of the Association for the Advancement of Applied Sport Psychology. Savannah, Ga.

Horn, T. S., & Hasbrook, C. (1986). Informational components influencing children's perceptions of their physical competence. In M. Weiss & D. Gould (Eds.), *Sport for children and youths* (pp. 81–88). Champaign, Ill.: Human Kinetics.

Horn, T. S., & Weiss, M. R. (1991). A developmental analysis of children's self-ability judgments in the physical domain. *Pediatric Exercise Science, 3,* 310–326.

Kleinfeld, J. (1975). Effective teachers of Eskimo and Indian students. *School Review, 83,* 301–344.

Malina, R. (1984). Physical growth and maturation. In J. R. Thomas (Ed.), *Motor development during childhood and adolescence* (pp. 2–26). Minneapolis, Minn. Burgess.

Markland, R. D., & Martinek, T. J. (1988). Descriptive analysis of coach augmented feedback given to high school varsity female volleyball players. *Journal of Teaching in Physical Education, 7,* 289–301.

Martinek, T. (1981). Pygmalion in the gym: A model for the communication of teacher expectations in physical education. *Research Quarterly, 52,* 58–67.

Martinek, T. (1988). Confirmation of a teacher expectancy model: Student perceptions and causal attributions of teaching behaviors. *Research Quarterly for Exercise and Sport, 59,* 118–126.

Martinek, T. (1989). Children's perceptions of teaching behaviors: An attributional model for explaining teacher expectancy effects. *Journal of Teaching in Physical Education, 8,* 318–328.

Martinek, T., & Johnson, S. (1979). Teacher expectations: Effects on dyadic interactions and self-concept in elementary age children. *Research Quarterly, 50,* 60–70.

Martinek, T., & Karper, W. B. (1982). Canonical relationships among motor ability, expression of effort, teacher expectations, and dyadic interactions in elementary age children. *Journal of Teaching in Physical Education, 1,* 26–39.

Martinek, T., & Karper, W. B. (1984). Multivariate relationships of specific impression cues with teacher expectations and dyadic interactions in elementary physical education classes. *Research Quarterly for Exercise and Sport, 55,* 32-40.

Martinek, T., & Karper, W. B. (1986). Motor ability and instructional contexts: Effects on teacher expectations and dyadic interactions in elementary physical education classes. *Journal of Classroom Interaction, 21,* 16–5.

Meyer, W. (1982). Indirect communications about perceived ability estimates. *Journal of Educational Psychology, 74,* 888–897.

Rejeski, W., Darracott, C., & Hutslar, S. (1979). Pygmalion in youth sports: A field study. *Journal of Sport Psychology, 1,* 311–319.

Rosenthal, R., & Jacobson, L. (1968). *Pygmalion in the classroom: Teacher expectations and pupils' intellectual development.* New York: Holt, Rinehart & Winston.

Schunk, D. (1984). Self-efficacy perspective on achievement behavior. *Educational Psychologist, 19,* 48–58.

Smith, R. E., Smoll, F. L., & Curtis, B. (1979). Coach effectiveness training: A cognitive-behavioral approach to enhancing relationship skills in youth sport coaches. *Journal of Sport Psychology, 1,* 59–75.

Smoll, F. L., & Schutz, R. W. (1990). Quantifying gender differences in physical performance: A developmental perspective. *Developmental Psychology, 26,* 360–369.

Smoll, F. L., & Smith, R. E. (1989). Leadership behaviors in sport: A theoretical model and research paradigm. *Journal of Applied Social Psychology, 19,* 1522–1551.

Thomas, J. R., & French, K. E. (1985). Gender differences across age in motor performance: A meta-analysis. *Psychological Bulletin, 98,* 260–282.

Thorndike, R. (1968). Review of Pygmalion in the classroom. *American Educational Research Journal, 5,* 708–711.

Ulrich, B. D. (1987). Developmental perspectives of motor skill performance in children. In D. Gould & M. Weiss (Eds.), *Advances in pediatric sport sciences* (vol. 2) (pp. 167–186). Champaign, Ill: Human Kinetics.

Weinstein, R. (1976). Reading group membership in first grade: Teacher behaviors and pupil experience over time. *Journal of Educational Psychology, 68,* 103–116.

Weinstein, R. (1989). Perceptions of classroom processes and student motivation: Children's views of self-fulfilling prophecies. In *Research on motivation in education: Goals and cognitions* (vol. 3) (pp. 187–221). San Diego, Calif.: Academic Press.

Leadership Effectiveness

Mimi C. Murray, *Springfield College*
Betty L. Mann, *Springfield College*

S ocial scientists and behavioral psychologists have studied leadership for many decades. With more than 350 definitions of leadership and thousands of empirical investigations of leaders (Bennis & Nanus, 1985), there still appears to be no generally accepted definition of leadership, nor is there clear understanding of what distinguishes successful leaders from less successful leaders or what distinguishes leaders from followers. Burns (1978), author of *Leadership*, a Pulitzer Prize–winning book, observes that leadership is one of the least understood phenomena on earth. Yet the search for qualities that lead to effective leadership is a quest that continues to occupy the attention of numerous investigators. Unfortunately, despite the varied interpretations and still incomplete analysis of leadership, there is a paucity of research and conceptual literature about leadership in sport situations.

When people are asked, "Who is a leader?" successful coaches such as Lombardi, Bryant, Schula, Landry, Stengel, Durocher, Lasorda, Auerbach, Wooden, Head-Summitt, Thompson, and Robinson are frequently included in their lists. Because coaches are leaders, coaching effectiveness can be maximized through understanding the concepts of leadership. Sport psychology consultants also serve in a leadership capacity, although from a different perspective than that of coaches. Thus, although this chapter is often written in the lexicon of the coach and may initially appear to be aimed exclusively at coaches, this is not the case. Knowledge of the basic principles of leadership presented in this chapter will help individuals in sport psychology deal more effectively with athletes; it will also help them to more fully understand effective coach–athlete communications and help coaches to become more effective leaders. This chapter describes several approaches to leadership and attempts to relate these theoretical frameworks to dimensions of leadership behavior in sports.

What Is Leadership?

Some authorities (Stogdill, 1974; Barrow, 1977) define leadership as the behavioral process of influencing the activities of an organized group toward specific goals and achievement of those goals. Others simply define leadership as the process whereby an individual influences others to do what he/she wants them to do. But leadership is often far more complex than the latter definition implies. Attempts to understand leadership should be concerned with *why* people comply as well as with how one person influences another.

Schein (1970) suggested that people comply because of a psychological contract. This hypothesis implies that individuals will do many things because they believe they should, and they expect reciprocation for what they do in the form of remuneration, perks, and privileges. Coaches and sport consultants need to be aware of the rewards or reinforcements their athletes expect. The athlete who complies with the wishes or demands of the leader might expect to win, to be positively reinforced, to get to play, or to receive a higher status. In essence, the cost–benefit ratio needs to balance. Consequently, both the leader and the athlete strike a bargain, or a psychological contract, with each other and with the team. Whether or not an athlete complies may be somewhat dependent on how she/he views authority. Individuals have learned to respond to authority through their experiences with parents, teachers, coaches, and other authority figures. Indirectly, individuals also learn how to respond to authority through the modeling portrayed in books, magazines, TV, and the movies. *Legitimate power* is often granted to coaches and sport psychology consultants when athletes feel it is right for these people to tell them what to do. In a later section of this chapter, we will discuss ways in which leaders can increase their potential influence or power.

Leadership Theories and Implication

Research on leadership has attempted to identify personal qualities and behaviors that are most likely to result in leader effectiveness and to determine what influence, if any, specific situational factors have on these variables. It was hoped that such knowledge could be used in both the selection and training of individuals who are likely to become effective leaders. Such research has resulted in testing trait, behavioral, situational, and transformational approaches to leadership theory.

Trait Approach

Assessing personality characteristics and traits to determine whether effective leaders have similar qualities is the same approach as one that was initially directed at trying to understand why certain people are successful athletes. The findings of trait or factor theory studies as applied to athletes and coaches have left us without conclusive results or information. No readily identifiable personality traits are related to leadership status or leadership effectiveness in *all* situations. A more viable explanation for effective leadership is that leadership qualities are situationally specific. Further, characteristics related to leadership do not operate separately but in combination.

If we could begin to address significant qualities or traits as *dispositional*, we might gain more valuable insights. "Dispositional" means that behavior associated with a given trait can vary from situation to situation, but individuals keep the same relative position regardless of the situation; that is, the most assertive individual will respond with the highest level of assertiveness. Research on dispositions associated with successful business executives indicates that these individuals are dominant, self-confident, assertive, high in levels of aspiration, and generally successful throughout life (Dunette, 1965). In 1971, Ghiselli found the following dispositions related to leadership success as determined by upward mobility and rated job success: self-perceived intelligence, initiative, supervisory ability, and self-assurance. For more information on traits associated with successful leaders, refer to Stogdill (1974) for an excellent review.

The work of Hendry (1974) and Ogilvie and Tutko (1966) established the stereotype of the typical coach/physical educator as someone who needs to be in control and is inflexible, domineering, and emotionally inhibited. Sage (1975) did not concur with these findings, which seemingly indicate that coaches are highly authoritarian, dogmatic, and manipulative. Sage's reservations were based on the small number of samples and the sampling techniques employed. Even if this stereotype is incorrect, these dispositions may be necessary for successful leadership under many situations found in sport, such as stressful game situations. For example, during a 30-second time-out the coach should be informing the athletes of the strategies to use when the game resumes. This is obviously not the time for participatory or democratic decision making. Further, authoritarianism in coaches may be only part of their sport personalities and is not necessarily present or apparent in other situations in their lives.

The authoritarian personality profile merits further explanation and understanding because it is a typical description of sport leadership—whether a false one or not. Authoritarians generally avoid unstructured situations because such situations are perceived as threatening. The inability to cope with ambiguous situations may result from the authoritarian's continuing use of old responses for new stimulus conditions, even when these responses provide less than satisfactory results. Such inability could help explain the "this is the way I was coached; it was good enough for me, and it is good enough for them" syndrome often found in coaching. Unfortunately, the practices of many coaches are frequently at odds with the most current sport knowledge in motor learning, sport psychology, exercise physiology, and biomechanics. Is it because many coaches cannot cope with change? This attitude may also explain why so many coaches can be threatened by insignificant social change such as longer hairstyles for men a few years ago and, more currently, male athletes wearing an earring. Those male authoritarians who are most threatened by social changes probably define their masculinity in and through sport. Thus, anything perceived as deviating from their masculine image, based upon their older, unchanged social values, might be difficult for them to understand.

Higher need for social approval, impulsiveness in decision making, and greater frequency in making errors have been noted as authoritarian traits (Podd, 1972). Some typically authoritarian coaches have been known to harass referees, humiliate players, and throw clipboards and chairs during a game. Can these aggressive behaviors be ethically justified, and do they provide an appropriate leadership role model?

According to Triandis (1971), authoritarians typically avoid introspection, approve of severe punishment, and tend to hold strong prejudices. Could this help explain why sport in some situations is still sexist and racist and is sometimes filled with physical and psychological abuses of athletes? A study of authoritarianism and associated attitudes sheds some light on the behavior of some male coaches and athletic directors toward females in sport. Males who were more concerned with winning at the expense of sportsmanship and who were also the highest in authoritarianism had neg-

ative attitudes about women, admired the traditional male roles, and were opposed to equality (Maier & Laurakis, 1981). A recent example of this type of behavior comes from remarks of Bobby Knight, Indiana basketball coach and U.S. coach for the 1984 Olympics: "I don't like people very well because most of them lack intestinal fortitude or they lack integrity. Women in particular bother me. I don't like women at all. I can't bear all the small talk and social amenities that women put you through." When asked what he said during an animated chat with a player, Knight responded, "I told him to take a picture of his testicles so he'd have something to remember them by if he ever took another shot like the last one. For you ladies, that's t-e-s-t-i-c-l-e-s."

Interestingly, Hendry (1972) and Ogilvie and Tutko (1966) found the personality profiles of successful athletes and coaches to be alike. Further, the profiles of coaches evidenced high levels of enthusiasm, need to achieve, and energy (Andrud, 1970; Gagen, 1971). In summary, the factor/trait approach to examining leadership has attempted to determine whether there is a universal personality for leadership success. This approach is also called the great person (man) theory of leadership. There are some common trends in that leaders have been described as being bright, confident, extroverted, and even tall, but the overall results of research on leadership personality characteristics and traits have been quite equivocal. Therefore, researchers directed their efforts toward examining characteristic behaviors of effective leaders rather than assessing distinguishing personality traits.

Behavioral Theories

Recent research on leadership theory has focused upon actual leadership behaviors, or how a leader leads rather than what a leader is. This approach examines the behavior of leaders and their group effectiveness, or the productivity and satisfaction of group members.

Researchers on behavioral theories have investigated the influence different leaders allow subordinates in decision making. From such research a classification system was developed by which leaders were described as *autocratic*, or dictatorial; participative, or democratic; or laissez-faire, or free rein. Little attention will be given here to leadership types because they are covered in Chapter 8.

The concern with leadership behaviors first emerged in business management areas, as did the factor trait approach to studying leadership. The majority of earlier studies (1940s and 1950s) were conducted by researchers at Ohio State University. From these studies, two leader behavior characteristics related to group effectiveness emerged. The first was consideration, and the second was initiating structure. "Consideration" reflects job relationships in which there is mutual trust, respect for others' ideas, and attention to others' feelings. Leaders who scored high in consideration had good rapport and communication with others. "Initiating structure" refers to how leaders define and structure their roles for goal attainment. Leaders who scored high in initiating structure were active in directing group activities, communicating, scheduling, and experimenting with new ideas. According to the Ohio State studies, successful leaders score high on both consideration and initiating structure.

After World War II some interesting studies on organizational effectiveness were conducted at the University of Michigan. The Michigan studies described a leader as being either production-centered or employee-centered (Stogdill, 1974) but not both. These classifications are self-evident. Later studies have revealed that leaders *can* be both employee-centered and production-centered, and the most effective leaders tend to score high on both behaviors.

When these various behavioral theories were applied to sport, it was found that the behaviors of coaches most desired by athletes were training for competitiveness, providing social support, and being rewarding (Chelladurai & Saleh, 1978). In a study of leadership and competitive rowers, Neil and Kirby (1985) found that less skilled and younger rowers preferred coaches who demonstrated person-oriented behaviors. Weiss and Friedrichs (1986) found that coaches of losing basketball teams were high on social support. Therefore, we cannot assume that social support leads to success. Massimo (1973) asked a large number of gymnasts what were the behaviors they desired most in a coach and found desired behaviors were ordered in importance from "use minimal verbiage," "have a sense of humor," "use individual psychology," and "have technical competency" to "appreciate the sociology of the team." We will use Massimo's statements and expand upon them. Al-

though the desirable leadership behaviors were initially identified for coaches and are expanded in coaching terminology, most of the behaviors are probably equally viable for sport psychology consultants and their interactions with athletes.

1. *Use minimal verbiage.* Too many people overcoach. This may be due to insecurity, to trying too hard, or simply to not knowing any better. An example of how to correct this is to select only one or two corrections for a group or an athlete to work on in each skill or effort. Once these corrections are selected, *briefly* verbalize the key analysis points for each correction and perhaps physically demonstrate the incorrect and correct movements. Then put the athletes in an appropriate drill.

2. *Have a sense of humor.* Although this behavior is desirable, one must be careful to not overuse humor. Sarcasm is not a desirable form of humor. Humor involves laughing at oneself and with others, not at another.

3. *Use individual psychology.* This implies dealing with each team member as an individual. Some athletes need considerable coaching and attention, and others can almost coach themselves. Fairness matters greatly to athletes, but there is no way a coach can appear to be completely fair. Some athletes will get more of the coach's attention on a given day than will others. Perhaps if the team understands why the coach is giving more time to a certain athlete, other members will be more understanding. This involves good communication skills. All athletes have different needs, and the coach should attempt to determine those needs and, within her/his own philosophy, provide for them.

4. *Have technical competency.* Anyone who is willing to learn and cares enough to take the time to understand correct movement mechanics, strategies, and fundamental principles of exercise physiology, motor learning, and psychology can effectively coach most sports. A person can acquire knowledge of a particular sport and factors influencing the learning process. This knowledge should not be equated with personal skill in performing. One can be a very effective coach and not be able personally to perform well, just as one can be an outstanding athlete and not have the

technical competencies and personal skills to be an effective coach.

5. *Appreciate the sociology of the team.* The coach must deal not only with the individuals on the team but also with how those individuals interact. This means that the coach should know what the team's "personality" is. The coach should not blow minor animosities between team members out of perspective, but if animosities go too far, then the coach should end them, diplomatically and emphatically.

Although there has been support for behavioral theories, there are sufficient inconsistencies in the literature to suggest that leadership is far more complex than to be relegated to explanations based upon traits or behaviors alone. It appears that both situational and individual factors, and the interactions of these factors, determine who will emerge as a successful leader.

Situational Theories

Some situational factors that are important to leadership success are the characteristics of subordinates, the organizational situation, and the demands of the specific situation. Of particular interest to those of us in sport are the interactions of coaches and sport consultants (leaders) with athletes (subordinates) in a specific situation. Fiedler (1967) in his contingency model argues that leadership style, the group, and the situation interact to affect group performance and satisfaction. Fiedler believes that a leader's style results from the leader's own needs and personality. He also suggests that leadership style is a stable personality characteristic that is well established. According to him, the two classifications of leadership style are people-centered or task-centered. Fiedler proposed that if leadership style is not flexible and the organization is not productive, the organizational structure should be changed or the leader replaced. If one accepts Fiedler's theory, then leadership style is generalizable regardless of the situation. According to Fiedler (1967), leadership can be improved in a given situation in two ways. The first is to change the leader's personality, not an easy task even if the leader wishes to change. The second is to change the situation, including the organizational structure, so that it is more compatible with the leader's personality. Personalities and situations should be matched and congruent for maximum leadership effectiveness. The studies in sport using Fiedler's contingency approach have proved interesting. Danielson (1976) found that the most effective coaching in ice hockey was person-oriented rather than task-oriented. In a study involving volleyball, Bird (1977) found that winning women's volleyball coaches in the more skilled Division I programs were person-oriented. The results were the opposite in less skillful Division II programs.

The application of Fiedler's model to sport might imply that a coach who is successful in one situation may not be so in another—for example, Perkins for Bryant. Ray Perkins had been a fairly successful professional football coach with the New York Giants; upon Bear Bryant's retirement at Alabama, Perkins took the helm and had a few fairly unsuccessful seasons. Conversely, there are examples of successful coaches in sport who have traveled from one team to another with success following each move. Pat Riley left a great Lakers team to lead the Knicks, with much improvement and success predicted for them. Is the difference because the situations for Riley are similar, moving from one professional basketball team to another, while Perkins moved from a professional to a collegiate team? Can Fiedler's model help explain this?

Fiedler's (1967) contingency theory posits that leaders' personality traits are relatively inflexible. Thus, leadership can be most effective when situations are favorable and compatible. In other situation-specific theories the focus is on the situationally specific *behaviors* of leaders and how these behaviors, rather than personality dispositions, affect followers. These other situation-specific theories to be briefly mentioned here are the life-cycle and path-goal theories.

Hersey and Blanchard (1969, 1977, 1982) proposed that effective leaders can and should adjust their leadership style to respond to the **life-cycle** needs of their followers and to the environment. Hersey and Blanchard (1982) suggested that an appropriate leadership style for a specific situation is determined by the maturity of the followers. Thus, the emphasis is on the subordinate and not the leader. Maturity is defined as "the ability and willingness of people to take responsibility for directing their own behavior (Hersey & Blanchard, 1982, p. 151). The behavior of the leader in relation to the follower(s) is then based on three variables: (1) the amount of guidance and direction a leader gives, or initiating behavior; (2) the amount of socioemotional support a leader gives, or consideration behavior; and (3) the maturity level of the followers as they perform a task. Case (1984) illustrates the importance of adapting leadership style to the needs of the followers within a particular situation by asking us to consider differences in leadership style that would be appropriate when coaching 9-year-old soccer players as compared to Division I collegiate soccer players. The experience, maturity, and skill level of the players may influence the leadership styles that would be most effective within the specific environment.

In the **path-goal theory** the leader is viewed as a facilitator who helps subordinates achieve their goals (House, 1971). As the term implies, the leader provides a path by which the followers can reach their goals. The specific characteristics of each situation should determine the leader behaviors that should most successfully aid the follower. A swim coach who determinines that her athlete wants to decrease her time in her event so she can qualify for a regional championship would provide the appropriate and specific conditioning and training program so that her swimmer could qualify for regionals. The coach would be operationalizing the path-goal theory of leadership by focusing on her athlete's goal. Further, by utilizing this theory one could predict that each athlete might prefer specific behaviors from his/her coach. Neither of these situation-specific theories, life-cycle or path-goal, has been applied to any great extent in sport. The results of the few studies that have done so are contradictory and inconclusive (Carron, 1987; Chelladurai & Carron, 1978; Chelladurai & Saleh, 1978; Von Strache, 1979). The potential for the application of these approaches to a better understanding of sport leadership is vast.

There appear to be no direct and simple answers to such questions as "Is group effectiveness caused by how a leader behaves, or does the leader behave in a certain way because of the group's performance?" It would be extremely difficult and unwise to assume any cause–effect relationships on the basis of the limited and somewhat contradictory research evidence available. Flexibility, which can be very disturbing for many authoritarians, would appear to be an ideal approach to coaching because of the situational nature of the varying sport milieu. Chelladurai reaches a similar conclusion in Chapter 8 when he discusses leadership style and decision making.

In *The Next American Frontier*, author Robert Reich's major emphasis is that traditional management in the United States is the greatest threat to American prosperity. Presently, management is bureaucratic, top-heavy, and authoritarian. Reich suggests we look at the management style in countries such as Japan, Germany, and France, which have the fastest-growing industries. The new, *flexible* management systems in these countries focus on smaller work teams and employee problem solving. As John Naisbitt (1984) believes, if people are to be affected by decisions, they should be part of the decision-making process. Workers, increasingly, are struggling for this recognition. The results of a study conducted in 1948 that asked workers and supervisors to rank in order of importance what workers want from their jobs are presented in Table 7-1. Interestingly, this study has been replicated several times over the past 30 years, and the results have been similar. Workers continue to seek appreciation for work done, want to be "in" on things, and seek promotion and growth, while supervisors perceive that workers are more interested in and motivated by wages and job security.

More recent interpretations of effective leadership reflect the needs of workers. We learn from Bennis and Nanus (1985), for example, that three major contexts shape a more responsive work environment: commitment, complexity, and credibility. These concepts refer to the nature of the work ethic, the dynamic changes of an information age society, and the need to be fair and trustworthy. Through their research, Bennis and Nanus discovered four strategies or themes that seemed to be common among competent leaders. They titled the first strategy "attention through vision." Jane Blalock, former Ladies Professional Golf Association superstar and currently a successful businesswoman, believes "you must dream in order to make things happen . . . keep striving but keep focused and your thoughts and dreams will become reality." A second strategy, according to Bennis and Nanus, is "meaning through communication." The competent leader has a vision, an intense focus on outcome and results, a realistic strategy to carry out the vision, and the ability to communicate the vision and rally the support of others. A third theme is "trust through positioning" and re-

Table 7-1 What Do Workers Want from Their Jobs?

	Supervisors	*Workers*
Good working conditions	4	9
Feeling "in" on things	10	2
Tactful discipline	7	10
Full appreciation for work done	8	1
Management loyalty to workers	6	8
Good wages	1	5
Promotion and growth with company	3	7
Sympathetic understanding of personal problems	9	3
Job security	2	4
Interesting work	5	6

Factors were rated from 1 to 10, with 1 being the highest priority.

flects the undeniable importance of trust and accountability. "Trust is the glue that maintains organizational integrity" (Bennis & Nanus, 1985, p. 44). The final strategy is the "deployment of self through positive self-regard." The competent leader realizes his/her sense of worth and creates in others a sense of confidence and high but reasonable expectations. In other words, leaders have a vision for the future that they can communicate, are trustworthy, and exhibit self-respect. Further, these powerful people accomplish much with tact and diplomacy. With their power, competence, and confidence, they empower others.

DePree (1989) commented that the "signs of outstanding leadership appear primarily among the followers. Are the followers reaching their potential? Are they learning? Do they achieve required results?" (p. 10). As previously described, researchers have attempted to identify situation variables that best explain and predict an effective, productive leader–follower relationship. House (1971) suggests that the personal characteristics of subordinates and task or job demands help determine the most appropriate leadership style. For example, a player with an internal locus of control who believes she is in control of her successes and her failures may perform better with the direction of a leader characterized as relationship-oriented. The individual with an external locus of control may be more compatible with a task-oriented coach. Hersey and Blanchard (1982) would suggest

that the coach needs to change her/his leader style (initiation or consideration) according to the maturity level of the followers to enhance satisfactory performance and satisfaction of the followers.

Another variable that has been studied by theorists for years (Weber, 1968; House, 1977) but is recently receiving increased attention is *charisma.* A study of transformational leadership, or charismatic leadership, may offer more insight into the question "What leader characteristics best facilitate the efforts and satisfaction of the worker?" Komives (1991) reminds us that research on charismatic leadership paralleled the fate of trait theories in the 1920s and 1930s. With renewed interest in the last 15 years, however, there is some agreement among researchers that transformational, or charismatic, leaders are those who inspire others to work to achieve a shared vision. Seltzer and Bass (1990) looked beyond the two behavioral dimensions of leadership, initiation and consideration, and found support for considering transformational leadership characteristics as important to a better understanding of leadership. They defined transformational leadership as superior leadership performance that is "seen when leaders broaden and elevate the interests of their followers, when they generate awareness and acceptance among their followers of the purposes and mission of the group, and when they move their followers to transcend their own self-interests for the good of the group" (pp. 693–694).

According to Komives (1991), both men and women are capable of scoring high as transformational leaders. Rosener (1991) found that women managers tended to view their leadership style as transformational, particularly those with managerial responsibilities in medium-size, nontraditional organizations. Rosener also found that women were more likely to be described as charismatic leaders. These findings further support the notion that the traditional male-oriented command and control style of managing may not be advantageous or the most suitable in all situations. While Rosener supports the value of an interactive leader style utilizing referent power rather than formal authority within an environment in which participation is encouraged and power is shared, she also recognizes the value in diversity of styles.

Women in Sport

The lack of women's involvement in sport leadership is of grave concern to many who are committed to increasing sport opportunities for girls and women. The number of women officiating, coaching, and administrating sport programs for girls and women has significantly decreased. This is a critical time, and in looking at the role of women in leadership, it may be time to reevaluate the qualities of leadership.

Researchers such as Acosta and Carpenter (1990), Hart, Hasbrook, and Mathes (1986), and Sisley and Capel (1986) have provided valuable information about the dramatic decrease in the number of women coaching females: a change from approximately 90% 15 years ago to less than 50% today. The writers view the this decline as more than unfortunate. Some investigators have attempted to explain the decrease in women coaching females (Eitzen & Pratt, 1989; George, 1989; Holmen & Parkhouse, 1981; Parkhouse & Williams, 1986). One explanation often presented is the "lack of qualified female coaches." The use of the term "qualified" is, of course, prejudicial. It is often assumed in sport that males, regardless of training or experience, are more qualified than females. Anderson and Gill (1983) found that hiring standards for male coaches of female teams were lower than for women or men coaching same-sex teams. Ironically, Eitzen and Pratt (1989) found most female coaches have physical education

backgrounds (which, we believe, is the ideal background from which to coach), whereas males coaching females were primarily from other areas in education.

Other researchers have explored gender coaching preferences of athletes. These studies have tended to find a pro male bias (George, 1989; Parkhouse & Williams, 1986; Weinberg, Reveles, & Jackson, 1984). We believe that this bias is due to sport being perceived as a male domain and to female gender socialization, as well as to the patriarchal nature of sport. These factors tend to devalue women; hence, female athletes may also devalue women.

One possible framework for understanding this decline and pro male bias in hiring coaches in sport can be found within Knoppers's (1987, 1989) application of Kanter's work on corporate organization in sport. Kanter believes that the workplace shapes the worker, while much of the literature states the opposite.

Kanter is an internationally recognized expert on corporate entrepreneurship and organizational change. She delineates, in her 1977 book *Men and Women of the Corporation*, the ways in which rigid job hierarchies can constrain employees. In particular, she demonstrates that subtle and overt discrimination affects performance. She shows that the problems and failures of women in management often stem from powerlessness, and she calls on companies to abandon rigid pyramidal structures and to empower employees, especially women.

Knoppers's application of Kanter's theory to sport relies on the same structural determinants that Kanter identifies as present in the workplace: opportunity, power and proportion of women. These factors are believed to determine work roles and may account for the decline in the number of female coaches. A few examples may help to illustrate this point.

First, to have opportunities is to have visible career ladders with the potential to experience more satisfaction than obstacles. What opportunities do neophyte women coaches perceive? Do they see opportunities for advancement to head coach or for administrative positions? The previously mentioned research on percentages of female coaches indicates that these opportunities are rapidly and dramatically declining. Second, to have power is to have access to resources and information. Are these available to women coaches? Although Susan Schafer, from the Department of Education in Colorado, has shown women in sport ways in which this access can be obtained, equal access to sport information in general remains an unrealized goal.

Third is the issue of proportion: The gender ratio for women in sport leadership positions is low. Through extrapolation, the percentage of full-time women coaches (at all ranks) would be about 25%. Coaching is male-dominated, and the skewness is increasing. This is in sharp contrast to other professions such as law and medicine where the number of women is steadily increasing.

Knoppers (1987, 1989) also says that institutional factors figure in the low number of women coaches. An example of such an institutional factor is homophobia, which, according to Lenskji (1986), precludes some women from getting jobs in coaching. This irrational fear is based on the false assumption that there are more lesbians in sport than in other professions. Perhaps more damaging is the false assumption that lesbians, as coaches, are more likely to seduce their female athletes. Although no involvement is or can be condoned between an athlete and a coach, it is worthwhile to note that, from the literature in psychology, the percentages of males compared to females who become sexually involved with their subordinates is considerably greater (Diesenhouse, 1989; Holroyd & Brodsky, 1977; Pope, Keith-Speigel, & Tabachnic, 1986).

Occupation stereotypes that grow out of gender typing are major barriers to women seeking leadership positions in sport. The generally lower self-concepts that females hold, as compared to males, often result in self-limiting behaviors that are expressed in phrases such as "I can't" or "I wonder if I am qualified." Another part of gender typing is stereotyping by which women view their tasks as of lesser value than male tasks. This belief is often confounded in organizational systems such as sport, which is traditionally defined as a male domain; therefore, women are assigned roles, if at all, in middle management levels in sport. These assigned roles result in organizational discrimination.

This phenomenon of organizational discrimination is paralleled in corporate America, where there exists a "glass ceiling" or invisible barrier that blocks women and minorities from top management jobs, despite legislative support for equal jobs. While there is rapid growth in the number of women and minorities entering the workforce, there is not a corresponding or proportional increase in these groups within senior vice-president levels and above. In fact, Gunas (1990/91) reported that 93% of the senior ranks are occupied by white males. Is there an explanation other than sociocultural conditions and discrimination? The glass ceiling initiative was created by the Department of Labor under the direction of former Secretary of Labor, Elizabeth Dole, to determine the nature and extent of job advancement and barriers and scrutinize hiring and promotional practices of U.S. businesses.

In sport, organizational discrimination is evidenced in fewer women coaching, officiating, and administering athletic programs. Discrimination is also shown by fewer women in high positions within sport governance such as the national governing bodies, the USOC, the state high school federations, and the NCAA. Self-limiting behaviors and organizational discrimination are among the components of occupational gender typing.

It would be beneficial for today's women to bring to the workplace, and in particular the sport workplace, their own unique and valuable qualities. Carole Oglesby has argued for the feminization of sport so that sport can be transformed into a more humane environment for all without lessening or decreasing (in fact, increasing) the skill levels and the physical prowess of our athletes.

Women in leadership need to use their female strengths rather than totally adopting what is alien to them: the male role. Women have the ability to create, to care, and to encourage growth in the context of concern for others. Women in sport need to approach leadership with courage, tolerance, and humor while addressing personal and organizational gender typing. This can be accomplished by communication with women and men about the negative aspects of gender stereotypes for both.

In sport it would be refreshing to see decisions questioned and well thought out from an ethical vantage point. The business world is addressing an outdated "macho" management style's detrimental effects and suggesting it be replaced with the teamwork concept, which involves trust, cooperation, point-of-view communication, and an emphasis on strengths, not weaknesses. Is this not the humanization of business? Could sport not benefit from this approach as well?

Evaluation of Leadership

There are basically two approaches to assessing leadership effectiveness in sport: behavioral observation and questionnaires. Research that focuses on determining the traits or factors of successful leaders through the administration of personality inventories is no longer popular. This is because the variation in a given trait from situation to situation can be so different that the notion of personality traits seems of little use in accounting for an individual's behaviors. However, it should be noted that within the larger field of personality psychology, there is some evidence to support the concept that individuals possess certain dispositions that appear constant, consistent, and immutable over time and across situations. These dispositions are anxiety level, friendliness, and eagerness for novel experiences. In examining the many personality inventories, three dispositions that were assessed in almost 50 scales are *extroversion* (sociability and activity), *psychoticism* (psychopathy, impulsiveness, desire to seek new and perhaps dangerous situations), and *neuroticism* (emotionality, anger, and anxiety). Interestingly, in his original work, Eysenck described these three factors as essential descriptors of personality. Often it seems as if the study of human behavior repeats itself. Presently there is a need for research that examines the relationships of these three dispositions to specific sport situations. Tentatively, however, it can be concluded that certain personality dispositions may impact on leadership.

Questionnaires

The disposition that has been most studied in sport psychology is neuroticism/emotionality—dealing with one's emotions, or "affect." In sport the most frequently used paper-and-pencil measures of personality have been the 16 Personality Factor questionnaire (Cattell, Eber, & Tatsouka, 1980) and the Eysenck Personality Inventory (Eysenck & Eysenck, 1968).

The measure designed to assess behavior of leaders that emanated from the Ohio State studies is the Leader Behavior Description Questionnaire

(LBDQ) (Hemphill & Coons, 1957). As previously mentioned, the researchers using this measure identified *consideration* between the leader and follower as characterized by behaviors such as friendliness, mutual trust, warmth, and respect. In addition to consideration, *initiating structure* is seen as another leadership quality characterized by identifying patterns, methods, procedures, and channels of communication. Consideration and initiating structures are seen as orthogonal and central to defining leadership behaviors.

The Coach Behavior Description Questionnaire (CBDQ) (Danielson, Zelhart, & Drake, 1975) was a modification of the LBDQ and the results obtained with this measure are reported in another section of this chapter. The Leadership Scale for Sport (LSS) (Chelladurai & Carron, 1981; Chelladurai & Saleh, 1978) was developed from the LBDQ. The LSS identifies five coaching behaviors—training behavior, autocratic behavior, democratic behavior, social support, and rewarding behavior. The results of studies using this scale (Neil & Kirby, 1985; Weiss & Friedrichs, 1986) can also be found in another section of this chapter. Because these assessments are based on athletes' perceptions of coaching behavior, they can be somewhat subjective.

Based on Fiedler's contingency theory (1967), the Least Preferred Co-Worker (LPC) scale was developed. This measure is used to determine a leader's sensitivity and empathy toward the subordinate the leader least prefers. A leader who scores high on the LPC is considered to be person- or relationship-oriented, meaning she/he can have positive and supportive feelings toward a follower or worker who is not liked or who may not be productive. Conversely, the leader who has a low score on the LPC tends to be more task-oriented. The study by Danielson (1978) described elsewhere is an example of the use of the LPC in sport to determine leadership motivation. Both the LBDQ (Hemphill & Coon, 1957) and the LSS (Chelladurai & Carron, 1983) have been used to test the efficacy of the life-cycle theory (Case, 1980). The LBDQ has also been utilized by Vos Stache (1979) to determine the efficacy of the path-goal theory in sport.

To assess transformational leadership, the Multifactor Leadership Questionnaire (Bass, 1985) was developed. It is completed in parallel form by the follower and the leader. The measure determines transformational (individual motivation or charismatic leadership, individualized consideration, intellectual stimulation, and inspiration), transactional (contingent reward and management by exception), and laissez-faire leadership behaviors. To our knowledge, there is a dearth of research using this approach to understanding sport leadership. Is this a direction for the future?

Behavioral Observation

The aforementioned techniques for assessing leadership are subjective, asking individuals to either describe their own or others' behavior. Individual perceptions are not always accurate. A more objective way to assess behaviors is through direct observation of the targeted behavior. The Coaching Behavior Assessment Scale (Smith, Smoll, & Hunt, 1977) enables the researcher to code and analyze actual behaviors as they occur in the natural setting. The behaviors are categorized as either reactive or spontaneous with subdivisions in each category. Smith, Smoll, and Curtis (1979) and Horn (1984) have demonstrated through their research that both positive and negative coaching behaviors can be identified and coded. This approach is beneficial in helping coaches understand their own behaviors as well as providing an effective vehicle for the training of coaches.

More research needs to be done in the assessment of leadership effectiveness in sport. The authors wish to encourage the combination of subjective and objective techniques as well as more qualitative assessment approaches and the further development of other techniques for evaluation. Ethically, the results of any evaluation should be shared with the individual who has been evaluated. Chapter 4 described how coaching behaviors and their consequences have been evaluated and then modified in order to increase leadership effectiveness.

How Leaders Can Increase Their Influence or Power

Power is the basis of followers complying with a leader's wishes. When a leader/coach is successful at influencing another person, he/she has demonstrated power. Power comes partly from being in a position of authority. The coach by virtue of

her/his position has control and is perceived as more valid than other members of the team. Consequently, the coach can exert a great deal of influence of either a positive or negative nature upon the behaviors of team members. To a lesser extent, the same can be said of a sport psychologist assigned to work with a team.

What specific measures can leaders take to ensure greater influence or power other than that granted by virtue of position? Paying attention to appearance, demonstrating self-confidence and expertise, appropriately allocating rewards and sanctions, and being an example to admire and emulate are all ways in which coaches and sport psychologists can increase their potential influence.

Appearance: First Impression

Visualize Tom Landry, the perennially successful, now retired, coach of the Dallas Cowboys. What were your first impressions of this great coach? He was always well-groomed, dressed in a tie and jacket at games; he appeared to be fit; he seemed to be in complete control of himself and his team regardless of the circumstances or intensity of the situation. At the other extreme, what are your impressions of a coach who never changes from a practice warm-up jacket and shirt, is overweight and out of shape, smokes on the sidelines, shouts obscenities at athletes and officials, and appears to be gearing up for a volcanic explosion in tense and close situations?

We may want to resist as "superficial" the notion that appearance is or should be important in effective leadership, and yet it is. Often our first impressions of people are inadequate and distorted, yet these approximations are critical starting points for predicting influence and the quality of social interaction to follow. Certainly, there are and have been successful coaches whose appearance and behavior have been less than exemplary, but they are the exceptions.

Pat Head-Summitt, women's basketball coach at the University of Tennessee, National Championship Coach, and U.S. Olympic coach, is another example to be admired. Athletes' immediate impressions of her are that she is extremely well-groomed, dynamic, enthusiastic, intense, fit, and in total control. Because of these first impressions and the influence that emanates from them, she must be a formidable recruiting force. The "Rosenthal effect," or a self-fulfilling prophecy, can be initiated by the coach who looks and acts like a winner. That is, the coach who behaves like a winner is more likely to become a winner.

Referent Power

Referent power (French & Raven, 1959) is based upon the attraction exerted by an individual on another person or on a group. The stronger the attraction, the greater the power will be. The influence occurs because people identify with one another. Referent power is task-specific and is more likely to occur when an individual such as a coach or sport psychologist demonstrates skill or competence at certain tasks or has expert power granted because of education, experience, and appearance. Identification with a leader occurs when the leader possesses personal characteristics and qualities valued by the group or team such as appearance, demonstrated knowledge, and the ability to express the values and concerns of her/his followers.

Charisma

Some leaders receive loyalty and commitment because they possess the illusive quality called **charisma**. This kind of influence is unique to the leader and group and thus cannot be transferred to another person. Political history is punctuated by charismatic leaders: John F. Kennedy, Martin Luther King, Jr., Adolf Hitler, Ghandi, Eleanor Roosevelt, and Gloria Steinem are a few examples.

Who would be on your list of charismatic coaches? If these coaches retired or resigned, would those who follow in their positions exhibit the same charisma? Obviously not. Unfortunately, in many instances the charismatic leader is the most difficult of all to replace. The most inappropriate and ineffective behavior for the new coach is to attempt to emulate or behave like the previous charismatic coach. Coaches need to develop and establish their own styles. How very different from one another were outstanding coaches from the past such as Lombardi, Bryant, Hayes, Auerbach, and Wooden—all uniquely distinct individuals. No one else could exactly duplicate their leadership style and charisma. We are all individuals, and our personalities differ greatly; therefore, we should not attempt to imitate someone else's behavior. Seltzer and Base (1990) noted that

charisma "operates at the leader-individual level rather than at the leader-group level" (p. 702). Charisma cannot be copied; it is individually created and perceived.

Allocation of Rewards and Sanctions

If a leader can influence others, it is frequently because others depend upon her/him. As previously discussed, this influence can arise from psychological identification because the leader has the power to allocate rewards or sanctions. The rewards can be objective or subjective. For example, some professional and college coaches have the authority to provide objective rewards such as salaries, tuition, room and board, books, and the like as well as subjective rewards such as approval or disapproval. The majority of coaches regularly give subjective, largely intangible rewards.

Some athletes are able to motivate themselves completely (internal motivation), whereas others need help from their peers, family, coach, and additional significant others (external motivation). The leader's role is much easier when he/she is involved with an athlete who is internally motivated. The leader's influence will be lessened if he/she does not appropriately motivate the athlete who needs external motivation. For example, when Jerry Kramer was asked how his coach, Vince Lombardi, motivated individual players, Kramer responded by saying that Lombardi knew who needed pats on the back, who needed to be kicked, and who needed various shades between the extremes. Lombardi had the ability to differentiate among the athletes and knew how to motivate each athlete effectively and at the proper time (Kaplan, 1983). (See Chapters 2 and 3 for specific suggestions regarding effective motivation.)

Role Model: An Example to Follow

A coach must not expect any more from an athlete than what the coach is willing to give or be. Athletes will emulate the coach's behavior. This means that the coach should be committed to exemplifying as well as enforcing the rules for the players. For example, if there is a punctuality rule, then the coach should abide by it too.

Control of emotions is another expectation most coaches have for their athletes. This is a worthy expectation, for people cannot function maximally in terms of physical performance or interpersonal relations if they lose emotional control. Decision making, information processing, speed and coordination, objectivity, reasonableness, and the acuity of the senses are just a few of the factors that are adversely affected by loss of emotional control. Coaches who lose emotional control are not performing at their optimal level, and they are also presenting a negative role model. If coaches can misbehave on the sidelines, why can't athletes misbehave on the sidelines or lose their tempers while performing?

Planning and commitment are also behaviors coaches expect from their athletes. In his autobiography, Lee Iacocca, "Chrysler's savior," stresses repeatedly that much of his managerial success is due to his own personal commitment to planning and his insistence that his employees also plan. Iacocca believes that the discipline of writing down one's goals is the first step toward making them happen.

Not only is goal setting appropriate and important for athletes; it is critical for coaches and sport psychology consultants. Setting goals is only the beginning. Goals also need to be evaluated, and progress in meeting goals needs to be appropriately reinforced. For example, Iacocca reviews and establishes goals on a quarterly basis. He feels it makes people accountable to themselves, while forcing leaders to reconsider their goals and not to lose sight of their dreams. Iacocca's quarterly review is a contract between a leader and follower and is signed by each. (For more detailed information on how to set effective goals and what strategies help to achieve these goals, see Chapter 13.)

Goals can be used to plan athletic practices down to the smallest detail. Such practices are extremely positive ways for a coach or sport leader to facilitate teaching and learning. During games, "Bear" Bryant carried reminders on a piece of paper. Among the things that he had written down were "Don't forget—use time-outs intelligently—double time-out—run clock down last play—ORDERLY BENCH."

In summary, having an appropriate appearance, exhibiting conduct that exemplifies the behavior expected from athletes, balancing the cost–benefit reinforcement ratio for complying with the leader's wishes, and complete planning and goal setting are specific behaviors all leaders can use to improve their credibility and influence. Improvement in any of these areas can potentially increase one's effectiveness as a leader.

Developing Leadership Within the Team

In identifying leaders within a team, a coach should be attuned to functional leadership that arises spontaneously in a climate of trust. Such a climate is present when coaches accept the uniqueness of each team member—including what might appear as deviant behavior, provided this behavior does not have a negative impact on the effectiveness of the team or the satisfaction of its members. Leadership within a team should go to the most competent. Natural leaders will usually surface if there is a climate of acceptance and if athletes are encouraged to provide input and leadership. A coach can help certain athletes demonstrate or develop their leadership abilities by giving those individuals responsibilities, small at first, and then positively reinforcing their successful attempts at leadership.

Human relations within a team can be improved if everyone is aware of expectations, if the rules and regulations are clearly stated, if team procedures are well written and available, and if responsibilities that do not overlap are clearly defined. Following are some suggestions for building effective team leaders:

1. Identify potential leaders and provide opportunities for leadership within the team.

2. Use these athlete leaders, as well as leaders such as athletic trainers, managers, and assistant coaches, wisely by delegating authority and responsibility to them.

3. Deal with all athletes and assistant leaders as individuals.

4. Keep communication open and direct rather than having team leaders serve as a "buffer" between the coach and other athletes.

Summary

Because of the significant role coaches play in the skill and personal development of their athletes, their influence, power, and effect cannot be negated. Being a good leader involves an appreciation of leadership theory and knowledge of how a coach can maximize influence and followership through positive role modeling, planning, preparation, and being true to oneself. Coaches must accept their athletes' as well as their own individuality. Coaches who fail miserably are often those who attempt to imitate or emulate other coaches. With insight, knowledge, and sensitivity toward individual differences, all coaches can be successful.

In leadership theory as well as coaching experience, it is evident that there are specific implications of what the coach as a leader should do:

1. Master and apply current knowledge of sport physiology, psychology, and biomechanics.

2. Develop interpersonal skills including the communication skills of speaking, writing, observing, understanding defensive mechanisms, motivating, and listening. Of all the communication skills, coaches are generally the weakest at listening. Interpersonal interactions are critical to sport success, and communication is the key (Mancini & Agnew, 1978). See Chapter 10 for a discussion of effective communication skills.

3. Eliminate all sexist, ageist, heterosexist, racist, ableist, and dehumanizing language.

4. Eliminate any attitude that involves the humiliation of losers and the glorification of winners.

5. Encourage the athletes as well as himself/herself to view the opponent as a challenge and not an enemy.

6. Understand the effects of social reinforcement on individual performance.

7. Control his/her own arousal level and be an example for the athletes of the emotionality needed for successful performance.

8. Help the athletes set their *own* goals. Emphasize the process (participation and playing as well as possible) and not the outcome goal (winning). This is an important concept because goals should be something that an individual can accomplish or control. Athletes can control their own performance but not the opponents'.

9. Live in the present. Do not constantly remind athletes of former winners or of the potential for team success two years hence.

10. Provide opportunities for success through well-planned practices, good game conditions, sensible scheduling, and a pleasant atmosphere. The administrative aspects of a coach's job cannot be overlooked. Planning, preparation, and budgeting are important functions that affect leadership performance. A coach must be a teacher, a leader, and an administrator.

11. Be rational and humanistic.

According to Maslow, the greatest leaders are those who are humble and flexible while also having the strength of character to make decisions that may not be popular (as cited in Sage, 1973). There seems to be a new concern for the humane aspects in sport. Fortunately, athletes are increasingly portrayed as people and are losing, somewhat, their superhero status. Kanter (1977, 1983, 1989) reminds us of the massive social changes we are constantly being bombarded with and that, with increases in technology and better understanding of the profile of the worker and the work environment, we must not forget the importance of personal touches—hi-tech/hi-touch. Bear Bryant was indeed a rare coach for he was able to change with the times. He was "the only one of his generation to coach as successfully in an era when football players used hair dryers in the locker room as he did when they wore crew cuts" (Phillips, 1980, p. 70). As coaches and sport consultants, we should commit to leadership in sport that is dedicated to the ethics and morality of positive growth for all athletes.

Study Questions

1. Why is leadership of particular interest to sport psychology consultants?

2. Describe your perception of the relationship between power and leadership.

3. Describe the authoritarian personality profile.

4. Distinguish between the trait and behavioral leadership theories.

5. Identify and describe five desirable leadership behaviors based on Massimo's (1973) study.

6. Describe in detail one situational theory. How do situational theories differ from trait and behavioral theories?

7. Identify the status of women in leadership positions in sport. In your discussion, describe causes and barriers to the existing status as well as prospects for the future.

8. List and describe three measurement tools used to evaluate leadership.

9. Explain the significance of a role model.

10. List four suggestions for building effective team leaders.

11. Identify factors, traits, and behaviors that you believe are important for the effective leader.

References

Acosta, R. V., & Carpenter, L. J. (1990). Women in sport: A longitudinal study—thirteen year update. Unpublished manuscript, Brooklyn College, N. Y.

Anderson, D. F., & Gill, K. S. (1983). Occupational socialization patterns of men's and women's interscholastic basketball coaches. *Journal of Sport Behavior, 6*, 105–116.

Andrud, W. E. (1970). *The personality of high school, college, and professional football coaches as measured by the Guilford-Zimmerman temperament survey.* Unpublished master's thesis, University of North Dakota, Grand Forks.

Barrow, J. C. (1977). The variables of leadership: A review and conceptual framework. *Academy of Management Review, 2*, 233–251.

Bass, B. M. (1985). Multifactor leadership questionnaire. Binghamton: State University of New York, School of Management.

Bennis, W., & Nanus, B. (1985). *Leaders.* New York: Harper & Row.

Bird, A. (1977). Team structure and success as related to cohesiveness and leadership. *Journal of Social Psychology, 103*, 217–233

Burns, J. M. (1978). *Leadership.* New York: Harper & Row.

Case, B. (1987). Leadership behavior in sport: A field test of situational leadership theory. *International Journal of Sport Psychology, 18*, 256–268.

Cattel, R. B., Eber, H. W., & Tatsouka, M. M. (1980). *Handbook for the Sixteen Personality Factor Questionnaire (16PF).* Champaign, Ill.: Institute for Personality and Ability Testing.

Chelladurai, P., & Carron, A. V. (1978). *Leadership.* Canadian Association for Health, Physical Education and Recreation, Sociology of Sport Monograph Series. Ottawa, Ont.

Chelladurai, P., & Carron, A. V. (1981). Applicability to youth sports of the Leadership Scale for Sports. *Perceptual and Motor Skills, 53*, 361–362.

Chelladurai, P., & Carron, A. V. (1983). Athletic maturity and preferred leadership. *Journal of Sport Psychology, 5*, 371–380.

Chelladurai, P., & Saleh, S. (1978). Preferred leadership in sport. *Canadian Journal of Applied Sport Sciences, 3*, 85–97.

Danielson, R. (1976). *Contingency model of leadership effectiveness: For empirical investigation of its application in sport. Motor Learning, sport psychology, pedagogy, and didactics of physical activity.* Monograph 5. Quebec City, Canada.

Danielson, R. R. (1978). Leadership motivation and coaching classification as related to success in minor league hockey. In D. M. Landers & R. W. Christians (Eds.), *Psychology of motor behavior and sport* (vol. 2). Champaign, Ill.: Human Kinetics.

Danielson, R. R., Zelhart, P. F., & Drake, C. J. (1975). Multidimensional scaling and factor analysis of coaching behaviors as perceived by high school hockey players. *Research Quarterly, 46*, 323–334.

DePree, M. (1987). *Leadership is an art.* New York: Doubleday.

Diesenhouse, S. (1989, August 20). Therapists start to address damage done by therapists. *New York Times*, p. 5.

Dunette, M. (1965). *Personnel selection and placement.* Belmont, Calif.: Wadsworth.

Eitzen, D. S., & Pratt, S. (1989). Gender differences in coaching philosophy: The core of female basketball teams. *Research Quarterly for Exercise and Sport, 60*, 152–158.

Eysenck, H. J., & Eysenck, S. B. (1968). *Eysenck Personality Inventory manual.* London: University of London Press.

Fiedler, F. (1967). *A theory of leadership effectiveness.* New York: McGraw-Hill.

French, J., & Raven, B. (1959). The bases of social power. In D. Cartwright (Ed.), *Studies in social power.* Ann Arbor: Research Center for Group Dynamics, University of Michigan.

Gagen, J. J. (1971). *Risk-taking within football situations of selected football coaches.* Unpublished master's thesis, Kent State University, Kent, Ohio.

George, J. J. (1989). Finding solutions to the problem of fewer female coaches. *The Physical Educator, 46* (1), 2–8.

Ghiselli, E. (1971). *Explorations in managerial talent.* Santa Monica, Calif.: Goodyear.

Gunas, P. J. (1990/91, Winter). The Department of Labor "Glass-ceiling" initiative. *Employment and Relations Today,* pp. 277–280.

Hart, B. A., Hasbrook, C. A., & Mathes, S. A. (1986). An examination of the reduction in the number of female interscholastic coaches. *Research Quarterly for Exercise and Sport, 57* (1), 68–77.

Hemphill, J. F., & Coons, A. E. (1957). Development of the Leader Behavior Description Questionnaire. In R. M. Stodgill & A. E. Coons (Eds.), *Leader behavior: Its description and measurement.* Columbus: Ohio State University Press.

Hendry, L. (1968). Assessment of personality traits in the coach athlete relationship. *Research Quarterly, 39,* 543–551.

Hendry, L. B. (1972). The coaching stereotype. In H. T. A. Whiting (Ed.), *Readings in sport psychology.* London: Kingston.

Hendry, L. (1974). Human factors in sport systems. *Human Factors, 16,* 528–544.

Hersey, P., & Blanchard, K. H. (1969). Life style theory of leadership. *Training and Development Journal, 23,* 26–34.

Hersey, P., & Blanchard, K. H. (1977). *Management of organizational behavior.* Englewood Cliffs, N.J.: Prentice-Hall.

Holmen, M. G., & Parkhouse, B. L. (1981). Trends in the selection of coaches for female athletes: A demographic inquiry. *Research Quarterly for Exercise and Sport, 52* (1), 9–18.

Holroyd, J. C., & Brodsky, A. M. (1977). Psychological attitudes and practices regarding erotic and nonerotic physical contact with patients. *American Psychologist, 32,* 843–849.

Horn, T. S. (1984). Expectancy effects in the interscholastic athletic setting: Methodological considerations. *Journal of Sport Psychology, 6,* 60–76.

House, R. J. (1971). A path–goal theory of leader effectiveness. *Administrative Science Quarterly, 16,* 321–338.

House, R. J. (1976). A 1976 theory of charismatic leadership. In J. G. Hunt & L. L. Larson (Eds.), *Leadership: The winning edge.* Carbondale: Southern Illinois University Press.

Iacocca, L., with Novak, W. (1984). *Iacocca.* New York: Bantam.

Kanter, R. M. (1977). *Men and women of the corporation.* New York: Basic Books.

Kanter, R. M. (1983). *The change masters.* New York: Simon & Schuster.

Kanter, R. M. (1989). *When giants learn to dance.* New York: Simon & Schuster.

Kaplan, E. (1983, January 30). The legend of Vince Lombardi. *Family Weekly.*

King, R. (1985). *Sex stereotyping and physical education.* New Zealand.

Knoppers, A. (1987). Gender and the coaching profession. *Quest, 39,* 9–22.

Knoppers, A. (1989). Coaching: An equal opportunity occupation? *Journal of Physical Education, Recreation, and Dance,* March, pp. 38–43.

Komives, S. R. (1991, March). Gender differences in the relationship of hall directors' transformational and transactional leadership and achieving styles. *Journal of College Student Development, 32,* 155–165.

Lenskji, H. (1986). *Out of bounds: Women, sport, and sexuality.* Toronto, Ont.: Women's Press.

Maier, R., & Laurakis, D. (1981). Some personality correlates of attitudes about sports. *International Journal of Sport Psychology, 12,* 19–22.

Mancini, V., & Agnew, M. (1978). An analysis of teaching and coaching behaviors. In W. Straub, (Ed.), *Sport psychology: An analysis of athlete behavior.* Ithaca, N.Y.: Mouvement Publications.

Massimo, J. (1973). *A psychologist's approach to sport.* Presentation to New England Gymnastic Clinic, Newton, Mass.

Naisbitt, J. (1984). *Megatrends.* New York: Warner Books.

NCAA. (1987, November 5). From the soccer press. *NCAA News.*

Neil, G. I., & Kirby, S. L. (1985). Coaching styles and preferred leadership among rowers and paddlers. *Journal of Sport Behavior, 8,* 3–17.

Ogilvie, B., & Tutko, T. (1966). *Problem athletes and how to handle them.* New York: Pelham Books.

Parkhouse, B. L., & Williams, J. M. (1986). Differential effects of sex and status on evaluation of coaching ability. *Research Quarterly for Exercise and Sport, 57*(1), 53–59.

Phillips, B. (1980, September 29). Football's super-coach. *Time.*

Podd, M. (1972). Ego identity status and morality: The relationship between two developmental contracts. *Developmental Psychology, 6,* 497–507.

Pope, K. S., Keith-Speigel, P., & Tabachnick, B. G. (1986). Sexual attraction to clients. *American Psychologist, 41*(2), 147–158.

Reich, R. (1983). *The next American frontier.* New York: Times Books.

Rosener, J. B. (1990, November-December). Ways women lead. *Harvard Business Review,* pp. 119–125.

Sage, G. H. (1973). The coach as management: Organizational leadership in American sport. *Quest, 19,* 35–40.

Sage, G. (1975). An occupational analysis of the college coach. In D. Ball & L. Loy (Eds.), *Sport and social order.* Reading, Mass.: Addison-Wesley.

Schein, E. (1970). *Organizational psychology.* Englewood Cliffs, N.J.: Prentice-Hall.

Seltzer, J., & Bass, B. M. (1990). Transformational leadership: Beyond initiation and consideration. *Journal of Management, 16,* 693–703.

Sisley, B. L., & Caper, S. A. (1986). High school coaching: Filled with gender differences. *Journal of Physical Education, Recreation, and Dance, 57* (3), 39–43.

Smith, R. E., Smoll, F. L., & Curtis, B. (1979). Coach effectiveness training: A cognitive-behavioral approach to enhancing relationship skills in youth sport coaches. *Journal of Sport Psychology, 1,* 59–75.

Smith, R. E., Smoll, F. L., & Hunt, E. (1977). A system for the behavioral assessment of athletic coaches. *Research Quarterly, 48,* 401–407.

Stogdill, R. (1974). *Handbook of leadership: A survey of theory and research.* New York: Free Press.

Stoner, J. H. F., & Freeman, R. E. (1989). *Management.* Englewood Cliffs, N.J.: Prentice-Hall.

Triandis, H. C. (1971). *Attitude and attitude change.* New York: Wiley.

Von Strache, C. (1979). Players' perceptions of leadership qualities for coaches. *Research Quarterly, 50,* 679–686.

Weber, M. (1968). *Economy and society: An outline of interpretive sociology* (originally published 1925). New York: Bedminster Press.

Weinberg, R., Reveles, M., & Jackson, A. (1984). Attitudes of male and female athletes toward male and female coaches. *Journal of Sport Psychology, 6,* 448–453.

Weiss, M. R., & Friedrichs, W. D. (1986). The influence of leader behaviors, coach attributes, and institutional variables on performance and satisfaction of collegiate basketball teams. *Journal of Sport Psychology, 8,* 332–346.

Styles of Decision Making in Coaching

P. Chelladurai, *Ohio State University*

*A*ll the activities carried out by a coach involve **decision making**, which is defined as the process of selecting an alternative from among many choices to achieve a desired end. For example, the coach has to decide what performance goals to pursue, what activities or programs will lead to the attainment of those goals, who of the available athletes should be selected, what should be the assignments for the selected athletes, and what are ways of motivating the athletes. In addition to these fundamental concerns, the coach needs to make decisions about practice and tournament schedules, travel arrangements and uniform selection, and other routine matters. Every decision the coach makes has a strong impact on the team and its performance. Thus, as has been said of management, coaching is in essence the art and science of decision making.

Apart from the concern with making good decisions, the coach is also faced with the question of how much participation in decision making he/she should allow the members of the team. This is an important concern since member participation may ensure that good decisions will be made and may also enhance the motivation of the athletes. Since the coach has sole authority over the degree and manner of members' participation,

he/she must have a clear grasp of the advantages and disadvantages of such participation and the conditions under which the participation will be most fruitful. This chapter focuses on the specific issue of participation in decision making and discusses theory and research on the topic.

Confounding Factors

First, the process of decision making must be isolated from factors that confound the issue. Three confounding factors in the coaching context are leader's personality, leader's mannerisms, and the substance of a decision.

Decision Making and Personality

The issue of decision styles in coaching has been clouded by the exclusive focus on the personality of the coach. For instance, a number of authors have suggested that coaches, influenced by their personality, tend to be either autocratic or democratic in all instances without reference to the nature of the problems facing them. In contrast, recent theorists suggest that instead of labeling coaches as autocratic or democratic, we should be analyzing the problem situation and designating it as calling for an autocratic or democratic decision-making style.

Decision Making and Leader's Mannerisms

One also must guard against confusing the coach's mannerisms and affectations with his/her decision style. For instance, consider a football coach who presents his playbook for the season to the quarterback with the apparently menacing command: "This is your bible. You better master it." In contrast, another coach may present his playbook with a smile and the comment: "Here is the playbook I drew up during the summer. You may get a kick out of reading it." The obvious difference in their mannerisms should not be allowed to mask the fact that both coaches autocratically decided on the plays.

Style and Substance of Decisions

An important issue regarding leadership style is that the "style" of decision making has been con-founded with the "substance" of the decision. For instance, in Fiedler's (1967) contingency model of leadership effectiveness, a leader is deemed to be either task-oriented or relations-oriented. In addition, the task-oriented leader is regarded as being relatively more autocratic and the relations-oriented leader as relatively more democratic.

Recently, however, there has been an attempt to separate the decision style of the leader from other leadership behaviors. To illustrate, five dimensions of leader behavior in coaching are identified and described in Table 8-1. Of these, training and instruction and positive feedback relate more directly to the task and its performance, whereas social support relates to the personal needs of the athletes. The remaining two dimensions refer to the social process of decision making. It has been found that experienced male athletes prefer more autocratic behavior and at the same time more social support than less experienced athletes (Chelladurai & Carron, 1982). The point is that in earlier leadership theories an autocratic style of decision making and socially supportive behavior were deemed to be negatively related, but recent theories and research indicate that these dimensions of leader behavior are independent of each other.

Table 8-1 **Leader Behavior Dimensions in Sport**

Dimension	Description
Training and Instruction	Behavior of the coach aimed at improving the athletes' performance by emphasizing and facilitating hard and strenuous training; by instructing them in the skills, techniques, and tactics of the sport; by clarifying the relationship among the members; and by structuring and coordinating the activities of the members.
Democratic Behavior	Behavior of the coach that allows greater participation by the athletes in decisions pertaining to group goals, practice methods, and game tactics and strategies.
Autocratic Behavior	Behavior of the coach that involves independence in decision making and stresses personal authority.
Social Support	Behavior of the coach characterized by a concern for the welfare of individual athletes, positive group atmosphere, and warm interpersonal relations with members.
Positive Feedback	Behavior of the coach that reinforces an athlete by recognizing and rewarding good performance.

From: Chelladurai & Saleh (1980).

Decision-Making Processes

Decision making as a significant component of leadership has been viewed from two perspectives: as a cognitive process and as a social process.

Decision Making as a Cognitive Process

The emphasis in decision making as a cognitive process is on the **rationality** of the decision. That is, the concern is with evaluating the available alternatives and selecting the best one to achieve a desired end. Decision makers can arrive at rational decisions only after defining the problem clearly, identifying relevant constraints, generating possible and plausible alternatives, evaluating and ranking the alternatives according to some selected criterion, and then selecting the best alternative in terms of some prespecified criterion. In this view, generating alternatives and evaluating them become crucial to decision making. Thus, the focus here is on the objective and optimal use of available information.

Decision Making as a Social Process

In the context of coaching the **social process** refers to the degree to which members of the team are allowed to participate in decision making and the varying degrees of influence the members have on the decisions. Thus, the social process of decision making may vary from strictly autocratic decision making by the coach to varying degrees of participation by members (e.g., consultation with one or a few members, consultation with all members, group decision making, and delegation). These variations have been called the **decision styles** of the coach (Chelladurai & Haggerty, 1978).

Participative Decision Making

Before discussing the theory and research concerning decision styles in coaching, we will first consider the advantages and disadvantages of team members' participation in decision making.

Advantages

Participation by athletes in decision making beneficially affects the team and its performance in three specific ways. First, such participation en-

hances the rationality of the decision insofar as there is more information available in a group to generate and evaluate alternate pathways to a goal. Thus, the quality of the decision is enhanced. Second, once a participative decision is made, the members feel that it is their own decision, and such feelings of ownership result in proper and efficient execution of the decision. Member participation increases the acceptance of the decision. Finally, participation in decision making is said to contribute to the personal growth of the members by facilitating their feelings of self-worth and self-confidence. This humanistic point of view has led several theorists to emphasize increased participation by members. In the athletic context, Sage (1973) advised that coaches should become more aware of the needs of their athletes and should allow greater participation in deciding on team membership, practice methods, team strategy, and so forth.

Disadvantages

Three notable disadvantages are associated with participative decision making. First, participative decisions are time-consuming. Anyone who has ever served on a committee has experienced tangential discussions and arguments over trivial issues.

A second disadvantage is that groups are relatively less effective in solving complex problems that require the decision maker(s) to keep a number of factors in perspective and to think through a series of steps and procedures that link all the relevant factors. Under such circumstances the group is less likely to make an optimal decision than the best member in the group.

Kelley and Thibaut (1969) provide a good example of the contrast between a simple and complex problem: the solution of a crossword puzzle versus the construction of a crossword puzzle. The solution of a crossword puzzle is a relatively simple problem in which the group will be more proficient than individual members. This is because the group can generate a greater number of alternatives, each of which can easily be judged as correct or incorrect according to the criteria provided. Furthermore, one need not be concerned with all the words in the puzzle at the same time. On the other hand, the construction of a crossword puzzle is more complex because the whole set of words and associated criteria must be kept in perspective and linked in a coherent and logical manner. According to Kelley and Thibaut (1969), the best individual in the group is likely to be more efficient than the group as a whole in this type of task.

A sport-specific example of the same concept would be to involve the defensive football squad in identifying why they are having trouble defending against a specific offensive pattern and then to have them follow up by planning what kind of practice is needed to correct the weakness. This relatively simple problem could easily be resolved by means of participative decision making. The decision would probably result in much more effective action by the players in resolving the problem than if the coach had merely told them what to do. Although there is merit in involving athletes in simple problems like this, it would probably be inefficient and ineffective to expect the defensive squad to deal with the more complex problem of drawing up the entire defensive game plan for an upcoming competition.

The third disadvantage of participative decision making is that its efficacy is heavily dependent upon the degree of integration within the group. If the group is marked by internal conflict and rivalry, participation in decision making may result in one of two negative outcomes. First, the internal conflict may be further accentuated; one subgroup may feel that it has won the argument, but the other may not accept the decision. This conflict is not conducive to effective implementation of the decision. The other possibility is that the subgroups may "smooth over" the issue and arrive at a compromise solution that is not optimal.

In addition to the disadvantages described above, which may be inherent in participation per se, a number of attributes of a problem situation may preclude or restrict member participation in decision making. Thus, it is necessary to analyze the mix of relevant characteristics of the situation before selecting the appropriate decision style. The following sections describe a framework purported to facilitate such analyses and the research results thereof.

A Normative Model of Decision Styles in Coaching

In 1978 Chelladurai and Haggerty proposed a normative model of decision styles in coaching, based largely on the works of Vroom and his associates (Vroom & Jago, 1974; Vroom & Yetton, 1973) and on heuristics. Briefly, their model identifies the following seven problem attributes deemed relevant to the athletic context:

1. *Time pressure.* Many of the decisions in the sport context, as in the case of military units in action, have to be made under great time pressure. The lack of time may preclude participative decisions.

2. *Decision quality required.* Some problems require optimal solutions (e.g., the selection of a quarterback in football), but in other cases the coach may be satisfied with any one of several minimally acceptable alternatives (e.g., the selection of a captain). Several members can carry out the functions of a captain. In fact, some teams elect a different captain for each game. But since the quarterback's function is more instrumental to the team's success, the best person(s) with the necessary abilities should be selected. Therefore, the coach should be more concerned about the quality of the decision in selecting a quarterback than in selecting a captain.

3. *Information location.* Information is the basis of high-quality decisions in any context. Such information in athletics relates to the strategies and tactics of the sport; its rules and their interpretations; and to the athletes, their capabilities, attitudes, needs, and preferences. The decision style adopted by the coach should allow for the participation of all those who possess the information so that a high-quality decision can be made. At the same time, the coach should guard against the "pooling of ignorance," which results when members without the necessary expertise and knowledge participate in decisions.

4. *Problem complexity.* On the basis of Kelley and Thibaut's (1969) work discussed earlier, Chelladurai and Haggerty suggested that the coach or one player with the necessary information is more likely to make the optimal decision than a group in the selection of plays where the relative abilities of team members and opponents, the sequence of events, and the various options and their consequences all must be held in perspective.

5. *Group acceptance.* It was noted previously that the acceptance of a decision by the group is

essential for effective implementation of the decision. However, acceptance of some decisions may not be critical. For instance, the decision to use a full-court press would be successful only if the players accept the press as appropriate and as within their capabilities. In contrast, acceptance of a decision to practice foul shots every day is not critical, as it is quite specific and its execution can easily be monitored.

6. *Coach's power.* The coach's power base may consist of one or more of the following: (a) control over rewards; (b) control over punishments; (c) the authority residing in the position of a coach; (d) the interpersonal liking and admiration the athletes have for the coach; and (e) the expertise, superior knowledge, and past performance of the coach. It should be pointed out that group acceptance emanating from the coach's referent and expert power is of real essence. The other three bases of power (reward, coercion, and legitimacy) only elicit compliance, not acceptance.

7. *Group integration.* Group integration encompasses the quality of interpersonal relations on the team and the relative homogeneity of members in ability and tenure. If the team is not integrated, the participative process will not yield optimal decisions and may weaken the already fragile team consensus and team spirit.

The next component of the normative model is the specification of the following three decision styles:

1. *Autocratic style.* In the autocratic style the coach makes the final decision. Although consultation with one or more players is included within the autocratic style in this model, other authors (Vroom & Yetton, 1973) prefer to treat this consultation process as a separate style of decision making.

2. *Participative style.* In participative decision making the group, which includes the coach as just another member, makes the decision.

3. *Delegative style.* In the delegative style the coach delegates the decision making to one or more members. The coach's involvement is restricted to announcing the decision and/or implementing it.

Having specified the attributes of a problem situation and the three decision styles, Chelladurai and Haggerty presented the model in the form of a flowchart as shown in Figure 8-1. The attributes are listed as questions at the top of the chart. The decision maker is required to follow the branches of the flowchart as indicated by the yes or no responses to the questions. At the terminal nodes the appropriate decision styles are indicated.

Although Chelladurai and Haggerty (1978) acknowledged that their model was fashioned after the framework provided by Vroom and Yetton (1973), there are considerable differences between the two approaches. Therefore, the results of empirical research carried out with the Vroom and Yetton model cannot be used to substantiate the Chelladurai and Haggerty model. Thus, the latter remains a heuristic model without any empirical base. Furthermore, the two studies conducted in this regard are not entirely supportive of the model. The next section further elucidates these research efforts.

Research on Decision Styles in Coaching

Early Studies at University Level

A study by Gordon (1983) was the only attempt to test the Chelladurai and Haggerty model in its entirety. Gordon's study was concerned with soccer coaches' self-reports on what decision styles they would use in any given situation and on what other coaches would use in the same situation, as well as with soccer players' preferences for a specific decision style in a given situation and their perceptions of what decision style their coaches would use in the same situation.

Chelladurai and Arnott's study (1985) was concerned only with the preferences of university-level basketball players of both sexes. Furthermore, their study included only four of the seven problem attributes (quality requirement, coach's information, problem complexity, and group integration). They argued that these four attributes were more critical in the determination of players' preferences.

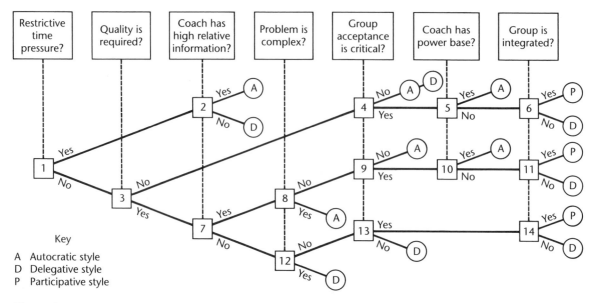

Figure 8-1 **A normative model of decision styles in coaching** *Source:*
Reprinted from "A Normative Model of Decision-Making Styles in
Coaching," by P. Chelladurai and T. R. Haggerty, 1978, *Athletic Ad-
ministration, 13*(I), p. B. Used with permission.

In both studies the categories of decision styles were autocratic, consultive, participative, and delegative. It must be noted that these authors, in contrast to Chelladurai and Haggerty (1978), separated the consultive style from the autocratic style. The consultive style was defined as the coach's making the final decision after consulting with one or more members of the team.

The results of the two studies are summarized in Table 8-2. The notable finding of both studies was that the delegative style was totally rejected by the respondents. Obviously, this finding is contrary to the normative model (see Figure 8-1), wherein the delegative style was prescribed in 7 of the 15 situations. The normative model prescribed the delegative style only under the simultaneous occurrence of the conditions that (1) the coach does not have the necessary information, which prohibits him or her from making the decision, and (2) the group is not integrated, which precludes the participative style. However, this line of reasoning overlooks the relative influences of team members in the three decision styles. For instance, Chelladurai and Arnott (1985) argued that the four decision styles could be placed on a continuum on the basis of the degree of the coach's influence in the decisions. That is, the coach's influence ranges from 100% in the autocratic style to 0% in the delegative style, as shown in Figure 8-2. However, from the players' perspective both the autocratic style and the delegative style exclude them from participation (see Figure 8-2).

Apparently, members would forego their influence in favor of the coach rather than in favor of another teammate(s). . . . One possible explanation for this result could be that sharing of the decision-making power with one or more (but limited) members from the group is antithetical to the egalitarian notion inherent in a team. That is, such delegation to a few athletes may be construzzed as preferential treatment by the rest of the team. (Chelladurai & Arnott, 1985, pp. 21–22)

High School Studies Based on Vroom and Yetton Decision Styles

Based on the earlier findings that delegation is not a viable option in team sports, Chelladurai, Hag-

Table 8-2 **Percentage Distribution of Decision Style Choices**

	Decision Styles			
	A	*C*	*G*	*D*
University Soccer (Gordon, 1983)				
Coaches' Own Choices	46.3%	33.3%	18.5%	1.9%
Coaches' Perceptions of Other Coaches	45.5%	41.2%	12.5%	0.8%
Players' Preferences	31.2%	41.9%	12.5%	0.8%
Players' Perceptions of Coaches' Choices	43.0%	39.6%	15.4%	2.0%
University Basketball (Chelladurai & Arnott, 1985)				
Players' Preferences				
Females	33.0%	18.1%	46.9%	2.0%
Males	38.9%	25.8%	34.1%	1.2%

A = Autocratic; *C* = Consultive; *G* = Group; *D* = Delegative

gerty, and Baxter (1989), and Chelladurai and Quek (1991) used the five decision styles prescribed by Vroom and Yetton for group problems. These five decision styles are described in Table 8-3.

Further, only five of the problem attributes specified by Chelladurai and Haggerty—quality requirement, coach's information, problem complexity, acceptance requirements, and team integration–were included in these two studies. Time pressure was excluded because its presence automatically led to the autocratic or delegative style based only on coach's information without reference to the other attributes. Coach's power was excluded since it was expected to be similar across comparable institutions (i.e., universities within one province).

The subjects in the Chelladurai, Haggerty, and Baxter (1989) study were 22 coaches (males = 15; females = 7), and 99 players (males = 53; females = 46) from university basketball teams in Ontario, Canada. The coaches indicated their choice of a decision style in specific situations, while the athletes expressed their preferences of a particular decision style in the same situations. Chelladurai and Quek's (1991) study was concerned with the decision-style choices of 51 coaches of high school

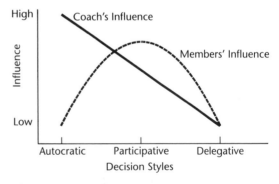

Figure 8-2 **Coach's and members' relative influence in three decision styles**

boys' basketball teams in and around Toronto, Canada.

The results of the two studies are presented in Table 8-4. Referring to the Chelladurai, Haggerty, and Baxter (1989) study, the distribution of decision-style choices was significantly associated with group membership (coaches, male players, and female players). Also, within each group the actual distribution was significantly different from

Table 8-3 Decision Styles in Coaching

Autocratic I (AI)	The coach solves the problem himself/herself, using the information available to him/her at the time.
Autocratic II (AII)	The coach obtains the necessary information from relevant players, then decides himself/herself. The coach may or may not tell the players what the problem is in getting the information. The role played by the players is clearly one of providing information to the coach, rather than generating or evaluating solutions.
Consultative I (CI)	The coach consults with the players *individually* and then makes the decision himself/herself. The coach's decision may or may not reflect the players' influence.
Consultative II (CII)	The coach consults with his/her players *as a group* and then makes the decision himself/herself. The coach's decision may or may not reflect the players' influence.
Group (G)	The coach shares the problem with his/her players. Then the coach and the players jointly make the decision without any influence on the coach's part.

Modified from: Vroom & Yetton, 1973.

Table 8-4 Percentage Distribution of Decision Style Choices

	Decision Styles				
	AI	AII	CI	CII	G
University Basketball (Chelladurai, Haggerty, & Baxter, 1988)					
Coaches	34.8%	20.2%	9.8%	20.2%	15.1%
Male Players	28.5%	16.8%	13.9%	21.3%	19.5%
Female Players	30.1%	14.0%	13.2%	25.8%	16.3%
High School Basketball (Chelladurai & Quek, 1990)					
Coaches	32.5%	15.4%	9.7%	1.3%	21.1%

the expected equal distribution across the five decision styles. The *AI* style (coach making decision alone) was chosen more often than any other style by each group. The *CII* style (consultation with all players on a group basis) was the second most popular choice in all three groups. It must also be noted that the participative style (*GII*) was chosen less than 20% of the times in all three groups. When the *AI*, *AII*, and *CI* styles are combined (be-

cause they involve minimal influence from the members), the total percentage amounts to 64.8% for coaches, 59.4% for male players, and 57.3% for female players.

The frequency distribution of the total choices in Chelladurai and Quek's (1991) study is presented in Table 8-4 along with those of Chelladurai, Haggerty, and Baxter (1989). Autocratic style without getting more information (*AI*) was the most preferred choice (32.5%) and consultation with a few individuals (*CI*) was the least preferred choice (9.7%) of the total decision-style choices.

Implication of the Research

The foregoing studies show that the autocratic style is preferred both by coaches and players to a greater extent than what is hypothesized by theorists. It must be recalled that the subjects in these studies were choosing a decision style in different situations involving the presence or absence of the problem attributes listed in Table 8-1. Both players and coaches changed their decision style preferences according to the variations in the situations. Thus, it is appropriate to dub the *situations* as democratic or autocratic rather than labeling the coaches as democratic or autocratic.

It must be noted that the preceding studies were concerned with team sports (soccer and basketball). The efficacy of specific decision styles needs to be verified in the context of differing types of sports (e.g., small versus large teams, open versus closed sports, individual versus team sports). For instance, the delegative style that was rejected by the soccer players (Gordon, 1983) and basketball players (Chelladurai & Arnott, 1985) could indeed be a viable decision style in individual sports that present a dyadic setting instead of a group setting as in the case of a team. That is, an individual sport team consists of numerous but distinct units consisting of the coach and each individual athlete, whereas there is only one unit in the case of a team sport (the coach and all athletes). Thus, the individual sport coach is not as much burdened with the task of coordinating the activities of the athletes as a team sport coach. Further, the individual sport coach need not be unduly concerned about consistency of his/her behavior toward all athletes. Therefore, delegating the decision-making authority to some athletes and not to others may be acceptable in individual sports.

It was alluded to earlier that the delegative style is antithetical to the egalitarian orientations of team sports. But the notion of egalitarianism may not be relevant in sports characterized by a hierarchical substructure that places one or more players in a superior position (e.g., the quarterback in North American football). Even in sports without a formal hierarchy, there may exist an in-

formal and socially acceptable "pecking order." Such stratified patterns of interactions may permit the delegation of decision making to those informal leaders.

There have been reports that females prefer more participation than males do (e.g., Chelladurai & Saleh, 1978). The two studies that included females yielded contradictory results. While Chelladurai and Arnott (1985) found that the females preferred more participation, Chelladurai, Haggerty, and Baxter (1989) did not find any gender difference. These latter authors argued that "the gender differences reported earlier were a function of less explicit description of the decision situations and the inclusion of fewer decision styles" (p. 213). Additional research is needed before any definitive statements can be made on this issue.

A significant finding was that both coaches and players preferred less participation when the quality requirement was not included and the problem was simple. More participation was preferred when one of these attributes was present in the absence of the other. These results suggest that the democratic selection of a captain and/or the starting five in basketball, for instance, may not have the desired effects. Such decisions may be considered trivial since the captain acts merely as a figurehead without any vested authority. With regard to the election of the starting five, there is no substance to the decision as long as the coach reserves the right to substitute players at the first whistle.

An overriding consideration in the choice of a decision style by a coach may be his/her inability to successfully engage in participatory procedures. As Vroom and Jago (1988) point out, the skills required to make autocratic decisions are different from those required to make participative decisions. To make an effective autocratic decision the coach must be able to identify alternatives, evaluate them, and then choose the best alternative. In more participative decision processes the coach needs the skills of a facilitator and a discussion leader. More specifically, the coach needs the skills to (a) state the problem in clear terms, (b) conduct the discussion making sure that it does not go off in tangents, and (c) assist the group in reaching a good decision without polarizing into cliques. Some coaches may choose more autocratic decisions because they feel that they do not possess the unique skills necessary to make participative decisions. It is important, therefore, that future research relate the decision-style choices of coaches to their abilities in participative procedures. It is also important that training in participative procedures become part of coach development programs.

Summary

Theories relating to the social process of decision making and the related research indicate that it is more useful to assume that situations call for autocratic or participative decision making rather than merely to categorize coaches as autocratic or democratic. This is not to deny the influence of the coach's personality but to point out that the coach's personality is only part of the total situation, which includes the team members' personalities and preferences and the type of problem involved.

There is a common tendency to view the autocratic style as something evil, indulged in only by despots and dictators as a device for furthering their own interests. Contrastingly, the participative style is viewed as a humanistic approach aimed at the welfare of the members. Coaches and athletes need to understand that these contrasting decision styles are not value-laden and that the autocratic style can be associated with humanism and benevolence.

Finally, research in the area of decision styles, although rather limited, clearly shows that the autocratic style is quite acceptable to the athletes in certain circumstances. It appears that coaches need to select a decision style appropriate to the particular situation rather than being guided by a belief that participative decisions are always superior and/or always preferred.

Study Questions

1. List and explain briefly three factors that may "cloud" the issue of participation in decision making.

2. Categorize each leader behavior dimension in Table 8-1 as task, social, or decision making-oriented.

3. Distinguish between the cognitive and social processes of decision making. Give examples from sport.

4. Describe the advantages and disadvantages of participative decision making in team sports.

5. List the seven problem attributes that Chelladurai and Haggerty (1978) deemed relevant to decision styles in the athletic context.

6. The results of a study showed that both coaches and players rejected the delegative style. How is this result explained in terms of coaches' and players' perceived influence across each of the three styles (autocratic, participative, and delegative)?

7. Give examples of situations where the coach should make a decision (a) without consultation (*AI*), (b) after consulting with the whole group (*CII*), and (c) jointly with group members (*G*). Explain why.

8. Give examples of how decision-style choices might differ in individual as opposed to team sport.

9. What factors within the coach make him/her more autocratic or more participative in decision making?

References

Chelladurai, P., & Arnott, M. (1985). Decision styles in coaching: Preferences of basketball players. *Research Quarterly for Exercise and Sport, 56*(1), 15–24.

Chelladurai, P., & Carron, A. V. (1982, May). *Task characteristics and individual differences, and their relationship to preferred leadership in sports.* Paper presented at the annual meeting of the North American Society for the Psychology of Sport and Physical Activity, College Park, Md.

Chelladurai, P., & Haggerty, T. R. (1978). A normative model of decision styles in coaching. *Athletic Administrator, 13,* 6–9.

Chelladurai, P., Haggerty, T. R., & Baxter, P. R. (1989). Decision styles choices of university basketball coaches and players. *Journal of Sports and Exercise Psychology, 11,* 201–215.

Chelladurai, P., & Quek, C. B. (1991). Situational and personality effects on the decision style choices of high school basketball coaches. Unpublished manuscript. University of Western Ontario, Canada.

Chelladurai, P., & Saleh, S. D. (1978). Preferred leadership in sports. *Canadian Journal of Applied Sport Sciences, 3,* 85–92.

Chelladurai, P., & Saleh, S. D. (1980). Dimensions of leader behavior in sports. Development of a leadership scale. *Journal of Sport Psychology, 2*(1), 34–45.

Fiedler, F. E. (1967). *A theory of leadership effectiveness.* New York: McGraw-Hill.

Gordon, S. (1983, July). *Decision-making styles in university soccer coaching.* Paper presented at the FISU conference, World University Games, Edmonton, Canada.

Kelley, H. H., & Thibaut, J. W. (1969). Group problem solving. In G. Lindzey & E. Arconson (Eds.), *The handbook of social psychology* (2nd ed.) (vol. 4) (pp. 1–101). Reading, Mass.: Addison-Wesley.

Sage, G. H. (1973). The coach as management: Organizational leadership in American sport. *Quest, 19,* 35–40.

Vroom, V. H., & Jago, A. G. (1974). On the validity of the Vroom-Yetton model. *Journal of Applied Psychology, 63,* 151–162.

Vroom, V. H., & Jago, A. G. (1988). *The new leadership: Managing participation in organizations.* Englewood Cliffs, N.J.: Prentice-Hall.

Vroom, V. H., & Yetton, R. N. (1973). *Leadership and decision making.* Pittsburgh, Penn.: University of Pittsburgh Press.

The Sport Team as an Effective Group

Albert V. Carron, *The University of Western Ontario*

*M*embership and involvement in groups is a fundamental characteristic of our society. We band together in a large number and variety of groups for social reasons or to carry out more effectively some job or task. Thus, each of us interacts daily with numerous other people in group settings—in the family, at work, in social situations, on sport teams. The result is a reciprocal exchange of influence; we exert an influence on other people in groups, and, in turn, those groups and their members have an influence on us. The following two examples illustrate just how powerful this influence can be.

In January 1980, Tony Conigliaro, a former Boston Red Sox baseball player, was driving with his brother when he suffered a massive heart attack—he experienced "sudden death." At least six minutes passed before CPR was administered and his heart was stimulated into activity. However, he remained in a coma for four days, and the prognosis for any significant recovery was bleak. A lack of oxygen to the brain for as few as four minutes can produce permanent brain damage. Also, people who are comatose for the length of time experienced by Conigliaro are almost never able to walk, talk, or look after themselves totally again.

Conigliaro's family refused to believe the prognosis. They were at his side constantly, talking, encouraging, providing love and affection. Slowly Conigliaro fought back, began to talk, and showed improvements that astounded his doctors. In fact, as Maximillian Kaulback, one of his doctors, stated, "This case is beyond science.... I wouldn't be surprised if someday it was proven that the input of the family in cases like this is significant" (quoted in McCallum, 1982, p. 72). The incident is powerful and moving; it also illustrates the importance of the family's positive influence—its love, concern, and physical and emotional support. The second illustration, however, shows another side of group influence.

On August 9 and 10, 1969, Charles Manson and four accomplices, three women and a man, brutally and senselessly killed seven people. Actress Sharon Tate, who was pregnant, and four others were killed the first night and Leno and Rosemary La Bianca the second. The two sets of victims were not related in any meaningful way, and there was no apparent motive for the murders. After the longest trial in American history, Manson and his accomplices were found guilty. The question of how such an atrocity could come about was more difficult to puzzle out. Psychiatrist Joel Hochman, commenting on the role of one of Manson's female accomplices, reported that "we might suggest the possibility that she may be suffering from a condition of *folie a famille*, a kind of shared madness within a group situation" (quoted in Bugliosi & Gentry, 1974, p. 461). Vincent Bugliosi, the prosecutor for the case, also felt that the influence of the group was significant. He described the Manson group as follows:

> There was also love, a great deal of love.
> To overlook this would be to miss one of the strongest bonds that existed among them. The love grew out of their sharing, their communal problems and pleasures, their relationship with Charlie. They were a real family in almost every sense of that word, a sociological unit complete to brothers, sisters, substitute mothers, linked by the domination of an all-knowing, all-powerful patriarch. (Bugliosi & Gentry, 1974, p. 484)

These anecdotes show the dramatic influence that groups can have on their members. In the Conigliaro case the influence was a positive one, whereas in the Manson case the influence was negative and destructive. The fundamental question is how groups can come to exert such influence. From a coaching perspective, insight into this issue could produce possible prescriptions for the development of a positive, productive sport group—an effective, cohesive team. In this chapter, both the nature of groups and group cohesion are discussed and some suggestions for the development of effective groups in sport settings are offered.

The Nature of Groups

Definition

Just what is a group? Of what does it consist? A number of definitions have been suggested, each highlighting some special feature or characteristic of a group. Some of the more important of these features of groups are a collective identity, a sense of shared purpose, structured patterns of interaction, structured methods of communication, personal and task interdependence, and interpersonal attraction (Carron, 1980).

A football team* can be used to illustrate each of these definitional components. For example, a

*This example is taken from Carron, 1981, pp. 246–247 and is used with the permission of Human Kinetics, Champaign, Illinois.

collective identity exists when individual team members, fellow teammates, and nonteam members all view the group as a unit distinguishable from other units: "We are teammates on the University of Xebec Scullers." The sense of shared purpose or objectives readily develops from the strong task-oriented nature of sport. With a football team this can vary from an awareness and agreement on short-term objectives (attend weight-training sessions in the off season) to long-term ones (win the championship).

Numerous examples are available for the structured patterns of interaction that exist within a team. The interrelated blocking assignments for various offensive plays and the defensive responsibilities under different alignments are unique task interactions within any specific team. Any newcomer to a football team requires some time to become completely familiar with its specific system. Similarly, the differentiation made explicitly or implicitly between rookies and veterans early in training camp (locker room assignments, uniform distinctions, hazing practices) is an example of the patterned social interactions existing within any sport team.

The argot of football in general—"blitz," "drive," "block," "fly," "curl," "trap"—and the way it is selectively used on particular teams provides an example of structured modes of communication. The specific terminology used to convey particular offensive and defensive assignments ("R-221," "Man," "Z-Curl") is another. Although members of a team can readily translate these apparently meaningless symbols into something meaningful, the nonteam member or uninitiated observer cannot.

Personal and task interdependence are inherent within the nature of sport itself; the rules of sport dictate the size, general structure, and organization of the sport team. Thus, an individual cannot play football alone, a specific number of players is permitted on the field at any given time, there are general rules on how they must be aligned, interaction with the opposition must conform to designated behavioral standards, and so on. In essence, then, each team member is inextricably bound to his/her teammates if competition is desired.

Finally, although there are documented exceptions, interpersonal attraction generally evolves from sport team participation. Therefore, attraction is usually present in some degree on most teams, although it is neither necessary nor sufficient to define a sport team.

Groups Versus Collections of Individuals

Individuals who study groups often make an important distinction between a group and a collection of individuals. Alvin Zander (1982), the former director of the Research Center for Group Dynamics at the University of Michigan, highlighted this issue when he pointed out that

> a group is a collection or set of individuals who interact with and depend on each other. A number of persons jointly engaged in an activity—traveling on a sightseeing tour, picking apples in an orchard, working in a personnel department, attending a seminar—are not necessarily a group, but it may become one. (pp. 1–2)

Zander went on to say that 10 characteristics that differentiate a group from a collection of individuals are that people in groups (1) talk freely, (2) are interested in the welfare of the collective as a whole, (3) feel that their associates are helpful, (4) try to assist those associates, (5) refer to the collection of individuals as "we" and to other collections as "they," (6) faithfully participate in group activities, (7) are not primarily interested in individual accomplishments, (8) are concerned with the activities of other members, (9) do not see others as rivals, and (10) are not often absent.

Sport teams possess all of these characteristics—they are groups in every sense of the word. And any group can become more effective. On a sport team, coaches or leaders must facilitate the development of the sense of "we" and reduce the importance of "I." Associated with the development of a stronger sense of "we" is an increase in group cohesiveness. The terms "cohesion" and "group" are tautological—if a group exists, cohesion is present.

Group Cohesion

Definition

Groups are dynamic, not static. They exhibit life and vitality, interaction, and activity. Their vitality may be reflected in many ways—some positive, others negative. For example, at times the group and its members may be in harmony; at other times, conflict and tension may predominate. Sometimes communication may be excellent between leaders and members, but at other times, it may be nonexistent. Also, commitment to the group's goals and purposes may vary over time. All these variations represent different behavioral manifestations of an underlying, fundamental group property that is referred to as "cohesiveness."

In an early, classic definition advanced by Festinger, Schachter, and Back (1950), **cohesiveness** was viewed as the sum of the forces that cause members to remain in the group. Subsequently, a second, classic definition was proposed by Gross and Martin (1951), who considered it to be the resistance of the group to disruptive forces. More recently, Carron (1982) proposed that cohesiveness is the "dynamic process which is reflected in the tendency for a group to stick together and remain united in the pursuit of its goals and objectives" (p. 124).

Two points should be made about this last definition. First, the use of the word "dynamic" is an acknowledgment that the way individual group members feel about one another and about the group and its goals and objectives changes over time and with experiences. Generally, the longer groups stay together, the stronger the bonding becomes. But cohesiveness is not static; it develops and then declines slightly, renews itself and increases again, and then declines slightly. This pattern is repeated throughout the course of a group's existence.

Second, the "goals and objectives" of all groups are complex and varied. Consequently, cohesiveness has many dimensions or aspects—it is perceived in multiple ways by different groups and their members. It has been proposed (Brawley, Carron, & Widmeyer, 1987; Carron, Widmeyer, & Brawley, 1985; Widmeyer, Brawley, & Carron, 1985) that these multidimensional perceptions of the group are organized and integrated by individual members into two general categories. The first category, **group integration**, represents each individual's perceptions of the group as a total unit, set, or collection. The second, **individual attractions to the group**, represents each individual's personal attractions to the group. Both of these categories of perceptions about the degree of unity within the group are also assumed to be manifested in two principal ways: in relation to the group's *task* and

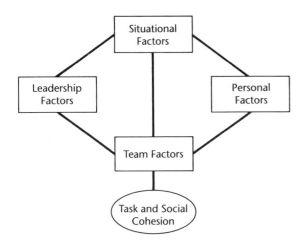

Figure 9-1 **A conceptual model for group cohesiveness** *Sources:* Brawley, Carron, & Widmeyer, 1986; Carron, Widmeyer, & Brawley, 1985; Widmeyer, Brawley, & Carron, 1985.

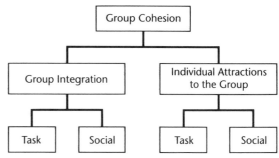

Figure 9-2 **A frame of reference to illustrate the factors contributing to cohesiveness in sport teams** *Source:* Adapted from Carron, 1982.

in terms of the *social* aspects of the group. This conception of cohesiveness is depicted in Figure 9-1. As the figure shows, cohesion within sport groups is considered to have four facets: individual attractions to the group—task, individual attractions to the group—social, group integration—task, and group integration—social.

The Antecedents and Consequences of Cohesiveness

Not surprisingly, because cohesiveness is multidimensional a wide variety of factors contribute to its development. A frame of reference, proposed by Carron (1982) can be used to organize these factors into four main categories (see Figure 9-2). One of these categories, **situational** (environmental) **factors**, is an acknowledgment that the social setting, the physical environment, and various structural aspects of the group contribute to cohesiveness.

Characteristics of individual team members also influence the nature and amount of cohesiveness that develops; the category **individual factors** represents these factors. **Leadership factors**, the third category, is an acknowledgment that decision styles, leader behaviors, and leader–member relations also influence group cohesiveness. The fourth category, *team factors*, represents the group-based aspects that produce a stronger bond, sense of "we," commitment to the collective. In the fol-

lowing sections, some of the main factors within each general category are identified and specific protocols, procedures, and techniques that might be used to enhance cohesiveness in sport teams are discussed.

Developing a Team Concept

Situational Factors

Individuals who are in close **proximity**, who are physically close to each other, have a greater tendency to bond together. Physical proximity by itself is not always sufficient for producing cohesiveness, but being in close contact and having the opportunity for interaction and communication do hasten group development. Some situations in sport that ensure physical proximity among group members include having a specific team locker room, residence, or training table. In youth sport situations, scheduling games that require the team to travel together in a bus or car is also beneficial. The important point is that group members should be placed in situations where interaction is inevitable.

A second situational factor that contributes to the development of cohesiveness is **distinctiveness**. As a set of individuals becomes more separate, more distinctive from others, feelings of oneness

Table 9-1 **Examples of Specific Strategies Suggested by Fitness Class Instructors to Enhance Group Cohesiveness**

Factor	Example of Intervention Strategies Used
Distinctiveness	Have a group name. Make up a group t-shirt. Hand out neon headbands and/or shoelaces. Make up posters/slogans for the class.
Individual Positions	Use three ares of the pool depending on fitness level. Have signs to label parts of the group. Use specific positions for low-, medium-, and high-impact exercisers. Let them pick their own spot and encourage them to remain in it throughout year.
Group Norms	Have members introduce each other to increase social aspects. Encourage members to become fitness friends. Establish a goal to lose weight together. Promote a smart work ethic as a group characteristic.
Individual Sacrifices	Use music in aqua fitness (some do not want music). Ask two or three people for a goal for the day. Ask regulars to help new people—fitness friends. Ask people who aren't concerned with weight loss to make a sacrifice for the group on some days (more aerobics) and people who are to also make a sacrifice on other days (more mat work).
Interaction and Communication	Use partner work and have them introduce themselves. Introduce the person on the right and left. Work in groups of five and take turns showing a move. Use more partner activities.

Adapted from: Carron & Spink, 1991; Spink & Carron, 1991.

and unity increase. Traditionally, distinctiveness is achieved through team uniforms and mottos, by having special initiation rites, by providing special privileges, or demanding special sacrifices. In an attempt to increase group cohesiveness in an exercise setting, Carron and Spink (1991) had fitness instructors engage in a team-building workshop. The instructors came up with a series of techniques and strategies that they used in their classes over a 13-week period (see Table 9-1). These techniques and strategies were highly effective in increasing the level of task cohesiveness of the groups. Subsequently, these same strategies and techniques were used in another set of exercise classes (Spink & Carron, 1991) and both individual adherence and task cohesiveness were positively affected.

Many of the factors that make athletes distinct from the general population are taken for granted. These include year-round intensive training programs and reduced time for social activities or part-time employment. The coach should highlight

such factors to develop a stronger feeling of commonality. Finally, emphasizing the sense of tradition and the history of the organization or team can contribute to the feeling of distinctiveness.

The team's *size* is also associated with the development of cohesiveness. Some recent research by Widmeyer, Brawley, and Carron (1990) has shown that there is an inverted-*U* relationship between social cohesion and team size in intramural basketball teams. That is, moderate-size groups showed the greatest cohesiveness, while larger and smaller groups exhibited the least. In research by Widmeyer and Williams (1991) using only the travel rosters of women's NCAA golf teams, however, social cohesion did not vary with team size.

In this same research with intramural basketball teams (Widmeyer, Brawley, & Carron, 1990), it was also shown that task cohesiveness decreases with increasing group size. Widmeyer and colleagues felt that this decrease could be attributed to the fact that it is more difficult to obtain consensus and task commitment in larger groups. In their research with women's NCAA golf teams, Widmeyer and Williams (1991) found that increasing team size was associated with increasing task cohesion. However, they only tested the 4–5 competitors on the travel rosters who were actually involved in the competition. The maximum team size among the teams examined was 12. Consequently, it is possible that the responses from the 7–8 golfers who were not on the travel rosters might have substantially altered the profile of the team's cohesiveness.

Personal Factors

One personal factor often cited as a contributor to cohesiveness is *similarity*—similarity in attitudes, aspirations, commitments, and ability. As Zander (1982) noted:

> Birds of a feather flock together, and create a more distinct entity when they do. People too form a better unit if they are alike, and an effective leader develops oneness within a set by encouraging likeness among members. To do this, she recruits persons who will interact well because of similar purpose, background, training, experience, or temperament…. Persons whose beliefs do not fit together well have a hard time forming a strong group. (p. 3)

In their study with golf teams, Widmeyer and Williams (1991) noted that similarity in terms of playing background (i.e., whether the golfer came from a country club or public courses) and number of years of experience on the team did not correlate with cohesiveness. Similarity in all aspects may not be critical in sport teams. On most teams, differences in personality, ethnicity, racial background, economic background, ability, and numerous other factors are inevitable. What the coach must do is work to develop a similarity in attitude about factors such as the group's performance goals, expectations for individual behavior, and codes of conduct for practices, games, and situations away from the sport environment.

The most important personal factor associated with the development of both task and social cohesiveness in sport teams is individual *satisfaction*. Satisfaction is derived from many sources in sport (Widmeyer & Williams, 1991). The quality of the competition is one element; having opportunities for social interactions with teammates is

another. Athletes also need to feel that they are improving in skill, or they are not satisfied. As well, satisfaction results from the recognition of others—parents, coaches, teammates, fellow students, the public. And, of course, the athlete's relationship with his/her coach is yet another potential source of satisfaction/dissatisfaction. When these elements are satisfying, cohesiveness is enhanced.

A personal factor associated with cohesiveness is *commitment* to the team. One technique for promoting commitment is to have more satisfied or prestigious team members make personal sacrifices for the group (Zander, 1982). This not only produces a sense of commitment and involvement in the individual, but it shows other team members how the welfare of the team is perceived by important group members. Some examples of the sacrifices generated by a group of fitness instructors to enhance the cohesiveness in their classes are presented in Table 9-1.

Leadership Factors

The interrelationships between the coach, the athlete, cohesiveness, and performance are complex. In a mutiny, for example, cohesion is high, the leader–subordinate relationship is poor (and the leader is excluded from the group), and performance from an organizational perspective is poor. One example of the complex interrelationship between coach, athlete, cohesiveness, and performance comes from a study by Widmeyer and Williams (1991). They had golf coaches rate the importance that they attached to task cohesion, the importance that they attached to social cohesion, and the number of techniques that they used to foster cohesiveness. These measures were not related to their athletes' perceptions of the amount of team cohesiveness. In short, in the Widmeyer and Williams study, coaches were not crucial to the development of group cohesion.

Another example of the complex relationship arises when a leader is on the fringe of the group from the perspective of cohesiveness—this can produce problems. The perceptions a group has about itself, about other groups, and/or nongroup members often become distorted with increased group cohesiveness. The group tends to be very favorable in its perception of its own members and to overvalue its own contributions, importance, and performance. Also, the group tends to undervalue the contributions, importance, and performance of other groups or nongroup members. This turning inward can lead to some difficulties for a new formally appointed leader such as a coach. The new leader may not be readily accepted, and any proposed changes to existing practices may be met with resistance (Jewell & Reitz, 1981).

This situation is often encountered in sport when a new coach replaces a highly popular, highly successful predecessor. The group makes constant comparisons between the two leaders' personalities, methods, and so on. And because a cohesive group tends to overvalue its own membership and undervalue outsiders, the new coach will encounter initial difficulties in being accepted.

When people have ownership over a decision, they tend to support that decision more strongly. Consequently, the coach's *decision style* can have an influence on the level of cohesiveness within the team. Team members engage in behaviors more persistently, with greater intensity, and for a longer duration when they have had an opportunity to participate in decision making. In short, a democratic decision style is better for cohesiveness than an autocratic decision style (Carron, 1988).

The *compatibility* between coaches and athletes (and the athlete and team as a whole) is also related to the level of cohesiveness. Carron and Chelladurai (1981) tested athletes and coaches from high school basketball and wrestling teams in their orientations/motivations toward the group activities. The three orientations examined were: task (individuals are motivated toward the group's goals), self (individuals are motivated toward personal rewards and outcomes), and affiliation (individuals are motivated to develop and maintain harmonious relationships within the group). The most important predictors of the athlete's perceptions of cohesiveness were compatibility between the athlete and his coach and between the athlete and his teammates in task motivation.

Team Factors

When a set of individuals is brought together for the first time (e.g., at training camp, at the first practice session, or at organizational meetings in the off season), a number of structural aspects characteristic of all groups begin to emerge. The four elements that make up a group's structure are

position, status, roles, and norms. These result from the interactions among individual members, their perceptions of one another, and their expectations for themselves, other individuals, and the group. The emergence of these structural characteristics is inevitable and essential if the set of individuals is to become a more cohesive group. Three structural characteristics that bear emphasizing are group positions, roles, and norms.

Group "**positions**" refers to the fact that when collections of individuals meet regularly, people typically begin to consistently occupy a specific geographic space. This fact alone contributes to a sense of continuity and unity and the development of perceptions of "we" versus "they." In the research by Carron and Spink (1991) that was discussed previously, fitness instructors drew on the principle that position stability contributes to cohesiveness and developed strategies and techniques for their classes (again, see Table 9-1). The result was that after 13 weeks, both task cohesiveness and adherence were improved.

A *role* is a set of behaviors that are expected from the occupants of specific positions within the group. Thus, when we think of the "role of a coach," a number of expectations for behavior come to mind: instruct athletes; set up the team's offensive and defensive alignments; communicate with parents, media, and the general public; organize practices, and so on.

Within every group there are two general categories of roles, formal and informal (Mabry & Barnes, 1980). As the term suggests, **formal roles** are explicitly set out by the group or organization. Coach, team captain, and manager are examples of explicit leadership roles within a team. Spiker and setter in volleyball; forward, guard, and center in basketball; and scrum half and prop in rugby are examples of explicit performance roles. The sport team as an organization requires specific individuals to carry out each of these roles. Thus, individuals are trained or recruited for these roles, and specific expectations are held for their behavior. On the other hand, **informal roles** evolve as a result of the interactions that take place among group members. Some examples of the informal roles that often emerge on a sport team are leader (which may or may not be the team captain), enforcer, police officer, social director, and team clown.

Not surprisingly, research has consistently shown that when individual group members understand their roles (which is referred to as *role clarity*), accept their roles (which is referred to as *role acceptance*), and attempt to carry out their roles to the best of their ability (which is referred to as *role performance*), the group's effectiveness is improved (Schriesheim, 1980). And, as previously indicated, role clarity, role acceptance, and role performance are also associated with task and social cohesiveness (Carron & Grand, 1982; Grand & Carron, 1982).

A National Hockey League coach once observed that the worst thing that could happen to a team was to have its "enforcer" score a few goals in successive games. The enforcer would then begin to see himself as and prefer the role of goal scorer, to the detriment of the team as a whole. The roles that individuals are expected to perform should be clearly spelled out. In other words, the behavioral requirements of a role should be made as explicit as possible because, as Merton (1957) pointed out, the occupants of a role generally have a different perspective of the role's requirements than do other members of the group. Thus, if the sixth-best player on a basketball team is to be used as a defensive specialist only, the coach should point this out. Otherwise, that person may see his/her role entirely differently.

In terms of role acceptance, it is also beneficial to set out any contingencies associated with role performance. "We plan to use you as a defensive specialist only. If you cannot or do not want to play this role, you will probably get very little playing time this year." Role acceptance is also enhanced when the coach minimizes the status differences among roles. Thus, the success of the total team and the importance of all roles for team success should be continually emphasized. When all group members perceive that their responsibilities are important and make a contribution to the common good, they more willingly accept and carry them out.

Both role clarity and role acceptance (and group cohesiveness) can be improved through an effective *goal-setting* program. Goal setting serves four important functions: It directs the individual's attention and actions toward appropriate behaviors, it motivates the individual to develop strategies to achieve the goal, it contributes to increased interest in the activity, and it leads to prolonged effort (Carron, 1984). All of these contribute to role clarity and acceptance.

The presence of *norms* is also associated with increased cohesiveness (see Table 9-1). A norm is a standard for behavior that is expected of members of the group. It may be task-irrelevant or task-relevant; in either case, a norm reflects the group's consensus about behaviors that are considered acceptable. The treatment of team manager or trainers by the athletes is one example of a task-irrelevant norm. On one team the manager might be regarded and treated as little more than an unpaid servant; on another team he/she might be considered a member of the coaching team. In both cases new team members quickly become aware of the standard of behavior considered acceptable in their interactions with the manager and begin to act accordingly.

The relationship between the presence of group norms and the degree of group cohesiveness is circular. The development of norms contributes to the development of cohesiveness. With increased group cohesiveness there is also greater conformity to group standards for behavior and performance. A recently formed group has minimal influence over its members. But as the group develops and becomes more cohesive, adherence to norms for behavior increases. Failure to conform can lead to different sanctions or types of punishment. For example, the group can control the amount of interaction it permits members, their degree of involvement in decision making, and their accessibility to task and social rewards. Controlling the opportunity to interact and to influence the group is probably the most powerful sanction the group possesses. As a group increases in cohesiveness, its members place increasing value on social approval and the opportunities to interact with other group members. Therefore, they show an increasing tendency to adhere to the group norms and to give in to the group influence—even if that influence is negative. Some examples of negative influence are the performance of deviant behavior (such as was the case in the Manson killings) or the maintenance of an inappropriately low work quota (low standards for productivity).

One of the best-known, most heavily researched issues relating to task-relevant norms is the **norm for productivity**. One example of this occurs in industrial settings when a level or rate of performance is established by the group as acceptable. Then productivity above ("rate busting") or

Table 9-2 Interactive Effects of Group Cohesiveness and Group Norm for Productivity on Individual and Group Performance

		Group Cohesion	
		High	Low
Group Norm for Productivity	High	Best performance (1)	Intermediate performance (2)
	Low	Worst performance (4)	Intermediate performance (3)

below ("malingering") that standard is not tolerated by the group. Cohesion and the norm for productivity jointly influence group productivity and achievement. Traditionally it was assumed that there is a direct, positive relationship between cohesion and productivity: As the former increased, the latter was improved. Research in management science, psychology, and sport, however, has shown that the picture is not quite that simple. For example, when Stogdill (1972) reviewed 34 studies that had been carried out with a variety of different groups, he found that cohesiveness was positively related to performance in 12, negatively related in 11, and unrelated to performance in 11. According to Stogdill, the key factor that influences the relationship between cohesion and performance is the group's norm for productivity (see Table 9-2). If group cohesiveness is high and the norm for productivity is high, performance will be positively affected (number 1). Conversely, if cohesion is high and the norm for productivity is low (number 4), performance will be low or negatively affected. When cohesiveness is low, groups with a high norm (number 2) will outperform groups with a low norm (number 3).

A group places a great deal of pressure on members to conform to its norms. In the movie *Chariots of Fire*, for example, the British sprinter Harry Abrahams was chided by his Cambridge dons for hiring a professional trainer—for becoming too serious. Similarly, when Pete Rose broke into major league baseball, he was nicknamed "Charlie Hustle" for the intensity he brought to all

aspects of his behavior on the field—sprinting to first base after a walk, for example. The implication was that he was too intense.

Another important aspect of group norms is their *stability*. It has been demonstrated experimentally that an arbitrary norm can persist for four or five generations after the original members have been removed from the group (Jacobs & Campbell, 1961). Thus, if a sport team develops negative norms, such as abusive behavior toward officials or other team members, a laissez-faire attitude toward training, a reliance on individual versus team goals, those norms could persist over a number of seasons unless steps are taken to eliminate them.

Establishing positive group norms is extremely important in sport teams, particularly if an inappropriate norm is in place. One technique that has been used successfully is to enlist the formal and informal leaders of the group as active agents. If group leaders (in addition to the coach) accept and adhere to specific standards, other group members soon follow.

In some instances the group leaders may be resistant to change. This poses a problem because on sport teams the formal and informal leaders are usually the most highly skilled. If this is the case, the coach must decide how important the new standard is to the long-term success of the organization. In the event that the new standard is considered to be very important, the coach may have to release the resistant team members.

Zander (1982) discussed a number of other methods for establishing and enforcing group standards. Some of the proposals advanced by Zander for the group leader (or coach in this case) include the following:

- Show individual team members how the group's standards can contribute to the achievement of desirable qualities in the team, more effective team performance, and a greater sense of team unity.

- Point out to all team members how their contributions toward developing and maintaining the standards can contribute to the team's success.

- Develop a method of assessing whether there is adherence to the group's standards, and then reward those team members who do adhere and sanction those who do not.

Another important group factor that influences the development of a team concept and task cohesiveness is the establishment of *group goals and rewards*. In most group activities, including track and field, swimming, baseball, and even basketball, hockey, and soccer, there is an opportunity for the gifted individual competitor to obtain special recognition and rewards. This is inevitable. However, to ensure that a concept of unity develops, the coach must emphasize the group's goals and objectives as well as the rewards that will accrue to the group if these are achieved. Individual goals and rewards should be downplayed.

Communication is also associated with increased group cohesiveness (see Table 9-1), but the relationship is circular. As the level of communication relating to task and social issues increases, cohesiveness is enhanced. And as the group becomes more cohesive, there is also increased communication. Group members are more open with one another, they volunteer more, they talk more, and they listen better. In short, the exchange of task information and social pleasantries increases with cohesiveness.

Yukelson (1984), in a discussion of group motivation, presented nine effective ways to enhance coach–athlete communication systems and team harmony:

- Open communication channels by providing opportunities for athlete input. Communication is a group process, and mutual

trust and respect are essential in order to keep the channels open.

- Develop pride and a sense of collective identity within the group by setting out realistic team, individual, and subunit goals. Feelings of pride and satisfaction develop when individuals and groups attain challenging but realistic goals.

- Strive for common expectations on what types of behavior are appropriate. "An organizational philosophy should specify not only the desired objectives the group is striving to achieve but also the strategy, operating procedures, or means to reach these goals as well" (pp. 236–237).

- Value unique personal contributions by emphasizing the importance of each of the roles that are necessary for group performance.

- Recognize excellence by rewarding exceptional individual performance. If realistic objectives are set out and each individual clearly understands his/her role, the outstanding execution of that role should be recognized to enhance feelings of pride and commitment in the group and its members.

- Strive for consensus and commitment by involving the total team in goal-setting activities.

- Use periodic team meetings to resolve conflicts. Many explosive situations can be resolved by encouraging open communication within the team.

- Stay in touch with the formal and informal leaders in the team. The team members with high prestige and status are not only a barometer for assessing the group's attitudes and feelings; they are also effective agents for implementing necessary changes.

- Focus on success before discussing any failures. A positive group climate is developed if the positive aspects of group and individual performance are highlighted before errors and omissions are discussed.

Not surprisingly, *performance success* is also associated with increased cohesiveness (Carron & Ball, 1977; Widmeyer & Williams, 1991). Again, as has been the case with so many other factors, the relationship is circular: cohesiveness contributes to performance success, and with performance success there is increased cohesiveness. Consequently, if it is at all possible, a coach should try to avoid an excessively difficult schedule early in a season.

Carron and Chelladurai (1981) suggested that the nature of the *sport task* may be an important element in the cohesion–performance aspect. They suggested that in sports where individuals perform alone and a team score is obtained by using the individual scores in some additive fashion (e.g., swimming, track and field, golf), cohesiveness is less important for performance than is the case in interactive sports (e.g., basketball, hockey). The rationale, of course, is that cohesiveness is a group property and therefore will have its most significant impact on performance when the group's task requires active cooperation among team members. Nonetheless, there is no doubt that even

in individual sports such as golf, greater cohesiveness is associated with a more effective team performance.

Group cohesion is also influenced by team stability (or individual member adherence). Again, this relationship is circular. When groups are together for a long time, their sense of unity (cohesiveness) increases. And, in turn, with increased cohesiveness there is increased stability in team membership—members do not voluntarily leave the team as readily, they are more punctual at practices, are absent less often, and leave practice before it's over less frequently (Carron, Widmeyer, & Brawley, 1988; Spink & Carron, in press). Consequently, to the extent that it is compatible with eligibility requirements and group needs, a coach should try to avoid excessive personnel turnover.

Summary

Groups are dynamic, not static; they exhibit life and vitality, interaction, and activity. Athletic teams are simply a special type of group. One important implication of this is that they are therefore subject to change, to growth, to modification, and to improvement. The coach is probably in the best position to influence change in a positive direction. To do this efficiently and effectively, it is beneficial to draw upon the wealth of research information that has been developed over a number of years in management science, social psychology, sociology, and physical education. Given the influence that groups have on their members, a knowledge of group structure, group dynamics, and group cohesiveness is essential for coaches. This understanding will provide an excellent base from which to weld athletes into a more effective team.

Study Questions

1. Using Carron's definition of a group, briefly describe the six features that characterize groups.
2. List at least six of Zander's characteristics that distinguish a group from a collection of individuals.
3. Define cohesiveness. What are the four specific facets of cohesion?
4. List the four factors that contribute to cohesiveness and give one specific example of each.
5. Discuss the relationship of team size to group cohesiveness.
6. Describe the situational, personal, and leadership factors that contribute to the development of cohesiveness.
7. The four elements that make up a group's structure are position, status, roles, and norms. Distinguish between each of these elements and describe how the elements might be manipulated or modified in order to enhance cohesiveness.
8. Describe and give complete, specific, concrete examples (using a sport of your choice) of at least five ways to enhance coach–athlete communication systems and team harmony.

References

Brawley, L. R., Carron, A. V., & Widmeyer, W. N. (1987). Assessing the cohesion of teams: Validity of the Group Environment Questionnaire. *Journal of Sport Psychology, 9,* 275–294.

Bugliosi, V., & Gentry, C. (1974). *Helter skelter: The true story of the Manson murders.* New York: Norton.

Carron, A. V. (1980). *Social psychology of sport*. Ithaca, N.Y.: Mouvement Publications.

Carron, A. V. (1981). Processes of group interaction in sport teams. *Quest, 33,* 245–270.

Carron, A. V. (1982). Cohesiveness in sport groups: Interpretations and considerations. *Journal of Sport Psychology, 4,* 123–138.

Carron, A. V. (1984). *Motivation: Implications for coaching and teaching*. London, Ont.: Sports Dynamics.

Carron, A. V. (1988). *Group dynamics in sport: Theoretical and practical issues*. London, Ont.: Sports Dynamics.

Carron, A. V., & Ball, J. R. (1977). Cause–effect characteristics of cohesiveness and participation motivation in intercollegiate hockey. *International Review of Sport Sociology, 12,* 49–60.

Carron, A. V., & Chelladurai, P. (1979). Cohesiveness as a factor in sport performance. *International Review of Sport Sociology, 16,* 21–41.

Carron, A. V., & Chelladurai, P. (1981) The dynamics of group cohesion in sport. *Journal of Sport Psychology, 3,* 123–139.

Carron, A. V., & Grand, R. R. (1982). Team Climate Questionnaire: Form B. In L. M. Wankel & R. B. Wilberg (Eds.), *Psychology of sport and motor behavior: Research and practice*. Edmonton: Department of Recreation and Leisure Studies, University of Alberta.

Carron, A. V., & Spink, K.S. (1991). *Team building in an exercise setting: Cohesion effects*. Paper presented at the Canadian Psychomotor Learning and Sport Psychology Conference, London, Ont.

Carron, A. V., Widmeyer, L. R., & Brawley, L. R. (1985). The development of an instrument to assess cohesion in sport teams: The Group Environment Questionnaire. *Journal of Sport Psychology, 7,* 244–266.

Carron, A. V., Widmeyer, W. N., & Brawley, L. R. (1988). Group cohesion and individual adherence to physical activity. *Journal of Sport and Exercise Psychology, 10,* 119–126.

Festinger, L., Schachter, S., & Back, K. (1950). *Social pressures in informal groups: A study of human factors in housing*. Stanford, Calif.: Stanford University Press.

Grand, R. R., & Carron, A. V. (1982). Development of a team climate questionnaire. In L. M. Wankel & R. B. Wilberg (Eds.), *Psychology of sport and motor behavior: Research and practice*. Edmonton: Department of Recreation and Leisure Studies, University of Alberta.

Gross, N., & Martin, W. (1951). On group cohesiveness. *American Journal of Sociology, 57,* 533–546.

Jacobs, R. C., & Campbell, D. T. (1961). The perpetuation of an arbitrary tradition through several generations of a laboratory microculture. *Journal of Abnormal and Social Psychology, 62,* 649–658.

Jewell, L. N., & Reitz, H. J. (1981). *Group effectiveness in organizations*. Glenview,Ill.: Scott, Foresman.

Mabry, E. A., & Barnes, R. E. (1980). *The dynamics of small group communication*. Englewood Cliffs, N.J.: Prentice-Hall.

McCallum, J. (1982). Faith, hope, and Tony C. *Sports Illustrated, 57,* 58–72.

Merton, R. K. (1957). *Social theory and social structure* (rev. ed.). New York: Free Press.

Schriesheim, J. F. (1980). The social context of leader–subordinate relations: An investigation of the effects of group cohesiveness. *Journal of Applied Psychology, 65,* 183–194.

Spink, K. S., & Carron, A. V. (1991, October). *Team building in an exercise setting: Adherence effects*. Paper presented at the Canadian Psychomotor Learning and Sport Psychology Conference, London, Ont.

Spink, K. S., & Carron, A. V. (in press). Group cohesion and adherence in exercise classes. *Journal of Exercise and Sport Psychology*.

Stogdill, R. M. (1972). Group productivity, drive and cohesiveness. *Organizational Behavior and Human Performance, 8,* 26–43.

Widmeyer, W. N., Brawley, L. R., & Carron, A. V. (1985). *The measurement of cohesion in sport teams: The Group Environment Questionnaire*. London, Ont.: Sports Dynamics.

Widmeyer, W. N., Brawley, L. R., & Carron, A. V. (1990). The effects of group size in sport. *Journal of Exercise and Sport Psychology, 12,* 177–190.

Widmeyer, W. N., & Williams, J. M. (1991). Predicting cohesion in a coaching sport. *Small Group Research, 22,* 548–570.

Yukelson, D. P. (1984). Group motivation in sport teams. In J. M. Silva & R. S. Weinberg (Eds.), *Psychological foundations of sport*. Champaign, Ill.: Human Kinetics.

Zander, A. (1982). *Making groups effective*. San Francisco: Jossey-Bass.

Communicating Effectively

David Yukelson, *Pennsylvania State University*

I n my work with intercollegiate sport teams and student-athletes I am often asked to address the topic of interpersonal communication and team harmony. The ability to express one's thoughts and feelings effectively and to understand the thoughts, feelings, and ideas of others is a key factor associated with individual and team success (Orlick, 1990; Rosenfeld & Wilder, 1990).

One day a football player came up to me following a meeting on communication and team harmony and remarked that, to him, communication is what teamwork and group chemistry are all about; it is tied to "oneness of thought and everyone being on the same page." He elaborated by saying, "If I can walk up to the line of scrimmage and know that the offensive tackle next to me is thinking the same thing I am, has internalized what he needs to do on this particular play, and gives me a nonverbal signal that we are going to take care of business, then communication has been transmitted and I know, with great confidence, we are going to execute with precise timing, efficiency, and cohesiveness."

His remarks reminded me that there is much more to communication than meets the ear. When my racquetball partner and I are playing well, for example, not much is said, but there is great chemistry and communication going on. We are familiar with each other's strengths, weaknesses, and playing style, and we give each other a lot of nonverbal reassurance. We are definitely "on the same page" with one another—we believe in each other, we communicate well, and, as a result, we play well together with great confidence, enthusiasm, and cohesiveness.

Coaches, athletes, and sport psychologists talk about the importance of effective communication, but relatively little has been written about the subject as it pertains to sport (Anshel, 1990; Connelly & Rotella, 1991; Harris & Harris, 1984; Henschen & Miner, 1989; Martens, 1987; Orlick, 1986; Rosenfeld & Wilder, 1990). Hence, the purpose of this chapter is to explore what effective communication is as it relates to sport, identify barriers to effective communication, and develop strategies for improving communication processes within athletic environments.

Sport Psychology, Communication, and Intercollegiate Athletics

Effective communication is one of the most powerful tools a coach, athlete, athletic administrator, or sport psychologist can possess. Open lines of communication can alleviate many problems that arise within athletic departments. Today coaches, athletes, athletic administrators, and various academic support personnel must adhere to a variety of new NCAA compliance issues regarding rules and regulations that include academic and athletic eligibility, financial aid stipulations, recruiting policies, travel, facility usage, and time restrictions. Without effective communication, policies and procedures will not be implemented consistently, resulting in a greater risk of infractions and fragmented services. Misunderstandings among all units create lack of trust, suspicion, territoriality, and breakdown in the team approach. Thus, coaches must work closely with athletic administrators and key academic support personnel. It is absolutely essential that open lines of communication exist, that administrators know what coaches and athletes are doing, that coaches feel administration supports their program and endeavors, and that everyone is working together toward the same goals.

In my day-to-day interactions I work with a variety of people within the intercollegiate athletic hierarchy; student-athletes, coaches, athletic administrators, academic counselors and support personnel, sport medicine doctors and athletic trainers, student trainers, team managers, cheerleaders, parents, alumni, etcetera. These people have a wealth of information and experience to draw upon. Everyone is different—all have their own personalities and comfort levels from which they work and communicate. There are certain protocols to follow, appropriate chains of command to work through, written and unwritten rules and policies that can't be violated. It is impossible to implement a thorough and effective sport psychology program if one is unable to gain the trust and support of key personnel at all levels of the athletic organization.

Similarly, it takes time and patience to integrate mental training techniques into already existing structures (Ravizza, 1988). Thus, sport psychologists working in applied settings should take time to develop rapport and establish a good working relationship with the people with whom they interact. Personally, I feel applied sport psychologists must first earn the trust and respect of the coaching staff before they can expect to work effectively on an individual or collective basis with their athletes. This can be accomplished by establishing open lines of communication with the coaching staff, by going slowly, being patient, and by listening and observing to learn as much as possible about the dynamics surrounding the team, including the coaches' philosophy, personality, and orientation toward the team itself. Gaining entry and building the trust of the coaching staff take time. It is import that the sport psychologist be able to relate easily with athletes and staff and be flexible, creative, and confident in the skills he/she has to offer (Orlick & Partington, 1987; Partington & Orlick, 1987; Ravizza, 1988).

Communication is also tied to a sport psychologist's ability to relate well with athletes (Gould et al., 1991; Orlick & Partington, 1987). As for my style and orientation, I have adopted an eclectic, personal-developmental approach to mental skills training (Danish, Petipas, & Hale, in press; Vealey, 1988) that looks at the total growth and development of student-athletes. At Penn State University I provide counseling and support in the areas of mental training for performance optimization in sport, motivation and stress management, intra-interpersonal skill development, and issues revolving around the academic growth and personal development of student-athletes.

I gain insight from listening to athletes and coaches. I ask a lot of questions, do a lot of listening. I listen to a variety of academic-athletic-interpersonal concerns, fears, frustrations, joys, and accomplishments. There are many insecurities, pressures, self-doubts, and daily hassles to work through. We spend a lot of time talking about confidence, concentration, consistency, composure, ideal performance states, awareness, and trust (Moore & Stephenson, 1991; Ravizza, 1984, 1986). Together we work on goal planning, visualization and mental imagery techniques, energy management, positive affirmations and cue-controlled relaxation strategies, constructive self-talk, preperformance routines, attentional control, and how to assume responsibility for one's actions. Based on individualized needs and concerns, we develop mental plans for training and competition (Orlick, 1986, 1990; Ravizza, 1990; Vealey, 1988) and talk about things that affect their lives outside of athletics. My goal is to teach student-athletes how to reconcile their role as both student and athlete, how to balance their academic, athletic, personal, and social needs effectively, trust the skills they have at their disposal, and in general feel good about what they are trying to accomplish both on and off the athletic field.

Communication Defined

Communication has been identified as a very important part of athletic success (Connelly & Rotella, 1991; Harris & Harris, 1984; Martens, 1987). Unfortunately, there seems to be no true consensus among researchers on what the word "communication" means. For instance, Dance and Larson (1976) surveyed a variety of journals and publications from a diversity of fields and found 126 different definitions in the literature. The *American Heritage Dictionary* (1983) refers to communication as the "transmission or exchange of thoughts, knowledge, ideas, and/or information by means of writing, speech, or signals." To communicate means to impart, transmit, "share" one's thoughts, feelings, or ideas. Communication has also been defined as a process by which we understand others and, in turn, endeavor to be understood by them (Anderson, 1959).

Communication is a dynamic *process* that constantly changes, shifting in response to the total situation. Communication can be expressed in many different ways: It can be interpersonal (verbal/nonverbal, symbolic/spontaneous, complementary/ parallel, one-on-one, group), intrapersonal (within one's organism, such as "self-talk"), written (books, diagrams, playbooks, other printed material), or visual (modeling, observational learning, pictures, video analysis).

Communication involves sending, receiving (encoding), and interpreting (decoding) messages through sensory channels (Harris & Harris, 1984). The message may be verbal (as in written or spoken communication) or nonverbal (such as facial expressions, gestures, eye contact, and body language) and can be distinguished in terms of content and emotion. The way a message is expressed will influence how the message is received and interpreted.

Much of our waking day is spent communicating, either verbally or nonverbally, through words, actions, body language, and gestures. When a person speaks, words are accompanied by volume, voice intonation, gestures, and body position. These accompanying characteristics are often referred to as the *nonverbal aspects of communica-tion*. Martens (1990) has identified five different categories of nonverbal communication: body motion (gestures, facial expressions), physical characteristics (physique, physical appearance), touching behavior that connotes positive reinforcement (pats on the back, arm on the shoulder), voice characteristics (pitch, resonance, inflections), and body position (personal space between you and others). The proximity of speakers to one another, the minute movements that constitute a gesture, the presence, absence, or degree of eye-to-eye contact, and "paralanguage" (e.g., grunts and groans) all constitute elements of nonverbal communication (Knapp, 1972).

Nonverbal communication is a very big part of sport. It can be very direct (hand signals), indirect (body language reflecting approval or disapproval), full of content (watching game films to prepare for an upcoming competition) and emotion (projecting a mentally tough, confident self-image), or very subtle (nonverbal communication between two athletes). For instance: Quarterback walks up to the line of scrimmage and senses a blitz, looks at the wide receiver in a certain way, receiver picks up nonverbal cue through experience and familiarity with the other's style of play, receiver goes up field on a streak pattern instead of short hooking route, they connect, touchdown!

Although our dominant communication channels are vision and hearing, we also communicate through the senses of touch, taste, smell, and kinesthetics. As human beings we are limited in our capacity to process information from our senses at any given time. The ability to process a certain amount of stimuli while filtering out irrelevant information or messages is called **selective attention** (Norman, 1976). Among the inherent structures of our sense organs that influence selective attention are **perceptual filters** (physiological limitations built into humans that cannot be reversed) and **psychological expectancies** (a psychological set or predisposition to respond in a certain way) (Tubbs & Moss, 1987).

In the process of interpreting verbal and nonverbal messages, information may be lost or distorted (Henschen & Miner, 1989). Sometimes we think we hear a person say one thing when in actuality he/she said something else. We then act on the basis of what we *think* the person said. Many communication problems are rooted in this kind of misunderstanding.

Past experience and emotional mood states can also have a strong effect on what we come to expect, anticipate, and choose to process or respond to. We hear what we want to hear and see what we want to see. Similarly, we can give off nonverbal signals that may be perceived by others differently (Wenburg & Wilmot, 1982). A coach in a good mood may respond positively to some athletes joking around; the next day, if the coach is stressed out, the same situation may be perceived differently. Thus, how individuals receive (decode) or construct (encode) messages is strongly influenced by past experience, emotional mood states, and their individuality. Martens (1987) provides a variety of examples of how "noise"—selective filtering, emotional mood states, and nonverbal cues and gestures—influences the way messages are received and interpreted.

Along these lines, Tom Perrin, a sport psychologist and assistant basketball coach at the University of Virginia, provides an illustration of how good intentions can be misinterpreted due to selective filtering or emotional mood states. An athlete misses a rebound and the coach compliments him for demonstrating good footwork and intensity. But the athlete, who is stressed over limited playing time the past two weeks, has two midterms coming up, and is upset over breaking up with his girlfriend the night before, processes the compliment as an insult. Many coaches stop there, dismiss the athlete's reaction as stupid, say something like "I can't control how he took it," and then storm off. Consequently, a wall is formed, communication blocked, the message never received.

Likewise, during the course of a long competitive season, coaches are susceptible to experiencing stress and burnout (Dale & Weinburg, 1990; Smith, 1986; Vernacchia, 1992). Their reaction to stress and the pressure of having to win can adversely affect how messages are transmitted and received. For instance, I recall a situation where a coach was not happy with the way the team had recently been playing. The coach's comments to one particular player were very demeaning and degrading; the nonverbal body language was so piercing, tone of voice so penetrating and hurtful, that the athlete felt devastated and completely tuned out anything positive that was said after that time. It was unfortunate because the athlete, very talented yet inexperienced and low in self-confidence, began to fear failure, was scared to make a mistake, and never quite recovered for the rest of the season.

Often the way a coach says something can be perceived and interpreted by the athlete to reflect the attitude and feelings the coach has toward the athlete (Henschen & Miner, 1989). *How* a coach says things is just as important as what the coach has to say, especially in stressful situations. A good rule of thumb is to become aware of verbal and nonverbal signals and make sure we "say what we mean and mean what we say."

Thus, communication is an attitude that goes beyond the content and emotion of what is said and done. Coaches who have good communication skills find many ways, verbally and nonverbally, to get their intended message across. A hundred people may each have a different perspective on what communication is, but it all seems to boil down to this: what was the *intent* of the message, *how* was it communicated, and how was it *received*. Coaches must make certain that the message conveyed is the message received.

Communication in Sport

With regard to sport, so much of what goes on in athletics revolves around communication. Communication affects motivation, confidence, concentration, and team dynamics. It has an impact on leadership, internalization of team goals and objectives, expectations coaches and athletes have for one another, and interpersonal processes, as well as individual attitudes, feelings, and behaviors. It affects strategy acquisition, teaching, skill development, and the ability to give feedback about performance effectively.

Research concerning communication in athletic settings has emphasized the importance of leadership style, methods of information dissemination, task and social cohesion, principles of reinforcement, and techniques to resolve conflict (Anshel, 1990; Carron, 1988; Connelly & Rotella, 1991; Martens, 1987; Orlick, 1986; Smith, Smoll, & Curtis, 1979). For instance, *leadership style* has been shown to influence the quality of an individual's athletic experiences (see Chapters 7 and 8; Martens, 1987; Wooten, 1992). Sensitivity and responsiveness to individual differences and creating a positive interpersonal climate have also been shown to be critical to effective communication in sport settings (Martens, 1990; Smith, Smoll, & Curtis, 1979). Martens (1987) has also stressed the importance of *communication style*, noting that clear, consistent, and direct communication with no hidden agendas is necessary for effective coach–athlete relationships and team culture.

Effective leaders possess appropriate interpersonal skills to move people to action. This could include a coach motivating a team, inspiring them to go out and give it their best, or an athlete challenging a coach or teammate, speaking up for betterment of the team, inspiring others to get the job done. Consequently, communication skills are essential to good leadership.

Whether you are a coach, athlete, administrator, or sport psychologist, effective communication depends on the process of mutual sharing and mutual understanding (Martens, 1987; Orlick, 1986). The foundation for effective communication skills is having *credibility* in the eyes of athletes and developing trust and mutual respect (Yukelson, 1984). Credibility is reflected in the athletes' attitude about the trustworthiness of what you say and do (Martens et al., 1981). *Trust* is linked to the concepts of honesty, integrity, sincerity, and truthfulness. Lack of honesty and betrayal of trust can lead to many interpersonal difficulties including apprehension, tension, hostility, resentment, and possibly backstabbing (Tubbs & Moss, 1987). It is very difficult to regain someone's trust once it is broken.

Respect is one of our deepest human needs and has a tremendous influence on an individual's motivation and self-esteem. The word "respect" comes from a Latin root that includes the notion of seeing or viewing. Respect is not often communicated directly in words but, rather, is demonstrated through one's actions, sense of genuineness, social influence, and orientation toward others (Egan, 1982).

Athletes are motivated most by coaches whom they respect (Halliwell, 1989). Many athletes lose respect for their coach when they feel betrayed or perceive they are not being listened to. I remember a situation where a coach heard "through the grapevine" that an athlete violated a long-standing team rule. The coach, who liked to be in control of everything, failed to garner all the facts, solicited information from other teammates as to what had happened, but never talked directly to the person in question. As a consequence, respect for the coach was shattered, and interpersonal relations among athletes were strained. A good rule to remember is to gather all the facts before passing judgment and to treat people exactly the way you want to be treated yourself!

Similarly, being able to put yourself in the shoes of others and "see" things from the other person's perspective (i.e., *empathy*) builds credibility and respect. Athletes expect to be treated with respect and dignity and want to feel that their input is valued and contributions appreciated.

I have observed that coaches who are good communicators have credibility in the eyes of their athletes. They establish open lines of communication; are truthful, fair, and consistent; accept individuals for who they are; care about athletes as people outside of athletics; and inspire athletes to reach for their best both on and off the athletic field.

Coaches who communicate well are great teachers as well as good role models. They observe performance analytically and are able to help athletes improve performance by providing specific behavioral feedback in a clear, constructive, nonthreatening manner (Smith, 1986; Martin & Hrycaiko, 1983). When they criticize, they criticize the specific behavior and not the person. For instance, instead of telling a volleyball player that he/she played poorly or like a dumb jerk yesterday, a coach who has good communication skills might say, "I noticed that you lost your concentration passing the ball midway through the second set. What disappointed me most was the fact that you failed to provide emotional support to your teammates the rest of the match."

Similarly, coaches who are good communicators explain, clarify, and individualize instruction to meet the athlete's needs and personality. The following communication from a coach to a fencer between bouts illustrates the point: "Kathy, you are too anxious on the strip. You are telegraphing messages to your opponent as to what your intentions are. Relax and trust your actions, lull your opponent into your spider web, play with it more, set up your actions, and when you see the window of opportunity, open up and go for it!" The importance of effective communication and giving constructive feedback in relation to goals an individual or team is striving to accomplish cannot be overstated.

Athletes react in various ways to how coaches communicate with them. They know the characteristics they like and dislike in coaches. In general, research in the area of youth sports indicates that young athletes like coaches who are supportive and encouraging, knowledgeable and instructive, honest and sincere, empathetic and understanding, enthusiastic and motivated, reliable, fair, and consistent (Martens, 1990; Martens et al., 1981; Smith, Smith, & Smoll, 1983). Personally, I believe the same thing holds true for older athletes as well.

In contrast, athletes dislike coaches who are judgmental, expressionless, capricious, and constantly negative. Judgmental coaches always seem to be passing blame, evaluating rather than instructing, making athletes feel intimidated and insecure. Expressionless coaches communicate no emotion at all, often leaving athletes unsure whether they are doing well or poorly. Capricious coaches are fickle and inconsistent, sending mixed messages (verbally and nonverbally) that confuse athletes. Coaches who are always negative, demeaning, and degrading run the risk of causing motivation problems among athletes, increasing their self-doubts, and undermining their self-confidence and/or self-image.

Communication and Groups

One of the most gratifying experiences a coach or athlete can have is to be a member of a team that gets along well and works together efficiently in a cohesive, harmonious, task-oriented manner (Orlick, 1990; Yukelson, 1984). When individuals work together in groups, communication, coordination, and interaction are essential (Carron, 1988). In fact, communication lies at the heart of group process. If a group is to function effectively, members must be able to communicate easily and efficiently with one another (Shaw, 1981).

Sport groups may be thought of as a collection of interdependent individuals coordinated and orchestrated into various task-efficient roles for the purpose of achieving some goal or objective that is deemed important for that particular team. A major role for the coach is to integrate the group into a smooth working unit that performs efficiently with a sense of pride, excellence, and collective identity (Yukelson, 1984).

Unfortunately, not every group functions cohesively. Interpersonal conflict is often the result of misunderstanding or miscommunication of

feelings. Henschen and Miner (1989) identify five types of misunderstandings that often surface within groups: (1) a difference of opinion resolvable by common sense, (2) a clash of personalities in the group, (3) a conflict of task or social roles among group members, (4) a struggle for power between one or more individuals, and (5) a breakdown of communication between the leader and the group or among members of the group itself.

Team building requires a group climate of *openness* where airing problems and matters of concern is not just appropriate but encouraged. It has been stated that the more open you can be with each other, the better are your chances of getting along and achieving both individual and team goals (Orlick, 1986). Orlick (1990) expounds by saying, "Harmony grows when you really listen to others and they listen to you, when you are considerate of their feelings and they are considerate of yours, when you accept their differences and they accept yours, and when you help them and they help you" (p. 143).

Coach–Athlete Communications

Since team dynamics are so complex, many interpersonal problems can arise due to misunderstanding or miscommunication between the coach and the team. Harris and Harris (1984) offer an interesting framework for examining communication processes and various lines of communication that occur in athletic teams: coach–team, coach–athlete, athlete–coach, and athlete–athlete.

From a coach–team perspective, it is important to obtain *consensus and commitment* on group goals and objectives, including appropriate means and methods for achieving them (Carron, 1988; Martens, 1987). Athletes unite behind common goals, so it is important to get athletes to think in terms of the coaching philosophy, values, operating procedures, and goals the team is striving to accomplish (Yukelson, 1984). Similarly, an important goal is to develop *homogeneity* in attitudes, thoughts, beliefs, and behaviors relative to the sport task. The degree of communication, the sharing, the conformity, is a measure of "one-mindedness."

In order to achieve these ends, it is suggested a coach adhere to the following communication principles: *Impart* relevant information regarding team goals and roles (share vision, get everyone on the same page, cultivate "oneness of thought," make sure everyone knows what is expected, outline strategies to reach goals and objectives); *inspire* athletes to reach for their best (motivate; inculcate pride, confidence, and team spirit; communicate with a sense of inspired enthusiasm; make people feel significant and valued); *clarify* (give people feedback on how they are doing in relation to individual and team goals); and *reinforce* (catch people doing things right; provide lots of positive reinforcement, support, and encouragement).

As for coach–athlete lines of communication coaches should build a psychological and social environment conducive for success and goal achievement. They should take the time to get to know their athletes as unique, goal-oriented individuals. Martens's (1987) ideas regarding transformational leadership and reciprocal influence seem to be very appropriate here, where athletes and coaches work together to meet each other's needs and common goals. Furthermore, it is a good idea to keep athletes informed of what is expected. Along these lines, coaches should be open and honest about various decisions that affect athletes directly (e.g., changes in line-up or strategy, role clarification). This will ease many misunderstandings or misinformation that can often lead to dissension or turmoil.

As for athlete–coach interactions, athletes need feedback as to where they stand and how they are progressing in relation to individual and team goals. Research indicates that *evaluative feedback* is a very important part of the goal-setting process (see Chapter 13 and Locke & Latham, 1990) and is directly tied to communication. Unfortunately, some coaches are not very good at giving feedback in a positive and supportive manner (Orlick, 1990). This can lead to motivation problems and performance inconsistencies. Similarly, many athletes have difficulty internalizing feedback for what it is, and, as a consequence, they take feedback personally as opposed to constructively.

In addition to needing tangible feedback regarding their efforts and accomplishments, many athletes will seek their coach out to talk about a variety of things outside of sport that may have an impact on their lives and self-esteem. A coach is often asked to take on many roles (i.e., teacher, counselor, confidant, friend, role model, and sometimes substitute parent). For these reasons it is important that lines of communication be open between coach and athlete.

As for breakdowns in coach–athlete communications, many occur when individuals restrict or distort communication due to lack of trust or respect, fear, conflict of interest, or other reasons. It is not unusual for something to happen between a coach and athlete where the athlete does not feel comfortable talking openly with the coach (e.g., personality clash, demotion to the second team, coach showing limited interest or appearing not to have time for "a peon like me"). Although it is common for coaches to have a so-called "open door policy," many athletes find it difficult to be honest with coaches who don't take the time to really listen to their concerns or who fail to reciprocate genuineness and respect. Connelly and Rotella (1991) note that some athletes go so far as to "fake honesty"—tell coaches or others what they want to hear so they don't have to deal with the situation at hand.

Coaches should create an environment that encourages athletes to initiate communication freely. Athletes must feel communication lines are truly open and thoughts can be voiced without reprisal. Similarly, it is suggested that coaches find out what their athletes' preferences are for communication at the competition site (Orlick, 1990). Some athletes appreciate a word of encouragement or a cue word to remind them to bring their best focus forward; others like to be left alone, to be given their own space to mentally prepare prior to the competition. Communication is a two-way street, and both the coach and athlete have a responsibility to make it work!

Anshel (1990) and Orlick (1990) offer several practical cognitive-behavioral interventions to facilitate coach–athlete communications. Some of these guidelines include being honest, positive, nondefensive, constructive, and empathetic. In addition, the following coaching tips for improving communication with athletes may prove helpful. If none of these suggestions works, it might be appropriate for a sport psychologist to intervene.

- To communicate successfully, you must understand that each person with whom you communicate has had different experiences than you.

- No one communication technique will meet all needs. Recognize individual differences in the way people respond to you. Do not assume that you (the communicator) and the receiver will interpret the information in the same way.

- Characteristics of effective communication include honest, clarity, consistency, and sincerity. Sarcasm, ridicule, and degrading or belittling comments are poor communication techniques. When coaches lose control, the emotional element of communication may override the content element.

- Use a style of communication that is comfortable for you. Whether you are laid back, animated, relaxed, vocal, or somewhere in between, communicate in a manner that is consistent with your personality and coaching philosophy.

- Learn how to become more empathetic. Put yourself in the shoes of your athletes. Show genuine concern for them as people, listen actively to their feelings and concerns, and work jointly with the athlete to find appropriate solutions.

- Reduce uncertainty—be supportive. As a coach you play a vital role in helping athletes feel worthy and important. Try to create a supportive atmosphere where athletes feel that their efforts and contributions to the team are appreciated and valued.

- Be positive when working with athletes. The positive approach to coaching is characterized by the liberal use of praise, encouragement, support, and positive reinforcement to strengthen desired behaviors. Discipline and corrective feedback are part of the positive approach when used correctly. The skillful use of positive reinforcement can increase motivation and strengthen self-esteem (see Chapters 2 through 4).

- Convey rationales as to why or why not athletes should do certain behaviors.

- Work to improve nonverbal communication skills.

- Be a good role model—influence by example!

- Remember the axiom "Your actions speak louder than words."

- If you have an open-door policy, show athletes (and your assistants) that you are sincere about using it!

- Solicit input from the team. Set aside time once a week at the end of practice to discuss openly how things are going (i.e., what is working; what is not; what you need more of, less of from coaches, teammates, trainers, etc.). This is an excellent way to build harmony, open up communication channels, and show athletes you care about their opinions.

As for athlete–athlete communication (interaction among athletes), it is important for teammates to establish and maintain good working relationships with each other both on and off the athletic field. Some of the closest and most cohesive teams I have ever been associated with had a special relationship (i.e., "bonding-together feeling") off the field that carried over into athletic success on the field, particularly in critical situations when they needed to trust each other the most.

Athletes are a great source of support for one another. They share common experiences that are unique to their own peer subculture, make sacrifices and work hard to achieve goals that are deemed important, spend a lot of time together, and in many cases are somewhat encapsulated in their own athletic world. Unfortunately, if interaction doesn't go well among team members, poor interpersonal relationships can be a great source of frustration and disappointment.

Athletic teams are very much like families. Some amount of tension, frustration, or even conflict should be considered normal. Several teams I have worked with have had their fair share of interpersonal communication problems and conflict. Problems have ranged from roommate problems (e.g., incompatibility, intolerance, needs not being met), interpersonal jealousies within the team, cultural differences, and freshman adjustment issues, to coach–athlete inequities (e.g., personality conflict; discrepancies in playing time; perceived injustices; or athletes feeling the coach does not listen, care, or appreciate their efforts). In situations like these, athletes often do not feel valued, accepted, appreciated, and/or respected. This can result in concentration and performance problems and lead to feelings of resentment and distrust, and possibly to withdrawal from the group itself.

Likewise, in a multicultural athletic environment some degree of conflict or misunderstanding is unavoidable. Whether defined in terms of racial, ethnic, religious, or socioeconomic differences, dissimilarities due to deeply rooted cultural systems often lead to intercultural misunderstandings (Tubbs & Moss, 1987). Since values, beliefs, relational roles, verbal and nonverbal communication systems, and attitudes in one culture are often different from those in another, when two people from different cultures initially get together, they sometimes feel uncomfortable simply due to these cultural differences.

As Orlick (1986, 1990) astutely points out, learning how to communicate effectively is an important first step in preventing and solving problems with coaches, athletes, and teams, whether the problems stem from cultural differences or from other factors. Expressing feelings, communicating clearly, being assertive, and listening well are psychological skills that must be practiced to be perfected (Connelly & Rotella, 1991; Orlick, 1990).

Often, people "clam up" when stressed or pressured, then expect others to be good at reading their minds and feelings (Orlick, 1986). Recognizing that it is difficult to be responsive to someone else's thoughts, feelings, ideas, and needs when you don't know what they are and that many of us have difficulty expressing ourselves adequately, I have found Orlick's writings on improving interpersonal relations and team harmony to be quite helpful. Although it is easier said than done, I am in total agreement with Orlick (1986) when he states: "The most important thing you can do to increase team harmony is to make a commitment to do so" (p. 98).

The following suggestions derived from Orlick and others may help improve interpersonal communication among coaches and athletes:

- Make sure everyone is pulling in the same direction (team comes first). Recognize that the more open you can be with each other, the better are your chances of getting along and achieving your goals.

- Discuss strategies for improving team harmony, including ways to support and help each other both on and off the athletic field. In addition, do whatever is necessary to make teammates feel valued, significant, appreciated, and accepted.

- Listen to others, and they will listen to you! Put yourself in the shoes of others; try to understand the other person's perspective.

- Learn how to give and receive feedback or criticism constructively. Listen to the *intent* of what is being said; avoid taking things personally.

- Learn how to tolerate each other better. Accept team members for who they are, including their flaws, personality quirks, idiosyncrasies, and funny little habits that make them unique.

- Avoid backstabbing and gossiping about teammates. Interpersonal cliques and petty jealousies will destroy team morale quickly.

- Keep confrontations private. Deal with the person directly (i.e., "Here is what your behavior is like, this is how your behavior makes others feel, here is how your behavior influences others and is perceived by others").

Not all conflicts can be resolved, but some can be managed more effectively. Perhaps the following tips for managing conflicts will be helpful:

- Identify and clarify the specific problem—try to be specific.

- Consider your relationship to those involved. If the relationship is important, you may wish to temper your response or choose your words carefully so minor conflicts do not become major ones.

- Think before you speak or react. Consider the possible consequences of what you say before you do anything.

- Discuss the issue but don't attack the person. Realize that other people have rights and feelings. Avoid degrading, personal attacks.

- Give others involved an opportunity to explain their side of the issue.

Assertiveness Training: The Need for Expression

In addition to the skills previously mentioned, athletes also need to learn how to stand up for what is important to them without infringing on the rights of others. **Assertiveness** refers to the honest and straightforward expression of a person's thoughts, feelings, needs, and goals in a socially appropriate way that does not violate the rights of others (Connelly & Rotella, 1991). Four major components of assertive response patterns include: the ability to say no; the ability to ask for favors; the ability to express both positive and negative feelings; and the ability to initiate, continue, and/or end general conversations (Lazarus, 1973).

People have difficulty being assertive for a variety of reasons, including fear of losing social approval (being hesitant to speak up for fear of what others might think), lack of awareness (never having been taught to be assertive or reinforced to speak up), lack of confidence to speak up (differences in cultural upbringing, social standing, race, gender, etc.), and risk of making oneself known (possible negative consequences associated with speaking up) (Connelly & Rotella, 1991; Egan, 1982). For instance, some freshmen may be afraid to speak up in team meetings for fear of looking bad in the eyes of upperclassmen or being perceived as a disruptive influence. Respect is earned, and it takes time to develop. Similarly, cultural and socialization factors may affect one's decision to be assertive. For example, it may be awkward for a person of Puerto Rican or Latin American descent to feel comfortable speaking up freely in new North American social surroundings.

Effective interpersonal skills like assertiveness cannot be taught in one session; rather, the process of shaping, refining, and reinforcing attitudes and behaviors continues throughout the season (Connelly & Rotella, 1991). Many of the techniques of a comprehensive mental skills training program (e.g., coping imagery, cognitive restructuring, thought stopping, goal setting, self-monitoring, observational learning) will be useful in teaching athletes how to assert themselves more effectively. The following "DESC" formula proposed by Greenberg (1990) is a good example of how people can verbally express themselves more assertively.

1. *Describe* the situation as you see it; paint a verbal picture of the other person's behavior or the situation to which you are reacting ("What I see happening is this . . . "; "When my play is criticized, . . . ").

2. *Express* your feelings regarding the other person's behavior or the situation you have just described ("When you do this, it makes me feel like . . . "; "I get angry and frustrated when you talk behind my back").

3. *Specify* what changes you would like to take place ("I would prefer you give me feedback in a more constructive, less degrading manner"; "I would appreciate it if you did not talk behind my back").

4. *Consequences* to expect ("If you don't get off my case, I will ask Coach to meet with us to straighten this situation out").

Sport Psychologists as Effective Communicators

Throughout the chapter I have talked about the importance of coaches and athletes developing good listening and communication skills. Likewise, it is important for sport psychologists to be good listeners and communicators. Often sport psychologists are asked to be facilitators or skilled helpers in dealing with teams. For example, sport psychologists are often asked to work with coaches and athletes on improving their communication skills. They might be asked to unobtrusively observe and critique a variety of on-court/field behaviors that may reflect breakdowns in communication, such as inconsistencies in body language, verbal and nonverbal statements of support or disapproval, various interactions among team members, and then report back to the coach on what they found. This can be a very important role, considering that communication is vital in all sports, particularly interactive sports like volleyball, basketball, lacrosse, field hockey, and tennis. Similarly, sport psychologists are often asked to facilitate team workshops on interpersonal communication and team cohesion.

Sport psychologists must have good interpersonal skills to work effectively with coaches and athletes on mental skills training. In order for sport psychologists to do a good job, they must be able to listen well, develop rapport, speak the appropriate sport language, and gain the trust of both the coach and athlete. In individual consultation, sport psychologists must be able to draw out strengths, weaknesses, and areas of concern and then individualize a mental skills training program based on the person's needs and abilities. This cannot be done without good communication skills.

Drawing from counseling theory, general communication skills that sport psychologists need in order to be effective helpers are genuineness, honesty, good listening and questioning skills, empathy, and the ability to help "clients" (in this case, athletes) generate alternative ways of looking at problems (Corey, 1977; Danish, D'Augelli, & Ginsberg, 1984; Egan, 1982; Ivey, 1983). A variety of communication skills, verbal and nonverbal, are essential in developing good helping relationships. However, it should be remembered that effective communication skills take time, patience, and practice to develop.

Sport Psychologists as Skilled Helpers

A helping relationship is a unique situation in which someone gives you permission to assist him/her. A good helping relationship fosters *trust* (being able to maintain confidences), *openness* (accepting others as they are, even if you don't agree with them), *comfort* (allowing people to feel and express whatever is true for them, whether it is sadness, happiness, anger, exhilaration, etc.), *empathy* (accepting and understanding the situation and feelings from the other person's point of view), and *genuineness* (responding honestly by adapting the helping skills to fit your own style and personality). In addition, a helping relationship is one that realizes that not all problems can be solved, not all people want to be helped, and you may not be the right person or in the right position to offer help.

Trust is essential to any helping relationship. It must be established before help can occur. There are many kinds of trust and many levels. For example, "social trust" refers to how much an individual trusts people in social situations. Some athletes reach out to new people more easily than others. "Emotional trust" refers to how easily an individual shares feelings with others. This could include whom an athlete feels comfortable revealing feelings to and which feelings he/she decides to share. "Physical trust" could include proximity (personal space between you and others) or territoriality (intrusions into one's personal space). Trust also means making a conscious effort to withhold judgment as to why the athlete feels a certain way (i.e., not pushing one's own viewpoint onto athletes). Often we quickly prejudge a person by actions alone without thinking about what might be behind the action (Pietsch, 1974).

Active Listening

Listening is an important communication skill because of its many uses. According to Rosenfeld and Wilder (1990), we listen for comprehension, appreciation, and evaluation; to empathize; and to gain self-understanding. Real listening means tuning into what the other person is feeling. Most of us have been trained to listen to "facts" rather than feelings (Pietsch, 1974). Thus, real listening means trying to discover what the other person is feeling.

Rosenfeld and Wilder (1990) identify three levels of listening, each representing a different degree of listening effectiveness. "Active listening" is the preferred mode of listening, where the listener is concerned about the content, intent, and feelings of the message being transmitted. This will be further elaborated on shortly. The second level of listening is minimal and is called "superficial" or "inattentive listening." In this situation, listeners often tune out after they think they have enough information as to what the speaker's intent is. While listeners at this level often grasp the basic meaning of the message, they often miss the emotional feeling and, subsequently, fail to comprehend the underlying concepts being communicated. Level-three listening is characterized by what I would call "arrogant listening." In this situation, listeners seem to be more interested in what they have to say as opposed to what the other person is saying. Thus, they listen now and again and wait for pauses in the conversation so they can jump in and hear themselves speak.

By far the most useful tool for improving listening is **active listening** (Martens, 1987). When people talk about themselves, they do so in terms of experiences (things that happen to them), behaviors (what they do or fail to do), and affect (the feelings and emotions that accompany and relate to experiences and behaviors) (Egan, 1982). Effective listening means demonstrating that we care enough to hear the other person's viewpoint (Pietsch, 1974).

Elements of good listening skills include attending to the person you are working with both physically and psychologically (e.g., adopt a posture that indicates involvement); listening and becoming aware of what that person is really trying to say (both verbally and nonverbally); encouraging self-exploration through judicious questioning and probing, paraphrasing, or clarifying to ensure your understanding is correct; and, finally, summarizing and communicating your understanding back in a respectful and empathetic way (Corey, 1977; Egan, 1982).

Reflective listening is one of the most powerful methods of demonstrating to the person you are working with (e.g., coach, athlete) that you are listening and understanding. It has been said that reflective listening is to verbal communication as video feedback is to physical skill instruction (Henschen & Miner, 1989). The skills of questioning, encouraging, paraphrasing, reflecting, and summarizing make up the basic listening sequence. The following reflective listening techniques (Egan, 1982; Ivey, 1983) may facilitate better communication between athlete and sport psychologist.

- *Questioning*: Use open questions to encourage the athlete to continue speaking ("How are you feeling about the injury?"; "Can you tell me more about what happened?"). At first, avoid asking "why" questions, which may put the person you are talking with on the defensive. Wait until he/she has reached an appropriate comfort level.

- *Clarifying*: Make clear to the other person what has been heard. Clarifying does not mean "I agree with your opinion," but, rather, it lets the speaker know you care enough to listen. Some good lead-ins include: "What I hear you saying is . . . "; "I am not sure I quite understand, but it sounds as if you are saying you are angry with your coach because she benched you. Is that it?"

- *Encouraging*: The counselor or sport psychologist can use a variety of verbal and nonverbal means to prompt athletes to keep talking. These include head nods, gestures, a phrase such as "uh-huh," or the simple repetition of key words the athlete has used.

- *Paraphrasing*: Check whether you have understood the message. Paraphrasing encourages the sharer to go on and explore his/her feelings and ideas further. Similar to reflective listening, it involves using one's own words, in short and concise comments, to feed back to the athlete the essence of what has just been said.

- *Reflecting*: Let the person know you hear the content and feelings of what is being said ("You're sad because . . . "; "You feel confident of your ability to play at this level but worry about getting in").

- *Understanding*: Express empathy, *not* sympathy ("It must be hard for you to sit and watch your teammates practice while you are recovering from arthroscopic knee surgery").

- *Summarizing*: Pull together all the main ideas and feelings of what has been said ("It sounds as if you have mixed feelings about the situation. On one hand, you have more time for yourself, but you are also apprehensive about getting your starting job back"). Summaries can be used to begin or end a conversation, for transition to a new topic, or to provide clarity when dealing with lengthy or complex issues or statements.

As for helping athletes generate alternative ways of looking at problems, it is important to remember that not all problems can be resolved and not all people want help. Thus, it is important to listen to what the athlete is asking for, then identify and define what the problem really is. The emphasis should be on the athlete's frame of reference.

First, gather information, role play, and brainstorm alternatives with the athlete you are working with. Incorporate the reflective listening skills discussed above. Point out the consequences of certain actions. Remember to check the forgotten factors (i.e., decisions are influenced by many factors including coaches, peer pressure, family pressure, attitudes, beliefs, feelings, risk levels, habits). Then identify an action plan and motivate the athlete to act. At the end, evaluate what went well and what didn't (Egan, 1982).

Effective helpers should be aware of things that could block effective communication processes. These could include information overload (saying too much at one time), telling people what they should do (e.g., "If I were you, I would . . ."), ordering or directing ("You should speak your mind to the coach"), warning or threatening ("You will regret it if you . . . "), or preaching and moralizing ("That's not right").

Empathy

The skills of attending, listening, and influencing are not always sufficient to provide quality relationships. Of primary interest is the factor of **empathy**. Empathy is a special kind of understanding. It means putting yourself in the shoes of the athlete, experiencing his/her world as if you were the athlete (i.e., moving into the athlete's frame of reference, understanding what the other person is experiencing from his/her own perspective).

Empathy is an acquired skill that comes with practice. More than merely sympathy or pity, it reflects an attitude of caring, concern, and general interest in other people. The attending skills previously mentioned, particularly paraphrasing and reflective listening, are deeply involved in developing basic empathy (Ivey, 1983). Empathy manifests itself when the counselor or sport psychologist truly understands what the athlete is going through and is able to paraphrase the athlete's main ideas accurately. Empathetic listeners reflect what they hear by restating the ideas in their own words or by asking good probing questions (Rosenfeld & Wilder, 1990). The following example gives two responses, one low and one high in empathy:

> *Athlete*: I really get mad when my coach criticizes me without letting me explain anything. It's not just because he criticizes me, but the way he does it is so degrading.
>
> *Sport psychologist* (low empathy): "You don't like being criticized."
>
> *Sport psychologist* (high empathy): "You get really mad when he criticizes you and his insulting manner makes you feel personally attacked."

The following is a summary of guidelines for effective listeners:

1   *Focus* on the person who is talking. Be attentive, genuine, and supportive.

2.   Listen for both *content* and *feelings*.

3.   Show that you *understand* what is being said.

4.   *Summarize* the main points.

5.   Promote new perspectives. Set *goals* based on action-oriented understanding. Work on role playing and coping rehearsal strategies to help prepare individuals for immediate action.

Need for Referral

Finally, sport psychologists must recognize when it is appropriate to make a referral. This is particularly true for those trained primarily in exercise and sport science. As an educational sport psychology specialist, I clarify at the outset what types of services I can and cannot provide. If a serious clinical issue arises, I will make a referral to an appropriate source of help. It is not unusual for an athlete seeking help in some performance enhancement area (e.g., concentration, confidence, anxiety management) to have some deeper, underlying personal problem (such as a recent death in the family, severe depression, drug abuse, eating disorder) that needs immediate counseling or therapy (see Chapter 21).

If an individual needs a referral, it is important to be open and honest about your own limits and the need to refer to a competent resource. Trust is a very important part of the process; thus, you should know as much as possible about the person(s) to whom you are referring. Give as much information as you can to the athlete about the person or place you are referring. Remember to follow up with the athlete to see how things are going. See Chapter 21 for guidelines regarding when it is appropriate to make a referral.

Summary

Communication is a multifaceted phenomenon that involves the transmission or exchange of thoughts, ideas, feelings, or information through verbal and nonverbal channels. Effective communication involves mutual sharing and mutual understanding. Its foundation is trust and mutual respect. Open lines of communication can alleviate many problems that arise within athletic environments.

Characteristics of effective and ineffective communication styles have been presented. Although there are many ways to motivate athletes, it has been suggested that coaches adopt a communication style that is consistent with their personality and coaching philosophy.

An important aspect of communication is the need to be honest, direct, and consistent. Since messages transmitted are not always received and interpreted as intended, it is important that coaches, athletes, and sport psychologists strive to be consistent in their verbal and nonverbal communications. Often, when incongruent messages are transmitted, the receiver can become confused as to the true meaning of the message, thus leaving the door open for miscommunication and misunderstanding.

Although much of this chapter focused on coach–athlete communications, many principles discussed carry over to the applied sport psychologist working within an athletic environment. Gaining entry, building rapport, developing trust, and individualizing a mental skills training program based on the coach's or athletes' needs and desires all require good listening and communication skills. Drawing from counseling theory, a variety of general communication skills that sport psychologists need to be effective in their work with coaches and athletes have been presented, with a strong emphasis placed on developing empathy and active listening skills.

Study Questions

1. Why is communication an important tool for a coach or sport psychologist to possess?

2. Since there is no agreed-upon definition of communication in the literature, how would you define communication in sport?

3. What kind of factors interfere with effective communication processes in sport?

4. Give some behavioral examples of verbal and nonverbal communication in sport.

5. What role does communication play in teaching mental skills to coaches and athletes?

6. What are some things a sport psychologist could do to improve coach–athlete communications?

7. As a coach or sport psychologist, how would you intervene if interpersonal conflict arose among team members that resulted in disruption of group cohesion and team harmony?

8. The volleyball team at Nike University has a tendency to clam up when the going gets tough (i.e., communication breaks down; team loses its intensity, enthusiasm, and focus in critical situations and fails to make appropriate adjustments to things that are going on during competition). How would you intervene as either a sport psychologist or coach to deal with this situation?

9. Why are active listening and empathy such important skills for a sport psychologist to develop in working with coaches and athletes?

10. What are some things one can do to become a better listener?

References

American heritage dictionary (1983). New York: Dell.

Anderson, M. P. (1959). What is communication? *Journal of Communication, 9,* 5.

Anshel, M. (1990). *Sport psychology: From theory to practice.* Scottsdale, Ariz. Gorsuch Scarisbrick.

Carron, A. V. (1988). *Group dynamics in sport.* London, Ont.: Spodym.

Connelly, D., & Rotella, R. J. (1991). The social psychology of assertive communication: Issues in teaching assertiveness skills to athletes. *The Sport Psychologist, 5,* 73–87.

Corey, G. (1977). *Theory and practice of counseling and psychotherapy.* Monterey, Calif. Brooks/Cole.

Dale, J., & Weinberg, R. (1990). Burnout in sport: A review and critique. *Journal of Applied Sport Psychology, 2,* 67–83.

Dance, F. E., & Larson, C. E. (1976). *The functions of human communication: A theoretical approach.* New York: Holt, Rinehart & Winston.

Danish, S., D'Augelli, A. R., & Ginsberg, M. (1984). Life development intervention: Promotion of mental health through the development of competence. In S. Brown & R. Lent (Eds.), *Handbook of counseling psychology* (pp. 520–544). New York: Wiley.

Danish, S. J., Petitpas, A. J., & Hale, B. D. (in press). A developmental-educational intervention model of sport psychology. In S. Murphy (Ed.), *Clinical sport psychology.* Champaign, Ill.: Human Kinetics.

Egan, G. (1982). *The skilled helper: Model, skills, and methods for effective helping.* Monterey, Calif.: Brooks/Cole.

Gould, D., Murphy, S., Tammen, V., & May, J. (1991). An evaluation of U.S. Olympic sport psychology consultant effectiveness. *The Sport Psychologist, 5,* 111–127.

Greenberg, J. S. (1990). *Coping with stress: A practical guide.* Dubuque, Iowa: Brown.

Halliwell, W. (1989). What sport psychologists can learn from coaches and athletes about the psychology of sport. *AAASP Newsletter*, p. 7.

Harris, D. V., & Harris, B. L. (1984). *Sports psychology: Mental skills for physical people*. Champaign, Ill.: Leisure Press.

Henschen, K., & Miner, J. (1989). *Team principles for coaches*. Ogden, Utah: Educational Sport Services.

Ivey, A. E. (1983). *Intentional interviewing and counseling*. Monterey, Calif.: Brooks/Cole.

Knapp, M. L. (1972). *Nonverbal communication in human interaction*. New York: Holt, Rinehart & Winston.

Lazarus, A. A. (1973). On assertive behavior: A brief note. *Behavior Therapy*, 4, 697–699.

Locke, E. A., & Latham, G. P. (1990). *A theory of goal setting and task performance*. Englewood Cliffs, N. J.: Prentice-Hall.

Martens, R. (1987). *Coaches guide to sport psychology*. Champaign, Ill.: Human Kinetics.

Martens, R. (1990). *Successful coaching*. Champaign, Ill.: Human Kinetics.

Martens, R., Christina, R. W., Harvey, J. S., & Sharkey, B. J. (1981). *Coaching young athletes*. Champaign, Ill.: Human Kinetics.

Martin, G., & Hrycaiko, D. (1983). Effective behavioral coaching: What's it all about? *Journal of Sport Psychology*, 5, 8–20.

Moore, W. E., & Stevenson, J. R. (1991). Understanding trust in the performance of complex automatic sport skills. *The Sport Psychologist*, 5, 281–289.

Norman, D. A. (1976). *Memory and attention: An introduction to human information processing*. New York: Wiley.

Orlick, T. (1986). *Psyching for sport*. Champaign, Ill.: Human Kinetics.

Orlick, T. (1990). *In pursuit of excellence* (2nd ed.). Champaign, Ill.: Human Kinetics.

Orlick, T., & Partington, J. (1987). The sport psychology consultant: Analysis of critical components as viewed by Canadian Olympic athletes. *The Sport Psychologist*, 1, 4–17.

Partington, J., & Orlick, T. (1987). The sport psychology consultant: Olympic coaches views. *The Sport Psychologist*, 1, 95–102.

Pietsch, W. V. (1974). *Human be-ing: How to have a creative relationship instead of a power struggle*. New York: New American Library.

Ravizza, K. (1984). Qualities of the peak performance in sport. In J. M. Silva & R. S. Weinberg (Eds.), *Psychological foundations of sport* (pp. 452–461). Champaign, Ill.: Human Kinetics.

Ravizza, K. (1988). Gaining entry with athletic personnel for season long consulting. *The Sport Psychologist*, 2, 243–254.

Ravizza, K. (1990). SportPsych consultation issues in professional baseball. *The Sport Psychologist*, 4, 330–340.

Rosenfeld, L., & Wilder, L. (1990). Communication fundamentals: Active listening. *Sport Psychology Training Bulletin*, 1(5), 1–8.

Shaw, M. E. (1981). *Group dynamics: The psychology of small group behavior* (3rd ed.). New York: McGraw-Hill.

Smith, N. J., Smith, R. E., & Smoll, F. L. (1983). *Kidsports: A survival guide for parents*. Reading, Mass.: Addison-Wesley.

Smith, R. E. (1986). Toward a cognitive-affective model of athletic burnout. *Journal of Sport Psychology*, 8, 36–50.

Smith, R. E., Smoll, F., & Curtis, B. (1979). Coach effectiveness training: A cognitive-behavioral approach to enhancing relationship skills in youth sport coaches. *Journal of Sport Psychology*, 1, 59–75.

Tubbs, S. L., & Moss, S. (1987). *Human communication* (5th ed.). New York: Random House.

Vealey, R. S. (1988). Future directions in psychological skills training. *The Sport Psychologist*, 2, 318–336.

Vernacchia, R. (1992). Preventing and reversing coaching burnout. In R. McGuire, D. Cook, & R. Vernacchia (Eds.), *Coaching mental excellence: "It does not matter whether you win or lose"* (pp. 127–139). Dubuque, Iowa: Brown.

Wenburg, J. R., & Wilmot, W. W. (1982). *The personal communication process*. Malabar, Fla.: Krieger.

Wooten, M. (1992). *Coaching basketball effectively*. Champaign, Ill.: Human Kinetics.

Yukelson, D. (1984). Group motivation in sport teams. In J. Silva & R. Weinberg (Eds.), *Psychological foundations in sport* (pp. 229–240). Champaign, Ill.: Human Kinetics.

Psychological Characteristics of Peak Performance

Jean M. Williams, *University of Arizona*
Vikki Krane, *Bowling Green State University*

*P*eak performances are those magic moments when an athlete puts it all together—both physically and mentally. The performance is exceptional, seemingly transcending ordinary levels of play. Privette defined peak performance as "behavior which exceeds one's average performance" (1982, p. 242) or "an episode of superior functioning" (1983, p. 1361). Competitively, these performances often result in a personal best. They are the ultimate high, the thrilling moment that athletes and coaches work for in their pursuit of excellence. Unfortunately, they also are relatively rare and, according to many athletes, nonvoluntary. But are they truly nonvoluntary? Can athletes be trained so that peak performances occur more frequently? If not to produce a peak performance, can they be trained so they consistently play closer to their optimal level?

To answer these questions, it is first necessary to know if there are any common characteristics that identify peak performances. For example, is there an ideal body/mind state associated with peak performance? If so, is this ideal state similar from one athlete to another or one sport to another? More importantly, if common qualities are identified, can they be trained?

First, it is safe to assume that peak performance is a consequence of both physical and mental factors. Mind and body cannot be separated. A precondition to peak performance is a certain level of physical conditioning and mastery of the physical skills involved in performance. For many decades, athletic and sport science communities have been devoted to improving physical training programs.

Obviously, the higher the level of physical skill and conditioning, the more potential control the athlete has over his/her performance. Within this minimal physical skill framework, one must realize that peak performance is relative—contingent upon each athlete's present level of ability. Thus, concern for enhancing peak performance may be as relevant to the coaches and sport psychologists who work with less skilled youth sport athletes as it is to coaches and sport psychologists who work with professional or elite amateur athletes.

Overview of Peak Performance

This chapter is not concerned per se with physical skill characteristics and physical training programs that enhance the likelihood of peak performance. Instead, its focus is on the mental side of peak performance and how the mind interacts with the body in ultimately producing performance. Most athletes and coaches will acknowledge that at least 40% to 90% of success in sports is due to mental factors. The higher the skill level, the more important the mental aspects become. In fact, on the elite competitive level, it is not uncommon to hear that the winner invariably comes down to who is the strongest athlete—mentally—on a given day! Rushall (1989) has stated that "psychology is the key to athletic excellence" (p. 165). For example, when the physical, technical, and mental readiness of Olympic athletes was assessed, only mental readiness significantly predicted Olympic success (Orlick & Partington, 1988). Additionally, in *Golf My Way*, Jack Nicklaus states that mental preparation is the single most critical element in peak performance. This is not a particularly surprising statement considering that Nicklaus believes golf is 90% mental.

If the mental side of performance is so important to success, then perhaps an ideal internal psychological climate exists during peak performance. Over the last 15 years, there has been a tremendous surge of research on psychological aspects of peak performance. The remainder of this chapter will reflect what has been learned from this research and from the insights of people who have worked with athletes in psychological training. Before identifying some of these research findings and insights, we must offer a caution. Do not think that the field of sport psychology has found all the answers. It certainly has not, and the evidence to support some of its answers is still quite tenuous. In addition to not having all of the answers, sport psychologists have probably not even identified all of the questions yet! There is, however, a growing foundation for understanding the mental side of performance and possibilities for improving performance through psychological skills training. This chapter, and the following chapters in this section, will attempt to reflect the latest state of knowledge and the current thinking and practices of those involved in mental training for peak performance.

The Peak Performance Psychological Profile

Before we can think in terms of psychological skills training, it is necessary to know if there is an opti-

mal psychological state for peak performance. If such a state can be identified for programs or for a given individual, then there is a foundation for developing a mental skills training program, provided these skills can be trained. There are at least three excellent sources for helping to identify the psychological characteristics underlying successful athletic performance. One is the data that have been generated from researchers who have asked athletes to recall their subjective perceptions during the greatest moment they ever had while participating in sport. The second source is the data generated from studies that have compared the psychological characteristics of successful and less successful athletes—for example, athletes who were Olympic qualifiers compared to nonqualifiers, or collegiate athletes who were successful compared to less successful collegiate athletes. The third source of information comes from people who have asked top athletes, coaches, scouts, and sport psychologists what they think it takes to be successful in sport.

Psychological Characteristics During Peak Experiences in Sport

Ken Ravizza (1977), the author of Chapter 12, was one of the first sport psychologists to publish a study on the subjective experiences of athletes during their "greatest moment" in sport. He interviewed 20 male and female athletes from a variety of competitive levels who related experiences in 12 different sports. Over 80% of the athletes reported having the following perceptions:

- Loss of fear—no fear of failure
- No thinking of performance
- Total immersion in the activity
- Narrow focus of attention
- Effortless performance—not forcing it
- Feeling of being in complete control
- Time/space disorientation (usually slowed down)
- Universe perceived to be integrated and unified
- Unique, temporary, involuntary experience

In trying to determine where "mental toughness" comes from and to answer other questions about the mental aspects of sports training, psychologist Jim Loehr interviewed hundreds of athletes. He asked them to describe how they felt when they were playing at their best. What were their psychological experiences prior to and during a peak athletic experience? The athletes gave surprisingly similar accounts. According to Loehr (1984), "It was," they said, "like playing possessed, yet in complete control. Time itself seemed to slow down, so they never felt rushed. They played with profound intensity, total concentration and an enthusiasm that bordered on joy" (p. 67). Loehr further clarified the relationship between optimal sport performance and confidence and arousal by compiling the following composite of athletes' interview statements:

> I felt like I could do almost anything, as if I were in complete control. I really felt confident and positive." [Regarding arousal,] "I felt physically very relaxed, but really energized and pumped up. I experienced virtually no anxiety or fear, and the whole experience was enjoyable. I experienced a very real sense of calmness and quiet inside, and everything just seemed to flow automatically. . . . Even though I was really hustling, it was all very effortless. (cited in Garfield & Bennett, 1984, pp. 37, 95)

Loehr concluded that the probability of good performance could be substantially increased if the following combination of feelings could be triggered and maintained: high energy (challenge, inspiration, determination, intensity), fun and enjoyment, no pressure (low anxiety), optimism and positiveness, mental calmness, confidence, being very focused, and being in control.

Loehr's research has been corroborated by Charles Garfield (Garfield & Bennett, 1984), president of the Peak Performance Center in Berkeley, California. In interviews with hundreds of elite athletes, Garfield identified eight mental and physical conditions that athletes described as being characteristic of the feelings they have at those moments when they are doing something extraordinarily well:

1. *Mentally relaxed.* This was described most frequently as a sense of inner calm. Some athletes also reported a sense of time being slowed down and having a high degree of concentration. By contrast, loss of concentration was associated with a sense of everything happening too fast and being out of control.

2. *Physically relaxed.* Feeling of muscles being loose with movements fluid and sure.

3. *Confident/optimistic.* A positive attitude, feelings of self-confidence and optimism. Being able to keep poise and feelings of strength and control even during potentially threatening challenges.

4. *Focused on the present.* A sense of harmony that comes from the body and mind working as one unit. No thoughts of the past or future. The body performs automatically, without conscious or deliberate mental effort.

5. *Highly energized.* A high-energy state frequently described as feelings of joy, ecstasy, intensity, and being "charged" or "hot."

6. *Extraordinary awareness.* A state of mind in which the athletes are acutely aware of their own bodies and of the surrounding athletes. They report an uncanny ability to know what the other athletes are going to do, and they respond accordingly. Also a sensation of being completely in harmony with the environment.

7. *In control.* The body and mind seem to do automatically exactly what is right—yet there is no sense of exerting or imposing control.

8. *In the cocoon.* The feeling of being in an envelope, being completely detached from the external environment and any potential distractions. Also a sense of complete access to all of one's powers and skills. Athletes "in the cocoon" are able to avoid loss of concentration and accelerated, tight-muscled, out-of-control feelings.

A recent study of competitive golfers (Cohn, 1991) further substantiated the previous findings. Collegiate golfers and touring and teaching professionals were queried concerning their peak performance experiences. Psychological characteristics associated with peak performance acknowledged by these golfers included:

- A narrow focus of attention, typically on one specific thought or action

- Feeling that performance was automatic and effortless—being immersed in the present
- Feelings of control over emotion, thoughts and arousal
- Feeling highly self-confident
- An absence of fear
- Feeling physically and mentally relaxed

Each of these qualities of peak performance was reported by at least 80% of the golfers interviewed. Many of the golfers associated this state with fun or enjoyment. These golfers also indicated that peak performance was considered a temporary phenomenon that typically lasted no longer than the length of a tournament (four rounds of golf).

Often associated with peak performance is the psychological construct **flow**. Csikszentmihalyi (1985) has considered flow the basis of intrinsically motivated experiences or self-rewarding activity. It is "the state in which people are so involved in an activity that nothing else seems to matter" (Csikszentmihalyi, 1990, p. 4). Flow is not analogous to peak performance. One may be in flow and not necessarily be having a peak performance; however, when an athlete experiences peak performance, he/she appears to be in a flow state. Jackson (1988) suggested that flow may be a precursor to or the psychological process underlying peak performance. Csikszentmihalyi (1991) defined the following conditions of flow: The challenges equal skill level; one knows what to do; one has clear goals, deep concentration, a sense of being in control, and loss of a sense of time; and activity becomes autotelic. In interviews with collegiate and elite athletes, Jackson (1991) found that athletes' descriptions of peak performances coincided with characteristics of flow: feeling in complete control, total confidence, complete absorption in the activity, and a sense of "could do no wrong." These athletes also reported that the experience of the performance was as affirming as the actual outcome. These characteristics are very similar to those reported to accompany peak performances.

Psychological Differences Between Successful and Unsuccessful Athletes

Another source of psychological peak performance information concerns research on why some indi-

viduals outperform others. These data primarily come from researchers who have used objective paper-and-pencil inventories to compare the psychological characteristics of successful and less successful athletes. In the mid-1970s, Mahoney and Avener designed an objective questionnaire to assess various psychological factors such as confidence, concentration, anxiety, self-talk, imagery, and dreams. Most of the questionnaire items employed an 11-point Likert-type scale. This basic tool, or variations of it, has been used by researchers to study athletes in the sports of gymnastics, wrestling, tennis, racquetball, and diving. When Mahoney and Avener (1977) compared 1976 U.S. Olympic qualifiers and nonqualifiers in men's gymnastics, they found that the finalists coped more easily with competitive mistakes, were better able to control and utilize anxiety, had higher self-confidence and more positive self-talk, had more gymnastics-related dreams, and had more frequent imagery of an internal versus external nature. **External imagery** occurs when a person views himself/herself from the perspective of an external observer, such as seeing oneself on television or videotape. **Internal imagery** requires an approximation much more like the actual perspective when the skill is performed physically, that is, imagining being inside the body and experiencing the same sensations as one might expect in actual physical execution.

Following are the results from a sampling of other studies that employed a design similar to Mahoney and Avener's. Better performers on the Memphis State University racquetball team, compared to less successful performers, had higher self-confidence in training and competition, reported fewer doubts, had more racquetball thoughts in everyday situations, and had dreams and imagery that were more likely to portray successful performance (Meyers et al., 1979). Canadian National Wrestling Team qualifiers compared with nonqualifiers were higher in self-confidence, closer to reaching their maximum athletic potential, more able to block anxiety one hour prior to and during competition, and experienced fewer negative self-thoughts one hour prior to competition (Highlen & Bennett, 1979). In a wrestling study comparing placers and nonplacers in a Big Ten wrestling tournament, the placers were more self-confident, closer to their athletic potential, more frequent users of attentional focusing to prepare for the meet, and more positively affected by seeing themselves as the underdog (Gould, Weiss, & Weinberg, 1981). The divers who competed successfully enough in Canada's National Championship to subsequently qualify for Canada's Pan American Diving Team had more self-confidence, higher concentration, lower anxiety during competition, and more self-talk and imagery than less successful divers. They also reported more vividness and better control of their imagery (Highlen & Bennett, 1983). Mahoney, Gabriel, and Perkins (1987) examined psychological differences in elite, preelite and collegiate athletes in a variety of sports. Elite athletes reported that they experienced fewer anxiety problems, had better concentration before and during competition, were more self-confident, used internal and kinesthetic mental imagery in their mental preparation, were more focused on individual rather than team performance, and were more highly motivated to do well than less elite athletes.

While questionnaire data have provided a solid foundation for understanding psychological characteristics of peak performance, interviews with athletes can extend and enhance these findings. Recently, Scanlan and associates (Scanlan, Ravizza, & Stein, 1989; Scanlan, Stein, & Ravizza, 1989) have provided an outstanding framework for conducting interview research in sport psychology. Their approach to the data analysis allowed themes to emerge from the data, as opposed to the more rigid structure of questionnaires. Their methods should serve as a model for qualitative research examining peak performance.

Gould, Eklund, and Jackson (1990) and Eklund (1991) utilized the methods suggested by Scanlan, Ravizza, and Stein (1989). In interviews with members of the U.S. 1988 Olympic wrestling teams, Gould, Eklund, and Jackson (1990) found certain psychological characteristics associated with athletes' best and worst performances. Eklund (1991) interviewed collegiate wrestlers and found almost identical results. These studies revealed that positive expectancies, total concentration, high confidence, a task-relevant focus, heightened arousal and intensity, and heightened effort and commitment were related to athletes' all-time best performances. In contrast, feeling listless, over- or underarousal, lack of concentration, irrelevant or negative thoughts, worries about losing, nonadherence to normal preparation routines, and negative physical feelings (e.g., tired, inadequate warm-up) were associated with all-time worst performances. Interestingly, unlike previous studies (Garfield & Bennett, 1984; Mahoney, Gabriel, & Perkins, 1987), Eklund (1991) noted that the collegiate wrestlers experienced some doubts prior to peak performances. However, the athletes' doubts turned into confidence during the match, suggesting that some temporary self-doubts do not necessarily rule out the possibility of a peak performance.

On the basis of the results of these studies and of similarly designed studies that have not been summarized here, there appear to be some commonalities in the psychological characteristics of more successful athletes. The most consistent finding is higher levels of self-confidence for the more successful competitors. Without exception, the researchers reported that the better athletes believed in themselves more than the less successful athletes. Most of the researchers also reported better concentration. Successful athletes were less likely to be distracted and kept a more task-oriented focus of concentration versus a preoccupation with outcome thoughts or thoughts of "messing up." Generally, the successful athletes also were more preoccupied with their sport and in a more positive way. This was reflected by more thoughts, imagery, daydreams, and dreams relative to their sport, with the content tending to be more positive. In a number of the studies, successful athletes were found to have less anxiety immediately before and during competition. Successful athletes were able to control their anxiety to a facilitative level and often were highly activated, which they interpret in a positive manner (e.g., "psyched up"). Most of the better athletes also had a higher ability to rebound from mistakes. One might conjecture that this could be a consequence of higher self-confidence, more optimal control of anxiety, and better concentration skills.

Psychological Skills and Peak Performance

Recent investigation of peak performance has focused on the mental preparation strategies and psychological skills utilized by successful elite athletes. Orlick and Partington (1988) conducted one of the most extensive investigations of Olympic athletes in their study of "mental links to excellence" with Canadian Olympic athletes. Seventy-five athletes were interviewed, and another 160 athletes completed questionnaires assessing factors related to optimal mental readiness and psychological elements of success. "Total commitment to pursuing excellence" (p. 129) was common to all of these elite athletes. Another distinctive characteristic was high-quality training that included daily goal setting, competition simulation, and imagery training. These athletes obviously cultivated their mental skills, as they had well-developed plans for competition, competition focusing, and coping with distractions. These plans typically included mental imagery, positive thoughts, and attentional focus strategies. Through postcompetition evaluations, which also were common among these athletes, their mental approach was continually refined.

As previously mentioned studies revealed, imagery was an important skill for peak performance in these Olympic athletes. Interviews with the best athletes (Olympic and world medalists) indicated that they had well-developed imagery skills, used an internal perspective, and used imagery on a daily basis. The questionnaire data revealed that 99% of the athletes reported using imagery as a mental preparation strategy. "On average, preplanned, systematic imagery was used at least once a day, 4 days per week, for about 12 minutes each time" (Orlick & Partington, 1988, p. 125).

Research with the Canadian Olympians also revealed three things that interfered with peak performance: changing preparation/performance patterns that worked, late selection onto the Olympic team, and an inability to refocus attention after distractions (Orlick & Partington, 1988). Olympic athletes with an ineffective focus of attention were preoccupied with self-doubts, concerns about competitors, concern with current standings or score, thoughts of the possible outcome, or were thinking too far ahead. This is in contrast to an effective focus of attention that zeroed in on the present task and was associated with an appropriate arousal level, positive self-statements, "clear and ever-present awareness of executing the task or plan without distraction" (Orlick & Partington, 1988, p. 126) and feelings of confidence, determination, power, and control.

The study of the 1988 U.S. Olympic wrestling teams (Gould, Eklund, & Jackson, 1990) also revealed many similar findings to Orlick and Partington's study of Canadian Olympic athletes concerning use of psychological skills. Four general dimensions of mental skills were utilized by the wrestlers. Imagery skills were the most frequently reported mental skill. Imagery was used to create positive images; mentally rehearse tactics, strategies, and techniques; relax; and reinforce goals and objectives. Thought control techniques such as thought stopping, self-talk, positive thinking, and prayer were common. Emotional control skills were used to regulate activation level and to create feelings associated with optimal performance states. Finally, behavioral preparation skills (e.g., separating self from others, distracting self with other activities) typically were used as mental preparation routines.

Gould, Ecklund, and Jackson (1990) also compared the responses of medalists and nonmedalists. The more successful Olympic wrestlers were able to effectively cope with distractions and unforeseen events and adhered to their mental preparation plans and precompetition routines more than the nonmedalists. The most salient difference between the medalists and nonmedalists was the extent that their coping strategies were practiced and internalized. The successful athletes had highly developed techniques for coping with distractions, which acted as "automatized buffers" that reduced the impact of negative unforeseen events or allowed the wrestlers to interpret these occurrences positively. Specific coping strategies of the successful wrestlers included using positive thinking; a narrow, specific focus of attention; and changing their environment (e.g., avoiding potential irritants, moving away from others). The less successful wrestlers, on the other hand, abandoned competitive plans when under pressure, lost competitive focus, and did not rigorously adhere to the mental preparation plans.

Eklund (1991) replicated the findings of Gould, Ecklund, and Jackson with collegiate wrestlers. Additionally, Eklund compared collegiate wrestlers' mental states at high, moderate, and low levels of performance, revealing somewhat of a continuum of mental states leading up to peak performance. Overall, as performance improved, wrestlers experienced an increase in positive affect and a concomitant decrease in negative affect. One of the clearest patterns was that task-relevant thoughts increased and irrelevant thoughts decreased as performances improved. The quality of task-relevant thoughts also improved, with a noticeable lack of focus in poor performances and an intense competitive focus in best performances. Additionally, activation levels changed as performance improved. Low levels of performance were associated with feeling listless and lethargic or "totally stressed out," moderate performance was associated with "more normal levels of nervousness" (Eklund, 1991, p. 275), while high levels of performance were associated with high positive activation and intensity. Changes in confidence were also evident. Low-level performance was accompanied by a lack of confidence and self-doubts, moderate-level performance was accompanied by low confidence and/or self-doubts, and high-level performance was accompanied by high and persistent confidence.

McCaffrey and Orlick (1989) corroborated the results of the previous studies. They interviewed top touring professional golfers, all of whom had won professional tournaments. The interviews revealed the following "elements of excellence" that nicely summarize the findings of the previous studies with elite athletes as well:

- Total commitment
- Quality rather than quantity of practice
- Clearly defined goals
- Imagery practice on a daily basis
- Focusing totally on one shot at a time
- Recognizing, expecting, and preparing to cope with pressure situations
- Practice and tournament plans
- Tournament focus plan
- Distraction control strategies
- Posttournament evaluation
- A clear understanding of what helps them play well versus play poorly

The use of psychological skills appears to help athletes achieve peak performances. As Csikszentmihalyi (1975, 1990) suggests, peak performance is most likely to occur when one's ability matches the challenges within a situation. Eklund's (1991) research indicates that as athletes become better versed in the use of certain mental skills, their ability may become more closely matched with high-level competitive challenges. Hence, they may also improve the likelihood of attaining peak performance. One important difference between the collegiate wrestlers and the Olympic athletes in the Orlick and Partington (1988) and Gould, Eklund, and Jackson (1990) studies was the lack of formalized precompetition routines used by the collegians. As Eklund (1991) noted: ". . . it seems that

the function of a mental preparation routine is to enhance the likelihood of the occurrence of optimal performance" (p. 260).

What Top Sport People Think It Takes to "Make It"

Another way to identify potential peak performance characteristics is to ask the best athletes, coaches, scouts, and sport psychologists what it takes to "make it" at the highest level in their sport. A study by Orlick (sport psychologist) and Reed (exercise physiologist) did just that (Orlick, 1980). They found disagreement from sport to sport regarding the *physical* attributes necessary for excellence but almost total agreement across sports on the necessary *psychological* attributes for success. Commitment and self-control were identified as the two key psychological ingredients for excellence.

For example, regarding **commitment**, when Orlick and Reed interviewed many of the top coaches and scouts in the National Hockey League, words like "desire," "determination," "attitude," "heart," and "self-motivation" were most often mentioned as the crucial factors that determine who does and does not make it at the professional level. Few athletes can reach high levels of excellence without high levels of personal commitment. One way for coaches and sport psychologists to assess levels of commitment and also to build commitment is to use the principles of goal setting (see Chapter 13). The level of commitment coaches can reasonably expect from athletes obviously depends upon the level and type of competition (e.g., youth sport participant, professional athlete, Olympic team member, nonscholarship compared to full-scholarship collegiate athlete). Regardless of the level or type of competition, those athletes who have the goal of being the best they are capable of or being one of the best in their sport need higher levels of commitment than athletes with less challenging goals. Achieving the highest standard possible requires that an athlete must want it more than others, be willing to train harder and longer (expending more hours and more effort and concentration during practices), and be willing to make sacrifices.

According to these top athletes, coaches, and scouts, high commitment alone is not sufficient to achieve real athletic success. Maturity and self-**control** are also needed. This means being able to perform well in big games and tight situations as well as in normal games and situations. This requires staying cool and confident and maintaining composure. One way top coaches and scouts assessed composure was to look at how athletes reacted to bad officiating calls. Athletes who remained cool and tried to calm their teammates under such circumstances were considered more desirable prospects. Being mature and positive, reacting well to mistakes, being able to accept criticism (even when undeserved), and not being afraid to fail (not holding back, having the courage to "go for it" in challenging situations) were other qualities used to describe self-control.

Mahoney, Gabriel, and Perkins (1987) had internationally renowned sport psychologists complete a psychological skills inventory "as they thought the ideal athlete would respond" (p. 183). Compared to elite athlete responses, the sport psychologists portrayed the ideal athlete as: "having less worry and performance anxiety, having fewer concentration problems, being more consistently self-confident, being more team focused, using more internally referenced mental preparations, and being more motivated to do well" (p. 189). This profile differed from elite athletes in that the psychologists viewed the ideal athlete as having fewer problems than occur in reality. However, the skills emphasized (anxiety management, concentration, motivation, mental preparation, and self-confidence) correspond with the descriptions of elite athletes throughout the studies reviewed in this chapter.

Limitations of Peak Performance Research

Can one assume that the psychological differences between the successful and less successful athletes were critical to performance differences? This may well be the case, but the design of the preceding studies does not permit that conclusion. Those studies were only correlational; they did not test a cause-and-effect relationship. Other untested history and selection variables might have caused the differences. For example, perhaps these psychological differences did not contribute to performance outcome so much as reflect previous experience and success levels (Heyman, 1982).

Additional limitations of peak performance research may include response bias due to previous knowledge of peak performance characteristics or performance outcome (Brewer et al., 1991). Brewer and colleagues (1991) utilized a novel approach to the study of peak performance in an experimental setting to test potential prejudices on retrospective recall. To test whether familiarity with descriptions of peak performance influenced recall, subjects (introductory psychology students) were exposed to different instruction sets prior to completing a peak performance questionnaire. Instructions included typical, atypical, or no examples of mental states associated with peak performance. Results revealed no differences in the responses of subjects receiving the different instruction sets. This suggests that prior knowledge of peak performance characteristics does not influence athletes' responses. This study also assessed the impact of performance outcome on peak performance descriptions. Subjects (introductory psychology students) completed a pursuit rotor task and were given "bogus" performance feedback. Those who received success feedback reported greater confidence and a clearer task focus than subjects who received failure feedback. Although this suggests that performance outcome may have an impact on peak performance descriptions, there are important factors that should be acknowledged. As Csikszentmihalyi (1990) states, a peak experience is an exhilarating and very positive experience rendering it undeniably favorable, regardless of the outcome.

Orlick and Partington (1988) noted that the Olympic athletes they interviewed were recalling an extremely important event in their lives. In this respect, athletes greatly differ from typical subjects in psychology studies, who have little investment in the topic of the investigation and may not have actually experienced a peak performance. Additionally, Orlick and Partington found the Olympic athletes often exhibited similar physical feelings (e.g., sweating, muscular tensing, increased heart rate) as they recounted their experiences as when they were actually in competition.

When conducting interviews with athletes, researchers incorporate many precautions to avoid potential biases. Orlick and Partington (1988) utilized the following controls to avoid bias in their interviews: the use of a standardized interview guide, pilot interviews in which athletes were asked (after the primary interview questions) if they were influenced in any way by the interviewer, use of probing questions to detect any misinterpretations of the athletes' statements, and a subsample of interview transcripts sent back to the athletes to be sure they accurately represented the athletes' accounts. Scanlan, Stein, and Ravizza (1989) had investigators independently identify themes among the data; then two investigators compared results and discussed their interpretations until a consensus was reached. When divergent views were presented, either one investigator would acquiesce when faced with a convincing argument, or the investigators would jointly recluster the themes. This process decreased

the potential bias and resulted in a more accurate representation of each athlete's experience (Scanlan, Stein, & Ravizza, 1989).

While Brewer and colleagues' caution should be heeded, it is also important to recognize controls taken by researchers to avoid potential biases. As Martens (1987) suggested, interview research methodology places much more responsibility on the researcher, who must utilize controls for unnecessary bias. Overall, the use of interviews can vastly enhance our understanding of athlete mental states accompanying or leading to peak performances by extending knowledge gained from objective questionnaire studies.

Summary

This chapter began with the questions "Is there an ideal body/mind state associated with peak self-control?" and "If so, is this ideal state similar from one athlete to another or one sport to another?" Regardless of the source of data or the nature of the sport, a certain psychological profile appears to be linked with successful performance. Although there are numerous individual variations, in most cases this general profile is depicted by the following characteristics:

- Self-regulation of arousal (energized yet relaxed, no fear)
- Higher self-confidence
- Better concentration (being appropriately focused)
- In control, but not forcing it
- Positive preoccupation with sport (imagery and thoughts)
- Determination and commitment

These commonalities in psychological qualities have led many researchers and practitioners to conclude that the presence of the right emotional climate helps mobilize physiological reactions that are essential to performing at one's best. A negative psychological climate, such as feelings of frustration, fear, anger, and worry, typically does the opposite. It may trigger reactions such as tight muscles and poor concentration. Thus, even though

adequate cause-and-effect data are lacking, current thinking and practice in applied sport psychology tend to assume that level of performance is a direct reflection of the way one is thinking and feeling rather than that the emotional state is a consequence of performance outcome. In actuality, both views could be correct: A circular relationship would be quite logical—that is, optimal mental states lead to better performance, and being successful enhances desirable mental states.

According to Loehr (1984) and others, this ideal performance state does not just happen. Top-level athletes have identified their own ideal performance state and have learned, intentionally or subconsciously, to create and maintain this state voluntarily so that their talents and physical skills thrive. Achieving one's own ideal internal psychological climate is not a simple task. The mental skills needed to trigger and sustain this ideal performance state are learned through knowledge and practice, just as the physical skills and strategies of the game are learned. It appears that some gifted athletes seem to be able to perfect these mental techniques on their own, but most athletes need to be taught specific training techniques. As Orlick and Partington (1988) stated, "Mental readying is derived from a number of learned mental skills that must be continually practiced and refined for an athlete to perform to potential and on a consistent basis" (p. 129). Many athletes who have been exposed to such systematic training believe that they have both improved their performance level and learned to perform more consistently at their best. For example, many of the Olympic athletes interviewed by Orlick and Partington stated that they could have obtained their best performances much sooner had they strengthened their mental skills earlier in their athletic careers. Olympic wrestlers also acknowledged the importance of sport psychology training as they voiced the need for more accessible sport psychology services, individualized mental training, and an integration of sport psychology with practices and competitions (Gould, Eklund, & Jackson, 1990). Fortunately, knowledge in applied sport psychology has advanced to the point that such techniques are now available. Although much still needs to be learned and tested, there is a sufficient base of knowledge to implement systematic mental skills training. The following mental skills were commonly used by elite athletes while achieving their peak performances:

- Imagery
- Goal setting
- Thought control strategies
- Arousal management techniques
- Well-developed competition plans
- Well-developed coping strategies (used when distracted or faced with unforeseen events)
- Precompetition mental readying plans

The remaining chapters in this section of the book specifically address the psychological states associated with peak performance and, when appropriate, provide techniques for learning to create and maintain desirable mental and physiological states. Chapter 12 is unique in that its purpose is to help coaches and sport psychologists learn how to assist each athlete in identifying his/her own internal psychological climate for peak performance and to identify those factors that tend to enhance or detract from this ideal climate. Such an awareness is the first step in mental skills training. In the chapters that follow, it becomes obvious that peak performance need not be a unique, temporary, involuntary experience. It is a product of the body and mind, and it can be trained. Just as improving physical skills, strategies, and conditioning increases the likelihood of peak performance, learning to control psychological readiness and the

ideal mental climate for peak performance also enhances performance.

Study Questions

1. Define "peak performance."
2. Briefly describe the three sources of data about peak performance.
3. List nine characteristics of peak performance compiled by Ravizza.
4. List nine characteristics of peak performance compiled by Loehr.
5. List eight characteristics of peak performance compiled by Garfield.
6. List the seven characteristics of peak performance of golfers found by Cohn.
7. Describe the four most consistent psychological differences between more and less successful athletes as found in questionnaire data.
8. List the "elements of excellence" that were found by McCaffey and Orlick.
9. Describe the characteristics of an effective focus of attention compared to an ineffective focus of attention.
10. Describe psychological attributes needed to "make it" in sports that were most commonly given by coaches, athletes, and scouts (Orlick).
11. Explain the limitations of questionnaire studies that look at the attributes of more and less successful athletes.
12. Explain the precautions taken by researchers to minimize bias during interviews concerning peak performance.

References

Brewer, B. W., VanRaalte, J. L., Linder, D. E., & VanRaalte, N. S. (1991). Peak performance and the perils of retrospective introspection. *Journal of Sport and Exercise Psychology, 8,* 227–238.

Cohn, P. J. (1991). An exploratory study on peak performance in golf. *The Sport Psychologist, 5,* 1–14.

Csikszentmihalyi, M. (1975). Beyond boredom and anxiety. San Francisco: Jossey-Bass.

Csikszentmihalyi, M. (1985). Emergent motivation and the evolution of the self. In D. Kleiber & M. Maehr (Eds.), *Advances in motivation and achievement* (vol. 4) (pp. 93–119). Greenwich, Conn.: JAI Press.

Csikszentmihalyi, M. (1990). *Flow: The psychology of optimal experience.* New York: Harper & Row.

Csikszentmihalyi, M. (1991). *Talent and enjoyment: Findings from a longitudinal study*. Keynote address at the annual meeting of the Association for the Advancement of Applied Sport Psychology, Savannah, Ga.

Eklund, R. C. (1991). *Pre-competitive and competitive cognition and affect in collegiate wrestlers*. Unpublished doctoral dissertation, University of North Carolina at Greensboro.

Garfield, C. A., & Bennett, H. Z. (1984). *Peak performance: Mental training techniques of the world's greatest athletes*. Los Angeles: Tarcher.

Gould, D., Eklund, R. C., & Jackson, S. A. (1990). *An in-depth examination of mental factors and preparation techniques associated with 1988 U.S. Olympic team wrestling excellence*. Unpublished final project report to USA Wrestling.

Gould, D., Weiss, M., & Weinberg, R. (1981). Psychological characteristics of successful and nonsuccessful Big Ten wrestlers. *Journal of Sport Psychology, 3*, 69–81.

Heyman, S. R. (1982). Comparisons of successful and unsuccessful competitors: A reconsideration of methodological questions and data. *Journal of Sport Psychology, 4*, 295–300.

Highlen, P. S., & Bennett, B. B. (1979). Psychological characteristics of successful and nonsuccessful elite wrestlers: An exploratory study. *Journal of Sport Psychology, 1*, 123–137.

Highlen, P. S., & Bennett, B. B. (1983). Elite divers and wrestlers: A comparison between open- and closed-skill athletes. *Journal of Sport Psychology, 5*, 390–409.

Jackson, S. A. (1988). *Positive performance states of athletes toward a conceptual understanding of peak performance*. Unpublished master's thesis, University of Illinois at Urbana-Champaign.

Jackson, S. (1991). *Examining flow experiences in sport contexts: Implications for peak performance*. Paper presented at the annual meeting of the Association for the Advancement of Applied Sport Psychology, Savannah, Ga.

Loehr, J. E. (1984, March). How to overcome stress and play at your peak all the time. *Tennis*, pp. 66–76.

Mahoney, M. J., & Avener, M. (1977). Psychology of the elite athlete: An exploratory study. *Cognitive Therapy and Research, 1*, 135–142.

Mahoney, M. J., Gabriel, T. J., & Perkins, T. S. (1987). Psychological skills and exceptional athletic performance. *The Sport Psychologist, 1*, 181–199.

Martens, R. (1987). Science, knowledge and sport psychology. *The Sport Psychologist, 1*, 29–55.

McCaffrey, N., & Orlick, T. (1989). Mental factors related to excellence among top professional golfers. *International Journal of Sport Psychology, 20*, 256–278.

Meyers, A. W., Cooke, C. J., Cullen, J., & Liles, L. (1979). Psychological aspects of athletic competitors: A replication across sports. *Cognitive Therapy and Research, 3*, 361–366.

Orlick, T. (1980). *In pursuit of excellence*. Champaign, Ill.: Human Kinetics.

Orlick, T., & Partington, J. (1988). Mental links to excellence. *The Sport Psychologist, 2*, 105–130.

Privette, G. (1982). Peak performance in sports: A factorial topology. *International Journal of Sport Psychology, 13*, 242–249.

Privette, G. (1983). Peak experience, peak performance, and flow: A comparative analysis of positive human experiences. *Journal of Personality and Social Psychology, 45*, 1361–1368.

Ravizza, K. (1977). Peak experiences in sport. *Journal of Humanistic Psychology, 17*, 35–40.

Rushall, B. S. (1989). Sport psychology: The key to sporting excellence. *International Journal of Sport Psychology, 20*, 165–190.

Scanlan, T. K., Ravizza, K., & Stein, G. L. (1989). An in-depth study of former elite figure skaters: I. Introduction to the project. *Journal of Sport and Exercise Psychology, 11*, 54–64.

Scanlan, T. K., Stein, G. L., & Ravizza, K. (1989). An in-depth study of former elite figure skaters: II. Sources of enjoyment. *Journal of Sport and Exercise Psychology, 11*, 65–82.

Increasing Awareness for Sport Performance

Kenneth Ravizza, *California State University at Fullerton*

Bases loaded, 3–2 count, two outs, game tied. This type of pressure situation frequently confronts athletes during performance, and all too often the coach's instructions are "Just relax" or Concentrate." This type of generalized advice tells the athlete that the coach has recognized a lack of concentration, and frequently this results in even more pressure.

The underlying basis of psychological interventions for performance enhancement involves teaching the athlete the importance of the recognition, or awareness, of the need to do something to gain control. Athletes will not be aware of the need to gain control unless they first identify their own ideal performance state (see Chapter 11) and can contrast that state with the present one. Thus, *awareness* is the first step to gaining control of any pressure situation. For example, the athlete must be aware of his/her emotional state, or arousal level, and adjust it as needed to reach the optimal arousal level for performance. Then the athlete must attend to the appropriate focal points that will fine-tune or lock in his/her concentration. For example, a softball player will only get two or three great pitches to hit in a game. The player must be fully focused on each pitch so that when the appropriate pitch comes, he/she is ready to make

solid contact. The lack of awareness demonstrated by many athletes is often a by-product of the sport socialization process, whereby the athlete is encouraged to follow orders and not to question the coach's authority. More and more, coaches are beginning to take a less dogmatic approach because they realize that dependency often results from a strictly authoritarian coaching style.

Furthermore, lack of awareness in athletes is almost always the result of excessive concern with achieving the end result. For example, the baseball player in the pressure situation focuses on the end result of getting a hit. Awareness and control are part of the process of skill execution—specifically, execution in the present moment. The anxiety lies in the end result. Thus, the baseball player must focus on key components of hitting, such as taking the signal, stepping into the box, taking the practice swings to get the rhythm, then focusing on the pitcher, then fine-tuning the concentration to the release area. At this point the athlete is totally focused on the task at hand and is ready to react spontaneously to the situation with controlled intensity. This type of appropriate *focus of attention* is essential in order to maximize performance.

The athlete's challenge is to focus on basic skills even when the athlete's pulse rate may increase significantly. The situation can be perceived as speeded-up or out-of-the-usual perspective because of the perceived threat of the situation. This chapter does not suggest a multitude of performance changes; instead, it suggests that the athlete be encouraged to become aware of his/her own ideal performance state and *routine* behaviors that he/she is already using to achieve this state. Many of the techniques we talk about in sport psychology are performed instinctively by the athlete. Awareness of these instinctive routines provides the athlete with something to focus on to regain control. Sport psychology consultants have contributed to enhancing performance by providing a structure or consistent framework for the various mental skills the athlete has often developed and practiced haphazardly.

This structure clarifies for the athlete the fact that there is a relationship between the various things that the athlete does to maximize performance. When the athlete can begin to understand that the imagery skills that are used for pregame preparation can also be used for concentration and relaxation training (as well as for academic studies), he/she has a better sense of control. *Control* is the key issue because the athlete's anxiety level tends to decrease with a feeling of control.

The purpose of this chapter is to discuss the importance of awareness in reaching peak performance in sport. Awareness will be presented as the first essential step in goal setting and self-regulation as it relates to skill development and the management of performance stress and other psychological factors. The final section will discuss specific methods that the athlete can use to develop heightened awareness.

The Importance of Awareness in Athletics

Every sport requires athletes to execute basic skills. The athletes must stand alone and accept the responsibility for their performance. During the off season, individual responsibility is an even more crucial aspect since it is then that athletes must put in hours of isolated, rigorous training and self-coaching to develop and refine essential skills. Athletes must perform the skills, reflect on the feedback gained from the performance, make correc-

tions and refinements, and then make the skills feel natural through a multitude of repetitions and refinements.

Athletes must recognize their strengths and weaknesses so that they can maximize their strengths and correct their weaknesses. Goal setting can be used to facilitate performance enhancement. At first, athletes want to be told what their goals should be, but it is essential that the athletes make the major contribution to establishing individual goals. This requires the athletes to reflect upon and evaluate their past performance. The coach gains a great deal of insight about the athletes' awareness on the basis of this evaluation of perceived strengths and weaknesses. The goals should be *performance* goals, such as "I will be more consistent at the foul line by shooting 50 shots a day with the goal of hitting over 60% by the end of two weeks and 65% after one month." This is different from an *outcome* goal, such as "I want to improve my foul shooting." The goals should be as specific as possible and of various duration; short-term, intermediate, and long-range. (See Chapter 13 for additional guidelines for goal setting and strategies for achieving goals.)

Goal setting requires awareness because the athlete first sets the goals, then strives to reach them, then proceeds to evaluate the performance feedback, and finally, adjusts the goals appropriately (Harris & Harris, 1984; McClements & Botterill, 1979).

Awareness as It Relates to Skill Development

Athletes must learn the difference between merely performing skills and experiencing skills. For example, try this exercise. Raise your right arm over your head five times—one . . . two . . . three . . . four . . . five—and halt. Now deeply inhale as you slowly raise your right arm over your head. Breathe slowly and steadily as you feel the movement, experience the muscles involved, feel the gentle stretch through the different muscles, feel that extension all through the arm, and now slowly let the arm down.

The difference between just going through the motions and really experiencing the skills hinges on the awareness involved. Feldenkrais (1972), a movement specialist, offers the following analogy:

A man without awareness is like a carriage whose passengers are the desires, with the muscles for horses, while the carriage itself is the skeleton. Awareness is the sleeping coachman. As long as the coachman remains asleep the carriage will be dragged aimlessly here and there. Each passenger seeks a different destination and the horses pull different ways. But when the coachman is wide awake and holds the reins the horses will pull and bring every passenger to his proper destination. (p. 54)

Like the coachman, athletes must gain control of muscles, emotions, and thoughts and integrate them into a smooth performance. When athletes are aware and focused upon the sport experience, they exert more control over the situation. They recognize sooner when their balance is off, when too much tension is present in certain muscle groups, or when thoughts have become self-defeating. Aware athletes are more attuned to subtle fluctuations in the flow of the contest and can adjust that much sooner. Aware athletes can conserve vital energy by exerting no more than the needed effort.

Learning the Basics

Awareness requires that athletes totally focus their attention on the task. This ability must be developed in practice. Coaches want their athletes to be intense and totally involved in practice because this aids in creating quality practice time. Many coaches also realize the importance of mental training for performance, but the challenge is to find time for it. For this reason, it is important to incorporate awareness training with the physical skills that are already being performed in practice. For example, coaches and sport psychology consultants should encourage athletes to develop concentration as they stretch before practice by feeling the stretch and breathing into it. This type of stretching develops concentration in that the athletes are tuned in to their body as they stretch.

With the 1984 U.S. Olympic Women's Field Hockey Team we established a set warm-up procedure for practice to aid the athletes in mentally and physically preparing for practice. The players began by stretching, then hit the ball back and forth to work out any kinks, and finally executed focused hitting. Focused hitting involves hitting the ball to exact locations—for example, to the receiver's right, middle, and left. This sequence is followed for five minutes. These are basic field hockey skills, but there is a difference when they are done with awareness. If the player's attention is on other aspects of the day, such as a party coming up or an argument with a friend, consistency in the focused hitting drill will be impossible.

This type of drill has two major advantages for the coach. First, visible objective performance demonstrates whether or not the athlete is concentrating. More importantly, awareness training is incorporated into the practice of basic skills. As a result, additional practice time is not required for mental training. This sophisticated approach to basic skills allows coaches to make the most of practice time by integrating mental or awareness skills training with basic fundamentals.

During one practice the Cal State Fullerton baseball team engaged in a focused bat and catch drill for 90 minutes because they had not been hitting exact locations consistently. This emphasis on basics was crucial because the players realized the coach was serious about executing the basics. The difference between performing the basics and focusing on the basics lies in the players' awareness. Athletes must learn to concentrate when the pressure is on, and the focal points for concentration become the task-relevant cues. Augie Garrido, Cal State Fullerton's baseball coach, gives the following example:

> We are really working on having the players clear their minds. Yesterday one player was given a bunt signal and he proceeded to pop out. His next time at the plate he was in a bunting situation and tried to bunt but missed. So I called him over and said, " You've tried two times and failed, and you are about to fail again because you still have the other two times on your mind. Give yourself the best chance to be successful by seeing the ball and bunting the ball. You can do that. Stay right with the ingredients of bunting. You've done it a hundred times, but you have to get the other times off your mind." The player proceeded to lay down a perfect bunt. (1982)

When athletes practice physical skills and mental skills together, their confidence increases because they are ready and experienced in the subtle skill of concentration.

The All-or-None Syndrome

Awareness develops in the process of participating in sport and this is where the athlete experiences self-control. Gymnasts learning new moves cannot expect to master them immediately. A series of progressions must be worked through. Often, in the midst of this process, gymnasts feel they have *either* hit the move *or* missed. If they hit it, they are delighted, but if they miss, frustration begins to set in. The challenge is to maintain motivation throughout the hours of practice.

At Cal State Fullerton we have established gradations of execution for the gymnasts to evaluate their skill development. For example, even if a move is "missed," certain aspects of the movement were probably successful, and it is important that they be identified. Similarly, in baseball a pitcher is told that he/she needs to raise his/her arm on a fastball release. The number 5 is given for the ideal release distance and a 1 is given for a side-arm release. After each pitch the player is asked to assign a numerical value from 1 to 5 to the arm location. It is essential that the athlete reflect on the position of his/her arm because this requires awareness. The coach can then give an evaluation from 1 to 5. This aids the athlete in beginning to adjust his awareness to what the proper position feels like (based on a principle from Gallwey, 1974). If a video recorder is available, the performance feedback is even more specific.

When athletes gain more awareness, they can make more accurate adjustments in their performance. This ability to refine the subtle intricacies of performance is a critical skill as athletes reach for maximum performance. In addition to improving self-control, the athletes experience a feeling of growing success. Even though the outcome is not perfect, players develop a more positive attitude about the skill and will keep their motivation level where it needs to be.

Playing the Edge of Peak Performance

To reach their full sport potential, athletes must learn to play the **performance edge**. For example, they must learn to control that delicate balance between power and grace. Every sport has components that must be balanced appropriately to maximize performance. This type of control necessitates that athletes be aware. They must monitor their performance in order to recognize when it is at its peak. In athletic training and conditioning, there are many times when athletes push too hard or do not push hard enough. At such times the athletes need to relate to their movement experience with the precision of a surgeon so that they can make needed adjustments. For example, runners constantly monitor their body for subtle messages so that they can make adjustments to reach that edge of peak performance.

One awareness technique I use with runners is the blindfold run. A blindfolded runner and a partner run a specified distance together, with the partner providing physical support and removing any dangers. The blindfold alters the runner's perspective, as the runner is now totally focused on the present moment. Usual thoughts and distractions are suspended by the new perspective. After about five minutes into the run, the athlete experiences running in a more aware fashion.

Coaches and sport psychology consultants are encouraged to discuss with their athletes this idea of "playing the edge" so that each athlete can begin to understand and identify where that edge is for him/her. Figure 12-1 and the chapter appendix suggest ways of keeping records of the mental aspects of performance.

Awareness in Managing Performance Stress

To move consistently toward peak performance, each athlete must know and be aware of his/her own experience of optimal performance. The athlete has to learn to control the excitement of the sport situation so that his/her energy can be channeled into the performance, or to reorganize when the arousal level is too low and activate it as needed. To gain this control the athlete must learn how competitive stress affects individual performance. (See Chapter 14 for more information on this topic.) The first step is to be aware of one's arousal level and then to adjust it as needed. The athlete must recognize which situations or stressors tend to negatively affect his/her performance. Knowledge of the stressful areas allows for the de-

PERFORMANCE FEEDBACK SHEET

Name _____

Opponent _____

1. What were your stressors for today's game?

2. How did you experience the stress (thoughts, actions, body)?

3. How was your level of arousal for today's game? What were your feelings at these various points?
   a. Bus ride to game:_____
   b. Warm-up on field, court, etc.:_____
   c. Just before the game:_____
   d. During the game:_____

   0 ————5————10
   Too Low   Perfect   Too High

4. What techniques did you use to manage the stress and how effective were you in controlling it?

5. How was your self-talk? (Describe.)

6. What did you learn from today's game that will help you in your next game?

7. What mental training techniques were most effective for you?

8. Briefly describe one play or segment of the game that you enjoyed.

9. How would you rate your play?_____

   1 ————5————10
   Terrible   OK   Great

10. Briefly describe how you felt about today's game.

11. Anything you want to say?

Figure 12-1 Sample performance feedback sheet.

velopment of a strategy to prepare and cope effectively with them. For example, playing in front of a crowd or in the presence of scouts is stressful; thus, the athlete can mentally prepare to deal with the situation to avoid surprise. The athlete has time to get support from teammates and the coaching staff and also to develop his/her own strategy.

Once the athlete understands the stressors, the next step is to be aware of the way that stress is experienced, because the manifestations of stress vary greatly among individuals. For example, "As the pressure mounts, my shoulders and neck tighten, my thoughts jump around, and I tend to get jittery." Changes in breathing are another bodily cue that often signals too much stress. Athletes should be trained to become sensitive to how their breathing responds to stress. For example, do they start to breathe more rapidly and shallowly? Do they hold their breath? Do they have difficulty breathing? These manifestations of stress may be perceived as problems, but they can be used as signals to provide feedback to the athlete as to whether the arousal level is appropriate. The athlete gains this personal knowledge by reflecting on previous performances and essentially using sport experiences like a biofeedback machine.

The athlete's consistent focus on his/her thoughts and feelings and use of appropriate interventions allows the athlete to maintain an optimal performance state. Interventions may include relaxation and activation techniques, concentration methods, thought control, and basic breathing techniques. (See Chapters 15–19 for specific techniques.) There are also times when the athlete must recognize that it is time just to flow with the experience and let it happen (Ravizza, 1984; Ravizza & Osborne, 1991). Once again, the sport journal described in the chapter appendix helps the athlete develop this awareness because it provides a mechanism for recording, evaluating sport performance, and processing the information learned from the act of participation.

Techniques for Developing Awareness

There are many techniques to increase awareness. One very valuable technique is keeping a sport journal. The sport journal provides a structured method to reflect on sport performances and to capitalize on the wealth of experiential knowledge gained from the performance. The journal guidelines in the appendix ask questions about stressors, manifestations of stress, and feelings associated with performance, concentration, and skill execution. After teams play a game, they can discuss what the members have learned so that, with the coach, they can establish new goals or modify earlier ones.

Following selected performances, coaches can give players feedback sheets similar to the one shown in Figure 12-1 so that they can process the subjective information gained from each contest. This procedure helps the players systematically learn from the experience and bring closure to their performance so that they can begin to focus on the next performance. This is particularly helpful in tournament play where the athletes have to perform many times during a short period, because it is critical to bring **closure**, or let go of one performance before beginning another.

With the athletes' permission, coaches and sport psychologists can read these journals and feedback sheets, using the information as a foundation for better understanding the athlete and what behavior or intervention might best facilitate performance and personal growth. Writing feelings in a journal or on a feedback sheet is often perceived by athletes as less threatening than actual verbal discussions. On the other hand, such writing often forges an understanding that promotes discussion. (In some cases, coaches have also worked with English teachers to capitalize on the athletes' interest in writing about the experiential aspects of sport performance to develop English writing skills.)

Some coaches and sport psychologists have helped athletes glean information regarding ideal psychological states for peak performance by having them fill out psychological questionnaires just before beginning performance. Ideally, this should be done prior to a number of competitions, enabling a comparison between performance and scores on the questionnaires. The intention is to find what psychological state(s) typically occurred when the athlete performed at his/her best. The Competitive State Anxiety Inventory-2 (CSAI-2) (Martens, Vealey, & Burton, 1990) is one example of an appropriate questionnaire for this purpose. The CSAI-2 assesses the athlete's current cognitive anxiety, somatic anxiety, and self-confidence. We know from the research discussed in Chapter 11 that each of these psychological states may be relevant to performance. See some of the questionnaires discussed in other chapters for additional examples of potentially appropriate instruments. It should be noted that not all sport psychology consultants find these questionnaires useful. It is critical that the consultant discuss the results with the athletes to determine if the information obtained is accurate for that athlete.

Monitoring relevant physiological systems is another tool for gaining awareness regarding ideal performance states. Purportedly, Eastern European sport psychologists frequently use this procedure when working with elite athletes. Heart rate, blood pressure, brain waves, muscle tension, galvanic skin response, and catecholamine levels are all examples of types of physiological monitoring that might be appropriate for identifying an athlete's psychological state and its relationship to performance. Research and interventions in this area are still in their infancy in North America. Work by Landers and his students provides one example of what the future might hold when sophisticated technology is more common (Landers et al., 1991; Salazar et al., 1990). Even without sophisticated technology, heart rate can be monitored right before a number of critical competitions and then compared with subsequent performance in order to determine an optimal pulse rate. According to Dr. Alexeev of the Moscow Research Institute of Physical Culture, this is one of the best ways to discover an athlete's optimal level of anxiety (Raiport, 1988).

Athletes who are good imagers can use imagery to gain awareness of their ideal performance state. This technique is particularly effective if the athletes are in the off season or in a situation where actual competition is not possible. Imagery is used to relive previous excellent performance, with particular attention given to identifying what feelings, arousal level, thoughts, muscle tension, attentional focus, and so forth might have occurred. There also may be merit in imaging previous bad performances in order to contrast their psycholog-

ical state with what appears to be a more optimal state.

Imagery can be an effective tool as well for creating awareness when filling out performance feedback sheets after an actual performance. Athletes who are unsure of exactly what happened can "replay" their performance to determine what they were thinking, feeling, and attending to at any given moment.

Group discussion is another method that coaches and sport psychology consultants can use to increase athlete awareness. Coaches should provide their athletes with an opportunity to discuss a performance by encouraging but not requiring them to do so. Sport psychology consultants should do the same thing after practice of certain mental training techniques. Sometimes coaches and sport psychology consultants can foster this form of communication through one-on-one discussions. Coach/sport psychology practitioners should share their perspective or expertise but also encourage the athletes to talk about the experience. They should ask questions about arousal and confidence levels, stressors, and manifestations. Every team is capable of this type of interaction, but such dialogue is frequently difficult to facilitate at first. As the athletes become much more aware of the needs of their teammates, team cohesion will be more likely to result. In turn, new insights into the athletes' own sport performance are gained. For example, one athlete responds to stress by withdrawing. An understanding of this by teammates relieves stress because other people now know that this is one method used to mentally prepare for performance. There is nothing "wrong" with an athlete who is quiet.

A good time to begin group discussions is after a positive experience because the feelings are nonthreatening. For example, after a great practice, the coach can ask the athletes to discuss what made the practice so good. How was it different from a nonproductive practice session?

In regard to specific methods of increasing awareness, it is important that the practitioner do what he/she is comfortable with. However, it is strongly suggested that coaches and sport psychology consultants slowly integrate the various methods discussed in this chapter.

Summary

Developing awareness is a critical element of peak performance because it provides athletes with the experiential knowledge to gain control of the performance. Awareness is the first step in raising self-control in sport participation. Initially, athletes need to become aware of their ideal performance state. Next, athletes need to recognize when they are no longer at that ideal state. As athletes develop the awareness skills, they will recognize earlier when they are not focused or aroused appropriately. This early recognition aids athletes in gaining control before it is lost. The sooner a deviation is recognized, the easier it is to get back on course. Athletes with a range of interventions can use them to get their mental-emotional and physical states to more nearly approximate what they have found leads to peak performance. Journal keeping, performance feedback sheets, assessing precompetitive performance states through psychological questionnaires and physiological monitoring, using imagery to relive past performances, and group discussions are all effective techniques for developing awareness. Depending upon the athlete's preferences and the circumstances, certain techniques may be more effective than others at any given moment.

Study Questions

1. Why is it important that athletes be aware of their ideal performance state?

2. What is the difference between merely performing skills and experiencing skills?

3. Why is it important to incorporate awareness training with the physical skills that are already being performed in practice?

4. Give an example of focused practice.

5. Describe how the all-or-none syndrome can be overcome.

6. What is meant by "playing on the edge?" What techniques can help an athlete become aware of this skill?

7. How can a sport journal and performance feedback sheets be used to increase awareness? Describe what might be included in a journal and feedback sheets.

8. How can psychological questionnaires and physiological monitoring be used to increase awareness of ideal performance states?

9. When might imagery and group discussion be used to increase awareness?

References

Feldenkrais, M. (1972). *Awareness through movement.* New York: Harper & Row.

Gallwey, T. (1974). *The inner game of tennis.* New York: Random House.

Garrido, A. (1982, December 7). Interview with author. Fullerton, Calif.

Harris, D., & Harris, B. (1984). *The athlete's guide to sport psychology: Mental skills for physical people.* New York: Leisure Press.

Landers, D., Petruzello, S., Salazar, W., Cruz, D., Kubitz, K., Gannon, T., & Han, M. (1991). The influence of electrocortical biofeedback on performance in pre-elite archers. *Medicine and Science in Sports and Exercise, 23,* 123–129.

Martens, R., Vealey, R. S., & Burton, D. (1990). *Competitive anxiety in sport.* Champaign, Ill.: Human Kinetics.

McClements, J., & Botterill, C. (1979). Goal setting in shaping of future performance of athletes. In P. Klavora & J. Daniel (Eds.), *Coach, athlete and the sport psychologist.* Champaign, Ill.: Human Kinetics.

Raiport, G. (1988). Red gold: Peak performance techniques of the Russian and East German Olympic victors. Los Angeles: Tarcher.

Ravizza, K. (1984). Qualities of the peak experience in sport. In J. Silva & R. Weinberg (Eds.), *Psychological foundations for sport.* Champaign, Ill.: Human Kinetics.

Ravizza, K., & Osborne, T. (1991). Nebraska's 3R's: One play-at-a-time preperformance routine for collegiate football. *The Sport Psychologist, 5,* 256–265.

Salazar, W., Landers, D., Petruzello, S., Han, M., Cruz, D., & Kubitz, K. (1990). Hemispheric asymmetry, cardiac response, and performance in elite archers. *Research Quarterly in Exercise and Sport, 61,* 351–359.

Guidelines for Keeping a Sport Journal

The sport journal is a tool to help you further develop your mental skills for sport performance. The first step in gaining self-control is to develop an awareness of your sport performance so that you can recognize when you are pulled out of the most appropriate mental state for you. The journal provides you with an opportunity to record the different intervention strategies that you experiment with to regain control. The long-range goal is to develop various techniques that you can implement in stressful situations to perform to your utmost ability.

If you choose to, the journal also can be a place where you can record your feelings and the personal knowledge that you are gaining about yourself, the game, your teammates, and any other factors. This is one of the few times in your life that you will ever direct so much energy toward one specific goal. There is a lot to learn from your pursuit of excellence. This journal will give you something to reflect back on after your high-level participation is completed.

The journal also can serve as a place where you can express your feelings in writing and drawings. It is beneficial to get these feelings out in some way so that they don't build up and contribute to unproductive tension. The use of colored pens is often helpful to express yourself. You do not have to make an entry every day, but date the entries you do make. The journal is an informal record of your thoughts and experiences as you train for high-level performance.

If you choose to have someone read your journal, please feel comfortable to delete any parts that you think are too personal to share. The intention of someone who is reviewing you should be to guide you and make *suggestions* that may facilitate your self-exploration in reaching your goals.

I would suggest that you try this technique, but it is not for everyone. If you choose not to, that is your choice. If you try the technique, assess the following areas with the accompanying questions/descriptors:

1. *Peak Performance.* What does it feel like when you play and/or practice at your best? Describe some of your most enjoyable experiences playing your sport. What have you learned from these moments when you are fully functioning?

2. *Stressors.* Outside the sport—write down your thoughts about various events outside your sport that are distracting to you. Parents, boy/girlfriends, peers, job hassles, financial issues, community (hometown expectations), etcetera. On the field—importance of contest, location, spectators, etcetera.

3. *Coaching Staff.* What do you need from your coaches? What can you give them in order to reach your goals? What can you do to make your relationship with your coaches more productive?

4. *Teammates.* What do you want from your teammates? What can you give them? How do you relate and work with your teammates? Write about your relationship with other teammates. Any unfinished business?

5. *Confidence.* At this time how confident are you in regard to achieving your goals?

What can you do differently to feel more confident? What can you ask of yourself, coach, and/or teammates?

6. *Manifestations of Your Stress.* How do you experience high levels of anxiety in performance? Assess your thoughts and physiological and behavioral reactions. What did you do to intervene and keep in balance?

7. *Awareness and Concentration.* What changes do you observe in your performance when you are aware? What concentration methods are you experimenting with? What are your focal points for various skills?

8. *Relaxation Training.* How are your relaxation skills developing? Are there any parts of your body that are more difficult than others to relax? What method is best for you? How are you able to relate this to your play? How quickly can you relax?

9. *Thought Control.* How is your self-talk affecting your performance? Write out some of your negative self-talk and make it positive.

10. *Centering/Concentration Skills.* What are you doing to concentrate appropriately before the contest and during the contest? What has

been successful? Unsuccessful? Describe your preperformance routine.

11. *Imagery.* How are your imagery skills developing? Do you see a TV screen-type image or is it more of a feeling image? At what point do you notice lapses in concentration? How clear are your images? Can you control the speed and tempo of the image?

12. *Controlling Your Arousal Level.* What are you doing to control your arousal level? What are you doing to increase arousal and intensity? What are you experimenting with to reduce arousal levels? What is working for you and what is not working?

13. *Pressure Situations.* How are you handling pressure situations? What are you doing differently? What are you doing to learn to cope more effectively?

14. *Quality Practice Time.* What do you do to mentally prepare for practice? How do you keep your personal difficulties from affecting your play? What are you doing to take charge? What works for you and what hasn't worked?

15. *Anything You Want to Address.*

Goal Setting for Peak Performance

Daniel Gould*, *University of North Carolina at Greensboro*

*I*n recent years a number of psychological strategies have been identified as ways of assisting athletes in achieving personal growth and peak performance. Goal setting is one such technique. In fact, goal setting has not only been shown to influence the performance of athletes of varied age and ability levels but has also been linked to positive changes in important psychological states such as anxiety, confidence, and motivation. It is clearly a technique that coaches and sport psychologists should regularly employ.

Unfortunately, goal setting is not always effectively employed by coaches and sport psychologists. It is falsely assumed, for example, that because athletes set goals on their own, these goals will automatically facilitate performance. This is seldom the case, however, as many athletes set inappropriate goals or do not set goals in a systematic fashion. Similarly, coaches and sport psychologists often forget to initiate the follow-up and evaluation procedures that are necessary if goal setting is to be effective. To use goal setting effectively coaches and sport psychologists must understand the goal-setting process and the many factors that can affect it.

*The author would like to thank Linda Bump, Linda Petlichkoff, and Jeff Simons for their helpful comments on early drafts of this chapter.

This chapter has a fourfold purpose. First, psychological and sport psychological research and theory on goal setting will be briefly examined. Second, a number of fundamental goal-setting guidelines will be discussed. Third, a system for effectively initiating goal-setting procedures with athletes will be presented. And, fourth, common problems that arise when setting goals will be identified and solutions will be offered. The principles and recommendations derived in this chapter are based both on research and on what sport psychologists have learned while utilizing goal-setting interventions with athletes in a variety of settings.

Goal-Setting Research and Theory

Before examining the research on goal setting and theoretical explanations for the relationships between goal setting and performance, we must first define goals and distinguish between various types of goals.

Defining Goals

Locke and his colleagues (1981) have generated the most widely accepted definition for the term "goal." For these investigators, a **goal** is defined as "attaining a specific standard of proficiency on a task, usually within a specified time limit" (Locke et al., 1981, p. 145). From a practical perspective, then, goals focus on achieving some standard, whether it be increasing one's batting average by 10 percentage points, lowering one's time in the 800 meters or losing 5 pounds. This definition also implies that such performance standards will be achieved within some specified unit of time such as by the end of the season, within two weeks, or by the end of practice.

Even though the definition by Locke and his associates provides a good general description of a goal, sport psychologists have at times found it useful to make specific distinctions between types of goals. McClements (1982), for instance, has differentiated between subjective goals (e.g., having fun, getting fit, or trying one's best), general objective goals (e.g., winning a championship or making a team), and specific objective goals (e.g., increasing the number of assists in basketball or decreasing a pitcher's earned run average in softball). Similarly, Martens (1987) and Burton (1983, 1984, 1989) have made distinctions between outcome goals, which represent standards of performance that focus on the results of a contest between opponents or teams (e.g., beating someone), and performance goals, which focus on improvements relative to one's own past performance, (e.g., improving one's time in the mile). These distinctions are important because evidence suggests that specific objective goals, as well as performance goals, are most useful when attempting to change behavior.

Goal-Effectiveness Research

Extensive psychological research has been conducted on the topic of goal setting (see Locke et al. (1981), and Mento, Steel, and Karren (1987) for extensive reviews). Typically, this research has involved a comparison of the performance of subjects who set goals or certain types of goals (e.g., specific-explicit goals) with the performance of subjects who are simply told to do their best or are given no goals. Studies sometimes manipulate other factors such as subject characteristics (e.g., race, educational level, personality) or situational variables (e.g., the presence or absence of feedback).

Psychological research on goal setting is impressive in that it has been conducted in a variety

of laboratory and field settings and has used a wide variety of tasks ranging from truck loading to brainstorming sessions; it has employed diverse samples of subjects including elementary school children, uneducated laborers, managers, and scientists. In addition, a clear pattern of results has emerged with ready implications for sport psychology specialists and coaches alike.

The most important result generated from this line of research is that goal setting clearly and consistently facilitates performance. In their excellent and comprehensive review of well over a hundred studies on goal setting, for example, Locke and colleagues (1981) concluded that "the beneficial effect of goal setting on task performance is one of the most robust and replicable findings in the psychological literature. Ninety percent of the studies showed positive or partially positive effects. Furthermore, these effects are found just as reliable in the field setting as in the laboratory" (p. 145). Thus, a review of the psychological research clearly shows that goal setting is a powerful technique for enhancing performance.

Given the abundance of research on goal setting and the consistent pattern of results found in the psychological literature in general, it is surprising that until recently the topic has been almost virtually ignored in the sport psychological literature. In fact, prior to 1985, only a few studies (Botterill, 1977; Burton, 1983, 1984) had been conducted on the topic.

Nevertheless, the results of these initial investigations showed much promise. Botterill (1977), for instance, had youth ice hockey players perform an exercise endurance task under various combinations of goal difficulty, goal explicitness specificity, and goal type (group, subject, or experimenter set) conditions. Consistent with the psychological literature, the results revealed that goal setting facilitated performance. Similarly, difficult goals were more effective in enhancing performance than easy goals, and explicit goals were more effective than general "do your best" goals. Finally, it was concluded that explicit, difficult, and group-set goals were most effective in enhancing endurance task performance.

In a more recent field investigation, Burton (1983, 1989) examined the effects of a goal-setting training program on the performance and cognitions (e.g., levels of self-confidence, motivation, and state anxiety) of male and female intercollegiate swimmers. In a five-month goal-setting program, performance as opposed to outcome goals were employed and an attempt was made to explain why goal setting influences performance by relating goals to other psychological constructs such as confidence and state anxiety. The results revealed that swimmers who participated in the goal-setting training program learned to focus highest priority on performance goals and that those swimmers high in goal-setting ability demonstrated better performance and more positive cognitions. Furthermore, a related study conducted with National Sports Festival swimmers supported these findings, demonstrating that goals were positively related to performance and positive psychological attributes (Burton, 1984).

Although goal setting was not widely studied by sport psychology researchers prior to 1985, increased attention has been placed on this topic in recent years. Much of this interest in goal-setting research was spurred by a 1985 *Journal of Sport Psychology* review article written by noted goal-setting researchers Locke and Latham, in which it was suggested that goal-setting research principles found in the general psychological literature were applicable to the sport context. This has led to a series of sport psychological studies testing Locke and Latham's proposition in the sport environment. (See Weinberg, in press, for an excellent review of these studies).

Recent sport psychology goal-setting research investigations have examined such issues as whether specific goals are more effective than general "do your best" goals, the effectiveness of long-term versus short-term goals, and the relationship between goal difficulty and task performance. Results have proven to be equivocal, with some studies supporting predicted relationships and others not. However, Robert Weinberg, the leading sport psychological researcher in the area, has indicated that these initial research efforts are characterized by a number of methodological problems such as the spontaneous setting of goals by control group subjects, competition between comparison group subjects, and the failure to control levels of subject motivation and commitment (Weinberg, in press). Hence, these methodological problems have limited the implications that can be derived from this research.

Despite the fact that the recent sport psychological goal-setting research has not been as fruitful as was hoped, it has shown that goal setting can and does influence performance in sport settings.

In addition, it reinforces a main contention of this chapter; that is, goal setting will only be effective when a systematic approach is adopted and a knowledgeable professional customizes the goal-setting process to his/her particular setting and athletes.

In summary, although not unequivocal, the results of the psychological and sport psychological research literature provide strong support for using goal-setting procedures to facilitate athletic performance. Moreover, these findings are further strengthened by the fact that they have been demonstrated in studies using varied tasks and largely different subject populations in both laboratory and field settings. A survey of leading sport psychology consultants working with U.S. Olympic athletes has also shown that goal setting is the most often used psychological intervention in both individual athlete–coach and group consultations (Gould et al., 1989). Data from Orlick and Partington's (1988) extensive study of Olympic athletes supports the survey results from the sport psychologists. The athletes reported daily goal setting as a part of their training program.

Theoretical Explanations for the Relationship Between Goal Setting and Performance

The old adage that there is nothing more practical than a good theory is an appropriate way to view the goal-setting process. It is important to know that goal setting influences performance, but it is equally important for coaches and sport psychologists to understand how and why goal setting is effective, especially when problems occur in goal setting and these individuals must assess the situation and make adjustments.

Three explanations have been proposed to describe how goals influence performance. Locke and his associates (1981) suggested a mechanistic theory to explain the goal-performance relationship in general. In contrast, Burton (1983) and Garland (1985) have proposed more cognitively oriented theories to explain how goal setting influences performance.

In their mechanistic theory, Locke and colleagues (1981) contend that goals influence performance in four ways. First, goals direct the performer's attention and action to important aspects of the task. For example, by setting goals, a basketball player will focus attention and subsequent action on improving specific skills such as blocking out under the boards or decreasing turnovers as opposed to becoming a better ball player in general. Second, goals help the performer mobilize effort. For example, by setting a series of practice goals, a swimmer will exhibit greater practice effort in attempting to achieve these objectives. Third, goals not only increase immediate effort but help prolong effort or increase persistence. As a case in point, the boredom of a long season is offset and persistence is increased when a wrestler sets a number of short-term goals throughout the year. Finally, research has shown that performers often develop and employ new learning strategies through the process of setting goals. Golfers, for instance, may learn new methods of putting in an effort to achieve putting goals that the golfers have set in conjunction with their coach or sport psychologist.

In contrast to the Locke and associates theory (1981), Burton's cognitive theory (1983) focuses solely on how goal setting influences performance in athletic environments. Athletes' goals are linked to their levels of anxiety, motivation, and confidence. That is, when athletes focus solely on outcome or winning goals, unrealistic future expectations often result; such expectations can lead to lower levels of confidence, increased cognitive anxiety, decreased effort, and poor performance. Unlike outcome goals, performance goals are both in the athlete's control and flexible. Moreover, when properly employed, performance goals assist the athlete in forming realistic expectations. This, in turn, results in optimal levels of confidence, cognitive anxiety, and motivation and, ultimately, in enhanced performance.

Like Burton (1983), Garland (1985) contends that goals influence one's performance through one's cognitive or thought processes. In particular, he contends that when an individual sets a task goal, that goal affects performance by influencing the individual's performance expectancy and performance valence.

Performance expectancy is an athlete's self-efficacy or confidence relative to reaching a range of performance levels. One aspect of performance expectancy is the athlete's confidence in achieving a specific goal. Moreover, it is predicted that the more confidence one has about achieving a specific task goal, the better he/she will perform. **Performance valence** refers to the range of satisfactions an athlete anticipates will be derived from

achieving various performance levels. Hence, an athlete anticipates certain satisfactions by setting a specific task goal and achieving a specific level of performance. When task goals are achieved, the person becomes more satisfied (performance valence increases), and the person becomes less motivated to improve performance.

Unfortunately, little research (particularly sport psychological research) has been conducted to directly test Garland's cognitive mediation theory. The theory does, however, provide researchers with some new ideas for explaining how goals may influence performance.

When setting goals, then, coaches and sport psychologists should make every effort to become aware of the mechanisms causing performance changes to occur. Simply stated, theorists indicate that performance changes occur because of the influence of goals on such psychological attributes as anxiety, confidence, satisfaction, and motivation; the directing of attention to important aspects of the skill being performed; the mobilization of effort; increases in persistence; and the fostering of the development of new learning strategies.

Goal-Setting Guidelines

The previously reviewed research clearly shows that goal setting facilitates performance. It is misleading to think, however, that all types of goals are equally effective in enhancing athletic performance. Research reviews conducted by Locke and Latham (1985) and Weinberg (in press) indicate that this is not the case. Their work has produced specific guidelines concerning the most effective types of goals to use. Similarly, sport psychologists (Bell, 1983; Botterill, 1983; Carron, 1984; McClements & Botterill, 1979; Gould, 1983; Harris & Harris, 1983; O'Block & Evans, 1984; Orlick, 1990) who have had extensive experience in employing goal-setting techniques with athletes have been able to derive a number of useful guidelines for those interested in utilizing such techniques, the most important of which are summarized below.

Set Specific Goals in Measurable and Behavioral Terms

Explicit, specific, and numerical goals are more effective in facilitating behavior change than general "do your best" goals or no goals at all. Therefore, it is of the utmost importance that in the athletic environment goals be expressed in terms of specific measurable behaviors. Goals such as doing one's best, becoming better, and increasing one's strength are least effective. More effective goals include being able to high jump 6 feet 5 inches by the end of the season or increasing one's maximum lift on the bench press to 240 pounds. If athletes are to show performance improvements, specific measurable goals must be set!

Set Difficult but Realistic Goals

Locke and his associates (1981) have found a direct relationship between goal difficulty and task performance. That is, the more difficult the goal, the better the performance. It must be remembered, however, that this relationship is true only when the difficulty of the goal does not exceed the performer's ability. Unrealistic goals that exceed the ability of an athlete only lead to failure and frustration. Thus, it is recommended that goals be set so that they are difficult enough to challenge athletes but realistic enough to be achieved (McClements, 1982).

Set Short-Range as Well as Long-Range Goals

When asked to describe their goals, most athletes identify long-range objectives such as winning a particular championship, breaking a record, or making a particular team. However, a number of sport psychologists (Bell, 1983; Carron, 1984; Gould, 1983; Harris & Harris, 1984; O'Block & Evans, 1984) have emphasized the need to set more immediate short-range goals. Short-range goals are important because they allow athletes to see immediate improvements in performance and in so doing enhance motivation. Additionally, without short-range goals, athletes often lose sight of their long-range goals and the progression of skills needed to obtain them.

An effective way to understand the relationship between short- and long-range goals is to visualize a staircase. The top stair represents an athlete's long-range goal or objective and the lowest stair his/her present ability. The remaining steps represent a progression of short-term goals of increasing difficulty that lead from the bottom to the top of the stairs. In essence, the performer climbs the staircase of athletic achievement by taking a step at a time, accomplishing a series of interrelated short-range goals.

Set Performance Goals as Opposed to Outcome Goals

North American society places tremendous emphasis on the outcome of athletic events. Because of this, most athletes are socialized to set only outcome goals (e.g., winning, beating a particular opponent). Unfortunately, outcome goals have been shown to be less effective than performance goals (Burton, 1984, 1989).

It has been theorized that outcome goals have several inherent weaknesses (Burton, 1984, 1989; Martens, 1987). First, athletes have, at best, only partial control over outcome goals. For example, a cross-country competitor can set a personal best but fail to achieve the outcome goal of winning because he/she came in second. Despite his/her superior effort, this runner could not control the behavior of the other competitors.

A second important weakness of outcome goals is that when they are employed by athletes, the athletes usually become less flexible in their goal-adjustment practices. For example, an athlete who sets an outcome goal of winning every game and loses the initial contest will often reject goal setting altogether. However, an athlete who sets an individual performance goal such as decreasing his/her 100-meter breaststroke time by five tenths of a second and fails to achieve this goal is more likely to reset the goal to one tenth of a second.

In summary, by emphasizing personal performance goals, coaches create greater opportunities for meeting the success needs of all athletes. Those highly gifted competitors who easily exceed the performances of their opponents learn to compete against themselves and, in turn, reach new performance heights. Similarly, the less skilled athletes on the team are no longer doomed to failure; they learn to judge success and failure in terms of their own performance, not solely on the basis of peer comparisons.

Set Goals for Practice and Competition

Setting goals that only relate to competition is a frequently made mistake when implementing a goal-setting program. This does not imply that setting competitive performance goals is inappropriate; rather, it suggests that *practice* goals should not be forgotten (Bell, 1983).

Common practice goals may include starting practice on time, making five sincere positive statements to teammates during practice, running to and from all drills, and achieving various performance standards. These are typically not the most frequently cited goals of athletes, but they take on special significance when one considers the amount of time athletes spend in practice as opposed to competition. Moreover, most athletes report that it is easier to get "up" and motivated for a game or match, whereas additional motivation is often needed for daily practices.

Set Positive Goals as Opposed to Negative Goals

Goals can be stated in either positive (e.g., increase the percentage of good first serves in tennis) or negative terms (e.g., decrease the percentage of bad first serves in tennis). Although it is sometimes necessary for athletes to set goals in negative terms, it has been suggested that, whenever possible, goals should be stated positively (Bell, 1983). That is, identify behaviors to be exhibited as opposed to behaviors that should not be exhibited. Instead of having goal tenders in ice hockey strive to decrease the number of unblocked shots, have them set goals of increasing the number of saves they can make. This positive goal-setting procedure helps athletes focus on success instead of failure.

Identify Target Dates for Attaining Goals

Not only should goals describe the behavior of focus in specific measurable terms, but they should identify target dates for goal accomplishment. Target dates help motivate athletes by reminding them of the urgency of accomplishing their objectives in realistic lengths of time.

Identify Goal-Achievement Strategies

All too often goals are properly set but never accomplished because athletes fail to identify goal-achievement strategies. That is, the athlete fails to understand the difference between setting goals and developing and initiating effective goal-achievement strategies. An important ingredient for any effective goal-setting program, then, is the

identification of ways of achieving goals. For example, a basketball player who has set a goal of increasing her field goal percentage by 5 percentage points may want to identify a goal-achievement strategy of shooting 25 extra foul shots after every practice. Similarly, a wrestler needing to lose 10 pounds prior to the start of the season should identify an achievement strategy of cutting out a midafternoon snack and running two additional miles a day.

Record Goals Once They Have Been Identified

It is easy for athletes to focus attention on their goals soon after those goals have been set. Over the course of a long season, however, goals are sometimes forgotten. Therefore, it is useful for athletes to record their goals in written form and place them where they will be seen (e.g., in their lockers). Additionally, Harris and Harris (1984) recommend that athletes keep notebooks recording goals, goal achievement strategies, and goal progress on a daily or weekly basis. Finally, Botterill (1983) suggests that the coach develop a contract stating all goals and goal achievement strategies for each athlete. Each athlete then signs his/her contract, and the coach keeps the contracts on file. Later the coach can use the contracts to remind the athletes of their goals.

Provide for Goal Evaluation

Based on their review of the research, Locke and his associates (1981) concluded that evaluative feedback is absolutely necessary if goals are to enhance performance. Therefore, athletes must receive feedback about how present performance is related to both short- and long-range goals. In many cases, feedback in the form of performance statistics like batting average, assists, goals scored, or steals made is readily available. Other goals, however, require that coaches make special efforts to provide evaluative feedback. For instance, a coach helping an athlete control his/her temper on the field may have a manager record the number of times the player loses his/her temper in practice. Similarly, a softball coach helping outfielders attain their goal of efficiently backing up one another may have an observer record the number of times players move into correct positions after the ball is hit. In Chapter 17, Bunker and Williams suggest that the sport psychologist trying to help an athlete become more aware of his/her negative thoughts might have the athlete put a box of paper clips in a pocket; then during practice the athlete transfers one paper clip at a time to another pocket for each negative thought.

Provide Support for Goals

A goal-setting program will not succeed unless it is supported by those individuals who are paramount in the athlete's life. This typically includes the coach, the athlete's family, and teammates. Therefore, efforts must be made to educate these individuals as to the types of goals the athlete sets and the importance of their support in encouraging progress toward the goals. For instance, if an athlete sets performance goals as opposed to outcome goals but significant others in the athlete's life only stress the outcome of the game or match, it is unlikely that performance goals will change behavior. Simply stated, significant others must understand the goal-setting process and support it!

A Goal-Setting System for Coaches

Goal-setting research and guidelines provide coaches with the information necessary for implementing goal-setting techniques with athletes. To be successful in implementing goal-setting procedures, however, coaches must develop and employ a goal-setting system. Botterill (1983) has outlined the essentials of such a system in detail. Of the many elements Botterill discusses, three seem paramount and can be incorporated into a three-phase goal-setting system: (1) the planning phase, (2) the meeting phase, and (3) the follow-up/evaluation phase.

The Planning Phase

Coaches will be ineffective if they attempt to set goals without first spending considerable time in planning them. Before discussing goals with athletes, for instance, coaches must identify individual and team needs. These needs may focus on any number of areas such as player fitness, individual skills, team skills, playing time, sportsmanship, and enjoyment.

Following this needs analysis, coaches must identify potential team and individual goals. Most

coaches can identify a large number of potential goals for their athletes, so it is important for them to consider how likely it is that their athletes will agree to and accomplish the goals. In doing so, coaches should consider the athletes' long-range goals, individual potential, commitment, and opportunity for practice. Finally, coaches must begin to consider possible strategies that they can use to help their athletes achieve their goals. For example, a segment of each practice could be devoted to the accomplishment of identified goals or extra practices could be held.

In essence, goal setting involves commitment and effort on the part of coaches as well as athletes. Therefore, coaches must be ready to initiate the goal-setting process with well-planned assessments of their athletes' abilities and established priorities.

The Meeting Phase

Once coaches have considered individual athlete and team needs, they should schedule goal-setting meetings. The first of these meetings should include the entire team. At the first meeting, coaches should convey basic goal-setting information (e.g., the value of setting goals, areas in which to set goals, types of goals to set, the importance of performance goals) and ask the athletes to think about their general objectives for participation, as well as specific team and individual goals. Coaches must then give the athletes time to reflect upon their reasons for participation and to formulate potential goals.

A few days after the initial meeting, a second meeting should be held for the purpose of discussing some of the athletes' goals. It is especially important to examine goals in respect to their importance, specificity, and realistic nature. It is also desirable to examine possible strategies for achieving these goals.

In most cases it will be impossible to set specific goals for each athlete during these initial group meetings. Therefore, coaches must also hold a number of meetings with individual athletes and small subgroup meetings (e.g., forwards, centers, and guards in basketball). In these meetings, individual goals should be recorded, specific strategies for achieving these goals identified, and goal evaluation procedures determined. Before and after practice are often the most effective times for holding such meetings.

The Follow-Up/Evaluation Phase

As previously stated, goal setting will not be effective unless evaluative feedback is provided to athletes. Unfortunately, because of the hectic nature of the season, this is often forgotten. It is therefore a good idea to schedule goal evaluation meetings throughout the season. At these meetings, subgroups of athletes should discuss their goals and progress made toward achieving them and reevaluate unrealistic goals or goals that cannot be achieved because of injury or sickness.

Finally, to facilitate goal follow-up and evaluation, coaches should develop systematic ways of providing feedback. Figure 13–1 contains such a system for the sport of basketball. Prior to the season, the coach prints goal achievement cards that are completed by the athlete during the preseason or seasonal meetings. These cards contain places for the athletes to rate their present skills, identify specific goals, describe goal achievement strategies, and develop goal evaluation schedules. In addition, performance evaluation cards are printed (see Figure 13–1) and used to evaluate performance on percentage scale (0% = poor; 100% = excellent). The evaluation cards are completed after various competitions and when combined with other available statistics serve as feedback for weekly goal follow-up meetings. Although written in the vernacular of the coach, this goal-setting system can also be used by sport psychologists as they work with athletes on goal setting. The suggestions are equally appropriate for goals in the physical and mental skills domains, but they may need to be somewhat modified for sport psychologists working with an individual rather than the entire team.

Common Problems in Setting Goals

Goal setting is not a difficult psychological skill to use. However, it would be a misconception to think that problems do not arise when setting goals. Some of the more frequently encountered problems include attempting to set too many goals too soon, failing to recognize individual differences in athletes, setting goals that are too general, failing to modify unrealistic goals, failing to set performance goals as opposed to outcome goals, understanding the time and commitment needed to implement a goal-setting program, setting only technique-related goals, and failing to create a

supportive goal-setting atmosphere. Each of these problems is addressed below.

Setting Too Many Goals Too Soon

A natural mistake that occurs when one first implements a goal-setting system is to set too many goals too soon. For example, it is not uncommon for coaches and athletes to set 5 or 10 specific goals. This usually has negative results. The athletes have so many individual goals that they cannot properly monitor performance or, if they do monitor performance, they find the record keeping to be overwhelming and lose interest. A more effective approach is to prioritize goals and focus on accomplishing the one or two most important ones. When these goals are achieved, the athletes then focus on the next most important prioritized goals. As the athletes become more experienced in goal setting, they also learn to handle greater numbers of goals more efficiently. In essence, coaches and sport psychologists must first teach their athletes how to set and accomplish goals so that later on the athletes can set goals independently.

Failing to Recognize Individual Differences

Not all athletes will be excited about setting goals, and some may even have negative attitudes about doing so. Coaches and sport psychologists must expect this and not overreact. *Forcing* athletes to set goals is ineffective, for individual commitment is needed. Rather, expose all of the athletes to goal setting and then work with those who show interest. Over time, their success will convince other less committed athletes to begin setting goals.

Setting Goals That Are Too General

Throughout this chapter the emphasis has been on the need for setting specific, measurable goals. Unfortunately, this does not always occur. Inexperienced goal setters will often set goals that are too general. Improving one's first serve in tennis, executing a better Yamashita vault in gymnastics, and lessening the frequency of negative thoughts are too vague. These goals are more effectively stated as increasing the number of good first serves from 50 to 55% in tennis, improving the Yamashita vault by sticking the landing 8 out of 10 times, and reducing negative thoughts to five or less during each practice session. When stating goals, always ask, "How can we make this goal measurable and specific?"

Failing to Modify Unrealistic Goals

In his extensive five-month study of goal setting, Burton (1989) found that competitive collegiate swimmers had problems readjusting goals once they were set. Although the swimmers had little difficulty raising their goals once they were achieved, a number of athletes failed to lower goals that became unrealistic because of illness or injury. Coaches must recognize this problem and continually emphasize the appropriateness of lowering goals when necessary.

Failing to Set Performance Goals

The work of Martens (1987) and Burton (1984, 1989) has demonstrated the value of setting performance goals as opposed to outcome goals. For too many athletes, however, winning or outcome goals are the only worthy goals. This is psychologically destructive and illogical but occurs because of the tremendous emphasis Americans place on winning. Coaches must be aware of this problem and continually emphasize the attainment of performance goals. For instance, coaches must continually remind athletes that great performances will typically lead to the best possible outcomes. Finally, coaches must realize that changing their athletes' perception of the importance of outcome versus performance goals may take a long-term effort.

Understanding the Time Commitment Needed to Implement a Goal-Setting Program

It is not uncommon for a coach to become interested in goal setting and to begin to implement a goal setting program with his/her athletes during the preseason or early season. However, as the season progresses, less and less time is spent on goal setting. By the end of the season the goal-setting program is all but forgotten.

Like other psychological skills, goal setting takes time to implement. It must be recognized that a good deal of commitment on the part of the coach is needed. When planning your goal-setting program, think about the busiest time of your team's season and how much time is available to commit to goal setting. It is much better to devote 20 minutes a week to goal setting throughout the season and follow through on that plan than to say you will devote 20 minutes a day to goal setting and not follow through on it. Similarly, time spent in preseason planning and organization (e.g., mass-producing goal achievement cards and goal evaluation forms) makes the goal-setting process much more efficient and realistic to implement.

Finally, consider program efficiency when organizing your program. One collegiate basketball coach, for example, simply had her athletes write down a practice goal on 3" by 5" index cards for the next day's practice. The coaching staff would then evaluate and provide feedback relative to these practice goals during each postpractice cool-down period. This was a time-efficient yet effective program that was easy to implement for the entire season.

Setting Only Technique-Related Goals

When setting goals with athletes, it is very easy to focus all of one's attention on technique-related goals (e.g., shooting statistics, faster running times). However, as previously mentioned, there are a number of other areas in which the performer may want to use goal setting. For example, a high school volleyball coach who was having trouble with his team's cohesion found it useful to have several key players set goals of giving sincere positive feedback to teammates at least five times per practice, and the team manager recorded the number of positive remarks made during practice. Similarly, an injured runner set specific goals relative to the number of times per week she would practice imagery. Finally, a football coach whose team seemed unenthusiastic and burned out at the end of a long season had considerable success asking the players to identify what elements of football were most fun for them (e.g., lineman throwing and catching the football) and then setting team goals to incorporate specified amounts of fun activities in every practice.

Failing to Create a Supportive Goal-Setting Atmosphere

To reiterate, coaches and sport psychologists cannot set goals for their athletes or force them to participate in the goal-setting process. The athletes

Goal Achievement Card—Basketball

Name _____ Date _____

Position _____ Years Experience _____

Skill/Activity	Strong	Average	Needs improvement	Specific Goal	Strategy	Target Date
Shooting • lay-ups • jump shots • free throws Ball handling Rebounding						

Performance Evaluation Card—Basketball

Name _____ Date _____

Position _____ Game _____

Skill/Activity	Available Statistics/Coach Performance Rating (0–100%)	Comments
Overall offensive play	80%	
Overall defensive play	94%	
Shooting	70%	
• lay-ups	2 for 2	
• jump shots	2 for 6	
• free throws	3 for 4	
Ball handling	90%	
• turnovers	1	
Rebounding	90%	

Figure 13-1 Sample goal achievement and performance evaluation cards for the sport of basketball

must be self-motivated and committed to the program. For this reason, the goal-setting leader needs to create a supportive goal-setting atmosphere, and in creating such an atmosphere, communication style is critical. Coaches and sport psychologists must act as facilitators of goal-setting discussions, not as dictators (Botterill, 1983). They must share

limitations with athletes and identify unrealistic goals, while simultaneously avoiding pessimistic remarks and putdowns. In essence, the leader must adopt a positive communication style that includes good listening skills, a sincere orientation, and a positive approach.

Summary

This chapter has provided strong empirical and experiential support for the utility of using goal setting in helping athletes attain personal growth and peak performance. Goals are effective because they influence psychological states such as self-confidence, direct attention to important aspects of the task, mobilize effort, increase persistence, and foster the development of new learning strategies. A number of recognized guidelines should be followed when setting goals with athletes. These include setting behaviorally measurable goals, difficult yet realistic goals, short-range as well as long-range goals, performance goals as opposed to outcome goals, practice and competition goals, and positive as opposed to negative goals. Equally important guidelines are identifying target dates for attaining goals, identifying goal achievement strategies, recording goals once they have been identified, providing goal evaluation procedures, and providing for goal support. Lastly, common problems that arise when goal setting must be recognized. These include setting too many goals too soon, failing to recognize individual differences, setting goals that are too general, failing to modify unrealistic goals, failing to set performance goals, not understanding the time and commitment needed to implement a goal-setting program, setting only technique-related goals, and failing to create a supportive goal-setting atmosphere. These problems can be easily avoided or controlled if they are recognized at the onset of the goal-setting process.

Like other psychological skills, goal setting is not a magic formula that guarantees success. Goal setting is a tool, a very effective tool, that when combined with hard work and discipline can help coaches, athletes, and sport psychologists reap the fruits of personal athletic growth and peak performance. It is highly recommended, then, that coaches and sport psychologists at all levels of competition engage in goal setting with their athletes.

Study Questions

1. Define what a goal is and differentiate between the following types of goals: (a) subjective, (b) general objective, (c) specific objective, (d) outcome, and (e) performance.

2. Briefly describe Locke and colleagues' (1981) mechanistic, Burton's (1983) cognitive, and Garland's (1985) cognitive mediation explanations for the relationship between goal setting and performance.

3. Identify and describe the 11 goal-setting guidelines presented in this chapter,

4. Describe the three phases of a goal-setting system for coaches and sport psychologists.

5. Indicate why failing to set a performance goal is a common problem when setting goals with athletes.

6. Is it easier to adjust goals upward or downward? Explain.

7. Give an example of goal setting that is not technique-related.

8. How can a coach create a supportive goal-setting atmosphere?

References

Bell, K. F. (1983). *Championship thinking: The athlete's guide to winning performance in all sports*. Englewood Cliffs, N.J.: Prentice-Hall.

Botterill, C. (1977, September). *Goal setting and performance on an endurance task*. Paper presented at the Canadian Psychomotor Learning and Sport Psychology Conference, Banff, Alb.

Botterill, C. (1983). Goal setting for athletes with examples from hockey. In G. L. Martin & D. Hrycaiko (Eds.), *Behavior modification and coaching: Principles, procedures, and research*. Springfield, Ill.: Thomas.

Burton, D. (1983). *Evaluation of goal setting training on selected cognitions and performance of collegiate swimmers*. Unpublished doctoral dissertation, University of Illinois, Urbana.

Burton, D. (1984, February). Goal setting: A secret to success. *Swimming World*, pp. 25–29.

Burton, D. (1989). Winning isn't everything: Examining the impact of performance goals on collegiate swimmers' cognitions and performance. *The Sport Psychologist, 3*, 105–132.

Carron, A. V. (1984). *Motivation: Implications for coaching and teaching*. London, Ont.: Sports Dynamics.

Garland, H. (1985). A cognitive mediation theory of task goals and human performance. *Motivation and Emotion, 9*, 345–367.

Gould, D. (1983). Developing psychological skills in young athletes. In N. L. Wood (Ed.), *Coaching science update*. Ottawa, Ont.: Coaching Association of Canada.

Gould, D., Tammen, V., Murphy, S., & May, J. (1989). An examination of U.S. Olympic sport psychology consultants and the services they provide. *The Sport Psychologist, 3*, 300–312.

Harris, D. V., & Harris, B. L. (1984). *The athlete's guide to sports psychology: Mental skills for physical people.* New York: Leisure Press.

Locke, E. A., & Latham, G. P. (1985). The application of goal setting to sports. *Journal of Sport Psychology, 7,* 205–222.

Locke, E. A., Shaw, K. N., Saari, L. M., & Latham, G. P. (1981). Goal setting and task performance. *Psychological Bulletin, 90*, 125–152.

Martens, R. (1987). *Coaches guide to sport psychology.* Champaign, Ill.: Human Kinetics.

McClements, J. (1982). Goal setting and planning for mental preparations. In L. Wankel & R. B. Wilberg (Eds.)., Psychology of sport and motor behavior: Research and practice. *Proceedings of the Annual Conference of the Canadian Society for Psychomotor Learning and Sport Psychology.* Edmonton, Alb.: University of Alberta.

McClements, J. D., & Botterill, C. B. (1979). Goal setting in shaping of future performance of athletes. In P. Klavora & J. Daniel (Eds.), *Coach, athlete and the sport psychologist.* Champaign, Ill.: Human Kinetics.

Mento, A. J., Steel, R. P., & Karren, R. J. (1987). A meta-analytic study of the effects of goal-setting on task performance: 1966–1984. *Organizational Behavior and Human Decision Processes, 39,* 52–83.

O'Block, F. R., & Evans, F. H. (1984). Goal setting as a motivational technique. In J. M. Silva & R. S. Weinberg (Eds.), *Psychological foundations of sport.* Champaign, Ill.: Human Kinetics.

Orlick, T. (1990). *In pursuit of excellence* (2nd ed.). Champaign, Ill.: Human Kinetics.

Orlick, T., & Partington, J. (1988). Mental links to excellence. *The Sport Psychologist, 2,* 105–130.

Weinberg, R. S. (in press). Goal setting and motor performance: A review and critique. In G. C. Roberts (Ed.), *Motivation in sport and exercise.* Champaign, Ill.: Human Kinetics.

Arousal–Performance Relationships

Daniel M. Landers, *Arizona State University*
Stephen H. Boutcher, *University of Wollongong*

Most athletes at some time or another have suffered from inappropriate levels of arousal. Consider, for a moment, the following illustrative examples. A U.S. Olympic weight lifter in international competition surprisingly deviates from his customary preparatory routine before a lift and totally forgets to chalk his hands. As might be expected, the lift is missed. A gymnast preparing for a high flyaway dismount from the still rings suddenly focuses on self-doubts concerning his ability to perform the stunt without the presence of a spotter. These doubts, coupled with an increased fatigue level brought about by a long routine, cause him to freeze and release the rings prematurely. Finally, a sprinter who appears lackadaisical and lethargic during precompetition workouts records one of her worst times during competition.

These are just a few examples of what athletes and coaches usually refer to as lack of concentration, "choking" under pressure, or failure to get the athlete "up" for competition. Sport competition can generate much anxiety and worry, which in turn can affect physiological and thought processes so dramatically that performance often deteriorates. In your own athletic or coaching experience, you have probably perceived a racing heartbeat, a dry mouth, butterflies in your stomach, trembling muscles, or an inability to clearly focus thoughts. In these situations you may have told yourself that you were "too tight" or tense or that you "couldn't think straight." Common expressions like these often prompt practical questions concerning whether the athlete should be "fired up" as much as possible or relaxed as much as possible before an important competition. Or perhaps there is some in-between state that should be sought.

These concerns are generally related to the topic of motivation and, more specifically, to the concept of arousal. Understanding arousal and its effects on athletic performance, finding ways to estimate the arousal demands of a particular sport, and assessing arousal levels of individual athletes form the focus of this chapter. In the first section we will describe arousal and its effects and outline a model for understanding its influence on athletic performance. In the second section we will describe the major hypotheses and research evidence for the arousal–performance relationship. Finally, in the third section we will describe a method whereby the coach or sport psychologist can estimate the optimal arousal level for a particular sport and for specific individuals within that sport.

The Nature of Arousal

Before considering how arousal is related to performance, it is necessary to clarify the nature of the arousal construct. This will be done by first defining arousal, followed by a discussion of its origin and how it is generated. Finally, various techniques for measuring arousal will be presented.

Defining Arousal

For our purposes, **arousal** will be viewed as an energizing function that is responsible for the harnessing of the body's resources for intense and vigorous activity (Sage, 1984). An individual's state of arousal is seen as varying on a continuum ranging from deep sleep at one end (as in a comatose state) to extreme excitement at the other (e.g., a panic attack) (Malmo, 1959).

An analogy used by Martens (1974) may be helpful in describing the concept of arousal. Imagine arousal as being equated with the engine speed of a stationary automobile. The engine may run very fast or just idle slowly. The intensity of the engine can be measured in revolutions per minute, whereas the intensity of the human engine is assessed by measuring the person's arousal level. The ideal intensity should match the requirements for the desired task outcome (e.g., quick acceleration) in order to produce the greatest performance efficiency. Sometimes, however, this is not the case. The human engine, just like the automobile, can be running very fast, but because it is in neutral or "park" gear, its effects may not be observed. At other times the engine may be racing with the car in forward gear but with the emergency brake on. This unnatural state is akin to what we will refer to later as a performance "disregulation," where extraneous influences (e.g., the brake or anxiety brought about by negative, self-defeating thought processes) interfere with the natural coordinative action of the skill being performed. The "human engine" refers to both the activation of the brain and the innervation of different physiological systems.

Unlike the car engine, our human engine cannot be turned off—at least while we are alive! Even as you sleep, there is electrical activity in your brain as well as small amounts in the muscles. Thus, arousal is a natural, ongoing state. However, when arousal levels become extremely high, you may experience unpleasant emotional reactions associated with the autonomic nervous system. This maladaptive condition is often referred to as "stress" or "state anxiety." As we will see in a later section of this chapter, anxiety reactions to competition can result in ineffective performance, faulty decision making, and inappropriate perception. Helping athletes harness arousal so that it will not become an uncontrollable anxiety response is one of the major preoccupations of sport psychologists. It is important to bear in mind that sport psychologists do not seek to make people unemotional zombies but instead attempt to teach skills that will enable athletes to better control arousal and, thereby, more effectively cope with anxiety.

Origin of Arousal States

The structures for controlling arousal are located in the brain and primarily involve the cortex, reticular formation, the hypothalamus, and the limbic system. These centers interact with the adrenal medulla and the somatic and autonomic systems to determine overall arousal. We can demonstrate the integration of these different systems in an athletic situation by means of the following example.

A field hockey goalie sits in the dressing room minutes before an important match. She is worried about the upcoming game because she doubts her ability to play well in the biggest match of the season. These thoughts lead to anxiety about performance. Her worrying may not be realistic, but to her body that does not matter. Technically speaking, the cerebral cortex and brainstem/midbrain reticular activating system signal the hypothalamus, which in turn releases hormones (CRT and ACTH) that trigger the pouring of another hormone (cortisol) and the catecholamines epinephrine and norepinephrine (also called adrenaline and noradrenalin) into the bloodstream (Krahenbuhl, 1975). The rapid increase in these stress amines and hormones prepares her body and mind for an emergency "fight or flight" situation. Autonomic nervous system measures, such as heart rate, blood pressure, and breathing increase, and muscles in general begin to tighten. Blood vessels in the hands and feet close down, and their blood supply is shunted to the larger, deeper muscles. The hockey goalie is now in an overly aroused or anxious state. Needless to say, we would not expect this athlete to perform well in this condition.

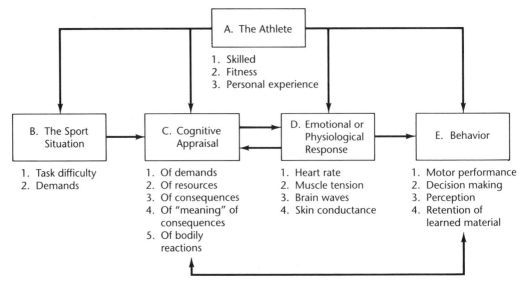

Figure 14-1 **A model illustrating factors that affect the arousal–performance relationship**

How Arousal Is Generated

From the foregoing example we càn see that the athlete's initial appraisal of the situation was the starting point of a chain reaction that ultimately led to the overly aroused state. This chain reaction along with the host of other factors involved in the arousal–performance relationship are outlined in Figure 14-1.

Our hockey goalie appraised the situation negatively and decided that her capabilities did not meet the demands of the upcoming game. This combination of an important, meaningful event and doubts about her ability was responsible for generating anxiety and worry. This is usually the first part of the arousal process,* which unless stopped will inevitably lead to the physiological reactions described in Figure 14-1 (see D.1–4). Once these physiological responses start to occur, she begins to appraise the feelings as well (C.5). Not

knowing how to cope with the physiological reactions can create even more worry and apprehension (C.1–4). Notice also that, once performance begins, aspects of the athlete's behavior (see E.1–4) are fed back for cognitive appraisal (C.1–5) that may further intensify anxiety. As we will see later, this process can be influenced by individual difference variables such as skill level, personality, physical and psychological fitness, and competitive experience.

Measurement of Arousal

Since arousal affects so many bodily functions, it appears to be an easy construct to measure. Unfortunately, this is not the case. We will discuss three areas of arousal measurement (see Table 14-1) and highlight the advantages and disadvantages of each.

Physiological measures. In sport psychology research much frustration has resulted from the lack of consistent agreement among different physiological variables and questionnaire measures of arousal. This situation has prompted investigators (e.g., Martens, 1974) to abandon physiological

---

*Although mental appraisal usually precedes the emotional reaction, it can sometimes follow it. This occurs in startle responses that can subsequently be interpreted to evoke anger or a good-natured response. It can also occur when the athlete is unknowingly doing something (e.g., stringing a bow before an archery competition) that may increase the level of physiological arousal.

Table 14-1 **Some Common Physiological, Biochemical, and Questionnaire Measures of Arousal**

Measure and Description

A. Physiological

  1. Central

     Electroencephalography (EEG). Changes occur in brain wave patterns from an alpha or relaxed state (8–13 Hz) to beta or a more aroused state (14–30 Hz).

  2. Autonomic

     Electrical properties of the skin. This measure assesses either the amount of skin conductance or resistance to an electric current. Elevations in arousal cause increased perspiration, which increases the flow of the current.

     Heart rate. Increases in heart rate, the pattern of beats, and heart rate variability can all be indices of arousal.

     Blood pressure. Increases in blood pressure are also associated with increased arousal levels and can be measured by cannulation or by the stethoscope and pressure-cuff method.

     Muscle activity. Muscle tension can be measured by electromyography (EMG), which measures the firing rate of motor units by means of surface electrodes attached to the muscle.

B. Biochemical

  1. Epinephrine. Epinephrine is released from the adrenal medulla during times of stress. This can be measured in the urine and blood.

  2. Norepinephrine. Also elevated during stressful activities, this catecholamine can be measured by the same techniques used for analyzing epinephrine.

  3. Cortisol. A steroid hormone that is released from the adrenal gland when the organism is confronted with either physical/emotional stressors or declining blood glucose levels.

C. Questionnaires

  1. Unidimensional measures
     State-Trait Anxiety Inventory (Spielberger, Gorsuch, & Lushene, 1970)
     Somatic Perception Questionnaire (Landy & Stern, 1971)
     Activation Deactivation Adjective Checklist (Thayer, 1967)
     Sport Competition Anxiety Test (Martens, 1977)

  2. Multidimensional measures
     Cognitive-Somatic Anxiety Questionnaire (Schwartz, Davidson, & Goleman, 1978)
     Competitive State Anxiety Inventory-2 (CSAI-2) (Martens et al., 1983, 1990)
     Sport Anxiety Scale (SAS) (Smith, Smoll, & Schutz, 1990)

measures in favor of questionnaires. Indeed, in the last decade, research concerning the relationship between arousal and sport performance has almost exclusively relied upon questionnaires despite evidence favoring physiological measures (Landers, Wang, & Courtet, 1985; Light & Obrist, 1983).

The low correlations found among physiological measures has been explained by Lacey, Bateman, and Van Lehn's (1953) principle of "autonomic response stereotypy." For example, in the same stressful situation, athlete A might display an elevated heart rate, while athlete B might show an increase in gastrointestinal activity. This principle suggests that averaging one physiological variable (e.g., heart rate) across a group of subjects may conceal individual arousal reactions.

To overcome this problem, Duffy (1962) has recommended the use of multiple physiological measures as an index of the arousal response. From these multiple measures, if Athlete A is found to be a heart rate responder when exposed to stressors like competition, this measure would be singled out for comparison of Athlete A in conditions varying in levels of perceived stress. By using each person's most responsive autonomic measure, greater differentiation can be achieved and thus more meaningful information can be gleaned.

The current view concerning physiological measures is that they are far more complex than first thought. However, with increased understanding of physiological processes and the continuing trend of cheaper, more sophisticated equipment, physiological measures have much potential as reliable indicators of the arousal response.

Biochemical measures. The adrenal glands are responsible for the release of epinephrine and norepinephrine into the bloodstream in times of stress. Also, a variety of corticosteroids enter the blood during high arousal. Increases in amines or cortisol have been examined chiefly by analyzing either the blood or urine. Blood analysis usually involves drawing blood from the subject by syringe or catheter. The analysis is complex and requires sophisticated equipment. Another disadvantage is that the drawing of the blood can be traumatic to certain subjects, thus confounding the results of the study. Urine analysis is less invasive but suffers from the same cost and time disadvantages as blood analysis. At this point it is also unclear how accurately these measures reflect the brain's overall hormonal levels.

Questionnaires. Many questionnaires are designed to assess the different effects of increased arousal. Some measure cognitive variables, some assess physiological responses, and others assess both dimensions in the same questionnaire (see Table 14-1). The advantages of questionnaires are that they are quick and easy to administer and relatively easy to analyze. One disadvantage is that they may be insensitive to changes in arousal levels by being susceptible to unwanted effects such as the social desirability response. Thus, athletes may complete a questionnaire with responses they perceive the coach or sport psychologist would like to see (e.g., Williams & Krane, 1989, in press). Another disadvantage is that questionnaires usually necessitate large samples to offset the inherent variability among subjects. This is often impossible with teams or small groups of athletes.

Many questionnaires are designed to assess both trait and state forms of anxiety. **Trait anxiety**

is a *general* predisposition to respond across many situations with high levels of anxiety. To assess trait anxiety, subjects are asked to rate how they generally feel. **State anxiety** is much more specific, referring to a subject's anxiety at a particular moment. People who are high in trait anxiety are expected to respond with higher levels of state anxiety, or situationally specific anxiety. The State-Trait Anxiety Inventory (Spielberger, Gorsuch, & Lushene, 1970) is a popular example of a well-researched questionnaire that assesses both dimensions of anxiety.

A new development in the construction of anxiety questionnaires is the trend toward more multidimensional instruments. Three questionnaires, one general (Schwartz, Davidson, & Coleman, 1978) and the others sport-specific (Martens et al., 1983, 1990; Smith, Smoll, & Schutz, 1990) have subdivided anxiety into the components of somatic and cognitive aspects. The CSAI-2 (Martens et al., 1983, 1990) has somatic and cognitive state anxiety subscales plus a self-confidence scale. The SAS (Smith, Smoll, & Schutz, 1990) has a somatic trait anxiety scale and two cognitive trait anxiety scales—one for worry and one for concentration disruption. Somatic or bodily anxiety is assessed by questions such as "How tense are the muscles in your body?" Cognitive anxiety would be indicated by affirmative responses to questions such as "Do you worry a lot?" It is believed that by subdividing anxiety into its component parts more will be understood about its nature and more effective therapies can thus be designed.

The Relationship Between Arousal and Motor Performance

In the motor behavior literature two hypotheses have been advanced to explain the relationship between arousal and performance. We will first consider the drive theory hypothesis and then the inverted-*U* hypothesis.

Drive Theory Hypothesis

Although this is not a consistently held view among all psychologists, for our purposes we will equate the term *"drive"* with *"arousal."* In other words, "drive" and "arousal" convey what we referred to earlier as the "intensity" dimension of behavior.

Drive theory, as modified by Spence and Spence (1966), predicts that performance (P) is a multiplicative function of habit (H) and drive (D): $P = H \times D$. The construct of "habit" in this formulation refers to the hierarchical order or dominance of correct or incorrect responses. According to this hypothesis, increases in arousal should enhance the probability of making the dominant responses. When performance errors are frequently made, as in the early stages of skill acquisition, the dominant responses are likely to be incorrect responses. Conversely, when performance errors are infrequent, the dominant response is said to be a correct response. Increases in arousal during initial skill acquisition impair performance, but as the skill becomes well learned, increases in arousal facilitate performance.

For example, a novice basketball player shooting foul shots only sinks 3 shots out of 10; therefore, the incorrect response (a miss) is dominant. The drive theory hypothesis would predict that given greater pressure, the novice player is likely to miss more than 7 shots out of 10. By contrast, the all-star basketball player may average 8 successful shots for every 10 attempted. In this case, because the dominant response is a correct response, an increase in arousal should enhance the player's chance of sinking more than 8 shots out of 10.

It is questionable whether a linear relationship between arousal and performance can be found for accuracy tasks such as foul shooting. However, Oxendine (1984) argues that linear relationships, as depicted in Figure 14-2, do exist for gross motor activities involving strength, endurance, and speed.

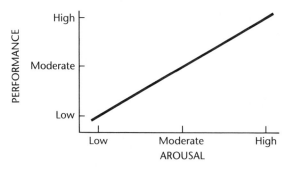

Figure 14-2 **The linear relationship between arousal and performance as suggested by drive theory**

These types of activities are typically overlearned, with strongly formed habit patterns. It seems likely, therefore, that a very high level of arousal is desirable for optimal performance in these types of gross motor skills. Anecdotal evidence regarding "superhuman" feats performed in emergency situations where unexpected physical strength, speed, or endurance was required (e.g., a mother lifting a station wagon off her trapped child) supports this view.

At first glance, these examples seem to provide ample evidence to support a drive theory explanation for sport skills involving strength, speed, and endurance. Contrary to Oxendine's analysis, however, we would like to argue on conceptual grounds that the "fight or flight" arousal responses produced in these emergency situations are not appropriate comparisons to the sport situation. The sport setting is highly structured, often involving complex decision-making and perceptual strategies, in addition to the performance of a motor skill. The surge of epinephrine resulting from an emergency situation may enhance strength in an uncontrolled manner, but this may actually be detrimental in actual sport performances. For example, there are many instances of overaroused sprinters recording false starts in intense competition. Similarly, many superenergized weight lifters have forgotten to chalk up or have lifted the barbell in a biomechanically inefficient way in major competitions. Thus, on experiential grounds it appears that even among weight lifters, sprinters, and long- or middle-distance runners there are limits to the amount of arousal the athlete can tolerate without suffering performance decrements.

The drive theory hypothesis has not fared much better when the experimental evidence from the motor behavior literature has been examined. For example, Freeman (1940) has shown that with high levels of arousal, reaction times are slower than when arousal levels are in the moderate range. Furthermore, in other arousal-producing situations (e.g., audience effects) where the drive theory hypothesis has received extensive support, it is now known that these effects were so small as to be of trivial practical significance (Bond & Titus, 1983; Landers, Snyder-Bauer, & Feltz, 1978). Thus, it appears that other hypotheses, such as the inverted-*U*, need to be considered to explain the highly complex network of skills characteristic of sport performance.

Inverted-*U* Hypothesis

The inverted-*U* relationship between arousal and performance is shown in Figure 14-3. The **inverted-*U* hypothesis** predicts that as arousal increases from drowsiness to alertness, there is a progressive increase in performance efficiency. However, once arousal continues to increase beyond alertness to a state of high excitement, there is a progressive decrease in task performance. Thus, the inverted-*U* hypothesis suggests that behavior is aroused and directed toward some kind of balanced or optimal state.

Although the exact shape of the curve does not exactly match the idealized pattern in Figure 14-3, the decrement in performance at high levels of stress does occur across studies with considerable regularity. For example, Martens and Landers (1970) found greater motor steadiness at intermediate levels of arousal as measured with a physiological measure. Wood and Hokanson (1965) have observed a similar inverted *U*-shaped pattern for performance when arousal has been experimentally produced by varying muscle tension. Babin (1966) and Levitt and Gutin (1971) have also found reaction-time performance curves resembling an inverted-*U* that were produced during total body exercise on a treadmill or bicycle ergometer of varying workload intensities and durations.

Inverted-*U* relationships have even been found in research studies that have used real-world sport skills. Fenz and Epstein (1969) have reported such relationships among physiological measures, self-report measures, and jumping efficiency of sport parachutists. Klavora (1979) found inverted-*U* performance patterns among high school basketball players as measured by coaches' performance ratings and self-reported anxiety measures by players for each game. Using questionnaire measures of state anxiety before each basketball game, Sonstroem and Bernardo (1982) were able to compare athletes' basketball performance in each of several games with their respective anxiety levels for these games. They found that a moderate level of arousal/anxiety was associated with a high level of overall performance in basketball. Other studies, which have employed intraindividual questionnaire measures of anxiety, have also confirmed the inverted-*U* relationship for pistol shooting (Gould et al., 1987) and swimming (Burton, 1988). However, the relationship was only found with measures of somatic, or bodily, arousal/anxiety and not with measures of cognitive arousal/anxiety.

Of course, some experiments do not show inverted-*U* curves (Murphy, 1966; Pinneo, 1961), but the weight of the evidence seems to support the inverted-*U* hypothesis. Overall, the findings suggest the following conclusions. First, the inverted-*U* hypothesis seems to generalize across field and experimental situations. Second, the same performance patterning generally exists for arousal induced psychologically or physically through drugs, exercise, or muscle tension.

Task characteristics. From an arousal perspective the characteristics of a skill or activity are essential determinants of performance. In the early 1900s it

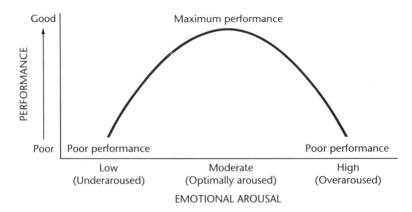

Figure 14-3 The inverted-*U* relationship between arousal and performance

was known that the optimal level of arousal varied among different tasks. Using laboratory animals, Yerkes and Dodson (1908) found that on more complex tasks the decrement in performance under increasing arousal conditions occurred earlier than it did for less complex tasks. The interaction of task complexity with arousal level is clearly illustrated in Broadhurst's (1957) experiment (see Figure 14-4). In this experiment, arousal was created by holding rats underwater for zero, two, four, or eight seconds prior to allowing them to swim underwater to complete a two-choice maze. In one condition the choice was made easier by making the correct escape door more obvious (brightly painted lines), whereas in the more difficult condition the doors were very similar. As shown in Figure 14-4, decrements in time to negotiate the maze occurred much earlier (after two seconds of submergence) in the more complex decision-making situation. Thus, higher levels of arousal can be tolerated on less complex tasks before performance is curtailed.

What does all of this mean for the performance of sport skills? Basically, the complexity characteristics of the motor skill need to be analyzed to determine how much arousal is optimal. A number of factors that must be considered appear in Table 14-2. Take, for example, the precision and steadiness characteristics required for successful execution of a skill. (See Figure 14-5.) For very precise fine motor skills that involve steadiness or control of unwanted muscle activity (e.g., golf), very little arousal can be tolerated without accompanying performance decrements. However for tasks such as weight lifting that involve mini-

mal fine motor precision, a much higher level of arousal can be achieved before performance is impaired.

In addition to considering factors associated with the motor act itself, it is important to consider the decisional and perceptual characteristics of the

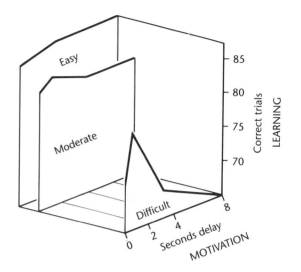

Figure 14-4 **A three-dimensional model illustrating the Yerkes-Dodson Law. Rats were held underwater and deprived of air for varying numbers of seconds, after which they were allowed to escape by selecting the correct door. The optimal level of motivation for learning depended on task difficulty** *Source:* Broadhurst, 1957.

Table 14-2 **The Complexity of Motor Performance**

Decision	*Perception*	*Motor Act*
Number of decisions necessary	Number of stimuli needed	Number of muscles
Number of alternatives per decision	Number of stimuli present	Amount of coordinative actions
Speed of decisions	Duration of stimuli	Precision and steadiness required
Sequence of decisions	Intensity of stimuli	Fine motor skills required
	Conflicting stimuli	

Source: Based on: Billing, 1980.

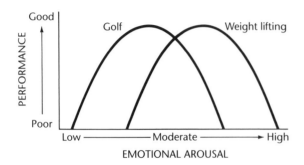

Figure 14-5 **Sport-specific optimal levels of arousal**

task. The underwater swimming of the rats in Broadhurst's (1957) experiment was an example of inverted-*U* performance curves when the complexity of alternative *decisions* was varied. Generally speaking, tasks with higher decisional demands require lower arousal levels for optimal performance compared to tasks with lower decisional demands.

The relationship of *perception* to the inverted-*U* hypothesis has been primarily studied in situations where subjects are attending to potentially conflicting stimuli. A number of studies (see Landers, 1978, 1980, for reviews) have shown that when dual tasks are performed, subjects will generally allocate more attention to one of them in order to maintain or better their performance. This strategy is typically chosen because it is believed that humans have very limited spare capacity for focusing attention on task-irrelevant cues when they are performing complex motor skills.

There are many examples of attention being shifted from secondary tasks to enhance the concentration necessary to perform the primary task. The experimental situation, called the "dual-task paradigm," involves creating differing levels of arousal while subjects are performing a primary task and at the same time periodically reacting to a tone or a visual stimulus (Landers, Wang & Courtet, 1985; Weltman & Egstrom, 1966).

From similar studies in which the dual-task paradigm has been used, Bacon (1974) offers the generalization that arousal effects depend upon the degree of attention the stimuli attract, with "sensitivity loss systematically occurring to those cues which initially attract less attention" (p. 86). Other investigators (e.g., Easterbrook, 1959) suggest that arousal acts to narrow the range of cue

utilization, which results in the inverted-*U* function previously described. The underaroused performer, for example, has a broad perceptual range and, therefore, either through lack of effort or poor selectivity, accepts irrelevant cues uncritically. Performance in this case is understandably poor. When arousal increases to a moderate or optimal level, perceptual selectivity increases correspondingly and performance improves, presumably because the performer tries harder or is more likely to eliminate task-irrelevant cues. Arousal increases beyond this optimal point result in further perceptual narrowing, and performance deteriorates in accord with the inverted-*U* hypothesis. For instance, a highly anxious football quarterback may focus attention too narrowly to detect task-relevant cues such as secondary receivers open in the periphery. The ideas of both Bacon (1974) and Easterbrook (1959) suggest that the effects of arousal impair one's performance through a loss of perceptual sensitivity by interfering with one's capacity to process information.

Individual Differences. The optimal level of arousal for a particular task is also dependent upon factors that are unique to the individual. Because of inherent personality differences and strength of dominant habits associated with the sport skill, some athletes can perform effectively at much higher levels of arousal than other athletes. People differ in the amount of prior experience with a task as well as the amount of practice they have had. As we discussed earlier, the strength of the correct habit response varies from one person to the next. The person who is more skillful—that is, has a stronger habit hierarchy—is more likely to offset the detrimental effects of increased arousal more effectively than the individual who is less skillful and possesses a weaker habit strength.

Of course, habit patterns may not always be appropriate. Landers (1985) has indicated that subtle changes in habit patterns may lead to **disregulations**, which are defined as a physiological measure of arousal that either negatively correlates with performance or creates some degree of discomfiture for the performer. For example, in our work with a world champion archer, we found that he had developed a habit of tightly squinting his nonsighting eye following the release of the arrow. At the end of several hours of shooting, this resulted in a tension headache. With the archer having to concentrate so much on the act of shooting, it was difficult for him to focus on the source of his problem. To correct this, it was necessary for us to bring the disregulation to his conscious awareness by providing an electromyographic signal of the electrical activity around his non-sighting eye. After several shots with this type of biofeedback, the squinting, which lasted for several seconds, was reduced to a blink and the headaches disappeared.

Perhaps the greatest individual difference factor is one's personality. The most relevant personality variables affecting one's optimal arousal level are trait anxiety and extroversion/introversion. As shown in Figure 14-6, if an athlete is high-strung and intolerant of stressful situations (i.e., introverted), even a small amount of arousal can put him/her over the top on the inverted-U curve. On the other hand, if the athlete is calm and collected (i.e., low trait anxiety or extroverted), he/she will be able to tolerate much higher levels of arousal without suffering a performance impairment.

Given individual differences in personality, habit patterns associated with the skills, and ability to cope with stress, it is clear that the relationship between arousal and performance is best assessed on an individual basis. Somewhere between the very diverse extremes of comatose state and panic attack, each athlete will have a "zone of optimal functioning" (Hanin, 1978). For some this arousal zone will be much higher than is evident for other athletes (Landers, 1981). The trick is to know where this zone is for each athlete and then to help the athlete to reproduce this arousal state more consistently from one competition to the next.

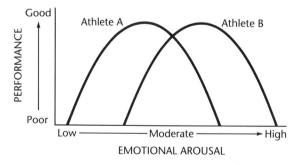

Figure 14-6 **Athlete-specific optimal levels of arousal**

Estimating the Relationship Between an Athlete's Optimal Arousal and Performance

As indicated above, the optimal arousal level will depend on task characteristics as well as individual difference factors. To help athletes learn to regulate arousal during the competition, it is important that the coach or sport psychologist compares the arousal demands of the sport task to the athletes' typical competitive arousal state. We recommend the following guidelines. Select a specific task such as playing the quarterback position in football. Avoid global activities such as gymnastics, football, or basketball, and be as task-specific as you can! Once you zero in on the task, answer the questions in Table 14-3. For example, high scores (3s and 4s) in the sport of archery on motor act characteristics (C.1–4) would produce high total scores. In short sprints, however, the decision/perceptual processes would in general receive low values (1s and 2s), and the gross motor nature of sprinting would keep the overall task score at a relatively low level. When using this table, bear in mind that it is only a rough guideline for estimating the complexity of your sport.

Total your scores and see where your chosen skill falls on the range in Table 14-4. If the skill has a low score, this indicates that the average athlete can be "psyched up" to a greater extent and still perform optimally. If an athlete performing this task is low trait anxious and typically responds to competition in a constantly "laid-back" fashion, you may need to supplement normal psych-up procedures by teaching the athlete some of the energizing techniques presented in Chapter 15. However, if the athlete scores over 32 in the specific skill you have selected, he/she will not usually be able to tolerate as much arousal. In this case it is important for the coach to overtrain the athlete in the basic skills so as to develop correct habits that are less susceptible to the debilitating effects of arousal/anxiety. For those more complex skills, coaches should particularly avoid implementing last-minute changes in technique since a weak habit strength for the skill will make the athlete more susceptible to the disruptive effects of arousal/anxiety.

In addition to reinforcing the strength of correct habits, it is also important in complex skills to

Table 14-3 **Estimating Complexity of Motor Performance**

A. Decision Characteristics of Skill

	0	1	2	3	4
1. Number of decisions necessary	None	Few	Some	Several	Many
2. Number of alternatives per decision	None	Few	Some	Several	Many
3. Speed of decisions	Not relevant	Very slow	Slow	Fast	Very fast
4. Sequence of decisions	Not relevant, only one decision	Sequence of 2	Sequence of 3	Sequence of 4	Sequence of 5 or more

B. Perception Characteristics of Skill

	0	1	2	3	4
1. Number of stimuli needed	None	Few	Some	Several	Many
2. Number of stimuli present	Very few	Few	Some	Several	Many
3. Duration of stimuli	More than 20 sec	More than 10 sec	More than 5 sec	More than 2 sec	Less than 2 sec
4. Intensity of stimuli	Very Intense	Intense	Moderately intense	Low intensity	Very low intensity
5. Clarity of correct stimulus among conflicting stimuli	Very obvious	Obvious	Moderately obvious	Subtle difference	Very subtle difference

C. Motor Act Characteristics of Skill

	0	1	2	3	4
1. Number of muscle actions to execute skill	1–2	3–4	5–6	7–8	9 or more
2. Amount of coordination of actions	Minimal	A little	Some	Several coordinative actions	A great deal
3. Precision and steadiness required	None	Minimal	Some	Considerable	A great deal
4. Fine motor skill required	None, only gross motor skill	Minimal	Some	Considerable	A great deal

pay greater heed to the relaxation, imagery, and cognitive coping strategies presented in Chapters 15, 16, and 17. Athletes who display consistent, high-level performance during practice or unimportant competition but then fail to perform efficiently in major competitions will have even more need to practice these coping techniques regularly.

To determine an optimal level of arousal for a given skill, each athlete should be examined individually. This is most easily done by administering one of the questionnaires listed in Table 14-1. By giving this to an athlete before each competition

Table 14-4 **Optimum Arousal Level and Complexity Scores for a Variety of Typical Sport Skills**

Level of Arousal	Complexity Score Range	Sport Skills
5 (extremely excited)	0–10	Football blocking, running 200 meters to 400 meters
4 (psyched up)	11–16	Short sprints, long jump
3 (medium arousal)	17–21	Basketball, boxing, judo
2 (some arousal)	22–31	Baseball, pitching, fencing, tennis
1 (slight arousal)	32+	Archery, golf, field goal kicking

Source: Based on: Oxendine, 1984, and Billing, 1980.

and noting his/her performance levels associated with the arousal/anxiety scores, a coach or sport psychologist should eventually be able to determine the athlete's zone of optimal functioning. Rather than completing the questionnaires at the time of competition, Hanin (1978) has recommended *retrospective* self-reports of arousal/anxiety. An athlete is asked to think back to a personal best performance and, while thinking about his/her psychological state at that time, to complete an anxiety scale. The anxiety score derived in this manner is taken as indicative of this athlete's zone of optimal functioning. Having this as a basis, the athlete's anxiety in a given competition can be compared to the anxiety score associated with a personal best performance. If these anxiety scores are discrepant, the coach or sport psychologist should use energizing techniques (Chapter 15) or relaxation, imagery, or other psychological skills (Chapters 15, 16, 17) to bring the athlete's arousal/anxiety levels in closer alignment with the predefined zone of optimal functioning.

Armed with the information in this chapter and the techniques described in Chapter 13, the athletes with whom coaches work will be better equipped to select, develop, and use the arousal self-regulation skills presented in Chapter 15.

Often coaches and sport psychologists want to identify athletes with inappropriate arousal levels for the tasks they are performing. Figure 14-1 suggests some areas that will serve as a guide in the identification process. The situation (B) of greatest interest, of course, is competition. The cognitive (C), physiological (D), and behavioral (E) response of athletes in the competitive situation can be compared to responses in noncompetitive situations (i.e., practice conditions). Marked discrepancies in these responses, accompanied by a poor competitive performance, may provide clues that the athlete is overaroused.

At the level of cognitive appraisal (C) the coach or sport psychologist should look for signs of distraction before competition. This is usually indicated by an athlete who is not paying attention to the coach's pregame instructions. The athlete may express more concern than is normal by making statements that indicate a certain degree of self-doubt about his/her ability to meet the competitive demands. This identification process is often simplified at a cognitive appraisal level when the athlete recognizes the excessive worry and comes to the coach or sport psychologist for help.

Even without this self-disclosure, many times it is possible to detect physiological or emotional responses (D) that relate to cognitive appraisal (C) in the way described in Figure 14-1. Where there is a consistent shift to poor performance from practice to competition, the coach or sport psychologist should look for obvious signs of emotional reactivity (e.g., flushed face, sweaty palms, dilated pupils). Another way of getting more direct verification of the arousal mismatch is to administer various measures of arousal/anxiety throughout the competitive season through use of unidimensional- or multidimensional-state anxiety measures (Table 14-1.C). All the questionnaires include questions that assess cognitive appraisal, physiological/emotional, or behavioral aspects. These measures have been successfully used to determine inverted-*U* patterns (Burton, 1988; Gould et al., 1987; Hanin, 1978; Klavora, 1979; Sonstroem & Bernardo, 1982). Some physiological measures are also quite easy for a coach or sport psychologist to use. For instance, Landers (1981) and Tretilova and Rodiniki (1979) tracked heart rates of top U.S. and Soviet rifle shooters and found an optimal heart rate increase above resting values where best performance scores were fired.

Finally, at a behavioral level (Figure 14-1.E) much can be gained from careful observation of the athlete's motor activity, actions, and speech characteristics. Hyperactivity before a performance can be gleaned from erratic behaviors such as pacing, fidgeting, and yawning. An unusually high or low energy level before or during competition may also indicate an inappropriate level of arousal. Rapid speech that sounds abnormal for a particular athlete may provide a reason for the coach or sport psychologist to inquire further into an athlete's arousal state.

The above-mentioned cognitive, physiological, and behavioral manifestations of arousal should not be the last step of the identification process. These factors are only indicators or clues that can serve as a basis for discussions with the athlete. Don't mistake fidgeting because the athlete needs to go to the bathroom as a sign of overarousal. Check out these possible signs of arousal to see what meaning the athlete gives to them. This interpretation is essential in the final determination of overarousal. As we will see in the next three chapters, interpretation is also important for designing interventions to help bring arousal levels under control.

Summary

In this chapter we have attempted to provide a basic understanding of arousal–performance relationships. The drive theory and inverted-*U* hypotheses were presented, the former theory emphasizing the development of correct habits to insulate the athlete against the effects of arousal and the latter hypothesis stressing the determination and maintenance of optimal arousal level for the task to be performed. To determine optimal arousal levels, several task characteristics must be considered as well as individual differences in state anxiety. We have provided guidelines to assist coaches and sport psychologists to estimate the arousal demands in reference to the complexity of the task to be performed. Finally, we have made suggestions to help in identifying athletes who are overaroused. We anticipate that, by increasing their understanding of arousal–performance relationships, coaches and sport psychologists will be able to better assess the task demands and more accurately determine appropriate arousal levels for their athletes.

Study Questions

1. Diagram the predictions of drive theory and the inverted-*U* theory under conditions of a well-learned skill (Figure A) and under conditions of a novice performer learning a new skill (Figure B). After diagramming, explain in words exactly where the two theories predict different performance outcomes.

2. In 1965, Zajonc proposed a drive theory explanation for the effects of a passive audience on an individual's performance. Zajonc hypothesized that an audience produced an increase in an in-

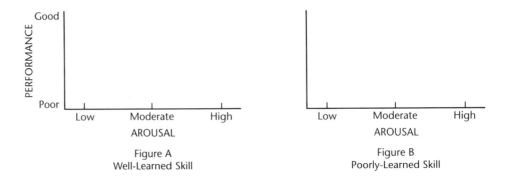

Figure A
Well-Learned Skill

Figure B
Poorly-Learned Skill

dividual's arousal level. Assuming that Zajonc was correct and arousal is increased by an audience, how would such an increase affect the performance of a novice performer and an elite performer? According to drive theory, would you desire an audience for the novice or elite performer?

3. Describe Easterbrook's theory of cue utilization and how it provides an explanation for the inverted-*U* relationship between arousal and performance.

4. You are aware of two athletes at your school who display markedly different patterns of emotional excitement when practicing and competing. The 200-meter sprinter becomes much more emotional than the golfer. They both seem to perform well in their respective psychological states. Describe why these vastly different states may make sense in terms of the inverted-*U* hypothesis.

5. Describe what is meant by the term "arousal." How does arousal relate to the term "anxiety"? Under what conditions might the arousal state of an individual trigger an anxiety response?

6. Describe the ways in which arousal/anxiety have been measured. What do you consider to be the strengths and weaknesses of these measures?

7. What two factors are known to modify the shape of the inverted-*U* relationship?

8. How would you go about determining the complexity of motor skills such as foul shooting in basketball versus maneuvering against three players to shoot a lay-up? According to the task complexity score, which task is more prone to the disruptive effects of arousal?

9. Which of the following athletes would you be most concerned about in terms of holding up under the effects of stress in an upcoming competition? Explain your choice.

- Athlete A is an outgoing individual who is relatively unskilled.
- Athlete B is an introverted person but is one of your most skilled players.
- Athlete C tends to be highly anxious and has recently made some changes in her tennis serving technique.
- Athlete D is low in anxiety and is also relatively unskilled.
- Athlete E is extroverted and is only moderately skilled.

10. According to the inverted-*U* hypothesis, a moderate or "optimal" level of arousal is needed for effective performance. Throughout the season, how would you go about helping an athlete achieve an optimal arousal state prior to each competition?

References

Babin, W. (1966). *The effect of various work loads on simple reaction latency as related to selected physical parameters.* Unpublished doctoral dissertation, University of Southern Mississippi, Hattiesburg.

Bacon, S. J. (1974). Arousal and the range of cue utilization. *Journal of Experimental Psychology, 103,* 81–87.

Billing, J. (1980). An overview of task complexity. *Motor Skills: Theory into Practice, 4,* 18–23.

Bond, C. F., & Titus, L. J. (1983). Social facilitation: A meta-analysis of 241 studies. *Psychological Bulletin, 94,* 265–292.

Broadhurst, P. L. (1957). Emotionality and the Yerkes-Dodson Law. *Journal of Experimental Psychology, 54,* 345–352.

Burton, D. (1988). Do anxious swimmers swim slower?: Reexamining the elusive anxiety–performance relationship. *Journal of Sport and Exercise Psychology, 10,* 45–61.

Duffy, E. (1962). *Activation and behavior.* New York: Wiley.

Easterbrook, J. A. (1959). The effect of emotion on cue utilization and the organization of behavior. *Psychological Review, 66,* 183–201.

Fenz, W. D., & Epstein, S. (1969). Stress in the air. *Psychology Today, 3* (4), 27–28, 58–59.

Freeman, G. L. (1940). The relationship between performance level and bodily activity level. *Journal of Experimental Psychology, 26,* 602–608.

Gould, D., Petlichkoff, L., Simons, J., & Vevera, M. (1987). Relationship between Competitive State Anxiety Inventory-2 subscale scores and pistol shooting performance. *Journal of Sport Psychology, 9,* 33–42.

Hanin, Yuri L. (1978). A study of anxiety in sports. In W. F. Straub (Ed.), *Sport psychology: An analysis of athlete behavior* (pp. 236–256.) Ithaca, N.Y.: Mouvement Publications.

Klavora, P. (1979). An attempt to derive inverted-*U* curves based on the relationship between anxiety and athletic performance. In D. M. Landers and R. W. Christina (Eds.), *Psychology of motor behavior and sport.* Champaign, Ill.: Human Kinetics.

Krahenbuhl, G. S. (1975). Adrenaline, arousal and sport. *Journal of Sports Medicine, 3,* 117–121.

Lacey, J. I., Bateman, D. E., & Van Lehn, R. (1953). Autonomic response specificity: An experimental study. *Psychosomatic Medicine, 15,* 8–21.

Landers, D. M. (1978). Motivation and performance:

The role of arousal and attentional factors. In W. Straub (Ed.), *Sport psychology: An analysis of athletic behavior*. Ithaca, N.Y.: Mouvement Publications.

Landers, D. M. (1980). The arousal–performance relationship revisited. *Research Quarterly*, 51, 77–90.

Landers, D. M. (1981). Reflections of sport psychology and the Olympic athlete. In J. Segrave & D. Chu (Eds.), *Olympism* (pp. 189–200). Champaign, Ill.: Human Kinetics.

Landers, D. M. (1985). Psychophysiological assessment and biofeedback: Applications for athletes in closed skill sports. In J. H. Sandweis & S. Wolf (Eds.), *Biofeedback and sport science*. New York: Plenum.

Landers, D. M., Snyder-Bauer, R., & Feltz, D. L. (1978). Social facilitation during the initial stage of motor learning: A reexamination of Marten's audience study. *Journal of Motor Behavior*, 10, 325–337.

Landers, D. M., Wang, M. Q., & Courtet, P. (1985). Peripheral narrowing among experienced and inexperienced rifle shooters under low- and high-stress conditions. *Research Quarterly*, 56, 57–70.

Landy, F. J., & Stern, R. M. (1971). Factor analysis of a somatic perception questionnaire. *Journal of Psychosomatic Research*, 15, 179–181.

Levitt, S., & Gutin, B. (1971). Multiple choice reaction time and movement time during physical exertion. *Research Quarterly*, 42, 405–410.

Light, K., & Obrist, P. A. (1983). Task difficulty, heart rate reactivity, and cardiovascular responses to an appetitive reaction time task. *Psychophysiology*, 20, 301–312.

Malmo, R. B. (1959). Activation: A neuropsychological dimension. *Psychological Review*, 66, 367–386.

Martens, R. (1974). Arousal and motor performance. In J. H. Wilmore (Ed.), *Exercise and sport science reviews*. New York: Academic Press.

Martens, R. (1977). *Sport competitive anxiety test*. Champaign, Ill.: Human Kinetics.

Martens, R., Burton, D., Vealey, R., Smith, D., & Bump, L. (1983). *The development of the Competitive State Anxiety Inventory-2 (CSAI-2)*. Unpublished manuscript.

Martens, R., Burton, D., Vealey, R. S., Bump, L. A., & Smith, D. E. (1990). Development and validation of the Competitive State Anxiety Inventory-2. In R. Martens, R. S. Vealey, & D. Burton, *Competitive anxiety in sport* (pp. 117–190). Champaign, Ill.: Human Kinetics.

Martens, R., & Landers, D. M. (1970). Motor performance under stress: A test of the inverted-*U* hypothesis. *Journal of Personality and Social Psychology*, 16, 29–37.

Murphy, L. E. (1966). Muscular effort, activation level and reaction time. *Proceedings of the 74th Annual Convention of the American Psychological Association* (p. 1). Washington, D.C.: APA.

Oxendine, J. B. (1984). *Psychology of motor learning*. Englewood Cliffs, N.J.: Prentice-Hall.

Pinneo, L. R. (1961). The effects of induced muscle tension during tracking on level of activation and on performance. *Journal of Experimental Psychology*, 62, 523–531.

Sage, G. (1984). *Motor learning and control*. Dubuque, Iowa: Brown.

Schwartz, G. E., Davidson, R. J., & Goleman, D. (1978). Patterning of cognitive and somatic processes in the self-regulation of anxiety: Effects of meditation versus exercise. *Psychosomatic Medicine*, 40, 321–328.

Smith, R. E., Smoll, F. L., & Schutz, R. W. (1990). Measurement and correlates of sport-specific cognitive and somatic trait anxiety: The Sport Anxiety Scale. *Anxiety Research*, 2, 263–280.

Sonstroem, R. J., & Bernardo, P. (1982). Intraindividual pregame state anxiety and basketball performance: A reexamination of the inverted-*U* curve. *Journal of Sport Psychology*, 4, 235–245.

Spence, J. T., & Spence, K. W. (1966). The motivational components of manifest anxiety: Drive and drive stimuli. In C. D. Spielberger (Ed.), *Anxiety and behavior*. New York: Academic Press.

Spielberger, C. D., Gorsuch, R. L., & Lushene, R. E. (1970). *Manual for the State-Trait Anxiety Inventory (STAI)*. Palo Alto, Calif.: Consulting Psychologists Press.

Thayer, R. E. (1967). Measurement of activation through self-report. *Psychological Reports*, 20, 663–679.

Tretilova, T. A., & Rodmiki, E. M. (1979). Investigation of emotional state of rifle shooters. *Theory and Practice of Physical Culture*, 5, 28.

Weltman, A. T., & Egstrom, G. H. (1966). Perceptual narrowing in novice divers. *Human Factors*, 8, 499–505.

Williams, J. M., & Krane, V. (1989). Response distortion on self-report questionnaires with female collegiate golfers. *The Sport Psychologist*, 3, 212–218.

Williams, J. M., & Krane, V. (in press). Coping styles and self-reported measures of state anxiety and self-confidence. *Journal of Applied Sport Psychology*.

Wood, C. G., & Hokanson, J. E. (1965). Effects of induced muscle tension on performance and the inverted-*U*. *Journal of Personality and Social Psychology*, 1, 506–510.

Yerkes, R. M., & Dodson, J. D. (1908). The relation of strength of stimulus to rapidity of habit formation. *Journal of Comparative Neurology of Psychology*, 18, 459–482.

Relaxation and Energizing Techniques for Regulation of Arousal

Dorothy V. Harris, *Formerly of Pennsylvania State University*

Jean M. Williams, *University of Arizona*

S omehow the misconception persists that if one practices and trains hard enough physically for a competition, everything else will magically come together. In fact, during a given competition, or between two competitions that closely follow each other, there is usually no marked change in an athlete's skill level, physiological capacity, or biomechanical efficiency. The fluctuation in performance is generally caused by the fluctuation in the athlete's mental control. The athlete simply does not lose and gain stamina, skill, strategy, or conditioning during the ebb and flow of a competition. What the athlete does lose is control of cognitive factors such as the ability to concentrate, to process relevant cues, to focus on positive self-talk, et cetera. In the final analysis, the athlete is inappropriately aroused.

Consistent high-level performance begins with the discovery of those factors and conditions that accompany superior performance. (See Chapter 12 for suggestions on how to discover what mental and bodily states are typically associated with an athlete's superior performance.) Beyond that, acceptance of the fact that each of us has control over our own behavior and arousal allows the athlete to learn and develop skills and strategies necessary to consciously regulate his/her responses in order to maintain an optimal level of performance.

Elmer Green and Alyce Green (1977) have studied the effects of the mental control of the *autonomic functions*, including the muscular and hormonal changes that occur in sport performance. In their experiments measuring the influence of the mental control of bodily functions, they studied yogis from India. The Greens found that yogis were voluntarily able to alter their brain waves, heart rate, breathing, blood pressure, body temperature, and other bodily processes that are generally regulated by the autonomic nervous system. The researchers also discovered that the ability to voluntarily control these processes could be taught to others with ease in a relatively short period of time. The Greens concluded that each of us possesses a highly complex, sophisticated, and effectively integrated network between the mind and body. They further concluded that every change in the mental-emotional state is consciously or unconsciously accompanied by an appropriate change in the bodily state. This conclusion provides strong support for the idea that we think with our entire body. Accepting this, we can learn to exercise much greater mastery and control over all of our functions and responses. Our bodies tend to do what they are told to do; the trick is to learn how to communicate with our bodies. This is the principle of learning how to regulate arousal and relaxation. The same principle applies to activating and "psyching" ourselves up to reach an optimal level of performance. Once an athlete has learned to identify which mental-emotional and bodily states and feelings accompany superior performance, he/she can learn to "program" these responses voluntarily to set the stage for another superior performance. Basically, that is all sport psychology is trying to do for the athlete.

Readiness, being psyched, energized, "wired," activated, aroused, or whatever is an integration of the mind–body feelings and thoughts that provide the athlete with a feeling of confidence, of mastery and control. The athlete can learn to reach this state voluntarily by practicing the skills and strategies included in this book; learning to regulate arousal level, the subject of this chapter, is one important part of the process. Once an athlete has identified his/her optimal level of arousal for maximizing performance, the athlete can use appropriate relaxation or energizing techniques and strategies to reduce or increase that arousal as needed. (See Chapter 14 for ways of determining optimal level of arousal for consistent, high-level performance and a discussion of the factors that influence optimal arousal level.)

Obviously, all athletes need a certain amount of arousal or motivation to accomplish a task; however, some need more than others to perform at the same level. Too much arousal is detrimental; that is more often the problem than needing a "win one for the Gipper" speech to psych up a team. Some athletes will respond positively to a highly charged motivational speech, whereas others will become overaroused. Most coaches and athletes have tended to emphasize the psyching up aspect of preparation for performance; most sport psychologists have focused on lowering arousal.

As noted in the preceding chapters, a combination of physiological, psychological, and behavioral responses occurs when an athlete is worried and afraid of not performing as desired. Each athlete has to learn his/her particular pattern of over-arousal resulting from worry and anxiety about performance. Learning to relax is essential to regulating these responses to avoid any detrimental effects on performance. When a muscle tenses up, as it does with worry and anxiety, it contracts or is shortened. This contraction involves nerves as well. Approximately half of the nerves alert the muscles to respond to the messages from the brain, and the other half carry the messages back to the brain. Human nerve circuits have no automatic regulators; there are no signals to alert one to too much tension.

Muscle tissue only works in one direction; it can only pull, which it does by shortening and thickening. Consequently, the voluntary muscles in humans (and animals) are arranged in pairs. When a muscle tightens, its opposite sets up a counter tension to hold the segment of the body in place. The double pull can build up formidable heights of tension over much of the body yet remain unidentified by most people. This double pull explains why a person can be scared stiff, become rigid with anger, be unable to move because of stage fright, and so forth. It also explains why an athlete shoots air balls, blows a short putt, passes with too much force, or overhits a tennis ball. The principle of the **double pull**, sometimes referred to as "bracing," has great significance for the athlete. When muscular tension occurs with anxiety and worry, it interferes with performance because it prevents appropriately coordinating movement. Proper form in any movement involves using just the right amount of tension in the muscle; too much tension interferes with the execution of the skill. We can learn to expend only those energies necessary to accomplish our purposes without waste. This is called **differential relaxation**.

Excessive muscular tension can be triggered by mental input generated by worry and anxiety about not performing well. When the nerve pathways are occupied by impulses alerting the system to "fight or flee," the impulses necessary for skillful, coordinated movement are inhibited to some degree. The more muscular tension in the body, the more difficult it is to execute good form or the proper coordination in any type of movement task. The following is an excellent technique for illustrating how excessive tension disrupts speed and coordination. Have your athletes rest their dominant forearm and hand palm down on a desk or tabletop. Now have them tense all the muscles in their hand and fingers and then try to alternately tap their index and middle fingers back and forth as quickly as possible. Then have them relax the muscles of the hand and fingers and repeat the exercise. Athletes quickly discover how too much tension makes their movements clumsy and slow!

To learn to avoid too much tension, athletes need to be taught how to relax. Total relaxation means letting go and doing absolutely nothing with the muscles so that no messages are traveling either to or from the brain.

As a coach or sport psychologist, you may be wondering why any athlete would want to be completely relaxed. Athletes need muscular tension and arousal to perform; some need maximal tension to accomplish their sport. However, in learning to train the muscles to relax totally, athletes develop a much greater sensitivity to their bodily feelings and responses. Once athletes become aware of bodily responses and learn to associate them with certain types of behavior and performance, they can learn to regulate different levels of tension to deal with the environment actively and effectively.

Once trained in relaxation, athletes can use this skill to lower general muscular tension under any condition. Relaxation can assist in removing localized tension such as that occurring with headaches or lower back pain or that surrounding injuries. Relaxation can facilitate recovery when athletes have only a short time between events or when they are fatigued. Relaxation also promotes the onset of sleep and reduces insomnia problems that plague many athletes prior to competition. Probably the most important contribution that relaxation can make to athletes is to teach them the regulation of muscular tension so that nerve pathways to the muscle are never overcharged.

In general, the techniques of relaxation can be divided into two categories. The first category includes techniques that focus on the bodily aspects, the "muscle to mind" techniques. Jacobson's (1930) scientific neuromuscular relaxation or progressive relaxation falls into this category. The objective is to train the muscles to become sensitive to any level of tension and to be able to release that tension. The second category of techniques includes the cognitive or mental approaches to relaxation; these work from "mind to muscle." Benson's relaxation response (1975), meditation, autogenic training, and imagery all approach relaxation from the mind-to-muscle perspective. Either approach is effective; the point is to disrupt the stimulus–response pattern of half of the nerves leading to the brain or away from the brain. It is immaterial whether the athlete focuses attention on the brain-to-muscle efferent portion of the cen-

tral nervous system or the muscle-to-brain afferent portion, which reduces the stimulation to the brain. Learning to reduce the sensation in either half of the circuit will interrupt the stimulation necessary to produce unwanted muscular tension.

Relaxation skills must be practiced on a regular basis just like any sport skill. When teaching relaxation to athletes, it is more effective to begin the training after a workout because it is easier to "let go" after having had some exercise. It is more difficult to hold muscular tension when physically fatigued. In addition, exercise is nature's best tranquilizer and tends to lower general anxiety and tension. Once the athletes are trained in relaxation skills, they should begin the practice workout with a brief period of relaxation to eliminate all unwanted muscle–brain–muscle stimulation so that they can focus their complete attention on the practice. When practices are conducted in this manner, their quality increases so that the amount of time necessary to reach the same level of accomplishment is reduced considerably.

Some athletes take longer to develop relaxation skills than others, but most should observe improvement after a few weeks of regular practice. Emphasize the fact that it takes time to develop the skills, and encourage the athletes to continue to practice for several weeks even though they will not detect immediate improvement.

The degree of relaxation attainable varies to some extent. Within that variation, athletes should learn how to relax and withdraw completely from the environment as well as to relax momentarily. The ability to relax completely serves a different function from relaxing momentarily. After a hard training session, before falling asleep at night, when fatigue sets in, or when an athlete is worried, sick, or under emotional stress, deep, complete relaxation is desirable. Learning to relax completely provides a reference point as the athlete learns what a "zero arousal" level feels like. It also provides an opportunity to increase awareness of both mental and physical responses and how integrated they are. In the process the athlete learns to recognize patterns of feelings, thoughts, and behaviors and how they affect performance. As a result, the athlete can develop procedures for changing behaviors that interfere with performance. The athlete can learn through deep relaxation how to become detached from the environment and be in full control without interference.

The ability to relax completely produces a positive, pleasurable, and beneficial experience that provides the central nervous system with a rest. That, in turn, allows regeneration of physical, mental, and emotional states with the athlete in control.

Finally, the ability to relax completely provides the foundation for learning the skill of **momentary relaxation** during practice or competition. Learning to relax momentarily is extremely important for athletes so that they can reduce overarousal at any point. When the nerves are carrying worry messages instead of the stimuli for smooth coordinated, integrated efforts, the performance suffers. With momentary relaxation, worry and anxiety stimuli are removed, resulting in an enhanced kinesthetic awareness. The momentary respite also allows the athlete to return to a point of controlled balance. Every aspect of performance is enhanced: concentration, attentional focus, awareness, confidence, precision, speed, and so on.

Momentary relaxation can be used just before and during warm-up. In fact, during stretching in preparation for competition is a good time to utilize the strategies of momentary relaxation and to focus on the upcoming game. The more uptight the athlete is prior to performance, the longer the session of momentary relaxation should be. After the competition, this type of relaxation can be used to return to the controlled, balanced state. During the competition, depending on the specific sport and/or position within the sport, brief periods or lapses in play allow for momentary relaxation as needed. The athlete must learn to become aware of tension and arousal levels and adjust them as necessary.

The learning of skills and strategies for a sport is enhanced when one is in a relaxed state, particularly if periods of learning are alternated with periods of relaxation. This is true for academic learning as well as athletic learning. Relaxation preparation is also necessary for concentration and imagery practice because it reduces and eliminates other thoughts and stimulation that interfere with the single-minded focus necessary for imagery practice.

Muscle-to-Mind Relaxation Skills and Strategies

Most athletes respond positively to muscle-to-mind techniques, perhaps because of their more

physical lifestyle. When learning these relaxation techniques, athletes should be in a comfortable position and in a quiet, warm environment. Once athletes are trained, they should be able to relax in any environment under any condition. Learning, however, should occur under ideal conditions.

Breathing Exercises*

Breathing properly is not only relaxing; it facilitates performance by increasing the amount of oxygen in the blood. This carries more energy to the muscles and facilitates the removal of waste products. Unfortunately, many individuals have never learned deep, diaphragmatic breathing, and those who have often find their breathing patterns disrupted under stress. Athletes who get uptight during a high-pressure performance situation find their breathing is usually affected in one of two ways—they either hold their breath or they breathe rapidly and shallowly from the upper chest. Both of these adjustments create even more tension and impairment of performance. A good technique for making athletes aware of what shallow, chest breathing feels like is to have them raise their shoulders way up and notice what happens to their breathing.

Fortunately, with practice, breathing is also one of the easiest physiological systems to control. Learning to take a deep, slow, complete breath will usually trigger a relaxation response. This relaxing, complete breath is the basis for a variety of breathing exercises. Suggestions for specific exercises for breathing control to increase relaxation follow. Depending on the exercise and how it is practiced, these techniques can be used for both deep and momentary relaxation. Some coaches and sport psychologists even "choreograph" specific breathing times into the performance of certain skills such as gymnastic and figure skating routines.

Complete breath. Proper breathing comes from the *diaphragm*, the thin muscle that separates the lung and abdominal cavities. During inhalation the diaphragm should move down slightly, thus pushing the abdomen out and creating a vacuum in the lungs. This fills up the lungs from the bottom. For practicing a deep, complete breath, have the athletes imagine that the lungs are divided into three levels or parts. Have the athletes concentrate

---

*Several of these exercises are adaptations from Mason, 1980.

on filling the lower section of the lungs with air, first by pushing the diaphragm down and forcing the abdomen out. Have them continue by filling the middle portion of the lungs by expanding the chest cavity and raising the rib cage and chest. Finally, have the athletes fill the upper portion of the lungs by raising the chest and shoulders slightly. All three stages should be continuous and smooth. The athletes should hold the breath for several seconds, then exhale by pulling the abdomen in (which pulls the diaphragm up) and lowering the shoulders and chest to empty the lungs. Finally, instruct the athletes to pull the abdomen in further to force out the last bit of air from the lungs. They should let go of all muscular action at the end of the exhalation so the abdomen and chest are completely relaxed.

Stress to the athletes that during the exhalation they should feel as if the air drains out of the bottom of the lungs, first emptying the upper part, then the middle, and finally the lower part. Repeat this exercise many times with instructions. Once athletes are comfortable with the sequential complete breath, emphasize that on the inhalation they should take a long, slow, deep inhalation through the nose, inhaling as much air as possible. Emphasize that the exhalation should be slow and complete and that the athletes should try to feel all tension leaving the body as the air is exhaled.

After learning the procedure, the athletes should take at least 30 to 40 deep breaths each day. Associating deep breathing with events that naturally occur during the day will facilitate practice. Suggest to the athletes that each time the phone rings, they should take a deep breath, exhaling fully and completely before answering. Some stress therapists suggest affixing to a person's wristwatch dial a tiny colored paper disc so that each time the person looks at the watch, he/she is reminded to relax by taking a deep breath. Another good time for athletes to practice this breathing exercise is during the time they are waiting for class to begin or when they need momentary relaxation, such as before a free-throw shot, tennis serve, or golf putt.

Sighing with exhalation. Sighing aids in reducing tension. Instruct the athletes as follows: "Inhale slowly and then hold your breath for 10 seconds, feeling the tension building in the throat and chest. Exhale through the mouth with a slight sigh as you let go of the tension in the rib cage. Do nothing about inhaling—let that happen naturally. Hold your breath and repeat the sigh with the exhalation as you force the air out of the lungs."

The quietest or calmest time of the breath is between the exhalation and inhalation. Stress that athletes feel the stillness at the moment directly after fully exhaling and sighing. If athletes can feel this quietness, they are learning how to relax. Practice again, but without holding the breath. As athletes exhale fully and completely, they should feel all the tension leaving the body. Be aware of the quiet time during the breath. Whenever athletes feel themselves getting too tense, they should try to recreate this moment of peace and calm by momentarily practicing this exercise.

Rhythmic breathing. Have the athletes inhale to a count of 4, hold for a count of 4, exhale to a count of 4, and pause for a count of 4 before repeating the sequence. You can alter the rhythm of their breathing by changing the count.

1:2 ratio. Have the athletes take a deep, full breath and then exhale fully and completely. Have them breathe again, only this time to a count of 4 on the inhalation and a count of 8 on the exhalation. If the athletes run out of breath before reaching 8, suggest that next time they take a deeper breath and exhale more slowly. Stress awareness of a full inhalation and exhalation. With more practice and deepened relaxation on the part of the athletes, you may need to change the count to 5:10 or 6:12. This exercise is a very powerful relaxer if done properly.

5-to-1 count. Instruct the athletes as follows: "Say to yourself and visualize the number 5 as you take a deep, full, slow breath. Exhale fully and completely. Mentally count and visualize the number 4 with your next inhalation. As you begin the exhalation, say to yourself, 'I am more relaxed now than I was at number 5.' Do not rush the thought. Inhale while mentally counting and visualizing the number 3. With the exhalation, say to yourself, 'I am more relaxed now than I was at number 4.' Allow yourself to feel the deepening relaxation. Continue until you reach number 1. As you approach number 1, you should feel totally calm and relaxed."

The complete exercise takes one to two minutes. If done properly, it should lead to more relaxation than practicing a single complete breath. This exercise can be used before or during practices and competition, depending on how much time is available and how much relaxation is needed.

Concentration breathing. Have the athletes concentrate on focusing their attention on their breathing rhythm. Tell them that if their mind wanders to some other thought between inhaling and exhaling to redirect their attention back to their next breath, letting the intruding thought disappear. Instruct them to think of becoming more relaxed with each exhalation. This is a good exercise for athletes to practice when they are having problems with distracting thoughts.

Progressive Relaxation Exercises*

Working under the assumption that an anxious mind cannot exist within a relaxed body, Jacobson (1930) developed the concept of **progressive relaxation (PR)**, another muscle-to-mind approach to relaxation. PR consists of a series of exercises that involve contracting a specific muscle group, holding the contraction for several seconds, then relaxing. The exercises progress from one muscle group to another. The purpose of the contraction of the muscle is to teach an awareness and sensitivity to what muscular tension feels like. The letting go, or relaxation phase, teaches an awareness of what absence of tension feels like and the acknowledgement that it can voluntarily be induced by passively releasing the tension in a muscle. The initial training program devised by Jacobson required much more time in training each muscle group than many of the modifications that have been developed over the years.

Approximately 30 minutes per instructional period is needed during initial practices. Once skill is acquired, shorter practice sessions can be used. The coach or others knowledgeable about relaxation should give the instructions. Tape recordings of instructions are available, but coaches and sport psychologists can make the instructions more relevant to a particular sport and situation. Encourage athletes to practice outside of the teaching session on their own to improve their skills. Be sure to mention that practice should not occur within an hour after eating a meal. Providing athletes with tapes or written handouts of relaxation exercises will facilitate their likelihood of practicing. With increased experience, these will not be needed.

*Several of these exercises are adaptations from Bernstein and Borkovec (1973).

When possible, the preferred practice is for the coach, sport psychologist, or designated individual to personally lead the PR exercises. This ensures that the athletes are practicing, and there is some evidence that live presentations are more effective than tape-recorded ones (Paul & Trimble, 1970).

Begin the relaxation session in a conversational tone. Over the course of the session, however, you should progressively reduce your voice volume while giving the relaxation phase instructions. This reduction in volume should be consistent with the progressive increase in relaxation in the athletes. At no time should you speak so softly that the athletes would have difficulty in hearing the instructions or that your voice becomes "whispery." In addition to speaking more softly as the session progresses, you should reduce the pace of speech so that you are speaking more slowly when giving relaxation instructions by the time the relaxation session is one-half to two-thirds completed. These changes in speed, tone, and inflection should be very subtle. In contrast to your delivery of the relaxation instructions, when giving the instructions to tense a muscle group, the voice *increases* in volume, speed, and tension. These changes in volume and speed during the relaxation and tension phases should be clearly perceptible to the athletes. They will help the athletes in distinguishing between relaxation and tension.

Pace the instructions by doing the exercises with the athletes. Pause about 20 to 30 seconds after each contraction so relaxation can continue for brief periods. Tense larger muscle groups longer than the smaller ones. Repetition is the key to learning, so continue to practice the same muscle groups until the athletes can relax quickly without producing additional tension. Before you begin, explain to the athletes exactly what they will be doing and what they can expect. For example, feelings of warmth and heaviness are common as the relaxation response increases. Also explain that muscle twitches and spasms are to be expected as muscle fibers begin to let go. If there is a great deal of tension, an entire muscle group may let go, producing involuntary movement. On occasion, this happens just before one falls asleep if there is a tremendous build-up of muscular tension. The flexor pair lets go before the extensors and they take up the slack, resulting in a sudden jerk throughout the body.

Restlessness is a signal to let go and relax further. If you are working with a single athlete or a small group, have the participants signal by raising a finger to indicate when they have followed instructions and accomplished the task. As they become proficient in relaxing, there is a tendency to not follow instructions. Emphasize the importance of following instructions passively. This is particularly true during the relaxation phase. Just let the relaxation happen—don't force it. Relaxation requires no effort. Any effort to relax causes tension.

PR can be done in either a sitting or lying posture. The latter is usually more conducive to relaxation, but athletes should sit up if they tend to fall asleep. The lying down position is on the back with the head, neck, and trunk in a straight line. The legs should be straight and slightly apart with the heels pointing inward and the toes pointing outward. The arms should be comfortably at the side with the hands a little way from the thighs, palms up, and fingers comfortably bent. A small pillow (rolled up "sweats" are a good substitute) can be put under either the knees or neck (not both) for additional comfort. If a chair is being used for the sitting position, athletes should sit upright, hips against the backrest, with the arms and legs uncrossed and the feet flat on the floor. The hands rest comfortably on the thighs (palms down). If no chairs are available, athletes can lean against the gymnasium wall.

Athletes wearing hard contact lenses can either remove them or keep their eyes open while practicing PR. They should also remove or loosen any constrictive clothing such as belts or shoes. The body should be completely supported by the chair, floor, mat, or whatever is being used. Regardless of which PR exercise is being practiced, the preceding protocol is a good one to follow.

Active PR. Read the following directions: "Sit or lie down in a comfortable position and try to put yourself in a relaxed state. Close your eyes and take a long, slow, deep breath through your nose, inhaling as much air as you can. Then exhale slowly and completely, feeling the tension leaving your body as you exhale. Take another deep breath and let the day's tensions and problems drain out of you with the exhalation. [Pause.] Relax as much as possible and listen to what I say. Remember not to strain to relax. Just let it happen.

"As we progress through each muscle group, you will first tense for approximately 5 to 7 seconds and then relax for 30 to 40 seconds. Do not start the tensing until I say "NOW." Continue to tense until I say "OK." [Note: The tensing and relaxing of each muscle group always are cued respectively with the words "NOW" and "OK." The directions and banter between "NOW" and "OK" should only last 5 to 7 seconds and between "OK" and "NOW" approximately 30 to 40 seconds.]

"Begin with tensing the muscles in the dominant hand and lower arm by making a tight fist NOW. Feel the tension in the hand, over the knuckles, and up into the lower arm. . . . OK, relax by simply letting go of the tension. Notice the difference between tension and relaxation [pause 20 to 30 seconds]. . . . Make another fist NOW [pause 5 to 7 seconds]. OK, relax. Just let the relaxation happen; don't put out any effort [pause 25 to 30 seconds].

"Next tense the muscles of the dominant biceps by pushing your elbow down against the floor or back of the chair. Tense NOW. Feel the tension in the biceps without involving the muscles in the lower arm and hand. . . . OK, relax and let it go. Just let it happen. . . . Tense the biceps NOW. . . . OK, release it. Notice the difference between tension and letting go into relaxation.

"With your nondominant hand, make a fist almost as tight as you can NOW. Feel the tension in your hand and lower arm. . . . OK, slowly relax, draining all of the tension out. . . . NOW tense again. . . . OK, relax and feel the difference between the tension and relaxation. . . . Also notice the different feeling for each new muscle group. . . . NOW push the elbow down to tighten the nondominant biceps. . . . OK, relax. . . . NOW tense the biceps again. . . . OK, notice the decrease in tension, drain it all out, and enjoy the feelings of relaxation. . . . Notice the sensations you have in the muscles of both arms and hands. . . . Perhaps there is a sort of flow of relaxation—perhaps a feeling of warmth and even heaviness in these muscles. Notice and enjoy this feeling of relaxation.

"Turn your attention to the muscles in your face. We will relax the face by progressing through three muscle groups. Begin by lifting the eyebrows just as high as you can NOW. Feel the tension in your forehead and scalp. [pause for only 3- to 5-second contractions with these smaller muscle groups]. OK, relax. Enjoy the spreading sensation of relaxation. . . . NOW frown again. . . . OK, relax. Release all the tension. . . . Your forehead should feel smooth as glass. . . .

"Next squint your eyes very tightly and at the same time wrinkle up your nose. Tense NOW. Can you feel the tension in the upper part of the cheeks and through the eyes? OK, relax. . . . NOW tense again. . . . OK, release all the tension. . . .

"Next pull the corners of your mouth back and clinch your teeth, but not so hard that your teeth hurt. Tense NOW. You should feel tension all through the lower part of your face and jaw. OK, relax. . . .

"Next tense and relax the muscles of the neck by trying to pull your chin downward toward your chest but at the same time preventing the chin from touching. That is, counter the contraction of the muscles in the front part of the neck with the contraction of the muscles in the back part of the neck. NOW tense. You may feel a bit of shaking or trembling in the neck muscles as you tense them. OK, relax. Drain all the tension from the muscles in the neck. . . . See if you can get your neck and face to feel completely relaxed. NOW tense the neck again. Feel the discomfort. . . . OK, relax. Drain all the tension out. . . Remember relaxation is simply the absence of tension. . . .

"Take a deep breath and hold it while raising your shoulders upward toward your ears. Tense NOW. Feel significant tension in the chest, the shoulders, and the upper back. . . . OK, relax. Drain all the tension out. . . . NOW hold your breath and raise your shoulders again. This may be a familiar sensation as most athletes raise their shoulders and/or hold their breath when they are uptight. OK, drain all the tension out. Let your shoulders drop completely. Enjoy the spreading sensation of relaxation. . . .

"Next tighten your abdomen as though you expect a punch while simultaneously squeezing the buttocks together. Tense NOW. You should feel a good deal of tightness and tension in the stomach and buttocks. . . . OK, release the tension, gradually letting it all drain out. Just let it happen. . . . NOW tense again. . . . OK, relax. Feel the sensation of relaxation spreading into those muscles. . . .

"Turn your attention to your right leg. Tighten the muscles in your right thigh by simultaneously contracting all the muscles of your thigh. Tense NOW. Try to localize the tension only to your thigh. . . . Note the sensation. OK, relax. Contrast the tension and relaxation sensations. Remember relaxation is merely the absence of tension; it takes no effort except merely releasing the tension. . . . NOW tighten the right thigh again. . . . OK, release the tension—just passively let it drain out. Enjoy the feeling of relaxation. . . .

"Next flex your ankle as though you are trying to touch your toes to your shin. Tense NOW. You should be feeling tension all through your calf, ankle, and foot. Contrast this tension with when you tensed the thigh. OK, relax. Simply release the tension; let go of any remaining tension. . . . NOW tense again. . . . OK, slowly release all the tension. . . .

"Tense the muscles in your right foot by either pointing the toes or curling your toes tightly inside your shoes, but don't tense very hard or you might cramp the muscles. Tense NOW. Particularly note the sensation of tension in your arch and ball of the foot. OK, relax. As all the tension drains out, feel the spreading sensation of relaxation. . . and perhaps warmth, heaviness, or even tingling. All of these sensations are normal. NOW tense again. . . . OK, slowly release all the tension. Let your foot, ankle, and calf feel very relaxed. . . .

"We will go through the same sequence with the left leg [provide appropriate commentary during the tensing and relaxation pauses]. Begin by tensing all the muscles of your left thigh NOW. . . . OK, relax. . . . NOW tense again. . . . OK, release the tension. . . .

"NOW flex your left ankle as though you are trying to touch your toes to your shin. . . . OK, release the tension. . . . NOW flex again. . . . OK, relax. . . .

"NOW point or curl your toes. . . . OK, release the tension. . . . NOW tense again. . . . OK, relax. . . . Both your left and right legs should feel very relaxed. If you feel any tension anywhere in your legs, simply release it.

"Relax all the muscles of your body—let them all go limp. You should be breathing slowly and deeply. Let all last traces of tension drain out of your body. Scan your body for any places that might still feel tension. Wherever you feel tension, do an additional tense and relax. You may notice a sensation of warmth and heaviness throughout your body, as though you are sinking deeper and deeper into the chair or floor. Or you may feel as though you are as light as air, as though you are floating on a cloud. Whatever feelings you have, go with them. . . . Enjoy the sensation of relaxation. . . .

"Before opening your eyes, take a deep breath and feel the energy and alertness flowing back into your body. Stretch your arms and legs if you wish. Open your eyes when you are ready."

After taking your athletes through their first few PR practices, take several minutes to discuss their reactions. Get them to identify what it felt like and how successful they thought they were at relaxing. For those who had difficulty in relaxing, stress again the importance of the absence of efforting, of being passive and just letting it happen. Also remind them of the need to practice regularly. Just like any physical skill, PR takes practice. See if any of the athletes became aware of places in their body where they tend to hold tension. The goal is to spot this tension and release it before it causes any pain, such as headaches and backaches, or performance problems.

Have the athletes practice this lengthy active PR exercise daily for one to two weeks. If less time is available, do only one repetition of each muscle group. Once athletes have achieved some skill in being able to relax at will, you can have them practice one of the following modifications or abbreviations.

Differential active PR. The differential active PR exercise is performed with the same sequence of muscle groups as the preceding exercise. The difference is in the amount of tension generated. Rather than doing an all-contraction twice for each muscle group, do an initial all-out contraction, then generate half as much tension, and then just enough tension to identify and let it go. If time is limited, use the preceding routine but combine the arms in the arm exercises and the legs in the leg exercises. You can also delete some of the smaller, less important muscle groups. Throughout the exercise, stress that tension should only occur in the muscle group being contracted.

This exercise is an important way to help athletes become aware of differential relaxation. As noted earlier, relaxing all muscle groups as completely as one can almost never occurs in sport. Neither does only total muscle contraction. Differential relaxation is far more common. **Differential relaxation** involves learning to relax all of the muscles except those that are needed for the task at hand. The muscles that are used should only be tensed to the level needed. Learning appropriate differential relaxation not only leads to better performance but also to less fatigue. With proper training in the active PR exercise, followed by practice of this exercise, athletes can better accomplish differential relaxation because they become more sensitive to tension in different muscle groups and more confident in their ability to control the level of tension.

Abbreviated active PR. Once the athletes have learned the PR technique, you can have them use a shorter procedure to achieve deep muscle relaxation quickly. Whole muscle groups can be simultaneously tensed and then relaxed; tense each group for 5 to 10 seconds and relax each for 20 to 30 seconds. Read the following directions:

"Make a tight fist with both hands, tighten the biceps and forearms, hold, and relax for 20 to 30 seconds.

"Tense all of the facial muscles while at the same time employing the tension procedure for the neck. . . . Relax. . . .

"Take a deep breath, hold it, and raise the shoulders while at the same time making the stomach hard and tightening the buttocks. HOLD. . . . Relax and let go. . . . [Give the instructions quickly so the tension build-up is continuous.]

"Tighten the muscles of both thighs at the same time curling the toes and tightening the calves. HOLD. . . . Relax and let go of all the tension. . . .

"A shortened version of this exercise is to put as much tension as you can in all muscle groups simultaneously, hold for 10 seconds, and let go, trying to maintain that tension-free, let-go position. Repeat this several times."

Passive PR. Once the athletes have learned the skill of deep muscle relaxation, they can relax the muscles without first tensing them. Many people find this passive form of relaxation more effective than the active form. With passive PR, the participant merely lets go from whatever level of muscular tension is in the muscle group. There is a slow progression from one part of the body to another as the participant relaxes each body part more deeply by letting go of any remaining tension. The same sequence of complete or abbreviated body parts can be used for passive PR as for active PR. (Some people prefer to progress from the feet up or from the head down.)

After a general lead-in to the exercise, progress through the specific body parts with directions such as the following: "Turn your attention to your dominant hand. Just tune in to how this hand feels. Become aware of any tension that might be in it and let go of the tension—even more and more. Let go of all the muscles in your dominant hand. Allow it gradually to become looser and heavier. Think about letting go further. Now go to your nondominant hand. Think of your nondominant hand getting looser, heavier, just letting go of the muscles in your nondominant hand. Let go further, more deeply, and now feel the relaxation coming into your left and right forearms. Feel your forearms getting looser and heavier. Enjoy the relaxation that is now coming into your forearms. . . ."

Quick body scan. The quick body scan is an abbreviated passive PR technique that is a helpful momentary muscle relaxation exercise best used during performance, such as just before serving, shooting a free throw, or batting. Quickly scan the body from head to toe (or toe to head). Stop only at muscle groups where the tension level is too high. Release the tension and continue the scan down (or up) the body.

Neck–shoulder check. It is very common for athletes to carry excessive tension in the neck and shoulders when they are worried or anxious. Once they have learned to spot tension and relax, instruct your athletes to scan their neck and shoulders periodically for any undue signs of tension. If they feel tension in the neck, they should release it passively or roll the neck around the shoulders. If the tension is in the neck, the athletes can drop (slump) the neck and shoulders. Releasing excessive tension in these two areas tends to spread relaxation to the rest of the body; it may also have a calming effect on the mind.

Mind-to-Muscle Relaxation Techniques

The majority of additional relaxation techniques and strategies focus on **efferent nerve control**, or the stimulation from the brain to the muscles. Among these techniques are meditation, visualization, and autogenic training. The techniques should be initially practiced in a comfortable position in a quiet environment. Any of the positions suggested for progressive relaxation practice can be used.

Meditation

The regular practice of meditation not only helps one teach a state of deep relaxation; it facilitates concentration by disciplining the mind. Four basic components are common to most types of meditation: a quiet environment, a comfortable posi-

tion, a mental device, and a passive attitude. A mental device, such as a mantra or fixed gazing at an object, helps to shift the mind from logical, externally oriented thought by providing a focus of attention on something that is nonarousing and nonstimulating. A **mantra** is a nonstimulating, meaningless rhythmic sound of one or two syllables that a person regularly repeats while meditating.

It is critical that athletes not worry about how well they are performing the technique because this disrupts effective meditation. Stress their adopting a "let it happen" attitude. The passive attitude is perhaps the most important element in learning to meditate. Distracting thoughts or mind wandering may occur, but this is to be expected and does not mean that the technique is being performed incorrectly. When these thoughts occur, simply redirect attention to the mental device, focusing on this cue and letting all other thoughts move on through consciousness with a passive attitude, making no attempt to attend to them.

The **relaxation response** developed by Herbert Benson (1975), a physician at Harvard Medical School, is an excellent meditative technique to teach athletes. This technique is a generalized version of a variety of Eastern and Western religious, cultic, and lay meditation practices. It has the advantage, however, of being a noncultic technique, with all reference to mysticism and unusual postures eliminated. In fact, the technique does not even need to be called meditation. For a mental device, Benson recommended the word "one." However, "one" is a very arousing, stimulating word for achievement-oriented athletes. A better word might be "calm" or "warm." The following are directions for meditation based upon a variation of Benson's relaxation response:

1. Sit quietly in a comfortable position.

2. Close your eyes.

3. Deeply relax all your muscles, beginning at your feet and progressing up to your face. Keep them relaxed.

4. Breathe through your nose. Concentrate on your breathing. As you breathe out, say the word "calm" or "warm" silently to yourself. For example, breathe IN . . . OUT, "calm"; IN . . . OUT, "calm"; and so forth. Breathe easily and naturally.

5. Continue for 10 to 20 minutes. You may open your eyes to check the time, but do not use an alarm. When you finish, sit quietly for several minutes, at first with your eyes closed and later with your eyes open. Do not stand up for a few minutes.

6. Do not worry about whether you are successful in achieving a deep level of relaxation. Practice the technique once or twice daily, but not within two hours after any meal, since the digestive processes seem to interfere with the elicitation of the relaxation response.

Visualization

If athletes have been trained in imagery and can visualize easily, visualizing being in a place conducive to relaxation is another successful technique for eliciting relaxation. For example, an athlete might visualize lying on a beach in the warm sun listening to the continuous rhythm of breaking waves. Other images might be sitting in the midst of a beautiful mountain scene or lying in a grassy valley by a gentle, gurgling stream. Whatever image provides the athlete with a sense of calm and relaxation is the one he/she should use.

Autogenic Training. **Autogenic training** was developed in Germany in the early 1930s by Johannes Schultz and has been used extensively with European athletes. The training consists of a series of exercises designed to produce two physical sensations, warmth and heaviness. Basically, it is a technique of autohypnosis or self-hypnosis. Attention is focused on the sensations one is trying to produce. As in meditation, it is important to let the feeling happen in a very passive manner. There are six stages in the training (see the summary below). Have the athletes learn each stage before progressing to the next stage. Some people suggest that trainees spend two weeks at each stage; however, the progression can be modified to suit the athletes' learning rate as well as the training program and length of season of the sport. It usually takes several months of regular practice of 10 to 40 minutes, one to six times per day to become proficient enough to experience heaviness and warmth in the limbs and to produce the sensation of a relaxed, calm heartbeat and respiratory rate accompanied by warmth in the abdomen and coolness in

the forehead. Once athletes have reached that level of training and can attain a relaxed state, they can use imagery to increase the depth of relaxation.

The first autogenic stage involves focusing attention in a passive manner on the dominant arm while silently saying, "My right (left) arm is heavy," three to five times during one minute. Have the athletes flex the arms and move the body about; then repeat the sequence with the nondominant arm, then with the dominant leg, followed by the nondominant leg. A sense of heaviness should take over the body. If the mind wanders, emphasize passively redirecting attention back to the task at hand. Some athletes may be able to produce a sense of heaviness immediately; others may take one or two weeks of three or more times of practice daily to accomplish the sensation. Instructions should follow the same general format for the warmth stage, which may take longer to achieve.

If athletes are having difficulty feeling the appropriate sensation, sometimes learning can be facilitated by having them physically experience the sensation. For example, if trying to achieve heaviness in the right arm, put a pillow over the arm and, if need be, a book or two on top of the pillow. For the warmth sensation, have the athletes immerse their hands in hot water or put a heating pad or hot water bottle over the hands while they initially do the exercise.

Regulation of the heartbeat is the third stage after mastering the heaviness and warmth exercises. Repeat the instruction "My heartbeat is calm and regular" three to five times during one minute. Take a brief break from the focus of concentration and then repeat the instruction again three to five times during one minute. Do a total of four repeats for the exercise. Follow the same procedures for the fourth, fifth, and sixth stages.

In summary, the stages for autogenic training are as follows:

Stage 1: Heaviness
My right arm is heavy.
My left arm is heavy.
Both arms are heavy.
My right leg is heavy.
My left leg is heavy.
Both legs are heavy.
My arms and legs are very heavy.

Stage 2: Warmth
Follow instructional format of stage 1.

Stage 3: Heart rate
My heartbeat is regular and calm.

Stage 4: Breathing rate
My breathing rate is slow, calm, and relaxed: "It breathes me."

Stage 5: Warmth in the solar plexis
My solar plexis is warm (hand placed on upper abdominal area).

Stage 6: Coolness of the forehead
My forehead is cool.

It may take anywhere from two months to a year to master these skills. As one becomes more proficient, the six stages can be combined by going through the above directions once, completing the entire series in a matter of minutes. At this stage, the appropriate phrases, respectively, for Stage 1 and Stage 2 are "My arms and legs are heavy" and "My arms and legs are warm." Regular daily practice for several minutes three or four times a day is recommended during training.

Autogenic Training with Visualization

After athletes have mastered the six stages of autogenic training and can induce the desired state in a few minutes and sustain it for 30 minutes to an hour, they are ready to move to the next phase of training, which combines autogenic exercises with visualization. The progression goes from first imagining the entire visual field being filled with one color to visualizing colors in movement or formations to holding an image of a particular object in a static position to visualizing some abstract concept such as happiness or confidence to reexperiencing through imagery some chosen state or feeling such as "flow," winning, or a peak experience when everything goes just right. The fourth and fifth elements of the progression enable athletes not only to practice self-regulation of arousal but also to reexperience thoughts, feelings, and states that led to optimal performance. The sixth and final element of the progression includes visualizing other people such as the coach, teammates,

and/or opponents. However, the athlete should begin visualizing neutral individuals first. This phase can ultimately lead to imagining successful sport performance in the competitive setting with all of the individuals involved.

As indicated earlier, autogenic training takes a relatively long time to master. As a result, it is less popular in the United States because athletes seldom train under the same coach for such long periods of time. In addition, the competitive seasons are frequently too short to introduce and learn autogenic training. However, it is used extensively in many European countries where athletes are housed in sport training centers for several years working with a relatively stable staff of coaches and sports medicine personnel. Despite the time required to become proficient in autohypnosis, many athletes find it a satisfactory means of training for relaxation and imagery. This approach will be particularly appealing to those athletes who respond to autosuggestion.

Skills and Strategies for Learning How to Increase Activation and Energy

Once athletes have been taught how to slow down the heart rate and respiration rate and to increase blood flow and temperature in the extremities, they can also learn to develop skills to speed up the heart rate and respiration rate, and to get the physiological systems ready for action. These skills are essential for generating energy on short notice or when brief bursts of energy are needed.

Just as there are a variety of effective techniques for decreasing arousal, there are many techniques for energizing or increasing arousal. Such skills and strategies should be used to build appropriate arousal when athletes are not psyched up enough for practice or for competition. They can also be used to reduce fatigue during practice and competition. The coach should encourage athletes to practice and develop these skills and strategies. Not only should athletes identify primary energizing techniques that tend to work for them, but they should also have back-up techniques in the event that the effectiveness of the primary techniques diminishes over time.

First, the athletes need to identify when energizing is generally needed in their particular sport or in specific positions or situations within the sport. The coach and sport psychologist should try to become sensitive to each athlete's optimal level of arousal; some athletes are much more likely than others to need energizing. The athletes also need to learn how to recognize signs and symptoms of low energy and activation and where they are located in the body. As an example, a track athlete may need to learn how to energize "dead legs" during a race. Or a weight lifter may want to put all available energy into the legs and arms to attain a particular lift.

We turn now to 10 specific skills and strategies that athletes can use to increase their activation and energy.

Breathing

Breathing control and focus work as effectively in producing energy as in reducing tension. Instruct your athletes to focus on a regular, relaxed breathing rhythm. Now have them consciously increase that rhythm and imagine with each inhalation that they are generating more energy and activation. With each exhalation, the athletes should imagine that they are getting rid of any waste products or fatigue that might prevent them from being at their best. Ask them to feel in full control, supplying sufficient oxygen and energy for any task that they have to perform. Have the athletes increase their breathing rate as they increase their level of energy generation. Along with the accelerated breathing rate, athletes may want to say "Energy in" with each inhalation and "Fatigue out" with each exhalation.

Using Energizing Imagery

Using imagery skills, have the athletes imagine that they are machines capable of generating energy at will. As an example, have them imagine that they are a train that is just beginning to move, building up steam, momentum, and power with each deep breath. There are literally hundreds of images that can be conjured up as cues for generating energy: animal images, machine images, forces of nature, etcetera. Instruct the athletes to develop a supply of imagery cues that work for them in various situations encountered in their particular sport. Instruct them to establish a plan for using these cues ahead of time and to practice

and prepare to use them on a regular basis. Some sports have lapses in action that are much more conducive to using cues for activation and energizing than others. Help your athletes to become aware of and to plan for the times when they can use these strategies with self-talk, concentration, and imagery. They are particularly effective when fatigue is beginning to set in, when a series of points have been lost, when a sudden burst of energy is needed to finish a play.

Formulating Energizing Verbal Cues

In the midst of a performance, depending on the sport or position, there are many occasions when the athletes do not have enough time to prepare imagery techniques to generate energy. In preparation for such times, think of word cues and images with which they can quickly associate energy buildup. Words such as "explode," "charge," "psych up," "go," and the like, as well as any image representing energy, can be used. Then have the athletes select the cues that are appropriate to their sport and to the tasks that they perform during competition. Athletes need to get to know themselves well enough to learn what types of thoughts, images, and cue words serve to activate and energize them during practice and competitive performance.

Combining Energizing Cues, Images, and Breathing

Raiport (1988), a former Russian sport psychologist, described in a recent book several exercises that Eastern European sport psychologists teach athletes to help them self-induce activation. Each of these exercises combines a verbal phrase with imagery and a certain breathing pattern. The breathing pattern is one of exhaling on the first part of the phrase and inhaling on the italicized part. For example, take the phrase "I've had *a good rest.*" The most meaningful part of the phrase (italics) is combined with the inhalation, which is physiologically connected with tensing up the muscles and thus facilitates energizing. When time permits, take a two-breath pause between each repetition of the phrase. The following exercises come from Raiport's 1988 book:

"I am breathing *deeper, inhaling energy*" (repeat twice). During the pauses between the phrases, visualize yourself inhaling a tiny cloud of white energy, which spreads throughout your entire body. [Some athletes may prefer an energizing color such as red or yellow.]

"My body is *becoming lighter*" (repeat four times). Imagine that the white cloud of energy you inhale is a very light gas, like helium. Feel your body becoming light and energized.

"Strength is *flowing into my body*" (repeat three times). Visualize a stream of vibrating energy pouring into your body with each breath. It fills you with freshness and vigor. Feel yourself overflowing with this purifying energy; it now radiates from every pore of your body. [Some athletes may benefit from giving the stream of vibrating energy an energizing color.]

"I am *vigorous and alert*" (repeat three times). Imagine strength, power, and a keen awareness of life expanding throughout your body.

"My muscles are *quivering with energy*" (repeat four times). Feel your muscles twitching in impatient anticipation for action. You feel energized yet relaxed. Strongly clench your fists and jaws several times.

Transferring Energy

Help your athletes learn to convert energy from other sources into a positive and useful force for athletic performance. Activation and arousal that result from aggression, anger, frustration, or some other emotion that tends to interfere with performance need to be converted into energy to accomplish performance goals.

Storing Excess Energy for Later Use

Many athletes have found that the strategy of storing excess energy that is frequently generated just prior to competition accomplishes two purposes: It provides them a means of transferring that energy somewhere else, and it provides a well of energy from which to draw upon at some later point. If an athlete has a problem with overarousal, suggest that the athlete store away that energy and use it later when he/she feels fatigued or discouraged.

Using the Environment

Some athletes have learned how to draw energy from the spectators to use for their own perfor-

mance. This type of strategy provides the home team with an advantage. Athletes need to learn how to take all types of energy available in the sport environment and put it to their own use through imagery, word cues, self-talk, and the like. They can even draw energy from their opponents, particularly when it appears that the opponents have the momentum going for them.

Listening to Music

Music is often a good energy provider. With the availability of cassette players and headphones, athletes can readily select and listen to the music that works best for them. However, the coach should ensure that the practice or competitive environment is not saturated with loud music that may detract from the optimal level of arousal for many athletes.

Improving Pacing

Athletes become underaroused in some sports because of fatigue. This tiredness is often caused by inappropriate pacing and unnecessary sources of energy drain. The alert coach can spot athletes who have difficulty in rationing out their energy over time. Appropriate physical practice plus teaching the athlete to become more sensitive to physical signs and symptoms can improve pacing. Pacing is also improved when unnecessary sources of energy drain are eliminated; these sources include too much muscle tension for a particular skill or situation, anger, frustration and undue response to officiating calls, and anxiety or worry over one's own performance or that of teammates.

Using Distraction

Another way to deal with underarousal caused by fatigue is to focus one's attention away from the state of fatigue being experienced. Most athletes do just the opposite; the more fatigued they become, the more they tune into it. This just increases the sense of fatigue as well as its detrimental effects on performance. Instead, suggest to the athletes that they apply their concentration skills and focusing ability on what is happening and about to happen within the performance setting. Remind the athletes to think about what they are doing rather than about how they are feeling.

Summary

It is the coach's and sport psychologist's responsibility to teach the athlete strategies and techniques for achieving an optimal level of arousal for practice and competition. Acquiring the ability to self-regulate arousal not only enhances one's learning and performance of athletic skills but also one's functioning in many nonathletic situations.

It is important for coaches to know that poor performance during competition is more frequently a consequence of overarousal than underarousal. All too often coaches assume the opposite and partially contribute to the continuation of the problem by berating athletes to try harder when intervening with some calming strategy would be much more appropriate. This chapter has described techniques for achieving total relaxation and momentary or partial relaxation. Such techniques rid the muscles of disruptive tension that interferes with performance and help "quiet" the rest of the body and the mind. They also promote confidence in the athlete's ability to lessen or eliminate the effects of undesirable thoughts and feelings.

Energizing skills and strategies that can be used to increase arousal and lessen the effects of fatigue were also described in this chapter.

No single control strategy is effective or desirable for all athletes. Consequently, coaches and sport psychologists will need to teach their athletes a variety of techniques. Athletes should be encouraged to identify and practice the primary techniques that tend to work best for them as well as some back-up techniques in the event that the primary ones lose their effectiveness.

Study Questions

1. Discuss how relaxation skills are useful to an athlete.

2. Compare conceptually the two major types of relaxation techniques ("muscle to mind" and "mind to muscle").

3. Give four examples of breathing relaxation techniques.

4. Briefly describe the technique of progressive relaxation (active, passive, differential).

5. Give an example of a meditation relaxation technique.

6. How can visualization be used to achieve relaxation?

7. What is autogenic training? Give an example of an autogenic relaxation technique.

8. Briefly describe and give an example of at least six different types of techniques for increasing activation.

References

Benson, H. (1975). *The relaxation response*. New York: Avon Books.

Bernstein, D. A., & Borkovec, T. D. (1973). *Progressive relaxation training: A manual for the helping professions*. Champaign, Ill.: Research Press.

Green, E., & Green, A. (1977). *Beyond biofeedback*. New York: Dell.

Jacobson, E. (1930). *Progressive relaxation*. Chicago: University of Chicago Press.

Mason, L. J. (1980). *Guide to stress reduction*. Culver City, Calif.: Peace Press.

Paul, G. L., & Trimble, R. W. (1970). Recorded vs. "live" relaxation training and hypnotic suggestion: Comparative effectiveness for reducing physiological arousal and inhibiting stress response. *Behavior Therapy, 1*, 285–302.

Raiport, G. (1988). *Red gold peak performance techniques of the Russian and East German Olympic victors*. Los Angeles: Tarcher.

Imagery Training for Performance Enhancement and Personal Development

Robin S. Vealey, *Miami University (Oxford, Ohio)*
Susan M. Walter, *Miami University (Oxford, Ohio)*

"The greatest discovery . . . is that human beings, by changing the inner attitudes of their minds, can change the outer aspects of their lives." — William James

Beth, a high school varsity tennis player, lacks consistency in her performance. In certain matches she plays brilliantly, yet in other matches she repeatedly commits unforced errors. When asked about her inconsistency, Beth shrugs and replies, "Some days you have it, and some days you don't." Beth's coach keeps telling her she needs to get "mentally tough."

Carl is a professional baseball pitcher in his rookie season. He is in peak physical condition and has been tagged by scouts as as a "can't-miss prospect," yet his performance is suffering because he is unable to concentrate effectively throughout the entire game. Carl's pitching coach prescribes extra pitching practice and tells him he's got to "keep his mind on the game."

Kim is the starting point guard for a major college basketball team. She does a fine job of handing out assists and running the team offense, but she is shooting poorly. Kim shoots well during practice, but in games she tends to freeze up. When Kim asks her coach what she can do to avoid "choking," her coach replies, "Just don't think about it! It'll come."

Beth, Carl, and Kim are physically gifted athletes. Yet their lack of psychological skill prevents them from performing well in sport. Like many athletes and coaches, they have no idea how to develop the psychological skills needed to improve their performance. Beth believes she has no control over psychological factors that influence her performance. Her coach admonishes her to get mentally tough yet does not tell her how to do this. Carl hopes to find a quick and easy way to learn to concentrate, and his coach expects that extra physical practice will help Carl's concentration. Kim has no idea how to avoid choking, and her coach believes that Kim's performance slump will go away if she avoids thinking about it.

Athletes and coaches spend thousands of hours in physical practice sessions attempting to develop physical skills to perfection. However, they devote very little time to the development of psychological skills because they believe these skills are innate and untrainable ("you either have it or you don't") or because they do not know how to practice psychological skills. Actually, psychological skills *are* trainable, and in this chapter the use of imagery as a psychological tool to facilitate sport performance and personal development is discussed. Imagery is a mental technique that "programs" the human mind to respond as programmed. All athletes possess the ability to use imagery effectively. In fact, many athletes use imagery, but they do not use it systematically and often are unable to control their imagery. Evidence supports the effectiveness of imagery in improving sport performance, but only through controlled, systematic practice.

Thus, the purpose of this chapter is to guide you in the systematic, controllable use of imagery in sport. First, a definition and some basic concepts of imagery are presented. Second, scientific and experiential evidence is cited to allow you to judge the effectiveness of imagery in performance enhancement. Third, various explanations for how imagery works to facilitate performance are overviewed. Fourth, some key considerations regarding imagery are identified as important to understand prior to the start of imagery training. The rest of the chapter is a "how-to" guide for implementing systemic imagery training. Four easy steps are outlined to enable you to set up the sport imagery program. These steps involve introducing imagery to athletes, evaluating their imagery ability, training them in basic imagery skills, and implementing a systematic imagery program. These steps are followed by an "imagery cookbook" containing "ingredients" such as uses, times, and methods for using imagery. Three sample imagery programs are outlined as examples of how to integrate different ingredients into a systematic imagery program. Finally, we revisit the cases of Beth, Carl, and Kim and use our new knowledge about imagery to propose a mental training regimen for these individuals based on their unique needs.

Understanding Imagery

Imagery may be defined as using all the senses to recreate or create an experience in the mind. This definition contains three keys to understanding imagery.

Imagery as Recreating or Creating

Through imagery we are able to recreate as well as create experiences in our mind. We *recreate experiences* all the time. Have you ever watched someone perform a flashy basketball move and then gone out and done it yourself? Or maybe you've improved your serve after watching a professional tennis player for a few hours? We are able to imitate the actions of others because our mind "takes a picture" of the skill that we use as a blueprint for our performance. In essence, this is imagery. Imagery is based on memory, and we experience it internally by reconstructing external events in our minds. Imagery is also useful to recreate your own performances after competition to evaluate your performance and identify strengths and weaknesses. Another powerful imagery technique is to recall previous outstanding performances and recreate them through imagery to increase confidence for an upcoming competition. Thus, imagery involves recreating experiences, or reconstructing external events in our minds, to imitate others or to recall our own past experiences.

We can also use imagery to *create new experiences* in our minds. Although imagery is essentially a product of memory, our brain is able to put the pieces of the "internal picture" together in different ways. As the programmer of your own imagery program, you are able to build an image from whatever pieces of memory you choose. Outstanding professional football quarterback Fran Tarkenton used imagery in this way to create offensive game plans. He viewed film of the opponent's defense and through imagery directed successful offensive patterns against that defense. Although Tarkenton may not have previously played that particular opponent, he was able to create images by combining his offensive plays with the defensive alignments he viewed on film.

Another example of using imagery to create new experiences in the Soviet Union's preparation of its athletes for the 1976 Summer Olympic Games. Prior to the start of the Games, representatives from the Soviet Union took photographs of the various Olympic sites in Montreal. The athletes studied the pictures. Although the Soviet athletes had not been to Montreal, they used the pictures to imagine themselves performing at those sites. Creating these types of images served to familiarize the athletes with the Olympic environment before they arrived.

Imagery as a Polysensory Experience

The second key to understanding imagery is realizing that imagery can and should involve all the senses, or that it is a ***polysensory*** experience. Although imagery is often termed "visualization" or "seeing with the mind's eye," sight is not the only significant sense. All of our senses are important in experiencing events. Images can and should include as many senses as possible including visual, auditory, olfactory, gustatory, tactile, and kinesthetic senses. "Auditory" refers to sound such as hearing the crack of the bat in baseball or the sweet sound of a perfect golf drive. "Olfactory" refers to smell such as a swimmer smelling chlorine in the pool. "Tactile" is the sensation of touch such as feeling the grip of a golf club or the textured leather of a basketball. "Gustatory" refers to the sense of taste such as tasting salty sweat in your mouth. "Kinesthetic" sense is the "feel" or sensation of the body as it moves in different positions. The kinesthetic sense would be important for a gymnast using imagery to practice a balance beam routine or a diver using imagery to feel the rotations before reaching for the water.

Using as many senses as possible may help athletes to create more vivid images. The more vivid the image, the more effective it is. Let's use the example of a wide receiver in football to stress the importance of using different senses. The receiver uses his visual sense to read the defense and focus on the ball before catching it. He uses his auditory sense to listen to the snap count barked by the quarterback. He uses his tactile and kinesthetic senses to run his pattern, jump in the air, catch a hard thrown ball, and touch both feet inbounds. He might also smell freshly mown grass and the sweat of his opponent's jersey when he is tackled. He may even taste the saltiness of his own sweat. All senses should be utilized when practicing imagery to create vivid images of sport experiences.

In addition to the senses just discussed, the *emotions* associated with various sport experiences are also an important part of imagery (Martens, 1987). In using imagery to help control anxiety, anger, or pain, athletes must be able to recreate these emotions in their minds. For example, athletes could recreate their thoughts and feelings experienced during competition to understand how and why anxiety hurt their performance. In using imagery to recreate past outstanding performances, athletes should feel the emotions associated with those experiences such as elation, satisfaction, pride, and self-esteem.

Imagery as the Absence of External Stimuli

The third important characteristic of imagery is that it requires *no external stimulus* antecedents.

Imagery is a sensory experience that occurs in the mind without any environmental props. Through imagery a golfer can hit an iron shot to the green while lying on a coach with his eyes closed. He needs no golf club in his hands, nor does he need to be out on the course for his body to experience hitting the shot. Research indicates that when individuals engage in vivid imagery and absorb themselves into the context of their images, their brain interprets these images as identical to the actual external stimulus situation (Richardson, 1983). This is what makes imagery so powerful. An Alpine skier can imagine herself skiing a downhill run, and her brain will interpret her images as if she was actually skiing the course. The power of imagery allows athletes to practice sport skills and strategies without physically being in the practice environment (e.g., pool, ski jump, gymnasium).

Evidence that Imagery Works

Scientific research studies and experiential evidence support the use of imagery as a means to enhance sport performance. The scientific evidence includes research on mental practice, preparatory imagery, packaged mental training programs, and incidence of imagery use. Experiential evidence includes examples of successful athletes who have used imagery and testimonials from athletes and coaches regarding its effectiveness.

Scientific Evidence

Mental practice research. **Mental practice** is the use of imagery to perform a specific sport skill repetitively in the mind. Richardson (1967a, 1967b) and Corbin (1972) conducted extensive reviews of studies in which the effects of mental practice on motor performance were evaluated. Although these reviews were qualified with certain conditions, the researchers concluded that mental practice is valuable in learning and performing sport skills. As a follow-up, Martens (1982) reviewed the imagery research related to sport and motor behavior from 1970 to 1982. He concluded that imagery is an effective technique to improve performance and documented improvement in the following sport skills through imagery practice: basketball free throw shooting, football place kicking, swimming starts, dart throwing, alpine skiing, karate skills, volleyball serving, tennis serving, and golf. Feltz and Landers (1983) conducted a review of the mental practice literature using meta-analytic procedures to provide some definitive answers to previous contradictory findings. Although these researchers identified several factors that serve to influence the relationship between mental practice and sport performance, they concluded that mental practice enhances performance and is better than no practice at all. It is also significant that mental practice has been shown to be effective in increasing the sport performance of both novice and experienced performers (Feltz & Landers, 1983).

Preparatory imagery. Research has also shown that using imagery immediately before performance can facilitate performance on that particular skill. Usually these studies employed imagery as one type of preparatory mental strategy either in combination with or in opposition to other mental strategies such as self-talk and attentional focusing. Imagery as a preparatory strategy used prior to performance has improved performance on strength tasks (Shelton & Mahoney, 1978; Tynes & McFatter, 1987), muscular endurance tasks (Gould, Weinberg, & Jackson, 1980; Lee, 1990), and golf putting (Murphy & Woolfolk, 1987; Woolfolk, Parrish, & Murphy, 1985).

Packaged mental training programs. Imagery has also been used along with other intervention techniques in packaged mental training programs that are implemented with athletes over a period of time to enhance performance, For example, a mental training program consisting of imagery, relaxation, and self-talk training was implemented with basketball players during the season to improve their defensive skills (Kendall et al., 1990). The program was clearly effective in enhancing the players' defensive skills in competition. Similar programs have been shown to be successful in enhancing performance in basketball shooting (Hall & Erffmeyer, 1983; Wrisberg & Anshel, 1989), gymnastics routines (Lee & Hewitt, 1987), figure skating (Mumford & Hall, 1985), tennis serving (Noel, 1980), and dart throwing (Straub, 1989).

Incidence of imagery use. The use of imagery by elite athletes seems to be widespread and provides additional evidence for the effectiveness of imagery as a means of performance enhancement. Of 235 Canadian Olympic athletes who participated in the 1984 Olympic Games, 99% reported using imagery (Orlick & Partington, 1988). These athletes estimated that during training they engaged in preplanned systematic imagery at least once a day, four days per week, for about 12 minutes each time. At the Olympic site, some reported engaging in imagery for two to three hours in preparation for their events. From a sample of 40 elite gymnasts, 92% reported using imagery to practice skills and strategies, to recall and control emotions, to improve concentration, and to set goals (Smith, 1987). Coaches attending a mental skills training workshop indicated that they used imagery more than any other mental training technique and felt that imagery was the most useful mental technique that they used with their athletes (Hall & Rodgers, 1989). Eighty-six percent of the U.S. Olympic sport psychology consultants in 1988 used imagery in their mental training programs with athletes (Gould et al., 1989).

Experiential Evidence

Perhaps it would be helpful to learn first-hand from athletes themselves about how imagery works for them. Several athletes who have at one time been the best in the *world* at their sport advocate the use of imagery. Dwight Stones, a three-time Olympian in the high jump, used imagery throughout his career. If you ever watched Stones compete, you may have noticed that he stood and stared intently at the bar before he began his approach. Stones believed in the power of imagery and used it before every jump.

Jack Nicklaus, perhaps the greatest golfer of all time, says that playing the ball to a certain place in a certain way is 50% mental picture, Nicklaus (1974) "goes to the movies" before every shot by using imagery to see three things. First, he sees the ball land in the target area. Second, he pictures the flight path of the ball to the target area. Finally, he vividly imagines himself using the appropriate swing for that particular shot. Certainly, Jack Nicklaus is successful because of his enormous physical talent. Yet experts feel that his concentration skills have carried him to a level above all other golfers. It may be that Nicklaus's systematic practice of imagery facilitates the concentration that is the key to his success.

Greg Louganis reached the pinnacle of his magnificent diving career at the 1988 Summer

Olympics by winning gold medals in both the springboard and platform events. Louganis believes in the power of imagery. He speaks of using imagery to practice each dive and of his particular technique of setting his dives to music as he practices them in his head.

Following is an excerpt taken from an interview with a Canadian Olympic diver:

> I did my dives in my head all the time. At night, before going to sleep, I always did my dives. Ten dives. I started with a front dive, the first one that I had to do at the Olympics, and I did everything as if I was actually there. I saw myself on the board with the same bathing suit. Everything was the same. . . . If the dive was wrong, I went back and started over again. It takes a good hour to do perfect imagery of all my dives, but for me it was better than a workout. Sometimes I would take the weekend off and do imagery five times a day. (Orlick & Partington, 1988, p. 112)

The list goes on. Fran Tarkenton, Chris Evert, Jean Claude Killy, O.J. Simpson—all of these athletes attest to using imagery to facilitate their performance. Coaches and teachers believe in the power of imagery, too. Tennis coaches are implementing imagery into their programs based on the recommendations of Gallwey (1976) in his book *Inner Tennis*. Pat Head Summitt, the highly successful women's basketball coach at the University of Tennessee, describes how her team uses imagery for relaxation before big games, mental practice of specific performance situations, and pregame preparation (Wrisberg, 1990).

Over all, there is a great deal of scientific and experiential evidence supporting the use of imagery as a means of performance enhancement. This leads to the question of how imagery works. How can a sensory experience in our mind enhance our ability to perform in sport? How can imagining clearing a high jump bar, skiing a cross-country course, or kicking a field goal help us to perform these skills better?

How Imagery Works to Facilitate Performance

Various theoretical explanations for how imagery facilitates performance have been advanced in the literature. In this section, four popular theoretical

explanations of imagery are presented and discussed in relation to sport performance. The theories presented include psychoneuromuscular theory, symbolic learning theory, bioinformational theory, and attentional-arousal set theory.

Psychoneuromuscular Theory: Muscle Memory

We know that as athletes engage in various sport movements, their brains are constantly transmitting impulses to the muscles for the execution of the movements. The **psychoneuromuscular theory** suggests that similar impulses occur in the brain and muscles when athletes imagine the movements without actually performing them. Thus, the psychoneuromuscular theory asserts that vivid imagined events produce innervation in our muscles similar to that produced by the actual physical execution of the event. It is helpful to use the term "muscle memory" when explaining this theory to athletes. Emphasize to them that through imagery they are strengthening their muscle memories by having the muscles fire in the correct sequence without actually physically executing the movement.

Scientific evidence supports the notion that vivid, imagined events produce similar innervation in our muscles as the actual physical execution of the event. Jacobson (1931) first supported this phenomenon. He demonstrated that the imagined movement of bending the arm created contractions in the flexor muscles of the arm. Jacobson's findings have been supported in the sport psychology literature (Hale, 1982; Harris & Robinson, 1986; Jowdy & Harris, 1990). Richard Suinn (1980) tested this phenomenon by having a downhill skier recreate a race using imagery. Suinn monitored the electrical activity in the skier's leg muscles as he imagined the downhill run. Suinn found that the printed output of muscle firings mirrored the terrain of the ski run. Muscle firings peaked at certain points during imagery that corresponded to times in which greater muscle contraction would be expected due to turns and rough sections on the course.

Thus, whether athletes actually perform movements or vividly imagine performing them, similar neural pathways to the muscles are used, although the muscle activity is far less during imagery as compared to actual movement. However, although research clearly supports that vivid imagery can produce low-level innervation of muscles, research has not demonstrated that this slight muscle innervation produced by imagery actually facilitates performance. Thus, the psychoneuromuscular theory has been supported in that imagery has been shown to elicit muscle innervation, but the occurrence of this low-level muscle innervation has not been shown to relate to performance improvement.

Symbolic Learning Theory: Mental Blueprint

The second explanation of how imagery may facilitate sport performance suggests that imagery may function as a coding system to help athletes acquire or understand movement patterns. All movements that we make must first be encoded in our central nervous system—we must have a blueprint or plan for this movement. The **symbolic learning theory** suggests that imagery facilitates performance by helping individuals to blueprint or code their movements into symbolic components, thus making the movement more familiar and perhaps more automatic. For example, a gymnast can use imagery to cue herself on the temporal and spatial elements involved in performing a balance beam routine. It is helpful to use the term "mental blueprint" when talking to athletes about this theory and emphasize that by using imagery they are strengthening their mental blueprint (or the mental code they use to perform the skill) to make the skill more automatic.

Symbolic learning theory was first proposed by Sackett (1934), who stated that imagery enables performers to rehearse the sequence of movements as symbolic components of a task. This theoretical position has been supported by studies that have demonstrated greater performance improvement through imagery on movement tasks that required cognitive coding as opposed to pure motor tasks (Feltz & Landers, 1983; Feltz, Landers, & Becker, 1988; Hird et al., 1991; Ryan & Simons, 1981, 1983; Wrisberg & Ragsdale, 1979). This theory has also been supported by research showing improved free throw shooting (Hall & Erffmeyer, 1983) and motor performance (Housner, 1984) when imagery is used to mentally encode modeled movement behaviors.

Bioinformational Theory: Response Set

Bioinformational theory is a newer theory of imagery that assumes that a mental image is an organized set of propositions that is stored in the brain's long-term memory (Lang, 1977, 1979). When individuals engage in imagery, they activate **stimulus propositions** that describe the content of the image for them and **response propositions** that describe what their responses are to the stimuli in that situation. For example, imagining shooting a basketball free throw in the final seconds of a close game would involve the stimulus propositions of the feel of the ball in the hand, the sight of the basket, and the sound of the crowd. The response propositions for this image might include muscular tension in the shooting arm, increased perspiration, feelings of anxiety, and the joyous sight of the ball swishing through the net. According to bioinformational theory, for imagery to facilitate sport performance, response propositions must be activated so they can be modified, improved, and strengthened. By repeatedly accessing response propositions for a particular stimulus situation and modifying these responses to represent perfect control and execution of a skill, imagery is predicted to enhance performance.

Research has supported that response processing during imagery facilitates performance on various tasks (Hecker & Kaczor, 1988). An important implication from this is that coaches, athletes, and sport psychologists involved in imagery training should include many response propositions when using imagery. Specifically, images should contain not just the conditions of the situation (swimming in a pool, rough water, championship meet), but also the athletes' behavioral (swimming strongly, right on pace), psychological (feeling confident, focusing on the race), and physiological (feeling energized) responses to the situation. When these positive response are included, the image will be more vivid and should result in psychophysiological changes in the body and thus improve performance.

It may be helpful to use the term "response set" when talking about this theory to athletes. Practically, imagery can be explained as a way of enhancing performance by programming personalized and appropriate responses to specific situations, or creating the perfect response set.

Emphasize that behavioral, psychological, and physiological responses should all be included in imagery. Another practical concern of bioinformational theory is that the meaning of particular images is very individualized so that response sets should be unique and personally meaningful to each athlete (Ahsen, 1984).

Attentional-Arousal Set Theory: Mental Set

The **attentional-arousal set theory** of imagery is a less sophisticated explanation for why imagery facilitates performance, yet it has intuitive appeal. The attentional-arousal set theory suggests that imagery helps the athlete to set the optimal arousal level and focus attention on the relevant aspects of the task. For example, a wrestler may use imagery prior to a match to either "psych up" or calm down and to focus attention on the particular strategy to be used against this opponent. The term "mental set" can be used to explain this theory to athletes and it can be emphasized that imagery can help them perform better by creating the right mental set (optimal arousal and concentration) for competition. The weakness of this theory is that it does not specifically explain *how* imagery optimizes arousal and attention, nor has the theory been validated by research. However, from an intuitive perspective, it is obvious that using productive imagery prior to competing can serve to facilitate performance.

Key Considerations in Using Imagery

Before we outline the sport imagery program, there are some key considerations about imagery that should be addressed. These considerations include imagery perspective, the use of imagery in conjunction with physical practice, and the imagery ability of athletes.

Imagery Perspective

Although Jacobson (1931) was the first to study differences in imagery perspective, Mahoney and Avener (1977) classified imagery as either internal or external. An **internal perspective** means that athletes see the image from behind their own eyes

as if they were inside their bodies, as opposed to an **external perspective** in which they see the image from outside their bodies as with a movie camera. Research has shown that elite athletes are more likely to practice imagery from an internal perspective as compared to nonelite athletes, who are more likely to practice imagery from an external perspective (Mahoney & Avener, 1977; Orlick & Partington, 1986; Rotella et al., 1980). Also, internal imagery has been shown to produce more neuromuscular activity than external imagery (Hale, 1982; Harris & Robinson, 1986).

Whether athletes should use an internal or external imagery perspective depends on the type of imagery being used. An internal perspective would seem to help a golfer become more aware of how the body feels during the swing and how the various parts of the swing look while making the shot. However, an external perspective might be a powerful tool to enhance a volleyball player's confidence if he/she uses imagery to step outside the body and watch his/her outstanding performance from the previous night. Athletes can use whichever perspective they feel most comfortable with at first, but if they have trouble with internal imagery, we advocate that they practice to get better at this perspective due to its importance in kinesthetic imagery. A suggested way to develop athletes' internal imagery ability is to have them actually perform a skill (e.g., serve a volleyball), then immediately close their eyes and try to replay the way the serve looked and felt from inside their body. This physical-mental practice routine should be repeated several times to strengthen athletes' internal perspective.

Use of Imagery in Conjunction with Physical Practice

It is important to remember that imagery does not take the place of physical practice. Nor is a combination of physical practice and imagery more effective than total physical practice within the same time frame (Hird et al., 1991). However, mental practice improves performance significantly more than no practice at all. Thus, think of imagery as a "vitamin supplement" that in addition to physical practice may give athletes an edge in competition. Imagery is valuable not as a *replacement* for physical practice but as a way to train the mind *in conjunction with* the physical training of the body. Imagery might be a useful substitution for physical practice when athletes are fatigued, overtrained, or injured. Clearly, imagery is valuable when athletes need to develop or enhance mental skills such as attentional control and arousal regulation. Traditionally, coaches have prescribed additional physical practice when athletes lack mental skills. However, imagery offers an attractive alternative to extra physical practice when attempting to enhance mental skills.

Imagery Ability of Athletes

The literature indicates that imagery is more effective when individuals are higher in imagery ability (Goss et al., 1986; Hall, 1985). This suggests that if athletes can improve the vividness and controllability of their images, performance may subsequently be improved. It is important to let athletes know that imagery is a skill that takes time to train, especially if they are not skilled in their initial attempts at imagery. Orlick and Partington (1988) document that even Olympic athletes did not initially have good control over their imagery, but they perfected their imagery skills through persistent daily practice. Systematic imagery training has been shown to be very effective in increasing both visual and kinesthetic imagery ability (Rodgers, Hall, & Buckolz, 1991). In the next section, a systematic imagery training program is outlined to help athletes develop the imagery skills needed to improve their performance.

Setting Up the Imagery Program

There are four phases in setting up the imagery program. First, the idea of using imagery must be sold to athletes. Second, the imagery ability of the athletes should be evaluated in order to develop the most appropriate type of program. Third, athletes must develop basic imagery skills. Fourth, a systematic program of imagery practice must be implemented and monitored.

Introducing Imagery to Athletes

Imagery only works for athletes if *they believe in it*. Thus, you must "sell" them on the idea that imagery can indeed help them to perform better. However, you should avoid unnecessary "hype" or unrealistic claims. Make sure they understand that imagery will not guarantee success. It is simply a training technique that has been proven to enhance sport performance.

An approach that we have found useful in introducing imagery to athletes is the analogy of *building a machine*. When athletes continuously practice a sport skill over and over, they are in essence attempting to build a machine. Divers attempt to fine tune their body to make their muscles react flawlessly in a dive. Shot putters work hours refining their technique in order to uncoil their body in maximum thrust. Coaches and athletes spend a great deal of time using drill and repetition attempting to build a flawless, automatic machine. Why not use imagery to help? Make the point that building a machine for optimal sport performance requires mental training as well as physical training.

The introduction of imagery can take place in an informal group setting if you are working with a team. We recommend that you spend no more than 30–40 minutes overviewing some important points about imagery. An introduction to imagery might include the following steps.

"Hook" 'em. You need to grab athletes' attention so they are intrigued by what you are going to talk about. Possibilities include (a) discussing the concept of building a machine, (b) asking them if they have ever "choked" in a crucial situation (even have someone describe his/her experience) and then introducing imagery as a means of combating choking in sports, (c) asking if any of them use imagery and have them describe what they do, (d) talking about famous and successful athletes in their sport who are known to use mental training techniques, or (e) anything you can think of to get their attention (explaining that sexual fantasies are a type of imagery always works for us!) Be creative!

Define and give evidence. Briefly explain what imagery is by using a definition such as "practicing in your head." Without bogging them down with scientific research, provide some brief evidence that imagery does work to enhance performance. It is helpful to use testimonials from famous coaches and athletes who believe in imagery. It is important at this point that they understand that imagery is not magic but simply a mental technique that they can use to help their performance.

Explain how it works. You should provide a simple and brief explanation for how imagery works to enhance performance. The amount of detail you get into here depends on the level of the athletes. We usually explain that imagery creates a mental blueprint of a particular skill and by using imagery they are ingraining or strengthening that mental blueprint to make their skills automatic or to build a machine. Although psychoneuromuscular theory has not been fully supported, athletes are always intrigued when they learn that their muscles are innervated during imagery similar to when they are performing the skill. Make sure you use terms such as "muscle memory," "mental blueprint," "response set," or "mental set" as opposed to scientific terminology.

To emphasize the way that imagery works, you may want to take your athletes through one or both of the following exercises so they can immediately experience the power of imagery. If correctly done, these exercises are extremely helpful in convincing skeptical athletes of the merits of practicing imagery.

String and bolt. Give each athlete a string approximately 14–16 inches long threaded through a heavy bolt (a neck chain and heavy ring also will work). Stabilizing the elbow, ideally on a table top, have each athlete lightly hold the two ends of the string between the thumb and forefinger with the weight suspended directly below. Focusing on the weight, each athlete in his/her mind's eye should imagine the weight moving right and left like the pendulum of a clock. Once most athletes have at least some movement right and left, have them change the image so the weight swings directly away from and then towards the chest. Again, once successful, change the image so the weight moves in a clockwise circle and finally in a counterclockwise circle. In discussing this exercise, you will find most athletes are absolutely amazed at how imagining the movement ultimately translates to the actual physical movement of the pendulum. Once completed, you can explain to the athletes that the subtle muscle innervation in the arm and hand created by the imagery is responsible for the movement of the pendulum.

Arm as iron bar. Pair each athlete up with a partner who is of similar height and strength. While directly facing each other, one partner extends his/her dominant arm straight out, palm up, so the back of the wrist is resting on the partner's opposite shoulder. The other partner cups both of his/her hands above the bend in the partner's elbow. The person whose arm is extended then maximally tightens all the muscles in the arm, trying to make it as strong as possible. Then the partner tests for strength by pushing down at the elbow with both hands, trying to see how much strength it takes to bend the arm. Then switch roles and have the other partner tested for strength. Afterwards, resume the initial position with the original partner. This time, to create strength, the partner is to close everything out of his/her mind and imagine that the arm is a thick steel bar. Not only is the arm a hard, steel bar, but it extends out through the opposite wall. Once the partner has created the image of an unbendable, strong steel bar, he/she indicates such by raising one of the fingers of the opposite hand. This signals the partner to again test for strength. Again, switch roles and have the opposite partner practice the image and be tested for strength. In follow-up discussion, you will find that most athletes will be amazed at how much stronger their arm was with the iron bar image.

Give specifics about how imagery will be used. At this point you want to let the athletes know exactly how imagery will be incorporated into their training. An important rule of thumb here is to keep it simple at first. For example, a basketball team could start initially by using mental practice for free throws and imagery to mentally rehearse specific team plays. It is a mistake to try to do too much too soon.

Evaluating Athletes' Imagery Ability

Before implementing an imagery program with your athletes, you must have an idea about their imagery ability. As discussed earlier, athletes need to be able to use all appropriate senses and their emotions when practicing imagery. Thus, it is important to have an idea about athletes' abilities to experience each of these through imagery.

One method of evaluation is to take the athletes through some of the "Basic Training" imagery exercises below. By discussing their images with them, you could determine if there are certain areas that need to be strengthened. A better idea is to administer the Sport Imagery Questionnaire to measure athletes' abilities to experience different senses, emotions, and perspectives during imagery. There are other inventories designed to measure imagery ability, but this instrument seems to be most useful to the coach/practitioner. The Sport Imagery Questionnaire appears as a chapter appendix.

Just as they differ in physical skills, athletes will differ in their ability to develop vivid and controllable images. For best results, direct athletes through the exercises in the questionnaire. Encourage athletes to answer honestly on the basis of their imagery ability. Administering the questionnaire should take approximately 15 minutes.

Basic Training

Imagery is a skill. Athletes differ in their ability to develop vivid and controllable images, just as they differ in physical ability. But, as with physical ability, athletes can increase their imagery ability through training. "Basic Training" is similar to a preseason physical conditioning program. By developing a foundation of strength and endurance, athletes are better equipped to fine tune their physical skills when the season begins. By strengthening their "imagery muscle" in Basic Training, athletes are more likely to benefit from the use of imagery during the season.

Basic Training includes three sets of imagery exercises. First, athletes need to develop *vivid* images. Like using a fine-tuning control on a television, increasing the vividness of images sharpens the details of the image. The vividness set includes exercises designed to strengthen the senses we have identified as important in sport performance. Second, athletes must be able to *control* their images. Controllability exercises involve learning to manipulate images by will. Third, athletes need to increase their *self-perceptions* of their sport performance. It is a skill to be able to "stand back and look at yourself" through imagery. This type of imagery enables athletes to practice being detectives investigating their own feelings and behavior in sport. This set of exercises will also increase athletes' vividness of emotional imagery as they try to graphically recreate their thoughts and feelings during competition.

It is important for athletes to gain proficiency in the type of exercises in each set. The example exercises purposely use vague descriptors to encourage you to develop your own imagery exercises that are tailored specifically for your athletes. It is

also helpful to develop additional exercises in areas in which athletes are having trouble. For example, kinesthetic imagery is usually the most difficult, so you should create kinesthetic imagery exercises based on the particular movements in your sport.

Vividness. Exercise 1: Pick a close friend or someone that you are around quite often. Have him/her sit in a chair in front of you. Try to get a sharp image of that person. Try to visualize the details of that person such as facial features, body build, mannerisms, clothes, etcetera. Now imagine that person talking. Still focusing on the face, try to hear his/her voice. Imagine all the facial expressions as he/she talks. See this person walk up to you and begin talking to you. Try to see this person from inside your body—from behind your own eyes. Think about how you feel about that person. Try to recreate the emotions you feel toward that person, whether it be warm friendship, deep love, or admiration and respect.

Exercise 2: Place yourself in a familiar place where you usually perform your sport (gym, pool, rink, field, track, etc.). It is empty except for you. Stand in the middle of this place and look all around. Notice the quiet emptiness. Pick out as many details as you can. What does it smell like? Now imagine yourself in the same setting, but this time there are many spectators there. Imagine yourself getting ready to perform. Try to experience this image from inside your body. See the spectators, your teammates, your coach, and the opponents. Try to hear the sounds of the noisy crowd, your teammates' chatter, your coach yelling encouragement, and the particular sounds of your sport (e.g., ball swishing through the net, volleyball spike hitting the floor). Recreate the feelings of nervous anticipation and excitement that you have prior to competing. How do you feel?

Exercise 3: Choose a piece of equipment in your sport such as a ball, pole, racquet, club, etcetera. Focus on this object. Try to imagine the fine details of the object. Turn it over in your hands and examine every part of the object. Feel its outline and texture. Now imagine yourself performing with the object. First, focus on seeing yourself very clearly performing this activity. Visualize yourself repeating the skill over and over. See yourself performing from behind your own eyes. Then step outside of your body and see yourself perform as if you were watching yourself on film. Now, step back in your body and continue performing. Next, try to hear the sounds that accompany this particular movement. Listen carefully to all the sounds that are being made as you perform this skill. Now, put the sight and the sound together. Try to get a clear picture of yourself performing the skill and also hear all the sounds involved.

Exercise 4: Pick a very simple skill in your sport. Perform the skill over and over in your mind and imagine every feeling and movement in your muscles as you perform that skill. Try to feel this image as if you were inside your own body. Concentrate on how the different parts of your body feel as you stretch and contract the various muscles associated with the skill. Think about building a machine as you perform the skill flawlessly over and over again.

Now try to combine all of your senses, but particularly those of feeling, seeing, and hearing yourself perform the skill over and over. Do not concentrate too hard on any one sense. Instead, try to imagine the total experience using all of your senses.

Once athletes have mastered these exercises, you might consider follow-up variations to imagine more complex skills, grouping skills together, or placing the skill in the context of competition (such as reacting to certain defenses, executing strategy, etc.).

Controllability. *Exercise 1:* Imagine again the person you selected for the first exercise in vividness. Concentrate on the person's face and notice all the different features. Now imagine this person getting up from the chair and walking about a room full of people. Watch the person walk about the room greeting and talking to different people. Continue watching as the person walks up and greets you. Create a conversation with this person.

Exercise 2: Choose a simple sport skill and begin practicing it. Now imagine yourself performing this skill either with a teammate or against an opponent. Imagine yourself executing successful strategies in relation to the movements of your teammate or opponent.

Exercise 3:   Choose a particular sport skill that you have trouble performing. Begin practicing the skill over and over. See and feel yourself doing this from inside your body. If you make a mistake or perform the skill incorrectly, stop the image and repeat it,

attempting to perform perfectly every time. Recreate past experiences in which you have not performed the skill well. Take careful notice of what you are doing wrong. Now imagine yourself performing the skill correctly. Focus on how your body feels as you go through different positions in performing the skill correctly. Build a perfect machine!

Self-Perception. *Exercise 1:* Think back and choose a past performance in which you performed very well. Using all your senses, recreate that situation in your mind. See yourself as you were succeeding, hear the sounds involved, feel your body as you performed the movements, and reexperience the positive emotions. Try to pick out the characteristics that made you perform so well (e.g., intense concentration, feelings of confidence, optimal arousal). After identifying these characteristics, try to determine why they were present in this situation. Think about the things you did in preparation for this particular event. What are some things that may have caused this great performance? Repeat this exercise imagining a situation in which you performed very poorly.

Exercise 2: Think back to a sport situation in which you experienced a great deal of anxiety. Recreate that situation in your head, seeing and hearing yourself. Especially recreate the feeling of anxiety. Try to feel the physical responses of your body to the emotion, and also try to recall the thoughts going through your mind that may have caused the anxiety. Now attempt to let go of the anxiety and relax your body. Breathe slowly and deeply and focus on your body as you exhale. Imagine all of the tension being pulled into your lungs and exhaled from your body. Continue breathing slowly and exhaling tension until you are deeply relaxed. Now repeat this exercise imagining a situation in which you experienced a great deal of anger, and then relax yourself using the breathing and exhalation technique.

Exercise 3: The purpose of this exercise is to help you to become more aware of things that happen during competition that bother you when you perform. Think about the times when your performance suddenly went from good to bad. Recreate several of these experiences in your mind. Try to pinpoint the specific factors that negatively influenced your performance (e.g., officials, teammates, opponent's remarks, opponent started to play really well). After becoming aware of these factors that negatively affected your performance, take several minutes to recreate the situations, develop appropriate strategies to deal with the negative factors, and imagine the situations again, but this time imagine yourself using your strategies to keep the negative factors from interfering with your performance. Reinforce yourself by feeling proud and confident that you were able to control the negative factors and perform well.

Additional sensory images. Remember, the exercises presented here are models to get you started. Be creative and provide meaningful images that are personally relevant to your athletes. Check the library for books on imagery if you would like other examples. Here are some additional sensory images that athletes may enjoy.

Visually, try to see various colors. Pick out objects of certain colors (e.g., a tomato) and then try to "paint the screen" in front of your face with that color (red). To practice auditory imagery, try to hear the beat of rain against a window, an automobile horn, the sound of a clock striking, applause from a crowd, and the sound of a train whistle. To practice kinesthetic imagery, try to feel yourself running up stairs, lifting a heavy weight, stooping down to tie your shoe, suspending your weight by your hands, nodding your head, and rising up from sitting in a low chair. To practice tactile imagery, try to feel velvet, wool mittens, a hot bath, the clasp of someone's hand on yours, a soft comfortable bed, a crisp dead leaf, and wet soap. To practice olfactory imagery, try to smell cigar smoke, roses, fresh paint, newly mown grass, leather, coffee, and your favorite cologne. To practice gustatory imagery, try to taste salt, chocolate, sugar, coffee, your favorite fruit, and a lemon. Although these images are not sport-specific in content, they are good practice in strengthening athletes' "imagery muscle" and also can be fun!

Implementing a Systematic Program

After Basic Training, athletes should be fairly proficient at experiencing vivid images, controlling these images, and using imagery to become more self-aware. They should also be somewhat proficient at using all senses and emotions to create a total sensory experience

Athletes are not ready to begin a *systematic* program of imagery. Keep in mind that imagery practice must be systematic to be effective. Your first concern is to build the imagery program into the athletes' routine. The imagery program must *not* be something extra but should instead be an integral part of training and practice.

Another key is to fit the needs of the athlete. The imagery program does not need to be long and complex. In fact, when first starting it is a good idea to keep it concise and simple. Initially, choose a sport skill or strategy that is easy to control. That is, choose a movement in which the environment is stable rather than reactive. For example, in basketball you could start with free throw shooting and in racquet sports with the serve. As your athletes become more proficient and accepting of the program, you can increase the variety of the program.

Imagery Cookbook for Coaches and Practitioners

It is impossible to design an imagery program that would be appropriate for all sports. For that reason, this section is designed as a "cookbook" in which the necessary "ingredients" of an imagery program are itemized. The ingredients listed include ways to use imagery, times in which imagery may be practiced, and methods of practicing imagery. It is up to you to choose which ingredients are most relevant for the needs of your athletes.

Uses

Athletes can use imagery in a number of ways to enhance sport performance. Uses of imagery can be categorized into three groups: (1) enhancing physical skills, (2) enhancing perceptual skills, and (3) enhancing psychological skills.

Enhancing physical skills. Learning sport skills. Imagery can be used to aid beginners in learning sport skills by helping to develop the appropriate mental blueprint of the skill (Feltz & Landers, 1983). Think of it as building a machine from scratch. It is advisable to combine imagery of this type with verbal triggers to ensure that correct technique is being imagined. **Triggers** are words or phrases that help athletes focus on the correct cues during imagery. The key to a trigger is its ability to program the proper image.

Sam Snead used the word "oily" to describe his fluid swing. A famous female golfer kept the word "oooom-PAH" written on her driver to program the image of an easy slow backswing and a vigorous downswing. A basketball player struggling with his shooting used the trigger "straight up" to perfect the image of his jump shot. A cross-country skier having trouble with her uphill technique used the word "quick" to symbolize the quick, short kick technique needed on hills. U.S. biathletes have used the trigger "Rock of Gibraltar" to program the steady body state they need to shoot effectively. Researchers advise the use of triggers by beginners when using imagery to emphasize the basic elements of the skill (Lane, 1980). Symbolic images are also effective aids for athletes learning sport skills. Golfers can imagine turning their body inside a barrel to ensure proper body rotation on the swing and can imagine their arms as a pendulum swinging from the shoulders for the proper putting stroke.

Practicing sport skills. Often termed "mental practice," imagery is used in this way to perform a specific sport skill repetitively in one's mind. Examples include using imagery to shoot free throws, execute a takedown, sprint over a set of hurdles, swing a golf club, hit a baseball, or perform a routine on the balance beam. Even when skills are well learned, imagery practice is important to make them automatic. Verbal triggers and symbolic images are also important in practicing well-learned skills as reminders of proper technique.

Problem solving (physical). It may be helpful for athletes to use imagery when they are mired in a slump or having technique problems. They can imagine themselves performing perfectly and try to analyze how their present technique is different from that perfect performance. It may be helpful for athletes to view videotapes of themselves performing well and then internalize that performance by using kinesthetic imagery.

Enhancing perceptual skills. *Learning strategy.* Although imagery can never take the place of physical practice, it is a helpful technique to use in conjunction with the physical learning of new strategies. For example, imagery could be used to help quarterbacks learn the different options of new plays or to help soccer players learn their positions in certain patterns. Lou Henson, men's basketball coach at the University of Illinois, reports that his team learned their offensive patterns more quickly and thoroughly as a result of a systematic imagery program.

Practicing strategy. Using imagery to practice strategies involves imagining types of team concepts or individual strategies. Example of this include using imagery to go through the options in a basketball offense, ski over a particular course to plan which techniques one will use, practice throws from the outfield based on where the runners are on base, and plan the type of shots one will play against a particular tennis opponent. As discussed previously, Fran Tarkenton used imagery in this way to prepare offensive game plans against specific opponents.

Problem-solving (perceptual). Similar to physical problem solving discussed previously, imagery can be used to solve perceptual problems such as analyzing why a certain strategy is not working. Coaches frequently use imagery in this way as they think through strategies and formations. By relaxing the mind and imagining the situation, one can often successfully determine how to correct problems.

Enhancing psychological skills. *Arousal control.* As discussed previously, research indicates that imagery is an effective technique to control precompetitive arousal levels. Athletes who need to increase their arousal, or psych up, for competition can imagine playing intensely and aggressively in front of a roaring crowd. Athletes who need to decrease their arousal prior for competition can mentally recall their preparation and good performances in practice and previous games and then visualize themselves handling the pressure and performing successfully in the upcoming competition.

Stress management. Arousal control is usually needed just prior to or during competition. Imagery may also be helpful to reduce stress that occurs due to sport demands as well as other life demands (e.g., job pressure, exams, deadlines). Athletes should have two or three relaxing images that they can use when they need to reduce stress. Examples might be images of a favorite place or a warm beach. Symbolic stress reduction images are also helpful. Fanning (1988) provides several useful images for stress reduction including the image of tightly twisted ropes untwisting, the image of hard and cold wax slowly softening and melting, or the sound of jackhammers becoming distant woodpeckers.

Goal setting. Athletes can use imagery to replay previous performances and set goals for improvement based on prior performance. Imagery is also useful for "goal programming," which involves using imagery to "program" goals by repeatedly imagining achieving goals in competition.

Self-confidence. Self-confidence is achieved by believing one is competent and successful. Imagery is a powerful technique to enhance confidence, as athletes should always see themselves as competent and successful in their images. It is especially useful to recreate past successful performances and internalize the positive feelings that accompanied those successes.

Attentional focusing. Imagery is very useful in helping athletes focus their attention on the relevant aspects of the upcoming competition. Terry Orlick (1986) advocates that athletes develop *focus plans* for competition that are practiced via imagery prior to using them in competitive events. Athletes should evaluate themselves and the specific demands of their sport to develop focus plans for competition. These plans outline where attention should be focused at different times during competition. By practicing focus plans repeatedly using imagery, athletes will be more likely to carry out the plans successfully.

Increasing self-perception. By systematically practicing imagery, athletes can become more aware of what is taking place within and around them. Just as an art teacher brings the subtle effects of shading to students' attention, a coach through imagery can help athletes relax and pay attention to sensory details. A runner may learn much about a previously run race by vividly recreating it in her mind.

A member of the U.S. Nordic Ski Team was having problems sustaining the level of concentration she needed throughout her races. By imaging her past races, she became aware that she was shifting attention to the wrong things toward the end of the race. All athletes can learn more about themselves and their sport if they "tune to the imagery channel."

Controlling physiological responses. Scientists are providing evidence that imagery can influence body functions previously thought beyond conscious control, such as heart rate, respiration, blood pressure, and skin temperature (Blakeslee, 1980; Schwartz & Beatty, 1977). Martens (1982) cites the example of the Indian yogis who are able to alter their heart rate, respiration, and brain waves through the practice of imagery. Why is this important in sport? Performance can be enhanced in many sports through the control of physiological responses. Biathletes must be able to reduce their body responses after strenuous cross-country skiing to achieve the static relaxation important in shooting. Jacque Mayol broke the world underwater diving record by using imagery and relaxation to reduce his autonomic body processes. Imagery can also be used by athletes to control and optimize physiological arousal prior to competition. We are only beginning to scratch the surface with regard to understanding the power of imagery in controlling our bodies.

Interpersonal skills. Imagery can be used for much more than performance enhancement. Athletes can practice the interpersonal skill of confrontation by imagining how they will approach the coach about a lack of playing time. Through imagery we can engage in self-reflection and examine how we engage with others in communication and behavior. As the title of this chapter indicates, imagery can enhance performance and also contribute to athletes' personal development. Many athletes who use imagery in sport testify to its benefit in other areas of their lives.

Recovery from injury. Imagery can be used to cope with pain, speed up recovery of the injured area, and keep physical skills from deteriorating. Injured athletes who attend practices and competitions but who cannot physically practice should imagine running through the drills and workouts just as though they were physically performing them. There are numerous stories of athletes who have used imagery and had remarkable recoveries from injury and quick returns to their former skill level.

Times

You now know some specific uses for imagery. But when is the most effective time to use it? Staying with our "cookbook" design, we offer three suggestions about when to use imagery.

Daily practice. A recurring theme throughout this chapter is the systematic use of imagery. To be systematic, daily imagery practice is advised. As you will see in the sample programs at the end of the chapter, this may require only 10 minutes per day.

First, imagery practice may be used *before actual physical practice sessions*. This fits imagery into the athletes' routine and may get them into the proper frame of mind for practice.

It may also be appropriate to practice imagery *after actual physical practice sessions*. This has been successful with groups in reaffirming the points emphasized in practice that day. Also, athletes are more relaxed at the end of practice and may be more receptive to imagery at that time.

There are certain times when imagery may be beneficial *during practice*. For example, if a basketball coach implements an imagery program to practice free throws, he/she may build in time for imagery practice prior to shooting free throws in practice.

Preperformance routine. It is helpful for athletes to go through a preperformance imagery routine *before every contest*. This routine should be individualized for each athlete and practiced in preperformance situations. To facilitate this, it is helpful to have a dark, comfortable room available to all athletes prior to competition. However, if no room is available, imagery can be practiced anywhere. Suggestions about the content of these precompetitive routines are included with the sample programs at the end of the chapter.

Also, there may be certain skills in sport that are conducive to a preperformance imagery routine *before actually performing the skill*. This is the type of routine that Jack Nicklaus practices before hitting each shot. "Closed" skills such as free throw shooting, field goal kicking, ski jumping, volleyball serving, or gymnastic vaulting are more easily practiced in this way, as opposed to "open" skills such as broken field running in football or executing a fast break in basketball.

Postperformance review. Another appropriate time to use imagery is after competition. Again, this should be an individual exercise, but coaches can monitor it by having the athletes complete *postcompetitive evaluation sheets* based on their postperformance imagery. Using imagery at this time facilitates increased awareness of what actually happened during the competition.

Methods

Now that we have examined some specific uses of imagery and times to use it, we turn our attention to methods of practicing imagery.

Individual versus group practice. It is beneficial to individualize imagery programs to fit the specific needs of each athlete. However, do not assume that this means giving athletes the information and letting them set up their own programs. Only the most conscientious athlete will take time to design an imagery program without the guidance (and gentle prodding) of a coach or sport psychologist. If there is time, meet with each athlete to implement individual imagery programs.

For team sports, group imagery exercises are most practical. Coaches can use the group setting to introduce imagery to athletes, evaluate their imagery ability, go through Basic Training, and then incorporate some of the ways of using imagery into a systematic program. If certain individuals want to set up an individual program to be practiced on their own, that's great!

Cassette tapes. Some athletes find it useful to buy commercially produced imagery tapes or make their own imagery tapes. There are several tapes on the market that utilize imagery to enhance psychological skills such as relaxation and concentration. Coaches and sport psychologists can make tapes for athletes that combine the practice of physical, perceptual, and psychological skills. The actual imagery practice should be preceded by a two- to three-minute relaxation exercise. This is normally followed by "guided" imagery practice, which means that the athlete listens to a prepared script of imagery sequences. When making imagery tapes for athletes, be sure to use specific verbal cues familiar to the athlete. Prior to making the tape, you should work with athletes to plan scripts that are personally meaningful and appropriate for their individual needs. Often, you can record an imagery tape as you are conducting an imagery session with an athlete. Keep in mind that athletes differ in their preference for tapes. Some find them limiting, yet others like the structure.

Imagery logs. To monitor imagery practice and improvement, it is useful for athletes to keep a log or written record of their imagery experiences. The log can contain different types of imagery exercises and self-evaluation forms to monitor individual progress in the program. The postperformance review exercise discussed in the last section could be included in the log. This is a means of emphasizing systematic practice and provides a way to monitor that practice.

Sample Programs

You now have the ingredients necessary to put together an effective imagery program. It is up to you to analyze the needs of your athletes and decide which ingredients will work best in your situation. To aid you in that endeavor, three specific imagery programs are outlined here as examples. The first program is for a team situation and provides examples of group exercises. The second program is for individuals in less structured situations. The third program is an example of skill acquisition in golf through imagery. These are only sample programs. You should develop your own program by using the ingredients and the samples provided.

Team Imagery Program

The coach or sport psychologist should begin the team imagery program well before the start of the competitive season so athletes are familiar with imagery and proficient in their imagery skills. Informational literature can be provided to more advanced athletes in the off season to introduce them to imagery. This reading material should be motivational and interesting so the athletes are intrigued and ready to learn more about imagery in the preseason.

First three weeks of preseason.

1. Introduce program (30 minutes).
2. Evaluate athletes' imagery ability (20 minutes).
3. Basic Training (each day for 10–15 minutes following practice). Begin Basic Training with the exercises suggested in this chapter; then add exercises that are appropriate for your team and sport (team patterns and strategies).

4. Provide individual imagery sessions for athletes who are interested. Also, invite athletes to meet with you individually to discuss personalized imagery training they can do on their own. Continue to provide individual sessions for athletes throughout the season if they want them.

Remainder of season (each day for 10 minutes prior to, following, or during practice).

1. Relaxation imagery*
2. Repetitive practice of simple sport skills*— perform them perfectly!
3. Repetitive practice of advanced sport skills*—perform them perfectly!
4. Competitive tactics and strategies in relation to specific needs of team and upcoming opponents*
5. Recreate past successful performance
6. Goal programming for future success

The imagery exercises marked with an asterisk should be included in *all* sessions. They are a warm-up for the other types of imagery. After these initial warm-up exercises, any types of imagery exercises can be used. Other suggested images might include:

- Fulfilling roles on the team
- Attentional focus (develop a team focus plan for different opponents)
- Using triggers and symbolic images
- Arousal control
- Correcting mistakes
- Precompetitive routine (should be practiced at least twice a week)

Precompetitive imagery routine. The suggested practice outline (the first six steps listed under "Remainder of Season") could be incorporated into individual precompetitive routines. Encourage each athlete to develop his/her own routine, and make available a preevent imagery room or specified area in which imagery can be practiced privately.

Postgame imagery review. Devise an event evaluation sheet that athletes will complete after each game. This sheet should ask the athletes to evaluate their performance in the following areas: physical skills, strategies, fulfillment of role, achievement of goals, arousal level, attentional focus, self-confidence, areas that need improvement, and strategies to improve these areas. Make the sheet concise and objective so the athletes will find it easy to complete (see Chapter 13 for a sample evaluation sheet).

Explain to the athletes that they should relax in a quiet setting, mentally recreate the competition, and complete the evaluation form. They can either keep the forms in a log book or turn them into you after each competition.

Individual Imagery Program

1. Education about imagery so basics of imagery are understood
2. Evaluation of imagery ability (use questionnaire)
3. Basic Training (twice a day for 20 minutes). Basic Training should include imagery practice in all areas. Also, this training should emphasize imagery exercises in areas found to be weak in the imagery evaluation phase.
4. Regular imagery sessions (throughout competitive season)

    Prepractice (10 minutes):
    Technique work
    Goal programming for practice
    Postpractice (10–15 minutes):
    Recreate practice performance
    Physical, perceptual, and psychological problem solving
    Psychological skills practice (according to individual need)
    Practice precompetitive imagery program
5. Competition day

    Preevent imagery (10–20 minutes)
    Use format suggested in Team Imagery Program
    Postevent review (10–20 minutes):
    Design personal event evaluation sheet or log

Golf Skill Acquisition Program

Skill acquisition exercises.

1. Set up in the correct address position. Stay there for a moment and concentrate on the *feeling* of your body and *how it looks* from where you stand. Be very sensitive as to how your body feels in this position. Repeat the set-up five times and work to develop a pattern each time you set up so that it will become automatic.

2. In slow motion take your swing to the top and hold. Be aware of the overall coiled feeling of your body and the tension in each body part. Repeat your backswing 10 times, attempting to replicate the arc of your clubhead each time. Build a machine!

3. Swing freely 10 times. Concentrate on the rhythm and feel of the swing as you come through each time. As you follow through with your hands high, track the imaginary ball you have hit in its flight.

Activity. Hit 10 balls, concentrating on swinging freely through each shot.

Triggers for full swing.

1. Firm left side (proper set-up technique)
2. Stake through your body (around which the body should rotate during the swing)
3. Control and explode (easy, controlled backswing and explosion of weight going forward into the downswing)

Imagery practice with triggers. Use each trigger to program the proper technique of the golf swing. Imagine performing the full swing five times using each trigger as a guide to proper technique.

Routine for each shot.

1. Prior to lining up, view your target area and imagine the ball there.
2. Visualize the flight path of the ball.
3. As you set up in the address position, use the triggers "firm left side" and "stake through your body" to reaffirm proper swing technique.

4. Imagine the perfect swing by thinking "control and explode."

5. Hit the ball.

Imagery exercise. Imagine this routine for different golf shots. Develop personal triggers or symbolic images for different shots.

Case Studies

Now that you understand the power of imagery and have seen examples of imagery programs for athletes, let's revisit the cases of Beth, Carl, and Kim that were described at the beginning of the chapter. As a test for yourself, go back and read about these athletes and jot down on paper how you would implement an imagery training program to help each of them. In this section, we overview how we hypothetically intervened with Beth, Carl, and Kim.

Beth

Initially we got to know Beth and talked with her about her perceived strengths and weaknesses as a player. We guided Beth through imagery in which she imagined her best and worst performances. After imagining each performance, she wrote down the characteristics of each, including how she felt during the performances, what she said to herself, how she prepared for the matches, and how she responded to performance errors. We then evaluated Beth's imagery skills, discussed her imagery ability with her, and recommended various Basic Training exercises in imagery with a special emphasis on controllability and refocusing after bad shots (as well as other weak areas that were identified).

We worked with Beth to develop a precompetitive imagery program in which she saw herself performing well, achieving her goals (goal programming), and refocusing after bad shots. After each match, Beth completed a competitive evaluation form in which she rated her performance and her ability to stay focused throughout the match. She identified what caused her to lose her focus and developed strategies to refocus in those situations. She mentally practiced this refocusing strategy and followed with some goal programming for

the next day's practice or match. Through imagery, Beth developed the mental skills to become a more consistent and successful tennis player.

Carl

Initially we got to know Carl and discussed his perceived strengths and weaknesses as a player. We introduced the concept of imagery to him and discussed his use of imagery when pitching. The key for Carl was becoming very systematic and consistent in his mental preparation and approach to pitching.

We evaluated Carl's imagery ability and provided Basic Training to enhance it. We worked with him to develop a prepitch routine that he followed before every pitch. This routine included specific behaviors to follow, but more importantly it included a mental routine of repeating to himself situational cues (e.g., number of outs, position of base runners, responsibilities on a bunt, etc.), focusing on the sign from the catcher, and mentally seeing the particular pitch smack into the mitt. At that point, Carl was urged to go to "automatic pilot" and see nothing but the catcher's mitt and feel himself exploding into the pitch. We also helped Carl develop a focus plan to use between innings in which he used imagery to relax his body yet keep his mind focused on the next inning. Carl evaluated his mental and physical pitching performance after each game to monitor his progress and developed additional strategies for improvement. Though his rookie inexperience showed at times, Carl became a much more focused pitcher and showed a great deal of improvement in refocusing and regaining his composure after bad innings.

Kim

We first got to know Kim and discussed her mental approach to the game. We guided her through some simple imagery exercises and evaluated her imagery ability. We had her recreate through imagery the times in which she had choked and shot poorly and gently pushed her to become more self-reflective and identify the thoughts and feelings that led to her choking. Through imagery we had her analyze differences in her thoughts, feelings, and behaviors during times when she choked as compared to times when she performed well.

During this time we also had Kim practice imagery extensively to become more skilled at controlling her images.

An important imagery skill needed by Kim was the ability to relax her body through imagery, so we worked with her to put together a personally meaningful imagery tape that would be effective in helping her to relax. We also worked with Kim in identifying her optimal level of arousal by having her evaluate her arousal levels after each game and identify the factors affecting those levels. Her daily imagery practice and precompetitive imagery routine included several images of increasingly stressful situations in which she was shooting the ball. She imagined herself in each situation using her coping strategies and performing successfully. If at any time she became anxious, she would go back to a less stressful situation and recreate it again. This imagery technique coupled with relaxation allowed Kim to keep herself calm in stressful situations on the court. After a while her confidence grew to the point where choking no longer was a worry for her. However, she continued using imagery to keep her mental skills sharp.

A Final Word

A story is told of a basketball player who was fouled in the closing seconds of a game with his team behind by one point. When the opposing team called time out, the player's coach advised, "Now is the time to use your imagery." The player frantically looked at his coach and exclaimed "Not now, coach! This is *important!*"

Many athletes will humor their coaches and themselves by going through the motions of practicing imagery. Yet, deep inside, these athletes really doubt that it can improve their performance. Besides being skeptical, many athletes are *afraid* of using imagery. They say that thinking too much will hurt their performance. That seems like an ostrich putting its head in the sand. The practice of imagery enables athletes to program proper technique, achieve optimal psychological skills, and correct problems and mistakes instead of hoping that things will work out by magic.

Imagery can only hurt performance if athletes build the wrong machine. That is, imagery will hurt performance if athletes imagine themselves choking at the free throw line, blowing game-winning field goals, or falling off the balance beam. Such negative images do occur in athletes at times, but, with practice, athletes can easily learn to control their images. Coaches and athletes must gain confidence in the effectiveness of imagery and learn to harness its powers. By believing in the power of imagery and implementing the programs discussed in this chapter, coaches and athletes can work together to elevate sport performance to new heights.

Summary

Imagery is defined as using all the senses to recreate or create an experience in the mind. It is a mental technique that "programs" the human mind to respond as programmed. The evidence supporting the positive influence of imagery on sport performance is impressive. Both scientific and experiential accounts of the use of imagery to enhance sport performance report positive results.

Four theories suggest how imagery may enhance performance. The psychoneuromuscular theory states that vivid, imagined events produce innervation in the muscles that is similar to that produced by physical execution of the event. The symbolic learning theory suggests that imagery facilitates performance by helping individuals blueprint or code their movements into symbolic components, thus making the movements more familiar and perhaps more automatic. Bioinformational theory indicates that individuals respond to imagery with response propositions that create psychophysiological changes in the body that positively influence performance. The attentional-arousal set theory suggests that imagery causes athletes to optimize arousal and focus their attention on relevant cues prior to competition.

All athletes possess the ability to use imagery to improve their performance. However, like physical skill, the psychological skill of imagery requires systematic practice to be effective. Setting up a systematic imagery program involves four steps. First, athletes should be educated about imagery and convinced about the merits of practicing imagery. Second, coaches must evaluate the imagery ability of the athletes in order to develop the most appropriate type of program. Just as athletes differ in physical skills, they will differ in their ability to develop vivid and controlled images. Third, coaches must train athletes in basic imagery skills. It is important for athletes to use all appropriate senses and their emotions when practicing imagery. In "Basic Training," athletes practice imagery exercises designed to develop their ability to mentally experience the sensations and emotions that are important in their sport. Fourth, coaches must monitor and implement a systematic program of imagery practice. Major concerns include building the imagery program into the athletes' routine and fitting the program to the needs of the athlete. Coaches and athletes can incorporate many uses of imagery and different methods of practicing imagery into this four-step program.

Study Questions

1. Briefly describe some of the evidence supporting the positive influence of imagery on sport performance.

2. Describe the four phases of setting up an imagery training program.

3. Vividness, controllability, and self-perception are three areas of Basic Training in the imagery training program. Define each of these and describe the role each plays in training an athlete to use an imagery program.

4. What are five different ways in which imagery can be used by athletes?

5. Identify and explain the four theoretical explanations provided in this chapter that address how imagery works to enhance sport performance.

6. Develop an imagery program for an athlete in your sport using the imagery "cookbook."

7. Why is imagery a polysensory experience?

8. What are three different times in which imagery can be used optimally by athletes?

9. What is the difference between external and internal imagery?

References

Ahsen, A. (1984). ISM: The triple code model for imagery and psychophysiology. *Journal of Mental Imagery, 8,* 15–42.

Blakeslee, T. R. (1980). *The right brain.* New York: Anchor Press.

Corbin, C. B. (1972). Mental practice. In W. P. Morgan (Ed.), *Ergogenic aids and muscular performance* (pp. 94–118). New York: Academic Press.

Fanning, P. (1988). *Visualization for change.* Oakland, Calif.: New Harbinger.

Feltz, D. L., & Landers, D. M. (1983). The effects of mental practice on motor skill learning and performance: A meta-analysis. *Journal of Sport Psychology, 5,* 25–57.

Feltz, D. L., Landers, D. M., & Becker, B. J. (1988). A revised meta-analysis of the mental practice literature on motor skill learning. In D. Druckman & J. Swets (Eds.), *Enhancing human performance: Issues, theories, and techniques* (pp. 1–65). Washington, D.C.: National Academy Press.

Gallwey, W. T. (1976). *Inner tennis.* New York: Random House.

Goss, S., Hall, C., Buckloz, F., & Fishburne, G. (1986). Imagery ability and the acquisition and retention of movements. *Memory and Cognition, 4,* 469–477.

Gould, D., Tammen, V., Murphy, S. M., & May, J. (1989). An examination of U.S. Olympic sport psychology consultants and the services they provide. *The Sport Psychologist, 3,* 300–312.

Gould, D., Weinberg, R., & Jackson A. (1980). Mental preparation strategies, cognitions, and strength performance. *Journal of Sport Psychology, 2,* 329–339.

Hale, B. D. (1982). The effects of internal and external imagery on muscular and ocular concomitants. *Journal of Sport Psychology, 4,* 379–387.

Hall, C. R. (1985). Individual differences in the mental practice and imagery of motor skill performance. *Canadian Journal of Applied Sport Science, 10,* 17S–21S.

Hall, C. R., & Rodgers, W. M. (1989). Enchancing coaching effectiveness in figure skating through a mental skills training program. *The Sport Psychologist, 2,* 142–154.

Hall, E. G., & Erffmeyer, E. S. (1983). The effect of visuo-motor behavior rehearsal with videotaped modeling on free throw accuracy of intercollegiate female basketball players. *Journal of Sport Psychology, 5,* 343–346.

Harris, D. V., & Robinson, W. J. (1986). The effects of skill level on EMG activity during internal and external imagery. *Journal of Sport Psychology, 8,* 105–111.

Heckor, J. E., & Kaczor, L. M. (1988). Application of imagery theory to sport psychology: Some preliminary findings. *Journal of Sport and Exercise Psychology, 10,* 363–373.

Hird, J. S., Landers, D. M., Thomas, J. R., & Horan, J. J. (1991). Physical practice is superior to mental practice in enhancing cognitive and motor task performance. *Journal of Sport and Exercise Pyschology, 8,* 293.

Housner, L. D. (1984). The role of visual imagery in recall of modeled motoric stimuli. *Journal of Sport Psychology, 6,* 148–158.

Jacobson, E. (1931). Electrical measurements of neuromuscular states during mental activities. *American Journal of Physiology, 96,* 115–121.

Jowdy, D. P., & Harris, D. V. (1990). Muscular responses during mental imagery as a function of motor skill level. *Journal of Sport and Exercise Psychology, 12,* 191–201.

Kendall, G., Hrycaiko, D., Martin, G. L., & Kendall, T. (1990). The effects of an imagery rehearsal, relaxation, and self-talk package on basketball game performance. *Journal of Sport and Exercise Psychology, 12,* 157–166.

Lane, J. F. (1980). Improving athletic performance through visuo-motor behavior rehearsal. In R. M. Suinn (Ed.), *Psychology in sports: Methods and applications* (pp. 316–320). Minneapolis, Minn.: Burgess.

Lang, P. J. (1977). Imagery in therapy: An information processing analysis of fear. *Behavior Therapy, 8,* 862–886.

Lang, P. J. (1979). A bio-informational theory of emotional imagery. *Psychophysiology, 16,* 495–512.

Lee, A. B., & Hewitt, J. (1987). Using visual imagery in a flotation tank to improve gymnastic performance and reduce physical symptoms. *International Journal of Sport Psychology, 18,* 223–230.

Lee, C. (1990). Psyching up for a muscular endurance task: Effects of image content on performance and mood state. *Journal of Sport and Exercise Psychology, 12,* 66–73.

Mahoney, M. J., & Avener, M. (1977). Psychology of the elite athlete: An exploratory study. *Cognitive Therapy and Research, 1,* 135–141.

Martens, R., (1982, September). *Imagery in sport.* Unpublished paper presented at the Medical and Scientific Aspects of Elitism in Sport Conference, Brisbane, Australia.

Martens, R. (1987). *Coaches guide to sport psychology.* Champaign, Ill.: Human Kinetics.

Mumford, P., & Hall, C. (1985). The effects of internal and external imagery on performing figures of figure skating. *Canadian Journal of Applied Sport Sciences, 10,* 171–177.

Murphy, S. M., & Woolfolk, R. (1987). The effects of cognitive interventions on competitive anxiety and performance on a fine motor skill task. *International Journal of Sport Psychology, 18,* 152–166.

Nicklaus, J. (1974). *Golf my way.* New York: Simon & Schuster.

Noel, R. C. (1980). The effect of visuo-motor behavior rehearsal on tennis performance. *Journal of Sport Psychology, 2,* 221–226.

Orlick, T., & Partington, J. (1986). *Psyched: Inner views of winning.* Ottawa, Ont.: Coaching Association of Canada.

Orlick, T., & Partington, J. (1988). Mental links to excellence. *The Sport Psychologist, 2,* 105–130.

Richardson, A. (1967a). Mental practice: A review and discussion (Part 1). *Research Quarterly, 38,* 95–107.

Richardson, A. (1967b). Mental practice: A review and discussion (Part 2). *Research Quarterly, 38,* 263–273.

Richardson, A. (1983). Imagery: Definitions and types. In I. B. Weiner (Ed.), *Imagery: Current theory, research, and application* (pp. 3–42). New York: Wiley.

Rodgers, W., Hall, C., & Buckolz, E. (1991). The effect of an imagery training program on imagery ability, imagery use, and figure skating performance. *Journal of Applied Sport Psychology, 3,* 109–125.

Rotella, R. J., Gansneder, B., Ojala, D., & Billing, J. (1980). Cognitions and coping strategies of elite skiers: An exploratory study of young developing athletes. *Journal of Sport Psychology, 2,* 350–354.

Ryan, D. E., & Simons, J. (1981). Cognitive demand, imagery, and frequency of mental rehearsal as factors influencing acquisition of motor skills. *Journal of Sport Psychology, 3,* 35–45.

Ryan, D. E., & Simons, J. (1983). What is learned in mental practice of motor skills: A test of the cognitive-motor hypothesis. *Journal of Sport Psychology, 5,* 419–426.

Sackett, R. S. (1934). The influences of symbolic rehearsal upon the retention of a maze habit. *Journal of General Psychology, 13,* 113–128.

Schwartz, G. E., & Beatty, J. (1977). *Biofeedback: Theory and research.* New York: Academic Press

Shelton, T. O., & Mahoney, M. J. (1978). The content and effect of "psyching-up" strategies in weightlifters. *Cognitive Therapy and Research, 2,* 275–284.

Smith, D. (1987). Conditions that facilitate the development of sport imagery training. *The Sport Psychologist, 1,* 237–247.

Straub, W. F. (1989). The effect of three different methods of mental training on dart throwing performance. *The Sport Psychologist, 3,* 133–141.

Suinn, R. M. (1980). Psychology and sport performance: Principles and applications. In R. M. Suinn (Ed.), *Psychology in sports: Methods and applications* (pp. 26–36). Minneapolis, Minn.: Burgess.

Tynes, L. L. & McFatter, R. M. (1987). The efficacy of "psyching" strategies on a weightlifting task. *Cognitive Therapy and Research, 11,* 327–336.

Woolfolk, R., Parrish, W., & Murphy, S. M. (1985). The effects of positive and negative imagery on motor skill performance. *Cognitive Therapy and Research, 9,* 235–341.

Wrisberg, C. A. (1990). An interview with Pat Head Summitt. *The Sport Psychologist, 4,* 180–191.

Wrisberg, C. A., & Anshel, M. H. (1989). The effect of cognitive strategies on the free throw shooting performance of young athletes. *The Sport Psychologist, 3,* 95–104.

Wrisberg, C. A., & Ragsdale, M. R. (1979). Cognitive demand and practice level: Factors in the mental rehearsal of motor skills. *Journal of Human Movement Studies, 5,* 201–208.

Sport Imagery Questionnaire*

As you complete this questionnaire, remember that imagery is more than just seeing or visualizing something in your mind's eye. Vivid images may include not only visualizing but experiencing many senses such as hearing, feeling, touching, and smelling. Along with these sensations you may also experience emotions or moods.

Below you will read descriptions of four general sport situations. You are to imagine the general situation and provide as much detail from your imagination as possible to make the image just as "real" as you can. Then you will be asked to rate your imagery in six areas:

1. How vividly you saw or visualized the image

2. How clearly you heard the sounds

3. How vividly you felt your body movements during the activity

4. How clearly you were aware of your mood or felt your emotions of the situation

5. How well you could control the image

6. Whether you could see the image from inside your body

After you read each general description, think of a specific example of it—the skill, the people involved, the place, the time. Next, close your eyes and take a few deep breaths to become as relaxed as you can. Put aside all other thoughts for a moment. Keep your eyes closed as you try to imagine the situation as vividly as you can.

*Adapted from Martens, 1982.

There are, of course, no right or wrong images. Use your imagery skills to develop as vivid and clear an image of the general situation described as possible. After you have completed imagining the situation described, please rate your imagery skills using the scales provided.

For items a–d:

1 = no image present

2 = not clear or vivid, but a recognizable image

3 = moderately clear and vivid image

4 = clear and vivid image

5 = extremely clear and vivid image

For item e:

1 = no control at all of image

2 = very hard to control

3 = moderate control of image

4 = better-than-average control of image

5 = complete control of image

Practicing Alone

Select one specific skill or activity in your sport, such as shooting free throws, performing a parallel bar routine, executing a takedown, throwing a pass, hitting a ball, or swimming the butterfly. Now imagine yourself performing this activity at the place where you normally practice (gymnasium, pool, rink, field, court) without anyone else present. Close your eyes for about one minute and try to see yourself at this place, hear the sounds, feel your body perform the movement, and be aware of your state of mind or mood. Try to see yourself from behind your eyes or from inside your body.

a. Rate how well you saw yourself doing the activity.   1 2 3 4 5

b. Rate how well you heard the sounds of doing the activity.   1 2 3 4 5

c. Rate how well you felt yourself making the movements.   1 2 3 4 5

d. Rate how well you were aware of your mood.   1 2 3 4 5

e. Rate how well you controlled the image.   1 2 3 4 5

f. Could you see the image from inside your body?   yes   no

Practicing with Others

You are doing the same activity but now you are practicing the skill with the coach and your teammates present. This time, however, you make a mistake that everyone notices. Close your eyes for about one minute to imagine making the error and the situation immediately afterward as vivdly as you can. Try to see the image from behind your eyes or from inside your body.

a. Rate how well you saw yourself in this situation.   1 2 3 4 5

b. Rate how well you heard the sounds in this situation.   1 2 3 4 5

c. Rate how well you felt yourself making the movements.   1 2 3 4 5

d. Rate how well you felt the emotions of this situation.   1 2 3 4 5

e. Rate how well you controlled the image.   1 2 3 4 5

f. Could you see the image from inside your body?   yes   no

Watching a Teammate

Think of a teammate or acquaintance performing a specific activity unsuccessfully in competition, such as missing a field goal, being passed by other runners, or falling from the rings. Close your eyes for about one minute to imagine as vividly and realistically as possible watching your teammate performing this activity unsuccessfully in a critical part of the contest.

a. Rate how well you saw your teammate in this situation.   1 2 3 4 5

b. Rate how well you heard the sounds in this situation.   1 2 3 4 5

c. Rate how well you felt your own physical presence or movement in this situation.   1 2 3 4 5

d. Rate how well you felt the emotions of this situation.   1 2 3 4 5

e. Rate how well you controlled the image.   1 2 3 4 5

f. Could you see the image from inside your body?   yes   no

Playing in a Contest

Imagine yourself performing the same or similar activity in competition, but imagine yourself doing the activity very skillfully and the spectators and teammates showing their appreciation. Now close your eyes for about one minute and imagine this situation as vividly as possible.

a. Rate how well you saw yourself in this situation.   1 2 3 4 5

b. Rate how well you heard the sounds in this situation.   1 2 3 4 5

c. Rate how well you felt yourself making the movements.   1 2 3 4 5

d. Rate how well you felt the emotions of this situation.   1 2 3 4 5

e. Rate how well you   1 2 3 4 5
    controlled the image.

f. Could you see the image   yes   no
    from inside your body?

Scoring

Now let's determine your imagery scores and see what they mean. Sum the ratings for each category and record them below.

Directions	Dimension	Score
Sum all "a" items	Visual	_____
Sum all "b" items	Auditory	_____
Sum all "c" items	Kinesthetic	_____
Sum all "d" items	Emotion	_____
Sum all "e" items	Controllability	_____
Sum all "yes" in "f" items	Internal perspective	_____

Interpret your scores in the visual, auditory, kinesthetic, emotion, and controllability categories based on the following scale: excellent (20–18), good (17–15), average (14–12), fair (11–8), and poor (7–4). Notice the categories in which your scores were low and refer to exercises in the chapter to increase your imagery ability in those areas. All of these categories are important for imagery training, so don't just rely on your visual sense. Work to improve the others!

If you used an internal imagery perspective in three or four of the situations, that is excellent. If you were unable to use internal imagery, refer to the instructions in the chapter to develop your internal imagery ability. Remember, it takes practice, but you can increase your imagery ability. Good luck!

Cognitive Techniques for Improving Performance and Building Confidence

Linda Bunker, *University of Virginia*
Jean M. Williams, *University of Arizona*
Nate Zinsser, *University of Virginia*

*T*he most consistent finding in peak performance literature is the direct correlation between self-confidence and success. Athletes who are truly outstanding are self-confident. Their confidence has been developed over many years and is often the result of positive thinking and frequent experiences in which they have been successful. Coaches and sport psychologists can probably identify many confident players with whom they have been associated. They are the people you would like to have come to bat when the game is at stake. They are the people whom you do not give up on even when they have lost the first set in a tennis match, fallen behind in a race, or been penalized in a competition.

Confident athletes think about themselves and the action at hand in a different way than those who lack confidence. What athletes think or say is critical to performance. Unfortunately, the conscious mind is not always an ally. We all spend vast amounts of time talking to ourselves. Much of the time we are not even aware of this internal dialogue, much less its content. Nevertheless, thoughts directly affect feelings and ultimately actions. Inappropriate or misguided thinking usually leads to negative feelings and poor performance, just as appropriate or positive thinking leads to en-

abling feelings and good performance (Rosin & Nelson, 1983; Dorsel, 1988, Kendall et al., 1990). The conscious mind—that remarkable, uniquely human instrument—is not automatically one's ally. It must first be trained to think effectively.

THOUGHTS→FEELINGS→BEHAVIOR

Confident athletes think they can and *they do*. They never give up. They typically are characterized by positive self-talk, images, and dreams. They imagine themselves winning and being successful. They say positive things to themselves and never minimize their abilities. They focus on successfully mastering a task rather than worrying about performing poorly or the negative consequences of failure. This prediposition to keep one's mind on the positive aspects of one's life and sport performance, even in the face of setbacks and disappointments, is a hallmark of the successful athlete, a trait Seligman (1991) refers to as "learned optimism." Having learned to be optimistic, these confident athletes get the most from their abilities. Their confidence programs them for successful performance.

If confidence is so critical to successful performance and personal growth, what can coaches and sport psychologists do to help promote self-confidence within their athletes? Many of the earlier chapters in this book have provided, either directly or indirectly, some answers to this question. For example, seeing improvement in physical skill is an obvious way to build confidence. Providing for a history of successful experiences builds both confidence and the expectation of future success. Coaches who observe the learning and performance guidelines outlined in Chapters 2 and 3 will be more likely to maximize successful skill development in their athletes. Effective coach–athlete interactions, as illustrated in Chapters 5, 6, 7, 8, and 9, are likely to enhance each athlete's sense of self-worth and self-esteem. Practices that maximize such growth in athletes, whether the growth be in physical skills or personal development, lead to a more positive self-concept and increased self-confidence.

In this chapter we discuss techniques for improving confidence and performance by learning to use and control thoughts or cognitions appropriately. It is important that athletes understand how the mind works, how it affects their feelings and actions, and ultimately how it can be disciplined. Initially thoughts may appear to occur spontaneously and involuntarily—thus, beyond control. With the skills of "intentional thinking," athletes can control their thoughts. They can learn to use self-talk to facilitate learning and performance. They can also learn to replace self-defeating thoughts with positive ones—thoughts that build confidence and the expectation of success. Such positive thought processes can become self-fulfilling prophecies.

Self-Talk

The key to cognitive control is **self-talk**. The frequency and content of thoughts vary from person to person and situation to situation. Anytime you think about something, you are in a sense talking to yourself. Self-talk becomes an asset when it enhances self-worth and performance. For example, such talk can help the athlete stay appropriately focused in the present, not dwelling on past mistakes or projecting too far into the future.

Self-talk becomes a liability when it is negative, distracting to the task at hand, or so frequent that it disrupts the automatic performance of skills.

Self-talk becomes especially destructive when an athlete engages in self-labeling or self-rating, the practice of evaluating oneself and then attaching a label to oneself (usually a negative label) based on that evaluation. It is through the use of negative self-talk that athletes label themselves as "losers," "choke artists," and the like. When athletes hold these negative perceptions of themselves, they will often behave in ways that will confirm these perceptions and thus prove to themselves that they are "right."

According to Albert Ellis and his colleagues (Ellis, 1988; Ellis & Dryden, 1987; Grieger & Boyd, 1980), evaluating and labeling oneself this way is both destructive to one's mental health and completely irrational. While it is possible and often desirable to rate one's *behavior* (such as test performance or execution of a sport skill), there is no logical or rational reason to label *oneself*, because what we call our "self" is a very abstract, theoretical concept and impossible to confirm with any certainty. Further, even if one's self could be empirically proven, it would include so many different traits, characteristics, and performances and would be so ever changing that rating and labeling it would be impossible. Athletes would be better off, Ellis argues, if they would eliminate self-rating and labeling altogether. This point will be further developed later in the discussion of irrational and distorted thinking.

The use of negative self-talk by athletes affects not only their immediate performance but also their overall self-esteem and, in extreme cases, can lead to acute depression. Seligman (1991) has described **depression** as nothing more than a disorder of conscious thought, and not a matter of brain chemistry or anger turned inward, as other theories maintain. Depressed people simply think awful things about themselves and their future; their symptom, negative self-talk, *is* their disease. Since depression results from consistently using negative thought, changing this habit will help cure the disease. The fastest way out of depression, and the fastest way to build one's self-esteem, is through consistently positive self-talk, in which the athlete continuously reminds himself/herself of past great performances, of skills and techniques that are performed well, and of a bright future ahead.

Raising self-esteem, however, takes time and patience. A conscientious effort to screen out negative memories and statements, to ignore so-called "experts" when they tell teams and players how good they can expect to be, and to focus the mind on present strengths and desired outcomes is required. Self-esteem begins and ends in the mind of the individual, with self-talk playing the primary and most powerful role in "feeding" the mind.

Before we address the matter of how specific types of self-talk can be used in different situations to help achieve excellence in learning and performance and to promote confidence, we want to remind you that the interview research reported in Chapter 11 found many athletes stating that their best sport performances occurred when they had no thoughts at all. The athletes were so immersed in the action that it just seemed to happen without conscious thought. Tim Gallwey, author of *The Inner Game of Tennis* (1974), and others have stressed that peak performance does not occur when athletes are thinking about it. Gallwey emphasizes learning to turn performance over to unconscious or automatic functions—functions that are free from the interference of thought.

It may be desirable to strive for such thought-free performance, but athletes usually *do* think both before and during most competitions, especially between points (as in tennis) or between plays (as in football). They also think during practices and outside of practices. Their thoughts affect their self-concept, self-confidence, and behavior. Therefore, it is important that coaches and sport psychologists teach athletes to recognize and control their thoughts. We concur with Keith Bell, author of *Championship Thinking* (1983), who supports this concept by emphasizing that it is not thinking itself that leads to substandard performance but inappropriate or misguided thinking. If used properly, thinking can be a great aid to performance and personal growth. The question should not be whether to think but what, when, and how to think.

The uses for self-talk are almost as varied as are the different types of sports. The effective coach and sport psychologist can use self-talk to aid athletes in learning skills, correcting bad habits, preparing for performance, focusing attention, creating the best mood for performance, and building confidence and competence.

Self-Talk for Skill Acquisition

The nature of thoughts and self-talk should change as performers become more proficient. During early learning, skill acquisition is usually aided when self-instructional talk is used to remind the performer of certain key aspects. For example, cue words might be used to describe a particular movement phase or to help in learning the appropriate sequencing of actions. Simple cues such as "step, swing" in tennis, "step, drop, step, kick" for a soccer punt, and "arms straight, elbows in" for the golf address are designed to foster cognitive associations that will aid the athlete in learning proper physical execution. Even on the beginning level, self-talk should be kept as brief and minimal as possible. Ororverbalization, by the coach or athlete, can cause paralysis by analysis.

As skills are mastered, self-talk becomes shorter, less frequent, and shifts from a focus on the mechanics of technique to a focus on strategies and optimal feelings. With learning, the goal is to reduce conscious control and promote the "automatic" execution of the skill. For most athletes this means less self-talk concerning the specific mechanics to be performed and more self-talk focusing on the desired feeling. Examples might be a distance runner using a phrase such as "smooth and fluid" to maintain a pace or a soccer player using the phrase "constant, accurate, and intense" to help her focus on the flow of play. Simple verbal cues like these may be used to trigger a desired, automatic action.

The effectiveness and content of self-talk while the athlete is learning skills also depend on the nature of the task. Skills that are self-paced—that is, initiated by the performer when he or she is ready—are positively influenced by thoughts just prior to performance. Examples include skills such as pitching, riflery, bowling, archery, golf, free throw shooting, and any kind of serve. Successful execution can be "programmed" by positive thoughts and images just prior to physical execution. If the skills are well learned, the nature of the self-talk should focus on what the performer is trying to achieve rather than the physical mechanics of the act. For example, in the book *Mind, Set and Match*, Bunker and Rotella (1982) suggest that a server in tennis should think or see "deep outside corner" to specify the landing area of the serve. Similarly, a pitcher might think "High and inside," or a free throw shooter might simply say, "Arch and swish."

Typically there is less time for this type of direct verbal-mental programming in reactive, externally paced skills such as spiking in volleyball, fast breaking in basketball, or volleying in tennis. With externally paced skills the performer needs to rely more on being able to automatically respond correctly, since there is not enough time to separately preprogram each movement. This being the case, athletes in these sports must learn to use the naturally occurring pauses in the game (changing sides of the court, time-outs, out-of-bounds) as opportunities to control their self-talk and set themselves up for success by focusing on what they want to achieve when the action begins again. For example, as a wrestler returns to the center of the mat after the action has taken him and his opponent out of bounds, his self-talk would ideally consist of a brief action plan for the next series of moves and a positive, emotionally charged cue word or phrase, such as "explode, fearless, continuous."

Self-Talk for Changing Bad Habits

Experienced athletes may wish to use technique self-talk when they want to change a well-learned skill or habit. In such cases the athlete must unlearn an automatic response that is no longer effective and replace it with a new one. In order to change a bad habit, it is usually necessary to intentionally force conscious control over the previously automatic execution. Self-talk can be an effective way to "deautomatize" the old skill and make way for a new response.

The more drastic the change, the more detailed the demands of self-talk in the relearning phase. For example, if a tennis player is attempting to change from a two- handed to a one-handed backhand, considerable *self-instruction* may be required. In this case the athlete must verbally redirect the entire swing motion. However, if the change is merely to get behind the ball and hit it a little bit earlier with more weight on the front foot, then a simple cue may be all that is necessary.

When an athlete uses self-talk to redirect technique or strategy, it is essential that the content of the statements focus on the desired outcome rather than on what the athlete is trying *not* to do. If a coach or athlete fails to focus on the desired goal and instead talks about avoiding the undesirable, the head is merely filled with the negative image. For example, saying, "Don't stay on your back foot" when hitting a backhand gives no direction to the swing pattern, and it emphasizes the negative. Effective self-talk would be using a cue such as "step-hit." In short, athletes should be trained to focus on what they want to happen, not

what they want to avoid. An additional bonus with this type of self-talk is that it reinforces the habit of making thoughts positive.

Self-Talk for Attention Control

Self-talk can also help athletes control their attention. It is often easy to be distracted during competition and practice. By using a specific set of verbal cues, athletes can keep their minds appropriately focused. Attentional control is particularly important in helping athletes stay in the present. As Hay (1984) puts it, "The point of power is always the present moment." The future cannot be controlled and the past cannot be erased or replaced, so it is essential that athletes learn to remain in the present. If athletes allow themselves to wander into the past (e.g., "If I had only made that last putt") or focus on the future (e.g., "If I birdie the next hole, I'll be leading the field"), they will have difficulty executing the present shot. Once again, focusing the mind on what is desired *right now* ("head down, smooth") gives the athlete the best chance of making the correct shot. Several books, including *Mind Mastery for Winning Golf* (Rotella & Bunker, 1981), have emphasized the importance of remaining in the present tense. (For further elaboration and specific examples, see Chapter 19.)

Self-Talk for Creating "Affect" or Mood

Researchers have found that affective cues can produce significant changes in performance. For example, runners who say "fast" or "quick" have been found to increase their speed (Meichenbaum, 1975). Golfers who use swing thoughts such as "smooth" or "oily" produce swings that appear smoother and more controlled (Owens & Bunker, 1989). Power words such as "blast," "hit," and "go" are important aids in explosive movements. A runner in the starting blocks should not be thinking about hearing the gun. It is much more effective to be saying "go" or "explode" so that when the gun sounds, it will directly trigger the desired movement (Silva, 1982). Otherwise, the athlete must process the fact that the gun went off and then start. For a long distance run, an athlete may wish to shift word cues throughout the race. During the initial portion, words that encourage consistent pace and energy conservation may be most appropriate. During the middle portion of the run, words that encourage persistence and tuning in to the body are important, while the final portion requires speed and power. Corresponding cues might be "easy," "responding," and "sprint." Each word has an emotional quality that is linked to the movement quality or content (Meichenbaum, 1975). Use of the right affective cues can ultimately help lead to the best potential for peak performance.

Self-Talk for Changing Affect or Mood

Similarly, self-talk can help angry or overaroused athletes refocus their energy so that it can be used constructively and can help bored or fatigued athletes mobilize the energy necessary for intense play. Golf legend Sam Snead learned that simply recalling the phrase "cool-mad" helped him control his temper so that it worked for him rather than against him (Rotella, 1984). Finn (1985) advises underaroused athletes to use a combination of self-talk and rapid breathing to reach a desired emotional state. Statements like "Come on, rev up, it's time to go all out!" alternated with rapid breathing or high-intensity running will increase the athlete's heart rate and produce a new mood state more favorable for peak performance. Use of the right affective cues can ultimately help lead to the best potential for peak performance.

Self-Talk for Controlling Effort

Self-talk can be an effective technique to help maintain energy and persistence. It may be difficult for some athletes to get started in the morning, at practice, or in the first few moments of a contest. Others may have difficulty changing tempo or maintaining effort. Phrases such as "go for it," "easy," "pace," "pick it up," "cool it," "hold onto it," "push," "stay," and so forth can be very effective in controlling effort (Harris & Harris, 1984).

Sustaining effort over a long training period is a typical problem for athletes. If practices become boring or fatigue sets in, athletes may begin to question their commitment or the value of that commitment. Athletes can use self-talk not only to direct action but also to sustain it. Such emphasis on effort control is essential because it helps athletes recognize the importance of hard work in

achieving success. And if by chance the athletes do not succeed, they are more likely to attribute failure to insufficient effort and therefore want to work harder in the future. Coaches should note that this is a much more productive attribution strategy than blaming lack of success on factors such as luck, poor officiating, or the weather.

Self-Talk for Building Self-Efficacy

The term "self-efficacy" refers to one's expectation of succeeding at a specific task or meeting a particular challenge. Self-efficacy can be considered a very specific form of self-confidence, the confidence to win a specific race, to make a particular shot, or to defeat a certain opponent. Efficacy expectations affect performance because they determine how much effort athletes will expend on a task and how long they will maintain effort when confronted with setbacks and obstacles. Many studies have shown that athletes with high self-efficacy outperform those with lower self-efficacy on strength, endurance, and skill tasks (Weinberg, Gould, & Jackson, 1979; Weinberg et al., 1981; Mahoney, Gabriel, & Perkins, 1987; Meyers et al., 1979). These studies illustrate how powerful efficacy expectations are and, just as importantly, demonstrate that an individual's preexisting expectations of efficacy can be enhanced to improve performance.

According to Bandura (1977), self-efficacy is influenced by verbal persuasion, both from others and from self in the form of self-talk. Mahoney (1979) also states that self-talk is a useful method for building the self-efficacy expectations of athletes. More recently Gould and colleagues (1989) found that elite college and national team coaches systematically encourage their athletes to develop positive self-talk. These coaches also rated the encouragement of positive self-talk as the third most effective strategy for developing self-efficacy, ranking physical practice first and the modeling of confidence by the coach himself/herself second. These studies indicate how effective positive self-talk is for enhancing self-efficacy.

A further area in which self-talk plays a crucial role in self-efficacy is rehabilitation from injury. Ieleva and Orlick (1991) found that athletes who recovered exceptionally fast from ankle and knee injuries had a significantly higher frequency of positive self-talk concerning the process of their recovery than did athletes who healed more slowly. Positive self-talk directly influences one's belief in the body's healing power and thus in the actual healing process itself.

Identifying Self-Talk

Appropriate use of the preceding kinds of self-talk will enhance self-worth and performance, but the same cannot be said for all types of self-talk. More specifically, negative or self-defeating self-talk will produce undesirable effects on performance (Rotella et al., 1980).

The first step in gaining control of self-talk is to become aware of what you say to yourself. Surprisingly enough, most people are not aware of their thoughts, much less the powerful impact they have on their feelings and behavior. By getting athletes to review carefully the way in which they talk to themselves in different types of situations, the coach or sport psychologist will identify what kind of thinking helps, what thoughts appear to be harmful, and what situations or events are associated with this talk. Once athletes develop this awareness, they usually discover that their self-talk varies from short cue words and phrases to extremely complex monologues, with the overall content ranging from self-enhancing to self-defeating. The key is to know both when and how to talk to yourself.

It is particularly helpful if athletes are instructed to identify specifically the type and content of thought associated with particularly good and particularly bad performances. For example, are there any usual thought patterns or common themes during different situations? Most athletes find different thinking during successful and unsuccessful performance. Identifying the thoughts that typically prepare an athlete to perform well and to cope successfully with problems during performance can provide a repertoire of cognitive tools for the enhancement of performance. The use of these same thoughts in future performance environments should create similar feelings of confidence and direct performance in much the same way. When an athlete can recreate these positive thoughts and bring them to the new environment, then the athlete can be said to be *taking control* of his/her mind.

Most athletes discover that during unsuccessful performance their mind actually programmed failure through self-doubt and negative statements. The body merely performed what the mind was thinking. Examples include an athlete's thinking before a competition, "I never swim well in this pool" or "I always play poorly against this opponent" and then going on to swim or compete exactly as prophesied. Obviously, future performance would be enhanced if athletes could eliminate dysfunctional and self-defeating thoughts that lead to worry and poor performance. Before such thoughts can be eliminated, they need to be identified. Three of the most effective tools for identifying self-talk are retrospection, imagery, and keeping a self-talk log.

Retrospection

By reflecting back to situations in which they performed particularly well or particularly poorly and trying to recreate the thoughts and feelings that occurred prior to and during these performances, many athletes are able to identify typical thoughts and thought patterns associated with both good and bad performance. It is also beneficial to recall the specific situation, or circumstances, that led to the thoughts and resulting performance. Viewing videotapes of actual past performances helps the athlete recount the action by heightening the memory of the event. If this technique is used, not only should the actual performance be taped but, ideally, the time before the contest begins, the time-outs or "breaks" during the contest, and even the time right after the contest ends. Thoughts during all of these times play a major role in performance, one's expectations regarding future performance, and even one's feelings of self-esteem or worth.

Imagery

Another technique is to have athletes relax as deeply as possible and then try reliving a past performance through visualization. This technique is much more effective if athletes have been previously trained in imagery (see Chapter 16 for suggestions). Athletes who are effective at imagery can usually describe exactly what happened during the competition and what thoughts and feelings preceded, accompanied, and followed the performance. After athletes have relived past performances through imagery, it may be helpful to have them write down the recalled thoughts, situations, and outcomes. If it is not disruptive, the athletes may even want to talk into a tape recorder as they are imaging.

Self-Talk Log

Not all athletes can use retrospection and imagery to remember accurately how they thought and felt or what circumstances triggered their thoughts and feelings. Even athletes who are comfortable using these tools run the risk of time and personal impressions distorting the actual thoughts and circumstances. Keeping a daily diary or self-talk log of thoughts and performance situations is an excellent tool for accurately creating awareness of self-talk. Thoughts should be transcribed as soon after they occur as possible. Athletes in sports such as golf, archery, rowing, and running have found it beneficial to have a tape recorder present while they perform so they can directly tape their thoughts and a description of the situation as they occur.

When keeping a log, the athlete should address such questions as "When I talk to myself, what do I say? What thoughts precede and accompany my good performances? Not only what thoughts, but how frequently am I talking to myself? When playing poorly, do I deprecate myself as a person? Do I call myself names and wish I were still sitting on the bench? Are my comments about how I feel about myself, about how others will feel about me, about how I may let down my friends and teammates, or about how unlucky I am?"

If there is a problem in thinking, the goal is to identify the problem and its boundary points in very specific terms. This means that each athlete must be able to answer questions such as "When do I have negative thoughts? Do I begin doubting myself even before I have a chance to perform? For example, when a whistle blows, do I automatically assume it is directed at me? If I have been fouled, do I start worrying from the moment the whistle blows until after I have shot the free throw or do I begin worrying only after I walk to the free throw line?" Athletes must be able to specify the initial cue that caused them to start worrying or thinking negatively. Also, when do they stop saying self-defeating things? Such detailed knowledge will help in planning an effective intervention. For instance, if worry begins with the referee's whistle, then this is the cue with which an alternate thought pattern should be linked.

It is as important to monitor self-talk during practice as it is during competition. The thoughts typically occurring prior to, during, and after practice play an important role in developing typical thought and behavior patterns. More specifically, the athlete should identify what is said after making mistakes, after teammates perform poorly, after having difficulty performing a new skill or strategy, when fatigued, and after the coach criticizes performance. Often the pattern of thoughts found during competition is merely a reflection of what occurs during practices. Learning to recognize and control the nature of self-talk during practices becomes the foundation for effective thinking during competition.

Techniques for Controlling Self-Talk

Using the preceding self-monitoring tools is an essential first step in the process necessary for producing performance-enhancing thoughts and eliminating disabling thoughts. However, the mere act of monitoring thoughts is usually not enough. In fact, paying too much attention to negative thoughts or thoughts associated with poor performance can be detrimental if they are not linked to some action or change process. Once awareness of negative talk and feelings is heightened, the coach or sport psychologist should immediately instruct the athlete in how to start dealing with these thoughts. Similarly, when good performance is analyzed, it should be with the intent of capitalizing on the state of mind that existed during that performance in the hope of being able to purposefully duplicate it in the future. In this section we present techniques for controlling self-talk.

Thought Stoppage

If an athlete's self-talk is constant and thus distracting, or if the talk produces self-doubt, it must be terminated. Getting rid of negative thoughts often makes it possible to break the link that leads to negative feelings and behaviors, just as stopping excessive or task-irrelevant talk facilitates the athlete's regaining a more appropriate attentional focus. The technique of **thought stoppage** provides one very effective method for eliminating negative or counterproductive thoughts (Meyers & Schleser, 1980). The technique requires *briefly* focusing on the unwanted thought(s) and then using a trigger to interrupt or stop the undesirable thought. The trigger can be a word such as *"stop"* or a physical action such as snapping the fingers or clapping one hand against the thigh. Each athlete should choose the most natural trigger and use it consistently. (Most athletes who use a verbal cue prefer the word "stop," but almost any cue is acceptable if it is used consistently.)

Thought stoppage will not work unless the athlete first recognizes undesirable thoughts and then is motivated to stop them. Developing the commitment necessary to improve the quality of an athlete's self-talk is not as easy for the coach and sport psychologist to accomplish as it sounds. This process requires the athlete to invest some time in monitoring the frequency and content of his/her self-talk and then truly deciding to change this for the better. For example, even after using the typical tools for creating awareness of thoughts, one young professional golfer would not admit negative statements were affecting her golf. As a method to convince her of the severity of the problem, she was asked to empty a box of 100 paper clips into her pocket. Each time she had a negative thought, she had to move a clip to her back pocket. At the end of the golf round she had shot an 84 and had 87 paper clips in her back pocket! The process of actually counting paper clips, each of which represented a negative thought, made her dramatically aware of her problem and motivated her to try thought stoppage (Bunker & Owens, 1985).

Thought stoppage is a skill, and, as with any other skill, it is best to experiment with it first during practice and become comfortable with it before using it in actual competition. An effective way to practice thought stoppage is to combine it with imagery. Athletes should be instructed to select a typical negative thought, or thought pattern, they would like to eliminate. Next they should close their eyes and as vividly as possible imagine themselves in the situation in which they usually have that negative thought. Once they have "recreated" the situation and negative thought, they should practice interrupting the thought(s) with whatever trigger they have selected for thought stoppage. They should do this over and over until the negative talk and accompanying feelings of worry and anxiety have been eliminated entirely. This will require time, patience, and a strong commitment to improving the quality of one's internal dialogue.

It is suggested that during the earlier stages of "physical" thought stoppage practice, athletes should "visibly" use their trigger. Saying "stop" out loud not only makes athletes more conscious of their wish to stop excessive or negative talk but serves several additional functions. It helps the coach to monitor whether athletes are doing what they were instructed to do. If an athlete's body language is showing frustration or disgust with play, his/her thoughts probably are too. The coach who sees no visible thought-stoppage trigger during these circumstances should directly confront the athlete by asking him/her what thoughts are occurring. This will serve to reinforce awareness and the need to stop negative talk immediately. The other advantage of visibly practicing the technique is that athletes realize they are not alone in their need to deal more effectively with self-talk. The technique is particularly effective when becoming more positive is a team effort and responsibility. Thus, this is a good time to encourage athletes to be supportive of one another rather than critical or sarcastic. When one high school basketball coach instituted such a program halfway though his season, he was so impressed with the outcome that he attributed a losing season's turning into a winning season to the athletes' learning to control negative talk and body language and becoming supportive rather than critical of one another.

Thought stoppage takes time to learn, particularly when negative thought patterns have become the dominant mode of response. Cautela and Wisocki (1977) have emphasized the importance of learning to turn off negative thoughts. Frustration over the recurrence of negative thoughts may be lessened if the coach or sport psychologist draws the parallel of trying to eliminate negative thoughts with trying to unlearn some well-established error in physical technique. Old habits change slowly, whether they are physical or cognitive, and they only change with considerable motivation and practice. The more practice an athlete employs, the less likely negative thought patterns are to recur.

Even with practice, it may not always be possible to avoid negative thoughts. When such thoughts do occur, good advice would be not to allow the mind to focus or dwell on them. Just let them pass on through and instead concentrate on some positive thought or some specific cue that can serve to trigger what the athlete wants to do next.

Athletes should learn to be disciplined enough not to allow the mind to focus or dwell on negative thoughts. This leads to the next technique for controlling thoughts—changing self-defeating thoughts to self-enhancing thoughts.

Changing Negative Thoughts to Positive Thoughts

Not only should negative thoughts be stopped; there is obvious merit in turning them into positive thoughts that either provide encouragement and support or appropriately direct attention. The coach or sport psychologist should instruct athletes to extinguish unwanted thought as soon as it is recognized and then immediately practice switching to a positive or more appropriate thought. If, for example, a gymnast finds himself saying, "This new move is really hard—I'll never get it right!" he should learn to follow this phrase immediately with "I've learned lots of hard moves before, so I know if I'm patient I can learn this one too."

Another advantage for teaching this technique along with thought stoppage is that it takes some pressure off athletes who initially doubt their ability to control their thoughts. Perhaps these athletes think they cannot control what thoughts enter their head, but they will accept their ability to control the last thoughts they have. For example, for the professional golfer who through use of the paper clip technique finally accepted that she had many negative thoughts that adversely affected her performance, the initial goal in working with cognitions was simply to reduce the negative statements that were not followed by self-enhancing statements. Not having to worry about the occurrence of a self-defeating statement took considerable pressure off of her. Each day she was able to reduce the number of paper clips that stood for negative thoughts not followed by positive thoughts, and in time she was able to get rid of the recurring pattern of negative talk.

Changing self-talk from negative to positive works best if coaches and sport psychologists have their athletes individually make a list of typical self-defeating things they say and would like to change. Often athletes can generate this list from the self-talk log discussed earlier. Meichenbaum (1977) has emphasized that it is important for athletes to specify when they make these self-

defeating statements and what causes them to make such statements. The goal is to recognize what the situation involved and why the negative thought occurred. Athletes should then design a substitute positive statement. It may be helpful to make a table with the self-defeating thoughts on one side and the preferred self-enhancing statements on the other side, directly opposite the negative thought (see Table 17-1).

Notice that the self-enhancing statements in the table always bring the athlete back to the present time and personal control of the situation. The positive self-talker sees a possibility in every problem, not a problem in every possibility.

The coach or sport psychologist may also want to couple relaxation techniques with changing self-defeating thoughts to self-enhancing ones. Most negative thoughts occur when an individual is under stress and therefore usually overly aroused physiologically. Instruct athletes to stop their negative thought and then take a deep breath. As they feel relaxation spreading with the long, slow exhalation, they should repeat the substitute self-enhancing thought.

There is nothing unusual about having negative thoughts, but winners do not store them away where they can build themselves into a mental block. Instead, they stop them and replace them with positive thoughts. The key is never to leave the negative thought in place. The last thought in any string or sequence of thoughts should be positive and self-enhancing.

Countering

Changing negative to positive self-statements probably will not achieve the expected behavioral outcome if the athlete still *believes* in the negative statements. For example, an athlete might change his/her talk from "I will never be able to run this offensive pattern; I'm just not quick enough" to "I can too; I'm as quick as anyone else." The athlete is merely going through the outward motions of being positive if the real belief system is still saying, "No, I can't; I really am too slow." Dysfunctional thought patterns will keep recurring if they have strong underlying bases that are not identified and refuted.

Heyman and Rose (1980) discussed the fact that athletes will rarely be able to accomplish something if they truly believe they cannot. Fur-

Table 17-1 **Examples of Countering**

Self-Defeating Thoughts	Change to Self-Enhancing Thoughts
I can't believe it's raining. I have to play in the rain.	No one likes the rain, but I can play as well in it as anyone else.
You dumb jerk.	Ease off. Everyone makes mistakes. Sluff it off and put your mind on what you want to do.
There's no sense in practicing. I have no natural talent.	I've seen good players who had to work hard to be successful. I can get better if I practice correctly.
This officiating stinks; we'll never win.	There's nothing we can do about the officiating so let's just concentrate on what we want to do. If we play well, the officiating won't matter.
Why did they foul me in the last minute of play—I'm so nervous, I'll probably choke and miss everything.	My heart is beating fast. That's ok, I've sunk free throws a hundred times. I'll take a deep breath to relax and then visualize the ball going in the basket "swish."
We'll win the meet only if I get a 9.0 on this routine.	Stop worrying about the score; just concentrate on how you're going to execute the routine.
The coach must think I'm hopeless. He never helps me.	That's not fair. He has a whole team to coach. Tomorrow I'll ask what he thinks I need to work on the most.
I don't want to fail.	Nothing was ever gained by being afraid to take risks. As long as I give my best, I'll never be a failure.
I'll take it easy today and go hard next workout.	The next workout will be easier if I go hard now.
Who cares how well I do anyway?	I care, and I'll be happier if I push myself.
This hurts; I don't know if it's worth it.	Of course it hurts, but the rewards are worth it.

ther, the motivation to even try will be eroded if there is no belief that one's efforts will ultimately yield success. Bell (1983) proposes that in such instances, merely directing one's thoughts toward desired actions may not be enough. Instead, the athlete may have to identify and build a case against the negative self-statements that are interfering with effective performance. Bell suggests using the tool of countering under these circumstances. **Countering** is an internal dialogue that uses facts and reasons to refute the underlying beliefs and assumptions that led to negative thinking. Rather than blindly accepting the negative

voice in the back of the head, the athlete argues against it.

When learning to use counters, it is important that the athlete actually describe the evidence necessary to change an attitude or belief. In the preceding example, the coach or sport psychologist might try helping the athlete identify issues such as "What makes me think I am slow? Have I ever in the past played with good speed? Am I as fast as any of the other athletes? If yes, are they successful at running this offense? What might be causing my slowness, and can I do anything to change it? If I am not quite as fast as some of my teammates, do I have any other talents that might compensate for this, such as using my good game sense to read the situation faster so I can react more quickly? What other skills do I have that might help me learn this offensive pattern?"

Any or all of the preceding approaches should lead to some evidence for refuting either the athlete's slowness or the importance of only speed in being successful at the offensive pattern. The more evidence and logic there is to refute the negative belief structure, the more effective the counters will be in getting the athlete to accept the positive statement; and the more firmly the athlete believes in the counters, the less time it will take to turn the thinking around. Later it may be possible for the athlete to identify the negative or irrational thought and simply dismiss it with such phrases as "No, that's not right," "Who says I can't? or just plain "bull."

In his discussion of countering, Bell (1983) makes another excellent point. Sometimes thinking is neither right nor wrong—it cannot be verified. Under such circumstances, Bell suggests challenging the utility of the thoughts in helping athletes reach their goals. Get the athletes to ask themselves, "Is this thinking in my best interest? Does this thinking help me feel the way I want to or does it make me worry and be tense? Does this thinking help me perform better?" When the athletes realize that thinking certain thoughts can only be detrimental, it becomes sensible, and thus easier, to use the tools of thought stoppage in order to change negative to positive self-statements. Helping athletes identify for themselves the value of these tools creates powerful motivation to use them.

Reframing

An additional technique for dealing with negative self-talk is **reframing**, described by Gauron (1984) as the process of creating alternative frames of reference or different ways of looking at the world. Because the world is literally what we make it, reframing allows us to transform what appears at first to be a weakness or difficulty into a strength or possibility, simply by looking at it from a different point of view. Gauron encourages athletes to cultivate the skill of reframing because it helps athletes control their internal dialogue in a positive, self-enhancing manner. Almost any

self-defeating statement or negative thought can be reframed, or interpreted from a different perspective so that it aids rather than hinders the athlete.

Should an athlete have the self-talk "I'm feeling tense and anxious about playing today," he/she can reframe the statement to "I'm feeling excited and ready." Similarly, an athlete dwelling on the "problems" of improving a skill or the "struggle" of a performance slump can turn these situations to his/her advantage and maintain a positive attitude by focusing on the "possibilities" of achieving a new level of skill and the "opportunity" present in each new performance. An important element of reframing is that it does not deny or downplay what the athlete is experiencing or encourage the athlete to ignore something troublesome. Instead, by reframing the athlete acknowledges what is happening and decides to use it to his/her best advantage.

Identifying Irrational and Distorted Thinking

In addition to dealing with negative self-talk and self-doubt, athletes need to realize that they may also be engaging in cognitive distortions and irrational thinking. According to Ellis (1982), athletes fail to reach their goals and perform below their ability primarily because they accept and endorse self-defeating, irrational beliefs. Ellis identifies four basic irrational beliefs that negatively affect athletes' performance. If athletes accept any of these beliefs (let alone two or three of them) or any of their variations, their progress and satifaction will be blocked. These four irrational beliefs are: (1) I *must* at all time perform outstandingly well, (2) others whom I hold significant to me *have to* approve and love me, (3) everyone has *got to* treat me kindly and fairly, and (4) the conditions of my life, particularly my life in sports, absolutely *must* be arranged so that I get what I want when I want.

Such thinking is counterproductive because it negatively influences self-concept, self-confidence, and performance. Once identified—a task that may take considerable soul-searching—these self-defeating beliefs need to be modified. Following are some irrational thoughts and cognitive distortions that are common among athletes (Gauron, 1984). Also provided are suggestions for modifying such irrational and distorted thinking.

Irrational and Distorted Thinking

Perfection is Essential

Catastrophizing

Worth Depends on Achievement

Personalization

Fallacy of "Fairness"

Blaming

Polarized Thinking

One-Trial Generalizations

Perfection is essential. One of the most debilitating irrational ideas for an athlete is that he/she must be competent and near perfection in everything attempted. No one can consistently achieve perfection. Athletes who believe they should be perfect will blame themselves for every defeat. Their self-concept will likely be lowered and they may start a fear-of-failure syndrome. Further, they will put such pressures upon themselves to do well that both their enjoyment and performance will likely suffer. There is always value in *striving* for perfection, but nothing is gained by *demanding* perfection. The same can be said for the thinking of the coach.

Castastrophizing. Castastrophizing often accompanies perfectionistic tendencies, as the athlete believes that any failure will be a humiliating disaster or that pleasing others (especially friends and parents) is the number one priority. Catastrophizers expect the worst possible thing to happen. Consequently, expecting disaster often leads to disaster! Individuals become plagued by "what ifs." "What if I lose today?" "What if my parents are embarrassed when I strike out?" "How will I ever be able to compete again?"

Perfectionistic thinking and catastrophizing can be combatted by realistic evaluations of the actual situation and the setting of appropriate goals. A careful assessment of the actual odds of success or failure as well as the objective nature of the possible outcomes or consequences is essential.

Worth depends on achievement. Another problem for some athletes is the belief that their worth depends on their achievements. Many young athletes believe that they are only as good as what

they win. Correspondingly, they think they must excel in order to please others. Try asking an athlete or coach to describe who he/she is without mentioning his/her sport or success rate! Athletes must learn to value themselves for more than what they do; worth as a human being is based on factors other than achievement outcome.

Personalization. The concept of personal worth is often linked with the self-defeating tendency to personalize everything. Unfortunately, some athletes believe that every time they walk past a crowd that is laughing, the crowd is laughing at them. Another example is athletes who think only their performance caused a team to lose. This essentially egocentric attitude does little to help foster self-worth and the ability to cope with potentially stressful situations.

Fallacy of fairness and ideal conditions. Some athletes believe they are entitled to fair treatment and ideal conditions. "Fair" is usually a disguise for just wanting one's personal preferences versus what someone else sees as being in the best interests of all concerned. "Ideal conditions" means that coaches should carve out the easiest possible path for athletes to follow. Athletes need to realize that it is irrational to think that things will come easily or that they will not need to be self-disciplined and to work hard. Rarely will athletes achieve any valuable gain without effort, pain, and sacrifice.

Blaming. Any feeling of unfair treatment can also produce blaming or external attributions. Nothing is gained by making excuses and/or assigning faults to others. This type of thinking allows the athletes to abdicate all responsibility—an absolutely nonproductive form of cognition. Athletes must learn to replace external attributions with attributions that are within their control: "Success comes from effort and working hard to develop my full potential, whereas failure comes from lack of effort or insufficient practice of key fundamentals." Athletes often learn their attributions from coaches. If coaches usually blame failure on external factors, athletes will too. This subtly leads athletes to expect failure under similar future circumstances, for example, bad weather, poor officiating. However, if coaches and sport psychologists provide appropriate internal attributions for individual athlete and team successes and failures, they will help athletes eliminate some of their feelings of external control and inappropriate, superstitious thinking. The more athletes realize they are personally responsible for and in control of their performance, the more their confidence will grow after good performance and the more confidence they will have in turning current failures into future successes.

On the other hand, if athletes accept complete responsibility for everything, they may be equally nonproductive. For example, some players are prone to taking sole responsibility for the entire team's performance. "We lost because I missed that last free throw." Accepting such irrational blame can lead to many potential problems, including further irrationalizations: "The coach and my teammates must really hate me." The answer to this kind of irrational thinking lies in helping athletes to be realistic and honest in evaluating performance outcome.

Polarized thinking. **Polarized thinking** is the tendency to view things and people in absolute terms. All-or-nothing thinking can lead an athlete to categorize everything as either successful or unsuccessful, good or bad rather than learning from each and every experience. Such thinking often leads to judgmental **labeling**—the identification or description of something or someone with a single evaluative word or phrase such as "choker," "butterfingers," "airbrain," "loser." Athletes and people who work with athletes need to recognize that such negative labeling is very detrimental because labels are often internalized and become, in a more or less permanent way, a part of self-concept and future expectations. Once established, labels are difficult to erase. Coaches and sport psychologists should instead stress the avoidance of any kind of negative evaluative language, judgmentalism, and absolute thinking. The personal behavior of the coach and sport psychologist should set the example for what they expect from their athletes.

One-trial generalizations. Perhaps the most dangerous cognitive distortions come from one-trial generalizations or superstitions. These are also among the easiest to desensitize. **Overgeneralizations** occur when a single incident causes athletes to link the situation with the out-come. Examples include statements such as "I never swim well in a pool without gutters" and "I can't golf well in the rain." If these conclusions are based on only one or two experiences, then some careful analysis can usually lead athletes to negate them. If they are based on many experiences, then they should merely be used to direct practice to overcome the apparent obstacle to performing well. Practicing under perceived negative conditions until success is achieved will often produce effective evidence to repudiate the initial negative generalization.

Modifying Irrational and Distorted Thinking

Irrational beliefs and distorted thinking often underlie much of the stress and resulting negative thoughts and feelings that athletes experience, both during athletic performance and life in general. Unfortunately, athletes often are unaware that the culprit is maladaptive thinking. Instead they think the circumstance or event caused the deleterious emotional reaction and behavior. For example, a basketball player misses a critical free throw in the final seconds of a game and ends up feeling worthless and fears being put in a similar circumstance in the future. The typical athlete probably thinks his thoughts and anxiety are caused by the missed free throw. In actuality it was the *assumptions* the athlete made about the event. In this case, irrational assumptions such as perfectionism, worth-depends-on-achievement, and/or personalization may have been the culprit.

The coach or sport psychologist can help athletes reduce their self-caused pressure and negativity by getting them to identify and dispute their irrational assumptions. Once these are identified and disputed, athletes can "program" themselves to think differently by substituting more rational self-statements and then practicing them. A substitute for perfectionistic demands might be "Succeeding is satisfying, *but it is human to make mistakes.*" A counter to worth-depends-on-athletic-achievement might be "It's great to be an athlete, *but I'm more than my athletic accomplishments.*" These phrases should be repeated daily until they are believed. Ideally athletes should incorporate one of the physical relaxation techniques discussed in Chapter 15 before repeating the phrase. Once relaxed and repeating the phrase, athletes might want to inhale with the first part of the phrase and exhale with the italicized part of the phrase. That way the key part of the phrase will be paired with when the athlete is most relaxed and thus most receptive to the thought. The phrase should be repeated at least three times with a two-breath-long pause after each repetition.

Less enlightened coaches and athletes might fear that modifying irrational beliefs such as perfectionistic demands and taking excessive responsibility for performance outcome may take the edge off an athlete's competitiveness. In actuality, whatever creates a better balance or puts athletics in the right perspective will usually improve performance by helping athletes stay physically relaxed and more positive in the potentially high-pressure situations that frequently occur in sport competition. To counter doubt about determining whether self-talk and underlying beliefs are rational or irrational, Steinmetz, Blankenship, and Brown (1980) offer the following five criteria:

1. Are the beliefs based on objective reality? That is, would a mixed group of people all agree that the event happened the way you perceived it or, do you exaggerate and personalize experiences?

2. Are they helpful to you? Self-destructive thoughts are usually irrational.

3. Are they useful in reducing conflicts with other people, or do you set up a me-versus-them situation?

4. Do they help you reach your short- and long-term goals, or do they get in the way?

5. Do they reduce emotional conflict, help you feel the way you want to feel?

Helping athletes eliminate irrational thinking and develop more adaptive thoughts will go a long way toward improving performance and, perhaps more important, personal growth.

Constructing Affirmation Statements

Feelings of confidence, efficacy, and personal control will be enhanced if coaches and sport psychologists assist athletes in constructing personal affirmation statements. **Affirmations** are statements that reflect positive attitudes or thoughts about oneself. For example, in 1985 Ivan Lendl had

a record of 9 wins and 12 losses against John McEnroe. Lendl then started writing each day in a notebook, "I look forward to playing John McEnroe." By early 1991 his record against McEnroe had improved to 19 wins and 15 losses, and Lendl had won the last 10 straight matches (Wishful Inking, 1991).

The most effective affirmations are both believable and vivid. They are also often spontaneous and thus capture the feelings of a particularly satisfying and successful experience (Syer & Connolly, 1984). "I am as strong as a bull," "I fly down the finish line," and "I really come through under pressure" are all good examples of positive affirmations. Note that each of these expresses a personal, positive message of something that is happening in the present.

Team slogans can also serve as affirmations: "Winners think they can and they do"; "See it, think it, believe it, do it"; "Say yes to success." Each slogan can become a recipe or formula for success provided it is internalized. As just noted, a good source of affirmations is positive statements that might naturally have occurred with previous successful performance. Another way to build affirmations is to have each athlete make a self-esteem list and a success list (Gauron, 1984). The **self-esteem list** contains all of the athlete's positive attributes—all of his/her perceived assets, strengths, and positive qualities. The **success list** contains all of the athlete's successes thus far. The goal is to use one's own personal history in an enabling way by reviewing, reexperiencing, and visualizing previous success experiences.

The self-esteem and success lists serve to remind the athlete of how capable he/she is and how deserving of being successful. This is not the time for modesty but for honest reflection on all of one's positive qualities and successes. Rushall (1979) has emphasized that once this positive frame of reference is established, the athlete should write specific affirmation statements that are *positive action-oriented* self-statements affirming his/her capabilities and what he/she would like to do. A positive action-oriented affirmation statement might be "I play well under pressure" rather than "I know I can play well under pressure." Affirmations should be in the present tense and worded in a way that avoids perfectionist statements that may be impossible to live up to, such as "I always . . ." or "I never. . . ."

Once formulated, how can these statements be maximally used to foster confidence and the desired goal of the affirmation? Gauron (1984) suggests having a number-one affirmation to work on each day, especially when feeling "bummed" or going into a slump. An athlete may want to write the statement 10 to 20 times each day on a piece of paper or on a card that can be carried around and pulled out and read during free moments. Once the affirmation becomes so integrated into the conscious mind that it is completely believed and made automatically, the athlete can select another affirmation to work on. Other techniques for utilizing affirmations are to post them (singularly or in combination) in places such as one's bedroom, bathroom, or locker. There is also merit in recording affirmations on cassette tape and playing them whenever possible, such as between classes or before going to bed.

Designing Coping and Mastery Self-Talk Tapes

Every individual has the capacity to program his/her mind for successful thoughts. Some athletes do it naturally; others must learn how to be effective thinkers. One very effective method for training the mind to think in a confident, success-oriented way is through the use of mastery and coping audiotapes. These are tapes on which the athlete records his/her own voice describing an outstanding performance where events proceed precisely as desired (mastery tape), and a performance in which the athlete successfully adjusts to, or copes with, a series of potentially distracting obstacles to achieve a desired level of performance (coping tape). Helping athletes design and produce these self-talk tapes is another strategy that coaches and sport psychologists can use to program confidence. According to Bell (1983), confident athletes focus their thoughts and images on coping with the environment and the opponent, on mastering the task, and on the rewards of success rather than worrying and catastrophizing about performing poorly and the consequences of failure. Mastery and coping tapes are tools that allow athletes to practice these specific skills.

To produce a **mastery tape**, an athlete first considers what a perfect performance would be like at his/her present level. Recalling a past great game or great day of competition may help the athlete

get started with this process. It is advisable to get the coach's opinion on what this perfect performance might be like in order to make the resulting tape more believable. Next, the athlete writes out a script describing this perfect performance, recording all of the positive thoughts and phrases that might occur if he/she were actually performing perfectly in a competitive situation that is progressing exactly as the athlete would wish. The concept with the mastery tape is always to be playing perfectly and always to be in complete control of the situation. If feasible, the mastery tape should be approximately the same length as an actual performance. For example, if an athlete is trying to master a perfect routine for free throw shooting in basketball, he/she would want a segment of tape about 15 to 30 seconds long. If the athlete needs to build confidence in the ability to handle time-outs being called before shooting, the tape might be the length of a time-out and include desirable self-talk for both this time and the preparation time before actually shooting.

If it is not feasible to produce a tape as long as the actual performance (as would be the case with many sports), the mastery script should consist of descriptions of important moments occurring throughout the competition, beginning early in the day and proceeding all the way to the end of the competition. For example, a lacrosse player might describe waking up the day of an important game, traveling to the field or stadium, dressing for competition, warming up, the opening face-off, key segments of the first two quarters of play, halftime, more key segments from the second half, and the game's end. At each of these moments, the athlete would describe his/her ideal thoughts, feelings, and emotions, making sure each moment proceeds exactly as desired. The greater the detail provided in these descriptions, the better, as this will enable the "programming" to work more quickly and effectively. Athletes should use sport-specifc terms and include specific descriptions of the weather, how the field or arena looks, how teammates and opponents are dressed, etcetera.

Once the athlete reviews this script with a coach, he/she records it onto an audiotape with a musical background that will help create the desired emotions. When recording the tape, it is important to speak slowly and provide pauses in order to allow the mind time to fully visualize each of the scenes that is described. Listening over and over to a mastery tape rendition of the perfect performance should "program" the conscious and subconscious mind for success by helping the athlete become comfortable with positive statements and associating these statements with his/her own voice and performance.

Since perfect performances are rare and because obstacles and setbacks are likely to occur in even the best of circumstances, producing and listening to a **coping tape** is an effective way of programming the mind to maintain one's confidence and focus in the face of difficulties. Coping tapes should allow the athlete to practice dealing with negative and anxious thoughts and situations. A coping tape is produced similarly to the mastery tape, but instead of imagining a performance in which the circumstances and conditions are perfect, an athlete producing a coping tape would imagine himself/herself in a difficult situation. The situation might be one in which he/she makes a foolish mistake and loses mental or emotional control. The athlete then rehearses the strategies needed to regain control and confidence. This is an excellent opportunity to practice thought stoppage, reframing, or any of the other techniques mentioned in this chapter and in other chapters, such as the arousal control techniques in Chapter 15.

Producing a coping tape requires an athlete to imagine all of the potential problems to be faced and how they might be handled successfully. Concern over such things as practice time, physical conditioning, environmental conditions, performance situations, pressures from other people, lack of sleep, unfriendly officials, and tough competition should all be considered. The coping tape includes a description of the negative situations and initial negative self-talk followed by rehearsal of an appropriate strategy and self-statements for dealing effectively with the situation(s) and feeling an optimal arousal level. It should be stressed that the emphasis on a coping tape is not on the stressful or distracting situation described but on the process by which the athlete regains control and confidence when confronted with these situations. At the conclusion of each segment of a coping tape, the athlete should feel that the situation has been resolved and that he/she is once again in complete control.

Listening over and over to this type of situational description and coping self-talk will help create a sense of well-being because if the same situations occur in real life, the athlete will already have practiced coping with them successfully. Once the athlete learns the skill of imagery, he/she can listen to the tape and actually visualize himself/herself successfully coping with what is described on the tape. Further guidelines on producing and using mastery and coping tapes are provided by Rotella, Malone, and Ojala (1985).

Summary

There is a direct correlation between self-confidence and success. Confident athletes think about themselves and the action at hand in a different way than those who lack confidence. The difference is that the confident athlete's self-talk and internal imagery are consistently positive and enthusiastic. The positive thinking of confident athletes is likely to lead to enabling feelings and good performance, just as the inappropriate or misguided thinking of athletes lacking in confidence is likely to lead to negative feelings and poor performance. Athletes can learn to use self-talk to build confidence and to facilitate learning and performance. The first step in an athlete's gaining control of thinking is to monitor self-talk to become aware of what kind of thinking helps, what thoughts are occurring that appear to be harmful, and what situations or events are associated with the talk. Three of the most effective tools for identifying self-talk are retrospection, imagery, and keeping a self-talk log.

Once awareness of self-talk and feelings is heightened, particularly of negative talk, the coach or sport psychologist can instruct the athlete in how to start dealing with these thoughts. Techniques such as thought stoppage, changing negative thoughts to positive thoughts, countering, reframing of irrational and distorted thinking, and constructing affirmation statements are possible tools for producing performance enhancing thoughts and eliminating disabling thoughts.

Using these tools will require an investment of time and faith on the part of the athlete, and there is no guarantee that immediate improvements will result. As with any other training method that truly enhances performance, the results of training the mind to think effectively will emerge gradually, in precise correlation to the athlete's persistence and commitment. Some athletes may be hesitant to take this step, just as there are athletes who do not use recent innovations in strength, endurance, and skill training. However, the athletes who do invest that persistence and commitment to improving their self-talk will find their efforts well rewarded.

Study Questions

1. Describe how the self-talk of a successful athlete is different from that of an unsuccessful athlete. Give five examples of the self-talk from each.

2. What is the relationship between (a) self-talk and self-esteem and (b) self-confidence and self-efficacy?

3. Name and describe the six uses for self-talk. Using any sport setting, provide an example of each.

4. Describe and give an example of the three techniques suggested for becoming more aware of one's self-talk.

5. Describe how a coach or sport psychologist might help athletes use the techniques of thought stoppage and changing negative thoughts to positive thoughts.

6. How does countering a negative self-statement differ from reframing? Give examples of both in response to the statement "I'm always getting beaten on my opponent's first serve."

7. List eight types of irrational and distorted thinking. According to Ellis, which types are particularly common for athletes? What might a coach or sport psychologist do to help an athlete modify his/her irrational and distorted thinking?

8. What are the guidelines for writing and repeating affirmations?

9. How does a mastery tape help an athlete develope appropriate self-talk?

10. What is the purpose of a coping audiotape, and how is this purpose accomplished?

References

Bandura, A. (1977). Self efficacy: Toward a unifying theory of behavior change. *Psychological Review, 8,* 191–215.

Bell, K. F. (1983). *Championship thinking: The athlete's guide to winning performance in all sports.* Englewood Cliffs, N.J.: Prentice-Hall.

Bunker, L. K., & Rotella, R. J. (1982). *Mind, set and match.* Englewood Cliffs, N.J.: Prentice-Hall.

Cautela, J. R., & Wisocki, P. A. (1977). Thought stoppage procedure: Description, application and learning theory interpretations. *Psychological Record, 27,* 255–264.

Dorsel, T. (1988). Talk to yourself: Realistic self-talk means less stress on the course. *Australian Golf Digest, 49,* 46–47.

Ellis, A. (1982). Self-direction in sport and life. In T. Orlick, J. Partington, & J. Salmela (Eds.), *Mental training for coaches and athletes* (pp. 10–17). Ottawa, Ont.: Coaching Association of Canada.

Ellis, A. (1988). Can we legitimately evaluate ourselves? *Psychotherapy Theory, Research and Practice, 25,* 314–316.

Ellis, A., & Dryden, W. (1987). *The practice of rational emotive therapy.* New York: Springer.

Finn, J. (1985). Competitive excellence: It's a matter of mind and body. *Physician and Sports Medicine, 13,* 61–72.

Gallwey, W. T. (1974). *The inner game of tennis.* New York: Random House.

Gauron, E. F. (1984). *Mental training for peak performance.* Lansing, N.Y.: Sport Science Associates.

Gould, D., Hodge, K., Peterson, K., & Gianni, J. (1989). An exploratory examination of strategies used by elite coaches to enhance self-efficacy in athletes. *Journal of Sport and Exercise Psychology, 11,* 128–140.

Grieger, R., & Boyd, J. (1980). *Rational emotive therapy.* New York: Van Nostrand.

Harris, D. V., & Harris, B. L. (1984). *The athlete's guide to sports psychology: Mental skills for physical people.* West Point, N.Y.: Leisure Press.

Hay, L. (1984). *You can heal your life.* Santa Monica, Calif.: Hay House.

Heyman, S. R., & Rose, K. G. (1980). Psychological variables affecting SCUBA performance: A reconsideration of methodological questions and data. *Journal of Sport Psychology, 4,* 295–300.

Ieleva, L., & Orlick, T. (1991). Mental links to enhanced healing: An exploratory study. *The Sport Psychologist, 5,* 25–40.

Kendall, G., Hrycaiko, D., Martin, G., & Kendall, T. (1990). Effects of an imagery rehearsal, relaxation, and self-talk package on basketball game performance. *Journal of Sport and Exercise Psychology, 12,* 157–166.

Mahoney, M. J. (1979). Cognitive skills and athletic performance. In P. C. Kendall & S. D. Hollon (Eds.), *Cognitive-behavioral interventions: Theory, research and procedure.* New York: Academic Press.

Mahoney, M. J., Gabriel, T. J., & Perkins, T. S. (1987). Psychological skills and exceptional athletic performance. *The Sport Psychologist, 1,* 181–199.

Meichenbaum, D. (1975). Toward a cognitive theory of self-control. In G. Schwartz & D. Shapiro (Eds.), *Consciousness and self-regulation: Advances in research.* New York: Plenum.

Meichenbaum, D. (1977). *Cognitive behavior modification: An integrative approach.* New York: Plenum.

Meyers, A. W., Cooke, C. J., Cullen, J., & Liles, L. (1979). Psychological aspects of athletic competitors: A replication across sports. *Cognitive Therapy and Research, 3,* 361–366.

Meyers, A. W., & Schleser, R. A. (1980). A cognitive behavioral intervention for improving basketball performance. *Journal of Sport Psychology, 2,* 69–73.

Owens, D., & Bunker, L. K. (1989). *Golf: Steps to success.* Champaign, Ill.: Human Kinetics.

Rosin, L., & Nelson, W. (1983). The effects of rational and irrational self-verbalizations on performance efficiency and levels of anxiety. *Journal of Clinical Psychology, 39,* 208–213.

Rotella, R. (1984). Untitled manuscript. University of Virginia. Charlottesville.

Rotella, R. J., & Bunker, L. K. (1981). *Mind mastery for winning golf.* Englewood Cliffs, N.J.: Prentice-Hall.

Rotella, R. J., Gansneder, B., Ojala, D., & Billing, J. (1980). Cognitions and coping strategies of elite skiers—an exploratory study of young developing athletes. *Journal of Sport Psychology, 1,* 350–354.

Rotella, R. J., Malone, C., & Ojala, D. (1985). Facilitating athletic performance through the use of mastery and coping tapes. In L. K. Bunker, R. J. Rotella, & A. S. Reilly (Eds.), *Sport psychology: Psychological considerations in maximizing sport performance.* Ithaca, N.Y.: Mouvement Publications.

Rushall, B. S. (1979). *Psyching in sports.* London: Pelham.

Seligman, M. (1991). *Learned optimism.* New York: Knopf.

Silva, J. (1982). Performance enhancement through cognitive intervention. *Behavioral Modification, 6,* 443–463.

Steinmetz, J., Blakenship, J., & Brown, L. (1980). *Managing stress before it manages you.* Palo Alto, Calif.: Bull.

Syer, J., & Connolly, C. (1984). *Sporting body sporting mind: An athlete's guide to mental training.* New York: Cambridge University Press.

Weinberg, R. S., Gould, D., & Jackson, A. (1979). Expectations and performance: An empirical test of Bandura's self-efficacy theory. *Journal of Sport Psychology, 3,* 320–331.

Weinberg, R. S., Gould D., Yukelson, D., & Jackson, A. (1981). The effects of pre-existing and manipulated self-efficacy on a competitive muscular endurance task. *Journal of Sport Psychology, 3,* 345–354.

Wishful Inking (January, 1991). *Special Report: On Sports,* p. 24.

Chapter 18

Concentration and Attention Control Training

Robert M. Nideffer, *President, Enhanced Performance Systems*

*T*he ability to control thought processes, to *concentrate* on a task (e.g., to "keep your eye on the ball") is almost universally recognized as the most important key to effective performance in sport. Mental control is typically viewed as the deciding factor in competition in both individual and team sports. In spite of the tremendous importance of concentration to performance, very little has been done either to define concentration or to systematically train athletes to concentrate more effectively.

One of the major roles of sport psychologists in the future will be to define "operationally" constructs such as concentration and arousal for both coaches and athletes. This chapter represents the beginning of the process. Only by operationally defining these concepts can we reach the point of being able to test scientifically our knowledge and the validity and utility of our training and counseling techniques. To define concentration operationally, we must define what it is behaviorally. In addition, we must begin to define those factors or conditions that affect the ability to concentrate. We must describe the conditions that affect concentration, and we must predict the behavioral effects (e.g., what specifically will happen to the ability to concentrate and to one's behavior or performance as a consequence).

Attention control training (ACT) is more than a technique (e.g., centering). It is a complex process that is theoretically based and involves: (1) assessment of attentional strengths and weaknesses; (2) assessment of the attentional demands of a given sport; (3) the assessment of situational and/or personal characteristics that are likely to affect arousal for an individual, and/or to dictate his/her behavior under pressure; (4) identification of situation specific problem areas and error patterns, and; (5) development of an intervention program. Although the training procedures are based on operational constructs, considerable research still needs to be conducted to evaluate and refine further both the attentional constructs and the training procedures.

Operationally Defining Concentration

How many times have you heard someone say, "Concentrate" or "Don't choke" and wondered just what that person was telling you to do or not do? When a coach tells an athlete to pay attention to the game, what is the coach really saying? Very often it isn't just the athlete who is confused; many coaches cannot even tell you what they mean. If they are asked for a definition of concentration, they sometimes get defensive. The thought of explicitly and behaviorally defining just what one should attend to does not seem to occur. Most coaches simply assume that an athlete is concentrating effectively if he/she is winning. Likewise, they assume that concentration is ineffective if performance is below their expectations. It is small wonder that it takes most people a very long time to develop good concentration skills and consistent performance under pressure! How can coaches possibly teach something that they have not thought about enough even to define?

In the next section we present a summary of the hypothetical principles that underlie attention control training. These principles begin the process of behaviorally and operationally defining concentration in sport.

Attention Control Training

The eight principles that underlie ACT are outlined here and elaborated upon in the subsections that follow.

1.   Athletes need to be able to engage in at least four different types of attention.

2.   Different sport situations will make different attentional demands on an athlete. Accordingly, it is incumbent upon the athlete to be able to shift to different types of concentration to match changing attentional demands.

3.   Under optimal conditions the average person can meet the attentional demands of most sport situations.

4.   Attentional characteristics are at times trait-like, having predictive utility across situations. At other times they are state-like, situationally determined and/or modifiable through training. Factors that determine the extent to which a given individual's attentional abilities are trait-like include biological and/or genetic predispositions and alterations in arousal. As arousal moves out of the "moderate range," the habit strength of the individual's more dominant attentional focus or style increases (Hull, 1951). Thus,

the individual's dominant attentional style becomes more trait-like and more predictive of behavior within a given situation.

5.   The individual's ability to perform effectively as the dominant attentional style becomes more trait-like depends upon two factors: (1) the appropriateness of his/her dominant attentional style and (2) the level of confidence he/she has within the particular performance situation (Carver & Scheier, 1989).

6.   The phenomenon of "choking," of having performance progressively deteriorate, occurs as physiological arousal continues to increase to the point of causing an involuntary narrowing of an athlete's concentration and to the point of causing attention to become more internally focused. This results in alterations in perception (time is speeded up) and interference with weight transfer, which affects the athlete's timing and coordination.

7.   Alterations in physiological arousal affect concentration. Thus, the systematic manipulation of physiological arousal is one way of gaining some control over concentration.

8.   Alterations in the focus of attention will affect physiological arousal. Thus, the systematic manipulation of concentration is one way to gain some control over arousal (e.g., muscular tension levels, heart rate, respiration rate).

Different Types of Concentration

When a coach tells an athlete to concentrate, the athlete is more likely to respond to the instruction if the coach specifically defines the type of concentration that he/she would like the athlete to engage in. To do this, it is necessary to think of attention as requiring at least two different types of focus. First, the athlete will need to control the *width* of his/her attentional focus. Certain sport situations require a fairly broad focus of attention because the athlete must be sensitive to several different cues. Other sport situations require a narrower type of concentration. Hitting a baseball, for example, requires a very narrow type of concentration. The second type of focus that needs to be controlled relates to the *direction* of the athlete's attention. In some situations, attention must be directed *internally* toward the athlete's own feelings and/or thoughts. At other times, attention must be focused *externally*, on the opponent, the ball, etcetera. Figure 18-1 presents the four different types of concentration that are required by different sport situations and that result when both width and direction of attention are controlled.

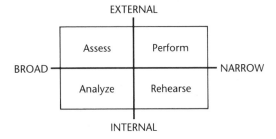

Figure 18-1 **Dimensions of attention**

Shifting Attention

Recall the second principle underlying attention control training: Different sport situations make different attentional demands on athletes. Thus, a position such as quarterback in football places a greater demand on an athlete to be able to develop a broad-external focus of attention (e.g., to be aware of the entire field) than a position such as guard, which requires a narrower type of concentration (e.g., to block a particular athlete on the other team). Beyond this difference, however, there are demands for shifting attention within a particular sport. An example from golf will illustrate the point.

When golfers step up to the ball prior to hitting a shot, they start off with a fairly broad-external type of attention. Golfers need to take in several different kinds of information. They need to be aware of the placement of hazards (trees, sand traps, out-of-bounds markers, water, etc.) and course conditions (dryness of the grass, amount and direction of wind). Once they have gathered this external information, golfers shift attention to a broad-internal focus to plan their shot. At this time, they should try to recall past similar situations, remembering how they played them and what the results were. Then they must think about any changes they may have made in the meantime, changes that might modify how they should now play this similar situation (e.g., have they changed their swing, gotten new clubs; are they in a different tactical position such as needing to be conservative or to take a risk). Analyzing all of this information allows golfers to select a particular club and to determine how they want to hit the ball.

Once golfers have formulated a plan, they shift to a narrow-internal type of concentration to monitor their own tension (e.g., making sure they are not too tight or too relaxed) and mentally rehearse the shot. They may picture in their mind what they want to feel and see as they execute the shot. Finally, golfers shift attention to a narrow-external focus as they address the ball and begin their backswing. At this time concentration is on the ball; to attend to other external or internal cues would only interfere with their execution of the shot.

This basic model can be applied to a great many sports. Thus, athletes are continually required to shift attention across the different dimensions listed even though some sports require more of one type of attention than others. In addition, in some sport situations coaches and/or other athletes can make up for attentional deficiencies of some players. As an illustration, in football the coach can select the plays for the quarterback. This limits the need for the quarterback to be able to develop a broad-internal type of attention.

It is essential during physical instruction and practice that coaches communicate to their athletes what type of concentration is appropriate. Then, when the coach tells an athlete to concentrate, the athlete will at least know what is expected. This knowledge, combined with attention control training, will lead to better concentration.

Individual Differences

The third and fourth principles underlying attention control training deal with an individual's ability to shift attention. The third principle indicates that if individuals are appropriately motivated and trained and if they have control over their level of arousal (so that it is neither too high nor too low), they are capable of effective concentration. They can control the width and direction of attention enough to be effective. The actual attentional demands of most sports are not so extreme that the average person cannot meet them! This means that there is hope for most athletes.

At the same time, the fourth principle indicates that it will be easier for some athletes to meet a given sport's attentional demands than for others. Just as we are willing to concede that there are physiological and biological differences among athletes, we should be willing to concede that there are attentional differences. As mentioned earlier, some of the differences seem to be learned (e.g., the result of social and environmental factors), whereas others seem to be genetic and/or biological. Research on attentional processes suggests the following differences, among others.

1. Different individuals have different capacities for developing a broad-internal type of attention. Thus, some individuals are better suited to analyzing large amounts of information than others.

2. Certain individuals appear to be more sensitive to environmental (external) information than others. The former read and react to other people more effectively.

3. Some individuals are more capable of developing a narrow, nondistractible type of attention.

Some superstars in sport seem to have been born for their particular event. There are sprinters with more fast-twitch muscle fibers than most other people, divers with a greater kinesthetic awareness, and so on. Likewise, some athletes are more attentionally suited to their sport. Their ability to focus narrowly makes it easier for them to be "dedicated" to follow through on a task, to be as selfish as they must be to make it to the top. Some athletes have the ability to deal with a great deal of information and not become overloaded and confused; this helps them to be more resistant to pressure and makes it easier for them to perform in critical situations.

Although a small percentage of the world's athletes may indeed have been born dedicated and resistant to choking, the majority have to learn to focus attention in order to achieve these goals. An increasingly important role for the sport psychologist and coach will be assisting athletes in recognizing the attentional demands of their sports, as well as helping athletes identify their own relative attentional strengths and weaknesses. The system-

atic assessment of attentional abilities and of the ability to shift from one type of attention to another will play a major role in the development of training programs. This assessment will aid the majority of athletes in developing concentration skills and/or compensating for any attentional problems they may have. Early attempts at this type of assessment have already begun and are listed in the references at the end of this chapter.

Playing to One's Attentional Strength

The fifth principle underlying attention control training indicates that athletes have a tendency to play to their strengths as pressure increases. This is true of almost all of us. We have an unerring capacity to become our own worst enemies, to turn what are normally strengths into weaknesses. For example, outgoing people who are normally appreciated because they also have enough sensitivity to know when to leave other people alone occasionally lose their sensitivity and become pests.

There is an unproven assumption in sport that good coaches do not make good athletes and vice versa. If this is true, one of the reasons might be that coaching makes a very heavy demand on an individual to be able to think and analyze. Coaches must be able to develop a broad-internal type of attention. In contrast, many sporting situations require athletes to shut off their analyzing. If they do not, we see the "paralysis by analysis" that coaches are so fond of talking about. The athletes think too much and fail to react to the sport situation. They are "in their head" at an inappropriate time. Athletes who ultimately become coaches are often the ones who were continually analyzing; they are not the brilliant broken field runners who reacted instinctively.

Take the pressure off most coaches and athletes and they can be either analytical or instinctive. Put them under pressure, however, and they play to their strengths. Analytical coaches become *too* analytical. They go inside their head and lose sensitivity to the athletes and the game situation. Often they attempt to communicate their analysis to the athletes, overloading them with information, getting them to think too much.

Instinctive athletes have a tendency to react too quickly. They may fail to analyze and plan when they need to. They lose their capacity to make adjustments, getting faked out by the same moves time and time again, not learning from their own mistakes. If arousal reaches the point of causing narrowing of attention and of increasing internal distractions, then the athletes' ability to process information deteriorates. At this time, coaches should be minimizing the amount of information that they are giving their athletes. The coaches should be providing as much structure and support as possible. If coaches are playing to their own strength, they fail. Instead of calling the play for their athletes, unsuccessful coaches ask the athletes what they think or give them several possibilities.

Another role of sport psychologists is to "team build" with coaches and athletes to get them to maintain effective communication under pressure. Sport psychologists do this by sensitizing coaches and athletes to their own and others' relative strengths and weaknesses. Sport psychologists help coaches and athletes identify the specific situations in which communication is likely to break down and help them plan alternative ways to behave. When no sport psychologist is available to help, coaches need to be sufficiently knowledgeable and aware to do this on their own.

As an example of the team-building process, consider a situation in which a coach tends to be more analytical and more assertive than the athletes (a normally ideal situation). As pressure increases, the coach becomes more analytical and more assertive and the athletes less so. At a certain point the athletes should be confronting the coach with the fact that they are being overloaded with instructions; they may behave in an even more outwardly compliant way, nodding their head to show agreement even when they are not hearing or when they are confused. The coach, thinking that he/she has a willing, even enthusiastic audience, feels encouraged to give still more information. The sport psychologist helps the athletes recognize their feelings of confusion and provides them with the support they need to confront the coach. Then all work together to develop ways of minimizing the problem. Perhaps insight is all the coach needs to decrease the amount of information he/she gives. Perhaps the coach's insight and an initial confrontation with the coach (e.g., "Coach, I can't take all of this right now") will provide all the encouragement the athletes need to be able to be honest with the coach in the future. The sport psychologist can usually give the coach suggestions for communicating the same information in a more simplified and structured way.

Operationally Defining Choking

Before we can examine the sixth principle underlying attention control training, we must define operationally the term **choking**. (Unfortunately, there is little agreement between most coaches and athletes regarding the definition of as critical a term as "choking." Thus, when a coach tells an athlete not to choke, the athlete may have no idea of what he/she is supposed to avoid.)

Given what we do know about the interaction between thought process (what we attend to) and physiological process, it is possible to come up with a definition of "choking" that can be very useful to coaches, athletes, sport psychology practitioners, and researchers alike.

Behaviorally, we can infer that athletes are choking when their performance seems to be progressively deteriorating and when they seem incapable of regaining control over performance on their own, that is, without some outside assistance—for example, the baseball player who follows a bobbled catch with a throwing error, or the diver or gymnast who lets an early mistake (e.g., on a dive or particular move) upset him/her to the point of making additional errors on other maneuvers.

Figure 18-2 illustrates the interaction that occurs between physiological and attentional processes under highly stressful conditions. The figure also shows how the changes that occur affect performance. By using Figure 18-2 and the section that follows, coaches should gain a more useful understanding of the choking process—an understanding that can help increase their ability to understand, predict, and control behavior in sport situations.

Prevention and Treatment of Choking

The seventh and eighth principles underlying attention control training suggest that by creating changes in what is going on either physiologically or attentionally, athletes can break the downward spiral associated with choking. Thus, if they eliminate the physical feelings associated with excessive tension (tight muscles, pounding heart), they will reduce the number of attentional distractors and improve their ability' to concentrate. Likewise, if coaches can get the athletes to either ignore or reinterpret their physical feelings (e.g., if they give a positive interpretation to being aroused, such as

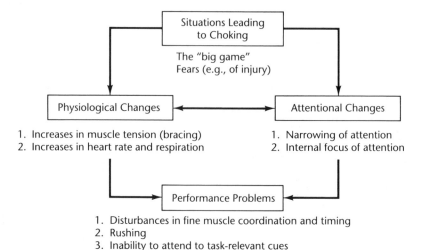

Figure 18-2 **Interaction between physiological and attentional processes under higly stressful conditions**

"I'm ready"), gradually the physical changes will be reduced and tension levels and heart rate will return to "normal" for the competitive conditions.

Under ideal conditions, we would be able to prevent choking from ever occurring. One of the unrealistic goals of many sport psychology programs is to prevent choking by teaching athletes some type of relaxation and/or rehearsal procedure. In truth, we probably can reduce the frequency of choking through better training and through some type of relaxation and rehearsal process. We can reduce the tendency to choke, but we cannot eliminate it. In addition, we are likely to be successful only if our program has a performance-specific focus. That is, we should teach the athletes to use the relaxation at a particular time (e.g., at bat) and we should train them to rehearse a particular performance situation (e.g., hitting under certain conditions).

By teaching athletes to relax, to monitor their own muscle tension levels, and to use their tension levels as a signal to employ some brief type of relaxation procedure, we can help them improve the consistency of their performance. By getting them to mentally simulate anticipated performance conditions and to systematically rehearse what they

will see and feel, we can begin to desensitize them, to reduce the newness of the experience, and to increase the likelihood that tension will not reach a level that will cause them to choke.

With a specific training focus we can reduce the frequency of choking and "season" athletes more quickly. Simulation and rehearsal can make up for some lack of experience. Nevertheless, there will always be unanticipated situations that we could not prepare for. If we tried to think of every contingency, we would overload ourselves and never make any progress. As a result, we must being to train athletes to recover quickly from the unexpected. Learning to recover once tension has already gotten out of control or once a mistake has been made is even more critical than trying to eliminate choking altogether.

Process Versus Outcome

Once athletes have made a mistake or once they become aware of the tension and the attentional distractions that are likely to interfere with performance, what they attend to becomes critical. In the prevention strategy discussed above, emphasis is placed on training the athlete to recognize and reduce physical tension, thereby improving concentration. Once mistakes have been made, however, many athletes find it difficult to directly challenge what is going on in their bodies.

Imagine a situation in which you have just double-faulted away a game in a critical tennis match. You know you are tight and you try to counter it by saying, "It's all right, just relax; the game isn't that important anyway," and a little voice inside of you immediately counters with, "Oh yes it is, you blew it, you can't do it."

Your lack of confidence created by the feelings and the failure causes you to doubt your own ability. Attempting to pick yourself up by your bootstraps, to take control directly, only creates more distractions and frustration. If you had a great deal of confidence in yourself, you could do that. You could challenge and confront yourself, using your frustration and anger to help you concentrate on the task. When you lack confidence, however, you must focus your attention on something else. You must become "process"-focused rather than "outcome"-focused.

During practice, especially in sports that require a great deal of training and sacrifice on the part of the athlete, individuals motivate themselves by thinking about outcome: "If we win the championship, I'll be a hero." "I am working this hard because I want to win a gold medal." "By making these sacrifices I can get the recognition and financial rewards I want." Once the competition begins, however, an outcome focus can become very negative.

To be thinking about how important the outcome of a contest is or about what one can win or lose during the actual competition typically generates additional physical and attentional changes that interfere with performance. One of the biggest contributors to choking is thinking about the outcome or the importance of a contest while involved in it. To help athletes break out of this thinking, sport psychologists are training them to recognize their tendency toward placing too much importance on outcome (during the competition) and to use those thoughts, when they occur, as signals to attend to "process." Coaches need to do the same thing. **Process cues** are related to the *process* of performing as opposed to the outcome. For example, swimmers might attend to some technical aspect of their stroke or the feeling of their body moving through the water. Often the focus is on

generating a rhythm. Over time, people learn that if they maintain this type of focus, the outcome will take care of itself. Then, as they have success and as confidence builds, they can begin to attend to outcome in order to motivate themselves to try harder. Thus, the athlete who has a lot of success and who becomes a little lazy or too relaxed needs to think about outcome to get the arousal up and to keep going.

The Process of Attention Control Training

In ACT, assessment of the athlete is an ongoing process. That process begins with administration of the Test of Attentional and Interpersonal Style (TAIS), whether there is a specific reason for referral or not (Nideffer, 1976). A description of the attentional and interpersonal characteristics measured by the TAIS is provided in Table 18-1. The TAIS is administered in advance of the training program, to both the coach and athlete. Subjects are told the instrument measures the attentional and interpersonal characteristics that are important determinants of performance and that information from the TAIS will be used to help design a training program. At this point, no attempt is made to control the subjects' response set (e.g., to ask them to respond in a sport-specific way, or to give them a comparison group).

Typically, subjects do not receive a formal report based on TAIS scores. Instead, information from the TAIS is used in the following ways: (1) It can help the workshop leader understand some of the factors that may be contributing to an already identified problem or, if a problem has not been identified, to provide direction for the trainer. Score patterns indicate areas of possible concern helping to focus interview questions and behavioral observations; (2) Information from the TAIS is used in the design of a training program and to provide an educational focus for the subject.

Scores on the TAIS for two different athletes are presented in Figure 18-3 and Figure 18-4. The individual whose scores are presented in Figure 18-3 (Pat) is a baseball player on a AAA team. This athlete was referred by the coach because of a particular problem. The athlete whose scores are presented in Figure 18-4 (Steve) is one of the best junior tennis players in the world. He participated

Table 18-1 **Test of Attentional and Interpersonal Style Scales**

Scale	Scale Description
BET	*Broad External Attention:* High scores indicate good environmental awareness and assessment skills ("street sense").
OET	*Overloaded by External Information:* High scores are associated with errors because attention is inappropriately focused on irrelevant external stimuli.
BIT	*Broad Internal Attention:* High scores indicate good analytical planning skills.
OIT	*Overloaded by Internal Information:* High scores are associated with errors due to distractions from irrelevant internal sources (e.g., thoughts and feelings).
NAR	*Narrow-Focused Attention:* High scores indicate the ability to remain task-oriented, to avoid distractions, and to stay focused on a single job.
RED	*Reduced Attention:* High scores are associated with errors due to a failure to shift attention from an external focus to an internal one, or vice versa.
INFP	*Information Processing:* High scores are associated with a desire for and enjoyment of a diversity of activity.
BCON	*Behavior Control:* High scores are associated with an increased likelihood of "acting out" in impulsive ways and/or a tendency to establish one's own rules rather than strictly adhering to the rules of others.
CON	*Interpersonal Control:* High scores are associated with both needing to be in control in interpersonal situations and with actually being in control.
SES	*Self-Esteem:* High scores are associated with feelings of self-worth and self-confidence.
P/O	*Physical Orientation:* High scores are associated with having been physically competitive and with the enjoyment of competitive activities.
OBS	*Obsessive:* This scale reflects speed of decision making, worry, and anxiety. High scores are associated with increased worry and difficulty making decisions.
EXT	*Extroversion:* High scores indicate an enjoyment of social involvements and a tendency to assume leadership in social situations.
INT	*Introversion:* High scores indicate a need for personal space and privacy.
IEX	*Intellectual Expression:* High scores indicate a willingness to express thoughts and ideas in front of others.
NAE	*Negative Affect Expression:* High scores indicate a willingness to confront issues, to set limits on others, and to express anger.
PAE	*Positive Affect Expression:* High scores indicate a willingness to express support and encouragement to others.
DEP	*Depression:* A high score is associated with situational (transient) depression.

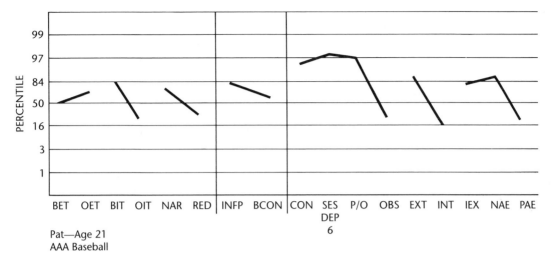

Figure 18-3 Pat's test of attention and interpersonal style (TAIS)

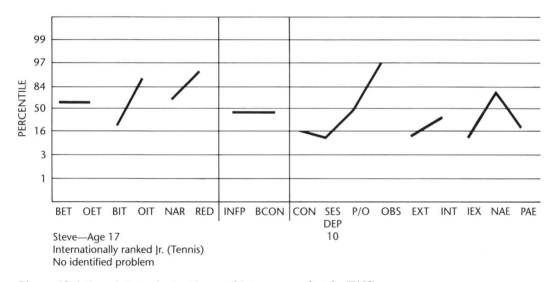

Figure 18-4 Steve's test of attention and interpersonal style (TAIS)

in a three-day ACT program for tennis players and at the outset of the program had no identified problem. Training programs differ when there are and are not specific problems or reasons for referral. By discussing the two cases separately, I can highlight those differences.

Case 1

Pat (see Figure 18-3) was described by his coach as a super kid. He has a great attitude, loves baseball and is all hustle. He tries harder than any other two kids on the team. Lately, his hitting has dropped off, particularly in situations where there are runners on the bases. He's trying too hard and it's affecting his confidence, though he says it isn't. I keep telling him to relax, but he can't seem to do it.

The coach had spoken to Pat about talking to "an expert on concentration," and Pat was eager to cooperate. He knew that he wasn't performing as well as he or the coach wanted in big situations. The coach gave him a copy of TAIS and asked him to complete it and to mail it to me. Arrangements were then made for me to spend three days with Pat and the coach during spring training.

I met briefly with both of them, explaining that to be helpful I needed to observe Pat in a game situation. In this meeting I emphasized my desire to help and at the same time attempted to subtly increase the pressure Pat was feeling by letting him know that I would be analyzing him. I wanted to create additional stress, so I could consensually validate the problem the coach had identified and so I could see for myself the physical consequences of "trying too hard."

Looking at Pat's TAIS profile had given me some insight into the types of problems that might be occurring:

1. The general attentional profile was that of an effective, analytical athlete who might become too analytical under pressure.

2. Pat's high need for control (CON), high level of self esteem (SES), and high score on the physical orientation scale (P/O) all indicated a high need to achieve. Thus, arousal would be likely to increase in any situation where Pat was not performing at the level he expected of himself.

3. A high score on the negative affect expression scale (NAE) combined with his high scores on control and self-esteem suggested Pat could become "his own worst enemy." Frustration at not performing well would be likely to lead to anger, which could cause him to tighten up and behave impulsively from time to time.

Observation session one. The game provided partial support for the information provided by the TAIS and the coach's reason for referral. Throughout the game Pat was enthusiastic and supportive of his team. He hustled and seemed to be a positive

force. At bat, however, the pressure he was feeling was obvious. In his first at bat he swung at the first pitch (a ball that was high), fouling out to the catcher. He knew he shouldn't have swung at the pitch and returned to the dugout mumbling about his stupidity.

In his second at bat there was no one on the bases. He concentrated a little better, waiting for "his pitch." He got on base with a walk. In his third at bat there was a runner on first. As Pat stepped into the batter's box, the tension in his neck and shoulder seemed much more noticeable. He continually moved his head and shoulders, trying to release some of the tension. He took the first pitch for a called strike (the third base coach had told him to take the pitch), and that increased the tension. He swung at the next pitch, a fast ball on the outside corner, but was very late. Then, he jumped at a pitch that was high and out of the strike zone.

Education session one. The opportunity to observe Pat in an actual playing situation was important for two reasons: (1) It served as another form of assessment, helping to consensually validate information gained through testing and from the coach; and (2) It provided Pat and me with a shared experience. Now I could use Pat's own behavior to make the points I wanted to make about the relationship between concentration, arousal, and performance. When talking about scores on the TAIS (e.g., the tendency to become angry in Pat's case), I could relate them directly to things observed in the game.

To facilitate the education process and to further validate the information already gained from the referral, the TAIS, and behavioral observations, I provide subjects with an ACT workbook that is sport-specific (Nideffer, 1989). There are several specific goals I hope to accomplish through education:

1. I make the subjects aware of the attentional requirements of their sport and of their own attentional strengths and weaknesses. This is accomplished through the use of the Inventory of Concentration and Communication Skills (ICCS) contained in the workbook. The subjects are asked a series of 15 questions relating to the four different attentional styles and to the different types of attentional distractions that can occur. In responding to the questions they are asked to answer each item as "it relates to your particular sport" and to compare themselves to "the average athlete you com-

pete against." Examples would include: "I am more capable of narrowing my attention, of shutting out distractions under pressure, of focusing my concentration on one thing, than ___% of the athletes I know." "___ % of my mistakes due to external distractions occur because I get bored (e.g., stare at other players, fans, etc.)." "___% of my mistakes occur because I get angry (e.g., at a call or opponent) and lose concentration." "___% of my mistakes due to external distractions occur because I rush my performance, failing to set up properly (e.g., getting pressured by my opponent's move)."

2. I teach athletes about the relationship between focus of attention, physiological arousal, and performance. My examples become highly situation-specific based on actual behavioral observations. To make sure the information is being absorbed, the athletes are asked to fill in a table like that shown in 18-2.

Pat's chart (Table 18-2) is instructive because he has identified two problems or responses to the pressure he feels. First, he's aware of tightening up. That's important because his awareness can be-

come a cue signaling him to use arousal control strategies. His thoughts at these times will also serve as cues. Not only does the awareness of a change in tension tell Pat he needs to make adjustments, but he's been able to identify those areas of tension that are most important to him (e.g., grip on the bat). He believes if he can relax his grip a little, the rest of his body will relax as well.

To this point, Pat's attempts to give himself instructions have served as distractors, keeping him from attending to the ball. He can't be in his head, consciously giving himself instructions, trying to problem solve, and attend to the release of the ball at the same time. In addition, many of his instructions are negative (e.g., "Don't blow it"), making him tentative or defensive. The end result is that he reacts too slowly and when he swings his weight is on his back foot. If he were more aggressive and his timing was on, there would be a transfer of weight from his back foot to his front foot as his bat makes contact with the ball.

In a game, when Pat finds himself being tentative and thinking too much, he gets angry and jumps from one problem to another. Anger makes him too aggressive; he rushes and swings early. His

Table 18-2 Observation of Case 1 Problem Response Patterns

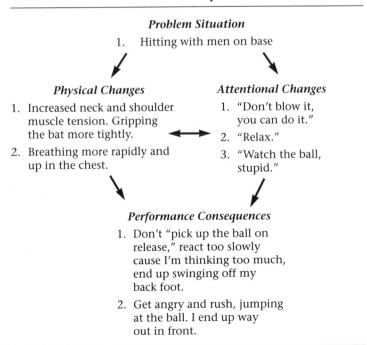

Problem Situation
1. Hitting with men on base

Physical Changes
1. Increased neck and shoulder muscle tension. Gripping the bat more tightly.
2. Breathing more rapidly and up in the chest.

Attentional Changes
1. "Don't blow it, you can do it."
2. "Relax."
3. "Watch the ball, stupid."

Performance Consequences
1. Don't "pick up the ball on release," react too slowly cause I'm thinking too much, end up swinging off my back foot.
2. Get angry and rush, jumping at the ball. I end up way out in front.

weight transfer occurs before the ball arrives. If he makes contact with the ball, he must rely on the strength in his arms instead of being able to use the weight of his entire body.

Observation session two. Once Pat had learned about the relationship between concentration and arousal, there was a second observation session. The purpose of this session was to provide Pat, myself, and the coach with an opportunity to validate previous findings. This is an important session for several reasons.

First, athletes in ACT are attempting to rate their concentration skills for the first time and may never have thought about these attentional dimensions before. Likewise, they may never have made direct comparisons between their concentration skills and those of other players. The second session provides them with an opportunity to make those comparisons. As a result, their initial impressions may change (Pat's did not).

In addition, the second observation session and discussions with the coach help to pinpoint specific performance cues that should and should not be attended to. The second session answers questions like "What specific thoughts increase (or decrease) muscle tension and/or arousal?" "What are the particular stimuli that remind you about outcome and the possibility of failure?" "What technical or tactical process cues should the athlete be attending to so he can perform more effectively?" As you might imagine, the technical and tactical knowledge of most sport psychologists is more limited than that of the coach and/or athlete. For this reason, the assistance of the coach and athlete in identifying critical task-relevant cues is essential. This is especially true with ACT because programs emphasize making specific behavioral changes within specific performance situations.

Pat's performance in the second observation session was different from the first, because he was observing his own behavior. He still did not have "good at bats." Mistakes were occurring, however, because he was too analytical and not watching the ball. Anger and rushing were not issues in the second session.

Pat learned that his coach and/or the third base coach had become distracting cues, causing him to tighten up. When there were runners on base, he was extremely sensitive to any anxiety on the part of the coach. He interpreted the coach's anxiety as a lack of confidence in his ability to get

a hit. Thus, attending to the coach would increase muscle tension and doubts (internal distractions).

Education session two. Following the second observation session, Pat filled out the information in Table 18-3. His goal, checked out with the coach, was to identify those feelings and thoughts that would result in a good at bat.

It's important to notice that as far as performance consequences are concerned, Pat didn't list "get a hit." To improve performance, Pat had to set reasonable goals. That meant controlling those things he has the power to control, mainly himself. A good at bat is one where you don't swing at bad pitches and do swing at good pitches. It is an at bat where you make good contact with the ball (e.g., hit a line drive), independent of whether the ball is caught and you are out or not.

Reasonable goal setting also means not expecting every single at bat to be a good one. Instead, Pat's goals involved reducing the frequency of errors due to not watching the ball, and/or rushing. It also involved learning to recover from errors more quickly (e.g., to avoid having one mistake lead to another).

Introduction of training techniques. In the second classroom session Pat was introduced to the concept of centering as a means for controlling physiological arousal and for disattending to negative and/or task irrelevant stimuli. To understand centering, you actually need to understand three terms: (1) "center of mass," (2) "centered," and (3) "centering."

Draw a vertical line from your head to your toes, which divides your body into two equal parts. Next, draw a horizontal line through your body so that 50% of your weight is above the line and 50% is below it. Where those two lines intersect (somewhere behind your navel) is your **center of mass**.

You are **centered** within a performance situation when your body weight is distributed about your center of mass in a way that feels comfortable (e.g., your body seems to communicate a physical readiness to perform). Exactly how your center of mass should be distributed varies from situation to situation. When you need to be more aggressive and/or alert, your center of mass is raised and slightly forward. The more relaxed and or immovable you need to be, the lower your center of mass.

Centering is the process used to adjust weight about your center of mass so you feel centered. Al-

Table 18-3 **Case 1 Response Patterns after Training**

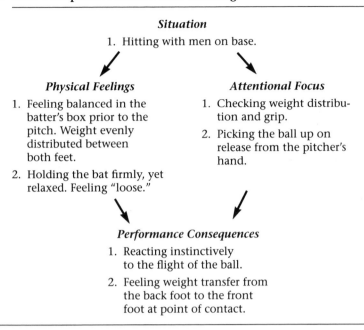

Situation

1. Hitting with men on base.

Physical Feelings

1. Feeling balanced in the batter's box prior to the pitch. Weight evenly distributed between both feet.

2. Holding the bat firmly, yet relaxed. Feeling "loose."

Attentional Focus

1. Checking weight distribution and grip.

2. Picking the ball up on release from the pitcher's hand.

Performance Consequences

1. Reacting instinctively to the flight of the ball.

2. Feeling weight transfer from the back foot to the front foot at point of contact.

terations in breathing and tension levels in various muscle groups (e.g., breathing from your abdomen instead of up in your chest, and relaxing neck and shoulder muscle tension) are used to make these adjustments.

Pat was instructed to use the centering technique immediately prior to each pitch when he was hitting with men on base. He was to time the end of his centering breath so that it was as close to the time the pitcher began his wind-up as possible. On the exhale he used two words to create the physical feelings and mental focus he wanted. He used the word "loose" to remind him of the feelings he wanted in his hands as he held the bat. He used the word "focused" to remind him to "pick up the ball on release."

The coach served as a facilitator for Pat in two ways. First, he acted as an external reminder, signaling Pat to use the centering procedure when there were base runners. Second, he reinforced Pat for good at bats rather than hits.

In addition to using the centering procedure in the games, Pat was encouraged to mentally rehearse. It's important to point out a couple of differences between mental rehearsal as used with ACT and mental rehearsal as used with other programs.

First, many mental rehearsal programs involve lengthy relaxation sessions before rehearsal. In ACT the athlete is shown how to use three deep breaths to quickly relax before rehearsal.

Second, many programs emphasize that the rehearsal perspective subjects use should be an *internal* one, as if they were actually engaging in the performance. Programs also emphasize that subjects should use all their senses (seeing, feeling, hearing, etc.) in the rehearsal process. Actual physical movements, however, are not overt in most programs. With ACT, athletes are encouraged to actually initiate and/or engage in the movements. This often facilitates imagery. In addition, some athletes are encouraged to rehearse with their eyes open. Many find this results in eye movements that also facilitate imagery.

Finally, subjects are encouraged to rehearse as frequently as they can, in the performance situation (when appropriate) and away from the performance situation. Pat, for example, was encouraged to rehearse in the dugout and in the on-deck circle.

Like many programs, rehearsal involved going through the entire situation including: (1) rehearsal of the thoughts and feelings associated with coming to bat with men on base, (2) rehearsal of tightening up, (3) rehearsal of remembering to center, (4) rehearsal of centering and redirecting attention, and (5) rehearsal of a successful experience.

The last thing accomplished in classroom session two involves putting the subject through a series of concentration tests designed to examine the subject's ability to control arousal and focus attention. These tests include using centering to make it impossible for someone to bend his/her arm, using centering to keep two people from lifting him/her off the ground, and using centering to focus attention in order to break a one-inch board.

The tests have two purposes. First, they provide subjects with support and motivation. Through the tests they can see the effectiveness of the procedure. Second, since few individuals master all three tests the first time, they demonstrate that centering to control concentration and arousal is a skill that must be continually practiced. Although the technique can be learned in a few minutes, the athletes cannot expect to execute successfully, particularly under pressure, without continued practice.

Third observational session. The final observational session provides the subject with an opportunity to practice what he/she has learned under supervision. Emphasis is on providing support and encouragement and on making corrections when necessary (e.g., if the subject is mentally rehearsing at the wrong time). Realistic goals are reemphasized, and, when appropriate, information from the TAIS is used to facilitate communication between the coach and athlete. For example, scores on the TAIS might indicate the athlete is easily overloaded with information (not Pat's case) and that the coach is highly verbal (high BIT and IEX). Under these conditions I would emphasize that coach and athlete need to find ways of keeping things simple, especially in the identified pressure situation.

Case 2

Steve, a 17-year-old tennis player, was one of the top juniors in the world and had been playing as a professional for over a year. He was tested with five other top juniors, all taking part in a three-day ACT program. Steve's TAIS scores are presented in Figure 18-4. There was no identified problem; all of the players were participat-

ing in the program because they had been told it would help them improve their concentration skills.

The workshop format was similar to the program used with Pat and included the following:

1. Brief introduction and program outline (1 hour)

2. Mini round robin tennis tournament to create competitive pressure and provide an initial observation session

3. Classroom session to work through the *ICCS*, educating players about concentration on the tennis court and its relationship to arousal and performance

4. A second tournament to validate findings from the first tournament and the players' responses in the classroom

5. Second classroom session to develop individualized intervention programs that used centering and rehearsal procedures

6. Third performance session giving players an opportunity to practice their ACT programs during competition

7. Testing of attention control and individual feedback sessions with each player and his coach.

TAIS results. Given that Steve was one of the best junior tennis players in the world, some of his scores on the TAIS were surprising. Normally I'd expect an athlete performing at Steve's level to score around the 77th percentile on TAIS scales measuring control (CON), self-esteem (SES), and physical competitiveness (P/O). Steve's scores on these scales were quite low (16%, 10%, and 50% respectively). In addition, Steve indicated he was internally overloaded (OIT) and not very expressive of thoughts and ideas. These scores generated several hypotheses:

1. Because Steve didn't express himself (IEX), had a low level of self-confidence, and was more introverted than extroverted, I doubted Steve's coach would be aware of his feelings and/or of the fact that he was overloaded.

2. Low scores on control, self-esteem, and physical orientation scales suggested Steve was not the "competitor" many other athletes were. It was my guess he needed a lot of support from the coach.

3. The overload, the low scores on self-esteem and intellectual expressiveness, and the tendency to ruminate and worry (OBS) indicated Steve would be an effective problem solver on court. He would need structure, and direction, instructions, and/or discussions prior to a match would have to be fairly simple.

4. Finally, one of the things creating stress for athletes low in confidence is positive expectations on the part of others. The more positive the situation for Steve, the more likely he would be to feel pressure.

First observation session. Coming into the training session, both Steve and the coach anticipated he would dominate the round robin tournament. As it turned out, Steve seemed to feel more pressure than any of the other players. He would start out well (e.g., win the first three or four games easily) and then begin to tighten up. He responded to the loss of points and/or games by becoming angry at himself, saying negative things, and then beginning to behave as if he didn't care (e.g., not moving for balls). The coach was surprised by Steve's performance. At the same time, he mentioned Steve had a "habit" of getting ahead of opponents ranked higher than he was and then losing the match.

Education sessions. As indicated by his TAIS profile, Steve was not very verbal during the classroom sessions. He listened and took notes but didn't contribute. He was uncomfortable and defensive in front of the other players, making it necessary to pull him aside in order to draw him out. In one-on-one conversations Steve was able to admit his anger when he wasn't "winning every point" against "people like these" (referring to the other five players). If he wasn't able to gain immediate control, he would "tank." When asked about playing against people "better than he was," he indicated that he usually started out well, but as soon as he would be in a "winning position," he would begin playing not to lose, rather than to win.

During these courtside talks, Steve was prepared for the material that would be presented in the classroom. He was told, for example, that "we will be identifying a problem situation for each athlete and then trying to see exactly what happens physically and mentally." Steve was told that

he should think about situations where he found himself ahead at the end of the first set and then begin to play conservatively during the second.

Though there were two different problems to be worked on, it was important to focus on one of them. Even if Steve didn't have a tendency to become overloaded, this would be true. The biggest factor keeping athletes from making significant changes is the fact they don't stay focused on one problem. A good coach would never dream of asking an athlete to work on several different technical or biomechanical issues at the same time. The same should be true of psychological or concentration issues. From a motivational standpoint it was important to let Steve pick the problem he felt was most important. He chose to work on situations where he was ahead of someone that he wasn't really expected to beat. Table 18-4 presents Steve's analysis of this problem.

Second observation session. Watching Steve play, I sensed that his arousal level dropped too low in pressure situations. The pressure of possible success seemed to result in an emotional shutting down. Steve would begin to appear lazy and/or preoccupied. There wasn't any evidence of muscle tension (e.g., low ball toss on serve, the inability to generate racquet head speed, difficulty bending). Instead, he simply didn't seem to be ready and/or attending to the task.

Steve was asked to imagine an arousal continuum:

> At one end of the continuum is a triangle standing on its base. The triangle represents the lowest level of arousal and the number you would assign to that arousal level is 1. When you're a 1, you are so relaxed you can't move. At the other end of the continuum is a triangle standing on its point. The number you assign to this triangle is a 10. When your arousal level is a 10, you are so wired your feet are hardly touching the ground. At a 10, your center of mass is too high; you don't feel solid. Where along this continuum are you when you are feeling most confident?

Steve indicated he felt most confident and ready when his arousal level was around a 7 or 8. When he was ahead, his arousal level seemed to drop to a 4 or 5. On the basis of his observations the centering procedures were modified during the training phase to help him increase his level of arousal every time he was in a winning position (e.g., at

Table 18-4 **Observation of Case 2 Problem Response Patterns**

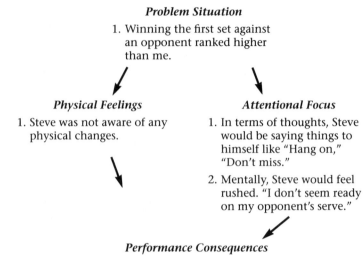

Problem Situation

1. Winning the first set against an opponent ranked higher than me.

Physical Feelings

1. Steve was not aware of any physical changes.

Attentional Focus

1. In terms of thoughts, Steve would be saying things to himself like "Hang on," "Don't miss."

2. Mentally, Steve would feel rushed. "I don't seem ready on my opponent's serve."

Performance Consequences

1. Steve was aware of the performance consequences because he and the coach had discussed them several times. He would become less aggressive, playing more from the baseline. He would be conservative on all of his shots, tending to hit back to the center of the court. He would not close as much on volleys and play farther behind the baseline. Often, he would be hitting shots off his back foot. At times he would let balls go, hoping they would be out.

the start of the second set, when he had break points). Table 18-5 provides a summary of the things that Steve was supposed to do in specific performance situations.

Because of Steve's tendency to become attentionally overloaded in pressure situations, however, and because he was alone on the tennis court, it was necessary to find ways to remind him to implement the ACT program. To help Steve remember and to encourage him to practice, he was given an "intention arousing device" (IAD). This is a small countdown timer that clips to a belt or pocket. The IAD can be set to time any interval from one minute to 24 hours. At the end of the time interval it vibrates, then resets itself and starts

timing the interval over again.* Steve was instructed to wear the IAD in those matches where he was playing opponents who were ranked higher than he was. He was also asked to wear it during the last half-hour of each training session. This was to get him to focus on controlling concentration and arousal (e.g., to use the centering and attentional refocusing) for a short period during each training session.

In the final feedback session with Steve and his coach, emphasis was placed on: (1) having the

*The IAD is marketed under the trade name of "MotivAider" and is available from Behavioral Dynamics, Inc., Box 66, Thief River Falls, Minn. 56701.

Table 18-5 **Case 2 Response Patterns after Training**

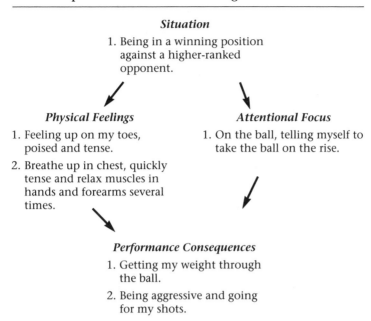

Situation

1. Being in a winning position against a higher-ranked opponent.

Physical Feelings

1. Feeling up on my toes, poised and tense.

2. Breathe up in chest, quickly tense and relax muscles in hands and forearms several times.

Attentional Focus

1. On the ball, telling myself to take the ball on the rise.

Performance Consequences

1. Getting my weight through the ball.

2. Being aggressive and going for my shots.

---

coach keep instructions relatively simple and structured, (2) getting the coach to draw Steve out to make sure he understood what was expected (e.g., by paraphrasing what the coach had said), and (3) encouraging Steve to do more of his own problem solving and to assume more responsibility in relatively nonstressful situations (like practice).

Because ACT programs are situation-specific, it's easy to evaluate the effectiveness of training. For Pat, success could be measured by an increase in the frequency of "good at bats." For Steve, positive change could be measured in terms of an increased frequency with respect to the number of times he would continue to "go for shots," take the ball on the rise, and get his weight through the ball when he was ahead in a match. Or, to put it the other way, progress was seen as occurring when there was a reduction in "tentative" shots.

Steve showed some immediate change, but the improvement was short-lived. Steve's lack of confidence meant that for lasting change to occur he would need considerable ongoing support from the coach. Unfortunately, the coach wasn't able to provide as much support as Steve needed.

Too often, athletes lacking in confidence are looking for a quick fix, or a miracle that's going to make them believe in themselves. They seem unable to accept the fact that real confidence must be based on real success. You need to be a winner to have the deep-seated conviction that you are a winner. Without that past history you can't expect to be free of doubts. To control those doubts under pressure requires practice. Athletes seeking to improve confidence or other concentration areas must use ACT or some other psychological training programs on a regular basis. They must practice the procedures just as they would practice anything else.

Several readings regarding the research, theory, and practice outlined in this chapter are listed at the end of the chapter. Specific techniques that coaches and sport psychologists can use to help train better concentration in athletes appear in Chapter 19.

Summary and Conclusions

All training programs recognize that there is some optimal level of arousal and that problems can occur on either side of the optimal level. In practice, however, most programs are designed to deal only with problems that result when arousal is too high. In addition, concepts like anxiety and arousal seem to be treated globally. It's as if a highly physiologically aroused individual is also anxious, worried, externally and internally distracted, and so forth.

The Importance of Greater Theoretical Specificity

ACT differs from the other programs in that the underlying theory is much more explicit. For example, concentration (attention) is behaviorally defined and so are the different types of concentration errors. Individuals can be highly aroused physiologically, without being anxious, worried, distracted, or impulsive. The greater differentiation allowed by the theory allows the practitioner to make predictions about the types of situations that are likely to be stressful to a given individual and to make predictions about the specific behaviors that are likely to occur under pressure.

The education phases of ACT teach participants to differentiate the types of concentration required within their particular sports. They are taught to think in terms of the width and direction of attention required. They learn to recognize when to shift from one focus to another. Greater definition allows them to be much more exact when it comes to describing problems and helps them learn more quickly. This behavioral specificity carries over into the assessment process, leading to the development of individualized, situation-specific training programs.

Assessment Differences

With ACT, assessment includes formal testing (use of the TAIS and the ICCS) to gather information about those attentional and interpersonal processes that are predictors of performance. Assessment also includes a structured interview that covers past performance history and repeated behavioral observations in actual performance settings.

The breakdown of attention on the basis of the width and direction of attentional focus leads to the identification and classification of the specific types of errors that occur within a performance situation (e.g., internal vs. external distractions, rushing and overaggressive responses as opposed to becoming tentative). This breakdown also leads to the identification (with the assistance of coach and athlete) of the technical, tactical, and/or motivational cues that should be attended to in the identified performance situation.

Although the literature is generally supportive of a variety of mental skills training programs, there are some special features of ACT that should influence its use. First, in contrast to most other programs, ACT was designed to be used with healthy, high-functioning individuals. An assumption that underlies the use of ACT is that the individual functions quite well the majority of the time. Thus, when problems appear to be fairly chronic and/or anxiety levels are high even in relatively low stress situations, ACT would be inappropriate.

ACT is especially appropriate when working with individuals for whom the "bottom line," or performance outcome, is critical. Most professionals—and in fact most high school and college athletes—are more concerned about winning than they are about "feeling good." In fact, for most of these athletes feeling good is tied to success. Because we are working with healthy, high-functioning individuals, the desire to be a winner is not an unreasonable goal. By the same token, healthy individuals are not likely to be so traumatized by failure that they can't confront it and grow. As you might imagine, the philosophy behind ACT, and to a lesser extent the procedures themselves, would appear to be less appropriate when working with younger athletes and/or recreational athletes.

Whenever possible, ACT programs involve the coach. First, the coach functions as a problem solver, identifying the most task-relevant cues the athlete should be attending to. Next, feedback from the TAIS (both coach and athletes) facilitates communication. Finally, the coach is shown how the ACT program should be integrated into both practice and competitive settings. Throughout the training process, everything possible is done to maximize the likelihood that the coach will encourage and support the athlete's use of the ACT procedures. Because ACT programs do involve the coach and because the first priority of the training program involves the improvement of performance, it is not the program of choice in clinical situations where athletes have relatively severe emotional problems.

Finally, ACT would appear to be the program of choice when some type of arousal and/or concentration intervention is required within an actual performance situation. This may mean training an individual to react to unexpected events (e.g., to recover quickly from a mistake or an accident). It may mean training the individual to overcome a problem that consistently appears within a particular situation (e.g., the tendency to become tentative when leading). Too many programs create (and/or add to) an artificial mind-body split, which affects the way many athletes and coaches see sport psychology. Programs that are developed and applied outside of the actual practice and/or performance setting feed the misconception that mental training is somehow separate from physical training. ACT programs are designed for implementation within the performance setting.

Study Questions

1. Describe the eight principles that underlie attention control training.
2. Diagram the figure depicting the four different types of attentional focus and then briefly describe and give an example of each.
3. What does it mean to "play to one's attentional strength"?
4. How is "choking" defined in terms of attentional focus?
5. Describe how to prevent and treat choking.
6. Explain the "process" versus "outcome" notion in regards to attentional phenomena.
7. In what types of situations and with what types of individuals might it be appropriate to use an ACT intervention?
8. Identify some specific problem in which ACT might be an appropriate intervention and then briefly describe the different processes you might go through in implementing an ACT intervention.

References

Carver, C. S., and Scheier, M. F. (1989). A control-process perspective on anxiety. *Anxiety Research, 1,* 17–22.

Hull, C. L. (1951). *Essentials of behavior.* New Haven, Conn.: Yale University Press.

Nideffer, R. M. (1976a). Test of attentional and interpersonal style. *Journal of Personality and Social Psychology, 34,* 394–404.

Nideffer, R. M. (1976b). *The inner athlete.* Los Gatos, Calif.: Enhanced Performance Services.

Nideffer, R. M. (1989). *Attention control training for sport.* Los Gatos, Calif.: Enhanced Performance Services.

Training Strategies for Concentration

Andrea Schmid, *San Francisco State University*

Erik Peper, *San Francisco State University*

C oncentration is essential for performing one's best. The major component of concentration is the ability to focus one's attention on the task at hand and thereby not be disturbed or affected by irrelevant external and internal stimuli. External stimuli may include an audience booing, music, bad officiating calls, and unsportsmanlike behavior from the opponents. Internal stimuli include distracting body sensations and thoughts and feelings such as "I'm really tired," "Don't be nervous," and "I blew it!"

Although external and internal stimuli appear to be separate categories, they continually affect each other. Almost every external event will trigger a cognitive and emotional shift in the athlete. Because this interaction occurs all the time, coaches and sport psychologists must train athletes to cope with these events under pressure situations such as a major competition. Unless this training has occurred and concentration skills have been mastered, performance will almost always suffer. Failure to develop or employ concentration skills has been the downfall of many athletes. According to Cox (1990), few areas in sport psychology are as important to the overall performance as the areas of concentration or attention.

For example, one 16-year-old U.S. rhythmic gymnast lost her poise and concentration and performed very poorly when a loud teenage voice yelled a lewd comment as she walked toward the mat to compete in an international meet. During the fifth game of a critical intercollegiate volleyball match the visiting team completely lost its composure when the home crowd began stamping their feet and clapping in unison whenever the away team was serving the ball, and a closely contested game with an 8–8 score ended 8–15 in favor of the home team. These examples illustrate the potential for distractions in a competitive environment. The ability not to react to or be disturbed by distractions such as these is achieved when athletes learn how to control their thoughts and appropriately focus their attention.

This learned mental control was demonstrated by gymnast Zoltan Magyar, the Olympic gold medalist, during the 20th gymnastics World Championship in 1979. At the finals of the pommel horse competition, Magyar was up after Nikolai Adrianov, the Olympic all-around champion. Adrianov missed two elements in his routine, and 10,000 spectators verbally reacted. Magyar was able to tune out all sound and distractions. He was also able to shut out defeating thoughts and to synchronize and harmonize the forces of his mind and body to defend his Olympic gold medal. According to the team physician, Magyar did not even realize that Adrianov had missed! Magyar was able to channel all of his energy into a productive performance. He had achieved the highest level of single-mindedness and exclusive concentration and attention (Schmid, 1982).

Many other performers, such as surgeons, artists, writers, and musicians, can equally achieve this kind of high level of concentration. For example, Walsh and Spelman (1983) reported that conductor Carlos Kleiber never noticed the earthquake rattling a giant chandelier when he was conducting Strauss's *Der Rosenkavalier* at La Scala. He was concentrating that intently! These examples illustrate how elite performers tend not to be disturbed by external factors, a skill not yet acquired by many developing performers.

Paradoxically, trying to concentrate is also not concentrating. Concentration means focusing, not forcing, one's attention on a task. At times this may be perceived as shielding ourselves from stimuli that might penetrate and disturb our focus of attention. Active shielding by itself would be a distraction. Thus, concentration is the learned skill of passively not reacting to or being distracted by irrelevant stimuli. Concentration also means being totally in the here and now, in the present. When our minds drift into the past or future, we are not as effective in our present performance. The ability to concentrate is a skill, and like any other skill it can be developed and improved through practice. We either learn to decrease attention to irrelevant stimuli or increase attention to relevant stimuli. In this process we learn **selective awareness**—the skill of selectively paying attention to relevant stimuli and ignoring irrelevant stimuli. In addition, when we become distracted, previous concentration training enhances our ability to rapidly refocus our attention on the task at hand without continuing to feel or think about the disturbance.

In Chapter 18, Nideffer identified the different types of attention or concentration that seem to be required in athletic situations. These types were described along two dimensions: broad versus narrow and internal versus external. The most appropriate type of focus, or attentional style, depends upon the sport skill and the demands of the specific situation. In concentration training, knowing what to focus on is as critical as knowing how to control one's focus. Athletes may have excellent concentration skills, but if they are focusing on the wrong things, the skills will not be very helpful.

In addition to providing athletes with techniques that help train better control of concentration, coaches and sport psychologists need to assist athletes in identifying different attentional styles and those most appropriate for their specific sport involvement. An excellent technique for helping athletes experience the different attentional styles is an "expanding awareness" exercise developed by Gauron (1984). Athletes can practice this exercise in its entirety or break the various segments into separate exercises. When practicing, athletes should sit or lie in a comfortable position. As you go through the steps yourself, you can see the relevance of the exercise for concentration training.

1. Focus on your breathing while continuing to breathe normally. For the next minute breathe more deeply and slowly while keeping the chest, shoulders, and neck relaxed. Return to normal breathing for three or four breaths and then back to deep breathing until the deep breathing is comfortable, easy, and regular. (The authors recommend monitoring the actual physiological changes, since in some cases subjects report relaxation while their physiology does not match the subjective experience.)

2. Now pay attention to what you hear by taking each separate sound, identifying it, and then mentally labeling it, such as footsteps, voices, or a cough. Next, simultaneously listen to all the sounds without attempting to identify or label them. They should listen to the blend of sound as they would to music, while verbal thinking drops away.

3. Now become aware of bodily sensations such as the feeling of where the chair or floor supports your body. Mentally label each sensation as you notice it. Before moving on to another sensation, let each sensation linger for a moment while you examine it; consider its quality and its source. Next, experience all these sensations simultaneously without identifying or labeling any particular one. This necessitates going into the broadest possible internal body awareness.

4. Attend now only to your emotions or thoughts. Let each thought or emotion appear gently, without being forced. Identify the nature of your thoughts and feelings. Remain calm no matter how pleasant or unpleasant they may be. Feel one, then another, then another. Now try to empty yourself of all thoughts and feelings. If this is not possible, tune in to only one and hold your attention there.

5. Open your eyes and pick some object across the room directly in front of you. While looking ahead, see as much of the room and the objects in the room as your peripheral vision will allow. Simultaneously observe the entire room and all the items in it. Picture now a broad funnel into which your mind is moving. Centered in the middle of the funnel is the object directly across the room from you. Gradually narrow your focus by narrowing the funnel so the only thing at the small end of the funnel is the object across from you. Expand your focus little by little, widening the funnel until you can see everything in the room. Think of your external focus as a zoom lens; practice zooming in and out, narrowing or broadening according to your wishes.

Besides helping athletes experience different attentional styles, the preceding exercise illustrates what it is like to keep focus in one place and then to change across the internal to external dimension and the specific to panoramic focus. This type of experience provides an excellent foundation for clarifying the most appropriate focus for specific athletic skills and situations.

In the remainder of this chapter we provide specific strategies and techniques that coaches and sport psychologists can use to train better concentration control in athletes. These strategies are divided into two sections: strategies to control distracting external factors and strategies to control internal distractions. The categorization is somewhat arbitrary, because external and internal stimuli continually affect each other. Because of this interaction, strategies in one category may be equally effective in correcting apparent lack of concentration in the other category.

External Factors: Strategies to Keep Concentration

Athletes need to be trained not to react (orient) to irrelevant external stimuli. In a competition these stimuli are situational factors that coaches often

expect the athletes to have learned by trial and error to control in previous competitive experiences. This "previous experience" strategy for developing concentration control has obvious limitations and false assumptions. Coaches need to realize that athletes can be systematically trained before a competition to be situationally independent. The concept underlying training is based upon Pavlovian conditioning. The novelty of the competitive environment, compared to the practice environment, tends to reduce performance. Through training, the novelty of the competitive environment can be minimized. In short, athletes need to experience simulated competition training in which they practice their physical skills while being exposed to all possible external stimuli that can occur during a real competition. This training follows similar procedures used by NASA and U.S. Air Force astronauts and pilots to cope with emergencies. For example, in flight training, pilots practice dead stick landings, pulling out of spins, recovering from stalls, and so forth. For athletes, strategies that reduce the novelty effect upon performance by conditioning an appropriate response include dress rehearsal practice, general simulation of competition experiences, and mental rehearsal of concentration training.

Strategy 1: Dress Rehearsal

Dress rehearsal is a particularly effective strategy for sports such as gymnastics, diving, synchronized swimming, and figure skating. Dress rehearsal is based upon the concept that ease in skillful competitive performance is unconsciously conditioned by the external and internal stimuli that surround the athletes during practice. The greater the number of different stimuli present during competition compared to practice, the more likely the performance quality will decrease. Stimuli can include things such as the athletes' uniforms, background illumination, announcers' voices, and music. Ironically, in order to make a good impression during the competitive event, athletes usually wear uniforms or costumes different from the ones they wore during practice. This means that an unconscious stimulus (the practice uniform) associated with the performance of the skill (response) is not elicited during the competition. Wearing a different or new uniform is a new stimulus and may inhibit performance. This may be one reason why some athletes tend to perform better during practice than during competition. Such athletes need to practice their complete competitive routines during practice in the same uniform they wear during actual competition. Dress rehearsal needs to be conducted frequently after the athletes have mastered a new skill and are practicing the whole routine for performance. This concept is important for any performer. For example, Mark Braunstein (1991), a violist with the Cleveland Orchestra, reported that he felt somewhat uncomfortable performing in his tuxedo in the orchestra after having practiced in his jeans at home. When he started dress rehearsal at home wearing his tuxedo he was able to concentrate more, feel more at ease, and improve his playing during concerts.

The reverse of this strategy can also be applied when an athlete is in a slump. In this case the athletes ceremoniously discard their uniforms and thereby symbolically disconnect from the slump associations and now practice with a new uniform. The athlete is metaphorically and ritualistically reborn.

Strategy 2: Rehearsal of Simulated Competition Experiences

Simulated competition experiences enable the athlete to become so familiar with the stimuli associated with competition that they are no longer distracting. This is the same concept that underlies dress rehearsal practice. The athletes are trained to concentrate and dissociate from the disruptive stimuli.

For example, in gymnastics, athletes might rehearse their routines in practice while a loud tape recording of a previous meet is played over the public address system. This tape would include another gymnast's floor exercise music, audience applause, and so on. A similar example for team sports such as football, basketball, and volleyball would be holding the week's practice before an away game with the public address system loudly playing hostile crowd noises and the opposing team's fight song. Such exercises reduce the effect of "meet-induced novelty," which tends to interfere with performance, and make the competitive experience seem just like practice workouts. We assume that a good example of not preparing for an extremely angry crowd was Zola Budd's slipping to a seventh-place finish after a strong lead during the 3000-meter finals in the 1984 Olympics. The thunderous booing of the hostile crowd must have demoralized her after the accident with Mary Decker from the United States.

When using this strategy, coaches and sport psychologists should overtrain athletes by including simulated practice of the worst possible scenario, such as having a basketball player ready to take a free throw shot and then having to wait the length of a time-out before shooting. "Wet ball" drills in football are based on the same concept. Many psychologically astute coaches turn the sprinklers on before practice and then soak the ball between plays when preparing for a football game during which rain is likely. As stated earlier, a similar approach is essential in the training of pilots and astronauts. They spend a significant amount of time practicing in very realistic flight simulators. In these simulators they are presented with numerous flight and equipment problems. The simulation trains pilots to maintain their concentration and appropriate responses in the face of disruptions or emergencies. Just as learning a physical skill takes time, learning the mental control of concentrating on the task while not reacting to external stimuli takes many hours of training.

Strategy 3: Mental Rehearsal

Most performers report that **visualization (mental rehearsal)** is an important ingredient in their success. Many discover this process serendipitously. A systematic training program was organized by Suinn (1980), who developed visual-motor behavioral rehearsal (VMBR) for Olympic biathlon, alpine, and nordic skiers. He reported impressive perceived results. Scientific findings confirm that skilled performers using mental rehearsal programs such as VMBR perform better than control groups (see Chapter 16).

Using mental rehearsal to practice concentration and to learn not to react to purposely induced external distractions is another useful strategy for athletes. Obviously, athletes can only benefit from this strategy after they have learned relaxation and imagery skills. Such a strategy might involve having athletes form pairs in which one member of the pair relaxes and mentally rehearses his/her sport while the other member attempts to distract the performer from the mental rehearsal. The distraction can be anything except touching. After this type of mental rehearsal the coach or sport psychologist might have the athlete rate his/her achieved concentration on a 0–6 scale. Thereafter the athletes reverse roles. In a study involving members of the U.S. national rhythmic gymnastic team (Schmid & Peper, 1982), the gymnasts practiced this pair distraction exercise daily for five days. On the first and fifth days they were asked to rate their concentration while mentally rehearsing their routine with a partner who attempted to distract them. They reported a significant increase in their concentration from the first day to the fifth day. Through this type of exercise, athletes learn how to detach and dissociate themselves from external distractions and resulting unwanted internal reactions (stimuli) while instead focusing on the task of mentally rehearsing their sport.

Just as the coach or sport psychologist can train athletes to use mental rehearsal to attain concentration, he/she can also train athletes to use mental rehearsal to *regain* concentration. For example, as soon as athletes realize their concentration has been disrupted by external factors such as crowd noises, they should stop themselves, take a deep breath to relax, and then bring their attention back by mentally rehearsing what they should be doing next.

The three strategies we have just outlined can be employed during regular physical practice sessions. Athletes are responsive to them and especially enjoy being involved in generating the distracting stimuli.

Internal Factors: Strategies to Stay Centered

The coach or sport psychologist must train the athlete's mind to exert control, because concentration inhibits distraction. Lapses in concentration invite fear and self-doubt, and the resulting worry and anxiety lead to further increases in lack of concentration, thus creating a vicious cycle that ultimately leads to failure. The effect of internal factors becomes more pronounced in high-pressure situations. As an analogy, consider what would happen if someone were to ask you to walk on a board 4 inches wide, 15 feet long, and 9 inches above the ground (like a practice beam in gymnastics). You would be able to do this without hesitation just by concentrating on the task of walking across the board. On the other hand, if the board were 60 feet off the ground you might become paralyzed by the fear of falling. Such fear inhibits per-

formance and increases the possibility of falling. Ironically, there is no difference in the physical skill required. The difference is in your psychological response to the perceived stressful event, and as a result your attention is on trying not to fall instead of on walking across the beam. In addition, if you had previously fallen off a beam, then everytime you thought about it or related the experience to someone, you might have unknowingly rehearsed all of the cognitive and motor events that led to failure.

Similar psychological processes occur during competition. For example, a field-goal kicker who normally hits his short kicks during practice may react quite differently during competition when he attempts to kick a short field goal and there are only a few seconds left on the clock and his team is behind by two points. He is even more likely to fear "blowing it" if he has recently missed a kick in similar circumstances. One professional football player, while kicking under such a high-pressure situation, described the goal posts as looking as though they had narrowed to less than a foot apart. It does not take much insight to figure out what happened to his kick!

One way to improve concentration is to reduce self-doubts and competitive anxiety and their resulting physical manifestations (i.e., increased arousal). (Arousal and cognitive control techniques are discussed in Chapters 15 and 17.) Unless an athlete has control over internal dialogue, his/her focus of attention will not be congruent with good performance, let alone peak performance. In addition to the specific arousal and cognition techniques found in preceding chapters, in our work with performers we have found the following strategies helpful in controlling internal dialogue and facilitating concentration and performance.

Strategy 1: Attentional Cues and Triggers

Athletes can use verbal and kinesthetic cues to focus their concentration and to retrigger concentration once it has been lost. These cues can help athletes center their attention on the most appropriate focus within the task at hand and thus help them to avoid distracting thoughts and feelings (Schmid, 1982). Similar observations have been confirmed by Nideffer (1981, 1987), who reported case histories in which athletes benefited from centering by using task-relevant cues.

Generally, it is best to find cues that focus on positives rather than negatives, the present (current or upcoming moment) rather than the past or future, and the process (proper form or execution) rather than the score or outcome. During a television interview on September 1, 1984, Greg Louganis, the Olympic diving champion, gave some excellent examples of effective attentional cues. He said, "I picture my dive as the judge will see it, then as I see it." In his forward three-and-one-half somersault dive, he uses the following word cues: "Relax, see the platform, spot the water, spot the water, spot the water, kick out, spot the water again." This helps him to concentrate and focus on the dive. Consequently, with his power to concentrate, he obtains a maximum result with a minimum of apparent effort. Coaches and sport psychologists should work with athletes to help them establish effective verbal and kinesthetic cues for triggering concentration. Such cues must be individualized, however. What is effective for one athlete may not be effective for another. Similarly, some athletes perform best with frequent cues and others with very few cues.

Strategy 2: Turning Failure into Success

Many athletes report that they commonly lose concentration after making a mistake. One way to deal with this problem is to train athletes to turn failure into success. This is a cognitive habit by which athletes mentally rehearse successful performance after a failure. As soon as possible after making an error (learning is only possible when errors occur), athletes should mentally rehearse executing the same skill perfectly rather than dwelling on the error. One component of successful performance is to avoid self-judgment or blaming others, which disrupts concentration, and to refocus on the performance. The power of not focusing upon the failure and just taking the challenge is illustrated by Lasse Viren during the 1972 Munich Olympic Games (Benagh, 1976). He won the 10,000-meter race and broke the world record despite the fact that he fell flat on his face as another runner ran over him. Even though he was down for three full seconds, he got up, composed himself, ran and came in first. Many others would have

given up because they would have assumed that they would be defeated.

More harmful than making a performance error is ruminating on the failed event. Each time athletes recite (verbally or mentally) a previous failure, they condition the mind to make the failure the preferred motor pattern. The verbal retelling to others or the chronic rumination on why one made a mistake is a type of global visual-motor behavior rehearsal in which one is training the mind to perform the same failure behavior again. Instead of reciting the error, the athletes might ask: "What was the problem?" "How could I have performed differently in the same situation?" or "What other skills do I need?" Then the athletes can mentally rehearse the previous conditions leading to the error but now change their behavior so that they imagine themselves performing the skill perfectly.

The coach or sport psychologist can also encourage athletes to do the same thing after an injury. When concerned friends and others ask what happened, athletes should avoid recounting the accident and instead focus on describing a perfect performance the next time. For example, after a 16-year-old downhill skier ran off the course and was seriously injured, her skiing improved remarkably when she stopped telling other people how she got injured. Whenever people asked her what happened, she described how she would now ski the race successfully. (When she felt herself going too fast, she would sink down into her skis and continue to breathe while setting the edges as she was going through a gate.) As she talked, she unconsciously rehearsed how to react successfully to the conditions under which she had previously fallen.

Strategy 3: Use of Electrodermal Feedback

The coach or sport psychologist can use electrodermal feedback devices in conjunction with peak performance training to (1) illustrate how thoughts affect the body and performance, (2) monitor physiological relaxation, (3) identify stressful components of the athletic performance during imagery rehearsal, and (4) facilitate concentration training (Peper & Schmid, 1983–1984). Such devices are available from biofeedback companies and businesses like Radio Shack.

An electrodermal activity (EDA) feedback unit measures and feeds back changes in skin conductance. **Skin conductance** measures the changes in sympathetic arousal as produced in the perspiration of the palmer surface of the hand. These changes correlate highly with the triggering of the "fight or flight" response. An increase in autonomic arousal usually results in an increase in skin conductivity. The feedback device reflects this change by increasing the pitch of the sound when conductivity and arousal increase and decreasing the pitch when conductivity and arousal decrease. The latency of the EDA response is about two seconds. It is important to note that EDA is a useful biofeedback tool with many athletes. However, some athletes do not respond in this physiological way. Instead, they may respond cardiovascularly, gastrointestinally, or muscularly (Peper & Williams, 1981). The following three techniques were developed and tested by the authors with gymnasts, skiers, synchronized swimmers, and musicians, and the performers reported enhanced concentration skills.

Technique A: Thoughts affect body. EDA feedback can be used to show that thoughts and feelings affect our performance. That is, each thought has a corresponding physiological effect—a concept that many athletes are unaware of. We often illustrate this concept in a group meeting in which one of the athletes is attached to a portable EDA feedback device. After the device is turned on, we ask the athlete to think of an anxiety-provoking event or we whisper something to him/her such as "You just blew your routine." Each time the person thinks of an embarrassing or anxiety-provoking situation such as imagining a difficult move, the pitch of the sound increases. After demonstrating the EDA feedback device, we ask the athletes to use it to experience how their thoughts and feelings affect their physiological state. This helps them to identify and stop disturbing thoughts and feelings, as well as to restructure their self-talk from negative to positive.

Technique B: Facilitating mental rehearsal. Athletes can use small portable EDA feedback units while they mentally rehearse their routine. These small feedback units fit in the palm of the hand, and the athletes receive auditory feedback. With the help of the feedback, athletes can more rapidly identify stressful, anxiety-provoking events or cues during imagery rehearsal of their routine or athletic event. In the case of the rhythmic gymnasts we worked with, some of their subjective experiences associated with the EDA feedback occurred during a hoop routine: "On a toss or catch that was risky, just when I was about to do a toss that I frequently miss, right before a toss, when I thought, 'You've got to make it!' so I tensed up just before the routine began." During a final assessment, most of the gymnasts reported that EDA feedback was helpful in learning to reduce their arousal during mental rehearsal. In fact, many of the gymnasts reported that within two weeks they had learned to inhibit the EDA feedback tone during imagery rehearsal.

Technique C: Enhancing concentration training. EDA feedback can be used to facilitate concentration learning in an enjoyable diadic practice similar to the one described earlier under the mental rehearsal strategy. In this practice, athletes again form pairs, with one member of each pair mentally practicing some competitive situation while receiving EDA feedback. Simultaneously, the other partner attempts to distract and arouse him/her so that there will be a change in the EDA feedback signal. After two to five minutes of practice, the athletes reverse roles. Athletes enjoy this competitive practice and at the same time learn awareness of their own internal cues of anxiety, as well as strategies to control their EDA response through passive attention. Through this competitive practice they learn the ability to detach and dissociate from external distractions and unwanted internal stimuli while focusing on the task.

Strategy 4: Increasing Focusing and Refocusing Skills

Focus training teaches performers to gently hold their attention on a predetermined task and, if the attention wanders, to gently bring the attention back. As Landers, Boutcher, and Wang (1986) state, failure to develop refocusing skills has been the downfall of many athletes. The key to avoiding these pitfalls is to perform in the present, that is, focus awareness in the "now" rather than the past or future. One must learn how to pass quickly from negative thoughts to a constructive performance focus. The dynamics of this strategy are similar to those of meditative practices, such as Raja yoga meditation in which a person focuses on a mantra and each time the attention wanders from the mantra the person gently guides the attention back to it. Using a similar approach, the following exercises can help performers improve their focusing skills.

Exercise A: Mindfulness. Sit quietly, close your eyes, and see how long you can focus on a single thought. For many activities this is very important. As Chris Evert (1988), a world-class tennis player, reported: "From the beginning, I realized you have to take one point at a time and lock into a kind of concentration zone. . . . If I concentrated, I could win a lot of points in a row while opponents were thinking about other things."

Exercise B: One pointing. Look at an action photo or an object from your sport. For example, if your sport is baseball, softball, or tennis, you might focus on the ball. If distracting thoughts enter your mind, bring your attention back to the ball. Don't shut out the thoughts or continue to explore the disruptive thoughts or feelings. Just gently bring the attention back to the ball.

Have athletes practice these two exercises daily for five minutes and chart their progress. Get them to time how long they can focus their attention on a single thought or on the picture. It is our experience that these home practices help athletes eliminate their concentration-breaking thoughts. Another similar exercise to practice focus training is Benson's relaxation response described in Chapter 15.

Exercise C: Grid exercise. Another training exercise for practicing focusing ability is the grid exercise (Harris & Harris, 1984). This exercise necessitates having a 10-by-10 block grid with each block containing a two-digit number ranging from 00 to 99 (see Figure 19-1 for a sample grid). The purpose of this exercise is to scan the grid and within a given time (usually one minute) find and put a slash through as many numbers as possible in numerical sequence starting with number 00. The same form can be used several times by starting with a number just higher than the highest number reached on the first attempt. New grids can be developed easily by simply relocating the numbers. According to Harris and Harris, athletes who

have the ability to concentrate, scan, and store relevant cues will usually score in the upper 20s and into the 30s during a one-minute timed trial. Those who cannot disregard everything except the task at hand do poorly. After initial practice, you can increase the difficulty of the exercise by creating distractions such as loud noises and verbal harassment to see if the performer can block out everything and concentrate fully on the grid. Besides training focusing skills, Harris and Harris report that this exercise has been used extensively in Eastern Bloc countries as a precompetition screening device for current level of concentration ability. Athletes are selected for competition on the basis of their performance.

Exercise D: Video games. There are many new video games that increase reaction speed, hand–eye coordination, and concentration. For example, Michele Mitchell, the 1984 and 1988 Olympic silver medalist in women's platform diving, attributed her consistent performance to good concentration enhanced by playing computer video games. As she said: "It helped me to be in the present." The advantage of the video games is that momentary lapses in concentration will result in immediate feedback—you *lose*. Practice these games in an arcade or at home on the personal computer.

Strategy 5: Developing Performing Protocols

Many athletes develop the ability to tune in to their ideal performance state by associating concentration with certain performance rituals. Preset behavioral protocols should be established during warm-ups, practice, and the actual competition. These protocols should be designed to cue both the body and mind. It will take time to help each athlete identify his/her own ideal preperformance concentration routine. Once a definite routine is developed, it should be practiced consistently. Over time these protocols will serve automatically to trigger the focused concentration athletes need for good performance. This is illustrated by the behavior of Eberhard Gienger, the 1974 world champion on the horizontal bar.

> To compete Gienger stood up, put on his suspenders, adjusted his gymnastic pants and slippers, chalked up, put on his hand guards,

GRID CONCENTRATION EXERCISE

Directions:
Beginning with 00, put a slash through each number in the proper sequence.

84	27	51	78	59	52	13	85	61	55
28	60	92	04	97	90	31	57	29	33
32	96	65	39	80	77	49	86	18	70
76	87	71	95	98	81	01	46	88	00
48	82	89	47	35	17	10	42	62	34
44	67	93	11	07	43	72	94	69	56
53	79	05	22	54	74	58	14	91	02
06	68	99	75	26	15	41	66	20	40
50	09	64	08	38	30	36	45	83	24
03	73	21	23	16	37	25	19	12	63

Comments:

Figure 19-1 Sample grid exercise form for training and assessing the ability
to concentrate

placed his warm-up jacket on his shoulders, turned his back to the competition apparatus, and concentrated on the upcoming routine with his eyes closed. . . . This ritual did not vary from event to event, nor from preliminaries to finals. (Salmela, 1976)

Systematic precompetitive behaviors enhance performance by getting the athlete ready for the task at hand. The authors, working with two synchronized swimmers for the 1988 Olympic competition, initially observed that their precompetition protocol was not well thought out. For example, when one swimmer put on her nose clip,

it irritated the other and triggered thoughts about non–task-related matters. After helping them analyze, plan, and carry out with minute detail their precompetition protocol, the authors observed that the swimmers had increased their focus on the task at hand. Similarly, Boutcher and Crews (1987) demonstrated that the use of a preshot concentration routine can improve putting performance of female golfers.

Finally, if attention lapses, performers can use their personal idiosyncratic protocols to refocus their attention. The small procedural steps are the triggers for concentration on the task.

Conclusion

The ability to control thoughts, arousal, and attentional focus appears to be the common denominator in the concentration of winning competitors. For example, the Canadian gold medal winner in rhythmic gymnastics at the 1984 Olympics reported that her goal was to perform to her best ability. Specifically, she reported: "I went out to perform and not worry about my scores. In fact, it helped me more not to know my scores at all. That way I didn't have anything to worry about. . . . I didn't care what anyone else was doing and I didn't want to know at all" (Botkin, 1984). She won by 0.050 of a point because she did not focus on winning. She was able to hold onto the present and to focus on her routine while the Rumanian girl who was leading the competition all three days lost her composure and made major faults in her last routine.

Many other athletes also report that peak performances occurred when they eliminated all thoughts about winning and their focus was instead on the process, the task at hand. This type of mental control allows athletes to be in the present. They do not ruminate over past performances, judge present performance, or anticipate future performances. To achieve consistency in performance, athletes need to develop and practice these mental skills in special practice sessions and then practice them throughout all physical workouts. Such a mental preparedness program should follow these steps to better concentration in order to achieve peak performance:

1. Learn personal strategies to attain optimal arousal for performance.

2. Learn to practice with a positive attitude versus self-doubt and negative talk.

3. Learn which attentional focus is best.

4. Associate concentration with certain triggers such as cue words or feelings.

5. Become aware of the competitive environment and practice exercises that will help one "habituate" to it.

6. Practice dissociation.

7. Develop protocols or rituals to trigger concentration.

Our current understanding of the influence of attention and concentration on performance depends largely upon self-report of performers. This will probably change in the next 10 years as direct psychophysiological measures of attention and concentration will be monitored during actual competition. Already clinicians are successful at training specific electroencephalographic patterns (EEG) in children with attention-deficit/hyperactivity disorders (Lubar, 1991). In this instance the EEG equipment monitors changes in attention/concentration and children learn through biofeedback mastery/control over their attention. Even more exciting is the recent work of monitoring with topographic EEG the arousal and attention of pilots in flight. Those data suggest that topographic EEG changes are related to flight performance (Sterman, 1991). Soon we would expect that on-line monitoring and feedback will assist the performer, coach, and sport psychologist in identifying lapses in concentration and giving feedback to refocus.

As electronic monitoring miniaturizes, becomes less invasive and technologically more sophisticated, it will be possible to monitor performers during their actual competition. Monitoring during competition is important because laboratory performance typically does not evoke the same thoughts, feelings, or movements as those associated with actual competition. Relatively little research exists on how to develop and maintain concentration or on how to avoid the disruption of concentration. We suggest that more research be conducted to identify the most effective components of the concentration training procedures. Psychophysiological assessment, such as EEG monitoring, will greatly complement the concentration knowledge derived from self-report and performance data.

In summary, concentration is the ability to direct one's full attention to appropriate cues in the present task instead of being controlled by irrelevant external or internal stimuli. Most top athletes have developed their own mental strategies for doing this. These strategies are often perceived as a component of natural athletic ability. In fact, they are not innate; they are skills that athletes acquire through regular practice of attention control training. The consistent control over one's attentional focus before and during competition is thus learned through practice, just as any difficult physical skill is learned.

Study Questions

1. Describe the potential interaction between external and internal stimuli in distracting a performer.

2. Describe a technique for helping athletes experience and distinguish among Nideffer's four attentional styles.

3. Briefly describe and give one example each of how dress rehearsal, rehearsal of simulated competition, and mental rehearsal can be effective strategies to keep concentration.

4. How can attentional cues and triggers be used to either initially focus or retrigger concentration?

5. Provide an example of how the technique of "turning failure into success" might be used and a brief description of why the strategy might be effective.

6. Describe the three techniques that use electrodermal feedback to stay centered.

7. Briefly describe the four exercises under the section "Increasing Focusing and Refocusing Skills."

8. Provide two examples of when and how developing performing protocols might be used to improve concentration.

References

Benagh, J. (1976). *Incredible Olympic feats*. New York: McGraw-Hill.

Botkin, M. (1984). Olympic gold makes topping oh so sweet. In *The 1984 Four Continents Rhythmic Sportive Gymnastics Championships Program*, pp. 4–5. Indianapolis, Ind.: USGF.

Boutcher, S. H., & Crews, D. J. (1987). The effect of a preshot attentional routine on a well-learned skill. *International Journal of Sport Psychology, 18,* 30–39.

Braunstein, M. (1991, October 21). *Interested in achieving peak performance?* Lecture/demonstration at San Francisco State University, San Francisco.

Cox, R. H. (1990). *Sport psychology: Concepts and applications.* Dubuque, Iowa: Brown.

Evert, C. (1988). Concentrated effort. *World Tennis, 36*(3), 29–30.

Gauron, E. F. (1984). *Mental training for peak performance.* Lansing, N.Y.: Sport Science Associates.

Harris, D. V., & Harris, B. L. (1984). *The athlete's guide to sports psychology: Mental skills for physical people.* New York: Leisure Press.

Landers, D. M., Boutcher, S. H., & Wang, M. Q. (1986). A psychological study of archery performance. *Research Quarterly for Exercise and Sport, 57,* 236–244.

Lubar, J. (1991). Discourse on the development of EEG diagnostics and biofeedback for attention-deficit/hyperactivity disorders. *Biofeedback and Self-Regulation, 16*(3), 201–226.

Nideffer, R. M. (1981). *The ethics and practice of applied sport psychology.* Ithaca, N.Y.: Mouvement Publications.

Nideffer, R. M. (1987). Psychological preparation of the highly competitive athlete. *The Physician and Sports Medicine, 15*(10), 85–92.

Peper, E., & Schmid, A. B. (1983–1984). The use of electrodermal biofeedback for peak performance training. *Somatics, 4*(3), 16–18.

Peper, E., & Williams, E. A. (1981). *From the inside out: A self-teaching and laboratory manual for biofeedback.* New York: Plenum.

Salmela, J. H. (1976). *Competitive behaviors of Olympic gymnasts.* Springfield, Ill.: Thomas.

Schmid, A. B. (1982). Coach's reaction to Dr. A. B. Frederick's coaching strategies based upon tension research. In L. D. Zaichkowsky and W. E. Sime (Eds.), *Stress management for sport* (pp. 95–100). Reston, Vir.: AAHPERD.

Schmid, A. B., & Peper, E. (1982). *Mental preparation for optimal performance in rhythmic gymnastics.* Paper pre-sented at the Western Society for Physical Education of College Women Conference, Asilomar, Calif.

Sterman, M. B. (1991). *Tracking arousal and attention in the cockpit.* Paper presented at the 22nd Annual Meet-ing of the Association for Applied Psychophysiology and Biofeedback, Dallas, Tex.

Suinn, R. M. (1980). Body thinking: Psychology of Olympic champs. In R. M. Suinn (Ed.), *Psychology in sports: Methods and applications.* Minneapolis, Minn.: Burgess.

Walsh, M., & Spelman, F. (1983, June 13). Unvar-nished symphonies. *Time*, p. 75.

Integrating and Implementing a Psychological Skills Training Program

Robert S. Weinberg, *Miami University*

Jean M. Williams, *University of Arizona*

*T*he authors of Chapters 11 through 19 have discussed peak performance characteristics, psychological theory, and exercises for training specific psychological skills. When sport psychologists began employing psychological skills interventions in the early 1980s, there were not many empirical data or controlled studies to help guide these initial attempts to improve performance. However, the last five to seven years have produced a number of field-based studies that have investigated the effectiveness of different psychological interventions to enhance performance. Although we have learned a great deal from these studies, many questions still remain. Some of the most important questions include the following: How old and skillful should athletes be before beginning psychological skills training? Who should conduct the training program—the sport psychologist or the coach? Is there an ideal time during the year for implementing a psychological skills training program? How much time is needed for psychological skills training? What specific components should be incorporated in training, and how should those components be sequenced and integrated? What ethical considerations should one be aware of

when implementing a program? In this chapter we address these questions and others, but first we must recognize that regarding some of these questions only preliminary data exist. Therefore, caution must be observed until more definitive studies are conducted.

Most comprehensive mental training programs stress the development of psychological skills and techniques such as anxiety management, imagery, goal setting, concentration, self-talk, thought stopping, routines, and confidence (just to name a few). The multitude of possibilities makes it very difficult to integrate all of the components into one comprehensive mental training program. In essence, situational constraints (e.g., the athlete or team only has a few weeks to learn and implement a psychological skills training program) do not always permit the implementation of a comprehensive mental training program, and thus it is often necessary to plan an abbreviated program. Furthermore, although a number of mental training programs have been recently developed (e.g., Boutcher & Rotella, 1987; Gordon, 1990; Kirschenbaum & Bale, 1980; Orlick,1986; Suinn, 1986), there still isn't general agreement among sport psychologists on how much time should be spent learning these techniques or what techniques are best for achieving certain objectives. For example, what technique should be used for an athlete who starts thinking ahead during competition to what might happen if he/she loses or wins the game?

Unfortunately, there are no ready-made solutions to questions of how coaches and sport psychologists can integrate and implement a psychological skills training program. The data base is only recently being developed, and thus new information is constantly changing the way that mental training programs are implemented. Nonetheless, if a mental training program is to be effective, strategies for putting all of the different components into place must be planned and well thought out. In this chapter we offer some suggestions and practical pointers for implementing mental skills training and for integrating various psychological skill components into these programs. Unless otherwise noted, these guidelines are the same for either the coach or sport psychologist, although we will discuss the pros and cons of taking on a dual role of coach/sport psychologist. Finally, we again caution you to view these recommendations only as suggested guidelines. In some cases the principles have not been empirically tested over time, and you should view this as an evolving area of study that probably will continue to change in the upcoming years.

Are Psychological Interventions Effective in Improving Sport Performance?

Probably the most important question that sport psychology consultants need to ask themselves revolves around the effectiveness of their psychological interventions in enhancing performance and personal growth. It is the same problem that has plagued clinical psychologists and counselors over the years—demonstrating that what they do makes a difference in the behavior and/or well-being of their clients. Defending the effectiveness of psychological skills training programs in improving sport performance and well-being requires the accumulation of well-controlled, outcome-based intervention studies conducted in competitive sport environments. These are traditionally

difficult to carry out due to time and money constraints, unwillingness of coaches and athletes to participate, and inability to adequately control the environment.

Fortunately, sport psychology researchers have been working hard to establish a data base concerning the effectiveness of these psychological interventions in improving performance. Along these lines, Greenspan and Feltz (1989) recently reviewed approximately 20 published studies that tested the effectiveness of various psychological interventions (23 different interventions in all) in competitive sport settings including such diverse sports as golf, karate, skiing, boxing, basketball, volleyball, gymnastics, baseball, tennis, and figure skating. The authors conclude that, in general, educationally based psychological interventions *are* effective in improving the performance of collegiate and adult athletes in competitive situations.

We should note that most of the studies reviewed were conducted with collegiate or adult populations, with few or no studies investigating elite athletes, youth athletes (under 18 years old), or special populations such as the physically disabled and mentally retarded. Following this review, there were a number of studies using elite and special populations. Most of these reports discuss the consultant's philosophy and implementation of psychological services. Few of the programs had formal assessment procedures other than athletes' verbal reports that they felt the intervention was helpful (see *The Sport Psychologist*, 1989, #4 and *The Sport Psychologist*, 1991, #4). Although these initial reports appear encouraging, we still need more controlled studies on these different groups before more definitive conclusions can be made.

Who Will Benefit from Psychological Skills Training

Many coaches and athletes misunderstand peak performance sport psychology. They think mental training strategies are only applicable to elite athletes or that these techniques can only fine tune the performance of the already highly skilled. In actuality, mental skills training should be beneficial for a variety of people, although, as previously noted, we need more studies across different skill and age groups and special populations. If beginning athletes are taught to set realistic goals, increase self-confidence, visualize success, and react constructively, we can expect their performance and personal development to progress faster than the performance and personal development of athletes who do not receive similar mental training. Special adjustments may be needed, however, based upon the population of athletes. For example, very young athletes may need adjustments such as fewer goals, shorter training sessions, simpler verbal instruction, and turning the exercises into games, but these athletes can still benefit from some sort of mental skills training provided they are interested in receiving it (Hellstedt, 1987; Orlick & McCaffrey, 1991; Smith & Smoll, 1982; Weiss, 1991).

The ideal time for initially implementing training may be when individuals are just beginning to participate in sport. As any experienced teacher or coach knows, it is far easier to develop proper physical technique in a beginner than it is to modify poor technique in a more experienced athlete. Although never empirically tested, the same phenomenon may be true for psychological skills. Furthermore, early implementation ensures the laying of a psychological skills foundation that will facilitate future achievement of full athletic potential, enjoyment, and benefit.

On the other hand, highly skilled athletes can certainly benefit from systematic psychological skills training programs. As athletes get better, physical differences tend to become smaller since less skilled, less gifted athletes usually drop out of formal competition. At this level, minute adjustments and differences can literally mean the difference between winning and losing. For example, Orlick (1986) provides a number of case studies of Olympic athletes who systematically employed a mental training program. The athletes report that their mental training and discipline were a critical component of their success. Their comments generally reflect the notion that everybody they were competing against was physically talented. The key difference was in their consistency of mental preparation and training. Let's look at an example of an Olympic skier in her second year of mental training:

> Last year I got angry with myself or so upset about not performing well. Initially if I didn't get angry or punish myself, I would feel guilty, as if I wasn't taking it seriously. This year I'm

keeping it in perspective and reminding myself what it's for. Now I'm thinking about enjoyment as well as intensity. This year for the first time ever, I pushed during a whole training camp. I never let up. I stayed interested and motivated. When I started to coast I stopped and went free skiing. I don't want to practice skiing at low intensity. (Orlick, 1986, p. 148)

Who Should Conduct the Psychological Skills Training Program

Ideally, a psychological skills training program should be planned, implemented, and supervised by a qualified consulting sport psychologist. The sport psychologist has the advantage of having more extensive special training and experience than a coach. Also, athletes may be more open in discussing difficulties with the psychological aspects of play because the sport psychologist does not decide who stays on the team and who gets to play. Even though it is desirable to have a sport psychologist administer the program, this is rarely feasible except perhaps at the highest levels of competition (and even here it is still a rarity for a sport psychologist to travel with a team throughout a season). The basic premise of this book is that it is also the responsibility of the coach to provide mental skills training and reinforce optimal psychological states; after all, who knows the athletes better and who works more closely with them? Thus, there are advantages to having mental skills training provided by the consulting sport psychologist *or* the coach.

When the mental training program is to be implemented by a sport psychologist, the selection of that person is critical. Who is qualified to be a sport psychologist? Fortunately, in 1991 the Association for the Advancement of Applied Sport Psychology (*AAASP Newsletter*, 1991) adopted criteria for certification for individuals working in the area of applied sport psychology. Basically, this certification requires individuals to have extensive backgrounds in both the sport and psychological sciences as well as some practical supervised experience implementing psychological skills with athletes and teams (see Chapter 1 for a more detailed explanation of AAASP certification). The U.S.

Olympic Committee also certifies educational and clinical sport psychologists, but only for working with Olympic or prospective Olympic athletes through the national governing bodies. The best choice is an individual who is certified by AAASP or the USOC since this ensures a certain experience, background, and competence in applied sport psychology. However, just because an individual is certified does not necessarily mean he/she has the type of orientation or experiential background that would best meet the needs of a specific team or coach. For example, will the person's focus be on dealing with personal and emotional problems (i.e., clinical approach) or teaching mental skills for enhancing performance (performance enhancement approach)? Does the person have experience with younger athletes or primarily elite athletes? Is he/she sufficiently knowledgeable about the sport in which the psychological skills are to be applied? How much time does the person have to spend with the team? Does the person have references from teams or individuals he/she worked with in the past developing psychological skills? These and other questions guide the selection of the sport psychologist who best suits the athletes' specific needs and goals.

If a sport psychology consultant conducts the program, we recommend that the coach, or coaching staff, attend most or all of the initial group training sessions. There are a number of reasons for this recommendation. First, the coach's presence tells the athletes that he/she thinks the sessions are important. Second, the sport psychologist will not be present during most of the physical practices and competitions; a knowledgeable coach can be a key person in ensuring the effectiveness of mental skills training by seeing that appropriate application of such training occurs. Ideally, the sport psychologist and coach should have special meetings to discuss ways for the coach to apply and reinforce whatever the sport psychologist emphasizes in mental skills training sessions. Third, misunderstandings regarding what the sport psychologist is doing will not occur because the coach will know exactly what is happening and will be providing feedback regarding what he/she perceives needs to be done. Ravizza (1990) in his work with professional baseball teams notes that in the early stages a good portion of his work with coaches was done in the locker room, hotel lobby, or at meals. As the relationship progressed, they set aside mutually

convenient times for formal meetings to discuss how individual players were performing as well as any other relevant issues.

Our understanding about how to conduct psychological skills training programs with athletes has increased rapidly in recent years. Along these lines, a number of sport psychologists have recently written about their consulting experiences with athletes and teams. In fact, separate issues of *The Sport Psychologist* (1989, #4; 1990, #4; 1991, #4) were devoted to psychological interventions with Olympic athletes, professional teams, and special populations (respectively). In these articles, sport psychologists described the specific programs they developed to help athletes enhance performance as well as personal growth in such sports and populations as baseball (Ravizza, 1990), tennis (Loehr, 1990), hockey (Botterill, 1990), gymnastics (Salmela, 1989), track and field (Nideffer, 1989), volleyball (Gipson, McKenzie, & Lowe, 1989), skiing (May & Brown, 1989), physically disabled (Asken, 1991; Clark & Sachs, 1991), and mentally retarded (Travis & Sachs, 1991).

Of course, the philosophy and implementation of mental training programs differ somewhat from one sport psychologist to the next. Each person has to understand the nature of the team or individual athletes he/she is working with and integrate that with his/her own background, training, and orientation. It's important for the sport psychologist to communicate his/her philosophy to the athletes and coaches at the outset and to make sure that everyone understands the parameters of the consultation.

It was previously noted that one of the drawbacks of having a sport psychologist conduct a psychological skills program is the difficulty in being with the athletes on a day-to-day basis. In many cases the sport psychology consultant cannot provide continuous services, either because the organization is diffused over a wide geographical area or because the consultant or athletic group cannot make the time commitment necessary to provide ongoing services. Coaches, of course, have the best access to athletes on a daily basis and are thus in a position to administer psychological interventions over the course of a season. An innovative consultation model has been developed by Smith and Johnson (1990) in their work with the Houston Astros minor league player development program. They call this model "organizational empowerment," and we will discuss it in some depth since it serves as an excellent prototype for sport psychology consultation.

In this model of service delivery, the sport psychology consultant trains one or more qualified individuals within the sport organization to provide psychological services to athletes and coaches. The consultant then oversees the program and provides ongoing supervision of the actual trainers. This approach thus empowers a sport organization to provide its own sport psychology services under the supervision of the consultant.

In setting up this program, one of the major challenges was to provide continuity to a major league baseball club that has minor league teams in several cities over a wide geographical area. Smith and Johnson strongly believe that one-shot or occasional psychological skills training, no matter how competently it is carried out, cannot be as effective as that provided on a continuous basis over an extended period of time. In addition, they feel there are real advantages to having someone identified with professional baseball as the service provider, given that the trainer has the requisite background in counseling and psychological skills training. A "baseball person" may have an easier time establishing credibility within what is still a very traditional baseball establishment and may find it easier to coordinate psychological skills training with the technical aspects of player development because of the deeper knowledge of the game and understanding of baseball life in general.

In their specific case, Smith (the sport psychology consultant) trained Johnson (a manager in the Astros organization with a master's degree in psychology). An intensive six-week training program was established prior to spring training in which Johnson was given a set of extensive sport psychology reading materials and Smith met with Johnson for several days concerning the use of psychological interventions in sport. In addition, Smith accompanied Johnson to spring training for 10 days of hands-on training plus a series of orientation workshops for staff and players. Weekly and sometimes daily telephone supervision continued throughout the remainder of spring training and the regular season, along with two additional 4-day blocks of personal contact. Once Johnson felt comfortable with his new skills, Smith worked with him to help put together a psychological skills

training program. Smith helped in overseeing the program, but it was Johnson who was in charge of implementing the day-to-day psychological exercises. With continued interaction and support between Smith and Johnson, the program enjoyed some initial success and is now ongoing.

When to Implement a Psychological Skills Training Program

It is generally agreed that the *least* desirable time to implement a psychological skills program is after the competitive season has started, when the athlete is facing a string of competitions in quick succession. At this time, mental training usually amounts to no more than a quick-fix, bandage approach and consequently is rarely, if ever, effective. One of the underlying principles of this book is that psychological skills are learned and therefore need to be practiced systematically, just like physical skills. Introducing a program in the middle of the season would not allow athletes time to learn these new mental skills and integrate them into their performance.

To draw an analogy, golfers or tennis players would not change their grip on the club or racket right before a tournament without extensively using the new grip in practice for several weeks or even months. If they did change their grip right before a tournament, performance would probably be worse, not better. Similarly, we should not expect athletes to be able to learn new psychological skills in such a short period of time. And even if there are benefits, the influence is probably only that of a short-term placebo—the athlete expects the psychological intervention to improve performance, and therefore it does. As soon as the novelty wears off, the athlete usually slips back into old ways of thinking, feeling, and performing.

For these reasons, most sport psychology consultants believe that the best time to initially implement psychological skills training is during the off season or preseason. During this period there is more time to learn new skills, and it is easier to try new ideas because this is the time of year when athletes are not so pressured with winning. Some athletes have reported that it took several months to a year to fully understand and integrate their new psychological skills into actual competitions. This underscores the importance of viewing mental training as an ongoing process that needs to be integrated with physical practice over a period of time.

When to Practice Psychological Skills

The rudiments of most psychological skills should first be taught and systematically practiced during special training sessions. The first or last 15 to 30 minutes of practice is often a good time for training. The content of the particular session will determine whether it is better held at the beginning or end of practice (see earlier chapters for suggestions on which training exercises are better practiced before or after physical workouts). Homework assignments also can be given, but unless the athletes are self-directed, it is better to have most mental training practice occur under someone's supervision.

As soon as possible the psychological skills practice should be integrated with physical skills practice. When integrating the two, the rehearsal of mental skills should have a performance-specific focus. For example, once athletes have learned the skill of relaxation and recognizing tension, they should be instructed to scan their muscles for harmful tension and practice appropriate differential relaxation while performing. Specific performance times should be identified—for example, always scan and relax before pitching, shooting a free throw, serving a tennis ball, or taking a shot in golf. Once relaxation skills have been effectively integrated into physical workouts, they should be tried during simulated or practice competition and later during actual competition. The same stepwise building of competence should occur for introducing and practicing other mental skills such as imagery and concentration. It is important not to proceed too quickly from learning to competition because the psychological skills may not be fully integrated and therefore performance decrements could occur. We have found that many athletes are often impatient and want to use their new skills almost immediately. But we must remember that this is not a quick fix, and learning new skills requires patience.

This progressive method of practice is also psychologically sound from a learning standpoint because it allows the athletes to gain knowledge and competence in using each mental skill as environmental demands slowly become more variable, challenging, and applicable. The ultimate goal is for the practice of mental skills to become such an integral part of all physical practices that the training program does not appear to be something extra. This type of systematic, consistent practice of mental skills is likely to achieve lasting optimal results rather than short-term placebo effects.

How Much Time Should Be Spent in Mental Training

By now it should be obvious that the time needed for practicing mental skills varies according to what is being practiced and how well it is learned. If a new mental skill is being introduced, special 15- to 30-minute training sessions three to five days per week may be needed. Some weeks no special sessions may be needed because all practice can occur along with physical workouts. As athletes become more proficient, fewer special training sessions are necessary. However, special sessions still may be advisable for individual athletes who are experiencing difficulty in learning the mental skills.

When separate times are not being designated solely for mental training, it is very important that the coaching staff or sport psychologist provide verbal reminders for integrating mental skills practice with physical skills practice. In addition, appropriate reinforcement for the use of these mental skills during practice is crucial for athletes' motivation since they are attempting to develop new habits and possibly break some old bad habits. This can be a difficult task, and a positive approach is important to keep spirits up, as well as providing informative feedback to help athletes integrate the mental skills into their physical performance.

The time frame we have just recommended may not be desirable if a sport psychology consultant is implementing the training, particularly when the sport psychologist has to spend time traveling to reach the team. Under such circumstances, fewer and longer mental training sessions are usually held unless a coach or other organization member is trained to carry out the mental training program. Most of the initial meetings should be group sessions in order to best use the sport psychologist's time. However, research has indicated that individual sessions and individualized training programs are needed to optimize the effectiveness of mental training programs (Seabourne et al., 1985). That is why most sport psychology consultants will typically start with some group or team sessions to lay down some general principles and state their philosophy before following up with individual meetings with athletes (e.g., Botterill, 1990; Halliwell, 1990). It is particularly critical that athletes are assigned training exercises to practice during the times the sport psychologist is not with the team. Successively longer intervals should be scheduled between sport psychologist–led sessions to allow for mastery and absorption of the techniques and coping strategies. The same stepwise building of competence that we described earlier should be observed here.

The traveling sport psychology consultant must design practice exercises in such a way that maximum feedback occurs from participation and that adherence to training is likely to occur. As noted earlier, in the absence of the consultant, the coach or an individual designated by the coach can play a major role in ensuring compliance and feedback if he/she assumes responsibility for personally conducting the training exercises or at least provides the time for athletes to practice. If this is not possible, the coach or designated individual should remind athletes of their homework assignments and briefly discuss the athletes' reactions to the exercises once the homework has been completed. However, maximum effectiveness is likely only when this individual and the sport psychologist work together as a team.

A logical question that arises after a mental training program has been put in place is "When can athletes stop mental skills training?" In the truest sense, mental skills training continues as long as athletes participate in sport. In this sense, mental skills are no different from physical skills. Retention will not occur without continued practice. Athletes who during physical practice allow their concentration to be sloppy, their mental attitude to be negative, or their arousal level to be too high or low invariably find the same behaviors occurring during competition. When we hear the names of such athletes as Larry Bird, Martina

Navratilova, Bo Jackson, Joe Montana, Jackie Joyner-Kersee, and Wayne Gretsky (just to name a few), we think of individuals who are highly skilled and great competitors. However, these same athletes are also known for their great practice habits, especially making sure that the mental aspects of their respective sports are integrated into their physical practice on an ongoing basis.

If athletes never stop mental skills training, what is the ideal length of time for their first exposure to a "formal" mental skills training program? Most sport psychology consultants would recommend an average of between three and six months since it takes time to learn these new mental skills, use them in practice, and then integrate them into actual competitive situations. The specific sport, time available, existing mental skills, and commitment of individuals are all factors that should be considered in determining actual length of time. For example, we have worked with athletes who simply needed to change a small part of their mental approach and were able to do that in under two months. On the other hand, Orlick (1986) has noted that many of the Canadian Olympic athletes that he has consulted with started practicing their mental training program a couple of years before the Olympic Games. Their psychological plans and mental preparation were extremely detailed and precise, as seen in the example provided in Table 20-1 for an Olympic alpine skier (Orlick, 1986, p. 34).

Setting Up a Mental Skills Training Program

Thus far we have discussed some important questions surrounding the use of mental training programs, including who will benefit, who should conduct the program, when to implement the training program, when to actually practice the mental skills, and how much time to spend on mental training. Although this information is important in understanding mental training programs, it does not really tell us exactly what to do in setting up such a program. Therefore, we will attempt to outline some of the critical components of implementing a mental skills training program. In order to accomplish this we will draw upon our own research and experience in consulting with athletes as well as those of other sport psychologists.

Table 20-1 **Prerace Mental Preparation Plan**

General Warm-up **Physical and Mental**	*Start Preparation* **Physical and Mental**
Night Before Race	
• Receive number, determine how many minutes after start I race.	• Arrive at start 20 minutes prior to my start.
• Figure out what time to awaken and leave for hill in the morning and approximately how many free runs or training course runs to have before start.	• First get race skis in snow, check them to see if all is ready; see rep. (equipment person).
• Estimate how long to put number on, stretch inside lodge.	• Begin stretching, running; think happy, relaxed thoughts.
• Spend ideally no more than 20 to 25 minutes in start area.	• Apply these comments to mental imagery.
Morning of Race	
• Light run, exercises, begin the morning on a positive or high note.	• Heavier physical preparation.
• Wake up feeling good about myself, be optimistic, flow.	• Get into skis, binding check.
• Important for me not to project (e.g., about outcomes); just feel good about myself for myself.	• More imagery of race focus and feeling—include correction imagery if needed.
• Free skiing and training courses to feel aggressive and pumped, yet calm and relaxed.	• Quicker physical activity.
• Focused and concentrated while skiing.	• 1 minute: Take coat, warm-ups off, intense, focused on task.
• Mental imagery (to know course and feel good about myself on the course).	• 30 seconds: Ready myself in start, think only of course and of myself.
	• Explosive start.

Discuss Your Approach—What You Do and What You Don't Do

We have found that many athletes are still fairly naive or uninformed about what sport psychology is and what sport psychologists do. Therefore, we believe it is important to spell this out right at the outset of the initial meeting. Although most ath-letes typically view sport psychology solely in terms of performance enhancement, they also should be made to understand its mental health aspects. In fact, as reflected in the title of this text, sport psychology has as much to do with personal growth issues as it does with achieving maximum performance. Therefore, these two different aspects need to be clearly communicated to athletes so they understand the broad focus that sport psychology can have.

In addition to conducting a brief discussion on what sport psychology is, it is equally critical that sport psychologists spell out their specific approach in dealing with psychological problems in sport and exercise. There are basically two approaches that sport psychologists take in working with athletes; clinical and educational. However, research and experience have indicated that the large majority of athletes consulting with sport psychologists require an educational approach as opposed to a clinical approach. Athletes typically need to develop some psychological skill like improving concentration or managing anxiety rather than to deal with a deep-seated, severe psychological problem. Therefore, we will focus on the educational approach, but it should be made clear that if an educational sport psychologist or coach comes across an athlete who has such a serious psychological problem that it is beyond his/her skills to treat, then the athlete should be referred to a qualified individual or counseling center. (See the following chapter for a discussion of when it may be appropriate to refer athletes for counseling or psychotherapy.)

Thus, the sport psychology consultant should tell the athlete what he/she does and does not do, as many people still believe that if athletes see a sport psychologist then something must be psychologically wrong with them. This is especially true of younger athletes, who can be extra sensitive to the idea that they "have to see a shrink." Rather, we try to emphasize that if an athlete stayed after practice to work with the coach on a particular move or physical technique, most people would applaud this extra effort to improve. Similarly, if an athlete realizes that he/she needs to work on some aspect of the mental game such as concentration skills, then this also should be applauded. In essence, working to improve mentally should not be looked on as a weakness but rather as simply another way for an athlete to improve performance as well as enhance personal growth.

Emphasize the Importance of Mental Training

Another important component to an initial meeting with athletes is convincing them of the need for systematic mental training and creating a positive belief structure regarding the effects of mental training. This can be done in many ways. One way to start is to have athletes identify how important their state of mind is in achieving success by having them decide what percentage of their game is mental. Then compare this percentage to the actual percentage of practice time spent training mental skills. The disparity is usually in the direction of the mental side of sport being very important, yet little or no time being spent specifically practicing these mental aspects. This usually will increase athletes' awareness of the importance of actually practicing these mental skills instead of simply focusing on physical skills.

Providing anecdotes about the importance of mental preparation from relevant, well-known amateur and professional athletes is another effective way to increase receptivity. The extensive coverage of the Olympic Games and other sport literature provide many personal stories of the positive effects of mental training. Such anecdotes are usually much more motivating than a recitation of the results of research studies on mental training. Along these lines, a recent study from the U.S. Olympic Training Center (Murphy, Jowdy, & Durtschi, 1990) revealed that over 90% of Olympic athletes surveyed regularly used some sort of mental preparation and training in preparing for competition. This type of information can help athletes realize that mental training does work and is being used by many of our very best athletes, although athletes of all ability levels can benefit from such training.

Fortunately, the popularity of applied sport psychology has evolved to the point that it is becoming easier to sell a mental skills training program to most athletes. Nevertheless, some athletes still will refuse to accept mental skills training. Most sport psychologists recommend not forcing unreceptive athletes to participate. Conversely, there also can be problems with athletes who are highly enthusiastic about mental training. For instance, occasionally this enthusiasm can lead to unreasonable expectations. Athletes, coaches, and sport psychologists must realize that no amount of mental training will substitute for poor mechanics, lack of practice, or limited physical aptitude. Also, good psychological skills cannot replace hard physical conditioning and training. Another problem may come from athletes who expect miracles from only a small investment of time. Excellent physical skills do not develop overnight and neither do mental skills. Once athletes recognize that good mental skills are acquired in the same way as good physical skills (i.e., through long-term, consistent practice), the foundation has been laid for appropriate mental skills training and practice.

Assessing Psychological Strengths and Weaknesses

Once athletes are informed of the approach the sport psychologist plans to take and are convinced of the importance of mental training, the next step in conducting any mental skills training program should be to determine the athletes' psychological strengths and weaknesses as related specifically to sport. A needs assessment helps reveal those psychological skills that are deficient or appear to have the most adverse effect on performance and personal satisfaction. In addition, it should also reveal the strong points of each athlete from a mental perspective. When something is bothering athletes or they are struggling with a specific problem, they often forget or overlook all the things that they do well, and these should not be forgotten.

In conducting the initial evaluation of athletes' psychological strengths and weaknesses, it is important that sport psychology consultants first understand that there are factors outside the psychological realm that influence performance (Boutcher & Rotella, 1987). These include such things as physiological conditioning, biomechanics (technique), strategy, and equipment. For example, a golfer who has a major flaw in his/her swing may attribute the resulting poor performance to ineffective concentration, whereas the underlying problem is biomechanical. The important point is that one must not try to interpret all aspects of performance from a psychological perspective. Thus, the need for input from experts such as coaches, biomechanists, and exercise physiologists must be recognized.

In terms of the actual psychological skills evaluation, we recommend an oral interview as well as written psychological inventories. In this way the athlete will have a chance to tell his/her story face to face as well as responding to some objective questionnaires. This also helps the consultant in looking for consistencies (and inconsistencies) between oral and written statements.

There are various approaches to conducting an initial interview, but the one we recommend is the semistructured interview, which is outlined in detail by Orlick (1980). Some general questions provide structure to this type of interview, but there is leeway to use the athlete's responses to form other follow-up questions. For example, some key questions might include the following:

- Summarize your involvement in your sport, noting important events both positive and negative (this is a good starting point as it lets athletes talk about themselves and become more comfortable).

- Describe what you believe to be your greatest psychological strength and your biggest weakness.

- Describe the boundaries of any specific psychological problem you are currently having (i.e., when, why, how).

- What is your relationship with your coach?

It is our experience that this interview should last approximately one hour. Of course, individual differences and time constraints can alter this time frame to some degree. The initial interview is very important not only to find out where the athlete needs help but also as a place to start building the trust that is critical for any therapeutic relationship. For a sport psychology consultant to be maximally effective, the athlete needs to feel comfortable and believe that the consultant is not only competent but cares about his/her particular situation. One thing that we have found important is that the consultant has a good working knowledge of the sport even if he/she does not have much actual playing experience. This helps build credibility from the athletes' point of view since it gives them a sense that the consultant not only understands psychology but also understands and appreciates the fine points of their sport.

In addition to the interview, most (although not all) sport psychology consultants use some paper-and-pencil psychological inventories to assess both psychological skills related to sport as well as more general mood states. Although many different inventories are utilized, some of the more popular ones include the following: Profile of Mood States (McNair, Lorr, & Droppleman, 1971), Sport Competition Anxiety Test (Martens, 1977), Competitive State Anxiety Inventory-2 (Martens, Vealey, & Burton, 1990), Test of Attentional and Interpersonal Style (Nideffer, 1976), Psychological Skills Inventory for Sport (Mahoney, Gabriel, & Perkins, 1987), and Trait-State Sport Confidence

Inventory (Vealey, 1986). In addition, a number of sport-specific inventories have been developed, such as the Tennis Test of Attentional and Interpersonal Style (Van Schoyck & Grasha, 1981), Anxiety Assessment for Wrestlers (Gould, Horn, & Spreeman, 1987), and the Riflery Attention Questionnaire (Etzel, 1979), that provide more directed questions toward a specific sport.

Once the interview and psychological inventories have been completed, we recommend that written feedback be provided to each athlete that highlights his/her psychological strengths and weaknesses as they relate to sport performance and participation. This assessment should be given to athletes in a second one-on-one meeting, and they should be provided with an opportunity to react to it. This provides an opportunity to get consensual validation from athletes in terms of the evaluation of the sport psychology consultant. At times we have found the oral interview and written assessments to be contrary, and this is a good time to bring any discrepancy up and have the athlete resolve it. The assessment should conclude with recommendations for the type of skills and intervention program that the consultant thinks would best suit the athlete's needs. Ideally, these recommendations are mutually decided and agreed upon by the athlete(s) and the sport psychologist.

If a sport psychology consultant is working with an entire team, it is essential that the coach be involved in the needs assessment because he/she is more likely to know the team's mental strengths and weaknesses over a period of time. This might, in turn, require different psychological approaches based on the team's history. For example, quite different psychological needs would probably be perceived for a team with a long history of losing compared to a team that climbed to the top and was currently experiencing the pressure of trying to maintain number-one status. A consultant working with the losing team might determine that the primary emphasis should be on developing a positive mental attitude. In such a case, systematic planning and strategies might be directed at getting the athletes to stop feeling like losers and begin thinking and feeling like they could win. Techniques for building confidence, monitoring and replacing self-defeating talk, and setting realistic goals might prove quite beneficial.

On the other hand, the coach or sport psychology consultant working with the highly successful team might perceive a primary need to develop skills for regulating arousal and maintaining concentration. Techniques would need to be planned for coping with the stress of being expected to win consistently, even when playing against excellent competitors who are always "up" for the defending champions. In addition, the team may need to focus on keeping sufficiently energized and focused when playing against clearly inferior competitors.

An obvious implication of this discussion on needs assessment is that the coach should be wary of anyone who presents a "canned" mental training program that does not provide for the specific needs of a given group of athletes. Although such a program may be better than nothing, optimal benefits for the investment in time will only come from training designed to meet the specific needs, maturation, and experience of the given group. It is, of course, more demanding and time-consuming for sport psychology consultants to individualize their programs based on specific needs of athletes, coaches, and teams. But for fostering the personal growth of athletes as well as helping them achieve maximum performance, the more attention that is paid to individual needs, the more likely it is that the program will be successful.

Determining What Skills to Include and How to Sequence Them

Once the assessment is complete and all needed psychological skills have been listed, the coach or sport psychologist must decide how many of these skills to emphasize. This decision should be based on when the program is first being implemented (e.g., preseason, practice season, competitive season) and how much time the athletes and coach are willing to devote to mental skills training. Several questions are pertinent at this point:

• How much practice time will be given up on the average each week for mental skills training?

• How many weeks of practice are available?

• Will there still be time to practice mental skills after the competitive season starts, or after the first couple of losses?

• How interested are the athletes in receiving mental skills training?

The answers to these questions will help provide a realistic perspective on the commitment to mental skills training and the time available for accomplishing psychological skill objectives. When there is not adequate time and/or commitment for a comprehensive training program, it is better to prioritize objectives and emphasize a few to work on initially rather than work superficially on all of the needed skills. The coach or sport psychologist may even wish to develop a two- to three-year plan (Gould, 1983; Orlick, 1986). When there is time, interest, and need for a comprehensive mental training program, what should be the main components of the program and how should the coach or sport psychologist sequence the teaching of all the different psychological skill components?

Although there is certainly no definitive answer as to what a psychological skills training program should include or in what sequence these skills should be taught, Vealey (1988) provides a thoughtful analysis of the nature of psychological skills training programs in the future. The first thing that Vealey notes is the need to differentiate between psychological skills and methods. **Skills** are qualities to be obtained, as opposed to **methods**, which are procedures or techniques employed in order to develop these skills. Although sport psychology consultants certainly use different models, it is useful to differentiate between skills and methods since this should encourage consultants to focus on the skill to be obtained and to then choose any method or combination of methods that will help attain this skill. At times, however, sport psychology consultants have become enamored with a particular method (e.g., relaxation) and use it indiscriminately instead of focusing on a skill that an athlete needs to develop. This type of approach may cause athletes to lose interest since the training is not directed specifically at meeting their individual needs.

Table 20-2 provides an overview of the methods that can be used to develop and enhance psychological skills. The basic psychological skills training methods include the four traditional techniques of goal setting (Chapter 13), imagery (Chapter 16), physical relaxation (Chapter 15), and thought control (Chapter 17). Physical practice and education are also included as foundation methods to emphasize that psychological skills are facilitated by productive physical practice and the understanding of the physical and mental processes that influence performance. In fact, most

Table 20-2 **Methods for Developing Psychological Skills**

Foundation Methods	Psychological Skills Methods
Physical Practice	Goal Setting
Education	Imagery
	Physical Relaxation
	Thought Control

Modified from: Vealey, 1988.

psychological skills training programs include an educational phase in which athletes are introduced to a number of basic sport psychology principles and concepts. This educational phase provides the needed information and background for athletes to move forward to the actual learning and implementation of specific psychological skills.

Using foundation and psychological skills methods, Vealey (1988) proposes a number of skills that can and should be developed in a well-rounded psychological skills training program (see Table 20-3). It's important to note that these skills reflect areas related to personal development as well as performance enhancement. Such a human development model (Danish & Hale, 1981) focuses on human growth and change and assists individuals in gaining control of their lives. This framework is an example of a holistic and personal development approach that emphasizes the need to first develop some basic skills before moving on to other sport and life skills.

The most basic skills are termed **"foundation skills"** and represent those qualities that are basic and necessary psychological skills. The first foundation skill is **volition**, which is concerned with one's internal motivation. Without an individual's desire to achieve success, there is little hope that any psychological skills program would be successful since it takes commitment to practice the skills and carry out the program. One good way to enhance athletes' motivation is through the use of goal setting (see Chapter 13).

The second foundation skill is **self-awareness**. Before athletes can start changing some of their previous bad habits, they need to understand and become aware of exactly when and where their problem behaviors occur and what they are think-

Table 20-3 **Psychological Skills**

Foundation Skills	Performance Skills	Facilitative Skills
Volition	Optimal Physical Arousal	Interpersonal Skills
Self-Awareness	Optimal Mental Arousal	Lifestyle Management
Self-Esteem	Optimal Attention	
Self-Confidence		

Modified from: Vealey, 1988.

Table 20-4 **A Sample of Psychological Skills Objectives and Outcomes**

Objective 1 **Positive Mental Attitude**	*Objective 2* **Coping with Mistakes and Failures**	*Objective 3* **Handle the High-Stress Situation**
Don't make negative statements at games or practices.	Accept the fact that mistakes and failures are a necessary part of the learning process.	Learn to interpret the situation as a challenge rather than a threat.
Change "I can't" statements to "I can" statements.	Don't make excuses. Appropriately accepting responsibility will help turn failures into success.	Recognize too much tension. Achieve appropriate differential relaxation.
Always give 100% effort.	Stay positive even after a stupid mistake.	Keep thoughts positive and focused on the task at hand.
Don't talk while coaches talk.	Be supportive of teammates even when they are making mistakes.	Image goal of performing well under high-stress situations.
Hustle during all plays and drills.	Keep focused concentration rather than dwelling on mistakes.	Focus concentration on appropriate cues.

Modified from: Gould, 1983.

ing and feeling at that time. In addition, athletes need to be aware of what they typically think and feel when performing at their best. That is, do they have an ideal performance state that is associated with peak performance? (See Chapter 11 for more detail on typical peak performance characteristics.) Keeping a sport journal is one way to increase awareness of performance states and understanding regarding how different situations bring about different emotional reactions. (See Chapter 12 for suggestions regarding how to keep a journal and implement other techniques for increasing awareness.)

If athletes are sufficiently motivated and have become aware of the relationship between their thoughts and feelings and behavior, then they can begin to develop their self-esteem and self-confidence. **Self-esteem** and **self-confidence** are not only critical to sport performance (Bandura, 1991) but are also central to a wide array of behaviors outside the world of sport and physical activity (Bandura, 1986). Thus, it would appear inappropriate to begin specific psychological skills training methods (e.g., imagery) until individuals learn a certain level of proficiency in the foundation skills.

The **performance skills** in Vealey's (1988) model are the traditional psychological skills that most sport psychology consultants attempt to teach. These skills are addressed in detail in various chapters throughout the text. The premise is that exceptional performance is most likely to occur when these skills are learned and integrated into an athlete's actual competitive performance.

Facilitative skills have unfortunately been left out of many psychological skill training programs in the past. Although these skills do not always directly influence sport performance, once acquired they can facilitate behavior in sport as well as other areas of life. For example, interpersonal skills are important for both athletes and coaches to have as they can enhance coach–athlete communication, which is an often-cited problem. In addition, communication breakdowns are often the cause of problems at work and in relationships, and thus developing interpersonal skills can help in a number of areas (see Chapter 10). Likewise, **lifestyle management skills** stress the personal development approach to psychological skills training (see Chapter 10). Providing athletes with lifestyle management skills allows them to organize and manage their lives more effectively by becoming more responsible for their actions, by managing their time, and by setting up career goals.

Regardless of the specific methods and skills to be included in any psychological skills training program, it will be more effective if psychological objectives appropriate to the athletes are identified (Silva, 1982; Seabourne et al., 1985). These objectives need to be defined in easily understood and measurable terms (see Table 20-4 for examples). Such definitions help clarify exactly what is meant by the objective and what outcomes are expected once the objective is achieved. The definitions also provide a clear foundation for planning strategies to accomplish the objectives and for assessing how effective the strategies were in achieving the objectives.

Evaluation of Program Effectiveness

It is not easy to evaluate the impact of a psychology skills training program, yet evaluation is essential for improving a training program and the skills of the person in charge of the program. In fact, evaluation should be an essential feature of any organizational as well as individualized intervention. Aside from the accountability demands that ethically oblige sport psychology consultants to evaluate the effectiveness of what they do (see Smith, 1989), there are practical considerations that are also important.

First, program evaluation provides consultants and/or coaches with the information needed to gauge the effectiveness of the various components of their programs and to make modifications where needed. Second, an evaluation provides the consumer with an opportunity to provide feedback concerning areas which he/she feels weren't included or to suggest changes in the way the program was conducted. Third, evaluation is the only way in which we can objectively judge whether the program achieved its intended objectives in changing some aspects of the individual's or team's behavior/performance.

It is important to note that evaluation should be a continuous process. Sport psychology consultants should assess the strengths and weaknesses of the content and delivery of their sessions, especially team sessions. Questions such as the following might be addressed: Did the session accomplish its objective(s)? Were explanations of psychological concepts and directions for practicing the training exercises adequate? What techniques appeared to work best? Was time allotted appropriately during the session? Are any additions or deletions warranted? How responsive did the athletes appear to be? Writing a critique is more beneficial than simply trying to remember strengths and weaknesses. Plans for future sessions may need to be modified on the basis of the results of each session evaluation.

A more formal, total evaluation should occur at the end of the mental skills training program. This evaluation might include team and individual discussions, as well as written evaluations by the athletes and coaches. The evaluation should focus on the players' assessment of the value of the program from both a psychological as well as performance perspective. Objective performance data should be used in addition to subjective reports from coaches and athletes. In addition, athletes should be asked how often they actually practiced their skills, because when psychological skills programs don't work, one of the major reasons is simply because athletes do not systematically practice what they have learned. Information should also be obtained on different aspects of the program such as group sessions, individual sessions, and written materials. Additional questions can be asked such as: What did athletes see as the major strengths and weaknesses of the mental skills training? What mental skills improved the most? What exercises were the most helpful? What suggestions do athletes have to make the program even better in the future? To help out new sport psychology consultants, Partington and Orlick (1987a, b) provide a sample sport psychology evaluation form as well as data on what makes a consultant effective from both the coaches' and athletes' point of view. But the key thing to remember is that we are continually learning, and thus our programs will continue to change and evolve.

Practical Pointers for Teaching Mental Skills

In the preceding chapters on mental skills training the authors have presented many excellent "pointers" for teaching specific mental skills. The following pointers apply either to the entire psychological training program or to its components.

Provide the What, Why, When, and How of Training

For mental skills to be of maximum value, the athlete must consciously and continually choose to utilize mental training methods. This necessitates a high level of commitment, an understanding of proper execution, and ultimately the ability to be self-sufficient in mental preparation. This can be accomplished in a number of ways. Athletes who are taught the what, why, when, and how of mental skills training are much more likely to acquire the necessary knowledge base to become self-sufficient in mental training as well as the motivation to follow the program through. At the beginning of each special mental training session,

the coach or sport psychologist should outline for the athletes the purpose, content, and approximate length of the session. The educational aspect of the program is critical to provide athletes with an understanding of what principles the program is based on and how it works. Similarly, before initiating practice on a new exercise or technique, the coach or sport psychologist should first explain the entire procedure so athletes know exactly what to expect and any questions can be answered. It is also a good idea to allot time for discussion and questions after practicing each exercise and at the end of each session. This type of learning atmosphere encourages open discussion and forthright self-examination. In addition to enhancing the learning process, such sharing often improves communication and understanding among teammates and leads to better group support and more team cohesiveness.

Stress Personal Responsibility

When it comes to performance, some athletes have the attitude "When you're hot, you're hot, and when you're not, you're not." These athletes view peak performance as more a consequence of fate than something under their own personal control. Implementors of mental skills training should teach the opposite attitude. Peak performance is not mysterious; it is a product of the body and mind, both of which can be controlled. This is why, with the right physical and mental training, athletes can learn to repeat their best performances more consistently. This means learning to be in control of oneself, instead of letting the environment or others do the controlling. The athlete must ultimately accept the fact that only he/she can take responsibility for being physically and mentally ready to compete. Therefore, no matter what mental skills are being taught or practiced, the coach and sport psychology consultant should continually emphasize that athletes must assume personal responsibility for their thoughts, feelings, and actions—because ultimately, in the heat of competition, athletes will have to rely on themselves to make positive things happen.

Be Flexible and Individualized

When teaching mental skills to a group of athletes, the best approach is to be flexible and individualized. All athletes do not learn mental skills in the same way and at the same pace any more than they do physical skills. Within reasonable time constraints, a variety of techniques should be introduced and practiced. Do not force everyone into a fixed pattern. Instead, encourage athletes to modify or combine techniques until they derive the most effective method for them. A back-up technique should also be identified and practiced for those times when the preferred one fails to accomplish its objective. Once a basic foundation of mental skills has been established, it is critical that the application of these skills be individualized on the basis of the specific psychological skill needs of the athlete and the requirements of his/her performance situation. Thus, the most effective coaches and sport psychology consultants will be those who can work simultaneously with the group and with individuals within the group.

Providing handouts and cassette recordings of exercises and specific concepts is another way to ensure that athletes have a variety of exercises with which to work and the knowledge base for making modifications and application. You might even consider making handouts or recordings of some of the exercises in this book. Although many athletes like to use recordings and handouts when they practice, be sure they do not become so dependent upon them that they cannot practice the mental skills without such props.

Use Goal Setting and Journal Assignments

You can also enhance and individualize the teaching of specific mental skills by using goal setting and journal assignments. This is one reason why many sport psychology consultants suggest that athletes be encouraged to keep a journal (see Chapter 12) and set goals (see Chapter 13) early in a training program. The following is an example of their use. After athletes have been taught to recognize tension and to relax, have them monitor muscle tension while performing and record in their journals any muscle groups that tend to carry too much tension, and when this is most likely to occur. Then instruct them to record in their journal a specific goal for getting rid of the disruptive tension as well as a strategy for achieving the goal. Finally, on succeeding days, they should record the progress they have made in achieving the goal.

In illustration, a runner identifies that he grimaces and his neck and shoulder muscles tighten when he is running under poor weather conditions, after experiencing the first signs of fatigue, and when a steep hill is coming up. He records this in his journal. Next, the runner sets a reasonable goal for correcting the problem: "In one week I will run a workout over hilly terrain keeping my face, neck, and shoulder muscles relaxed throughout the run." After he records the goal, he plans and records a strategy for reaching the goal: "(1) Do five minutes of progressive relaxation (PR) each day on just the face, neck, and shoulder muscles. (2) After PR practice, visualize running fluidly over hilly terrain. (3) When running, frequently scan the face for tension—if needed, relax the face so the forehead is smooth as glass and the jaw is slack. When the face is relaxed, scan neck and shoulders for unwanted tension. If tense, relax by slowly rolling the head and/or dropping the shoulders." Each day the runner records his progress in achieving the goal. Once the runner feels he is consistently achieving the goal, he may want to establish a slightly more difficult goal and repeat the process.

Encourage a Passive State of Mind Versus a Forcing Attitude

It is essential that coaches and sport psychology consultants help athletes understand that maintaining a passive state of mind facilitates the learning of most of the mental skills addressed in earlier chapters. A **passive state of mind** means letting things happen rather than forcing them to happen. Trying too hard, exerting effort to the point of trying to force it, is generally counterproductive. For example, in Chapter 19, Schmid and Peper state that "concentration is the learned skill of passively not reacting to or being distracted by irrelevant stimuli." Active attempts at forcing concentration (e.g., "I will not let myself be distracted by the spectator's booing") are usually ineffectual. A more effective, passive approach to a distracting audience is to focus instead on the desired goal (e.g., shooting a free throw) by keying on cue words that trigger the desired skill and/or by imaging the performance.

Unfortunately, the typical athletes' past athletic environment has done little to foster skill in using a passive state of mind to correct a problem. When they are failing or having difficulty performing, most athletes are admonished by coaches to try harder. Thus, excessive effort often becomes the conditioned response when one is having performance difficulties. Coaches will be more effective if they first assess the motivation level of the athlete having difficulty. Then, unless there is reason to believe an athlete is undermotivated, give the athlete directions on how to focus in a positive way on cues or images for performing the task at hand. This more passive approach will lead to better learning and performance of both mental and physical skills.

Precompetition and Competition Plans

The ultimate goal of psychological skills training is for each athlete to learn how to create consistently at competition time the ideal performance state (thoughts, feelings, bodily responses) typically associated with peak performance. Rarely will this occur if precompetition preparation and competition behaviors are left to chance or good and bad breaks. Athletes get ready for competition in a variety of ways, but more often than not they do not have a consistent pattern of readying procedures. Performance is likely to be enhanced if an athlete's preparation becomes more systematic. Implementors of psychological skills training programs can help athletes develop effective behavioral plans that can be used regularly as precompetition and competition readying procedures.

One of the objectives of precompetition planning is to arrange the external and internal world in a way that maximizes the athlete's feelings of control. The athlete's **external world** consists of the actual physical surroundings, what is happening in these surroundings, and the physical things the athlete does. The **internal world** is the athlete's thoughts, feelings, and mental images. The greater the familiarity, routine, and structure in the external environment, the easier it is for the athlete to be in control of his/her internal world. The external world can be stabilized in a number of ways—for example, eating similar meals with the same time lapse before each competition; always arriving at the contest site with a set amount of time for precompetition preparation; establishing a set dressing ritual; and following the same equipment check, taping, and warm-up procedures.

Maintaining a constant and familiar external world is even more critical with away competitions. This is more easily accomplished when athletes diligently adhere to elaborate and consistent precompetition plans before both home and away games. The coach can also increase familiarity with the site of away games by taking the athletes to the site before the competition begins, ideally at least a day before. Some coaches and sport psychology consultants even advocate getting films of the away facility, including the locker rooms, and showing these films to their athletes well before a competition (see Chapters 16 and 18 for further elaboration on how such films can be used and why they are effective in improving performance).

The best precompetition and competition plans consist of procedures that ready the athlete physically and mentally for competition. Most coaches already prepare their athletes well physically for competition by tapering heavy workouts on the days prior to competition and conducting warm-up exercises and technique drills before the start of a competition. However, these physical preparations should be supplemented with emotional and cognitive readying procedures if athletes are to maximize their chances of being ready to peak at competition time. This entails planning procedures for monitoring and controlling the task at hand as competition nears. It also means monitoring and controlling emotions so that the energy and excitement for competing builds slowly. But this should be done without the athlete becoming energized too soon or becoming overenergized and thus producing feelings of anxiety and worry rather than excitement and challenge.

Mental monitoring and readying procedures should be integrated with certain external markers such as waking up the morning of competition, traveling to the competition, arriving at the competition site, getting dressed, doing warm-up exercises and technique drills, and dealing with the short time between physical warm-ups and the beginning of competition. For example, some athletes have found it effective to wake up slowly in the morning and then, before getting out of bed, to relive through imagery a previous best performance. These athletes believe that this type of imagery starts the competition day with a winning feeling and expectancy of success. When some athletes arrive at a competition site, they like to find a quiet place where they can practice 5 to 10 minutes of relaxation exercises such as deep breathing or passive progressive relaxation. Such athletes believe that these relaxation procedures have the benefit of bringing them to the same starting point prior to each competition before they begin the rest of their on-site preparation. Other athletes combine their dressing ritual with cognitive focusing techniques designed to narrow attentional focus to what the athletes want to do during the competition. Often athletes end their dressing ritual or precede their physical warm-up with a 5- to 10-minute imagery exercise of exactly what they want to feel and perform during competition. Some athletes even use *all* of these readying procedures.

The most effective readying procedure is individual; this means that the length, content, and sequencing of behavioral protocols vary greatly from one player to another—even when the players are on the same team. Such variability stems partly from different needs in creating an ideal performance state and different preferences for the mental training exercises. Much trial-and-error experimentation, accompanied by consultations with a coach or sport psychology consultant, may be necessary before each athlete identifies the most effective precompetition ritual for performing well.

Ultimately, it is important that each athlete develop a definite routine that he/she systematically goes through for every competition. The particular routine should be the one that best helps the athlete to get in touch with thoughts, feelings, and bodily responses and to make whatever adjustments are necessary so that when the time for competition arrives, the athlete is as near his/her ideal performance state as possible. A good starting point in developing a routine is to examine what athletes are already doing in their precompetition preparation. The more experienced, successful athlete may already have an effective preparation ritual, although it may not be identified as such or be used systematically. It may be best to leave this athlete alone, except to have him/her consciously identify existing preparation behaviors that are effective and then commit to using these procedures consistently before each competition. The less experienced or less effective athlete will need more assistance and experimentation until the most effective readying procedures are identified.

No athlete should be forced to use precompetition or competition readying procedures. Although most athletes find such structured rituals to be an effective way to enhance level and consistency of performance, some athletes are not comfortable with such techniques or feel they are not

beneficial. Other athletes may need only a very abbreviated readying procedure. For example, Jimmy Connors has said, "Because I'm familiar with the games of most players on tour, I never think far ahead about what I'm going to try to do in a match. . . . Before playing a tournament match, I just like to go off by myself somewhere private for five minutes or so to collect my thoughts" (Connors, 1984, p. 34). One important implication of the diversity in effective readying preferences is that many coaches may need to allow athletes much more flexibility in precompetition preparation procedures than is currently observed in many sports.

Some excellent examples of precompetition and competition planning come from the work of Orlick (1986) with Canadian Olympic athletes. Orlick has the athletes he works with develop very specific precompetition and competition plans. However, in addition, his athletes also develop precompetition and competition *refocusing* plans in case things don't go exactly as they originally planned. This is extremely important since often things out of an athlete's control can throw off his/her plans at the last second. And, as Jack Donohue, Canadian Olympic basketball coach, says, "What happens to you is nowhere near as important as how you react to what happens to you." A refocusing plan is aimed at helping athletes refocus away from unwanted external distractions or internal distractions such as worries, self-doubt, and self-putdowns. A good example of precompetition and competition refocusing plans for an Olympic speedskater is provided in Table 20-5.

Stress Application to Other Life Pursuits

One tremendous bonus that comes from implementing a mental training program is that the skills learned are applicable to life in general as well as to athletics, and the benefits last long after the competitive year is over. The training program can assist athletes in applying their new mental skills by suggesting relevant uses in nonathletic settings. For example, suggest that athletes learn to do their homework more quickly by using mental training concentration skills. With these skills, athletes can become more aware of when their mind is wandering and can bring their focus of attention back to the task at hand. If an athlete gets so uptight before tests that he/she cannot remember what was

Table 20-5   **Refocusing Plans for an Olympic Speedskater**

Worries about Competitors Before the Race

- They are human just like me. We'll see what they can do in the race, not in warm-ups or in training. I need to focus on my *own* preparation.
- All I can do is my best. Nobody can take that away from me. If my performance is good, I'll be happy. If it's not so good and I try, I shouldn't be disappointed.
- I'm racing for *me*. It's *my* max that I want.

Worries about Competitors During the Race

- If I start to think about others during the race, I'll shift my concentration to *my* race, *my* technique—"Stay low, race your race."
- "I have the potion—I have the motion."

Pre-event Hassles

- Skate blades don't cut the ice—carry a small sharpening stone to pass over the blades.
- Delay in start—if I'm already on the ice and it's likely to be a short delay, jog around, keep moving, stay warm, do a mini warm-up with some accelerations. Follow normal prerace plan when approaching the line.
- Windy or snowy conditions—it's the same for everyone. Just go out and do what you can do.

Worries During Competition

- Poor start—no problem, it can happen. It's not the start that determines the final results. Follow your race plan. Push your max.
- Not hearing a split time—it's ok. Just skate well and race your race.
- Pain in legs—shift focus to the specifics of the task being done, the steps in the turn, pushing the blade to the side, pushing hard to the finish line.

From: Orlick, 1986, pp. 165–166.

learned, the same relaxation and positive thinking skills that athletes are taught to control competitive anxiety can be used for test-taking anxiety and many other stressful situations people face in life. Another application of mental training is to visualize a speech or an important job or TV interview in advance to give oneself confidence. The potential benefits that come from increased self-control, confidence, mastery, and so on are limitless. When athletic programs offer both physical and mental skills training, they provide a better argument that participating in competitive sport can also be a valuable educational experience.

Practice It Before Teaching It

Before teaching any of the mental training exercises to athletes, sport psychology consultants and coaches should take the time to practice each technique themselves. Personally experiencing an exercise is an excellent way to increase one's ability to teach a specific technique and to answer any questions athletes may have about it. An additional bonus of practicing the exercises, particularly if the practice is systematic and long-term, is that the practitioner will accrue psychological benefits similar to those that the athletes receive from the practice. After all, athletes are not the only people who can benefit from learning skills such as effectively setting goals, planning strategies for goal achievement, handling stress, and maintaining concentration and confidence under even the most demanding situations.

Teach by Example

In regard to psychological control—or any type of behavior—good coaches and sport psychology consultants teach and lead by example. If the person leading the mental training program does not exemplify what he/she is teaching, it is highly unlikely the athletes will model it either. The coach who appears calm, confident, and in control during a competition usually has athletes who act the same way. Players are more likely to offer encouragement and support toward one another when they have a leader who models encouragement (Wescott, 1980). But research on modeling need not be cited to illustrate the importance of teaching by example. All one has to do is watch a ball game. The next time you see athletes consistently losing control and concentration after poor officiating calls, look to the bench, and you probably will see the coach behaving similarly. Watch how athletes react to poor performance. Athletes who become negative or rattled after mistakes are often led by coaches who react similarly. For psychological training to be maximally effective, the coaches and sport psychology consultants must exemplify in practice and competition the behavior they expect from athletes.

Observe Practices and Competitions Whenever Possible

As noted earlier, one of the disadvantages of a sport psychology consultant conducting a mental training program with teams is his/her lack of day-to-day availability. Despite this limitation, it is critical that the consultant attempt to attend some practices and competitions. We have found that this is particularly important at the beginning stages of the intervention. Listening and reading about an athlete's problem cannot substitute for actually being there to observe it. This firsthand view can provide the consultant with critical information that might not be evident from an interview or paper-and-pencil measure. As noted earlier, the problem might be biomechanical or physical in nature rather than psychological, and this would not likely show up in an interview or a test. And perhaps even more important than the information the consultant gains is the trust that will be built up as athletes know that the consultant really cares about them, since he/she is taking the time to actually see them perform. In surveys evaluating the effectiveness of sport psychology consultants (Gould et al., 1989; Partington & Orlick, 1987a), a critical component to the perceived effectiveness of sport psychology consultants that directly impacted the building of trust between the athlete and consultant was the amount of time they spent being with and observing the athletes.

Emphasize Strengths as Competition Nears

Behavior by the coach and sport psychology consultant prior to and during competition is particularly critical. The nearer the time to competition, the more important it is that they are reassuring and complimentary toward athletes. This is not the time to be critical of technique or anything else. Besides, it is too late to change weaknesses, so there is no reason to focus on them. Instead, if at all possible, get athletes to think they are looking great and help build their confidence. In short, now is the time to build from what is positive, to play to strengths rather than weaknesses. Such behavior by the coach and sport psychology consul-

tant will help athletes build and maintain confidence rather than self-doubt prior to competition. This usually means better performance.

Most coaches automatically do this, even if they do not know why—they just know it works. Unfortunately, some coaches naturally tend to be critical right up to and through game time. Often these coaches are not even aware of their unsupportive behavior and its potential negative impact on players' self-confidence, self-esteem, and enjoyment. Other coaches succeed in staying positive in pregame preparation and during a game until something goes wrong. They then jump all over the athletes (often because they have lost emotional control) rather than being reassuring and directing behavior in a positive way toward what needs to be done. Using the self-monitoring and/or outside monitoring described in the next section should help coaches and sport psychology consultants assess their behavior prior to and during competition.

Monitor Your Behavior

In Chapter 12, Ravizza suggests that athletes become more aware of their behavior, thoughts, and feelings through self-monitoring. The same awareness on the part of coaches and sport psychology consultants can help them become more effective in working with athletes. For example, by means of self-monitoring, coaches and sport psychology consultants can become more conscious of how they communicate with athletes during different situations. They should monitor what they say as well as what they communicate with their body language. They should ask themselves such questions as: "How is my behavior likely to change in certain situations?" "Am I a good role model for the mental discipline and psychological control I wish to teach?" "Am I behaving in a way that facilitates the personal growth and performance of my athletes, or is my behavior towards them disabling?" The awareness created by conscientious and objective self-monitoring is a necessary first step in becoming more effective in working with athletes.

There is also merit in having someone else observe and evaluate one's behavior. For example, if a coach has a sport psychology consultant working with the team, he/she would be an ideal person to observe the coach's behavior during practices and games. Coaching behaviors should be analyzed on the basis of the principles for desirable behavior elaborated in earlier chapters. Evaluation would be facilitated if special forms were designed (e.g., Tharpe & Gallimore, 1976; Smith, Smoll, & Hunt, 1977). The information presented in earlier chapters can be used to help plan a specific strategy for modifying a coach's behavior in a direction that is more likely to facilitate the performance and personal growth of his/her athletes. A prospective sport psychology consultant's behavior could be assessed through a supervised internship working with athletes on mental skills training.

Ethical Considerations for the Coach and Sport Psychology Consultant

Sport psychology is a relatively young profession, and the people practicing applied sport psychology in the 1970s and early 1980s had little to guide them in terms of ethical issues. The purpose of this section is to call attention to some basic ethical concerns involved in implementing mental skills training. This brief discussion should not be construed as a complete presentation of the many complex ethical issues and interrelationships involved in psychological skills training. A more thorough discussion of these topics can be found in Danish and Hale (1981, 1982), Nideffer (1981), Nideffer, Feltz, and Salmela (1982), Heyman (1984), and Rotella and Connelly (1984).

Recently, sport psychology associations such as the Association for the Advancement of Applied Sport Psychology (AAASP), the North American Society for Sport Psychology and Physical Activity (NASPSPA) and the Canadian Society for Psychomotor Learning and Sport Psychology (CSPLSP) have developed modifications of the American Psychological Association's Ethical Standards (1981) that should guide the conduct of sport psychology consultants. At the core of these standards is the general philosophy that sport psychology consultants respect the dignity and worth of the individual and honor the preservation and protection of fundamental human rights. In addition, consultants are committed to increasing the knowledge of human behavior and of people's understanding of themselves and others in sport environments. The essence of this philosophy is that the athlete's welfare must be foremost. There are nine principles outlined in the American Psychological Association's ethical guidelines (1981), but space only permits us to highlight them briefly.

Principle 1: Responsibility

Consultants maintain the highest standards of their profession. They accept responsibility for the consequences of their acts and make every effort to ensure that services are used appropriately. Thus, sport psychology consultants would be expected to do things such as accurately communicating the limitations of various services they have to offer; developing a clear, concise service contract; and making sure that research findings are not misleading.

Principle 2: Competence

Consultants recognize the boundaries of their competence and the limitations of their techniques. They only provide services and only use techniques for which they are qualified by training and experience. They maintain knowledge of current scientific and professional information related to the services they render. Consultants accurately represent their competence, education, training, and experience.

Principle 3: Moral and Legal Standards

Consultants' moral and ethical standards of behavior are a personal matter to the same degree as they are for any other citizen, except as they may compromise the fulfillment of their professional responsibilities or reduce the public trust in sport psychology. Consultants will not allow the needs of an organization or team to override their concerns for the physical and emotional health of athletes or physical activity participants.

Principle 4: Public Statements

Public statements, announcements of services, advertising, and promotional activities serve the purpose of helping the public make informed judgments and choices. Consultants accurately and objectively represent their professional qualifications and affiliations. Consultants also represent, in a professional manner, those institutions and organizations with which they are affiliated. The limits and uncertainties of present psychological knowledge and techniques are taken into account in any public statement providing psychological information, professional opinion, or information concerning psychological testing and services.

Principle 5: Confidentiality

Consultants respect the confidentiality of information obtained from persons in the course of their work. They reveal such information to others only with the consent of the person or as required by law. Consultants, where appropriate, inform their clients of any limits to confidentiality. When using psychological tests, consultants do not share the results of test information with anyone unless the person tested has agreed to such disclosure.

Principle 6: Welfare of the Client

Consultants respect the integrity and protect the welfare of the people and groups with whom they work. When conflicts of interest arise between clients and the consultants' employing institution, consultants clarify the nature and direction of their loyalties and responsibilities and keep all parties informed of their commitments. Consultants fully inform consumers as to the purpose and nature of an evaluative treatment and educational or training procedure, and they freely acknowledge that clients, students, or participants in research have freedom of choice with regard to participation.

Principle 7: Professional Relationships

Consultants act with due regard for the needs, special competencies, and obligations of their colleagues in other sport-related professions (coaching, training, etc.). They respect the prerogatives and obligations of the institutions with which these other colleagues are associated.

Principle 8: Assessment Techniques

In the development, publication, and utilization of assessment techniques, consultants make every effort to promote the welfare and best interests of the client. They guard against misuse of assessment re-

sults. In applied settings, clients have a right to know why they are being tested, the results of the testing, and the conclusions drawn on the basis of test results. Test users avoid imparting unnecessary information that would compromise test security or confuse or needlessly upset the athlete, coach, or participant organization. Consultants do not use tests to discover problems but instead use them to focus on specifically (behaviorally) defined questions or concerns.

Principle 9: Research with Human Participants

The decision to conduct applied research is based on a professional's judgment with regard to how he/she can best contribute to psychological science and human welfare. In all research, the investigation is carried out with respect and concern for the dignity and welfare of the people who participate and with cognizance of state, federal, and provincial regulations and professional standards.

Potential Problem Areas

Although the potential benefits of implementing a psychological skills training program are clearly demonstrable, there are of course some problems that a consultant or coach will have to deal with throughout the process. Each situation, naturally, will offer its own unique set of problems. For example, working one on one with individual athletes is quite different from working with an entire team. Working with Olympic athletes or professional athletes might present an entirely different set of problems than working with high school athletes. However, a number of common problems have been identified by athletes, coaches, and consultants when it comes down to practically implementing these mental training programs. If not adequately dealt with, these problems can severely reduce the effectiveness of the program. Some examples of common problems include the following:

- Overcoming player reluctance about participating in a mental training program
- Lack of time spent with individual athletes in a team setting
- Gaining the trust of the athletes

- Making sure athletes systematically practice their skills
- Consultant's lack of knowledge about the specific sport
- Maintaining contact with athletes throughout a competitive season
- Getting full cooperation from coaching staff/organization

A sport psychology consultant needs to be aware of these potential problem areas and be ready to deal with them if necessary. It has taken most of us several years to learn many of these things in a trial-and-error fashion. Many of us made mistakes in our early years of consulting because we simply weren't aware of, or hadn't experienced, many of these nuances of setting up and implementing a mental training program. A lot of homework and planning should be a prerequisite for any sport psychology consultant considering working with athletes and teams. However, with good preparation, careful thought, and a sense of commitment, this can be a very rewarding experience. After all, helping individuals reach their potential both inside and outside the world of sport is what it's all about.

Summary

In this chapter we have addressed many general issues relating to the integration and implementation of a psychological skills training program. In summary: (1) There are advantages to having either a coach or a sport psychologist implement a psychological skills training program, (2) athletes of all types and age and skill levels can benefit from mental training, (3) mental skills training should continue for as long as an athlete participates in sport, (4) the initial mental skills training program should probably be three to six months in length and start in the off season or preseason, (5) a psychological skills needs assessment should be made in order to determine the specific components to be incorporated in training and the psychological objectives to be achieved, (6) there is no one best way to sequence and integrate psychological components even though one was proposed, (7) once basic mental skills are acquired they should have a performance-specific focus and be integrated with practice of physical skills, and (8) real benefits from psychological skills training will only occur with long-term systematic practice.

We have also suggested practical teaching pointers that apply to either the entire psychological training programs or to many of its components. Stress that athletes accept self-responsibility for their mental state. Be flexible, eclectic, and individualized in planning training techniques. Emphasize employing a passive state of mind when learning psychological skills. Stress personal growth and how to use mental skills in nonathletic settings. Practice techniques before teaching them. Teach by personally exemplifying the mental skills being taught. Finally, we concluded the chapter with ethical considerations that all psychological training implementors need to be aware of and observe in their own behavior.

This chapter and the earlier chapters on psychological skills training have emphasized that the rewards are many for those who choose to teach and practice mental training in their dedication to the pursuit of excellence. Benefits will accrue not only in athletic performance but in performance outside of the athletic setting and, perhaps more importantly, in general personal growth and in enhanced sense of self-worth.

Study Questions

1. Discuss who will benefit most from psychological skills training.

2. Are psychological skills intervention programs effective in enhancing performance? Provide evidence to support your answer.

3. What are some advantages and disadvantages of a coach or sport psychology consultant conducting a mental training program?

4. How much time should be spent in mental training?

5. When is the best time to practice psychological skills?

6. When is the best time to implement a psychological skills training program?

7. Discuss what would be covered in a first interview with an athlete.

8. Discuss the use of psychological inventories to help assess athletes' psychological skills.

9. Discuss Vealey's distinction between psychological methods and psychological skills. What are the different categories of psychological skills? What impact does this distinction between methods and skills have on the implementation of a psychological skills training program?

10. Discuss how a psychological skills program might be evaluated.

11. Discuss five practical pointers that may help make a psychological skills program more effective. Cite specific practical examples and research to support your points.

12. Discuss the importance of ethics in conducting psychological intervention programs with athletes. What do you believe are the five most important ethical principles pertaining to applied sport psychology, and why?

References

American Psychological Association (1981). Ethical principles of psychologists. *American Psychologist, 36,* 633–638.

Asken, M. J. (1991). The challenge of the physically challenged: Delivering sport psychology services to physically disabled athletes. *The Sport Psychologist, 5,* 370–381.

Association for the Advancement of Applied Sport Psychology Newsletter (Winter, 1991, vol. 6).

Bandura, A. (1986). *Social foundations of thought and action: A social cognitive theory.* Englewood Cliffs, N.J.: Prentice-Hall.

Bandura, A. (1991). Perceived self-efficacy in the exercise of personal agency. *Journal of Applied Sport Psychology, 2,* 128–163.

Botterill, C. (1990). Sport psychology and professional hockey. *The Sport Psychologist, 4,* 369–377.

Boutcher, S., & Rotella, R. J. (1987). A psychological skills educational program for closed-skill performance enhancement. *The Sport Psychologist, 1,* 127–137.

Clark, R. A., & Sachs, M. L. (1991). Challenges and opportunities in psychological skills training in deaf athletes. *The Sport Psychologist, 5,* 392–398.

Connors, J. (1984, December). *Tennis,* pp. 33–35.

Danish, S. J., & Hale, B. D. (1981). Toward an understanding of the practice of sport psychology. *Journal of Sport Psychology, 3,* 90–99.

Danish, S. J., & Hale, B. D. (1982). Let the discussions continue: Further considerations on the practice of sport psychology. *Journal of Sport Psychology, 4,* 10–12.

Etzel, J. F. (1979). Validation of a conceptual model characterizing attention among international rifle shooters. *Journal of Sport Psychology, 1,* 281–290.

Gipson, M., McKenzie, T., & Lowe, S. (1989). The sport psychology program of the USA Women's National Volleyball Team. *The Sport Psychologist, 3,* 330–339.

Gordon, S. (1990). A mental skills training program for the Western Australia cricket team. *The Sport Psychologist, 4,* 386–399.

Gould, D. (1983). Developing psychological skills in young athletes. In N. Wood (Ed.), *Coaching science update,* Ottawa, Ont.: Coaching Association of Canada.

Gould, D., Horn, T., & Spreeman, J. (1983). Competitive anxiety in junior elite wrestlers. *Journal of Sport Psychology, 5,* 58–71.

Gould, D., Tammen, V., Murphy, S., & May, J. (1989). An examination of the U.S. Olympic sport psychology consultants and the services they provide. *The Sport Psychologist, 3,* 300–312.

Greenspan, M. J., & Feltz, D. F. (1989). Psychological interventions with athletes in competitive situations: A review. *The Sport Psychologist, 3,* 219–236.

Halliwell, W. (1990). Providing sport psychology consulting services to a professional sport organization. *The Sport Psychologist, 4,* 369–377.

Hellstedt, J. C. (1987). Sport psychology at a ski academy: Teaching mental skills to young athletes. *The Sport Psychologist, 1,* 56–68.

Heyman, S. R. (1984). Cognitive interventions: Theories, applications, and cautions. In W. F. Straub & J. M. Williams (Eds.), *Cognitive sport psychology* (pp. 289–303). Lansing, N.Y.: Sport Science Associates.

Kirschenbaum, D., & Bale, R. (1980). Cognitive-behavioral skills in golf: Brain power golf. In R. Suinn (Ed.), *Psychology in sports: Methods and applications* (pp. 275–287). Minneapolis, Minn.: Burgess.

Loehr, J. (1990). Providing sport psychology consulting services to professional tennis players. *The Sport Psychologist, 4,* 400–408.

Mahoney, M. J., Gabriel, T. J., & Perkins, T. S. (1987). Psychological skills and exceptional athletic performance. *The Sport Psychologist, 1,* 181–199.

Martens, R. (1977). *Sport competition anxiety test.* Champaign, Ill.: Human Kinetics.

Martens, R., Vealey, R. S., & Burton, D. (1990). *Competitive anxiety in sport*. Champaign, Ill.: Human Kinetics.

May, J. R., & Brown, L. (1989). Delivery of psychological services to the U.S. Alpine Ski Team prior to and during the Olympics in Calgary. *The Sport Psychologist*, *3*, 320–329.

McNair, D. M., Lorr, M., & Droppleman, L. F. (1971). *EDITS manual for POMS*, San Diego, Calif.: Educational and Industrial Testing Service.

Murphy, S., Jowdy, D., & Durtschi, S. (1990). Imagery perspective survey. Colorado Springs, Colo.: U.S. Olympic Training Center.

Nideffer, R. M. (1976). Test of attentional and interpersonal style. *Journal of Personality and Social Psychology*, *34*, 394–404.

Nideffer, R. M. (1981). *The ethics and practice of applied sport psychology*. Ithaca, N.Y.: Mouvement Publications.

Nideffer, R. M. (1989). Psychological services for the U.S. track and field team. *The Sport Psychologist*, *3*, 350–357.

Nideffer, R. M., Feltz, D., & Salmela, J. (1982). A rebuttal to Danish and Hale: A committee report. *Journal of Sport Psychology*, *4*, 3–6.

Orlick, T. (1980). *In pursuit of excellence*. Champaign, Ill.: Human Kinetics.

Orlick, T. (1986). *Psyching for sport: Mental training for athletes*. Champaign, Ill.: Human Kinetics.

Orlick, T., & McCaffrey, N. (1991). Mental training with children for sport and life. *The Sport Psychologist*, *5*, 322–334.

Partington, J., & Orlick, T. (1987a). The sport psychology consultant: Olympic coaches' views. *The Sport Psychologist*, *1*, 95–102.

Partington, J., & Orlick, T. (1987b). The sport psychology consultant evaluation form. *The Sport Psychologist*, *1*, 309–317.

Ravizza, K. (1990). Sportpsych consultation issues in professional baseball. *The Sport Psychologist*, *4*, 330–340.

Rotella, R. J., & Connelly, D. (1984). Individual ethics in the application of cognitive sport psychology. In W. F. Straub & J. M. Williams (Eds.), *Cognitive sport psychology* (pp. 102–112). Lansing, N.Y.: Sport Science Associates.

Salmela, J. H. (1989). Long-term intervention with the Canadian Men's Olympic Gymnastic Team. *The Sport Psychologist*, *3*, 340–349.

Seabourne, T., Weinberg, R. S., Jackson, A., & Suinn, R. M. (1985). Effect of individualized, nonindividualized and package intervention strategies on karate performance. *Journal of Sport Psychology*, *7*, 40–50.

Silva, J. M. (1982). Performance enhancement in competitive sport environments through cognitive intervention. *Behavior Modification*, *6*, 443–463.

Smith, R. E. (1989). Applied sport psychology in the age of accountability. *Journal of Applied Sport Psychology*, *1*, 166–180.

Smith, R. E., & Johnson, J. (1990). An organizational empowerment approach to consultation in professional baseball. *The Sport Psychologist*, *4*, 347–357.

Smith, R. E., & Smoll, F. L. (1982). Psychological stress: A conceptual model and some intervention strategies in youth sports. In R. A. Magill, M. J. Ash, & F. L. Smoll (Eds.), *Children in sport* (pp. 153–177). Champaign, Ill.: Human Kinetics.

Smith, R. E., Smoll, F. L., & Hunt, E. (1977). A system for the behavioral assessment of athletic coaches. *Research Quarterly*, *48*, 401–407.

Suinn, R. M. (1986). *Seven steps to peak performance*. Toronto, Ont.: Luber.

Tharpe, R. G., & Gallimore, R. (1976, January). What a coach can teach a teacher. *Psychology Today*, 75–78.

Travis, C. A., & Sachs, M. L. (1991). Applied sport psychology and persons with mental retardation. *The Sport Psychologist*, *5*, 382–391.

Van Schoyck, S. R., & Grasha, A. F. (1981). Attentional style variations and athletic ability. The advantages of a sports-specific test. *Journal of Sport Psychology*, *3*, 149–165.

Vealey, R. S. (1986). Conceptualization of sport-confidence and competitive orientation: Preliminary investigation and instrument development. *Journal of Sport Psychology*, *8*, 221–246.

Vealey, R. S. (1988). Future directions in psychological skills training. *The Sport Psychologist*, *2*, 318–336.

Weiss, M. R. (1991). Psychological skill development in children and adolescents. *The Sport Psychologist*, *5*, 335–354.

Wescott, W. L. (1980). Effects of teacher modeling on children's peer encouragement behavior. *Research Quarterly*, *51*, 585–587.

When to Refer Athletes for Counseling or Psychotherapy

Steven R. Heyman, *University of Wyoming*

*F*or the most part, the chapters in this text focus on what has become known as "educational sport psychology" (Berger, in press), which involves approaches to help sport participants maximize their skills and enjoyment. This is probably typical of most of the recent volumes in sport psychology. There has been some attention in the literature to more serious psychosocial problems affecting athletes and sport participants (May & Asken, 1987; Tricker & Cook, 1989), but there has been little overlap between writings on educational sport psychology and what has become known as "clinical sport psychology."

This gap between educational and clinical sport psychology creates problems for us here. In the space of a chapter it is impossible to describe for readers with diverse backgrounds precise methods for the assessment of an individual's problems and ways to resolve them. The goal of this chapter, then, is to provide a set of *guidelines* that people working with athletes and sport participants can use as reference points *for referring individuals for professional counseling or psychotherapy*. Some suggestions will also be provided about making appropriate referrals for varying circumstances. It should also be noted that both an educational *and* a clinical/counseling sport psychologist can work with an individual at the same time.

Because sport psychology is a new and interdisciplinary field, the reasons for some of the difficulties in finding guidelines for referral are embedded within the field's current situation. As Berger (in press) notes, many of the individuals working in sport psychology have received their graduate degrees from physical education/kinesiology programs. Although they have studied research methods and performance enhancement approaches, such individuals may have difficulty obtaining backgrounds from graduate courses in counseling/psychotherapy, personality, or psychological assessment. Also, such coursework may not be of interest to individuals more concerned with performance. This would be similar to the position of industrial psychologists, who may be concerned with performance issues but who usually do not have particular training in issues relating to counseling or psychotherapy.

As sport psychology began to develop in the 1970s, traditionally trained psychologists attempted to distance it from more clinically oriented approaches. Many individuals reported coaches and athletes being wary of "shrinks" and the association with psychosocial problems. Although the reference could not be located, there was a discussion in *The Monitor*, the publication of the American Psychosocial Association, in which elite athletes were described as "supernormal," with an almost blanket denial that such individuals could have problems. Certainly this does not seem to be the case (May & Asken, 1987; Ryan et al., 1981). Some athletes and sport participants at all levels are likely to have psychosocial problems, although no recent research exists to indicate whether at greater or lesser frequency than in other populations.

Sport participants have often been described in personality research as "tough minded" (Singer, 1972), and such individuals are not likely to want to acknowledge psychosocial problems. Similarly, the sport world has for a long time been dominated by a tough-minded, hypermasculine mindset that would see problems as a reflection of personal weakness and that probably would prefer to deny or ignore them.

Although our society at large has become more psychologically minded in the last 50 years and many issues of psychosocial distress are recognized as issues requiring help, often stigmas are still attached to those in counseling or therapy. Athletes who seek the services of sport psychologists, even if merely to enhance performance, are no exception. For example, Linder, Pillow, and Reno (1989) found that athletes who consulted a sport psychologist to improve performance were derided by the public as compared to athletes who attempted to resolve the same issues by working with their coaches. It is important to understand that as humans we all experience difficulties and that counseling or psychotherapy, particularly if intervention is sought early enough, can be an important part of personal growth and development, not a mark of personal failure. Athletes and sport participants, who may be subjected to particularly strong personal and interpersonal stressors, should be given resources to help them deal with the issues they confront as part of their growth and development. Perhaps over time, as sport psychology continues to grow and develop as a field, educational sport psychologists will have a better understanding of these issues, there will be more clinical/counseling sport psychologists available, and resources will be developed not only for performance enhancement but also for personal growth and development (Rejeski & Brawley, 1988). There are books (e.g., Etzel, Ferrante, & Pinkney, 1991) and articles (e.g., Lanning, 1982; Wittner et al., 1981) dealing with athletic counseling, but generally these relate more to surface issues and day-to-day problems such as study skills than to deeper personal and interpersonal issues.

Differentiating Performance Enhancement from More Problematic Personal Issues

In much of the performance enhancement literature, problems in performance are related to issues like competition anxiety, poor self-talk, motivational issues, and burnout (Greenspan & Feltz, 1989; Straub & Williams, 1984). Determining whether other factors might be involved requires understanding a number of interrelated issues.

Naturally, it is recognized that an athlete coming to a coach or an educational sport psychologist may be uncomfortable if an interview probes personal areas. Likewise, the sport counselor may be reluctant to ask highly personal questions. It is possible, however, to get at least a feel for some of the salient issues in typical discussions of sport performance factors. It is natural for the sport psychology consultant or coach to build rapport by asking people about themselves. This can lead not only to understanding an athlete's performance or motivational problem but also to an understanding of the whole person.

Fortunately, an overwhelming majority of requests for assistance with performance will be just what they appear to be. The next sections will try to help identify those less common requests that may reflect issues that might require additional professional assistance to help the athlete grow and develop.

First, how long a problem has existed, its severity, and its relationship to other issues in the person's life become important. A problem that is more recent, that is not severe in its emotional implications, and that does not have strong overlaps with other aspects of a person's life is less likely to require professional assistance. Thus, for example, an athlete who is facing a tough competitive situation and who experiences mild to moderate anxiety, fear, and negative self-talk is not likely to require referral. However, a person for whom each athletic competition becomes an all-or-nothing battle for a sense of self, whose emotional state is dependent on these outcomes, and where strong anxiety, depressive states, or substance abuse may also be involved is more likely to need a referral, although certainly performance-related issues can still be addressed by the educational sport psychologist.

Second, unusual emotional reactions may also need to be considered. Anxiety that generalizes to situations beyond the athletic arena may signal that other issues are present and that interventions may be needed to help deal with other areas of the person's life. Depression, in particular, is an important emotional reaction to monitor. Athletes often experience depression following a loss or a failure to perform as hoped or expected. If the depression is particularly severe or seems to last longer than is typical, it may well be that the athlete needs help to get through the sense of loss or disappointment. In many cases, however, individuals may hide their depression from others or may mask it through the use of alcohol or other substances.

Individuals experiencing depression may show a personal and social withdrawal. They may also show a hopelessness, a loss of self-esteem, and a slowing in or withdrawal from physical activities. Verbalizations indicating depression, hopelessness, or poor self-esteem should be monitored. Overt and covert signs may signal an individual's call for help. With depression there is always the risk of suicide or suicidal gestures, which may take the form of unusual risk taking. Particularly within the sport environment, some individuals will take their depression and turn it outward, against others, in the form of physical aggression.

Anger or aggression is likely to be an issue presented by an athlete only if it has become a problem to others. Unfortunately, it may take the form of fights with strangers, which sometimes involves legal complications, as well as familial abuse issues. In other cases an athlete may lose control within the competitive context, and this can be a performance threat in that the person becomes a liability in terms of penalties, ejections from the game, or an emotional reaction that may inhibit otherwise good performance.

Third, it may also be important to examine the effectiveness of more traditional performance-enhancement interventions. For example, perhaps an athlete has not disclosed the full extent of the issue or is not aware of it. It may be that the person working with the athlete did not come to understand the nature and extent of the problem. If more traditional interventions, such as working on self-talk and visualization, do not seem to be working, there are several possibilities to consider. Perhaps the athlete did not respond to the particular intervention—for example, not all individuals can visualize. It may also be that the sport-related problem was not accurately assessed or was stronger than initially assumed. It may also be, however, that the sport-related issue is, in fact, related to other issues in the person's life and may have deeper, stronger, or more chronic patterns. These possibilities should be investigated.

It is important that the athlete not be treated as a failure; rather, with the goal of developing a better relationship, coaches or educational sport psychologists should seek to understand the person and his/her issues more clearly. Although they may not be trained as counselors or interviewers, they are help givers. As they come to understand a person, the person may disclose personal, and at times, troubling issues. It is important for help givers to become comfortable with such revelations.

Certainly, the patterns described above are only a sampling of possibilities. Any unusual emotional reactions, particularly if they are deep, chronic, or related to other issues in the athlete's life, may warrant further consideration.

When Performance-Enhancement Approaches Seem to Create Problems

As previously indicated, when an individual is not responding to a more traditional performance-enhancement intervention, there may be a number of issues to consider. Sometimes, however, a more serious situation emerges. In medical terms, there are "iatrogenic complications." This means that the *treatment itself* causes additional problems.

In a milder situation, an attempted intervention may fail due to an unclear relationship between the athlete and the person working with the athlete. For example, an individual attempting an intervention involving relaxation may not have achieved a sufficient sense of rapport with the athlete for the person to consider relaxing. In other cases, for example, an athlete referred by a coach may feel coerced and will not be a willing participant.

Some situations activate personal issues for the athlete. Someone who feels a great need for personal control or who has a great fear of losing control may respond with increasing levels of anxiety when asked to relax. This pattern can also emerge with other interventions, such as visualization and biofeedback.

Although the use of hypnosis has been addressed in other writings (Heyman, 1984), I have a particular concern about individuals attempting to use hypnosis without having been adequately trained in its uses as well as in some of its more serious considerations. Although many individuals are not at all responsive to hypnosis, and most of those who are will not have any negative reactions, there have been cases in which negative reactions have occurred. With a highly responsive person who has deeper or more severe issues that are activated or exacerbated by hypnosis, much more traditional psychotherapy might be required to resolve the issues. Aside from referring readers to Heyman (1984), I would suggest strongly that individuals not attempt to utilize hypnosis unless they have been appropriately trained.

Another consideration is somewhat more complicated to explain without writing at great length but needs to be addressed. Some of the interventions most commonly used in educational sport psychology are clearly drawn from cognitive-behavioral psychology (see Straub & Williams, 1984). These include cognitive restructuring, self-talk, etcetera. Usually these techniques address more conscious issues and can be evaluated and responded to by an athlete fairly quickly and directly. Other approaches, however, such as visualization, relaxation, and hypnosis, require that a person is able to loosen conscious controls, and they may allow preconscious or unconscious material more access to consciousness. Although problems with these approaches are rare, someone working with these techniques over time with a large number of individuals should be sensitive to the possibilities. First, a person may become uncomfortable with memories or associations that emerge. One case on which I consulted involved an athlete who had a particularly negative relationship with a coach when the athlete's performance slumped. The coach, utilizing visualization and imagery, unknowingly activated memories of childhood physical abuse that had been denied and repressed. The athlete at first tried to hide these but became increasingly fearful of the relaxation and imagery sessions. It was necessary to locate a professional who could work with the athlete around the childhood issues.

In another case in my experience, individuals working with performance-enhancement approaches became concerned when an athlete seemed to become "increasingly flaky" as an approach was used. Adding to the performance-enhancement specialists' confusion was the fact that the athlete's performance seemed to be improving! The athlete had always been considered somewhat eccentric, and the eccentricities seemed to increase following the intervention. Again, it was clear that the athlete should be evaluated and monitored by a clinical/counseling psychologist, who would work with the performance-enhancement specialists.

Likewise, other reactions such as anxiety, depression, anger, and the release of bottled up memories or emotions should be noted if they seem to result from more traditional performance-enhancement interventions. The educational sport psychologist—or anyone else working with an athlete—must be able to talk with the athlete about these reactions and to have a sense of when a consultation or referral might be appropriate.

More Specific Athlete-related Issues

Sometimes, in addition to performance issues, or related to them, other issues confronting athletes may surface. Again, these have been reviewed in other volumes (Asken & May, 1987; Tricker & Cook, 1989), as well as chapters within this volume (e.g., Anshel, Chapter 22).

Identity Issues

One of the most problematic issues for many athletes is that their whole sense of self has revolved around their role as an athlete. This may be particularly true for those at elite levels or in more glamorous sports, but it can occur for any person in any sport. Very often the athlete's hopes for the future and social support from others may revolve around the sport and the athlete's success at it. For someone working with these issues, attempts at performance enhancement may take on an extreme urgency, as the athlete's sense of self may well be riding on the outcome.

In many cases these identity issues do not become manifest unless performance is threatened (e.g., the competition becomes more threatening) or the career ends. Chapter 25 discusses career termination issues in that context. Increasingly, elite and professional sport organizations try to prepare athletes for career termination, but each year tens of thousands of graduating high school athletes will confront these issues, as will thousands of collegiate athletes. I can remember when I first began teaching at a small, regional university, watching academic involvement decline and substance abuse increase among football players who were cut after their first year on the team. Many of them had been playing football since elementary or junior high school and had received most of their personal and interpersonal valuing from this participation. When it was gone, they seemed empty and confused. Performance-enhancement approaches used with such individuals may evoke a desperate, and perhaps an all-encompassing, driven quality. It is not simply a question of a need to win: It can express a desperate need to give a meaning and direction back to one's life.

Negative Identities

There are several other related entity issues I would like to discuss, at least briefly. While we normally think of the identity of "athlete" as something both an individual and peer groups see as positive, valuable, and rewarding, there are also versions of this that become negative identities (Erikson, 1968). In essence, a **negative identity** is the acceptance and valuing of an identity that is generally disapproved of by society. For example, the "dumb jock" is one such negative identity. Individuals and subgroups may determine that athletes shouldn't care about school or shouldn't do well, and so forth. This negative identity, while disapproved of by many, may become important to an individual or subgroup.

Similarly, the "tough jock" identity becomes problematic. Being an athlete—most commonly for men but increasingly for women—means being tough, and it often involves intimidating others verbally or physically.

Substance abuse issues also can become part of negative identity patterns. To be a successful "jock"

one may need to be able to consume a great deal of alcohol or other drugs. In some cases I have seen, this is done covertly, with an eye to the "clean cut" image that has to be maintained for public relations purposes.

As with many other human issues, unless a person sees these as areas that are problematic and that he/she would like to change, it may only be possible for the coach or educational sport psychologist to communicate concern for these areas and to point a person in the direction of someone who can help him/her work on these issues.

Sexual Orientation and Gender Role Issues

Although there is much mythology about sexual activities and athletes (Ziegel, 1979), surprisingly little research seems to have been done, although some recent articles are beginning to address important issues (e.g., Butt, 1990; Rotella & Murray, 1991).

Athletes and sport participants, particularly those in their adolescent and early adult years, will confront a number of issues relating to their sexuality, gender role, and interpersonal relationships. These may present thorny issues not only for the athlete but also for individuals working with them, if the help givers have conflicts or biases in these areas.

Gender roles have been dealt with a little bit more than have sexuality issues (Harris & Harris, 1984). Within our society the athlete role has been more compatible with expectations of male behavior than with female behavior. Is it not classic, after all, for a coach to say derisively to a group of men on a team, "You're behaving like a bunch of girls." That conveys a very powerful message about attitudes toward males and females. If we assume we are all capable of non–gender-specific behaviors, any roles that force us to suppress a segment of ourselves are self-limiting and self-defeating.

Male athletes and sport participants can express aggressive, achievement-oriented, and other "masculine" traits but have been more likely to suppress more nurturing, compassionate, or "feminine" traits. This is partly due to a homophobic attitude prevalent in our society, which will be discussed in terms of working with athletes shortly.

As women's sports become more popular and widespread, the demands on women may also change. Whether women in sport will be asked to be "masculine" on court but "feminine" off court, or will be asked to be "masculine" in both settings, or will be allowed an androgynous option is not yet clear. Certainly for a long time women in sport have been haunted by homophobic specters. Why would a woman be in sport unless she were a lesbian? Fearsome myths abound about predatory coaches and players. Some coaches and administrators of women's sports are reputed to avoid recruiting women they see as being lesbians or even those who have too masculine a physical appearance! Optimally, in society in general and in the sport environment in particular, a person's sexual orientation will cease to be a matter of concern.

In recent years our society has been trying to deal with gender role issues and with homophobia. One might ask, how do these relate to the issues of when to refer? A regrettable example was recently reported by Garnets and colleagues (1991) in a report on issues in psychotherapy with lesbians and gay men.

> A 19 year old male client . . . had been receiving therapy from a University athletic department's sport psychologist. . . . The student-client developed transference toward the psychologist and in the seventh session shared with the psychologist his affection/positive feelings—referring to being "surprised that he could feel love for a man that way." The psychologist became angry, immediately terminated the session and all therapy. (p. 967)

If the above report is accurate, there would certainly be clear ethical issues about the psychologist's behavior (American Psychological Association, 1989). Even worse, the original report of this incident (APA Committee on Lesbian and Gay Concerns, 1990) went on to state that the sport psychologist "broke confidentiality by telling the client's coach he was gay. The client sat out the rest of the games that season and was asked to not return the next season as 'his problem was unacceptable'" (p. 34).

In working with athletes and sport participants, particularly during adolescence and young adulthood, one may encounter people who experience conflict or confusion about sexuality and gender roles. I was asked by a coach to talk with a football player whom I will call Matt. Matt was a great player but rarely interacted with his teammates outside of practice or games. He also seemed aloof and "stand-offish" when he was around

them. There was a perception that he was a "snob," and tensions were building. After several sessions, Matt affirmed that he was gay and that he was afraid if his teammates knew this they would verbally and physically harass him, and his chances for a professional career would be limited. We were able to work on these issues and to help him be more comfortable and confident in his interactions with his peers, preparing for but not fearing disclosure, although he elected not to volunteer information about his sexual orientation.

A coach or an educational or clinical sport psychologist who is homophobic or who has biases about gender role behaviors (for example, negative attitudes toward women who are assertive) may have great difficulty when encountering issues of sexual orientation or gender roles. If so, such a person should seek help; he/she cannot truly be of help to others who have conflicts with these issues. A person who is open and accepting of others, however, will convey an important message to the athlete and will increase the likelihood of accepting an appropriate referral.

Sexuality and HIV-related Issues

The disclosure of Magic Johnson's status as HIV positive has, at least temporarily, affected much of society's thinking about AIDS. Given the general homophobia in society and sports, the unfortunate association of AIDS with gays may legitimize the stigmatization and abuse of gay and lesbian athletes and may feed into fears about disclosure. It is very likely that coaches and others working with athletes and teams may need to know more about the myths and realities of HIV transmission to allay fears.

At the same time, issues relating to sexuality and drug use must be dealt with. Athletes at all levels may have increased opportunities for anonymous sexual encounters. Whether Wilt Chamberlain's accounting of "20,000" women is accurate or not, sport "groupies" exist. Sexually transmitted diseases were curable before, and perhaps considered a laughing matter if not a badge of honor as a true sexual athlete, but AIDS has changed that. Athletes and sport participants may well suffer from fears and anxieties about AIDS and may need to talk with a help giver who can refer them to someone more knowledgeable, if necessary.

At the same time, it must be understood that sharing needles, in addition to sexual behaviors, is a high risk factor for HIV infection. Steroids can be injected, and often in gyms or locker rooms several athletes may use the same syringe. Again, athletes or sport participants may need to talk with someone about their behaviors and their fears. This person should be knowledgeable and should also be able to make referrals for more specific issues.

Eating Disorders

Although only very sketchy research exists, it has been assumed that athletes concerned with their weight for competition purposes may be more vulnerable to developing eating disorders. Coaches, educational sport psychologists, and others working with athletes should be aware of preoccupations with weight and food that athletes might have. The anorexic pattern of severely limiting food intake will likely show in poor health, although in some groups of athletes—for example, marathoners—this may be less obvious.

More commonly, athletes have been thought to have bulemic patterns, composed of episodes of binging and purging. An individual overeats, often foods that are fattening, and then induces regurgitation. There are a number of physical and psychological hazards connected with this pattern. In the course of working with an athlete when weight concerns are also discussed or when unusual eating patterns are observed or discussed, it might be necessary to raise this issue in a caring, concerned way. Again, referral to someone more specialized in this area might be necessary.

Alcohol and Substance Abuse Issues

Due to the public attention to celebrities' problems with alcohol and drugs, this is perhaps one domain in which athlete's problems have received extensive attention. Authors in this book (Anshel, Chapter 22) and in other volumes (Asken & May, 1987; Tricker & Cook, 1987) have considered these areas. Due to the association within our culture of masculinity and drinking (as well as the ability to consume large amounts of other substances), athletes may be more vulnerable. In addition, individuals inclined to take risks, or "sensation seekers," as Zuckerman (1979) has called them, are also likely to indulge in greater amounts of alcohol and drug use. Certain sports may disproportionately attract sensation seekers.

Someone working with athletes should recognize the general symptoms of excessive alcohol or drug use. Most commonly, these involve chronic use or binges, a centering of life events around this usage, personality changes during usage, and usage interfering with other life activities or relationships. Unfortunately, high school and college life in general, and often the athletic environment, will cloak problem usage with different forms of social acceptability. Given denial and defensiveness around issues of alcohol and drug use, a coach or educational sport psychologist concerned about these issues can note his/her concern, but not in a lecturing or threatening manner. The availability of individuals to whom to refer an athlete is important, particularly if the athlete becomes concerned about this usage and would like to seek help.

Anger and Aggression Control

In many competitive sports we encourage psychological attitudes of toughness and competitiveness and see the opponent as an enemy to be defeated. In contact sports in particular, but in other sports as well, physical aggression is sanctioned. Most athletes are able to control their anger and aggression both on the field and off, although some require a little time after competition for the person's behavioral controls to reset.

There are individuals, however, who experience difficulty with anger or aggression control and for whom a referral might be appropriate. Some individuals may have always had a reputation for conflict. For men, this may have a negative identity component that cloaks the problem in an acceptable way for a peer group. The athlete may be tough on and off the field, someone "not to mess with." Unfortunately, the frequency and severity of conflicts may escalate to harmful levels.

In other cases, someone going through a personally difficult time may be less able to control anger or aggression. This may be expressed either on or off the field. Particularly when anger and aggression have not been issues for a person before, they might be discussed with the athlete, and a referral made.

Alcohol and drug use may also be related to such behaviors. In general, when people are intoxicated, bottled-up anger or rage may be expressed more easily. In recent years, in addition, "roid rages," or violent reactions in some individuals who are taking steroids, have been noted (Gregg & Rejeski, 1990).

There are ways to help individuals deal with anger (e.g., Novaco, 1975), as well as with aggression (Heyman, 1987). It is easier to help someone resolve conflicts and reestablish controls if he/she has had a reasonably good history of anger and aggression control. Helping athletes with more problematic histories is possible, but it may be a slower process.

A myth that needs to be addressed is the fear that therapy will take away whatever makes an athlete great. Coaches, athletes, and others might wonder whether an athlete who is driven by conflicts may suffer diminished abilities if the conflicts are resolved. Since there is virtually nothing in the literature about this, I will comment from a more personal perspective. Physical abilities and skills cannot be lost due to the resolution of conflicts, any more than any kind of ability, intelligence, or creativity could be lost. Could the direction or expression be changed? Perhaps. Cases I have seen have involved individuals who expressed their abilities in hostile, aggressive ways but who found equally skillful but more personally and socially acceptable ways to express these talents as conflicts were resolved. It would be naive to assume, however, that coaches working with aggressive football players or boxers should have no fear that if conflicts relating to anger or aggression were to be resolved, the athletes might not be as successful or might choose a different expression for their talents. Such cases, however, would be extremely rare. As someone desiring to help people develop and grow, my goal would be to help athletes become free to choose their own direction.

Relationship Issues

Athletes and sport participants are likely to have relationship problems similar to those of others in their peer groups. There are some problems, however, that might be somewhat unique to athletes, although similar to others who are celebrities or who are dedicated to a demanding activity in which the partner may not be involved.

Many athletes have to be away from friends or family for extended periods of time. This can cause loneliness, anxiety, and depression, both for the athlete and the family members. There may be conflicts in the relationship, or fears or suspicions, and these can manifest themselves in decreased performance, increased anger or aggression, or a number of other ways.

At the same time, practice and competition place demands on the athlete's time even when he/she is at home, and this, too, may be problematic for the partner. For many marathoners, who may not be elite or competitive athletes, for example, the months taken to train may disrupt family or relationship patterns. Someone who spends years involved in training and competition may need a very understanding or mutually involved partner.

Given the glamour and celebrity status that can surround athletes, as well as long travels away from home, there is the opportunity for infidelity. Even where an athlete is not unfaithful, the partner may have fears about this when the athlete is away, or the athlete may have fears about the partner left behind.

It is not always easy to identify these issues. In some cases, when performance becomes problematic, the athlete will indicate the source is interpersonal or a relationship problem. In other cases, a relationship problem may manifest itself in changes in mood; the expression of anger, depression, or anxiety; or increases in alcohol or drug use. Often teammates will be told of the situation, and they may discuss it with a coach or others.

The athlete or sport participant may need to talk with someone individually, in order to understand personal reactions better and to make decisions about commitments and behaviors. In other cases, marital, relationship, and/or family counseling or therapy might be required.

When to Refer: A Summary

Throughout the chapter I have tried to address a variety of issues involved in deciding when to refer an athlete for professional counseling or psychotherapy. In most situations, referral will not be necessary. I hope that this chapter has provided helpful clues for recognizing when an athlete presents issues beyond the scope of the usual sport psychologist–client interaction. It is also important, however, for individuals working on performance-enhancement issues, whether educational sport psychologists, coaches, or others, to recognize that there has to be a sensitivity to the athlete's personal issues, and there must be a caring and concern in making appropriate referrals. These helping individuals must also be sensitive to their own issues and values as they might affect their ability to work with and to be sensitive to the issues others might have.

Referral: To What?

Early in the chapter it was suggested that, while we have become more accepting of personal and psychosocial conflicts, society in general and the sport world more particularly might have difficulty acknowledging and dealing with some issues.

Early in this century, as the nature of human conflict was recognized, there was a shift from blaming individuals or family backgrounds for problems to a "medicalization" of problems. In an attempt to understand people and treat them more compassionately, psychiatry and psychoanalysis (led by physicians) came up with the concept of mental illness, diagnosis, treatment, etcetera. In the 1960s Thomas Szasz (1961) suggested, rather, that we again shift perspective to see conflict issues as problems in living.

There are many different theories of personality and approaches to counseling and psychotherapy. Individuals may have conflicts ranging from mild through severe. These do not have to be seen as illnesses or personal failings, but they may require the help of a trained professional. Increasingly the medical model is fading, as models of growth and development replace it. At the same time, it must be recognized that a small percentage of athletes, much like a small percentage of the general population, will have severe problems that may seriously affect their own functioning and their interpersonal relationships but that may not interfere with the performance of their athletic activities. Many therapists have worked with individuals who are highly successful in some domains of their lives, while having significant personal problems or disturbances in other domains.

Referral: To Whom?

There are many different types and levels of professional counselors, psychologists, psychiatrists, and psychotherapists. If a coach, trainer, athlete, or educational sport psychologist has not developed a working relationship with someone to whom they can refer, it may be necessary to investigate resources within the community. Most colleges have counseling centers, and many high schools have counseling personnel. It is possible to meet with them to find who may have a particular background in working with athletes or who might be interested in developing such a specialization. Similarly, individuals in private practice within a community or working at community mental health centers may be well suited for sport referrals.

Individuals who are licensed or certified by a state as counselors, psychologists (clinical or counseling), psychiatrists, or social workers have met certain educational requirements, although this does not speak to the quality of their work. In many states, however, the term "psychotherapist" is not legally defined. In essence, therefore, anyone can take out an advertisement and declare himself/herself to be a therapist. Some individuals will be trained, usually at the master's level. Perhaps the best advice for someone who is not familiar with these complex issues is to consult a licensed or certified psychiatrist, counselor, social worker, or psychologist for help in locating appropriate individuals to whom to refer.

To make things even more complicated, it may be necessary to know more than one professional. For example, a psychotherapist may work well with certain personal or interpersonal issues but might not be skilled with eating disorders or substance abuse. Perhaps one person works well with anxiety and depression but not with patterns of anger or aggression. In many cases, counselors and therapists know the areas in which they are not as well trained or experienced and are able to refer to others. In other situations, however, the coach or educational sport psychologist may want to develop a personal listing of individuals with different skills.

It is important to understand the nature of *confidentiality* in counseling relationships. The coach or person referring the athlete to the professional may want feedback, but the professional may not be able to report much, or even any, information. There are very clear ethical issues on confidentiality that the person referring the athlete and the professional should discuss in developing a working relationship. The therapist likely cannot disclose the issues discussed with the athlete or even whether progress is being made.

Similarly, the athlete may not want to discuss the general or specific issues being explored in counseling or therapy. Over time, however, it is likely that a sense will develop of how helpful a therapist is and perhaps with what types of problems. A significant hallmark is the referral of one athlete by another to a person he/she has found helpful.

Final Thoughts

This has been a difficult chapter to write because there are many complex issues to discuss, or at least to acknowledge. Many of these could easily merit chapters on their own. Until sport psychology develops more interdisciplinary training programs, acknowledgement in the literature that athletes confront issues that can benefit from professional help must be forthcoming. This chapter has explored ways to help those not trained in counseling or psychotherapy to recognize these issues and to facilitate such referral.

Study Questions

1. Why has it been difficult for sport psychology to address more serious personal and interpersonal problems athletes might have?

2. What are three patterns someone might note as indicating more serious problems when working with an athlete on performance enhancement?

3. How can performance-enhancement approaches themselves sometimes cause problems?

4. How does homophobia in society and in the sport world contribute to problems for athletes who may be struggling with identity issues around their sexuality?

5. How might a concern with food and/or making weight reflect more serious eating disorder problems?

6. What are the general symptoms of alcohol or drug abuse? Why might athletes be more vulnerable to developing problems in this areas?

7. What are some signs that aggressiveness in an athlete has become problematic? Is it likely that an athlete who has been driven by anger will become less successful if underlying conflicts are resolved?

8. What factors related to sport can cause or exacerbate relationship problems for athletes?

9. How might a coach or an educational sport psychologist find professionals to whom to refer athletes for counseling or psychotherapy?

References

American Psychological Association (1989). *Ethical principles of psychologists*. Washington, D.C.: American Psychological Association.

APA Committee on Lesbian and Gay Concerns (1990). *Bias in psychotherapy with lesbians and gay men*. Washington, D.C.: American Psychological Association.

Berger, B. G. (in press). Sport and exercise psychology. In M. G. Wade & J. Baker (Eds.), *Kinesiology, the study of activity*. Dubuque, Iowa: Brown.

Butt, D. S. (1990). The sexual response as exercise: A brief review and theoretical proposal. *Sports Medicine, 9*, 330–343.

Erikson, E. (1968). *Identity: Youth and crisis*. New York: Norton.

Etzel, E. F., Ferrante, A. P., & Pinkney, J. (1991). *Counseling college student athletes: Issues and interventions*. Morgantown, W.Va.: Information Technology.

Garnets, L., Hancock, K., Cochran, S., Goodchilds, J., & Peplau, L. A. (1991). *American Psychologist, 46*, 964–972.

Greenspan, M. J., & Feltz, D. L. (1989). Psychological interventions with athletes in competitive situations: A review. *The Sport Psychologist, 3*, 219–236.

Gregg, E., & Rejeski, W. J. (1990). Social psychologic dysfunction associated with anabolic steroids: A review. *The Sport Psychologist, 4*, 275–284.

Harris, D. V., & Harris, B. L. (1984). *The athlete's guide to sports psychology: Mental skills for physical people*. New York: Leisure Press.

Heyman, S. R. (1984). Cognitive interventions: Theories, applications, and cautions. In W. F. Straub & J. M. Williams (Eds.), *Cognitive sport psychology*. Lansing, N.Y.: Sport Science Associates.

Heyman, S. R. (1987). Counseling and psychotherapy with athletes: Special considerations. In J. R. May & M. J. Asken (Eds.), *Sport psychology: The psychological health of the athlete*. New York: PMA.

Lanning, W. (1982). The privileged few: Special counseling needs of athletes. *Journal of Sport Psychology, 4*, 19–23.

Linder, D. E., Pillow, D. R., & Reno, R. R. (1989). Shrinking jocks: Derogation of athletes who consult a sport psychologist. *Journal of Sport and Exercise Psychology, 11*, 270–280.

May, J. R., & Asken, M. J. (1987). *Sport psychology: The psychological health of the athlete*. New York: PMA.

Novaco, R. (1975). *Anger control: The development and evaluation of an experimental treatment*. Lexington, Mass.: Heath.

Rejeski, W. J., & Brawley, L. R. (1988). Defining the boundaries of sport psychology. *The Sport Psychologist*, 2, 231–242.

Rotella, R., & Murray, M. M. (1991). Homophobia, the world of sport, and sport psychology consulting. *The Sport Psychologist*, 5, 355–364.

Singer, R. N. (1972). *Coaching, athletics, and psychology*. New York: McGraw-Hill.

Straub, W. F., & Williams, J. M. (1984). *Cognitive sport psychology*. Lansing, N.Y.: Sport Science Associates.

Szasz, T. (1961). *The myth of mental illness*. New York: Harper & Row.

Tricker, R., & Cook, D. L. (1989). *Athletes at risk: Drugs and sport*. Dubuque, Iowa: Brown.

Wittner, J., Bostic, D., Phillips, J., & Waters, W. (1981). The personal, academic, and career problems of college students: Some possible answers. *Personnel and Guidance Journal*, 60, 52–55.

Ziegel, V. (1979). Is there fight after sex? *The Ring*, 58(11), 28–31.

Zuckerman, M. (1979). *Sensation seeking: Beyond the optimal level of arousal*. Hillsdale, N.J.: Erlbaum.

Drug Abuse in Sport: Causes and Cures

Mark H. Anshel, *University of Wollongong*

Much has been written in recent years about drug use among sport competitors, particularly use of performance-enhancing drugs (e.g., anabolic steroids) and "recreational" drugs (e.g., hallucinogens, such as cocaine). Considerable anecdotal evidence and, to a lesser extent, scientific data have surfaced indicating that drug abuse among athletes is more common than previously recognized. Perhaps no source of information influenced this perception more than the frequent media reports revealing the extent of drug abuse and the positive results of drug tests by high-profile, elite athletes. Yet, despite this evidence, official reaction to drug use has been inconsistent. Indeed, the absence of assertive and consistent responses to drug abuse by sport administrators and coaches has likely contributed to its proliferation. As Strauss (1987) points out, "Sports officials voice unequivocal disapproval of performance-enhancing drugs and formally ban them. Yet, when violations are uncovered, punishment is inconsistent" (p. 13).

The term "drug" means different things to different people. Some competitors ingest performance enhancing drugs such as anabolic steroids, while others abuse "recreational" drugs such as cocaine, heroin, or marijuana. Obviously, the reasons for ingesting recreational and performance-enhancing drugs vary. The objective of recreational drug users is to alter the state of mind, with no intention of improving performance. Users of drugs such as steroids, on the other hand, feel a need to improve performance to gain a competitive advantage. These different rationales for ingesting drugs must be taken into account when developing strategies to reduce or eliminate such behaviors.

What drugs are banned by sport organizations? Why break the rules and chance expulsion from a team and sport organization? Why risk severe health problems? The purpose of this chapter is to address these questions and to suggest cognitive and behavioral strategies that coaches, parents, and sport psychology consultants can use to combat drug abuse in sport. Only when causes for drug usage are identified can cognitive and behavioral strategies be devised to help prevent and perhaps eliminate this problem.

Brief Review of Drugs Banned in Sport

The International Olympic Committee (IOC) refers to the act of ingesting banned drugs as "doping" (Prokop, 1990). **Doping** has been defined as "the administering or use of substances in any form alien to the body or of physiological substances in abnormal amounts and with abnormal methods by healthy persons with the exclusive aim of attaining an artificial and unfair increase of performance in competition" (Prokop, 1990, p. 5). The IOC has classified five doping categories that are banned from international competition: anabolic androgenic steroids, stimulants (including hallucinogens), narcotic analgesics, beta-adrenergic blockers, and diuretics (Chappel, 1987; Park, 1990). Central nervous system depressants that serve to reduce anxiety (e.g., alcohol, barbiturates, and sedative hypnotics), local anesthetics, and corticosteroids (anti-inflammatory drugs that relieve pain) are not on the IOC list but are tested for in selected international competitions (Chappel, 1987; *Drugs in Sport*, 1990). Typically, however, these substances are considered illegal. In addition, the technique of blood doping has been banned. The reasons for banning such drugs in sport are understandable given their psychophysiological effects (see Mottram, 1988; Park, 1990; Strauss, 1987; Weinhold, 1991; and Williams, 1983, for complete reviews of these drugs). Not banned by the IOC and therefore not against policies of national and international sport organizations, at least for mature-age athletes, are depressants (e.g., alcohol), nicotine, diet regimens (e.g., carbohydrate loading or any other food-ingestion habits), amino acids, and vitamins. However, excessive caffeine—at least 15 micrograms per milliliter of urine—is banned (Chappel, 1987).

Anabolic Steroids

Some athletes use **anabolic steroids** to increase strength and power. The function of anabolic steroids is to increase the male hormone androgen and decrease the female hormone estrogen. These effects explain why steroids have a masculinizing effect (e.g., increased facial and body hair, lowered voice, increased muscular bulk and strength, and interference with reproductive function) for both sexes. Prolonged steroid use may cause cancer of the liver and lymph system, heightened aggression, premature heart disease, and death (Donald, 1983; Strauss, 1987; Cohen, Noakes, & Benade, 1988; Lubell, 1989). The negative side effects can be even greater for individuals who have not yet reached physiological maturity. Another concern about steroids is their addictive properties, both

psychologically and sometimes somatically, or physically (Weinhold, 1991).

There is considerable controversy concerning the benefits of anabolic steroids on athletic performance. It would appear that steroids may improve performance only when strength is a primary component of the sport (e.g., weight lifting, shot putting) and when steroid usage is combined with an intensified training program. These benefits primarily occur because steroids promote the synthesis of proteins that are used to build skeletal muscle tissue (Williams, 1983).

Stimulants

Stimulant drugs increase the rate, and hence the work capacity, of the heart, central nervous system, and respiratory system. Stimulants are divided into three groups: **psychomotor** (e.g., amphetamines, cocaine, and most diet suppressants); **sympathomimetic amines**, which stimulate the sympathetic and autonomic nervous systems; and miscellaneous **central nervous system (CSN) stimulants** (e.g., drugs such as ephedrine that are found in many prescription and over-the-counter cold remedies). Ostensibly these drugs improve athletic performance by increasing alertness through inhibition of mental and physical fatigue.

Another category of stimulant is **hallucinogens**. Often referred to as "recreational," "mind-altering," or "street" drugs (Bell & Doege, 1987; Julien, 1981), hallucinogens alter the perceptions of incoming stimuli. The IOC does not place hallucinogens in a separate banned drug category because they are stimulants or narcotic analgesics, both banned by the IOC. Because they inhibit response and decision-making time and attentional focus, these drugs impair rather than enhance sport performance. Marijuana (a sedative) and LSD, PCP, and cocaine (stimulants) are examples. The use of these drugs is also against the federal laws of most countries.

Narcotic Analgesics (Anti-inflammatories)

Narcotic analgesics are used by athletes for their pain-killing properties, to slow or stop the inflammation and swelling of tissue, to reduce fever, and to produce feelings of well-being or invincibility. As pain suppressants these drugs enable an injured competitor to continue playing despite tissue damage and injury. Anti-inflammatories can actually reduce performance effectiveness in some sports due to their sedative effect. All analgesics are toxic in large doses. Examples of narcotic analgesics include codeine, heroin, morphine, and opium. Harmful effects of analgesics include gastrointestinal disturbances, physical and psychological dependence, and depressed respiration—including respiratory arrest. Nonnarcotic analgesics such as aspirin and acetaminophen, which are not habit-forming and do not affect the central nervous system, are not banned.

Beta-Adrenergic Blockers

Perhaps best known for the treatment of high blood pressure and some forms of heart disease, **beta blockers** are among the few drugs banned by the IOC that do not induce dependence. They aid performance by slowing the heart rate, decreasing anxiety, and steadying natural body tremors. These are desirable outcomes in sports such as rifle and pistol shooting, archery, bowling, and golf. Adverse effects of beta blockers include bronchospasm, CNS disturbances, hypotension, and impotence.

Diuretics

Diuretics increase the rate at which water and salts leave the body as urine. Athletes such as jockeys, wrestlers, and boxers use diuretics in order to "make weight" for a competition. Other athletes use diuretics to overcome fluid retention—often to modify the excretion rate of urine in order to alter the urinary concentrations of banned drugs such as anabolic steroids. The rapid depletion of body fluids in general and of potassium in particular can produce heart arrhythmias. Nausea, heat exhaustion or stroke from impaired thermoregulatory control, blood clotting, reduced blood volume, and muscle cramps are other possible outcomes (Russell, 1990).

Depressants

Depressants relieve tension, reduce anxiety, and have a steadying effect on the nervous or fearful athlete, such as reducing arm tremor in shooters. They also, however, impair reaction time, hand–eye coordination, balance, and judgment. Thus,

for the most part, depressants inhibit rather than enhance sport performance. Because they are addictive, the heavy and prolonged use of depressants may result in severe withdrawal symptoms. Barbiturates, sedative-hypnotics, and alcohol are examples of this form of drug.

Blood Doping

Blood doping involves removing approximately one liter (about two units) of the athlete's blood one to two months before the competition and appropriately freezing and storing it. The athlete's frozen red blood cells are then infused back into the competitor shortly before competition, thus producing increased red cell mass and hemoglobin of up to 15%. The effect may last as long as two weeks. This technique increases oxygen uptake—the blood's oxygen-carrying capacity—thereby improving aerobic (endurance) performance. Despite these apparent benefits, the results of studies on the effects of blood doping on actual endurance performance have been equivocal. However, the failure to find beneficial performance occurred primarily in studies employing improper procedures. There are few medical dangers if doping is performed by a careful and knowledgeable physician. Still, blood doping is unethical and falls into the IOC's definition of banned drugs by ingesting a substance in an abnormal quantity or the improper route of entry into the body for the purpose of artificially fostering physical performance.

Rationale for an Antidrug Policy in Sport

Why do antidrug policies exist in competitive sport? Why not allow all athletes to take whatever substances they wish? Typical reasons for banning drugs concern legal considerations, ethical issues related to cheating and creating an unfair performance advantage, and medical problems. Equally important is the need to protect athletes from themselves—that is, many athletes will take any drug, no matter how harmful, to enhance their performance (*The Australian*, 1991).

Legal Considerations

Certain drugs, particularly in the hallucinogens category, are against federal law. For example, smoking marijuana or ingesting cocaine can result in a fine or incarceration. In addition, because such drugs slow information processing and distort visual perception, they can have a dangerous effect on the athlete's personal safety. Further, media exposure of the problem will embarrass the user and organization responsible for monitoring the conduct of its players, often resulting in termination of sponsorship or removal of leaders. Substance abuse also is often accompanied by criminal activity, violence, and a drain of personal and community financial resources (Anshel, 1990a).

Ethical Issues

One important reason drugs have been banned by sport organizations is because they may facilitate athletic performance (Weinhold, 1991). Athletes who ingest performance-enhancing banned drugs are cheating by gaining an unfair competitive advantage (Strauss, 1987). This is an ethical issue. From a philosophical perspective, conference presenter Lawrie Woodman (in Anshel, 1990a) reports that "strict control of drug taking in sport begins with establishing equality among participants. If sport is to continue as we know it, then athletes must not have an unfair advantage" (p. 51).

Medical Problems

Perhaps the most important problem with drug use in sport is the potential lethal effect on health and well-being. The literature abounds with research indicating unequivocal evidence on the detrimental medical effects of drug taking (e.g., Chappel, 1987; Donald, 1981; Julien, 1981; Strauss, 1987). Anecdotal evidence has shown that athletes are literally dying from using so-called performance-enhancing drugs (*Drugs in Sport*, 1989, 1990). For example, as reported in the *Sydney* (Australia) *Daily Telegraph* (October 26, 1989), a 23-year-old bodybuilder died of cardiac arrest hours before entering the Mr. Australia contest. Police reports indicated he ingested 20 tablets of potassium chloride and 11 diuretic tablets within 24 hours. This incident shows the extent to which some athletes will go to succeed, literally at all costs.

Widespread media reports in recent years on deaths and terminal diseases of elite athletes due to drug taking attest to the potentially lethal medical side effects of drug abuse. The causes of death from sport-related drug abuse are both acute (e.g., dehy-

dration, heat stroke, cardiac arrest) and chronic (e.g., liver cancer, lymphoma, cardiovascular disease). Less lethal physical maladies (e.g., kidney stones, irregular heart beat, sterility, hypertension) and psychological problems (e.g, heightened anxiety, suicidal tendencies, short attention span, depression, aggression, and schizophrenia) have been reported as well (Corrigan, 1988; Donald, 1981; Lamb, 1984; Weinhold, 1991). Another problem with the use of drugs is their addictive properties. According to Julien (1981), "A person physically dependent on a drug requires that drug in order to function normally" (p. 24). For example, the sudden stoppage of stimulants depletes neurotransmitters and is followed by a period of depression, irritability, and increased fatigue. Clearly, society has an obligation to protect the public in general and sport participants in particular by prohibiting certain practices that sooner or later may lead to serious physical and mental problems.

How Widespread Is Drug Abuse in Sport?

It is impossible to determine the exact extent of drug abuse in sport. The two primary sources of drug usage, anecdotal evidence and scientific research studies, have serious limitations. Anecdotal reports, among other serious shortcomings, fail to provide concrete evidence documenting the usage of drugs. Scientific studies suffer from underreporting because ethical and legal considerations make drug taking a largely clandestine behavior. Keep these limitations in mind when examining the following information.

Anecdotal Evidence

Anecdotal evidence consists of information provided by individuals based on their own experiences or perceptions. For example, former American Olympic gold medal hurdler Edwin Moses (1988) asserts that "at least 50 percent of the athletes in high-performance sports such as track and field, cycling, and rowing would be disqualified if they weren't so adept at beating the tests" (p. 57). Australian Olympic team runner Gael Martin told the Australian Senate Standing Committee (*Drugs in Sport*, 1989) that "30 percent of [Australia's] track and field athletes were using steroids" (p. 188), herself included, while training at the Australian Institute of Sport.

In an unusually candid confession (Alzado, 1991), former National Football League star Lyle Alzado admitted to extensive anabolic steroid use during his athletic career. Alzado, suffering from a terminal brain tumor, contended that his nonstop use of steroids caused this condition. He claimed that he passed drug tests by stopping drug intake a month before testing. Did the coaches know he was taking drugs? Alzado said that "the coaches knew guys were built certain ways, and knew those guys couldn't look the way they did without taking stuff. But the coaches just coached and looked the other way" (p. 25). At the very least, Alzado's story accurately illustrates the sacrifice that elite athletes are prepared to make for success in sport. Perhaps of greater concern is Alzado's contention that "Ninety percent of the athletes I know are on [steroids]" (p. 21).

In another example of self-reported drug use, a story in *Sports Illustrated* (Chaikin & Telander, 1988) detailed the effects of prolonged steroid use on Tommy Chaikin, a skilled football lineman with the University of South Carolina. His prolific steroid taking almost took his life. The result was heightened chronic aggression, severe acne, backache, insomnia, testicular shrinkage, hair loss, depression, poor vision, inability to cope with stress, chronic anxiety, poor concentration, and, even more serious, hypertension, heart murmur, and benign tumors. Surgery, immediate cessation of taking steroids, and counseling saved his life.

In a self-effacing report on the factors that led to his "addiction" to anabolic steroids, Chaikin provides significant insight into numerous psychological and social pressures that foster drug use in sport. According to Chaikin, "I felt I had the coaches' encouragement . . . he told me 'do what you have to do, take what you have to take.'" (p. 88). He contends that "college athletes feel tremendous pressure to succeed" due to the expectations of others. "Nobody wants to sit on the bench and be a failure" (p. 88). Unspoken sanctioning of drug use by coaches and sport administrators is reflected by the absence of team rules and other forms of communication that discourage drug taking. Perhaps not surprisingly, Chaikin says the coaches never called him in the hospital, nor did the university offer to pay any medical expenses. The university claimed his health problems were not related to playing for the team.

Other anecdotal evidence exists to show that some coaches actually sanction drug use. Their encouragement of drug use takes one of two courses: direct (e.g., advising, "Taking steroids is the only way to stay competitive") or indirect (e.g., requiring that the participant reach an unrealistic body weight by a certain time; requiring a particularly demanding performance goal; or ignoring drug-taking behavior, thus sanctioning its use). For example, Canadian world-class sprinter Ben Johnson, after having his gold medal taken away, strongly asserted to a Canadian government inquiry that his coach knowingly gave him a substance that was banned by international sport organizations (*Time*, 1989). "Charlie [Francis] was my coach. . . . If Charlie gave me something to take, I took it" (p. 57). In fact, this coach's testimony at the same inquiry supported Johnson's contention. Francis told Johnson (and other sprinters) that "drugs marked the only route to international success and admitted that he provided such chemicals to his charges" (*Time*, 1989, p. 57).

Anecdotal evidence indicates team physicians also have contributed to drug abuse among athletes. For example, Ye Qiaobo, a Chinese speed skater, was sent home in disgrace from the 1988 Olympics after testing positive for steroids. A later inquiry revealed that she unknowingly had been taking steroids prescribed by the team doctor. A segment on CBS's coverage of the 1992 Olympics revealed the extensiveness, as far back as preparation for the 1976 Olympics, of East Germany's experimentation with steroids. Team doctors, under orders from the highest political powers, prescribed steroids for athletes, even 13-year-old girls, and then kept careful records regarding the effects of different dosages on performance and the length of time needed in order to test "clean."

Scientific Evidence

Scientific research on drug use in sport has centered primarily on performance-enhancing drugs, particularly anabolic steroids. Pope, Katz, and Champous (1988) investigated the prevalence of anabolic steroid use in American college males. Of the 1,010 respondents, only 17 (2%) reported using steroids. Four subjects used steroids primarily to improve personal appearance, while the goal of the other respondents, all competitive athletes, was to improve sport performance. The authors admit to the problem of underreporting in comparing their results with other studies in which a far higher percentage of steroid use—as high as 20%—is reported among university competitors (e.g., Dezelsky, Toohey, & Shaw, 1985; Heitzinger et al., 1986).

A study of over 3,000 male American high school seniors found 6.6% used anabolic steroids, with over two-thirds of the user group first taking drugs when they were 16 years of age or younger (Buckley et al., 1988). Out of 4,064 Australian athletes surveyed by the Australian Sports Drug Agency over a three-year period, only 39 respondents (1.0%) admitted to using anabolic steroids (Australian Sports Medicine Federation, 1989).

Other studies of specific sport populations, particularly ones involving strength and/or endurance, report higher drug usage. For example, an Australian government inquiry (*Drugs in Sport*, 1989) indicated that about 70% of Australia's elite swimmers and Olympic track and field squad have ingested a performance-enhancing aid. A survey of 93 National Football League athletes showed that 60% admitted to using amphetamines to improve performance (Cohen, 1979). Perhaps no sport has received more recognition for abusing anabolic steroids than weightlifting. According to an Australian government inquiry (*Drugs in Sport*, 1990), positive drug tests—and disqualifications—occurred with two Canadian weightlifters in the Pan American Games (1983), two weightlifters at the Canadian Weightlifting Federation Competition (1984), eight finalists at the Seoul Olympic Games (1988), and the gold medal winner and two other finalists at the 1990 Commonwealth Games. In addition, after a positive drug test finding for the Bulgarian bantamweight gold medalist at the 1988 Olympic Games, the entire Bulgarian weightlifting team left for home and refused additional drug tests.

In a study with a slightly different slant, Martin and Anshel (1991) examined the attitudes of 94 elite adolescent male and female Australian athletes toward ingesting various drugs (e.g., anabolic steroids, anti-inflammatories, hallucinogens, alcohol) related and unrelated to sport performance. The authors found that athletes were inclined to say they agreed with using alcohol and tobacco before and during the competition season and with using anti-inflammatories in response to an injury. In contrast, athletes voiced disagreement with the use of anabolic steroids, but not unconditionally. According to their replies, if these athletes were of-

fered a performance-enhancing drug, they were more likely to avoid drug taking if the substance was detectable by testing. Thus, at least for younger elite competitors, testing inhibits drug abuse. Whether these results can be generalized to older athletes is far less certain.

In another study, Anshel (1991a) conducted personal interviews with American university athletes, 94 males and 32 females, competing in nine sports. In order to overcome the inherent dangers of underreporting found in related literature, information about the participants' personal use of drugs was not solicited. Of the 126 athletes surveyed, 81 (64%) revealed "known" drug use on their team. More specifically, 68 (72%) of the 94 male subjects and 13 (40%) of the 32 female subjects contended that teammates took a drug that the user knew was illegal or banned from their sport. Forty-three percent (494 of the athletes' 1,156 responses) acknowledged that athletes use drugs for the purpose of enhancing performance as opposed to recreational use. These report rates far exceed admitted drug use in other surveys.

Likely Causes of Drug Abuse in Sport

Athletes abuse many types of drugs, and for different reasons. Hence, any discussion on the likely causes of drug abuse in sport should differentiate among the types of substances ingested. Based on a review of the anecdotal and scientific literature and on my own professional interaction with athletes as a sport psychology consultant in the United States and Australia, I conclude that the causes of drug use lie within three categories: physical, psychological/emotional, and social.

Physical Causes

Given the extensive pressure on skilled athletes to succeed and "be competitive," a view held and often communicated by their coaches, it is not surprising that performers explore all possible avenues to reach—perhaps even go beyond—their performance potential. The sources of this pressure are rarely identified in combating drug use. As indicated earlier, coaches (and sponsors) can and often do contribute to the competitors' dilemma by reinforcing the need to win at any cost. The expectations of parents, media, and peers only fuel the pressure to maximize performance by artificial substance abuse (Chappel, 1987; Lamb, 1984; Williams, 1989).

Enhance sport performance. The most common physical cause for ingesting drugs is attempting to enhance performance. Depending upon the drug being taken, the athlete may be seeking benefits such as increased strength, endurance, alertness, and aggression or decreased reaction time, fatigue, anxiety, and muscle tremor. (See the earlier discussion of banned drugs for a more comprehensive list of potential physical and performance effects of specific types of drugs.)

Cope with pain and injury rehabilitation. Athletes also ingest drugs to psychologically cope with physical discomfort (*Drugs in Sport*, 1990) and to expedite recovery from injury (*Drugs in Sport*, 1990; English, 1987; Goldman, 1984). For example, athletes may feel that medical treatment is not sufficient to eliminate pain. They will take drugs to attenuate pain with no prescription and without the coach's knowledge (Donald, 1983), usually for the reason of not disappointing the coach or to avoid losing starting status (a tendency more typical of the male subjects) (Anshel, 1991a; Donald, 1983).

Weight control. Amphetamines are often used to control appetite and diuretics to reduce fluid weight. These drugs quickly reduce weight, allowing the athlete to compete in a lower, more favorable weight group (Donald, 1983) or at a weight deemed more facilitative to success.

Psychological Causes

By far the most common rationale for using recreational drugs among athletes is psychological and emotional (Anshel, 1991a; Wragg, 1990). For some athletes, mind-altering drugs provide the most convenient escape from unpleasant emotions. There also are psychological causes for taking drugs believed to be ergogenic aids.

Stress and anxiety. Emotions such as stress, tension, and anxiety may be antecedent causes of ingesting drugs, particularly hallucinogens and beta blockers. Drug taking attenuates the stress and tension associated with the pressures to succeed over

a prolonged time period, a full season or longer. Thus, recreational drug use may reflect a short-term approach to managing stress and anxiety or be a vehicle for escaping an unpleasant present situation (Donald, 1983; Egger, 1981).

Boredom. For many individuals, experimentation with recreational drugs, often ingested in group (social) situations, can help overcome boredom (Julien, 1981). This type of drug use appears to be more prevalent on weekends or when team-related activities are unplanned, especially when traveling. Athletes can also become bored by redundancy in the team's practices or in some other aspect of their participation (Anshell, 1991b; Egger, 1981).

Personal problems. Drug taking may be a response to a personal problem independent of sport involvement. The athlete's personal life can be a potential source of support—or of extreme stress. Orlick and Partington's (1986) interviews with 16 Canadian Olympic athletes showed that elite athletes, like any other individuals, need the love, acceptance, and support of their immediate family. When this support is lacking, the competitor may be less capable of coping with sport demands and more susceptible to the mental escape that certain drugs provide.

Low self-confidence. Many athletes use drugs to build self-confidence (Anshel, 1991a). This use reflects the athlete's doubt about his/her own skills ("They make me feel better about my ability") or concern about staying competitive ("I'm sure 'so and so' are taking them" or "If I'm going to perform at 'X' speed, I have to take these"). As an example, competitors may use steroids to foster aggressive behavior and increase body size and strength to overcome low self-confidence, especially in contact sports.

The "Superman" complex/experimentation. Some athletes feel impervious to any potential negative side effects of drugs (Collins et al., 1984). According to Don Weiss, executive director of the National Football League: "It is not easy to convince pro football players that they are vulnerable to the negative health effects of steroids. Some of these young men are such great physical specimens with such great athletic ability that they think they'll be like that forever" (Shroyer, 1990, p. 115). According to Nicholson and Agnew (1989), athletes who exhibit the "Superman complex" do not feel constrained by the deleterious effects of drugs, even after obtaining valid information about possible detrimental effects to their health.

Perfectionism. Some individuals are never pleased with their accomplishments, even with the appropriate recognition and adulation of others. For these people, "good" is never quite good enough. A **perfectionist** is someone who has trouble discriminating between realistic and idealized standards (Hewitt & Flett, 1991). He/she bypasses attainable excellence in pursuit of unattainable perfection. It would appear that the perfectionist athlete is a "ripe" candidate for drug abuse (Hewitt, Mittelstaedt, & Flett, 1990). Some athletes may be driven to seek consistent, perfect performance through anabolic steroids or other performance-enhancing drugs. Inversely, these individuals may need to mentally escape the pressures of their unrealistically high goals with mind-altering drugs. Although perfectionism has not been studied among athletes who take drugs, it would not be surprising to find that certain drug-taking competitors fit the profile of this unhealthy psychological state.

Social Causes

Perhaps there is no greater cause of succumbing to drug ingestion than response to social—and societal—pressures.

Peer pressure and acceptance. Pressure from peers, or the need to gain group acceptance, is a likely cause of drug taking among sport participants (Nicholson, 1989; Wragg, 1990). From the perspective of psychological maturation and development, the need for social acceptance and pressure to conform make adolescents particularly susceptible to peer influence. Wragg (1990) describes the peer group as "a critical agent of socialization as dependence on the family is reduced and the young person seeks to belong and fit into new relations with peers" (p. 237). Hence, in their eagerness to attain social acceptance, adolescents become aware of the types of approval-earning behaviors—the need to please other people— that will facilitate popularity. Wragg (1990) concludes that these developmental characteristics, "coupled

with a setting or contest where (drugs) are readily available, clearly implies that adolescence is a time of increased susceptibility to risk from drug use" (p. 238). Attitudes of strongly rejecting drug use should be developed early in life, *before* drug taking occurs.

Models. According to Gill (1986), modeling occurs when we learn by demonstration or change our behavior to imitate behaviors we have observed. Modeling has a particularly influential effect during adolescence. Accordingly, the development of appropriate (e.g., training and effort) and inappropriate (e.g., cheating, drug taking) behaviors of young athletes is often derived from the modeling of older, more experienced counterparts (Chu, 1982). The modeling effect is reinforced by media reports that publicize incidences of drug abuse by professional athletes (Collins, Pippenger, & Janesz, 1984). It is highly likely that reports of drug use by "established" sports stars influence the use of performance-enhancing drugs among interscholastic and intercollegiate athletes, many of whom aspire to compete at higher (i.e., Olympic or professional) levels. Perceptions are common that elite athletes ingest drugs and "if it doesn't hurt so and so, it won't hurt me" (*Drugs in Sport*, 1989; Nicholson, 1989; Nicholson & Agnew, 1989). Thus, for many athletes, drug use is "sanctioned" through observing their elite models.

Social support. Athletes may ingest a banned substance to gain social support. For example, the increase in muscle size and strength from steroid use may result in acceptance and approval among peers and coaches (*Drugs in Sport*, 1989, 1990). Social support is a primary need of athletes, particularly from teammates. Rosenfeld, Richman, and Hardy (1989) operationally define **social support** in a sport context as involving a network of personal ties to meet a recipient's needs for venting feelings, providing companionship and reassurance, reducing uncertainty during stressful times, aiding mental and physical recovery from stress and fatigue, and improving communication skills. Their findings indicate that coaches in particular are not providing listening support, emotional support, or shared social support. Statements from their subjects such as "No one ever tells me I'm doing a good job" or "There's no one to turn to when I need to talk to somebody" indicate the lack of social support. Perhaps more than any other rationale for drug use among athletes, the absence of social support can create drug dependency in athletes for either enhancing performance (i.e., to gain needed recognition from others) or as a vehicle to cope with stress or relieve boredom (i.e., reasons to use recreational drugs).

Strategies for Controlling Drug Abuse

The effectiveness of strategies to prevent or eliminate drug taking in sport is often a function of factors such as the individual's perceived needs for using drugs (e.g., gaining self-confidence, overcoming pain, improving strength), the type of drug usage (e.g., performance-enhancing versus mind-altering), the sport's physical demands (e.g., those requiring improved aerobic capacity, strength, and steadiness), and situational factors (e.g., boredom, stress, or the expectations of others). However, athletes share similar types of experiences, psychological demands, and performance requirements. Therefore, many of the issues described here can be applied to most competitors.

An array of techniques is available in the antidrug "arsenal." However, these techniques are only as effective as the individuals who implement them. It is important to recognize the role of coaches, parents, teachers, and sport psychology consultants in providing initiative, leadership, and expertise for successfully using these strategies. Coaches in particular have a far greater influence in regulating athlete behavior and attitude than any other individuals in the competitor's sport domain (Orlick & Partington, 1986). Anshel (1986, 1990a) and Smith (1983) contend that the coach is the most important agent in preventing drug use on the team—yet coaches tend not to be concerned with the athlete's behaviors away from the competitive environment in general and with drug-taking behaviors in particular (Anshel, 1986; Rosenfeld, Richman, & Hardy, 1989). Coaches' reticence to engage in actions that they believe might constitute intrusiveness into the private lives of others is understandable. However, the coaches' feelings would be more justifiable if drug use among athletes was not so common and medically unsafe. Appropriately trained sport psychology consultants might assist coaches by helping them develop and implement their team's drug policy

and by providing guidance on how to meet privately and confidentially with team members to discuss these delicate issues. Consultants have the additional role of helping athletes modify certain feelings and behaviors that might predispose them to drug use.

The two approaches taken in this chapter for combating drug use in sport center on cognitive and behavioral strategies. **Cognitive** strategies deal with influencing the athlete's behaviors and attitudes intellectually and psychologically through verbal and nonverbal communication. **Behavioral** techniques, on the other hand, involve two components: (1) setting up situations that foster certain desirable responses from the athletes, and/or (2) using verbal and nonverbal techniques that reinforce favorable behaviors or performance outcomes (Martin & Lumsden, 1987). The following suggestions were derived from anecdotal and scientific literature, media reports, and my own experiences as a sport psychology consultant.

Cognitive Approaches

The primary objective of cognitive strategies in controlling substance abuse in sport is to appeal to the participants' maturity, intellect, and need for self-actualization and personal fulfillment, both individually and collectively as a group of competitors (Donald, 1983; Egger, 1981). Individual issues concern the health and well-being of the competitor, while team issues reflect social support and group success.

Provide education. Education is the most widely used strategy for preventing drug abuse. Traditionally, the primary objective of drug educational programs was to disseminate accurate information about the negative consequences of drug taking. However, the effectiveness of drug education programs on drug-taking behaviors has been less than optimum. For example, data gathered from 1981 to 1986 on 9,891 U.S. college athletes by the drug education consulting firm Heitzinger and Associates (1986) indicated that "drug education deterred [only] about 5% of the regular users from experimenting with drugs; drug testing and knowledge of punishment deterred 5% of the social users" (p. 158).

Marcello, Danish, and Stolberg (1989) initiated a drug prevention program for university student athletes in the United States. Their program, directed toward performance-enhancing and recreational drugs, consisted of skill training in the areas of decision making, risk assessment, stress management, assertiveness training, resisting peer pressure, and transferring learned skills to outside settings. The findings indicated that the program did not lead to reduced drug use. The program developers later decided the amount of time spent teaching resistance to peer pressure was overemphasized. Apparently, "pro-usage attitudes are influenced by parental modeling, media advertising, cultural, ethnic and religious factors, and peer influences prior to their arrival at college," as opposed to the assumption that the school environment fosters drug abuse (p. 208). Assessment of other knowledge-based approaches also shows no significant effect on the frequency or extent of drug use (Hanson, 1980; Kinder, Pope, & Walfish, 1990; Stuart, 1974).

According to Nicholson and Agnew (1989), there are at least two underlying factors that may explain the limited success of education programs in controlling drug use. First, education is based on the tenet that people use drugs because they have no knowledge of any deleterious effects. Consequently, once educated about these deleterious effects, the individual is expected to develop a negative attitude toward drug use that, in turn, will dictate desirable behavior. Apparently the learner's knowledge increases after educational programs, but rarely is the person's attitude or drug-taking behavior influenced. In fact, the person's curiosity about the effect of drugs may be awakened by these programs, possibly leading to increased drug experimentation (Marcello, Danish, & Stolberg, 1989; Stuart, 1974). A second factor is that knowledge of the negative health consequences of drugs does not tend to decrease its use (Reilly, 1988). For example, many athletes continue to use drugs such as steroids because they do not see sufficient evidence that the medical damage is as great as depicted. The result is lost credibility among physicians and educators who are perceived as overstating the negative effects of drugs. This second factor is flawed for the same reason as the first assumption: Drug users do not usually make rational judgments based on the advantages and disadvantages of drug use.

It has become apparent that educational programs should be only one of several components in drug prevention programs (Marcello, Danish, & Stolberg, 1989; Strauss, 1988). Still, Ryan (1982) suggests that the "education of athletes to prevent

them from starting drug abuse or to reclaim them from it has probably been successful to some degree. It is impossible to measure the effects exactly, but without drug education the situation would probably be much worse" (p. 50).

Following are some suggestions for educational programs. Invite specialists to discuss topics of current or future interest to the athletes such as stress management (preventive measures, coping with pressure), assertiveness training (how to deal with peer pressure to experiment with drugs), and academic tutoring (to reduce stress from demands of classes). Professional athletes would find discussions on financial investment, legal issues, and facts about retirement of great interest. Other appropriate topics might come from specialists in the fields of medicine (e.g., the short-term and long-term somatic responses to drug use or a discussion of different types of drugs), law (e.g., the legal implications in sport and the community in general), psychology (e.g., addiction, dependency, anorexia, bulimia, or the psychological causes of drug use), and nutrition (e.g., proper food intake for optimal energy without ingesting artificial substances). Another source of information could be former athletes whom the athletes can identify with, such as members of previous teams or well-known university or professional athletes.

Bell and Doege (1987) feel that physicians, particularly, should have a primary role in the drug education effort. They also feel that physicians should refrain from prescribing anabolic steroids, amphetamines, and other potentially harmful substances; should educate colleagues and the public about the problem; and should support the development of programs to reduce the illegal prescription and distribution of drugs.

Show concern. Coaches and parents must not deny the existence of possible drug taking by their athlete or child. It is common to assume that a problem does not exist. Many coaches have told me, "There is no drug problem on my team." Sadly, based on confidential interviews with the players of these same coaches, they are often wrong. It is essential that athletes realize their coaches are aware of the dangers of drug taking and that coaches communicate their concern about the problem to each participant. This means more than indicating disapproval. It also entails expressing to each athlete a thought-out and rational explanation for a policy that strictly forbids drug use.

Coaches must be aware of their players' mental status. Like anyone else, an athlete may have a troubled life away from the sport arena. Difficulties with academic pursuits, poor family or social relationships, or the lack of a meaningful relationship with the coach or family members may foster drug use. In addition, all healthy children seek the approval of their parents. Parents must give it unconditionally! If athletes think they are improving and meeting the expectations of coaches and parents without drugs, then taking foreign substances will be perceived as unnecessary.

Discuss ethical issues. According to media reports, world champion track and field athlete Carl Lewis contends that drug taking has three negative effects: (1) The athlete will never know his/her real full potential, (2) there is a health risk, and (3) the drug-induced athlete is quitting on himself/herself. Coaches must inform their athletes that drug taking is depriving them of knowing their performance potential. What does cheating reflect? What is the purpose? Where is the satisfaction? Parents in particular have a role in providing their children with healthy alternatives to drugs (e.g., developing skills, using mental skills training) and removing the need to "do absolutely anything" to succeed as athletes.

Provide communication outlets. Often the head coach cannot be readily accessible to all team members, and supervising all player behavior on and off the field is virtually impossible for one person. Yet, athletes often need— and warrant— personal contact and communication with team leaders. Coach availability may help players deal more effectively with personal and sport-related issues. The risk for ingestion of recreational and other types of drugs may increase from a lack of such contact. Assistant coaches, athletic trainers, team counselors, other school teachers or professors, team captains, and even wives or close acquaintances of the coaching staff can act as an athlete's communication outlets for emotional support or as a liaison with the team's head coach. Parents also play a vital role in this communication process. Parent–athlete communication should primarily consist of allowing the athlete, son or daughter, to set the agenda of items for conversation and to do most of the talking. Active listening is an important skill here for par-

ents as well as the rest of these "providers" (see Chapter 10).

Be aware of the athletes' mental status. Athletes are people too. Their personal life may or may not be very fulfilling which may lead to mental stress and burnout; drugs may provide the escape route. Coaches should know their players as individuals as well as competitors. However, coaches' awareness of their athletes' feelings cannot be automatically assumed. According to Hanson and Gould (1988), coaches are somewhat minimally aware of the attitudes, feelings, and overall mental status of their players, particularly before a contest. Coaches and team consultants should be sensitive to various aspects of the athletes' life (e.g., a divorced or deceased parent, poor school grades, a lack of social fulfillment, end of a personal relationship or friendship). Personal information can be obtained simply by asking the athlete.

Part of this awareness strategy is for coaches and parents to look for signs of drug use. Signs of drug use can take physical, emotional, behavioral and cognitive forms, and are listed in Table 22-1.

Teach coping skills. The ability to cope with stress and to maintain self-control are among the most salient required mental skills of successful athletes (Orlick, 1990; Orlick & Partington, 1986). The athlete's ability to cope successfully with the array of stressors in his/her sport career and personal life will likely make a significant contribution toward avoiding the influence of drugs. (See earlier chapters for suggested physical and cognitive strategies for managing stress and anxiety and attaining optimal arousal.)

According to Tobler's (1986) personal development program model, low self-esteem and low self-confidence are other reasons for drug ingestion. However, the results of selected past research have not shown a strong relationship between self-esteem and drug use, at least in nonsport situations (Gerslick et al., 1987; Kandel, 1978). Polich and colleagues (1984) found that programs based on overcoming personal mental deficiencies have yielded inconclusive results. The relationship between completing these programs (particularly in attempts to increase self-esteem) and avoiding drug abuse has not been proven to date.

Still, coaches and parents can play key roles in helping athletes feel better about their ability and performance by having realistic expectations, providing instruction and informational feedback on skill execution, and offering praise for both desirable outcomes and optimal effort. The key objective is increasing and solidifying the participant's self-esteem, which in turn will decrease the athlete's self-appraisal of inadequacy. At the same time, threats, sarcasm, and other forms of negative communication have a counterproductive influence on the player's mental status and self-esteem (Anshel, 1990c). Sport psychologists can help athletes with low self-esteem and self-confidence by teaching them the cognitive techniques found in Chapter 17.

Provide counseling. Coaches do not typically have training in counseling, but the coach is often the first—and most important—person to whom an athlete comes to discuss personal or team-related concerns (Anshel, 1990c; Rosenfeld, Richman, & Hardy, 1989). Team members need private and confidential access to their coach. Coach–athlete discussions can help reduce the many pressures and other factors that underlie the athlete's need to ingest drugs. The sport psychologist, who should have training in at least basic counseling skills, can be another effective confidant and facilitator in helping athletes deal with their pressures and problems. The availability of counseling from a licensed professional is also important. Coaches and sport psychologists should identify a person who may offer professional psychological guidance to team members who need it (see Chapter 21 for guidelines on referral). However, it must be understood that all counseling issues are confidential.

Professional counselors, sport psychologists, nurses, physicians (particularly in the sports medicine area), and other medically trained personnel should be available either to work with the team on a consistent basis or to respond to a drug crisis, whether it is an acute drug response (emergency) or acknowledgement of a positive drug test.

Promote the perception of a meaningful team role. Athletes who perceive themselves as valued team members will more likely remain loyal to the coach and maintain proper health (Anshel, 1991a). Conversely, feelings of irrelevance and the absence of a clearly identified team role may lead to feelings of group detachment. Athletes who feel detached may be more likely to engage in rule-

Table 22-1 **Physical, Behavioral, Emotional, and Cognitive Signs of Drug Use**

Physical Signs
- Blood-shot eyes
- Dark circles under eyes
- Profuse sweating
- Heightened sensitivity to touch, smell, and sound
- Chronic fatigue
- Trouble maintaining normal body temperature (always hot or cold)

Behavioral Signs
- Unusually secretive behavior
- Increased tardiness to practice and school
- Apathetic attitude about school
- Poor school performance
- Social isolation
- Often broke or out of money
- Irresponsible
- High risk-taking behaviors
- Change in dress style
- New circle of friends
- Marked changes in usual or normal ways of behaving

Emotional Signs
- Extreme mood swings
- Irritability
- Highly reactive
- Less affectionate
- Chronic physical fatigue
- Heightened aggression/hostility
- Recurrent depressive episodes

Cognitive Signs
- Decreased mental capabilities
- Disordered thinking
- Increased forgetfulness
- Thinks that others are out to get him/her
- Denial of problems
- "Superman complex" (i.e., sense of invulnerability)
- Shortened attention span
- Thoughts of suicide

breaking behaviors due to reduced coach loyalty. And, in their view, they have less to lose by engaging in risk-taking behaviors. Ideally, each player should feel wanted and needed.

One approach to enhancing team-role meaningfulness is to solicit input from the participants on making decisions about various issues directly affecting them (e.g., team policy or game strategies)—or at least to discuss issues with the coach before decisions are made. These strategies would likely promote team loyalty and athlete accountability for their actions. It also reflects a coach's respect for his/her players, a perception that is very important in promoting team cohesion and a supportive team climate (Fisher et al., 1982).

Behavioral Strategies

As indicated earlier, the primary objective of a behavioral approach is to shape the environment to control and influence subsequent behavior, a system referred to as "contingency management" (see Martin & Lumsden, 1987, and Rushall & Siedentop, 1972, for explanations and guidelines). Specifically, behavioral techniques involve (1) setting up situations that foster certain desirable responses from the athletes and/or (2) using verbal or nonverbal techniques that reinforce favorable behaviors or performance outcomes (Martin & Lumsden, 1987).

Teach sport skills. Athletes, perhaps more than most other individuals, are driven to achieve the virtually impossible task of performing consistent and error-free skilled movements. It is in the athletes' best interests to acknowledge the boundaries of human performance in general and perhaps their own capabilities and limitations in particular. If most athletes who take drugs do so to facilitate their performance, then this objective can be met without drugs if they make use of properly implemented conditioning programs and are taught sport skills and strategies. Good coaches are good teachers (Anshel, 1990b). Athletes will feel they can stay competitive and be less in need of artificial means to perform at superior levels when they experience quality conditioning and instructional programs. The key objectives for the coach are to: (1) make skill and conditioning improvement apparent to the athlete, and (2) positively reinforce desirable performance changes by verbally and nonverbally communicating approval (Martin & Lumsden, 1987).

Avoid boredom. Boredom usually leads to inappropriate actions. My own confidential discussions with elite competitive skiers reveal that redundant and prolonged skiing and conditioning drills often lead many competitors to engage in recreational drug use at private parties (Anshel, 1987). Egger (1981) suggests that sports should be "an alternative high" (p. 26). Coaches should plan exciting practice sessions and work with athletes to set and reach challenging performance goals (e.g., "I think you can run 0.5 seconds faster after another month of training").

Another way to counter boredom is to provide, *during* the season, recreational programs that are unrelated to the sport. For example, one team in the National Hockey League has traditionally sponsored a trip to Las Vegas for the players and their wives over a three-day break in their schedule (Anshel, 1990c). Perhaps a camping trip or some other recreational pursuit will reduce stress and burnout. My informal discussions with over 200 college athletes revealed that more nonsport recreational opportunity—and relatively less practice time, especially during the last half of the season—is highly desirable. Thus, coaches can reduce boredom by providing alternative activities for their players away from team-related events.

Be aware of the athletes' life away from sport. What type of activities do the athletes engage in during off hours, and with whom? If the athletes' peers take drugs, there is an increased likelihood that the athletes will do so as well. Other questions about athletes that team leaders and sport psychologists should ask include: How are they doing in school? Do they have any friends? Do they have a satisfying family and social life or is it in turmoil? Are they receiving proper attention and recognition from others? Are they nearing the end of their playing career? If any of these issues are unpleasant or stressful, how are they coping? Although there are limits to the coach's and sport psychologist's intrusions into an athlete's personal life, this information can signal potential concerns. Problems can be avoided if action is taken relatively soon. Coaches, particularly, can help create a supportive environment away from sport to reduce the probability of drug use.

Develop and implement a drug policy and plan of action. The widespread information about the dangers of drugs in sport requires teams and sport organizations to develop a drug policy and a vehicle to inform athletes about banned drugs and the consequences of taking them. Failure to do so, in effect, actually sanctions drug use—or gives the impression that sport leaders do not care. For example, a study conducted by the newspaper *USA Today* (1990) showed that "only 54 percent of coaches said their school has an anti-steroids drug policy" (p. 1B).

Athletes need to know the limits, or boundaries, between acceptable and unacceptable behaviors. The coach and parents must jointly assert that "taking drugs is not allowed." Responsible, mature individuals in secure and nonthreatening situations can often make this distinction themselves. However, many others—athletes among them—cannot, particularly when they are self-centered, psychologically immature, and/or have low self-esteem.

Strict limit setting is equally important for responding effectively to an infringement of the policy. This is especially relevant following a positive drug test. The team's response to breaking team rules is the most important element in protecting each player and maintaining the coach's (and organization's) integrity. Probably the toughest response to drug abuse in sport has been recently introduced by the British Olympic Association. According to a report appearing in *The Australian* newspaper (1991), "anyone caught using illegal substances will be banned for life from British Olympic teams" (p. 64). This policy, announced in advance, alerts athletes to the dire risks of engaging in behaviors that are inappropriate and that will not be tolerated. The policy also relieves the athlete of feeling pressured to engage in behaviors that are illegal, unethical, and detrimental to their physical and mental health.

Should a drug-taking incident occur, coaches should know whom to call—physicians, school administrative personnel, a counselor, legal advice, perhaps a religious leader, and so on. For example, should parents be notified if their son/daughter is involved in drugs? All team leaders and athletes should know *in advance* the necessary steps in responding to a player's drug problem. This policy should be an integral part of an overall crisis management plan. Medical and psychological support services should be in place and ready to respond in an emergency 24 hours a day. A management-by-crisis approach must be avoided.

Respecting the competitor's confidentiality and privacy is another important ingredient to an effective plan of action. Cases of drug abuse need not be publicized nor handled publicly. The objective of an effective response to drug abuse is to extinguish the probability of future undesirable behaviors by responding efficiently to an emergency. Effective crisis management consists of anticipating the likelihood of a drug problem and being ready to react accordingly.

Have a continuous drug testing program. Drug policies and educational programs should also emphasize drug testing and sanctioning processes. While drug-testing programs have heretofore been relatively infrequent, it has now become a more common reality for intercollegiate and elite athletes—probably so much so that, in some settings, drug testing programs and sanctions now contribute to the effective prevention of drug use. Drug testing can be a particularly powerful behavioral controller when the threat of dismissal or some other serious penalty accompanies a positive drug test.

One benefit of drug testing and sanctions is that athletes are provided with a genuine counterargument to resist social pressures that encourage drug taking. According to Anshel (1991b), athletes can respond this way to their drug-using peers: "Look, if I get caught with drugs, the league says I'll be suspended for the remainder of the season and the whole team will be hurt!" Thus athletes can maintain their integrity while assertively stating their opposition to drug use.

Three principles contribute to an effective drug-testing program:

1. *Announce the policy in advance.* All team personnel should become aware of the team's or league's rules and guidelines from the first day of participation. Only in this way can participants effectively be held accountable for their actions. However, the actual testing procedure should *not* be announced in advance. To reduce costs, **random testing**—in which only a percentage of the team's athletes, rather than all players, are selected—has been shown to deter, though not eliminate, drug abuse (*Drugs in Sport*, 1989, 1990).

However, the urine sample must be provided under direct observation of the authority figure.

2. *Be consistent in implementing the policy.* The least effective approach to enacting a drug policy is responding to one athlete differently than to others. Unfortunately, team rules will likely be tested by group members. If the coach or league officials are serious about drug abuse prevention and control, they must react vigorously and consistently to the team's most and least talented players. Otherwise, any credibility the policy has will be destroyed.

3. *Link test results to sanctions.* The coach's or league's responses to positive drug tests can be very restrictive (e.g., player dismissed from the team) or more flexible (e.g., counseling and monitoring). However, the least appropriate response is to have a policy that includes sanctions that are not implemented or used inconsistently. Athletes, not unlike others in a subordinate position, need to realize that behaviors that are illegal, unethical, and medically unsafe cannot be tolerated.

Use behavioral contracting. A **contract system**, often called a "performance contract," is among the most sophisticated forms of contingency management. It is a preplanned agreement between two parties (the coach or administrative unit and athlete in this case) that a specified reinforcement will occur to the athlete following the occurrence of a particular action (Rushall & Siedentop, 1972). Contracts can be verbal or, perhaps more effectively, be in written form, signed by the parties involved. This technique is used in management,

education, and counseling to promote a person's accountability for his/her actions. One key to the effectiveness of behavioral contracting in implementing a drug policy is the coach's willingness to meet the contract's obligations completely and consistently for all athletes.

Use a support group. Palmer's (1989) study on the effectiveness of educational programs on drug use revealed that high school seniors served as excellent peer educators and role models in drug prevention among fellow student athletes and nonathletes. Among the first structured attempts at dealing with drug abuse on a sports team, particularly at the elite level, was one conducted by the Cleveland Browns football team (Collins, Pippenger, & Janesz, 1984). In addition to medical and psychological treatment programs, the team owner hired a psychiatrist to conduct group and individual therapies and establish self-help meetings for players and their wives. The core of the program consisted of a subgroup called "The Inner Circle," which consisted of a group of identified drug-involved players. According to the authors:

> Group discussions typically dealt with who was relapsing and why and the need for changes in the individual's lifestyle to support staying "clean. . . ."Rather than participating in cover-ups and deceptions, the players saw that relapses were "contagious," and that when one member was in trouble, others would soon follow. . . . The group eventually became responsible for much of its own therapeutic work in keeping its individual members away from drugs (Collins, Pippenger, & Janesz, p. 490).

Conclusions

The causes of drug taking among athletes are multidimensional, as evidenced by the taking of different performance-enhancing and recreational drugs. Although personal characteristics and sport demands play a relevant role in drug taking, situational and environmental issues also contribute by exacerbating the pressures placed on athletes to achieve sport success. Examples include unreasonable expectations by others, particularly the coach; defining success as a function of outcome rather

than performance improvement; peer pressure; the perception of social acceptance through media reports of high profiled athletes who take drugs; and, at the elite level, the financial incentives for success. Given the extent and persistence of pressures to win, perhaps it is not surprising that education, threats, and even drug testing alone are not efficient means of eliminating drugs in sport.

Winning should not be at the expense of the athletes' health and psychological well-being. It is true that athletes, rather than their coaches and other sport leaders, must take the primary responsibility for their actions, particularly when those actions are illegal and unethical. However, athletes also need protection and a support network to help cope with sport-related pressure and stress (Rosenfeld, Richman, & Hardy, 1989). When a player attaches his/her self-esteem to sport success, the probability of using drugs increases. Such players need help in meeting the responsibilities of competition because they often do not have the psychological resources to cope. Protection from this pressure must come from team coaches, sport psychology consultants, parents, and other team and organizational personnel (e.g., athletic trainers, counselors, teammates).

It is unrealistic to expect athletes to eliminate the problem of drug abuse without external support. Particularly warranted are implementation of team and league drug policies; drug educational programs; drug testing; psychological skills training; counseling; activities to counter boredom; and closer monitoring of the athletes' attitudes and behaviors by coaches, sport psychology consultants, and sport administrators. Sadly (and surprisingly), research on the effectiveness of cognitive and behavioral strategies and educational programs in reducing drug use among athletes is lacking. The author hopes this will change as drug policies and educational/intervention programs become more commonplace.

Conference presenter Lawrie Woodman of the Australian Sports Commission (see Anshel, 1990a) places the problem of drug abuse in perspective. He says,

> The root of the problem is people. The misuse of drugs in sport is a people problem; it is not just the system or the rules. The issue is ultimately one of codes of conduct or standards and it is people who set standards. If we fail to recognize and confront the drug problem in sport, the concept of athletic competition will change as we now know it. (p. 51)

Nothing less than the integrity of sport is at stake.

Study Questions

1. How does the IOC define doping?
2. List the five doping categories banned by the IOC. Give an example of drugs under each category and indicate why athletes might take such a drug.
3. Identify the different health concerns for ingesting drugs from the different doping categories.
4. What is the rationale for an antidrug policy in sport?
5. Using both anecdotal reports and evidence from scientific studies, give some indication of the extensiveness of drug abuse in sport.
6. Discuss the physical, psychological/emotional, and social causes of drug abuse in sport.
7. Distinguish between cognitive approaches and behavioral strategies in controlling drug abuse in athletes. Provide examples of both types of interventions.
8. Discuss the three main components of an effective drug-testing program.

References

Alzado, L. (1991, July 8). I'm sick and I'm scared. *Sports Illustrated, 75,* 21–25.

Anshel, M. H. (1986, May/June). The coach's role in preventing drug abuse by athletes. *Coaching Review, 9,* 29–32, 34–35.

Anshel, M. H. (1987, November 15). *Coaching strategies for managing drug abuse in sport.* A presentation to coaches of the United States Olympic Ski Team, Colorado Springs, Colo.

Anshel, M. H. (1990a). Commentary on the national drugs in sport conference—1989. Treating the causes and symptoms. *Australian Journal of Science and Medicine in Sport, 22,* 49–56.

Anshel, M. H. (1990b). *Sport psychology: From theory to practice.* Scottsdale, Ariz.: Gorsuch Scarisbrick.

Anshel, M. H. (1990c, January). *Suggested cognitive and behavioral strategies for reducing/preventing drug abuse in sport.* A paper presented at the 1990 Commonwealth Games Conference, Auckland, New Zealand.

Anshel, M. H. (1991a). Causes for drug abuse in sport: A survey of intercollegiate athletes. *Journal of Sport Behavior, 14,* 283–307.

Anshel, M. H. (1991b). Cognitive and behavioral strategies for combating drug abuse in sport: Implications for coaches and sport psychology consultants. *The Sport Psychologist, 5,* 152–166.

Australian Sports Medicine Federation (1989, October). *Survey of drug use in Australian sport* (2nd ed.). Canberra, A.C.T. (Australia): Australian Sports Drug Agency.

Badewitz-Dodd, L. (1990). *Drugs and sport.* Crows Nest, N.S.W. (Australia): IMS.

Bell, J. A., & Doege, T. C. (1987). Athletes' use and abuse of drugs. *The Physician and Sportsmedicine, 15,* 99–106, 108.

Buckley, W. E., Yesalis, C. E., Friedl, K. E., Anderson, W. A., Streit, A. L., & Wright, J. E. (1988). Estimated prevalence of anabolic steroid use among male high school seniors. *Journal of the American Medical Association, 260*(23), 3441–3445.

Chaikin, T., & Telander, R. (1988, October 24). The nightmare of steroids. *Sports Illustrated,* pp. 84–93, 97–98, 100–102.

Chappel, J. N. (1987). Drug use and abuse in the athlete. In J. R. May & M. J. Asken (Eds.), *Sport psychology: The psychological health of the athlete* (pp. 187–212). New York: PMA.

Chu, D. (1982). *Dimensions of sport studies.* New York: Wiley.

Cohen, J. C., Noakes, T. D., & Benade, A. J. S. (1988). Hypercholesterolemia in male power lifters using anabolic-androgenic steroids. *The Physician and Sportsmedicine, 16,* 49–50, 53–54, 56.

Cohen, S. (1979). Doping: Drugs in sport. *Drug Abuse and Alcoholism Newsletter, 8*(1).

Collins, G. B., Pippenger, C. E., & Janesz, J. W. (1984). Links in the chain: An approach to the treatment of drug abuse on a professional football team. *Cleveland Clinic Quarterly, 51,* 485–492.

Corrigan, B. (1988, October–December). Doping in sport. *Sports Coach, 12,* 11–17.

Donald, K. (1983). *The doping game.* Brisbane, Australia: Boolarang.

Drugs in sport: An interim report of the Senate Standing Committee on Environment, Recreation and the Arts (1989, May). Canberra, A.C.T.: Australian Government Publishing Service.

Drugs in sport: Second report of the Senate Standing Committee on Environment, Recreation and the Arts. (1990, May). Canberra, A.C.T.: Australian Government Publishing Service.

Egger, G. (1981). *The sport drug.* Boston: George, Allen & Unwin.

English, G. (1987). A theoretical explanation of why athletes choose to use steroids, and the role of the coach in influencing behavior. *National Strength and Conditioning Association Journal, 9,* 53–56.

Fisher, A. C., Mancini, V. H., Hirsch, R. L., Proulx, T. J., & Staurowsky, E. J. (1982). Coach–athlete interactions and team climate. *Journal of Sport Psychology, 4,* 388–404.

Gerslick, K., Grady, K., Sexton, E., & Lyons, M. (1981). Personality and sociodemographic factors in adolescent drug use. In D. J. Lettiers & J. P. Ludford (Eds.),

Drug abuse and the American adolescent (pp. 81–116). Rockville, Md: U.S. Department of Health and Human Services, National Institute on Drug Abuse, Research Monograph No. 38.

Gill, D. (1986). *Psychological dynamics of sport.* Champaign, Ill.: Human Kinetics.

Hanson, D. (1980). Drug education, does it work? In F. Scarpitti & S. Datesman (Eds), *Drugs and youth culture: Annual reviews of drug and alcohol abuse* (vol. 4) (pp. 212–236), Beverly Hills, Calif.: Sage.

Hanson, T. W., & Gould, D. (1988). Factors affecting the ability of coaches to estimate their athletes' trait and state anxiety levels. *The Sport Psychologist, 2,* 298–313.

Heitzinger & Associates (1986). *1981–1986 data collection and analysis: High school, college, professional athletes alcohol/drug survey.* 333 W. Miflin, Madison, Wis.

Hewitt, P. L., & Flett, G. L. (1991). Perfectionism in the self and social contexts: Conceptualization, assessment, and association with psychopathology. *Journal of Personality and Social Psychology, 60,* 456–470.

Hewitt, P. L., Mittelstaedt, W., & Flett, G. L. (1990). Self-oriented perfectionism and generalized performance importance in depression. *Individual Psychology Journal of Adlerian Theory, Research and Practice, 46,* 67–73.

Julien, R. M. (1981). *A primer of drug action* (3rd ed.). San Francisco: Freeman.

Kinder, B. N., Pope, N. E., & Walfish, S. (1980). Drug and alcohol education programs: A review of outcome studies. *International Journal of the Addictions, 15,* 1035–1054.

Lamb, D. R. (1984). Anabolic steroids in athletics: How well do they work and how dangerous are they? *American Journal of Sports Medicine, 12,* 31–38.

Lubell, A. (1989). Does steroid abuse cause—or excuse—violence? *The Physician and Sportsmedicine, 17,* 176, 178–180, 185.

Marcello, R. J., Danish, S. J., & Stolberg, A. L. (1989). An evaluation of strategies developed to prevent substance abuse among student-athletes. *The Sport Psychologist, 3,* 196–211.

Martin, G. L., & Lumsden, J. A. (1987). *Coaching: An effective behavioral approach.* St. Louis, Mo.: Times Mirror/Mosby.

Martin, M. B., & Anshel, M. H. (1991). Attitudes of elite junior athletes on drug-taking behaviors: Implications for drug prevention programs. *Drug Education Journal of Australia, 5,* 223–238.

Moses, E. (1988, October 10). An athlete's Rx for the drug problem. *Newsweek,* p. 57.

Mottram, D. R. (Ed.) (1988). *Drugs in sport*. London: Spon.

Murray, D., & Perry, C. (1985). The prevention of adolescent drug abuse: Implications of etiological development, behavioral and environmental models. In C. Jones & R. Battjes (Eds.), *Prevention*. Rockville, Md.: U.S. Department of Health and Human Services, National Institute and Drug Abuse, Research Monograph No. 56, 77–126.

Nicholson, N. (1989, July). The role of drug education. In S. Haynes & M. H. Anshel (Eds.), *Proceedings of the 1989 National Drugs in Sport Conference—Treating the causes and symptoms*. University of Wollongong, Wollongong, N.S.W., Australia.

Orlick, T. (1990). *In pursuit of excellence* (2nd ed.). Champaign, Ill.: Human Kinetics.

Orlick, T., & Partington, J. (1986). *Psyched: Inner views of winning*. Ottawa, Ont.: Coaching Association of Canada.

Palmer, J. (1989, Fall). High school senior athletes as peer educators and role models: An innovative approach to drug prevention. *Journal of Alcohol and Drug Education*, 35, 23–27.

Park, J. (1990). Analytical methods to detect dope agents. In J. Park (Ed.), *Proceedings of the International Symposium on Drug Abuse in Sports (doping)* (pp. 51–70). Seoul, Korea: Korea Institute of Science and Technology.

Pope, H. G., Katz, D. L., & Champoux, R. (1988, July). Anabolic-androgenic steroid use among 1,010 college men. *The Physician and Sportsmedicine*, 16, 75–77, 80–81.

Prokop, L. (1990). The history of doping. In J. Park (Ed.), *Proceedings of the International Symposium on Drug Abuse in Sports (doping)* (pp. 1–9). Seoul, Korea: Korea Institute of Science and Technology.

Reilly, C. (1988). *An evaluation of the peer support program*. (Report No. A 88/5). Sydney, N.S.W. (Australia): N.S.W. Department of Health.

Rosenfeld, L. B., Richman, J. M., & Hardy, C. J. (1989). Examining social support networks among athletes: Description and relationship to stress. *The Sport Psychologist*, 3, 23–33.

Rotella, R. J. (1984). Psychological care of the injured athlete. In L. Bunker, R. J. Rotella, & A. S. Reilly (Eds.), *Sport psychology: Psychological considerations in maximizing sport performance* (pp. 151–164). Ithaca, N.Y.: Mouvement Publications.

Rushall, B. S., & Siedentop, D. (1972). The development and control of behavior in sport and physical education. Philadelphia: Lea & Febiger.

Russell, D. G. (1990). *Drugs and medicines in sport*. Wellington, New Zealand: Royal Society of New Zealand.

Ryan, A. J. (1982). Advantage, drug-free athletes. *The Physician and Sportsmedicine*, 10, 50.

Shroyer, J. (1990). Getting tough on anabolic steroids: Can we win the battle? *The Physician and Sportsmedicine*, 18, 106, 108–110, 115, 118.

Smith, G. (1983). Recreational drugs in sport. *The Physician and Sportsmedicine*, 11, 75–76, 79, 82.

Steroid Trafficking Act of 1990 (1990, August 30). Committee of the Judiciary, 101st Congress, 2nd Session, Report No. 101–433.

Strauss, R. H. (1987). Anabolic steroids. In R. H. Strauss (Ed.), *Drugs and performance in sports* (pp. 59–68). Philadelphia: Saunders.

Strauss, R. H. (1988, October-December). Drug abuse in sports: A three-pronged response. *Sports Coach*, pp. 12, 23.

Stuart, R. (1974). Teaching facts about drugs: Pushing or preventing? *Journal of Educational Psychology*, 66, 189–201.

Tobler, N. (1986). Meta-analysis of 143 adolescent drug prevention programs: Quantitative outcome results of program participants compared to a control or comparison group. *Journal of Drug Issues*, 16, 537–567.

Tricker, R., Cook, D. L., & McGuire, R. (1989). Issues related to drug abuse in college athletics: Athletes at risk. *The Sport Psychologist*, 3, 155–165.

Weinhold, L. L. (1991). Steroid and drug use by athletes. In L. Diamant (Ed.), *Psychology of sport, exercise, and fitness: Social and personal issues*. New York: Hemisphere.

Williams, M. H. (1983). *Ergogenic aids in sport*. Champaign, Ill.: Human Kinetics.

Williams, M. H. (1989). *Beyond training: How athletes enhance performance legally and illegally*. Champaign, Ill.: Leisure Press.

Wragg, J. (1990). The impact of adolescent development: Implications for the timing, evaluation and development of drug education programs. *Drug Education Journal of Australia*, 4, 233–239.

Athletic Staleness and Burnout: Diagnosis, Prevention, and Treatment

Keith P. Henschen, *University of Utah*

"Fatigue makes cowards of us all!" (Vince Lombardi)

*T*he phenomenon of "fatigue," "burnout," "staleness," or whatever label is used to identify it is very real. Picture, for example, a team that performs very well from the beginning of the season through the third quarter of the schedule, then just seems to be going through the motions. Physically each player is in peak shape, but something is lacking. There is no excitement, no feeling, no motivation, just a lackluster performance. While other teams seem to be peaking, this team proficiently stagnates. Eventually a team with much less talent but more "heart" defeats our talented team. Why? What has happened? How can individuals with so much physical talent become so apathetic during performance? The answers to these questions are as complex as the phenomenon itself.

Athletic staleness occurs frequently, but most coaches and players appear to be at a loss to diagnose, prevent, and treat this malady. Considering the high demands placed upon today's athletes and the length of most sport seasons, it is not surprising that many athletes and coaches have difficulty avoiding performance slumps and, at times, total burnout. In this chapter we will discuss what causes staleness; what physiological and psychological factors are typically associated with periods of athletic stagnation; and what techniques are available to diagnose, prevent, and treat staleness and burnout.

Definitions and Diagnosis

What do we mean by the terms "burnout," "staleness," and "slumps"? What do they have in common and how do they differ? The term "burnout" first appeared in the literature concerning job stress. **Burnout** is defined as a state of mental, emotional, and physical exhaustion brought on by persistent devotion to a goal whose achievement is dramatically opposed to reality (Freudenberger & Richelson, 1981; Maslach, 1982; Pines, Aronson, & Kafry, 1981). Burnout afflicts overly dedicated, idealistic men and women who are motivated toward high achievement and who work in unrewarding situations (Maslach & Pines, 1977; Pines, Aronson, & Kafry, 1981). In other words, individuals most prone to burnout are "those who work too hard, too long, too intensely and are extremely dedicated to what they are doing" (Fender, 1989). Considering the type of person susceptible to burnout, it is easy to understand why many athletes may be at risk. Feigley (1984) noted that the circumstances of job stress and athletic stress show remarkable parallels even when comparisons involve children as young as age 10.

Burnout's devastating states of physical, mental, and emotional exhaustion result in the development of negative self-concepts; negative attitudes toward work, life, and other people; and a loss of idealism, energy, and purpose (Freudenberger, 1980; Freudenberger & Richelson, 1981; Maslach, 1982).

Burnout is the long-term end result of emotional and/or physical exhaustion, lower productivity and depersonalization, while **staleness** may be described as a symptom of ensuing burnout, or an early warning sign of the negative state to come (Fender, 1989). If athletic staleness is ignored, burnout will eventually follow. However, if staleness is recognized by the athlete, coach, or sport psychologist, the devastating path to burnout may be averted. A **slump** may occur along with staleness or may be a result of staleness. The term "staleness" refers to an overall physical and emotional state, whereas the term "slump" indicates a more specific performance-related phenomenon.

According to Feigley (1984), certain personality characteristics and behavioral patterns increase an individual's susceptibility to burnout. Shank (1983) identified the following characteristics and behaviors as predisposing certain people to burnout: (1) perfectionism, (2) being "other-oriented," and (3) lack of assertive interpersonal skills. Perfectionists are at risk because they are overachievers who tend to set high standards for themselves and others (Freudenberger & Richelson, 1981). They also may tend to invest more time and effort on a task than are necessary. Other-oriented people have a strong need to be liked and admired and are often extremely sensitive to criticism. They tend to be generous with everyone but themselves. People who lack assertive interpersonal skills find it difficult to say no or express negative feelings such as anger without feeling extremely guilty.

Feigley (1984) also noted that, ironically, coaches often find quiet, concerned, energetic perfectionists to be ideal athletes. Care must be taken to make sure burnout does not cause these people to quit their sport before they can reach and enjoy their full potential. Coaches and sport psychologists should not persuade these athletes to curtail their commitment to athletics but persuade them to achieve a better balance. "While dedication to a sport is essential for high-level success, if one's focus is too narrow, too intense, or too prolonged at too early an age, the likelihood of burnout increases dramatically" (Feigley, 1984, p. 112).

Staleness and slumps, or periods of poor performance, can also be caused by a multitude of psychological or environmental factors and physical problems. Athletes who attempt too much, worry continually, and adhere to poor health habits (especially poor nutrition) frequently manifest the staleness syndrome. Also, many athletes who experience staleness attribute the situation to attitudinal problems or a general lack of motivation. Factors such as chronic fatigue, anxiety, and boredom are normally precursors to staleness. Physical symptoms such as minor body aches, stomach upsets, headaches, and eating disorders usually accompany staleness. Thus, both physiological and psychological characteristics contribute to and are manifestations of athletic staleness. Assessment of staleness should take into account both types of manifestations (Wilson, Haggerty, & Bird, 1986; Wilson & Bird, 1988).

The psychological factors may be more difficult to detect than the physiological ones and are much more difficult to treat. Table 23-1 lists some physiological and psychological characteristics of staleness.

Coaches or sport psychologists can use the Profile of Mood States (POMS) (McNair, Lorr, & Droppleman, 1971) to diagnose the onset of staleness in sports. The POMS measures six transitory affective states (tension, depression, anger, vigor, fatigue, and confusion) by rating 65 adjective states on a five-point scale ranging from "not at all" to "extremely." Successful athletes have been found to differ psychologically from unsuccessful athletes. Psychological mood states typically associated with top-level athletic performance form what Morgan has called an "iceberg profile" (Morgan & Johnson, 1977, 1978). That is, more successful athletes tend to score high on vigor and low on tension, depression, anger, fatigue, and confusion.

In carefully documented research with swimmers and wrestlers, Morgan and colleagues (1987) found that the psychological mood state profile of "stale" athletes was the opposite of successful athletes. Specifically, as the season progressed, the iceberg profile of stale swimmers and wrestlers "in-

Table 23-1 **Characteristics of Staleness**

Psychological	Physiological
Sleep disturbances	Higher resting heart rate
Loss of self-confidence	Higher systolic blood pressure
Drowsiness and apathy	Delayed return to normal HR
Quarrelsomeness	Elevated basal metabolic rate
Irritability	Elevated body temperature
Emotional and motivational imbalance	Weight loss
Excessive weariness that is prolonged	Impeded respiration
Lack of appetite (anorexia)	Subcostal aching
Fatigue	Bowel disorders
Depression	
Anxiety	
Anger/hostility	
Confusion	

verted." There was a stepwise increase in the group's mood disturbance that coincided directly with increases in training, and decreases in the training regimen (i.e., tapering) were associated with improvements in mood state.

These findings suggest that astute coaches and sport psychologists should be cognizant of mood swings in their athletes because these swings can indicate the possible onset of athletic staleness. Workout modifications such as tapering in swimming and making practice less intense or allowing time off in other sports might be dictated if athletes appear to be "flattening" or inverting on their optimal psychological mood state profile. Additional suggestions for avoiding undesirable shifts in psychological states appear in the next section.

Sport psychologists, coaches, and athletes should learn to recognize the initial signs associated with staleness. By the time many of these signs are in full bloom, the battle is half lost. The most important challenge is to eliminate the possibility of staleness ever securing a firm foothold. A word of caution: When an athlete consistently experiences most of the psychological characteristics of staleness, simultaneously and at high levels, with or without accompanying physical symptoms, the coach should consider referring the athlete to a professionally certified counselor or psy-

chologist. Under such circumstances, the coach should not try to play amateur psychologist. (See also Chapter 21.)

Prevention

To make a plan for preventing athletic staleness, one needs to understand how this phenomenon is associated with training and competition. Innumerable factors contribute to athletic staleness. Some are listed in Table 23-2.

Obviously, there are a few main contributors to staleness or burnout that coaches can help eliminate. Possibly the most significant factor promoting staleness is the length of the season. Most high school and college sport programs have seasons that are virtually year-round. This hurts the athlete. The length of a season is dictated by high school activity associations and appropriate national governing body (college), but many coaches ignore or circumvent these time constraints. An example of this occurs in college basketball. The NCAA states that practice cannot begin officially until October 15 of each year. In any major college in the country, practice typically (officially) begins on the first day of school (around the first week of September). After six weeks of illegal "condition-

Table 23-2 **Causes of Staleness**

- Length of total season
- Monotony of training
- Feelings of claustrophobia
- Lack of positive reinforcement
- Feeling of helplessness
- Abusiveness from authorities
- Stringent rules
- High levels of competitive stress
- Perceived overload
- Boredom
- Perceived low accomplishment

ing," practice legally begins. By the first week in March of the following year, a basketball team has practiced for approximately 25 weeks. After the season is over, most teams informally condition, weight train, and illegally practice until the following September, when the cycle is repeated. No wonder staleness occurs. Many college athletes spend more time at their sport activities than do their professional counterparts. Coaches need to seriously consider cutting back on the amount of time the athlete is in the sport while providing more quality practice time.

Another prime contributor to athletic staleness is the monotony of training. Far too many athletes are forced to participate in practice situations that are pure drudgery. Many coaches are guilty of embracing the philosophy of "the more the better." If one hour of practice is sufficient, then two hours would be more beneficial, four hours would be even better, and so on. Motor learning research unequivocally refutes this practice, but these coaches ignore the research findings and continue to adhere to their mistaken philosophy. Staleness is frequently the final outcome.

Other environmental factors present during practice can also hasten the onset of staleness. Feelings of being locked in with no other place to go, a constant lack of positive reinforcement, abusiveness from those in authority, and unreasonable institutional rules are factors that predispose an athlete to staleness. All of these factors interact to structure a situation in which the athlete feels out of control or trapped in a hopeless circumstance.

The logical result is "going through the motions," a characteristic of staleness.

When the preceding factors are combined with high levels of emotional stress and the typical young age of the athlete, a volatile no-win situation often develops, the end result being staleness. Sport competition involves a great deal of emotional stress, and young athletes are often unequipped to handle it effectively. Unless the athlete achieves constant success, or a variable ratio of success, a common outcome is staleness.

What can be done to prevent this ailment before it begins to occur? Obviously, the coach should keep the season's length in proper perspective and formulate practice sessions that eliminate boredom. Coaches should also strive to make practices and actual game time more rewarding (Dale & Weinberg, 1989). Coaches can also take five additional steps to prevent staleness:

1. Schedule time-outs.
2. Allow athletes to make some choices.
3. Control outcomes.
4. Plan mental practice periods.
5. Handle postcompetition tension.

Time-outs

It is essential for people's mental wellness to experience periods of time away from a continual stressor. Athletes are no exception. They need time away from competition and practice. Business has realized this concept by providing for vacations, holidays, and even weekends away from the work environment. Many people in the athletic establishment have yet to realize the value of time-outs for performance. Many teams practice or compete every day from the beginning to the end of the season. It is hard to understand why some coaches believe that a break is a sign of weakness. A time-out period used appropriately will refresh and invigorate the athletes.

There are some very creative ways to use time-out periods. In my high school basketball-playing days, our coach once did something very unusual. Our team had been practicing from the start of the season for about four weeks. Our first game was approximately one month away. We were a veteran team and thought all of the practice was a waste of time. Consequently, our commitment to practice was not great. After going through the motions of practicing the first month, we found that our coach had posted a message on the locker room door stating that there would be no practices until further notice. All of the players felt this was a little strange, but we enjoyed the first few days away from practice. Finally, during the second week of no practice, the coach called a team meeting. When the meeting started, the coach asked us if we had enjoyed our two-week vacation and if we were ready to start practice again. We all emphatically assured him that we were ready, eager, and willing to do anything he wanted. The season's first game was only two weeks away. Needless to say, our practices from then on were crisp, sharp, and intense. As players, we were convinced that we were behind the other teams who had continued to practice while we vacationed. Actually, that season was one of the best our school ever experienced. Years later I asked the coach what his rationale was for our not practicing for those two weeks. His explanation was very enlightening:

> That team was as stale as any team I had ever coached. You guys were a veteran team who needed shaking up. Your attitudes were lousy, and I needed to do something to get you recommitted to our program. You were all good kids, but the spark of enthusiasm was missing. I probably could have waited until we lost a game and then somehow got you back into my way of thinking, but I decided to gamble a little. I just felt you boys needed a break to get your heads screwed back on. Boy, did you guys come back. I look back at that as one of my finest decisions.

This example is evidence of what happens after a time-out period. Staleness can be replaced by enthusiasm (Jones, 1981).

Choices

Another procedure that is effective in alleviating staleness is allowing the athletes to participate in some of the decision making. By permitting input from the athletes and using their suggestions, the coach helps to solidify the players' commitment. This procedure allows the athletes to make their involvement on the team a primary instead of a secondary commitment. If the team becomes a primary force in the lives of its players, the team members will do almost anything to ensure its suc-

cess. If, on the other hand, a secondary association is formed, the resultant commitment will be partial and sporadic. A person actively participating in any endeavor does not have the time or energy to dwell on the negative for long. When a person's decisions or choices are being utilized and subsequently evaluated, he/she will do everything possible to ensure success.

One way to involve athletes in making decisions is to have them form committees to decide which offenses or defenses they should use in upcoming games. Have the players demonstrate to other team members what the opponent will be doing and how to nullify the opponent's strengths. Again, providing an atmosphere in which the athletes' choices are considered important is crucial to eliminating staleness.

Control of Outcomes

Research on overtraining and burnout indicates that a prime contributor to these conditions is the feeling of no control over what is happening (Morgan, 1984). When athletes perceive a hopeless situation in which they are physically present but not totally involved, staleness is normally inevitable. Provide an environment that allows the athletes to feel that they have some control over their own destiny, and you will diminish the likelihood of staleness. (This procedure is similar to the previous one.)

Mental Practice Periods

Another way to prevent staleness is to add variety to practice and training in order to increase motivation and interest. One way you can accomplish this is by incorporating periods of mental practice within the physical training sessions. This accomplishes two things: (1) It breaks up the monotony of the practice session, and (2) it allows the body to recuperate physically without jeopardizing practice time. Though the body may be fatigued, the mind can continue almost indefinitely. By alternating periods of physical practice and mental practice during training sessions, the likelihood of fatigue is greatly lessened. The University of Utah's women's gymnastics team (which as of this writing has won seven NCAA championships during the last decade) has used this technique for the past 14 years. Three or four times each day the team (as a group) takes 10 minutes to relax and mentally rehearse individual routines. When these mental practice periods are completed, the gymnasts continue their physical training in a much more refreshed state. Again, mental practice periods are a form of "change," which prevents staleness. (See Chapter 16 for suggestions on how to develop mental rehearsal skills and the different ways in which mental rehearsal can be used.)

Postcompetition Tension Management

What is **postcompetition tension**? How are contemporary coaches handling this psychological phenomenon, and what is its relationship to staleness? Many coaches may not even be aware that this phenomenon exists, but an understanding of the relationship between postcompetition tension and athletic staleness is crucial to preventing staleness.

For years, researchers have been accumulating evidence indicating that some ingredient is lacking in the psychological training and treatment of athletes (Henschen, 1973). The final buzzer does not stop or ease many of the intense psychological variables that a sport contest evokes. Postgame quarrels, fights, drinking binges, and so forth are instigated by athletes who have pent-up emotions that the end of the game has failed to relieve. Other responses include withdrawal and depression. Many coaches seem to spend unlimited hours preparing athletes psychologically to compete but at the conclusion of the contest leave it to the athletes to devise a means of relieving the excess emotion caused by the competition. Coaches should have a similarly intensive program for dealing with postcompetition tension as they do for precompetition preparation because athletes who remain constantly frustrated will eventually experience burnout (Caccese & Mayerberg, 1984).

Research indicates that most athletes experience one of three emotional states at the conclusion of a contest regardless of the outcome: (1) depression, (2) euphoria, or (3) intrapunitive or interpunitive aggression (Henschen, 1973). Any of these emotions left unchecked for a period of time will rapidly contribute to a state of staleness. These emotions can quickly drain an athlete's energy.

Handling postcompetition tension is as important for the reserves as it is for the starters. In

Table 23-3 Techniques for Handling Postcompetition Tensions

1. Provide a supportive atmosphere immediately following a contest.
2. Concentrate on your players' emotions, not your own.
3. Try to be with your team after a contest (not on the radio or TV).
4. Converse with players as they are dressing.
5. Provide an unemotional yet realistic assessment of each athlete's performance.
6. Talk to all team members, even those who did not get to play.
7. Once athletes have dressed, have a team group activity (e.g., postgame meal, swimming, bowling, movie).
8. Keep athletes away from well-meaning peers and parents.
9. Do not allow team members to gloat over success or be depressed over a loss.
10. "Get on with the program" and encourage your players to do the same.
11. Begin preparation for the next opponent at the very next practice.

fact, the athletes for whom the coach should be most concerned are probably the substitutes who have not received an opportunity to play. These athletes experience increased frustration because they have not seen any game action.

Because postcompetition tension and its relationship to staleness is a relatively new area of concern within the athletic establishment, you may find the suggestions in Table 23-3 useful in your attempts to alleviate this situation.

The Fun Factor

A few final thoughts concerning the prevention of staleness seem to be in order. All of the prevention procedures we have just reviewed fundamentally involve *enjoyment*. Possibly the best way to prevent staleness is to ensure that the athletes are having fun. Years ago the Western Electric studies convinced psychologists that *any* type of change would increase productivity of assembly-line workers (Roethlisberger & Dickson, 1947). Behaviorists embraced the concept that if an activity is followed by a pleasurable feeling or reward, it is likely to be repeated (Rotter, Chance, & Phares, 1972). People continue to do things that they enjoy. Far too many coaches, through improper reinforcement and motivational techniques, make athletics into drudgery and work. When this is the perception, then athletes become bored, stale, or burned out. Something does not have to hurt to be good. "No gain without pain" is a myth.

Treatment

By this time you should be able to recognize the symptoms of staleness and also be aware of a variety of techniques that you can use to prevent it. Now comes the real test: How do you treat a team or individual who has already demonstrated a degree of staleness?

Remember that each case is unique and should be treated as such. As a general rule, however, the most effective way to treat athletic staleness is a psychological reprogramming. Initially, the coach needs to reassess his/her entire season, determine the most likely contributors to the staleness syndrome, and progress from that point. Realistically, only two courses of action are available: (1) Remove the athletes from the situation—have them withdraw completely from the activity for an appropriate period of time or (2) devise a program that will alleviate the staleness syndrome. The first course of action can provide some great benefits, but it is not a feasible solution in most athletic situations. Therefore, only reprogramming holds any real promise in sports. You might try any or all of the following suggestions to reprogram an individual, but be aware that not all of these procedures will work for every athlete; do not become discouraged if one method is not always successful.

The best method of eliminating, or at least reducing, staleness is to digress a few steps and *reestablish goals for both practice and competition* (O'Block & Evans, 1984). Good goal setting keeps us on the road to success. The type of goal setting needed to treat staleness is very simple. Set short-term goals and provide rewards or incentives every time a goal is accomplished. For many athletes experiencing staleness, their only goal is just getting through the season. New, meaningful, exciting goals will take their minds off the long, sometimes

dreary season and put some "pizzazz" back into playing. Success in meeting short-term goals will contribute to a better success–failure ratio and to the athlete's positive self-concept.

Each sport is different, but having fun goals in the late stages of a season is very beneficial. A key point is to set fun goals for practice as well as for competition. Almost all goals seem to be competition oriented. Most coaches and players appear to forget that nine-tenths of participation time in sports is spent in practicing, not competing in games. Performance goals are necessary, but enjoyable practice and training goals are essential to mental well-being (e.g., mastering a skill each day). Be sure that the rewards for attaining goals are meaningful to the athletes and that the rewards are greater toward the end of the season than at the beginning. When staleness occurs, you should break down the season into subphases and subgoals.

Another procedure for treating staleness is to *teach the athletes how to relax*. As noted earlier, one of the prime contributors to staleness is frustration. A common remedy from frustration is self-relaxation. Whether you select autogenic training, modified autogenic training, self-hypnosis, or progressive relaxation is irrelevant. The important point is that each athlete has one of these techniques at his/her command. Athletes who can control themselves usually do not demonstrate staleness. For many athletes a simple progressive relaxation technique is quite useful (see Chapter 15).

You can use other methods to aid in *mental reprogramming*. The objective is to "eliminate any physical causes and then learn to disregard mental distractions" (Harris & Harris, 1984). A simple procedure is to teach athletes the method of *self-talk*. This has the effect of putting things back into a proper perspective. Self-talk should always be positive and concerned with the correct maneuver or skill. Self-talk will become almost automatic if practiced diligently (see Chapter 17 for specifics). Stopping negative thoughts and only concentrating on the positive can change an athlete's outlook and thus lessen the effects of staleness.

One final suggestion for the treatment of athletic staleness through reprogramming is the use of *imagery*. A perceptive coach will turn inward to an athlete's thoughts to treat staleness rather than resort to more physical overtraining, which just compounds the situation. Many rich benefits await the athlete who uses imagery (Tower & Singer, 1981):

- A differentiated sense of identity and self-awareness.
- A gain in self-confidence and security
- High levels of self-control
- More positive affective experiences
- Augmented resources for dealing with stress (better coping strategies)

Even though mental imagery can provide many benefits, some athletes have difficulty achieving it. Imagery is a skill and like all skills must be learned and perfected. Once this skill is mastered, it is readily apparent how it can be utilized to treat staleness. Coaches can encourage imagery by having the entire team practice it together during regular practice time. This is often helpful because the athletes are in the same environment in which athletic performance will take place. Having the athletes develop a practice routine for imagery every day is a good idea. Examples of imagery exercises follow.

Exercise A: Interaction between tension and relaxation (Davis, McKay, & Eshelman, 1983). Close your eyes. . . . Be aware of the tension of your body . . . and imagine that it is filled with different colored lights, for example, a soft blue light for relaxation and a red light for tension. . . . Allow the lights to change from blue to red, or from red to blue, and be aware of any physical sensations you may experience while this is taking place. . . . Pause. . . . Change all the lights in your body to a soft blue and experience the overall feeling of relaxation.

Exercise B: The happiness room. Imagine you are standing at the bottom of a staircase. Look up toward the top of the stairs and see a large door. Grasp the handrail and slowly climb the stairs. When you reach the top, grab the doorknob and open the door. When the door is open, imagine a totally vacant room. As you are standing in the doorway, decorate this room with everything that pleases you. Carpets (plush), lights, wall hangings, waterbed, girlfriends or boyfriends, refrigerator,

etcetera. Money is no object. Everything in this room is there to please you. This is your happiness room and there is no other room like it in the world.

Position yourself very comfortably in front of one wall. On this wall of your happiness room is a three-foot by three-foot television screen. It is only about one inch thick. Take your remote control and turn on the television. The picture on the television screen is you performing your sport. Watch yourself very carefully. You are performing perfectly. Imagine how good it feels to perform so well. You are excellent.

After watching yourself perform for a little while, turn off your television. Look around your happiness room and experience how good it feels. Walk to the door, open it, turn off the lights, and slowly descend the stairs. When you reach the bottom of the stairs you will be fully awake and rejuvenated.

Athletes should practice this simple guided imagery exercise daily for optimum results. The happiness room allows athletes to watch and feel themselves performing perfectly without any negative reinforcement.

Exercise C: Music listening. Get into a comfortable position and close your eyes. . . . Allow yourself to flow with the music. . . . Permit the music to let various thoughts float through your mind. Do not dwell on any of the thoughts. Passively allow them to float in and out of your mind. As one thought seems to disappear, another takes its place. Ignore all negative ideas and concentrate only on the positive thoughts. Allow the music to relax you deeply. . . . As you are listening to the music, think of a special friend. Experience yourself talking to your friend. You and your friend are going to examine the tension and stress in your life. . . . Ask your friend what is causing your tension and stress. . . . Ask your friend, "How can I become less tense and deal with stress better?" You and your friend will meet and discuss this problem daily. After a few days, your friend will suggest a number of solutions to your problem. . . . Again, allow yourself to flow with the music and become relaxed.

This imagery exercise is best accomplished if the athletes are allowed to select the music they will listen to. The music should be instrumental (without words) and relaxing to the individual athletes.

The three preceding exercises are examples of modes for stimulating imagination: visualization, guided imagery and listening to music. Some athletes will respond better to one mode than the others. Most important is the fact that almost all athletes can use imagery, and this is an ideal method for the treatment of staleness.

Summary

Staleness and burnout are very real psychological and physiological phenomena. Burnout has been defined as a state of mental, emotional, and physical exhaustion brought on by persistent devotion to a goal whose achievement is dramatically opposed to reality. Burnout afflicts overly dedicated athletes who are motivated toward high achievement and who work in rather unrewarding situations (Perlman & Hartman, 1982). It results in negative attitudes and negative self-concepts. Individuals who are perfectionistic, other-oriented, and lacking in assertive interpersonal skills are more susceptible to burnout. Burnout is a reaction to chronic stress, and when this occurs a previously enjoyable activity becomes an aversive source of stress (Smith, 1986). Symptoms of burnout are both physiological and psychological.

Staleness can be described as a precursor or early warning sign of burnout. Staleness is characterized by a variety of psychological and physiological variables. Causes of staleness include: length of total season, monotony of training, feelings of claustrophobia, lack of positive reinforcement, feelings of helplessness, abusiveness from authorities, stringent rules, and high levels of competitive stress.

Generally, thoughts concerning the prevention of staleness and burnout center around the concept of enjoyment. Preventive measures include:

- Proper planning and pacing of training
- Creative designs
- Scheduling time-outs
- Ample positive reinforcement
- Management of pre- and postcompetitive stress
- Holding mental practice periods
- Controlling the athletes' success–failure ratio
- Allowing athletes to make choices and control outcomes

Study Questions

1. Describe the differences between burnout, staleness, and slumps.
2. What are the personality characteristics and behavioral patterns of individuals most susceptible to burnout?
3. List the physiological and psychological characteristics of staleness.
4. What six transitory affective states are assessed by the Profile of Mood States (POMS)?
5. List a number of causes of staleness.
6. Discuss five steps that coaches can take to prevent staleness.
7. What are three emotional states that athletes experience at the conclusion of a contest?
8. Present and discuss five techniques for handling postcompetition tension.
9. Once staleness has set in there are realistically only two courses of action available—what are they?
10. What are the benefits of using imagery?
11. Discuss a number of preventative measures for burnout and staleness.

References

Caccese, T. M., & Mayerberg, C. K. (1984). Gender differences in perceived burnout of college coaches. *Journal of Sport Psychology, 6,* 279–288.

Dale, J., & Weinberg, R. S. (1989). The relationship between coaches' leadership style and burnout. *The Sport Psychologist, 3,* 1–13.

Davis, M., McKay, M., & Eshelman, H. (1983). *The relaxations and stress reduction workbook.* Oakland, Calif.: New Harbinger Publications.

Feigley, D. A, (1984). Psychological burnout in high-level athletes. *The Physician and Sportsmedicine, 12,* 109–119.

Fender, L. K. (1989). Athlete burnout: Potential for research and intervention strategies. *The Sport Psychologist, 3,* 63–71.

Freudenberger, H. J. (1980). *Burnout.* New York: Doubleday.

Freudenberger, H. J., & Richelson, G. (1981). *Burnout: How to beat the high cost of success.* New York: Bantam Books.

Harris, D. V., & Harris, B. L. (1984). *The athletes' guide to sports psychology: Mental skills for physical people.* New York: Leisure Press.

Henschen, K. P. (1973, December). Coaches beware: Post-competition tension. *Scholastic Coach,* 52–53.

Jones, J. W. (Ed.) (1981). *The burnout syndrome.* Park Ridge, Ill.: London House Management Press.

Maslach, C. (1982). Understanding burnout: Definitional issues in analyzing a complex phenomenon. In W. S. Paine (Ed.), *Job stress and burnout: Research, theory, and intervention perspectives* (pp. 29–40). Beverly Hills, Calif.: Sage.

Maslach, C., & Pines, A. (1977). The burnout syndrome. *Child Care Quarterly, 6,* 100–114.

McNair, D. M., Lorr, M., & Droppleman, L. F. (1971). *EDITS manual for the Profile of Mood States.* San Diego, Calif.: Editorial and Industrial Testing Service.

Morgan, W. P., Brown, D. R., Raglin, J. S., O'Connor, P. J., & Ellickson, K. A. (1987). Psychological monitoring of overtraining and staleness. *British Journal of Sports Medicine, 21,* 107–114.

Morgan, W. P., & Johnson, R. W. (1977). Psychologic characterization of the elite wrestler: A mental health model. *Medicine and Science in Sports, 9,* 55–56.

Morgan, W. P., & Johnson, R. W. (1978). Personality characteristics of successful and unsuccessful oars-men. *International Journal of Sport Psychology, 9,* 119–133.

O'Block, F., & Evans, F. (1984). Goal setting as a motivational technique. In J. Silva & R. Weinberg (Eds.), *Psychological foundations of sport.* Champaign, Ill.: Human Kinetics.

Perlman, B., & Hartman, E. A. (1982). Burnout: Summary and future research. *Human Relations, 35,* 283–305.

Pines, A., Aronson, E., & Kafry, D. (1981). *Burnout: From tedium to personal growth.* New York: Free Press.

Roethlisberger, F. J., & Dickson, W. J. (1947). *Management and the worker.* Cambridge, Mass.: Harvard University Press.

Rotter, J. B., Chance, J. B., & Phares, E. J. (Eds.) (1972). *Applications of a social learning theory of personality.* New York: Holt, Rinehart & Winston.

Shank, P. A. (1983, March). Anatomy of burnout. *Parks and Recreation, 17,* 52–58.

Smith, R. E. (1986). Toward a cognitive-affective model of athletic burnout. *Journal of Sport Psychology, 8,* 36–50.

Tower, R. B., & Singer, J. L. (1981). The measurement of imagery: How can it be clinically useful? In P. C. Kendall & S. Hollon (Eds.), *Assessment strategies for cognitive-behavior interventions* (pp. 221–222). New York: Academic Press.

Wilson, V. E., & Bird, E. (1988). Burnout in coaching—Part two. *S.P.O.R.T.S., 8,* No. 9.

Wilson, V. E., Haggerty, T., & Bird, E. (1986, September). Burnout in coaching. *S.P.O.R.T.S.,* Ottawa, Ont.: Coaching Association of Canada.

Stress, Injury, and the Psychological Rehabilitation of Athletes

Robert J. Rotella, *University of Virginia*
Steven R. Heyman, *University of Wyoming*

W hen the original draft of this chapter was completed in 1986, there had been a few studies dealing with factors that might predispose athletes to injury (e.g., Coddington & Troxell, 1980; Passer & Seese, 1983), but there was little systematic relationship between them and no real attempt to integrate them in a meaningful way for the athlete, coach, sport psychologist, or trainer. In the intervening years, not only have there been more studies in this area (see Williams & Roepke, in press, for an excellent overview), but models have been generated (e.g., Andersen & Williams, 1988). Yet one problem remains: Often the research makes generalizations across a number of individuals but does not present information about how to individualize approaches. While everything possible should be done to reduce the factors that might cause injury, unfortunately, injuries will still occur. It is therefore also important to address the different psychological reactions athletes will have to injury and to describe ways to proceed with the psychosocial components of the rehabilitation process.

Also, although some more clinical articles appeared before 1986 discussing athletes' psychological reaction to injury (e.g., Nideffer, 1983; Yaffe, 1983), their practical implications were not clear. Again, since the appearance of the original version of this chapter a number of articles have appeared

(e.g., DePalma & DePalma, 1989; Smith, Scott, & Wiese, 1990). This chapter will try to incorporate this newer material but also retain its focus on integrating theory and practice, using case examples, in a way that can be of use to athletes, coaches, trainers, sport psychologists, and others working in the sport environment.

It is assumed in this chapter that the injured athletes will be returning to their sport. It is recognized, however, that in some cases injuries will be so severe, or the damage so permanent, that an athlete will not be able to return to her/his sport. It is beyond the scope of this chapter to discuss the psychological issues involved when this happens, but the reader is directed to the chapters by Henschen (Chapter 23) and by Ogilvie and Taylor (Chapter 25) in this volume, as well as to several chapters in May and Asken (1987).

Psychological Readiness to Return After Injury

Historically, sport medicine specialists have concerned themselves primarily with the physical aspects of injury rehabilitation. As a result, athletes who attained a prescribed level of physical rehabilitation were assumed to be fully prepared for a safe and successful return to competition. Gradually it has become clear that this assumption is not valid for all athletes. Certainly, some athletes psychologically adapt to injury quite readily. If these athletes are provided with physical rehabilitation combined with support, encouragement, and the assurance that it is safe to return to competition, they are ready for a confident return.

However, other athletes, despite physical readiness, are not psychologically ready to return to competition. To them even the suggestion of returning is a questioned challenge. Doubts, fears, and anxieties surface. Despite assurances from trainers, physicians, and coaches, these athletes do not feel ready. Fears mount concerning the possible risk of returning too quickly. The mind and body get overloaded with thoughts and images of further injury. Sleep is interrupted by recurring dreams of a disastrous return to the playing field or by vivid recall of the feelings of the original injury.

It appears that the frequency with which these apprehensive responses occur has increased as (1) surgical techniques have reduced the time period required for physical rehabilitation, thereby reducing the time frame available for psychological adjustment; and (2) athletes have become more aware of the importance of taking care of their bodies. As a result, the future will demand that injury rehabilitation include both physical and psychological components. It will no longer suffice to argue that athletes who appear to be physically ready to return but who do not feel prepared psychologically are malingerers, mentally weak, or lacking in toughness. The old-school approaches of challenging desire and commitment to the team; inducing guilt for letting the team down; or using scare tactics to foster fear, shame, and embarrassment will have to change. These strategies cause more problems than they cure. For example, upon an athlete's initial return to competition, anxiety and tension can lead to one or more of the following:

- Reinjury
- Injury to another body part
- Lowered confidence resulting in a temporary performance decrement
- Lowered confidence resulting in a permanent performance decrement
- General depression and fear of further injury, which can sap motivation and the desire to return to competition

Today's athletes are well educated. They usually see through coercive strategies and will distrust individuals who use such approaches. The athletes may respond by simply refusing to return to competition by confidently claiming that they are not ready or by finding other indirect ways to undermine their performance and/or physical rehabilitation. As a result, everyone suffers—the athletes, the team, the coach, and the sport psychologist.

Old approaches to rehabilitation will have to be replaced by sound educational approaches. Coaches, athletic trainers, and sport psychologists will have to teach athletes how to respond psychologically to injury in a positive and growth-oriented way rather than in a negative and self-defeating one. We must realize that it is unnatural to be psychologically ready to return to competition after physical rehabilitation is complete unless that rehabilitation takes place naturally. In a world that uses special equipment to shorten the time needed for physical recovery, we need to find special techniques to facilitate an equally rapid psychological adjustment.

Athletes are stronger, quicker, and presumably sturdier than the rest of us. They seem blessed. We forget that what they do is hard. We so rarely see them at their most vulnerable—in pain and out of commission. And we almost never hear, from their perspective, about those injuries that disrupt their existence and play havoc with their futures.
Harry Stein, "Brought to His Knees"
Sport, September 1984, p. 64

Factors That Predispose Athletes to Injury

Common sense, which is important in most situations, can at times cause us to overlook important but subtle relationships when injury occurs. Common sense would seem to tell us that accidents occurring outside of practice and athletic injuries occurring during practice or a game are the result of unfortunate but physically tangible events. Can there be more than just a sequence of physical events relating to an accident or injury?

Research within the general population (e.g., Levenson et al,, 1983) and within the athletic population (e.g., Bramwell et al., 1975; Coddington &

Troxell, 1980; Cryan & Alles, 1983; Guttman et al., 1984; Passer & Seese, 1983; Smith, Smoll, & Ptacek, 1990) suggests that certain specific psychological factors may predispose some individuals to injury and reinjury. In addition, more applied research (Suinn, 1967; Yaffe, 1983) suggests other factors that can influence injuries, illness, and missed practices.

It is important to recognize the use of the word "predispose." By this we mean that although we cannot predict with complete accuracy who will or will not suffer from a particular problem, we can reasonably predict the group from which those likely to have a problem will come. Even though we still need to develop and more precisely refine our predictive abilities, identifying populations predisposed to injury allows us to target specific interventions to the group most likely to need them. Identifying predisposed populations also enables us to watch for the earliest signs of the particular problem concerning us.

Life Stress Events

Life stress events—specifically, the amount of change and upset experienced in the year prior to a competitive season—are the most specific factors cited in predisposing some athletes to injury. Most of the early studies in this area involved only football players (Bramwell et al., 1975; Coddington & Troxell, 1980; Cryan & Alles, 1983; Passer & Seese, 1983). More recent studies continue to document the stress–injury relationship in football (Blackwell & McCullagh, 1990) as well as in other sports such as alpine skiing (May et al., 1985); elite and intercollegiate gymnastics (Kerr & Minden, 1988; Petrie, in press); intercollegiate track, baseball, and softball (Hardy & Riehl, 1988); and high school wrestling, basketball, and gymnastics (Smith, Smoll, & Ptacek, 1990). Over all, Williams and Roepke (in press) reported 18 of 20 studies found a positive relationship between life stress and athletic injuries.

Most of the research instruments used in these studies, lists of potentially stressful life events, were modified for athletes by also including stressors specific to athletic participation. Events related to general life stress included death of family members and changes in residence, whereas events related to sports included trouble with coaches and being dropped to a lesser play status (Bramwell et al., 1975).

A coach, trainer, or sport psychologist working with athletes individually or with a small team may be aware of these events for his/her athletes; the coach, trainer, or sport psychologist of a larger team may be less aware of such events unless he/she specifically asks about them. The use of a screening instrument can help to identify individuals who may well be "at risk" for injury. (We will discuss this in more detail later in the chapter.) Once these athletes are identified, we can provide preventive interventions that vary from more formal programs to allowing athletes to ventilate their feelings instead of holding them in and allowing the pressure to intensify. For example, some at-risk individuals are good candidates for a stress reduction program. (See Chapter 15 for stress intervention techniques.) Such a program might include techniques such as relaxation training or cognitive restructuring. In some cases it may be most useful for concerned individuals to form support groups in which athletes can get together and share their concerns (Hardy & Crace, 1990; Oglesby, 1984). Finally, where levels of stress appear to be extreme, professional counseling may be necessary (see Chapter 21).

A coach or other individual working with teams should understand the nature of psychological tests before administering stress inventories. Otherwise, these tests may be misinterpreted and misused. Coaches or teammates who are aware of the results of an athlete's stress score might also add additional pressure with their concerns, comments, expectations, or actions. They may even help to create a self-fulfilling prophecy if they have not been trained in the use and interpretation of tests.

Although life stress was the factor studied most consistently in the research, other factors have been discussed. Sanderson (1977) lists a number of these, including the athlete for whom injury serves as a potent weapon ("You pushed me too hard; now I'm hurt and you feel guilty") or as an excuse ("I really did not want to do this; now I cannot"). If we can understand and anticipate these responses, we may be able to help athletes eliminate injury and its unpleasant consequences.

Ogilvie (1983) also mentions the frustrations of the remorse-ridden athlete who tries to assuage some inner sense of guilt. Even where there is success, it is often hollow and bitter. In some cases the push toward even greater achievement results in physical injury, but in other cases the injury is more indirect. One of the authors has seen in clinical practice of psychotherapy a number of successful high school and college athletes who abuse alcohol and drugs and seem to do so because of the hollowness and bitterness that their very accomplishments force them to recognize. Along these same lines, athletes who are uncertain and lacking in self-esteem may be placed in greater conflict as successes increase. These individuals are more and more afraid that they will not be able to continue to perform at the levels others expect.

Although the factors of life-stress research and case study evidence of reasons for injury seem to be different, the basic processes are, in fact, similar. If we return to our concept of predisposition, what the different researchers agree on is that internal conflicts can create stresses that make injury more likely. Some (e.g., Nideffer, 1983) point to the decreased athletic, cognitive, and emotional flexibility that athletes may confront while under stress. Others (e.g., Sanderson, 1977) point to more individual ways in which an injury resolves a conflict situation. All would probably agree, however, that an understanding of these factors is essential for coaches, sport psychologists, athletes, and other people concerned with athletic performance and injury. Knowledge of these factors allows for a more integrated understanding of the rehabilitation process, as well as for a remediation of problem situations before the negative consequence occurs. Perhaps even more important, it allows for the possibility of prevention through early detection and intervention.

We must keep in mind when using a life-events measure that the same stressful event will be experienced differently by different individuals. Several factors are involved. A person's coping mechanisms are critical—some people have more effective coping methods. A recent study found that injured volleyball players had lower coping resources than noninjured volleyball players (Williams, Tonymon, & Wadsworth, 1986). Social support from family, friends, and significant others, a group likely to include coaches and teammates, is very important. Experience with similar stressors can also be important. Along related lines, Williams and Roepke (in press) cite that Hardy and colleagues (1987) found that athletes who were higher in social support had a lower incidence of injury, even when controlling for levels of life stress, although other studies have reported inconsistent or partial relationships between social support, life stress, and in-

jury (Hardy, Richman, & Rosenfeld, 1991; Smith, Smoll, & Ptacek, 1990; Compas et al., 1987). Smith, Smoll, and Ptacek (1990) also found that injury vulnerability increased when high-stress athletes had few psychological coping skills to deal with arousal, concentration, and thought control.

Athletes sometimes experience both internal and external pressure to cope with stress by denial or repression—in essence trying to make believe the stressors are not there. Of some athletes, an observer might say, "There's no problem; they're dealing well in their situation," whereas, in fact, the opposite is true. The use of life-events measures, which can be modified for more individualized needs, insights, and experiences of coaches and sport psychologists, may be very helpful.

Social support is a concept involving the numbers and types of relationships people have. Research has suggested that certain types of social support systems are helpful in moderating the effects of life stress. In essence, while a greater number of supportive relationships may be desired, the *quality* of such relationships is also important. For example, a popular member of the team may be very important to other members and may seem to have a large number of relationships. It may be, however, that although others come to this individual as a resource, he/she may not see others as being similar resources. It may also be that a role traps an individual in relationships in unfulfilling ways. On one football team a young man with fairly strong religious values felt he had to go out, drink, and chase women with his teammates in order to receive their support and friendship. Although he achieved an external measure of support, the relationships were unfulfilling for him and added to his level of stress. It was, in fact, through a classroom discussion of stress that the athlete sought out someone with whom to discuss his conflicts. Both his coach and his teammates were unaware of the nature and range of his stress. After he successfully resolved the conflicts, his coach commented that he was a "much freer person and player." This probably resulted from increased flexibility due to decreased stress. The athlete may well have been an accident that *did not* happen.

Experience and Personality

Previous experience with stress may be potentially useful, but it can also be a liability. Having experienced a specific or similar situation before may make a person feel better able to deal with a recurrence. On the other hand, if a person's coping mechanisms have been previously taxed or eroded by a stressful situation, then another stress or crisis may increasingly impair functioning.

One factor that makes athletes valued competitors may also make them more vulnerable to injury: the willingness to take risks. Several research studies (Dahlhauser & Thomas, 1979; Vaillant, 1981; Cohen & Young, 1981) have suggested that this is the case for competitive athletes, particularly when this willingness, even desire, to take risks is related to externally oriented motivations. Some external motivations vary from a desire to please others to a belief that one's fate is controlled by external sources.

It would be very useful to have a specific "personality" test to predict the more injury-prone athlete. Unfortunately, from those studies that have used measures of more basic, stable personality patterns (with instruments such as Cattel's 16 Personality Factors Questionnaire or the California Personality Inventory), no consistent results have emerged. It may well be that by the time athletes are in high school or college they are able to integrate basic patterns with sport demands. Life stress, on the other hand, taxes athletes' coping abilities and offsets previously established equilibrium, hence predisposing them to injury. Similarly, counterphobics or excessive risk takers, if not held in check or changed, would propel themselves into situations for which they do not have adequate coping skills. As a result, they are more vulnerable, not only because of the excessive physical demands but because the added stress causes an additional drain on the ability to respond.

Substitutes May Be Particularly Vulnerable

Coaches and trainers need to keep an especially close lookout for borderline starters and substitutes who mask pain and play through injury. Often such players feel that a missed day of practice will lead to reduced playing time or a missed game may mean losing their position and game time. These players may believe that acting tough and masking injury are their only ways to get playing time, and they may be very fearful of losing what they had to work so hard to earn.

Athletes' Reactions to Injury

Regardless of the best efforts of coaches and trainers, injuries still occur. The second step involved in serving the athletes' best interests involves an understanding and appreciation of the psychology of injury rehabilitation.

Predictable Psychological Reactions to Injury

The loss inflicted by an athletic injury will always lead to a period of grieving (Pederson, 1986; Weiss & Troxell, 1986). It is helpful for athletes to realize that the resulting thoughts and feelings are a normal and useful part of the effective rehabilitation process.

Following injury, athletes commonly experience a sequence of predictable psychological reactions similar to those outlined by Kubler-Ross in her classic *On Death and Dying* (1969). These reactions include (1) disbelief, denial, and isolation; (2) anger; (3) bargaining; (4) depression; and (5) acceptance and resignation while continuing to remain hopeful about the eventual return to competition. Athletes initially respond by believing that there is no damage, that the injury is less serious than originally thought, or that the injury will be healed in a day or two. However, when they realize that the injury will prevent practice and competition for an extended time period, athletes often respond by feeling isolated and lonely. As they attend to their injuries, they typically become irritated with themselves and others. Anger is followed by a true sense of loss. Normal comfort and freedom are gone, as are the abilities to enjoy and display physical prowess on center stage. Although each step does not always progress as exactly and routinely as presented here, depression is usually followed by acceptance and hope of a successful return to competition. However, coaches and sport psychologists should be aware of a variety of factors that may intervene and, if not properly managed, delay or prevent this important final adjustment step from occurring.

Perceptual Responses to Injury

Athletes perceive injury in various ways. Some view it as a disaster; others see it as an opportunity to display courage; and still others welcome it as a relief from the drudgery of practice or the embarrassment and frustration of poor performance, lack of playing time, or a losing season.

It is not uncommon for injured athletes to feel concerned about whether they will ever completely recover and return to their previous form. They must be prepared for a quick return to action, a delayed recovery, or the end of their career. Only a positive and enthusiastic response will ensure the best possible chance of complete rehabilitation both physically and mentally.

Because of the importance of athletic performance to many athletes, physical injury often spreads to the self-image. Emotional and irrational thinking often become dominant. Athletes responding in this manner may increasingly become lost in the "work of worry" and eventually become overwhelmed by anxiety. Such interfering thought patterns can further delay or sabotage effective rehabilitation.

When athletes think irrationally, they may exaggerate the meaning of the injury; disregard particularly important aspects of the injury; oversimplify the injury as good or bad, right or wrong; overgeneralize from this single event; or draw unwarranted conclusions when evidence is lacking or contradictory (Beck, 1970; Crossman & Johnson, 1985). Athletes may, for example, feel sorry for themselves and perceive that training room personnel give preferential treatment to "major sport" athletes or to "mens' team" athletes. They may exaggerate and catastrophize that their career is ended. They may become discouraged after 10 days of therapy even though they have been told that recovery will take at least two to three weeks. Injured athletes may decrease their motivation for rehabilitation and increase their anxiety by focusing on other athletes with similar injuries who failed to recover rather than thinking of numerous other athletes who fully recovered. Some injured athletes may, out of fear, decide they are injury-prone. This thought can lead athletes to grow increasingly anxious and thus actually cause them to become more frequently injured.

Identity and Injury

Previous writings dealing with athletes' emotional reactions to various stressful situations (Heyman, 1987) and some recent research (Brewer, Van Raalte, & Linder, 1990, 1991) have focused on an athlete's personal sense of self. For many athletes, but particularly for those who are intensely involved with their sport and those who achieve notable success, the whole focus of their identity, their sense of self, may be in this role as an athlete. The reader no doubt recognizes that similar issues can occur with injury as occur with career termination or retirement. Perhaps a case can illustrate the points.

> Matt was a star basketball player who suffered a serious injury, requiring him to be hospitalized for several weeks, and whose recovery would take several months. Although at first he seemed to be doing well, involved in his physical rehabilitation, his schoolwork, and with his friends, he became increasingly withdrawn. Finally, in talking with his trainer, he discussed feelings of meaninglessness, of being a "was." It wasn't that basketball was everything: It was the *only* thing. His whole life, and his whole sense of self, had centered on basketball.

> It was clear that Matt was going to recover and return to sport. It was also recognized, however, that at some point in time he would face the end of his career. His coach knew that Matt enjoyed working with children, but rather than trying to involve him in coaching a youth sport, which would have kept him, again, closely tied to sport, he helped him to become a "big brother." The boy with whom Matt worked came from a troubled family, and as they spent mutually enjoyable time together, Matt became increasingly interested in the problems of children and adolescents. Over time, he planned to take more psychology and counseling courses, and he also volunteered to work in several community agencies.

> When he returned to basketball he was again a star player. He also knew, however, that when his career ended he would become a school counselor, or perhaps a marriage and family counselor. He had a greater sense of himself as a person and of what he could do with and for others.

If someone has only one basis for a sense of self or the different components of identity are tied to one sphere (Erikson, 1968), if that sphere is threatened, so will be the entire person. To as great an extent as possible, we should encourage athletes to develop themselves in as many domains as possible. Unfortunately, the reality of many situations, if not mitigating against expansion of self, may cause it to be overlooked.

What we can expect is that the more narrowly focused an injured athlete's sense of self is, the more threatened the athlete will be. Such a person, depending on the severity of the injury, may be more vulnerable to feelings of anxiety, depression, or hopelessness (Smith et al., 1990). He/she might be more motivated to return to sport and possibly might also try to return prematurely. The coach, trainer, or others involved in the rehabilitative process should be sensitive to these issues. It may be appropriate to help the athlete to come to see himself/herself as more fully a person, with many potentials, and to explore other possibilities—not to replace the sport or athlete identity, but to complement it.

In comparing the perceptions of the seriousness of illness of athletes and trainers, Crossman and Jamieson (1985) found that athletes in general perceived injury as more serious. A group they defined as "overestimators" experienced even greater pain, more anger, loneliness, and apathy. They noted: "Such athletes might benefit from psychological support and counselling about how to cope with their injury. . . those athletes who overreact to an injury may also show slower recovery" (p. 1133).

While referral for counseling or therapy may not be necessary as part of reframing the athlete's understanding of and reaction to an injury (Smith, Scott, & Wiese, 1990), there may be the opportunity to discover *positive* implications of the injury (Ermler & Thomas, 1990; Frankl, 1963), not in a "Pollyannaish" way but as a source of self-understanding, self-growth, and discovery. Ermler and Thomas (1990) note that individuals who can develop positive meanings from injury adjust and cope significantly better than those who do not. These findings are similar to those of Bulman and Wortman (1977), who examined coping in severely injured individuals.

The question of referral for counseling and psychotherapy is always problematic (see Chapter 21 for a detailed discussion of when to refer). Not all sport psychologists are trained as counselors or psychotherapists, and not all counselors and psychotherapists will be sensitive to the particular issues confronting athletes. Although an increasing number of professional and college teams do have consulting relationships with counselors and psychotherapists, or have in-house sport psychologists, many colleges and certainly most high schools do not.

Ermler and Thomas (1990) discuss how important it might be for an athlete to develop listening and communication skills as part of becoming able to talk about the injury, the sense of self, and recovery from injury. Although it would be helpful for an athletic department or staff to have someone trained in basic counseling skills, referral sources, again, can be important.

Reacting to Injured Athletes

Reaction to an injured athlete can spring thoughtlessly from "old-school" attitudes about toughness in sport or can proceed naturally from a philosophy that embraces the concept of the athlete as a whole person, not just a sport participant. The first reaction not only can impede an athlete's recuperation from injury; it can arguably *predispose* an athlete to sport accidents. The second reaction approach deals with short- and long-term aspects of an injury situation in a way that greatly increases the chances of an athlete's return to healthy sport participation.

Potentially Dangerous Attitudes

In an effort to help athletes develop into successful competitors, many coaches and athletic trainers have unknowingly fostered erroneous attitudes concerning successful injury rehabilitation. A clear understanding of these potentially dangerous attitudes is crucial to a complete appreciation of the psychological aspects of injury and rehabilitation.

Act tough and always give 110%. Athletes have been systematically taught that mental toughness and "giving 110%" all of the time are necessary for success in sports. Although mental toughness and giving one's best are important to success, we must realize that when taken to *extremes*, these actions can foster injury and failure.

Certainly, athletes must be capable of "playing through" some kinds of pain. Seldom, however, do we educate athletes about the necessity of learning which kinds of pain to ignore and which kinds of pain to listen to and respond to appropriately. The same holds true for learning the amount of pain one should tolerate.

Many highly motivated athletes learn to endure almost any amount or kind of pain. This ability may make for a "tough" athlete, but it may also make for a vulnerable, often injured athlete who never plays in a fully healthy state. Such athletes often have short-lived careers and a lifetime of suffering.

Especially in many contact sports, tough athletes are given bountiful rewards. Unfortunately, the rewards often lead to an extreme psychological reaction by athletes wishing to win the admiration and respect of coaches, trainers, teammates, and fans. The athletes may thoroughly enjoy the rewards, and they may become increasingly involved in earning more rewards by proving and continually displaying their dedication.

With time, the well-intentioned appearance of dedication and commitment develops into the projection of a false image of invulnerability. As athletes attempt to live up to this impossible image, both psychologically and physically, problems begin to appear. Soon, it is accepted as fact that tough athletes never need a rest, never miss a play, never go to the training room, and never let an injury keep them from playing. Failure to live up to the expectations fostered by this image is judged as a sign of weakness.

Eventually, athletes begin to believe in the image of invulnerability off, as well as on, the playing field. They believe that they only deserve the right to feel proud if they give 110%. No one points out to them that giving 110% is impossible or that trying to do so can cause performance at 50% of optimal ability. This belief system persists in spite of the fact that athletes who adhere to these attitudes are unable to perform at their best because they are chronically overtired, playing in pain, and adjusting their style of play to their injuries.

Finally, the athletes become extremely vulnerable and totally unprepared for the incapacitating injury or lifelong pain that will likely follow. A major change in attitude is required to ensure a healthy adaptation to injury and life. Without this change in attitude, athletes will not be able to accept injuries and respond positively to them. As a result, athletes will fail to develop to their fullest potential, and in so doing their coaches and trainers will also fail. True professionals must realize the hazards of these mistaken attitudes of the past before they can use to the fullest the specific psychological strategies that we present later in this chapter.

Injured athletes are worthless. Some coaches have been led to believe that the best way to foster a rapid recovery from injury is to make injured athletes feel unimportant as long as they are injured. This is, to say the least, a counterproductive approach. Coaches who hold this view clearly communicate to their athletes that they only care for them as performers. Some coaches communicate this message by isolating injured athletes from healthy team members. Some refuse any form of verbal communication while using body language to suggest that injured athletes should feel guilty for being injured and not helping the team win. Others talk behind the injured athletes' backs and suggest that the athletes are malingerers, lack mental toughness and desire, or are not fully committed to the success of the team.

Leaders in sport must realize that the time during which athletes are recovering from injury is crucial for either developing or destroying trust. It is during this time that leaders have a chance to demonstrate care and concern and show that they are as committed to their athletes as they ask their athletes to be to them.

Most contemporary athletes are intelligent and sophisticated. They realize that actions speak louder than words. Athletes have learned to respect their precious physical gifts, and they expect their coaches and trainers to do likewise.

Successful leaders of athletes must help the athletes realize that attitudes such as desire, pride, and commitment are beneficial at the right time and place but that these attitudes may also be hazardous to present and future health if taken to the extreme. The key is for leaders to do what is in the *best interest* of injured athletes. When this approach is followed, athletes, coaches, trainers, and

---

Montreal Expo's President John McHale attempted to describe Andre Dawson's response to the injury and pain in his knee. "Andre is a very unusual man . . . I'll tell you what's happening here. What's happening is that even with the year he's had, his pride and his commitment to his job are such that he won't *take himself out or even excuse himself."*

Andre's view was "I'm just not the sort to throw in the towel. I don't know, maybe that's just the way I was raised."

Harry Stein, "Brought to his Knees"
Sport, September 1984, pp. 64, 66

teams alike will have the best possible chance of attaining their fullest potential. When this approach is not followed, there is still a chance that the athletes themselves will put sport in a proper perspective. But they will do so out of *distrust* rather than trust. This will often lead athletes to decide that sport is unimportant and a place for personal abuse rather than positive growth and fulfillment.

Whole-Person Philosophy

Danish (1986) makes an excellent point when he reminds us to respond to athletes as people, not just injuries. He also describes a helping skill model that can be of use to those working with athletes.

Crisis intervention model. If we consider the nature of injury to athletes, particularly injuries that are painful, sudden, and moderate to severe in their effects, another model comes to mind: the crisis intervention model. **Crisis intervention** is a short-term intervention method most often used when individuals' coping abilities are overwhelmed or when others recognize that those who are injured are not aware of the extent to which their normal patterns have been impaired and overwhelmed. Crisis intervention consists of getting people through crises until their normal coping abilities return or until more long-term help can be implemented.

Crisis intervention models follow a similar pattern and can be learned fairly easily; they form the basis of most volunteer hotlines. In the case of

---

"I went to the doctor with Andre Dawson a couple of times," Pete Rose was saying now...The conversation rapidly turned to the gruesome but unavoidable subject of permanent injury. "Listen," said Rose, "I know a guy who fought the whole organization because he didn't want to jeopardize his health— Johnny Bench. He told them, 'I will not catch anymore, period. I don't plan to be a cripple when I'm through.'"

Rose paused. . ."And I'm not gonna sit here and tell you that someone who says that is wrong. I mean, hell, when you finish playing this game, you've still got half your life in front of you."

Harry Stein, "Brought to His Knees"
Sport, September 1984, p. 63

---

working with injured athletes, such models can help coaches and sport psychologists to become more aware of the meaning of injuries to athletes, to be appropriately reassuring, to help athletes attend to immediate and practical concerns rather than to more distant worries, and to see injury and the problems it poses in manageable units as opposed to an overwhelming, engulfing catastrophe.

Crisis intervention courses vary in length from 15 to 50 hours. As Gluck (1983) notes: "The person who helps to carry a player off the field is as important as the individuals who administer first aid and cardiopulmonary resuscitation. In most instances, a stretcher may be unnerving to the injured player and to his family" (p. 333). A person who is trained in crisis intervention can deal not only with athletes but with family members as well. The injury is truly a crisis, and without appropriate responses the bottomless fears, the searing emotions may well set a very poor direction that will need to be countered in subsequent rehabilitation attempts. Crisis training also helps coaches to recognize more clearly the intellectual and emotional limitations the injury may create for injured athletes: the extreme pessimism or optimism that must be accepted and worked with until a more stable balance can be achieved. If crisis intervention is successful, it can lay the groundwork for later psychological rehabilitation strategies.

Social support. Social support, as mentioned previously, is critical in the rehabilitation process, particularly with moderate to severe injuries. If the athletic identification has been strong, family and friends may have come to respond to the athletes primarily through their role as athletes. In many cases, friendships are based exclusively along these lines, particularly with other teammates or with other athletes. Suddenly these important ties may be ruptured. Injured athletes may no longer be seen and may no longer see themselves as athletes. Activities around which their lives centered now move along without them. No one quite knows how to relate to these athletes except perhaps in terms of their past glory or possible future—but not to the injured people in the present.

Coaches and sport psychologists must help ensure that normal contacts are maintained. They should be as reassuringly optimistic about recovery of past abilities as possible, and they should also encourage injured athletes to discover other bases of support for themselves. These actions serve more than some obscure long-term need, as Eldridge (1983) notes. They also help to reestablish and maintain a sense of equilibrium. This will not be the same equilibrium as prior to the injury; it can be an even better one.

While social support and the reintegration of the injured athlete are important parts of the rehabilitation process, there are two problems with this "double-edged crutch" that may need to be confronted. First, an injured athlete may present a conscious or unconscious threat to others: "If it could happen to them, it could happen to me." This fear may evoke anything from a mild feeling of discomfort to an almost phobic avoidance of the injured player. This effect may even be exacerbated when a physical disfigurement or highly visible disability is present.

Second, although cooperation and cohesion are part of teamwork, so is competition. An athlete's injury may present an opportunity to another person. The "second string" player, for example, may have a chance for glory. There may be mixed feelings by some team members in terms of providing emotional support and encouragement for a rapid return.

There is no easy way for a coach, trainer, sport psychologist, or athlete to proceed. The first scenario is probably easier to manage. Modeling warmth, openness, and acceptance will be very helpful. Showing at conscious and unconscious levels that the injured person should not be feared will set an important tone in the athletic environment. At the same time, the message "You will recover and rejoin us" is a powerful message for all concerned.

The second situation is more difficult. Even where it is recognized, it may be difficult to respond to it. Where possible, the competition should be appropriately focused on the athletic situation, and not personalized. Tensions within the system (a polarization of teammates into factions around the competing athletes) should be surfaced and discussed. If not, the situation may fester and grow worse. One cannot ignore the realities of competition. One can, however, try to maintain as positive a climate as possible.

Addressing the whole person. As we know, the mind and body function together. When we consider the involvement of injured athletes in the physical rehabilitation program (Danish, 1986;

Sanderson, 1978), we must also understand what, if any, attempts are made in the psychological arena. How motivated will athletes be in the journey to recovery? How well will they deal with the often minute steps forward or the reverses that are a part of rehabilitation? How will they manage their fears of lost abilities when they return to competition or their fears of reinjury? Unfortunately, these questions are often met with silence or not asked out loud by athletes. Consequently, they echo internally, and in the echo fears may grow.

What we have been describing is the backdrop to a more holistic view of the psychological rehabilitation process. It is not an attempt to fix an injured part but to address the whole. It seems likely that in most cases athletes' participation and commitment to the physical rehabilitation program will be contingent on psychological factors, and the interaction will form a continuing, holistic pattern.

Teaching Specific Psychological Rehabilitation Strategies

Coaches and sport psychologists must encourage athletes to view injury from a self-enhancing perspective rather than a self-defeating one. They need to teach athletes that when an injury occurs, it is reasonable and appropriate to think the injury is unfortunate, untimely, and inconvenient and to feel irritated, frustrated, and disappointed. It is *unreasonable* for athletes to convince themselves that the situation is hopeless, that injuries are a sign of weakness and should be hidden, or that their season or career is over.

Nancy Mayer, a star guard for the University of Virginia basketball team, describes the role her coaches and trainers played in helping her through a year and a half of rehabilitation following a serious knee injury.

> The trainers, Joe Gieck and Sue Halstead Shapiro, helped me step by step. They taught me patience. They did more than they think. Our assistant coach Gino Auriemma really helped me get my head up when I was frustrated. It was easy to get down and his reinforcement meant a lot. . . . It was scary. I felt very awkward. I was scared to find out if I was as good as I was before, if I could still play well. (Ratcliffe, 1983)

Athletes with emotional self-control will be able to cope with injury more effectively by responding rationally to it. They can best exert self-control if they have knowledge of the injury and the rehabilitation process. It is difficult, if not impossible, for intelligent athletes to be positive and relaxed if they lack knowledge, are anxious, and wonder why they are doing what they are doing in the training room. Much anxiety results from uncertainty, misconceptions, or inaccurate information. If uncertainty persists, athletes may have trouble getting through the denial and isolation phases of rehabilitation. Honest and accurate information coupled with hope helps athletes move into the acceptance phase (Kavanaugh, 1972). In addition, athletes who realize the purpose of rehabilitation are more likely to work hard and to provide useful information about their progress.

However, emotional control must not be misrepresented to athletes as they progress through the stages of the grief process identified by Kubler-Ross (1969). Athletes must be helped to realize it is acceptable and appropriate to honestly express distressing emotions. During the depression stage, coaches or sport consultants must not negate disturbing feelings by urging athletes to "pick their spirits up." They should honestly explain to athletes that these feelings are normal and actually a sign of progress toward recovery psychologically and emotionally. During the acceptance stage, athletes may benefit from sharing experiences with other athletes who have successfully recovered from similar injuries and effectively returned to competition. For more seriously injured athletes, support groups for sharing and discussing concerns, fears, and difficulties may be helpful (Silva & Hardy, 1991; Wiese & Weiss, 1987). If, in spite of such support, prolonged detachment, lack of spontaneity, and disinterest in activities and people persist, professional counseling or therapy may be necessary (Wehlage, 1980).

Thought Stoppage

What athletes say to themselves following an injury helps determine their subsequent behavior. Athletes can be taught coping skills to control their inner thoughts. Then when faulty or self-defeating internal dialogues occur, the athletes can use an intervention strategy such as thought stoppage. (See Chapter 17 for more information on thought stoppage and other techniques for controlling thoughts.)

As an example of the importance of inner

dialogue, consider an injury-related situation in which an athlete is in the training room receiving treatment and going through rehabilitation exercises while experiencing a great amount of pain and little apparent improvement in the injured area. If her inner dialogue becomes self-defeating, the athlete worries and questions the benefit of treatment and exercise.

> This is awful. This hurts too much to be beneficial. These exercises will probably cause me more harm. Besides, I've been doing this for three days now, and I can't see any progress. It would be a lot easier to just let the injury heal on its own. I don't think I'll come tomorrow. If it's really important, the coach will call me. If she doesn't, it will mean I was right. It really doesn't matter if I get treatment.

The athlete does not get much out of today's treatment and begins to develop excuses for not continuing therapy.

On the other hand, if the athlete's inner dialogue is self-enhancing, she worries and questions the benefits of treatment and exercise but then thinks:

> Stop. These exercises hurt, but it's OK—they'll pay off. I'm lucky to have knowledgeable people helping me. I'll be competing soon because I'm doing these exercises. I must not let the pain bother me. If the pain gets too severe, I'll speak up and tell the coach. She'll want to know. Otherwise, I'll live with it and think about how happy I'll be to be competing again.

The athlete has a good treatment session and prepares herself to continue for as long as necessary. She develops rapport with the coach, who feels good about the athlete.

By learning a mental self-control strategy such as thought stoppage, athletes can often shorten the time period needed to advance from disbelief to acceptance to a safe and successful return to competition.

Imagery

Athletes' imaginations can greatly influence their response to injury. Many imagine the worst that could happen. Athletes can be taught to control their visual images and to direct them productively to reduce anxiety and to aid in rehabilitation. Imagery strategies include visual rehearsal, emotive imagery rehearsal, and body rehearsal (Lazarus, 1974; Moss, 1979). (See Chapter 16 for more detailed information on what imagery is and techniques that can be used to teach and enhance imagery skills.)

Visual rehearsal. Visual rehearsal may include both mastery and coping rehearsal. Mastery rehearsal fosters motivation for rehabilitation and confidence upon return to competition. While disabled, athletes may visually rehearse returning to competition and performing effectively. For athletes who experience difficulty viewing themselves vividly in their mind, relaxation exercises should precede the imagery session. Some athletes visualize better with the aid of recordings or video replays of their most effective game performances.

In coping rehearsal, injured athletes visually rehearse anticipated problematic situations or obstacles that may stand in the way of their successful return to competition and then rehearse effectively overcoming these obstacles. Coping rehearsal is the more realistic of the two visual rehearsal methods and prepares athletes for difficulties that might occur.

Emotive rehearsal. Emotive rehearsal enables athletes to feel secure and confident that rehabilitation will be successful. The athletes rehearse various scenes that produce positive, self-enhancing feelings such as enthusiasm, self-pride, and confidence. Athletes may, for instance, rehearse feeling excited about their first game following injury or rehearse thoughts of the admiration coaches, teammates, and friends will have for them on their return from injury. Athletes can also be instructed to think of other athletes like themselves who have overcome similar injuries and then generate other scenes that produce positive feelings.

Body rehearsal. In body rehearsal the athletes vividly envision what is happening to the injury internally during the rehabilitation process. To do this, the athletes must receive a detailed explanation of their injury. Whenever possible, color pictures should be used to help the athletes develop a mental picture of the injury. The healing process and purpose of the rehabilitation techniques are then explained. After visualizing the healing process, athletes are asked to imagine in vivid color

the healing occurring during treatment sessions and at intervals during the day. Although there is a need for further research to determine the effectiveness of body rehearsal, it appears to be a beneficial strategy for aiding the healing process.

Goal Setting

Throughout the rehabilitation process it is most helpful for the rehabilitation team to work actively with the injured athlete at setting specific short-term and long-term goals for recovery, return to practice and competition, and day-to-day rehabilitation that include time, place, and activities (DePalma & DePalma, 1989). Athletes should be actively involved in this process as much as possible, with more seriously injured athletes more actively involved.

It is essential that these goals are important to the athlete (Danish, 1986), and this is best accomplished if time is taken to explain to the athlete the relationship between staying focused on and committed to agreed-upon goals and successful rehabilitation and return to competition.

Psychological Skills for Performance Preparation

In the contemporary world of sport it is increasingly important that athletes are psychologically ready to return to competition with the level of confidence they had prior to the injury. During recovery, athletes can benefit from using imagery strategies to rehearse effective performance upon

---

When Philadelphia Phillies pinch-hitter Len Matuszek unloaded against the Chicago Cubs Tuesday night, he released six weeks of frustration.

In his second at bat since coming off the disabled list, Matuszek cracked a leadoff, pinch-hit home run in the seventh inning to give the Phillies a 3-2 victory over the Cubs. He hit the first pitch into the right-field bull pen. "That was all I had on my mind during my time on the disabled list. I kept envisioning some ways to help this team win a game. Even with the injury, my attitude has been good."

"Phillie Unloads Frustration on Cubs"
The Daily Progress, July 24, 1984, p. D3

---

their return to competition. Whenever possible, athletes in team sports should attend practice and stay up to date on offensive and defensive strategies as well as scouting reports. Doing so will serve the purpose of once again getting the mind focused and prepared for competition and increase the chances of a successful return.

Athletes Are Human

Injuries can be major or minor. It is important to remember that the seriousness of an injury does not necessarily determine the ease or difficulty of psychological rehabilitation. And psychological rehabilitation is necessary to ensure a healthy future for athletes, a future that must include more than just their playing careers.

Rehabilitation is both a mental and physical process. Because athletes are human, this process includes an emotional component that will change from day to day. It is crucial to strive to make this process a positive experience in which athletes are actively involved.

The following example highlights the importance of appreciating this emotional component. A university-age athlete was drafted out of high school by a professional baseball team but chose to go to college before turning professional. In the fall of his freshman year in college he tore ligaments in his throwing arm, which required surgery. The following advice and program were outlined for him as he psychologically prepared for his return to practice the following spring. The program was designed to facilitate a safe return and a successful future.

The athlete, a pitcher, was reminded of how excited he would be on the first day of spring practice to find out if he still "had it," if he could still throw hard. He was reminded of the need to be smart, emotionally controlled, disciplined, and patient in order to control himself when his personal excitement over being back on the field with his teammates was combined with the high of a beautiful spring day following a long winter. He was also told that he would feel great and have an almost overpowering urge to overthrow on the first day his arm felt good. In addition, he would want to try all of his different pitches. The desire to help his teammates be successful and the thrill of getting back on stage and becoming a star again would be highly motivating. He was told of the im-

portance of realizing the temptation of these feelings and cautioned not to fall victim to them.

Together, this athlete, his coaches, and his trainers outlined a specific plan. They decided on a set number of throws each day, the distance of the throws, the approximate speed of the throws, and the kinds of throws. For the first three weeks the athlete's catcher and a coach would help make sure that the plan was adhered to on a daily basis. Short-term and long-term goals were detailed so that by the fifth game of the year, the athlete would be ready to return to the pitching mound for three innings of relief pitching.

A similar plan was detailed for physical treatments. Both plans were reinforced by coaches, trainers, and teammates, as well as by daily visualization of the good feelings and results that would occur from sticking to the plan. Despite many days of questioning, doubt, and uncertainty, the athlete generally remained positive, stayed with the plan, and made a highly successful return to competition one week later than planned.

As with many other athletes, the process from injury to return to competition was a challenge to this athlete's mind and body. Because the process was managed properly, it allowed for a positive and bright future.

The Injured Athlete: Lessons to Be Learned from Combat Reactions

Modern sports, particularly many competitive and contact sports, have their roots in war and combat. As we conclude our consideration of the psychological rehabilitation of injured athletes, we can learn valuable lessons from the principles used with those injured in combat. Kardiner (1959) notes:

> The soldier lives in an atmosphere of continuous fatigue, anxiety, and boredom, deprived of sex and opportunity for complete relaxation. Moreover, his weaknesses are exposed to public gaze and his failure to be an effective member of a team may inflict a blow to his self-esteem from which he may never recover. (p. 248)

Certainly these sound like some of the factors others have linked to predisposing athletes to injury.

More extensive symptoms of a problem process include poor appetite, carelessness, unusual jumpiness, irritability, inability to relax, and nightmares, which in their frequency of appearance may indicate the extent of stress athletes are experiencing.

In response to the trauma of war or of injury in sport, some people will seek to avoid situations that they assume produced stress. Others will try to adapt themselves to their new, narrowed world. Still others will show signs of psychological disorganization. They may be unable to derive pleasure from sport and nonsport activities. Their thoughts and dreams will often force them to return to the traumatic event.

Within the war situation the most important consideration is keeping soldiers close to their unit, with a return to regular duty as quickly as possible. What has occurred and the soldier's reactions to it are to be kept tied together so they do not become separated psychologically and thus more difficult to resolve. This also prevents soldiers from building up the feared situation to overwhelming proportions in the absence of the real stimuli. More recent research from combat situations confirms these general principles (Solomon & Benbenishty, 1986), although it should be noted that while group cohesion is often important for the rehabilitation of soldiers (Labuc, 1986), in some sport situations, competition or conflicts within a team might be problematic.

The same factors that predispose soldiers to a psychological breakdown may predispose athletes to injury. This is not where the similarities end. The more significant the injury and its meaning to athletes, the more similar the recovery process will be to that experienced by soldiers. Soldiers feel bound to duty by external motivations: patriotism, peer evaluation, and so on. Athletes often tie their identity to sport, and thus when sport is taken away, life's meaning is shaken in direct relation to the importance of sport to them. Smith and colleagues (1990) confirm that, in a related way, the most seriously injured group of athletes, as compared with less seriously injured athletes, experience more tension, depression, and anger, while also manifesting less vigor, and they tend to have a longer-lasting mood disturbance.

In war, separating soldiers from their unit exacerbates feelings of letting others down and also ruptures important social ties. Not only do athletes experience these feelings; they often also fear being replaced. The longer athletes are kept away by injury, the longer these feelings and fears fester.

Perhaps an example will further clarify these relationships. Frank, a high school second-string quarterback, injured his knee and was to be out of practice and games for a month. Frank was an average student, and most of his special recognition as a person came during the games in which he played. His coach knew he was highly motivated and always gave his best. Frank felt he had to do this; others were waiting to take his place, and he desperately wanted to be the starting quarterback in his senior year. Given the importance of athletics to Frank, the depression he experienced after being injured was not surprising. It was also not surprising that his dreams involved reliving the accident or seeing himself walk away uninjured.

The pressures under which Frank played may have predisposed him to the injury, although there is no sure way to ascertain this. His rehabilitation, however, was modeled very much along the lines of soldiers' rehabilitation. As soon as he was able to join his team at practice, he did—even if it meant just helping out. Frank changed clothes with the rest of the team, was there through practice, and showered with the team. He was on the sidelines for games. As he was able, he gradually resumed all of his usual activities. When he had to run slower or lift less weight, he did, but his routine approximated his normal routine. The dreams ceased and the depression lifted relatively quickly. Although at times he wanted to move more quickly than was advisable, the coach underscored the importance of Frank's appropriate recovery to the team. As Frank gradually returned to activity, he had virtually no fear of reinjury when he faced full practice and his first game because he had been close to this in previous practice.

Too often, when athletes are kept away because of injury, they feel that their teammates and time have marched on. There are new jokes, new alignments—in essence a new situation that excludes injured athletes and into which they must try to reintegrate themselves. By being there, other athletes have grown and developed with the situation.

We would go so far as to say that as soon as athletes can rejoin a team—even if on crutches or bandaged—they should do so. It is sometimes too much to ask someone to get back on a horse after being thrown, but a modified approach allows a

Duke Snider, the Hall of Famer who broadcast games for the Montreal Expos, comments on Andre Dawson's desire to keep playing despite suggestions that he should stop and have surgery. Snider himself had his career subverted by a severe injury at the age of 31.

"After the injury I was a shell of my old self. . . I sit up there every day and I see one of the best young players in such pain he simply can't do the job he's trying to do. I see his knee buckle when he swings. I see him overswing to try and compensate. . . hobbling down the first base line, and being unable to slow down to make a slide—so many little things."

"It's easy for me to say, but I think he shouldn't play the rest of the year."

But it was pointed out, Dawson doesn't want to sit out the year.

Snider nodded. "Andre has an awful lot of pride, and I respect him for it. But common sense and judgment have to enter into it, too." He stopped. "The thing is you still think *you can do what you've always done. It takes a while for it to sink in that you can't." He stops again. "The truth is, when Arthur— that is, arthritis—comes to live in your knee, he never leaves."*

Harry Stein, "Brought to His Knees"
Sport, September 1984, p. 67

gradual remount while preventing the consolidation of fears of overwhelming obstacles.

For many individual sport athletes the case is somewhat different. There is usually not the same group support system or as much fear of replacement. There is still involvement with others, however. The basic process of separation from an activity that means a great deal remains. So does the opportunity for the separation of event and feelings and the consolidation of fears. Thus, as soon as possible after injury, athletes should develop routines similar to prior training and competition. If this is not possible, coaches should consider involving recuperating athletes in the training of others.

As this section ends, it is important to return to our original example of soldiers and athletes. To underscore the important similarities, let us remember that while we may say soldiers fight "for something" and "against others," competitive athletes certainly do no less. The psychological wounds of battle are not inflicted by others on soldiers but by the soldiers themselves, and such wounds affect rehabilitation. Helping soldiers gain control over this situation is a critical part of the rehabilitation process. The reaction of athletes to injury is also something personally created. The rehabilitation process for athletes, as for soldiers, must prevent the development and exacerbation of damage and must provide them with the tools to move forward and live healthy and successful lives.

Summary

Sport medicine has made great advances in the physical rehabilitation of injured athletes, but little attention has been given to the psychological rehabilitation of these athletes. Although some athletes have effective psychological responses, others do not. This chapter focuses on factors that may predispose athletes to injuries, patterns of negative reactions to injuries, and ways in which coaches and sport psychologists can help athletes respond psychologically to injuries in positive, growth-oriented ways.

Although no clear injury-prone personality has been identified, some factors such as high life stress and low social support and psychological coping skills are predictive of injury. These and other factors related to injury are described, and possible preventive interventions are presented. More and less adaptive responses to injury are illustrated, including comparisons to Kubler-Ross's model of loss. Crisis intervention responses, systems of social support, and cognitive-behavioral interventions are ways to help injured athletes respond to injury in a more positive psychological way.

Study Questions

1. What are key factors that may predispose some athletes to injury? How can the sport or team environment be modified to reduce risk factors and enhance buffering factors?

2. List five responses that may occur as a result of anxiety and tension associated with an injury upon an athlete's initial return to competition.

3. How and why might personal growth possibilities become an important part of the psychological rehabilitation of the injured athlete?

4. List five problematic results of an athlete returning to competition following an injury if not psychologically prepared.

5. Identify and briefly explain the five predictable psychological reactions to injury similar to those first outlined by Elizabeth Kubler-Ross.

6. Identify specific ways in which irrational thinking may distort an athlete's perceptual response to an injury.

7. Explain the differences amongst visual rehearsal, body rehearsal, and emotive rehearsal.

8. Describe what other psychological strategies might be used to hasten rehabilitation and to prepare for returning to competition.

9. In what ways might an injured athlete be like a soldier injured in a combat situation, and what are important differences?

References

Andersen, M. B., & Williams, J. M. (1988). Psychological risk factors: Injury prediction and preventative measures. In J. Heil (Ed.), *The sport psychology of injury*. Champaign, Ill.: Human Kinetics.

Beck, A. (1970). Cognitive therapy: Nature and relation to behavior therapy. *Behavior Therapy, 2*, 194–200.

Blackwell, B., & McCullagh, P. (1990). The relationship of athletic injury to life stress, competitive anxiety and coping resources. *Athletic Training, 25*, 23–27.

Bramwell, S. T., Masuda, M., Wagner, N. N., & Holmes, T. H. (1975). Psychosocial factors in athletic injuries. *Journal of Human Stress, 2*, 6–20.

Brewer, B. W., Van Raalte, J. L., & Linder, D. E. (1990, May). *Development and preliminary validation of the Athletic Identity Measurement Scale*. Paper presented at the North American Society for the Psychology of Sport and Physical Activity, Houston, Tex.

Brewer, B. W., Van Raalte, J. L., & Linder, D. E. (1991, June). *Construct validity of the Athletic Identity Measure-ment Scale*. Paper presented at the annual meeting of the North American Society for the Psychology of Sport and Physical Activity, Monterey, Calif.

Bulman, R. J., & Wortman, C. B. (1977). Attributions of blame and coping in the "real world": Severe accident victims react to their lot. *Journal of Personality and Social Psychology, 33*, 351–363.

Campas, B. E., Davis, G. E., Forsythe, C. J., & Wagner, B. M. (1987). Assessment of major and daily stressful events during adolescence: The Adolescent Perceived Events Scale. *Journal of Consulting and Clinical Psychology, 55*, 534–541.

Coddington, R. D., & Troxell, J. R. (1980). The effects of emotional factors on football injury rates—a pilot study. *Journal of Human Stress, 7*, 3–5.

Cohen, D. A., & Young, M. L. (1981). Self-concept and injuries among female high school basketball players. *Journal of Sports Medicine and Physical Fitness, 21*, 55–61.

Crossman, J., & Jamieson, J. (1985). Differences in perceptions of seriousness and disrupting effects of athletic injury as viewed by athletes and their trainer. *Perceptual and Motor Skills, 61*, 1131–1134.

Cryan, P. D., & Alles, W. F. (1983). The relationship between stress and college football injuries. *Journal of Sports Medicine, 23*, 52–58.

Dahlhauser, M., & Thomas, M. D. (1979). Visual disembedding and locus of control as variables associated with high school football injuries. *Perceptual and Motor Skills, 49*, 254.

Danish, S. J. (1986). Psychological aspects in the care and treatment of athletic injuries. In P. E. Vinger & E. F. Hoerner (Eds.), *Sports injuries: The unthwarted epidemic* (pp. 345–353). Littleton, Mass.: PSG.

DePalma, M. T., & DePalma, B. (1989). The use of instruction and the behavioral approach to facilitate injury rehabilitation. *Athletic Training, 24*, 217–219.

Dunn, R. (1983). Psychological factors in sports medicine. *Athletic Training, 18*, 34–35.

Eldridge, W. D. (1983). The importance of psychotherapy for athletic-related orthopedic injuries among athletes. *International Journal of Sport Psychology, 14*, 203–211.

Erikson, E. (1968). *Identity: Youth and crisis*. New York: Norton.

Ermler, K. L., & Thomas, C. E. (1990). Interventions for the alienating effect of injury. *Athletic Training, 25*, 269–271.

Gluck, J. M. (1983). The doctor's bag. *Orthopedic Clinics of North America, 14*, 323–336.

Guttman, M. C., Knapp, D. M., Foster, C., Pollack, M. L., & Ropowski, B. L. (1984). *Age, experience, and gender as predictors of psychological response to training in Olympic speedskaters.* Paper presented at the 1984 Olympic Scientific Congress, Eugene, Ore.

Hardy, C. J., & Crace, R. K. (1990, May/June). Dealing with injury. *Sport Psychology Training Bulletin, 1,* 1–8.

Hardy, C. J., Richman, J. M., & Rosenfeld, L. B. (1991). The role of social support in the life stress/injury relationship. *The Sport Psychologist, 5,* 128–139.

Hardy, C. J., & Riehl, M. A. (1988). An examination of the life stress–injury relationship among noncontact sport participants. *Behavioral Medicine, 14,* 113–118.

Kardiner, A. (1959). Traumatic neuroses of war. In S. Arieti (Ed.), *American handbook of psychiatry* (vol. 1) (pp. 246–257). New York: Basic Books.

Kavanaugh, R. E. (1972). *Facing death.* Los Angeles: Nash.

Kerr, G., & Minden, H. (1988). Psychological factors related to the occurrence of athletic injuries. *Journal of Sport and Exercise Physiology, 37,* 1–11.

Kubler-Ross, E. (1969). *On death and dying.* New York: Macmillan.

Labuc, S. (1986, July). *Psychological stress, morale, and military efficiency: Minimizing stress reactions.* Paper presented at the 21st International Congress of Applied Psychology, Jerusalem, Israel.

Lazarus, A. (1974). Psychological stress and coping in adaptation and illness. *International Journal of Psychiatric Medicine, 5,* 321–333.

Levenson, H., Hirschfeld, L., Hirschfeld, A., & Dzubay, B. (1983). Recent life events and accidents: The role of sex differences. *Journal of Human Stress, 10,* 4–11.

Lysens, R., Auweele, Y. V., & Ostyn, M. (1986). The relationship between psychosocial factors and sports injuries. *Journal of Sports Medicine and Physical Fitness, 26,* 77–84.

May, J. R., Veach, T. L., Reed, M. W., & Griffey, M. S. (1985). A psychological study of health, injury, and performance in athletes on the U.S. alpine ski team. *Physician and Sports Medicine, 13,* 111–115.

Moss, R. H. (1979). *The crisis of illness: An overview in coping with physical illness.* New York: Plenum Medical Book Co.

Nideffer, R. M. (1983). The injured athlete: Psychological factors in treatment. *Orthopedic Clinics of North America, 14,* 374–385.

Ogilvie, B. C. (1983). The orthopedist's role in children's sports. *Orthopedic Clinics of North America, 14,* 361–372.

Oglesby, C. (1984, June). Personal communication with author.

Pedersen, P. (1986). The grief response and injury: A special challenge for athletes and athletic trainers. *Athletic Training, 21,* 312–314.

Passer, M. W., & Seese, M. D. (1983). Life stress and athletic injury: Examination of positive versus negative events and three moderator variables. *Journal of Human Stress, 10,* 11–16.

Petrie, T. A. (in press). Psychosocial antecedents of athletic injury: The effects of life stress and social support on female collegiate gymnasts. *Behavioral Medicine.*

Ratcliffe, J. (1983, June 19). Saga of UVA Blue CHipper. *The Dailey Progress,* p. D3.

Rotella, R. (1984). Psychological care of the injured athlete. In L. Bunker, R. J. Rotella, & A. S. Reilly (Eds.), *Sport psychology: Psychological considerations in maximizing sport performance.* Ithaca, N.Y.: Mouvement Publications.

Sanderson, F. H. (1977). The psychology of the injury-prone athlete. *British Journal of Sports Medicine, 11,* 56–57.

Sanderson, F. H. (1978). The psychological implications of injury. *British Journal of Sports Medicine, 12,* 41–43.

Silva, J. M., & Hardy, C. J. (1991). The sport psychologist: Psychological aspects of injury in sport. In F. O. Mueller & A. Ryan (Eds.), *The sport medicine team and athletic injury prevention* (pp. 114–132). Philadelphia: Davis.

Smith, A. M., Scott, S. G., O'Fallon, W. M., & Young, M. L. (1990). Emotional responses of athletes to injury. *Mayo Clinic Proceedings, 65,* 38–50.

Smith, A. M., Scott, S. G., & Wiese, D. M. (1990). The psychological effects of sports injuries. *Sports Medicine, 9,* 352–369.

Smith, R. E., Smoll, F. L., & Ptacek, J. T. (1990). Conjunctive moderator variables in vulnerability and resiliency life research: Life stress, social support, and coping skills, and adolescent sport injuries. *Journal of Personality and Social Psychology, 58,* 360– 369.

Solomon, Z., & Benbenishty, R. (1986). The role of proximity, immediacy, and expectancy in frontline treatment of combat stress reaction among Israelis in the Lebanon War, *American Journal of Psychiatry, 143,* 613–617.

Suinn, R. M. (1967). Psychological reactions to disability. *Journal of the Association for Physical and Mental Rehabilitation,* 13–15.

Vailant, P. M. (1981). Personality and injury in competitive runners. *Perceptual and Motor Skills, 53,* 251–253.

Wehlage, D. F. (1980). Managing the emotional reaction to loss in athletics. *Athletic Training, 15,* 144–146.

Weiss, M. R., & Troxell, R. K. (1986). Psychology of the injured athlete. *Athletic Training*, *21*, 104–154.

Wiese, D. M., & Weiss, M. R. (1987). Psychological rehabilitation and physical injury: Implications for the sport medicine team. *The Sport Psychologist*, *1*, 318–330.

Williams, J. M., Haggert, J., Tonymon, P., & Wadsworth, W. A. (1986). Life stress and prediction of athletic injuries in volleyball, basketball, and cross-country running. In Le. E. Unestahl (Ed.), *Sport psychology in theory and practice*. Orebro, Sweden: Veje.

Williams, J., Tonymon, P., & Wadsworth, W. A. (1986). Relationship of stress to injury in intercollegiate volleyball. *Journal of Human Stress*, *12*, 38–43.

Williams, J. M., & Roepke, N. (in press). Psychology in injury and rehabilitation. In R. N. Singer, M. Murphy, & L. K. Tennant (Eds.), *Handbook of research in sport psychology*.

Yaffe, M. (1983). Sports injuries: Psychological aspects. *British Journal of Hospital Medicine*, *27*, 224–232.

Career Termination in Sports: When the Dream Dies

Bruce Ogilvie, *Los Gatos, California*

Jim Taylor, *Nova University*

O nly in recent years have educators, coaches, and sport administrators seriously examined their responsibility for the long-term physical and mental health of their athletes. This is not to imply that there has been a general lack of caring, but more a reflection of how they set their priorities in terms of their primary role in the lives of their athletes. The issues that will be treated in this chapter will focus mainly upon the career termination of athletes who have made sport participation a major investment in their lives. The term 'elite athlete' will be used to distinguish such athletes from recreational sport participants.

History and Background

The termination effects of referred university, national, and professional athletes first captured the attention of sport psychologists. Interest in the topic had been stimulated during meetings between the leading professionals in the field in western Europe who were consultants for their various national teams. It was a rare occasion when experienced professionals such as Miroslav Vanek, Paul Kunath, Ferruccio Antonelli, Lars-Erik Unestahl

and John Kane did not at some time express concern about adjustment to a life after sport. In addition, attention from the media (Bradley, 1976; Jordan, 1975; Kahn, 1972; Plimpton, 1977) and early scholarly, though anecdotal, writings (Broom, 1982; McPherson, 1980; Ogilvie & Howe, 1986) brought to light some of the significant concerns associated with career termination among athletes.

Along with these nonempirical considerations of this issue, research emerged in the 1970s that produced data about many concerns related to career termination (Haerle, 1975; Hill & Lowe, 1974; Snyder & Baber, 1979). These and more recent studies examined issues related to career termination for athletes at different sports and levels of competition.

Twenty years ago, most attention to these concerns was found in the Eastern European countries. The discussions concerned the serious maladaptive patterns on the part of athletes who were slow to make the transition from elite sportsperson to "average" citizen. The impression at that time was that the Eastern European nations were accepting more responsibility for preparing their national athletes for a career beyond sport. The team psychologists in these countries appeared to have a greater sensitivity to these issues because they typically had long-term relationships with the team members. Frequently these relationships were established during pre- or early teens and endured throughout their athletic careers until the athlete's middle 30s.

In addition, educational and vocational counseling were an integral part of the athletes' developmental process. Also, a large proportion of these athletes were studying in fields related to sport participation, such as coaching, motor learning, exercise physiology, and physical therapy. Those athletes who could combine their love of sport with a professional career after retirement from their sport rarely seemed to exhibit problems of adaptation to a life as noncompetitors.

In addition, European elite athletes typically had a longer competitive history and were, therefore, older than U.S. national athletes. This is a function of population size and the relatively limited pool of talent they were drawn from. Most countries do not have the vast talent pool available to the national governing bodies (NGB) and professional leagues in the United States. As a result, it was expected that European athletes would compete longer for their national teams and would retire at a later age.

The decentralized nature of sports in the United States has made it difficult to identify the incidence of adjustment problems that elite athletes experience and to address them in an organized way. Unlike in other countries, which often have national training centers for elite sports preparation, the primary development pools leading to world-class and professional competition in the United States are the collegiate athletic programs and private sports clubs such as those found in swimming, figure skating, and gymnastics.

As a result of decentralization, the opportunity to address possible postcareer needs of elite athletes has proven to be most difficult. The difficulties include a variety of issues, including the limited contact with athletes by trained professionals such as sport psychologists and career counselors. Until recently, sport psychologists rarely had the opportunity to evaluate the need for such services to elite athletes. Additionally, there has been little time to explore postathletic career concerns with them. For example, the primary settings for contact by sport psychologists working with NGBs is short-term training camps and at competitions,

neither of which provide conditions conducive to discussion of career termination issues.

In addition to the organizational/structural obstacles to addressing career termination, wide differences in philosophy among coaches and administrators with respect to athlete retirement may hinder further exploration of these concerns. For example, head coaches may sabotage career counseling programs because they interpret them as distracting the athletes from their primary focus of winning.

Despite these barriers, the U.S. Olympic Committee and the individual NGBs have recently established an ongoing career counseling program available to all Olympic-caliber athletes (USOC, 1988). These career counseling seminars were extremely well received by national team members (Gould et al., 1989; May & Brown, 1989; see Case Study #1).

Similar development also appears to be occurring at the professional level. The players' associations of the National Football League (NFL) and the National Basketball Association (NBA) have recently offered career counseling services to their members. However, the extent of use by the athletes is unclear. In fact, research indicates that relatively few elite athletes consider postathletic career concerns (Arviko, 1976; Haerle, 1975; Lerch, 1981). It may be that the high salaries accorded these athletes—for example, average salaries of $500,000 for NBA players (Cohen, 1989)—and the presence of agents-counselors (Garvey, 1984) may provide a false sense of security to the athletes (Hill & Lowe, 1974). Thus, postathletic career planning holds a low order of priority for them.

It should also be noted that as amateur sports become "professionalized" in the form of prize money and attendance incentives, chronological age difference between nations will begin to be less evident. When international-level amateur competitors are able to earn meaningful livings within sport, the incentive to continue the athletic career is great.

Causes of Career Termination

The causes for termination of an athletic career are most frequently a function of three factors: age, deselection, and injury. These factors influence a variety of psychological, social, and physical issues that contribute to the likelihood of postcareer distress.

Age

The influence of age on career termination is a function of both physiological and psychological factors. The career-limiting effects of age have significant ramifications for both young and older athletes. For athletes participating in sports where peak performance occurs during adolescence, career termination may result while they are still teenagers. This will be particularly evident for those sports such as gymnastics and figure skating, in which puberty often signals elite competitive participation is nearing an end. At that point the alterations in physiology restrict rather than contribute to motor skills and performance.

Physiological restrictions are also evident with older athletes in sports such as baseball, football, and tennis that require size, strength, and precise motor skills. Athletes in these sports may compete effectively into their 30s or later. However, due to the natural physical deterioration that accompanies approaching middle age, athletic performance will decrease commensurately (Fisher & Conlee, 1979). Efforts to slow this process may be made (Mihovilovic, 1968), but the process is inevitable.

Deselection

One of the most significant contributors to the incidence of termination is the nature of the selection process that occurs at every level of competitive sports. This process, which follows a Darwinian "survival of the fittest" philosophy, selects out only those athletes capable of progressing to the next level of competition and disregards those who do not meet the necessary performance criteria. Most organized youth programs still place the highest priority on winning, and this same philosophy predominates throughout high school, university, and professional sport. Data indicate that only one in five scholastic athletes receive college scholarships and only 1% of those play professionally (Ogilvie & Howe, 1986). Selection camps in the NBA exemplify dramatically the severity of the deselection process at the professional level. These young players often spend four years dreaming of playing professionally, are invited to camps, and then summarily released based on a brief period of evaluation. The powerfully

negative emotional impact of this experience is clear (see Case Study #2).

Injury

The occurrence of injury, whether severe or minor, may force athletes to end their athletic careers. National figures have estimated that between three and five million recreational and competitive athletes experience a sport-related injury (Kraus & Conroy, 1984). The proportion of these injuries that result in career termination for athletes is unclear. However, the research to date indicates that 14%–32% of the athletes that were studied were forced to end their careers prematurely because of injury (Allison & Meyer, 1988; Hare, 1971; Svoboda & Vanek, 1982; Werthner & Orlick, 1986). Furthermore, it has been suggested that severe injuries may result in a variety of psychological difficulties including fear, anxiety, and loss of self-esteem (Rotella & Heyman, 1984), depression, and substance abuse (Ogilvie & Howe, 1986; Rotella, 1984).

Free choice

One cause of career termination that is not often considered is that of free choice (Coakley, 1983). This cause is the most desirable because it is within the control of the athlete. Athletes choose to end their careers voluntarily for a variety of personal, social, and sport reasons including a change in values and motivations and the desire to pursue new interests and goals (Greendorfer & Blinde, 1985), to spend more time with family and friends, and because they no longer find their sports participation rewarding (Werthner & Orlick, 1986).

Reactions to Career Termination

Career termination can be conceptualized as a complex interaction of stressors. Whether the stressors are financial, social, psychological or physical, their effects may produce some form of trauma. The number of athletes who exhibit some form of trauma when forced from their sport is not known precisely. Those who have published their concerns and experiences with such individuals have mainly been clinical sport psychologists who provide services to the more elite end of the athletic continuum. Though each poses the question as to whether we are just seeing the tip of the iceberg, they are consistent in their grave concern for what might be the hidden significant number of such athletes throughout the competitive world (May & Sieb, 1987, Rotella & Heyman, 1986, Ogilvie, 1982, 1983).

Despite the concerns expressed by professionals working at the elite level, the extant literature has not produced widespread evidence of termination trauma at all levels of sport participation. Notably, there is little evidence of difficulties in athletes concluding their scholastic and collegiate careers (Blinde & Greendorfer, 1985; Coakley, 1983; Greendorfer & Blinde, 1985). As Coakley (1983) suggests, "the transition out of intercollegiate sports seems to go hand-in-hand with the transition . . . to . . . other roles normally associated with early adulthood" (p. 4). However, significant problems have been reported for world-class amateur and professional athletes (Arviko, 1976; Mihovilovic, 1968; Weinberg & Arond, 1952). Identity crises (Ball, 1976; Pollack, 1956), attempted suicide (Beisser, 1967; Hare, 1971), and alcohol and drug abuse (Arviko, 1976; Ogilvie & Howe, 1986; Newman, 1991) are some of the maladaptive reactions that have been reported.

Factors Contributing to Reaction

The particular reaction that emerges upon career termination will depend upon a variety of personal, social, environmental, and developmental factors. These factors influence the meaning of the termination to the athletes and dictate its practical implications for life after sport.

Available Resources

A significant contributor to the reaction of athletes to career termination involves the assets they have available to assist them adapting to the change. Three primary resources appear to have the greatest influence: coping skills (Lazarus & Folkman, 1984; Meichenbaum, 1977), social support (Sarason & Sarason, 1986; Smith, 1985), and preretirement planning (Coakley, 1983; Pearson & Pettitpas, 1990).

Coping skills can be characterized as cognitive, emotional/physiological, and behavioral. Cognitively, an important aspect of career termination is the perceptions that the athletes hold

about the experience. The ability of athletes to reorient their perceptions in an adaptive manner that is consistent with their new situation is critical (Bruning & Frew, 1987; Meichenbaum, 1977; Moleski & Tosi, 1976). In addition, it is important for retiring athletes to effectively manage the anger, anxiety, and sadness that are generated by the termination process (Browning, 1983; May, House, & Kovacs, 1982). Finally, a wide repertoire of behavioral skills need to be fostered because such skills enable athletes to address the manifest adjustments required by career termination (Lange & Jakubowski, 1976; King, Winett, & Lovett, 1986).

Social support is another resource that will facilitate the career termination process. Research indicates that two types of support are important in this transition. First, emotional support from family and friends acts as a buffer against the stressors of termination (Coakley, 1983; Svoboda & Vanek, 1982). Evidence has shown that athletes who receive emotional support demonstrated less distress following career termination (Mihovilovic, 1968; Reynolds, 1981). Second, several investigators have reported that institutional support prior to, during, and after career termination was related to effective transition (Gorbett, 1985; Manion, 1976; Schlossberg, 1981).

An important component of institutional support is the organizational endorsement and availability of preretirement planning for athletes during their competitive careers. These programs may include continued education, off-season job training, and financial planning. These preparations may ease the difficulties associated with career termination by broadening self and social identities and by enhancing the athletes' perceptions of control. Research has indicated that most athletes give little consideration to postathletic career concerns (Svoboda & Vanek, 1982; Weinberg & Arond, 1952; Werthner & Orlick, 1986). Additional investigations have shown that preretirement planning is related to more effective adaptation following career termination (Hill & Lowe, 1974; Kleiber & Thompson, 1980; Rowen & Wilks, 1987).

Intrapersonal Factors

The available resources described above will influence several intrapersonal factors that will, in turn, affect the athletes' reactions to career termination. These personal characteristics are self-identity, perceptions of control, and social identity. Each of these may determine the extent to which the individual is vulnerable when forced to confront the reality of the end of a sport career.

"Self-identity" related to career termination refers to the degree to which the athletes define their personal worth in terms of their achievements as an athlete. It has been suggested that athletes who become overly invested in their sport may be seen as "unidimensional people" (Ogilvie & Howe, 1986) and may be unhealthily dependent upon their sports participation for self-validation (Pearson & Pettitpas, 1990).

The degree of perceived control that athletes have over the end of their careers will also contribute to the quality of the reaction to career termination (Blinde & Greendorfer, 1985; McPherson, 1980). This issue is particularly meaningful because three of the four primary causes of career termination—age, deselection, and injury—are outside of the control of the athletes.

There is considerable evidence outside of sport that perceptions of control may influence many aspects of human functioning, including motivation (Wood & Bandura, 1989) and self-competence (Deci, 1980), and the emergence of psychological difficulties such as anxiety (Garfield & Bergin, 1978) and depression (Alloy & Abramson, 1982). In addition, research within sport indicates that retiring athletes experience a loss of perceived control (Mihovilovic, 1968; Werthner & Orlick, 1986).

Athletes whose social identities are limited to their athletic environment may also cause adjustment difficulties upon retirement. These athletes' social identities affect them at two levels. First, if their early development occurred largely in this setting, the athletes may be "role restricted," that is, they may only know how to interact effectively with members of the athletic community (Ogilvie & Howe, 1986). Second, due to their role restriction, they have no social support resources outside of the sports setting.

Commitments to sport may create forms of psychological or social dependency that the individual can come to believe are irreplaceable. In terms of ego psychology, their sense of self can become integrally bound in the expression of a single aspect of their nature (Ausubel & Kirk, 1977). Such an identity may express only a very limited number of attributes or qualities in terms of the individuals' true potential. In turn, these limitations

increase athletes' vulnerability to distress associated with career termination.

Prevention and Treatment of Career Termination Trauma

Effectively addressing career termination issues is not something to be left to sport psychologists when the end of an athletic career approaches. Rather, preparation for retirement is a long-term process that may be initiated at the beginning of an athletic career and continued through the athletic years and only concluded when a successful transition to a postathletic career and lifestyle has been made.

Prevention

The prevention of career termination crises may begin in the early stages of athletic development. It is becoming increasingly clear that sport participation may have a significant effect upon personal and social development (Ogilvie, 1987). There is, in fact, considerable evidence indicating the deleterious effects of deselection upon children's self-esteem (Scanlan, 1985; Smith, Smoll, & Curtis, 1979).

Of primary concern is the need for parents, coaches, and youth sport administrators to engender a more holistic approach to youth sports participation in which personal and social development holds precedence over athletic success (Pearson & Pettitpas, 1990). Similar commitment must also be found in the education system. It has been suggested that scholastic and collegiate sports programs develop and reinforce attitudes and behaviors that increase the vulnerability of athletes to career termination trauma (Remer, Tongate, & Watson, 1978). For example, these programs limit athletes' opportunities to develop diverse self and social identities and impede their social support systems.

What is most important to emphasize to the athletes as well as those who influence them is that sport participation need not be restrictive. Rather, sport involvement may be a significant means by which athletes may develop attitudes and skills that will successfully serve them in other areas of their lives (Scanlan, Stein, & Ravizza, 1989).

In sum, children should not be placed in a situation where their sport participation and achievement arrest the development of personal and social attributes that are necessary for effective functioning in nonsport aspects of their lives. Ideally, sport may become a meaningful setting in which young athletes may take psychological and social risks that will serve them well in other areas of their lives.

Treatment

Despite the best efforts made in the prevention of career termination trauma, crises may still arise when the reality of the end of an athletic career is recognized. The experience of career termination crises may adversely affect athletes cognitively, emotionally, behaviorally, and socially. As a result, it is important to address each of these areas actively and constructively.

The most significant aim of intervention is for sport psychologists to assist the athletes in preserving their sense of self-worth while establishing a new self-identity (McPherson, 1980). Additionally, Ogilvie and Howe (1986) have suggested that athletes progress through a grieving process similar to the one proposed by Kubler-Ross (1969). Consequently, it is important for sport psychologists to help athletes come to terms with the anger, sadness, and frustration they may experience during career termination (Yalom, 1980).

Also, athletes may be assisted in dealing with the stress associated with career termination and be shown that the skills they used to master their sport may be used as effectively in overcoming the challenges of a new career and lifestyle (Meichenbaum & Jaremko, 1983). Finally, the sport psychologist may aid athletes in expanding their social identity and social/behavioral repertoires and developing new social support systems outside of the sports environment (Ogilvie & Howe, 1986).

Two case studies provided examples of (1) a positive scenario of support for athletes in preparing for postathletic competition careers and (2) a negative scenario of harsh disregard for the pressures of Darwinian deselection.

Case Study #1: Programmatic Career Counseling

The U.S. National Men's Volleyball Team was the first NGB to establish a structured career counseling program prior to the 1984 Summer Olympics.

The NGB of volleyball had come to the conclusion that duplicating the training and development philosophy of their Eastern colleagues was imperative if they were to produce internationally competitive teams. Once the team selection had been made, it was decided that these individuals could not be expected to sacrifice four years of their lives to this program without some consideration for their future economic welfare. Such programs rarely can succeed without the support of the coaching staff, and in this case the head coach, Doug Beale, was supportive of his athletes and their interest in career development. He believed that the program would contribute to rather than detract from the ultimate success of the team.

The program became an integral part of the training regimen and included time and support staff to assist the athletes in learning about postathletic career development, setting postcareer goals, and pursuing those aims. The career counseling program was both well received and actively utilized by the members of the team. Furthermore, it seemed to enhance rather than inhibit motivation and concentration toward their performance goals.

Case Study #2: The Trauma of Deselection

The selection process typically used by NBA teams exemplifies the potential for trauma due to deselection. This setting illustrates the selection process in its purest Darwinian form. The purpose of this example is to demonstrate the severity of life in the world of professional sports.

An NBA team brought to rookie training camp between 18 and 22 players. The athletes brought to this camp were a highly select sample of talented players. These included draft choices and highly selected athletes who had not been drafted but who were judged to have sufficient potential to play in the NBA. Each had passed the scrutiny of the director of player personnel and his scouting staff. They were players who often had been the best on their team or best in their conference in college. With few exceptions, they were from NCAA Division I basketball programs. Most had been recognized talents since high school and all had been supported by collegiate athletic scholarships.

The selection process included several performance opportunities. There were six structured sessions divided into two-a-day practices. During these practices all aspects of their skills were evaluated by the coaching staff. Every moment the athletes were "under the microscope." The pressure to perform well was significant, and it manifested itself in inconsistent play and periodic outbursts of anger and frustration.

Following the practices there was an evening intrasquad game to which the community fans were invited. This competitive setting provided the coaches with a final opportunity to evaluate the players under game conditions and gave players the chance to either further demonstrate their abilities or to redeem themselves from poor practice performance.

Players were informed immediately after the intrasquad game about the coaching staff's decision about team selection. At that time, four to six players were invited to participate in their summer league program. The remaining players were thanked for their efforts and then given plane tickets home—thus, at best, delaying the start of their professional careers or, at worst, ending their athletic careers and their dreams of being professional athletes.

Summary

This chapter has reviewed the relevant literature pertaining to career termination among athletes. From this overview, several conclusions can be drawn.

1. First, the extant research suggests that career termination crises are more likely to occur to world-class and professional athletes than scholastic or collegiate athletes. This occurrence appears to be due to the greater ego involvement and personal investment of the former group of athletes and to the fact that retirement from world-class and professional sport participation typically occurs outside of the normal developmental process.

2. Second, distress due to career termination will not necessarily occur. Rather, the emergence of trauma is due to a variety of developmental, psychological, and social factors including early life experiences, coping skills, perceptions of control, self and social identities, social support, and preretirement planning.

3. Addressing career termination issues may begin at the earliest stages of sport participation. This process involves having parents, coaches, and youth sport administrators create an environment that will enable young athletes' sport involvement to be a meaningful vehicle that will engender healthy personal and social development.

4. Despite the best efforts to eliminate crises that arise due to career termination, trauma may still occur when athletes fully recognize that their sport careers are over. This distress may manifest itself psychologically, emotionally, behaviorally, and socially. It is important that each of these areas is addressed directly and constructively by a trained professional.

Study Questions

1. Compare the American and Eastern European methods of athlete development and their implications for career termination.

2. Briefly describe the causes of career termination and indicate how each factor would affect athletes' adaptation to retirement.

3. Indicate the types of athletes who have retirement difficulties and the nature of the distress that is commonly experienced.

4. Describe the three primary resources available to athletes to help them during the career termination process and give examples of how they influence retiring athletes.

5. Discuss the intrapersonal factors that affect athletes' reactions to retirement and how they are related to the athletes' adaptation.

6. Indicate the role that early development has on

athletes' reactions to retirement and give an example of an ideal upbringing for healthy career termination.

7. Identify the primary areas that sport psychologists must address in working with a retiring athlete and describe some of the techniques that could be used.

References

Alloy, L. B., & Abramson, L. Y. (1982). Learned helplessness, depression, and the illusion of control. *Journal of Personality and Social Psychology, 42*, 114–116.

Arviko, I. (1976). *Factors influencing the job and life satisfaction of retired baseball players.* Unpublished master's thesis, University of Waterloo, Ont., Canada.

Ausubel, D., & Kirk, D. (1977). *Ego psychology and mental disease: A developmental approach to psychopathology.* New York: Grune & Stratton.

Ball, D. W. (1976). Failure in sport. *American Sociological Review, 41*, 726–739.

Beisser, A. (1967). *The madness in sports.* New York: Appleton-Century-Crofts.

Blinde, E. M., & Greendorfer, S. L. (1985). A reconceptualization of the process of leaving the role of competitive athlete. *International Review of Sport Sociology, 20*, 87–94.

Botterill, C. (1982). What "endings" tell us about beginnings. In T. Orlick, J. T. Partington, & J. H. Salmela (Eds.), *Proceedings of the Fifth World Congress of Sport Psychology* (pp. 164–166). Ottawa, Canada: Coaching Association of Canada.

Bramwell, S. T., Masuda, M., Wagner, N. N., & Holmes, A. (1975). Psychological factors in athletic injuries. Development and application of the Social and Athletic Readjustment Scale (SARRS). *Journal of Human Stress, 2*, 6–20.

Broom, E. F. (1982). Detraining and retirement from high level competition: A reaction to "retirement from high level competition: and "career crisis in sport." In T. Orlick, J. T. Partington, & J. H. Salmela (Eds.), *Proceedings of the Fifth World Congress of Sport Psychology* (pp. 183–187). Ottawa, Canada: Coaching Association of Canada.

Browning, E. R. (1983). A memory pacer for improving stimulus generalization. *Journal of Autism and Developmental Disorders, 13*, 427–432.

Bruning, N. S., & Frew, D. R. (1987). Effects of exercise, relaxation, and management skills on physiological stress indicators: A field experiment. *Journal of Applied Psychology, 72*, 515–521.

Coakley, J. J. (1983). Leaving competitive sport: Retirement or rebirth. *Quest, 35*, 1–11.

Deci, E. L. (1980). *The psychology of self-determination.* Lexington, Mass.: Heath.

Duda, J. L., Smart, A. E., & Tappe, M. K. (1989). Prediction of adherence in the rehabilitation of athletic injuries. *Journal of Sport and Exercise Psychology, 11*(4), 367.

Eitzen, D. S., & Sage, G. H. (Eds.). (1982). *Sociology of American sport* (2nd ed.). Dubuque, Iowa: Brown.

Garfield, S., & Bergin, A. (1978). *Handbook of psychotherapy and behavior change: An empirical analysis* (2nd ed.). New York: Wiley.

Gorbett, F. J. (1985). Psycho-social adjustment of athletes to retirement. In L. K. Bunker, R. J. Rotella, & A. Reilly (Eds.), *Sport psychology: Psychological considerations in maximizing sport performance* (pp. 288–294). Ithaca, N.Y.: Mouvement Publications.

Greendorfer, S. L., & Blinde, E. M. (1985). "Retirement" from intercollegiate sport: Theoretical and empirical considerations. *Sociology of Sport Journal, 2*, 101–110.

Hare, N. (1971). A study of the black fighter. *The Black Scholar, 3*, 2–9.

Henschen, K. P. (1986). *Athletic staleness and burnout: Diagnosis, prevention and treatment.* In J. M. Williams (Ed.), *Applied sport psychology: Personal growth to peak performance.* Palo Alto, Calif.: Mayfield.

Hill, P., & Lowe, B. (1974). The inevitable metathesis of the retiring athlete. *International Review of Sport Sociology, 4*, 5–29.

King, A. C., Winett, R. A., & Lovett, S. B. (1986). Enhancing coping behaviors in at-risk populations: The effects of time-management instruction and social support in women from dual-earner families. *Behavior Therapy, 17*, 57–66.

Kleiber, D., & Thompson, S. (1980). Leisure behavior and adjustment to retirement: Implications for pre-retirement education. *Therapeutic Recreation Journal, 14*, 5–17.

Kraus, J. F., & Conroy, C. (1989). Mortality and morbidity from injuries in sport and recreation. *Annual Review of Public Health, 5*, 163–192.

Kubler-Ross, E. (1969). *On death and dying.* New York: Macmillan.

Lange, A. J. & Jakubowski, P. (1976). *Responsible assertive behavior.* Champaign, Ill.: Research Press.

Lazarus, R. S., & Folkman, S. (1984). *Stress, appraisal, and coping.* New York: Springer.

Manion, U. V. (1976). Preretirement counseling: The need for a new approach. *Personnel and Guidance Journal, 55,* 119–121.

May, E., House, W. C., & Kovacs, K. V. (1982). Group relaxation therapy to improve coping with stress. *Psychotherapy: Theory, Research and Practice, 19,* 102–109.

May, J. R., & Sieb, G. E. (1987). Athletic injuries: Psychosocial factors in the onset, sequelae, rehabilitation, and prevention. In J. R. May & M. J. Asken (Eds.), *Sport psychology: The psychological health of the athlete* (pp. 157–186). New York: PMS.

McPherson, B. P. (1980). Retirement from professional sport: The process and problems of occupational and psychological adjustment. *Sociological Symposium, 30,* 126–143.

Meichenbaum, D. (1977). *Cognitive-behavior modification.* New York: Plenum.

Meichenbaum, D., & Jaremko, M. (1983). *Stress reduction and prevention.* New York: Plenum.

Mihovilovic, M. (1968). The status of former sportsman. *International Review of Sport Sociology, 3,* 73–96.

Moleski, R., & Tosi, E. J. (1976). Comparative psychotherapy: Rational-emotive therapy versus systematic desensitization in the treatment of stuttering. *Journal of Consulting and Clinical Psychology, 44,* 309–311.

Murphy, S. M., Abbot, S., Hillard, N., Pettitpas, A., Danish, S., & Holloway, S. (1989). *New frontiers in sport psychology: Helping athletes with career transition process.* Presented at the annual meeting of the Association for the Advancement of Applied Sport Psychology, Seattle, Wash.

Newman, B. (1991, March 11). The last return. *Sports Illustrated,* pp. 38–42.

Ogilvie, B. C. (1982). Career crises in sports. In T. Orlick, J. T. Partington, & J. H. Salmela (Eds.), *Proceedings of the Fifth World Congress of Sport Psychology* (pp. 29–32). Ottawa, Canada: Coaching Association of Canada.

Ogilvie, B. C. (1983). When a dream dies. *Women's Sports Magazine, 5*(11).

Ogilvie, B. C. (1987). Traumatic effects of sports career termination. In *Proceedings of the National Conference of Sport Psychology,* Washington, D.C.: U.S. Olympic Committee.

Ogilvie, B. C., & Howe, M. (1982). Career crisis in sport. In T. Orlick, J. T. Partington, & J. H. Salmela (Eds.), *Proceedings of the Fifth World Congress of Sport Psychology* (pp. 176–183). Ottawa, Canada: Coaching Association of Canada.

Orlick, T. D., & Botterill, C. (1975) *Every kid can win.* Chicago, Ill.: Nelson Hall.

Pearson, R., & Pettitpas, A. (1990). Transition of athletes: Pitfalls and prevention. *Journal of Counseling and Development, 69,* 7–10.

Pollock, O. (1956). *The social aspects of retirement.* Homewood, Ill.: Irwin.

Remer, R., Tongate, R. A., & Watson, J. (1978). Athletes: Counseling for the overprivileged minority. *The Personnel and Guidance Journal, 56,* 622–629.

Reynolds, M. J. (1981). The effects of sports retirement on the job satisfaction of the former football player. In S. L. Greendorfer & A. Yiannakis (Eds.), *Sociology of sport: Perspectives* (pp. 127–137). West Point, N.Y.: Leisure Press.

Rotella, R. J., & Heyman, S. R. (1986). Stress, injury, and the psychological rehabilitation of athletes. In J. M. Williams (Ed.), *Applied sport psychology: Personal growth to peak performance* (pp. 343–364). Palo Alto, Calif.: Mayfield.

Rowen, R. B., & Wilks, S. (1987). Pre-retirement planning, a quality of life issue for retirement. *Employee Assistance Quarterly, 2,* 45–56.

Sarason, I. G., & Sarason, B. R. (1986). Experimentally provided social support. *Journal of Personality and Social Psychology, 50,* 1222–1225.

Scanlan, T. K. (1985). Sources of stress in youth sport athletes. In M. R. Weiss & D. Gould (Eds.), *Sports for children and youth* (pp. 75–89). Champaign, Ill.: Human Kinetics.

Scanlan, T. K., Stein, G. L., & Ravizza, K. (1989). An in-depth study of former elite figure skaters: II. Sources of enjoyment. *Journal of Sport and Exercise Psychology, 11,* 65–83.

Schlossberg, N. (1981). A model for analyzing human adaptation to transition. *The Counseling Psychologist, 9,* 2–18.

Smith, R. E. (1985). A component analysis of athletic stress. In M. Weiss & D. Gould (Eds.), *Competitive sports for children and youths: Proceedings of the Olympic Scientific Congress* (pp. 107–112). Champaign, Ill.: Human Kinetics.

Smith, R. E., Smoll, F. L., & Curtis, B. (1979). Coach effectiveness training: A cognitive-behavior approach to enhancing relationships skills in youth sport coaches. *Journal of Sport Psychology, 1,* 59–75.

Svoboda, B., & Vanek, M. (1982). Retirement from high level competition. In T. Orlick, J. T. Partington, & J. H. Salmela (Eds.), *Proceedings of the Fifth World Congress of Sport Psychology* (pp. 166–175). Ottawa, Canada: Coaching Association of Canada.

Thornton, J. S. (1990). Feast or famine: Eating disorders in athletes. *The Physician & Sport Medicine, 18, 4,* 116–121.

Weinberg, K., & Arond, H. (1952). The occupational culture of the boxer. *American Journal of Sociology, 57,* 460–469.

Werthner, P., & Orlick, T. Retirement experiences of successful Olympic athletes. *International Journal of Sport Psychology, 17,* 337–363.

Wood, R., & Bandura, A. (1989). Social cognitive theory of organizational management. *Academy of Management Review, 14,* 361–384.

Yalom, I. D. (1980). *Existential psychotherapy.* New York: Harper/Collins.

Author Index

Seefeldt, V., 36, 59-61
Seese, M. D., 338, 340
Seligman, M., 225, 226
Seltzer, J., 88, 93
Shank, P. A., 329
Shapiro, D. C., 16
Shapiro, E., 37
Shapiro, S., 37
Shaw, M. E., 127
Shea, J. B., 16
Sheier, M. F., 244
Shelton, T. O., 203
Shrauger, J. S., 39
Shroyer, J., 317
Sieb, G. E., 359
Siedentop, D., 322, 324
Silva, J., 228, 287, 348
Simons, J., 176, 181, 205
Singer, R. N., 12, 300
Sisley, B. L., 89
Skinner, B. F., 30
Slater, P., 38
Smith, A. M., 338, 344
Smith, D. E., 173, 174, 203
Smith, G., 318
Smith, N. J., 127
Smith, R. E., 26, 27, 29, 30, 36-40, 42, 43, 45, 46, 52, 60, 92, 74, 75, 125-127, 173, 164, 276, 277, 278, 287, 294, 336, 340, 341, 344, 351, 359, 360
Smoll, F. L., 26, 27, 30, 36-40, 42, 43, 45, 46, 52, 60, 74, 75, 78, 92, 125-127, 173, 174, 276, 294, 360
Snow, R., 68
Snyder-Bauer, R., 175
Solomon, Z., 351
Sonstroem, R. J., 176, 181
Spelman, F., 263
Spence, J. T., 175
Spence, K. W., 175
Spielberger, C. D., 173, 174
Spink, K. S, 114, 116, 120
Spreeman, J., 284
Stein, G. L., 141, 145
Stein, T. K., 360
Steinmetz, J., 238
Stephenson, J. R., 123
Sterman, M. B., 272
Stern, R. M., 173
Stogdill, R. M., 39, 82, 83, 85, 118
Stolberg, A. L., 318, 319
Straub, W. F., 7, 9, 203, 300, 302
Strauss, R. H., 310, 311, 313, 319
Stuart, R., 319
Suinn, R. M., 4, 204, 265, 274, 340
Svoboda, B., 358, 359

Swann, W. B., 39
Swinnen, S., 21
Syer, J., 238
Szasz, T., 307

Tabachnic, B. G., 90
Tatsouka, M. M., 91
Telander, R., 314
Tesser, A., 39, 40
Tharpe, R. G., 32, 294
Thayer, R. E., 173
Thomas, C. E., 344
Thomas, J. R., 78
Thomas, M. D., 342
Thompson, S., 359
Thoreson, C. E., 46
Thorndike, E. L., 18, 19
Thorndike, R., 68
Titus, L. J., 175
Tobler, N., 320
Tom, D. Y. H., 68, 69, 71
Tongate, R. A., 360
Tonymon, P., 341
Tosi, E. J., 359
Towbridge, M. H., 18
Tower, R. B., 335
Travis, C. A., 277
Tretilova, T. A., 181
Triandis, H. C., 84
Tricker, R., 299, 302, 305
Trimble, R. W., 190
Troxell, J. R., 338, 340, 342
Tubbs, S. L., 124, 126, 130
Tutko, T., 83, 84
Twentyman, C. T., 45
Tynes, L. L., 203

Ulrich, B. D., 76

Vaillant, P. M., 342
Van Lehn, R., 173
Van Raalte, J. L., 343
Van Schoyck, S. R., 284
Vanek, M., 6, 358, 359
Vealey, R. S., 123, 153, 173, 164, 283-287
Vernacchia, R., 125
Vevera, M., 176, 181
Vincent, W. J., 18
Von Strache, C., 87, 91
Vroom, V. H., 102-107

Wadsworth, W. A., 341
Walfish, S., 319
Walsh, M., 263
Walter, C. B., 18, 20, 21
Wandzilak, T., 39

Subject Index